For Rex,

With many thanks
& best wishes

Mitch

—30—
THIRTY YEARS OF JOURNALISM AND DEMOCRACY IN CANADA

THE MINIFIE LECTURES, 1981-2010

© 2009 Canadian Plains Research Center.

All rights reserved. No part of this work covered by the copyrights hereon may be reproduced or used in any form or by any means—graphic, electronic, or mechanical—without the prior written permission of the publisher. Any request for photocopying, recording, taping or placement in information storage and retrieval systems of any sort shall be directed in writing to Access Copyright.

Printed and bound in Canada at Friesens.
The text of this book is printed on 100% post-consumer recycled paper.

Edited by: Mitch Diamantopoulos
Cover and text design by Duncan Campbell, CPRC.
Editor for the Press: David McLennan, CPRC.

Library and Archives Canada Cataloguing in Publication

30 : thirty years of journalism and democracy in Canada : the Minifie lectures, 1981-2010 / edited by Mitch Diamantopoulos.

(University of Regina publications ; 26)
Includes index.
ISBN 978-0-88977-225-0

1. Journalism—Canada. 2. Journalism—Canada—History.
I. Diamantopoulos, Mitch, 1966– II. University of Regina. Canadian Plains Research Center III. Title: Thirty years of journalism and democracy in Canada. IV. Title: Minifie lectures, 1981–2010. V. Series: University of Regina publications ; 26

PN4903.T45 2010   071'.1   C2009-907530-X

Canadian Plains Research Center
University of Regina
Regina, Saskatchewan
Canada, S4S 0A2
tel: (306) 585-4758   fax: (306) 585-4699
e-mail: canadian.plains@uregina.ca
web: www.cprcpress.ca

We acknowledge the financial support of the Government of Canada through the Book Publishing Industry Development Program (BPIDP) for our publishing activities. We also acknowledge the support of the Canada Council for the Arts for our publishing program.

 Canadian Heritage   Patrimoine canadien   Canada Council for the Arts   Conseil des Arts du Canada

Ron Robbins (1915–2009)

To Canada's working journalists, who serve as watchdogs against democracy's many foes, and to their public, who, in turn, defend press freedom from its many adversaries. It is largely to their very special relationship, and solidarity, that we owe the democratization of the modern world.

And to the memory of Ron Robbins (1915–2009), the founding director of the School of Journalism at the University of Regina. He gave the best years of his life to the pursuit of excellence in journalism and journalism education.

And, finally, to the over 700 graduates of the School of Journalism, its staff and its faculty, and its many, many friends. They have helped to realize Ron Robbins' vision of a more engaged, enlightened and empowered Canadian public.

CONTENTS

Remembering James M. Minifie — XI

*Introduction Extending the Democratic Frontier:
Canadian Journalism and the Public Interest, 1981–2010*
MITCH DIAMANTOPOULOS — XIII

LECTURES

–1981–
*Cleopatra, Harlots and Glue:
The Importance, Standards and Ethics of Modern Journalism*
KNOWLTON NASH — 1

–1982–
Back to Basics: The Enemy is Us
CLARK DAVEY — 19

–1983–
*Phantom Lovers, Secrecy and the Right to Know:
The Modern Journalistic Experience, Its Perils and Opportunities*
WILLIAM STEVENSON — 31

–1984–
How Celebrity Corrupts Journalists, and Other Tall Tales
CHARLES LYNCH — 47

–1985–
Journalism: It's Not Minding Falling Off an Elephant
JOE SCHLESINGER — 59

–1986–
Images, Self-Images, and the Long String
HELEN HUTCHINSON — 69

–1987–
Mutual Ignorance: Canada and the United States
ALLAN FOTHERINGHAM — 81

–1988–
Fuddy-Duddy Journalism: I'd Rather not Rather
ANN MEDINA — 91

–1989–
What I Know Now that I Didn't Know in the Days When I knew Everything…
PETER GZOWSKI — 99

–1990–
The Great Canadian Identity Mystery
PATRICK WATSON—117

–1991–
Recipes for Sacred Cow
ERIC MALLING—129

–1992–
Reflections on Television:
The Other Side of the Screen
PAMELA WALLIN—143

–1993–
The Journalist as Advocate
JUNE CALLWOOD—161

–1994–
Can Professional Journalists
Survive Corporate Authoritarianism?
ARTHUR KENT—173

–1995–
The Ring of Truth:
The Trials and Tribulations of Interviewing
VALERIE PRINGLE—187

–1996–
Canada without CBC News:
A Win or a Loss?
PETER MANSBRIDGE—201

–1997–
News Media in the Next Millennium:
Outrunning the Bear
LLOYD ROBERTSON—213

–1998–
Cries and Whispers:
Late Twentieth Century Journalism
REX MURPHY—225

–1999–
The Art of the Once-Over
ADRIENNE CLARKSON—239

-2000-
My Life as a Dinosaur
WENDY MESLEY—253

-2001-
The Sixth Estate
LINDEN MACINTYRE—263

-2002-
Are Canadian Media Living Up to Their Mission?
HAROON SIDDIQUI—277

-2003-
Kyoto: The Real Goods on Climate Change
ALANNA MITCHELL—287

-2004-
Values, Meaning, and Feeding the Beast Called Media
EVAN SOLOMON—299

-2005-
Is Journalism Worth Believing In Anymore?
KEVIN NEWMAN—311

-2006-
*Iraq and the U.S. Media:
A Tragic Failure*
DAVID HALTON—321

-2007-
*Terror and the Press:
The Same Old Story*
EDWARD GREENSPON—333

-2008-
The Canadian Narrative: Time for a Rewrite
CAROL OFF—351

-2009-
*The Unseen Muzzle: How Timidity, Self-Censorship
and Libel Chill Work Their Magic*
TERRY MILEWSKI—361

-2010-
*Turning the World Back On:
Journalism and the New Global Reality*
TONY BURMAN—375

Photo Credits—389

Index—391

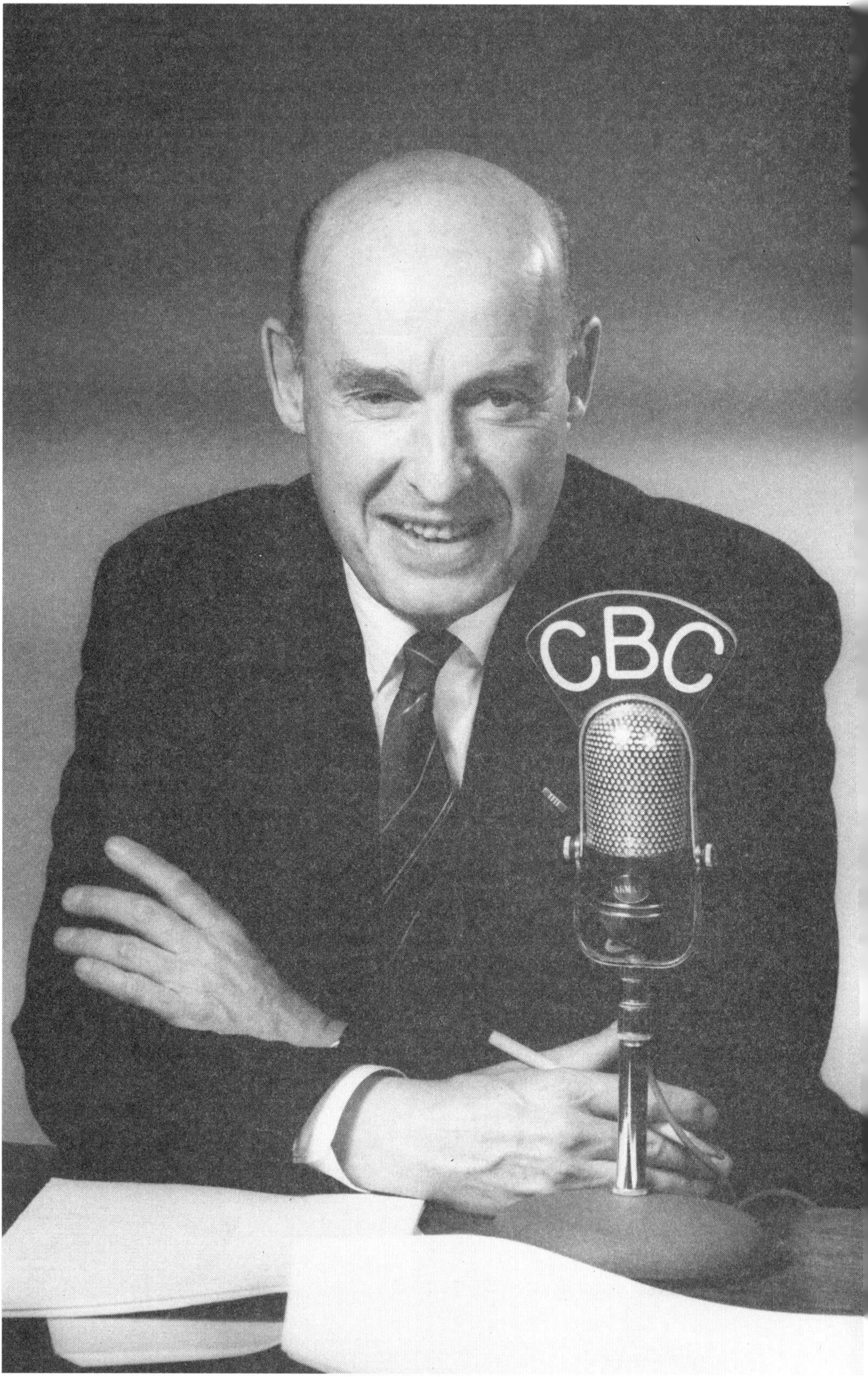
CBC

REMEMBERING JAMES M. MINIFIE

James M. Minifie, one of Canada's most courageous journalists, was born in Burton-on-Trent, England, in 1900. His father was a hay and feed dealer who joined the adventurous pioneers then emigrating to Canada in 1909. The family homesteaded at Vanguard, near Swift Current, Saskatchewan.

As a boy, James M. Minifie shared in the sparse comforts and many hardships of early prairie life. His father had led the campaign for the tiny school where young James attended lessons after early morning farm chores. At the age of 16, he talked his way into the Canadian Army, serving in Europe during the First World War.

On his return to Canada at the conclusion of hostilities, he attended Regina College, forerunner of the University of Regina. He went on to the University of Saskatchewan, graduating in 1923; studied at Oriel College at Oxford as a Rhodes Scholar; and finished his education at the Sorbonne in Paris.

Minifie's career as a journalist began in 1929 when he joined the staff of the *New York Herald Tribune* as a reporter, subsequently becoming their Paris correspondent. During the Spanish Civil War, he was captured by Franco's forces and returned to Paris when released. Later, he went to Rome to report on Benito Mussolini, the Italian dictator.

In the Second World War, Minifie reported the Battle of Britain from London. While watching an air raid during the Blitz, shattered glass from the blast of a German bomb cost him an eye. Transferred to Washington, he joined the Office of Strategic Services and at war's end was awarded the American Medal of Freedom for his contributions to the Allied cause.

Then began James M. Minifie's long association with the Canadian Broadcasting Corporation as their Washington correspondent. For 15 years, first on radio, then on television, he built up a large following of devoted listeners and viewers who waited for the famous, "This is James M. Minifie . . ."

He wrote several highly regarded books before being overtaken by illness in 1968. Moving to Victoria, B.C., because of poor health, he died in 1974.

In June 1980, the James M. Minifie Fund was set up to help support the launch of western Canada's first journalism education program, the School of Journalism at the University of Regina. The fund has provided the school with modern facilities for classes in all aspects of journalism, and makes possible the annual James M. Minifie Lecture. Tax deductible donations are welcome—for details please contact the Head of the School of Journalism.

INTRODUCTION

EXTENDING THE DEMOCRATIC FRONTIER:
Canadian Journalism and the Public Interest, 1981–2010[1]

Since 1981 Canada's most outstanding journalists have been invited to deliver the annual James M. Minifie Lecture at the University of Regina's School of Journalism. This thirtieth anniversary retrospective brings their statements together in one collection. It is a showcase for the sharp insight, eloquence and wit that define the journalistic imagination—and enable and enliven democratic societies.

However, this volume represents more than a 'who's who of Canadian journalism' or a mere showcase of literary talents. It is a chronicle of three decades of Canadian history, and journalism history, too. In the pages that follow, 30 leading journalists have tackled many of the public issues that most mattered to Canadians from 1981 to 2010. From war to climate change to our ongoing constitutional crisis, these addresses provide a unique front row view of history as it happened.

Indeed, the Minifie Lectures are a kind of annual audit of our 'common sense'[2] and our shared values as Canadians. Each address reflects a fleeting moment in the infinite unfolding of the Canadian idea, bearing witness, as Carol Off suggests in her talk, to the continuous 're-writing of the Canadian narrative.'

Importantly, these pages also tell the inside story of Canadian journalism itself. For in this age of media globalization, deregulation, and crisis, the state of the mass media system too has become a pressing public issue.[3]

Drawing these threads together, this anthology provides a valuable documentary record of the essentially intertwined recent history of Canadian politics, culture and journalism. Presented in language that is accessible and incisive, these talks are a pleasure to read—and a welcome reprieve from the encrustations of disciplinary jargon and hyper-specialization that too often overgrow the academy. This kind of truly 'public' language is increasingly important in an age of increased mobility, social fragmentation, and the retreat into private life and the tribalism of identity politics. American media sociologist Todd Gitlin has mourned the rise of this post-democratic dystopia—governed by apathetic resignation and withdrawal—as a 'twilight of common dreams.'[4]

There remains, nonetheless, more to the world than the shadowy bureaucratic dictates of the state and the merciless blind passions of the marketplace. As journalism's very existence attests, history is made by people—preferably alert, informed, and engaged people filled with civic virtue and democratic ambition. As Raymond Williams reminds us, "what we call a society is not only a network of political and economic arrangements, but also a process of learning and communication."[5] It is in this spirit of sustaining and reinvigorating the public life that is the currency of our democracy that Peter Mansbridge makes his case below for public broadcasting: as a conduit for the "national conversation." Similarly, Edward Greenspon reminds us of Arthur Miller's apt quip: "a good newspaper is a nation talking to itself." Among other things, these lectures emphasize that the history of a country simply can't be separated from the conversations its citizens have about the public good. A nation's journalism therefore both records, and inspires, its history.

Canadians often debate political and economic matters across the kitchen table, discussions invariably informed by news reports. Yet, we don't take this popular process of 'learning and communication' as seriously as perhaps we should. This 'blindspot'[6] also prevents us from taking journalism seriously.[7] The derogation of journalism is a serious problem for any democratic society, for journalism is nothing if not a powerful form of popular pedagogy in our media age. It's a pedagogy that—at its best—teaches us to be well-informed, thoughtful and engaged citizens. Like quality schools, much depends on quality journalism.

For example, in an era when our modernist faith in 'progress' collides with unprecedented threats of imminent ecological disaster, our species needs to learn, communicate and then act on these lessons quickly. Like the paradigm shifts in our worldviews provoked by the works of Galileo and Darwin, Alanna Mitchell argues in her lecture that climate change science requires a similar, but swifter, shift in popular consciousness to drive the necessary political commitments. For this reason, we need journalists to help us 'rewrite the legends' of how society should work, in better accordance with the facts and findings of science.[8]

Who can deny that our national conversation would have been poorer over the last 30 years without the voices of the journalists profiled in these pages? The contributors assembled in this volume are some of Canada's most important and influential public intellectuals.[9] Their urgent task has been to help us make sense of history as it is being made. For journalism provides more than a 'first draft of history,' for the mere convenience of academic historians. More importantly, as Pamela Wallin suggests in her chapter, it provides the public with 'working drafts' of history at the constitutive moments[10] of that history. These are the times of decision, when ideas, culture and the popular will come together—in informed choices—to shape the future.

In these times we have needed all the help we can get to make sense of our 'runaway world.'[11] Since 1981, Canada has been re-made once again—by global economic restructuring, by the revolution in information and communication technology, by climate change, by resource and religious wars, by growing inequality, poverty, and hunger, and by the most serious economic collapse since the Great Depression. It has been an extraordinary period of upheaval and confusion, calling forth both catastrophic media failures and heroic, challenging journalism. The pages which follow are a testament to both the value, and vulnerability, of this most precious democratic resource.

This collection illuminates the war for the hearts and minds of this professional community, as waged by working journalists themselves. It tells a larger story about the re-invention of journalism in our age, from the inside out. This is a backstage view of how our journalism has evolved, for better and for worse, and a textbook of contemporary issues in journalism. Knowlton Nash issues a prophetic warning of the dawn of 'show business values' in the news. June Callwood launches a trenchant critique of *faux* objectivity. Arthur Kent and Tony Burman lament the eclipse of foreign news. These thirty interventions weave an important, wide-ranging, diverse and colourful tapestry of critical perspectives on Canadian journalism.

The *publication* (literally 'making public') of these lectures is an effort to extend the audience for these important voices. It is also an effort to bring those voices together into a larger dialogue—so they can be compared, contrasted, and quarreled with by an emerging public. We hope this conversation about some key issues in Canadian journalism—a conversation thirty years in the making, will extend and deepen the public's conversation about the next thirty years. In particular, we hope this intervention will strengthen the conversation begun, and sustained, at the Minifies, between the press corps[12] and its historic patron, the democratic citizenry. That's a particularly urgent task in a period of crisis in the media industries, uncertainty for the journalistic profession, and informational emergency for the Canadian public.

In this sense, the chapters of this book reflect much more than the chronological passing of the seasons. They reflect the press corps' relentless pursuit of that quintessential moving target, the truth. For 30 years and more, the contributors to this volume have struggled to make sense of their craft. They have confronted its challenges and its adversaries. And they have done this in rapidly changing conditions, with dwindling staff and resources, and under the constant pressure of the newsroom deadline. Like the 'speed-up' of the assembly line, these journalists, too, have had to deal with the accelerating and increasing demands of the 24 hour news-cycle and the Internet. Their contributions, therefore, embody an important part of Canadian journalism's struggle for clarity, coherence and the creation of a collegial memory. For, as Zelizer[13] has argued, the press is an 'interpretive community' in which meanings matter and debate is important. These chapters represent hard fought for lessons from the frontlines of journalistic inquiry, but with implications also for the public sphere of democratic citizenship which our journalism so crucially informs.

THE PRESS, THE PUBLIC AND POPULAR RULE

Most of all, this is a book about journalism and democracy.

It is a cornerstone of democratic theory that a free press is a necessary guardian of the public interest. It is a watchdog against those who would deceive the public, and subvert the peoples' best interests. This is why press freedom enjoys constitutional protections in democratic societies around the world. You may be a wonderful writer, a gifted artist, or a capable stenographer without being defined by this central democratic commitment. But you will not be a journalist.

This collection must also, therefore, be a book about 'the public.' For journalism implies responsibilities to the public. The public is the moral justification for a free press in a democratic society; it is the historic *force motrice* and *raison d'être* of journalism. That is why we often refer to journalism as a 'public trust' rather than simply an industry or a literary art. Like the achievement of mass literacy and public schooling, independent journalism, too, is a form of popular learning that had to be fought for by the public, and which needs to be defended by the public.

Simply put, quality journalism is a necessary condition of democratic self-governance in modern societies. For people are not born citizens. We all need to learn about public issues, and to participate in informed debate to develop the capacity for rational and autonomous reasoning. We largely learn these lessons through the conversation that journalism convenes. Journalism is as crucial to modern citizenship as diagnosis is to medical treatment.

Unlike the face-to-face democracy of the Athenian city-state, modern citizens deliberate over public issues in what C. Wright Mills has described as a 'second hand world'[14]—from the comfort of our living rooms; not in the *agora* or the town square. Citizens need a thriving free press to help them form their opinions about the peoples' business. But today, more than ever, we rely on journalists to deliver quality information, diverse views and to facilitate strenuous debate. Nowhere is the modern citizen's dependence on media[15] greater than in the sparsely populated expanse of Canadian Confederation.

It is because of this defining commitment to the democratic process that James Carey has argued that the public is journalism's 'God-term.'[16] Indeed, it is the central preoccupation of our professional faith: to advance public understanding, to inform public opinion, to raise the level of public debate, and to defend the public interest. At the very epicentre of the journalistic mission, always, are the civil rights of the public: to be informed, to be heard and to participate in democratic life. Without journalism at its service, we know the public would be less able to effectively reflect and deliberate, and then collectively decide on a course of democratic action. And when the public is confused, distracted or disengaged, cliques, oligarchs—and worse—will fill that void.

If journalists had the equivalent of a Hippocratic oath,[17] it would not simply be "to do no harm." It would be to empower the public, "to do the most good." For journalism, democracy and our public culture have a special, co-dependent relationship. The Minifie Lectures are also, therefore, an extended meditation on what journalism is, what journalism should be and why there is often so wide a gap separating the rhetoric and *realpolitik* of the press.

These thirty veteran reporters have their differences, as journalists must in an open, pluralist society.[18] But they have all struggled to report the truth as best they could about things that matter to the public. This, as Chomsky has argued, is the essence of intellectual responsibility.[19] Raising the level, and expanding the scope of debate within the press corps—and sustaining the dialogue between the public and the journalism at its service—are democratic achievements of which many less free societies would be rightly envious, and of which Canadians should be duly proud. They may be less obvious or quantifiable than an increase in the GDP or a decrease in housing starts, but it is through these advances in our 'learning and communication' that we define our shared future.

Yet, one notes the heavy hand of history, and celebrity, in this collection. Of the first thirty Minifie Lecturers, men out-number women by a ratio of two to one, most clearly skewing the tenor and the topics in the early years. At a ratio of fifteen to one, visible minority voices are also muffled. Notably silenced in the first thirty years of the Minifie Lectures are the non-celebrity voices of Aboriginal journalists, queer journalists, and the ranks of the alternative media. This School has pushed hard to build diverse classrooms, diverse newsrooms and diverse media forms in recent years, and to promote a healthy skepticism toward privilege and authority. Nevertheless, the leading journalists of this period are creatures of their times and privileged position. A relatively closed circle, they necessarily reflect the structure and institutionalized values of established journalism. They tend to therefore also voice the concerns and perspectives of a comfortable minority, mostly based in Toronto. Try as they may to criticize the structure of power in the industry or celebrity culture, and many do very ably, they are themselves defined by it. Efforts by the rich and powerful to 'keep their enemies close' by conferring honours, and extending assorted invitations to favoured journalists may further compromise even the most well-meaning and determined of independent spirits. "Fame corrupts," Charles Lynch argued in his 1984 address: "we can be fearless in print about everything except our own business, where our inhibitions show."

But dissenting voices are well represented here, as they always are when great journalism is at issue. This volume is a window on three decades of soul-searching, social critique and professional self-criticism. Indeed, in the best critical spirit of the journalistic tradition, many contributors are deeply, even ruthlessly, critical of the failures and shortcomings of corporate journalism and public broadcasting in our age. No one escapes the critical gaze: not owners, not advertisers, not policy makers, nor even the public at large or the profession itself.

THE CRITICAL TRADITION, SCHOOLING AND POPULAR EDUCATION

The sustained critical reflection and discussion made possible by this series of public talks over the last three decades owes much to the leadership of three wise men:[20] a leading journalist, a critical communications scholar and a pioneering journalism educator. Without their distinct contributions, the conversation this collection represents would not have been possible. They are James M. Minifie, Dallas Smythe and Ron Robbins. Through their stories, we can learn much about the history of journalism in Canada in the post-war period.

MINIFIE'S LEGACY: COURAGE TO USE OUR INTELLECT

This special publication marks the 30th anniversary of the Minifie Lectures, a series named in honour of James M. Minifie. Minifie was a crusading journalist, and an outspoken advocate of the twin Enlightenment causes of truth and the freedom to tell it. Minifie's contemporaries included people like George Orwell and Ernest Hemingway, who also hastened to cover the Franco dictatorship and popular resistance in Spain. They were a generation of journalists shaped by the horrors of war and fascism. Minifie was captured by Franco's forces in the Spanish Civil War. In London, during the Second World War, he lost an eye to the shattered glass from the blast of a German bomb while watching an air raid. Like Orwell and Hemingway, Minifie, too, helped defend independent thought and democratic freedom in a world wracked by ultra-nationalism, censorship and propaganda.[21] Together, their generation provided a bright light and a moral compass for a public struggling to make its way. They cleared a path through the trauma and rubble of a world that had been blown asunder by greed, hatred, and empire. They helped Canadians leave behind the painful twilight of Enlightenment hubris without abandoning the core values of the Enlightenment ideal.

The conversation that is democracy would be incalculably poorer without the Minifies, the Orwells, and the Hemingways. The Canadian, British and American publics they respectively addressed relied on their dispatches to understand the forces that were redefining their world. The Minifie Lectures, in short, salute that courageous reporter from Vanguard, Saskatchewan, and what his legacy represents: the importance of Canadian journalism to our democratic society. It is a public lecture. It is a free lecture. And it is a lecture about the public interest. For thirty years, leading journalists and the public have come together in Regina to address the great issues of the day. Not one Minifie Lecturer has received a speaker's fee. Such is the higher calling of 'the public' to great journalists.

It is, therefore, also worth noting that all of these contributors, in some cases represented by heirs and executors, have donated their fees for this book to advance the studies of a young journalist. In this age, when we are told that people only act on the basis of self-interest, and when public service is widely denigrated, the Minifie Lecturers' Scholarship is a potent symbol. It symbolizes the profession's higher calling to the public interest and the widely and deeply felt need for a rigorous journalism education—to meet the new challenges posed to democracy in this brave new world.

Minifie would be pleased.

SMYTHE'S LEGACY: THINKING CRITICALLY ABOUT COMMUNICATIONS AND SOCIETY
Long before the School of Journalism was established at the University of Regina in 1980, others were laying the foundations to take Minifie's craft more seriously at the academy. Indeed, Canadian communications theorists like Harold Innis, Irene and Graham Spry and Marshall McLuhan occupy important roles in the pantheon of twentieth century thinking about culture, communications and democratic life.[22] One of the leading architects of the emerging University of Regina in the sixties was the brilliant and irrepressible Dallas Smythe. He was one of the world's leading communications theorists and researchers. As Economist at the Federal Communications Commission from 1943 to 1948, Smythe pioneered the regulation of U.S. broadcasting. As Research Director for the National Association of Educational Broadcasters from 1948 to 1953, he helped secure educational channels in the U.S. He worked with other groundbreaking, critical communication theorists, George Gerbner and Herbert Schiller, at the University of Illinois from 1948 to 1963. In fact, Smythe taught the first class ever in the political economy of communications.

Smythe became an economic advisor to Canada's Fowler Commission on Broadcasting, from 1956 to 1957, before being recruited to the University of Regina by Graham Spry.[23] Spry was the legendary leader of the Canadian Radio League and the father, thereby, of Canadian public broadcasting.[24] Smythe spent a decade at the University of Saskatchewan, Regina Campus[25] from 1963 to 1973, authoring its famous Regina Beach Statement (1963), and involving himself in the highly contentious debates on the New World Information and Communications Order at UNESCO from 1969 to 1973. Over the course of his career, Smythe wrote hundreds of articles, reports and monographs, including the influential book *Dependency Road: Communications, Capitalism, Consciousness and Canada*. To this day, the Union for Democratic Communications[26] awards the Dallas Smythe Award to a leading practitioner or academic who lives up to his lofty example.[27]

Smythe was drawn back to his childhood home by the open, progressive spirit of social innovation that defined Saskatchewan in the sixties. Named for Queen Victoria, Regina is situated on the ancestral homelands of the Plains Cree, ceded with Treaty Four. It is the bloody terminal point for both the Riel Rebellion in 1885 and the On-to-Ottawa Trek of the unemployed in the thirties. The legendary home of agrarian socialism and Medicare, Regina is the only city I know of to have both a Riot and a Manifesto as its namesakes. Located in Saskatchewan's capital city, the University of Saskatchewan, Regina Campus, expressed this rich legacy. Its media did not. As Lynch reminds us, the Co-operative Commonwealth Federation never received a fair shake in Saskatchewan news columns. Smythe arrived hot on the heels of the famous doctors' strike of 1962.[28]

By 1980, a new journalism school would sink its roots into the fertile soil of a vibrant and critical campus culture. The sixties played a formative role in that culture, and the student newspaper featured prominently.[29] The distinct history and democratic vitality of this community would enfold the Journalism School. It is not surprising that, from its very inception, the Minifie Lectures would be a flagship for the important relationship between the community and the School, a tribute to the very public nature, and importance, of its mission.

Although Smythe retired from the University of Regina seven years before the School of Journalism was established, his imprint on the university's institutional culture,[30] and his path-breaking, critical communications studies left important legacies.[31] Smythe argued the mass media were not well understood due to their relative youth, historically speaking, but that they were central to the very structure of modern life, consciousness, and democratic possibility. They were, in his pithy trademark phrase, a "blindspot."[32]

Certainly, the establishment of a journalism school reflected the reality of an expanding media industry in the West, and the demand for skilled labour, through the seventies. It also reflected an increased scholarly focus on mass communications within the academy, which, in turn, raised the profile of journalism. A specific debt is owed to Smythe for 'illuminating the blindspot.' This attention created the intellectual conditions for a different kind of journalism school, firmly grounded in the liberal arts and a critical conception of communications. It emerged long before any other journalism schools in the Canadian West.

More generally, Smythe laid the basis for a culture of innovation at the University of Regina. Long before it became commonplace, his emphasis was on inter-disciplinarity, and on the social context and consequences of education.[33] This implied an independent and critical approach to journalism, rather than simply being captive to industry interests or conventional wisdom. Smythe argued forcefully against the cultural invasion of the university by a stripped-down, market-driven technical rationality that was unhinged from social ethics and social criticism. There was, therefore, a deep distrust of the notion that a journalism school might simply churn out graduates, in an assembly-line fashion, to meet the narrow needs of profit-focused employers. The fact that the School was designed the way it was, and embodied the liberal arts mission and critical spirit which it did, largely reflects Smythe's enduring influence.

ROBBINS' LEGACY: JOURNALISM EDUCATION AND DEMOCRATIC VITALITY

You may be surprised to discover that—despite the utter centrality of journalism in the functioning of modern democracies—the first journalism school in the world was established only a century ago.[34] Compared to formal instruction in mathematics or philosophy or astronomy—which go back thousands of years—journalism education is a relatively young field. To establish this School in 1980 was, therefore, no small or easy achievement.

This courageous enterprise was led by the School's first director, Ron Robbins. Robbins was no stranger to Canadian journalism. After leaving behind his wartime military service and a stint of reporting for the Press Association and the BBC as a young man, Robbins went to work for the Canadian Press wire service. Over the span of 26 years with the Canadian Broadcasting Corporation, he coordinated the public broadcaster's staff training, was responsible for provincial and federal election coverage and supervised the CBC's overseas bureaus. He rowed against the relentless current of vocational thinking—that training for journalism could be reduced to a set of technical skills.[35] He faced an industry that doubted the relevance of anything other than on-the-job apprenticeship. He met resistance, too, from working journalists. Not without reason, they distrusted the corrosive influence of middle class professionalism on their democratic mission to 'afflict the comfortable and comfort the afflicted,' as A. J. Liebling once put it.[36] Undaunted, Robbins' school did not even consider applicants to the two year program without a degree already in hand, or at least two years of pre-Journalism liberal arts courses. Robbins ensured a generation of journalists would graduate with a solid grounding in the social sciences, humanities ... and in critical thinking. This was no small service to the public interest at the time. More depth, rigour and context were demanded from the press corps by an increasingly complex, rapidly changing world—and an increasingly well-educated public.

At the same time, Robbins did not lose sight of the need for practical, hands-on instruction and mentorship in the field. In fact, his school established the strongest internship program in the country. Spanning a full 13 weeks, this paid internship remains the envy of journalism schools across the country. It moved the School well beyond the bipolar disorders of a narrow vocationalism, on the one hand, and a disconnected academicism, on the other. Rather than turning out stenographers or essayists, Robbins' school emphasized the full sweep of academic, professional and democratic rigours and responsibilities. As the School's graduates fanned out, they played an important, vanguard role in redefining modern journalism across the Canadian West and well beyond.

Robbins' vision judiciously balanced the worlds of theory and practice, knowledge and skill, and classroom and studio work. He was well ahead of his time.[37] The program at the University of Regina quickly became well-known and respected as one of the leading schools in the country. It succeeded despite early doubts that such an ambitious program could be launched "in the middle of nowhere." The School sank deep roots in the region and cultivated its own distinctive, and intensive, approach to journalism education–accepting only 26 new students per year. It also overcame the hinterland churn of Eastern journalism school graduates in the West. Typically, these migrant young journalists brought neither background in local issues nor long-term commitment to building local knowledge, sources and expertise. Creating an innovative centre of gravity 'outside' the regional and doctrinal mainstream of Canadian journalism was perhaps the greatest contribution of the new school on the Prairies. Certainly, Robbins believed in that vision to his dying breath, leaving his entire estate to endow a student scholarship in perpetuity at the journalism school he founded. Named for his wife Kay, it was a final act of affection and democratic conviction.

Minifie, Smythe and Robbins all made distinct contributions to the contemporary practice of journalism on the Prairies. And there is a lesson in that. For the realization of excellence in journalism is a social achievement. It depends on the efforts of journalists, media scholars and journalism educators alike. It takes excellence in the field, excellence in cultivation of the craft, and excellence in our thinking about journalism to secure the basis for quality popular learning and communication. Sound thinking and craft skill guide solid journalism. Solid journalism enables well-informed democratic action. Strong democratic cultures and press freedoms support each other, and create the conditions for academic freedom and better scholarship. This is the virtuous circle that enlivens journalism, democracy and critical thought alike. Undermine any one of these fragile foundations and the whole intellectual and cultural superstructure of democratic society teeters.

THE LESSONS OF HISTORY AND THE RE-INVENTION OF JOURNALISM
In this age of consumerism, fast food culture, and celebrity journalism, we are too apt to forget the formative and defining relationship between democracy and journalism. We forget that the emergence of a modern 'public' depended crucially

on the rise of journalism as its eyes, ears and voice. Without journalism, the struggle for hearts and minds would be conducted in dark silence and democracy would surely be lost. That's why the state of journalism is not simply a concern for media owners or journalists. It is very much the peoples' business.

It is too easy to forget, too, in our age of instantaneous electronic communication and 24-hour news channels, that journalism was a crucial lever in the creation of the modern world. Like the pamphleteers of the Reformation, the newspaper war against Britain that preceded the American Revolution, and the tracts that prefigured the French Revolution, the emergence of journalism was a crucial marker in the transition from the mediaeval superstition and despotism of the Dark Ages to the Enlightenment promise of modern democracy. While the rediscovery of democracy was painful and the early press, too, had its spectacular failures, an important principle of social life emerged in the pages of the early newspapers. Through rational public dialogue, the people would now govern themselves. Against the arbitrary rule of aristocrats, clerics and monarchs, journalism made public the facts, the debates and the decision-making powers that were previously the preserve of elites. Journalism was inherently, and essentially, a popular and democratizing practice.

The journalists of early modernity forced power to account and subjected tradition to the sustained, withering gaze of critical reason. Men (and they were mostly men) like Jonathan Swift,[38] Charles Dickens,[39] Karl Marx,[40] Mark Twain,[41] Thomas Paine[42] and William Lyon Mackenzie [43] shook the world from its slumber. While without democracy there can be no journalism, it is surely also and equally true that without journalism there can be no democracy. That's why American revolutionary Thomas Jefferson famously declared "if it were left to me to decide whether we should have a government without newspapers, or newspapers without a government, I should not hesitate a moment to prefer the latter." [44]

Yet, we forget at our peril that journalism, like democracy, has always had, and will always have, enemies. In the early eighteenth century, the English popular press faced bans on reporting on parliament, newspaper taxes, and seditious libel laws—all designed to contain the ability of the restless many to inform themselves and to create a democratic public.[45] The last thing the *ancien regime* wanted was the majority of peasants, workers and merchants, the so-called 'third estate,' conversing about their interests and developing a democratic agenda.[46] This is why its democratic ally, the press, encountered such resistance. When, in the second half of the nineteenth century, working class societies attempted to finance a militant working class press, English authorities again attempted to suppress this new journalism. The so-called security system required publishers to raise financial bonds. This was an attempt to exclude 'pauper' ownership of the press. Press taxes also placed papers beyond the reach of working class consumers.[47] The historic 'fourth estate,' continues, to this day, to encounter the animosity of dictators and elites everywhere.

Over the centuries, many have been persecuted, arrested, exiled and murdered for exercising the basic press freedoms which we too casually take for granted in Canada today. Many continue to put themselves in harm's way. Forty-two journalists were killed in 2008 alone.[48] Throughout the modern era, despots large and small have sought to crush journalism: to preserve their privileges, to pre-empt popular enlightenment, and to prevent the popularization of democratic ideas that threaten their interests.

Contemporary efforts to muzzle, co-opt and defang the press have been far-reaching and persistent. As a result, many journalists today turn their critical gaze at the industry itself. They identify with a 'fifth estate,' a press club reserved for the explicitly independent and oppositional ranks of the 'true believers'[49] outside corporate journalism altogether. Indeed, a central preoccupation throughout these pages is the menace corporate concentration of ownership, editorial centralization and commercialization pose to independent, investigative journalism and the media diversity upon which democratic functioning depends. Arthur Kent denounces corporate authoritarianism and management run amok. Charles Lynch and June Callwood both skewer proprietors who prevent journalists from exercising their freedom of expression but use their holdings as political playthings.[50] Clearly, it is not only the state that poses a menace to independent thought and action. Increasingly, journalism is laid siege by market forces and media barons themselves. They are eager to lure and pander to affluent audiences (and the advertising revenues that follow) with skewed representations of the world, to monopolize markets, and to wring cost-savings from staff reductions.[51]

The state of journalism today is, rightly, a source of some consternation. From the eradication of poverty to the blights of racism or environmental degradation, our journalism continues to condition our historical possibilities. It can shrink or expand our world. For the quality of our society ultimately depends on the quality of the decisions we make about our future. This, in turn, pivots on the quality of the dialogue in which citizens engage. Journalism is the critical nexus where popular power to change the world meets the difficult questions that require investigation, reporting and popular illumination. The quantity, quality and diversity of journalism crucially extends, or limits, the ability of citizens to act intelligently and ethically. It raises or lowers the bar on our expectations of elected representatives. It defines the character and vibrancy of our democracy. It can shape a culture of hope and democratic engagement, or it can shape a culture of fear and authoritarian reaction.[52] It is for these reasons that journalism deserves to be taken seriously by serious democrats.

TAKING DEMOCRACY SERIOUSLY

This collection profiles the best of Canadian journalism. Its contributors seek to alert, to inform and to protect the people against those who would conceal or distort the truth. In other words, this is also a book about the ongoing struggle for democratic vitality and press freedom in Canada from 1981 to 2010. To paraphrase Chomsky, it is an artifact of journalism's continuing, epic struggle to "speak the truth and expose lies"[53]; to provide the public with an "intellectual self-defence"[54] against censors and spin-doctors alike. The themes of each lecture range widely, as the cultural environment has evolved over the last thirty years, but that central journalistic mission to inform a more vibrant and critical public culture underwrites them all. In that sense, this collection also profiles the best of Canadian democracy.

Media cynics would be wise to heed Nobel Prize winning economist Amartya Sen's observation that there has never been a famine in a country with free opposition parties and a free press.[55] The press holds the powerful to account and mobilizes the public to act against preventable disasters. It acts as a distant early warning system and mechanism for public accountability. Sometimes, that saves lives.

Yet, journalism also casts a long, dark shadow. For when our journalism fails us, or we fail it, the consequences can be catastrophic. One need only consider, as does Alanna Mitchell, the world's slow awakening to the tragedy of global warming or, as David Halton suggests, the decision to go to war in Iraq on the false pretext that Saddam Hussein's regime had weapons of mass destruction and was linked to the 9/11 terror attacks. Indeed, while a free press may prevent famines, it remains incapable of mobilizing wealthy countries to arrest chronic and persistent hunger in the under-developed world. It too often seems disinterested in action against growing poverty and social exclusion in the ranks of the advanced economies.[56] The scandal of global poverty, through which more than 800 million people go to bed hungry and 50,000 people die every day from poverty-related causes,[57] stands as a scathing indictment of journalism's fidelity to the democratic purpose. It begs the question of *which publics* journalism really serves.

Certainly, journalistic investigation and discovery offer great promise to global peace and prosperity. However, an ill-equipped press corps—under-staffed, harnessed to a machine that places sensation and celebrity before depth and context, speed over accuracy, and commercial gain over the citizen's need for meaningful perspective—threatens to place us in equally grave peril. Democracy and the public interest are inextricably bound together. If we care about the public's quality of life, and its democratic rights to strive for a better life, we must also be always vigilant about the quality of the journalism placed at its service.

Looking ahead, press freedoms face many new challenges. This is a new world, where the ranks of public relations staff now statistically outnumber the press corps.[58] This has given rise, in Linden MacIntyre's phrase, to a 'sixth estate' of spin and organized deception. Complex issues now require quick research, analysis and investigation to counter state and corporate efforts to manipulate the public—from genetically modified foods to climate change to economic policy options.

In this new context for journalism, independent reporting faces many economic and legal threats[59] and media failure can have high-stakes consequences.

James Minifie insisted on the role of a free press in securing a democratic future. Ron Robbins understood that it is precisely because not everyone in this unequal and highly specialized society has the privilege of advanced study of the issues of our times that our journalists should have the broadest and most sound preparation possible for public service. And Dallas Smythe grasped that it is because media power has become so pervasive, so recently, that it needs to be more widely studied, and rigorously analyzed. This *troika* for a critical new Canadian journalism has much to teach. Perhaps the most enduring and important lesson is that both advanced journalism education for the press and critical media literacy[60] for the rest of us are crucially important. And they are particularly important in an age when monopolies of knowledge, sponsored expertise and systematic disinformation are increasingly used as weapons—both against under-staffed and overwhelmed newsrooms and the public interest.

Without journalists well-schooled in researching, analyzing and investigating the most well hidden facts, and critical media consumers—and active citizens—on their guard against spin and propaganda, the public can only be further disenfranchised. Indeed, the public's intellectual self-defences are frequently breeched by the overwhelming force of the bureaucratic battalions of the public relations state,[61] the army of front-groups, think tanks and smokescreens behind which vested interests so frequently lurk,[62] and the increasing use of media in the 'psychological operations' of the military.[63]

For democrats, much weighs in the balance of raising the level of public debate. The cultivation of journalists is a crucial pivot and mechanism for raising up—or dumbing down—that public debate. Excellence in media and journalism studies will not, in itself, change the world. But journalists who think critically and act courageously always have.

Similarly, critical media literacy provides a crucial lever in the public's abilities: to resist the manipulations of the sixth estate; to read between the lines of systemic media bias; and to effectively defend journalists' rights to freedom of expression—on which our own freedoms and self-realization ultimately depend.

The Minifie Lectures are a recognition that this popular process of 'learning and communication'—the process of intellectual and cultural development that we call democracy—is a journey which the press corps and the public it serves need to take together . . . just as it has always been.

Bon voyage and good reading.

Mitch Diamantopoulos
Department Head, School of Journalism, University of Regina
November 7, 2009.

ENDNOTES:
1. Thanks to those who commented on an earlier draft of this Introduction: Patricia Bell, April Bourgeois, Gennadiy Chernov, John F. Conway, Patricia Elliott, Isobel Findlay, Robin Lawless, David McLennan, Brian Mlazgar and James M. Pitsula. Also, a special thanks to Shelley Kessel for her diligent efforts to help pull the transcripts and speaker permissions for this collection together and to Robin Lawless and Duncan Campbell for their assistance in assembling photographs. An extra special thanks to David McLennan and Brian Mlazgar at the Canadian Plains Research Center for making this initiative both a possibility and a pleasure.
2. As Antonio Gramsci, the Italian journalist, political philosopher and father of cultural studies who died in one of Mussolini's jails, argued, 'common sense' is no substitute for 'good sense.' The former must constantly be interrogated by the latter. Journalists occupy a special place in this ongoing process of intellectual and cultural reflexivity and renewal, as do public talks like the Minifie Lecture.
3. One need only consider the number of hearings convened on the media during this period by Royal Commissions, House and Senate committees and the Canadian Radio-television and Telecommunications Commission to get a sense of the importance, and political difficulty, involved. They have all struggled to balance competing claims of industry advocates for media market deregulation, on the one hand, and public interest advocates' claims for social regulation to limit excessive concentration of ownership, etc. on the other hand. These debates include the Senate Committee on Mass Media, which reported in 1970, the hotly contested 1981 report of the Royal Commission on Newspapers, the Lincoln Committee's 2003 report on broadcasting and the Senate hearings which issued their report on news media in 2006. At the international level, the 1980 MacBride Report on global information flows led to calls for the right to regulate and intervene in media markets to protect cultural sovereignty at UNESCO. Deregulationist advocates of free markets and a 'free flow' of information objected to the proposed infringement on 'press freedom' and in 1984 the U.S., under Reagan, withdrew in protest. In 1985, the U.K., under Thatcher, followed.
4. Gitlin, T. (1995). *The Twilight of Common Dreams*. Henry Holt and Company, New York.
5. Williams, R. (1962). *Britain in the Sixites: Communications*. Baltimore, Penguin. p.11
6. Smythe, D. (1981). "Communications: Blindspot of Economics," in Melody, H.W., et. al. (Eds). *Culture, Communication and Dependency: the Tradition of H. A. Innis*. Ablex, Norfolk, N.J., pp. 111–125. Smythe, D. (1983). "Communications: Blindspot of Western Marxism," *Canadian Journal of Political and Social Theory*, Vol. 1, No. 3, pp. 34–39.
7. Zelizer, B. (2004). *Taking Journalism Seriously: News and the Academy*. Sage, London.
8. To put this more formally, environmental reporting provides one instance of the pivotal position of journalism in the 'reflexivity' of modern societies. Unlike traditional societies, where practices are sanctioned by the mere fact that they are part of the established way of doing things, modern societies are defined by their reflexivity, i.e., by their ongoing critical self-examination of those practices based on the scientific rules of evidence and logic. "The reflexivity of modern social life consists in the fact that social practices are constantly examined and reformed in light of incoming information about those very practices, thus constitutively altering

their character." In democratic societies, it is largely through the critical scrutiny and reportage of journalism that conventions are revised, and popular will informed to make necessary changes. Giddens, A. (1990). *The Consequences of Modernity.* Stanford University Press, Stanford. pp. 36—45.

9. Todd Gitlin describes the public intellectual as "an intellectually serious writer who knows about culture, the arts, politics and writes or speaks for public clarification . . . and public enlightenment." Gitlin, T. (Summer 2006). "The Necessity of the Public Intellectual." *The Raritan Review.* Vol. 18. No. 3. pp. 85—103. As Jacoby has argued, the public intellectual may be an endangered species. See Jacoby, R. (1987). *The Last Intellectuals: American Culture in the Age of Academe.* Basic Books, New York.

10. I borrow this conception from Starr, P. (2004). *The Creation of the Media: Political Origins of Modern Communications.* Basic Books, New York.

11. Giddens, A. (2003). *Runaway World: How Globalization is Reshaping Our Lives.* Taylor and Francis, London.

12. The term 'press' is used in an inclusive sense: to encompass journalism as it practised across all technological platforms. This choice of term reflects the historic connection of modern democracy and the newspaper and the ethic of journalism as a democratic craft. In my view, there are precious few terms that capture these democratic and historical connotations as well as 'the press.'

13. Zelizer, B. (2004). *Taking Journalism Seriously: News and the Academy.* Sage, London.

14. Indeed, "the *first rule for understanding the human condition,*" American sociologist C. Wright Mills argued, "is that men (*sic*) live in second hand worlds" (my emphasis). Mills, C.W. (n.d.) "The Cultural Apparatus" in *Power, Politics and People.* Ballantyne Books, N.Y. pp 405—422.

15. In late modernity, we increasingly learn more from 'mediated interaction' such as telephone, social media and e-mail, and 'quasi-mediated interaction' such as mass media programming, than we do from face-to-face interaction. Thompson, J. (1995). *The Media and Modernity: A Social Theory of the Media.* Stanford University Press, Stanford, Calif.

16. Carey, J. W. (2007). "A Short History of Journalism for Journalists: A Proposal and an Essay." *The Harvard International Journal of Press / Politics.* Vol. 12, No. 1. pp. 3—16.

17. In fact, several efforts at professional re-definition have recently helped put journalism on a firmer, more reflexive ethical footing. These include the Committee of Concerned Journalists' 1997 'Principles of Journalism:' *www.journalism.org/resources/principles*, and the International Communications Forum's 2000 'Sarajevo Commitment:' *www.icforum.org/Sarajevo.html*.

18. See, for example, Linda McQuaig's vigorous critique of Eric Malling's controversial and politically consequential report for W5 on the New Zealand experience with debt reduction in Feb., 1993. Malling's report drew an audience of 1.6 million but also provided politicians with a justification, that McQuaig characterizes as specious, for drastic social program cuts. McQuaig, L. (1995). *Shooting the Hippo: Death by Deficit and other Canadian Myths.* Viking, Toronto.

19. The role of the intellectual should be to "find out and tell the truth, *as best one can,* about things that matter, to *the right audience.*" Chomsky, N. (1996). *Perspectives on Power.* Black Rose Books, Montreal. p. 55.

20. The history of women in Canadian journalism has only recently begun to be written. Minifie's contemporary, Gladys Arnold, provides a good place to start: Arnold, G. (1987). *One Woman's War*. James Lorimer and Company, Toronto.
21. This struggle, of course, was far from simple. Like Orwell, Minifie found himself torn between wartime patriotism and his own intellectual independence and democratic principles. Ironically, Orwell—the author of such classic tracts against totalitarianism and the police state as *Animal Farm* and *1984*—actually informed on suspected communists to the British anti-communist propaganda unit of the Foreign Office in 1949, the year before his death. He was disdainful of leftists who ignored evidence of Stalinist atrocities. In 1943, after his injury in London, Minifie found himself working for the Psychological Warfare Branch with the Office of Strategic Services, the intelligence service that would later become the Central Intelligence Agency. Yet, just as Orwell's scathing indictments of authoritarianism, left and right, gained intensity from his personal experience of the impossible moral conflicts it imposed, Minifie too struggled to reassert his post-war intellectual independence and democratic commitments against the repressive regime of Cold War doctrine. Part of Minifie's Washington beat for the *International Herald Tribune* at war's end was Senator Joe McCarthy's hearings, to which he listened in "silent outrage." Minifie, J. M. (1976). *Expatriate*. Macmillan of Canada. Toronto. p. 189. As his books, and Lynch—in this collection—remind us, Minifie was ultimately a "foe of the CIA, of Joe McCarthy and Richard Nixon" as surely as Orwell rejected the politics of both capitalism and Stalinism.
22. Babe, R. E. (2000). *Canadian Communication Thought: Ten Foundational Writers*. University of Toronto Press, Toronto.
23. Babe, R. E. *op cit*. p. 117.
24. *Op cit*., pp 39—55. Also, see: McChesney, R. W. (1999). "Graham Spry and the Future of Public Broadcasting: The 1997 Spry Memorial Lecture." *Canadian Journal of Communication*. Vol. 24., Vol 1. Interestingly, Spry and Smythe shared in common the experience of 'exile' as intellectuals with strong democratic commitments in the repressive, anti-communist climate of their time. Spry helped organize the Mackenzie-Papineau Battalion which fought against the Francisco Franco dictatorship in the Spanish Civil War. He was branded a 'Red' for this, and his involvements in the League for Social Reconstruction, the Co-operative Commonwealth Federation (CCF), and the drafting of the Regina Manifesto. Unemployable in Canada, he spent much of his working life in the U.K. Smythe also faced the anti-communist hysteria of the era for his support for the Republican cause in Spain. He was dubbed a 'premature anti-fascist' by security agents and left the U.S. in part, to escape the intellectual chill of McCarthyism on critical research (Babe, R. E., *op cit*, p. 114).
25. The University of Regina gained its formal independence in 1974. Pitsula, J. (2006). *As One Who Serves: The Making of the University of Regina*. McGill-Queen's University Press, Montreal.
26. The Union for Democratic Communications describes itself as "an organization of communication researchers, journalists, media producers, policy analysts, academics and activists dedicated to: critical study of the communications establishment; production and distribution of democratically controlled and produced media; fostering alternative, oppositional, independ-

ent and experimental production; development of democratic communications systems locally, regionally and internationally." Downloaded, October 14, 2009 from *http://www.democratic-communications.org/about.html*.
27. This biographical detail is drawn from Babe, R. W. (2000). *Op cit*. pp. 112- 139.
28. Spry served as Agent-General for Tommy Douglas's government in London from 1946 to 1968, playing a key role in enlisting British doctors to help secure Medicare against the doctors' strike of 1962. (Babe, R. E., *op cit*, p. 42).
29. Pitsula, J. (2008). *New World Dawning: The Sixties at Regina Campus*. Canadian Plains Research Center, Regina.
30. Pitsula, J. (2006). *As One Who Serves: The Making of the University of Regina*. McGill-Queen's University Press, Montreal.
31. Wasco, J. et. al. (1993). *Illuminating the Blindspots: Essays Honouring Dallas W. Smythe*. Ablex Publishing, Norwood, New Jersey; Smythe, D.W. and Guback, T. H. (1994). *Counter-clockwise: Perspectives on Communication*. University of California Press, Berkeley.
33. Pitsula, J. (2006). *As One Who Serves: The Making of the University of Regina*. McGill-Queen's University Press, Montreal.
34. The Missouri School of Journalism was established in 1908. *http://www.journalism.missouri.edu/about/history*
35. Against the notion that journalism is not a field that requires academic training, that it is 'a-theoretical,' Gasher argues "Journalism schools already subscribe—uncritically—to a theoretical framework that informs even the most practical courses; the problem is that these theories are rarely made explicit, they are rarely called into question, and when they are identified at all, they are rarely presented in the context of competing, alternate theories. The conventional theoretical framework is comprised of, among other beliefs, the democratic theory of the press (whereby journalism serves democracy, as opposed to serving economic and political power); a reflection theory of the media (whereby the media reflect, rather than construct, society); a theory of objectivity (which fails to account adequately for human subjectivity); and a theory of liberal pluralism (whereby truth emerges by giving voice to a range of diverse viewpoints)." Gasher, M. (2005). "Commentary: It's Time to Redefine Journalism Education in Canada." *Canadian Journal of Communication*. Vol. 30. pp. 665—672.
36. Steward expresses this aversion to the notion of journalism schools as uncritical, industry-sponsored 'channelling colonies:' "I do long for the days when newsrooms were full of extraordinary people, many of them eccentric to be sure, but so much more sceptical and rebellious than the university-educated, professionalized, middle-class journalists that fill today's newsrooms. I believe that education, that familiarity with orthodoxy, made it easier for the executives at head office to implement the changes they imposed from the top in the name of a better bottom line and return on revenue. Many journalists of the 1980s easily digested all the marketing jargon, too, because it was developed at business schools and universities just like the ones they had attended." Steward, G. (1996). "The Decline of the Daily Newspaper." In Holmes, H. & Taras, D. (Eds.). *Seeing Ourselves: Media Power and Policy in Canada*. Harcourt, Brace and Co., Toronto.

37. This theory-practice dualism in the field of journalism education was at the heart of the 2002 debate around the Columbia Graduate School of Journalism and the wider debate about the need to move from a craft orientation to a more critical, liberal arts embedded model. For contrasting Canadian views in this debate, see Ward, S. J. A. "Journalism Schools—Time to Join the Academy" & Hayes, D. "Journalism Education—Keep it Practical." *University Affairs*, Oct., 2003, pp. 24–28. For a more detailed perspective on the debate about journalism education, see: Skinner, D., Gasher, M. & Compton, J. (2001). "Putting Theory to Practice: A Critical Approach to Journalism Studies." *Journalism: Theory, Practice and Criticism.* Vol. 2. No. 3., pp. 341—360.
38. Swift, J. (1902). *The Prose Works of Jonathan Swift: Contributions to The Tatler, The Examiner, The Spectator, and The Intelligencer.* G. Bell, New York.
39. Slater, M. (1994). *Dickens' Journalism, Vol. 1: 'Sketches By Boz' and Other Early Papers, 1883—39.* Ohio State University Press, Columbus.
40. Ledbetter, J. (2007). *Karl Marx. Dispatches for the New York Tribune: Selected Journalism of Karl Marx.* Penguin Books, London.
41. McWilliams, J. (1997). *Mark Twain in the St. Louis Dispatch, 1874—1891.* University of California, Berkeley.
42. Nelson, C. (2007). *Thomas Paine: Enlightenment, Revolution and the Birth of Modern Nations.* Penguin, New York.
43. Kilbourn, W. (1964). *The Firebrand: William Lyon Mackenzie and the Rebellion in Upper Canada.* Clarke, Irwin and Co., Toronto.; Rosner, C. (2008). *Behind the Headlines: A History of Investigative Journalism in Canada.* Oxford University Press, Don Mills, ON. pp. 20 -35.
44. In Hargreaves, I. (2005). *Journalism: A Short Introduction.* Oxford University Press, Oxford. p. 95.
45. Curran, J. (1982). *Power Without Responsibility: The Press and Broadcasting in Britain.* Routledge, London. p. 221.
46. Popkin, J. (1990). *Revolutionary News: The Press in France, 1789-1799.* Duke University Press, London.
47. Curran, J. *Op cit.* p. 222.
48. These deaths were directly related to their work as journalists. "They either died in the line of duty or were deliberately targeted for assassination because of their reporting or their affiliation with a news organization." Downloaded Oct, 14, 2009 from *http://cpj.org/deadly/2008.php*. This high-risk environment has fuelled the development of professional defence organizations such as PEN Canada (*http://www.pencanada.ca/*) and Canadian Journalists for Free Expression (*http://www.cjfe.org/*).
49. Cockburn, A. and St. Clair, J. (2007). *End Times: The Death of the Fourth Estate.* Counterpunch and AK Press, Oakland, California.
50. There is a veritable cottage industry in profiles of politically motivated media proprietors. Two Canadian examples from the period under investigation here are Siklos, R. (1995). *Shades of Black: Conrad Black and the World's Fastest Growing Press Empire.* Reed Books, Toronto.; Barlow, M. and Winter, J. (1997). *The Big Black Book: The Essential Views of Conrad and Barbara Amiel Black.* Stoddart, Toronto.; Edge, M. (2007). *Asper Nation: Canada's Most Dangerous Media Company.* New Star Books, Vancouver.

51. Some leading critics of market-driven journalism include: Bagdikian, B. (1992). *The Media Monopoly*. Beacon Press, Boston.; Winter, James P. (1997). *Democracy's Oxygen: How Corporations Control the News*. Black Rose Books, Montreal.; Kent, T. (1992). "The Times and Significance of the Kent Commission." In Holmes, H. & Taras, D (Eds.). *Seeing Ourselves: Media Power and Policy in Canada*. Harcourt, Brace and Jovanovich Canada, Toronto. and; McChesney, R. W. (2007). *Communications Revolution*. The New Press, New York.
52. Glassner, B. (1999). *The Culture of Fear: Why Americans are Afraid of the Wrong Things*. Basic Books, New York; Giroux, H. (2006). *Beyond the Spectacle of Terrorism: Global Uncertainty and the Challenge of the New Media*. Paradigm Publishers, Boulder.
53. Chomsky, N. (1996). *Perspectives on Power*. Black Rose Books, Montreal.
54. Chomsky, N. (1989). *Necessary Illusions: Thought Control in Democratic Societies*. Anasi, Concord, ON.
55. Sen, A. (2000). *Development as Freedom*. First Anchor Books, New York. pp. 180—188.
56. Swanson, J. (2001). *Poor Bashing: The Politics of Exclusion*. Between the Lines, Toronto. pp. 90—105.
57. In the Canadian context, almost 5 million Canadians live in poverty and one in six Canadian children is poor. Canada's child poverty rate (15 per cent) is three times as high as the rates of Sweden, Norway or Finland. *http://www.makepovertyhistory.ca/en/the-issues*.
58. Hargreaves, I. *op cit*. p.95.
59. The editor of the U.K.'s *Guardian* newspaper provides a timely case study of deceptive corporate practices, libel chill and the failure of financial journalism in the context of the 2009 stock market crash and global recession: Rusbridger, A. (2009). "A Chill on *The Guardian*," New York Review of Books. Vol. 56., No. 1. *www.nybooks.com/articles/22245*.
60. Kellner, D. and Share, J. (2005). "Toward Critical Media Literacy: Core Concepts, Debates, Organizations, and Policy." *Discourse: studies in the cultural politics of education*. Vol. 26, No. 3, September 2005, pp. 369–386.
61. Davis, A. (2002). *Public Relations Democracy: Public Relations, Politics, and the Mass Media in Britain*. Sage, London.
62. Dobbin, M. (1998). *The Myth of the Good Corporate Citizen*. Stoddart, Toronto. Gutstein, D. (2009) *Not a Conspiracy Theory: How Business Propaganda Hijacks Democracy*. Key Porter Books, Toronto; Carey, A. (1997). *Taking the Risk out of Democracy: Corporate Propaganda versus Freedom and Liberty*. University of Illinois Press, Urbana.
63. Osgood, K. (2006). *Total Cold War: Eisenhower's Secret Propaganda Battle at Home and Abroad*. University Press of Kansas, Kansas City. Saunders, F. S. (1999). *The Cultural Cold War: The CIA and the World of Arts and Letters*. The New Press, New York; Simpson, C. (1994). *Science of Coercion: Communication Research and Psychological Warfare, 1945–1960*. Oxford University Press, Oxford.

-LECTURES-

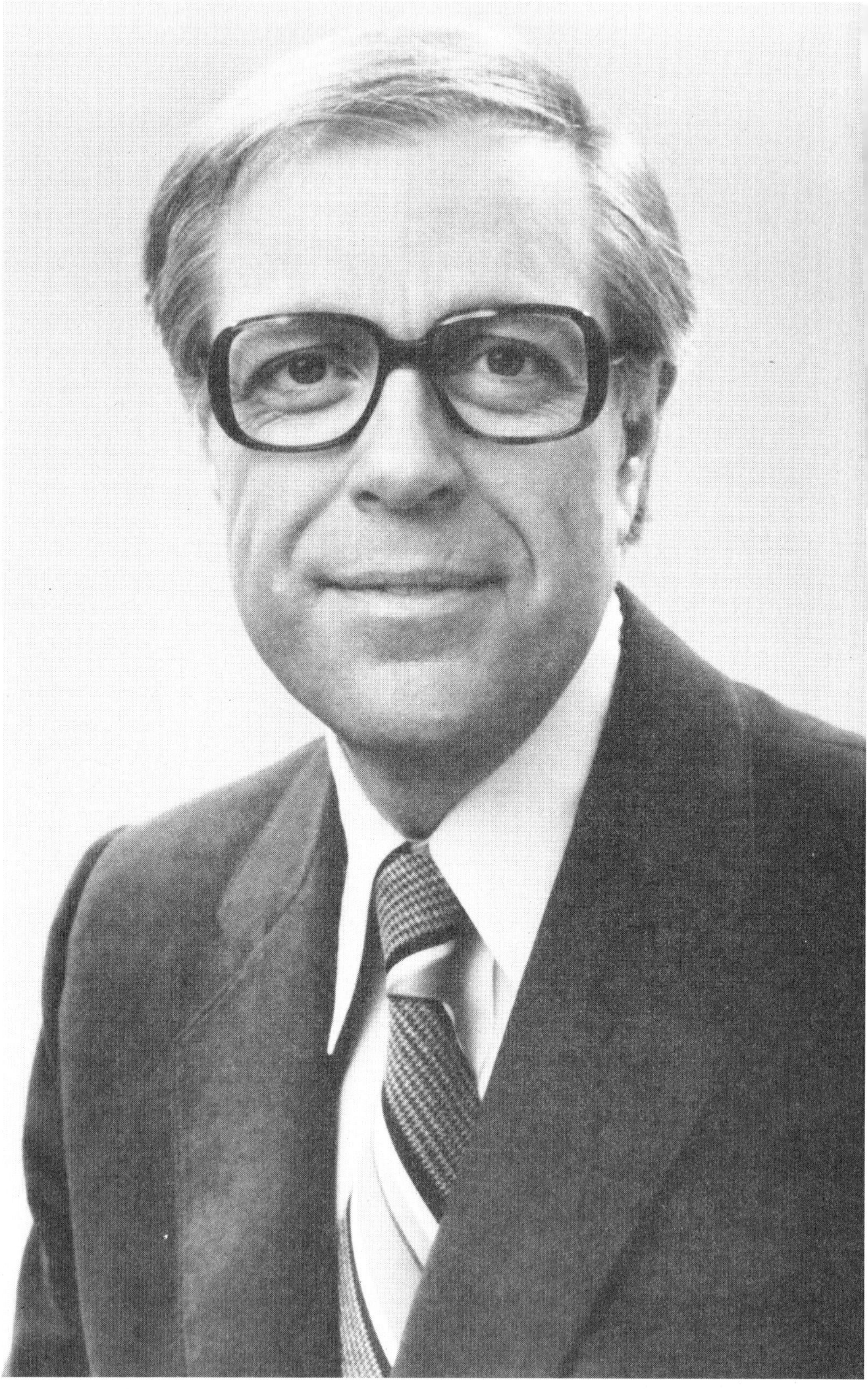

—1981—
KNOWLTON NASH

Knowlton Nash began his career with *The Globe and Mail* before becoming an editor with the British United Press, freelancing for the *Financial Post* and *Maclean's* and becoming CBC's Washington correspondent. In Washington, Nash covered the Cuban missile crisis and the assasination of John F. Kennedy. He interviewed Che Guevara, five U.S. presidents, seven Canadian Prime Ministers, and four Prime Ministers of the United Kingdom. He joined CBC management as head of news and information programming in 1968, and became anchor of *The National* in 1978. Nash was named to both the Order of Canada and the Order of Ontario. He received the President's Award of the Radio and Television News Directors' Association in 1995, and was inducted to the Canadian News Hall of Fame in 1996. He holds four honorary doctorates. In 1992 he was the Max Bell Professor at the University of Regina School of Journalism. In 2006, Nash accepted a lifetime achievement award from the Canadian Journalism Foundation. He is the author of nine books, and was on the founding advisory board for the University of Regina's School of Journalism.

CLEOPATRA, HARLOTS AND GLUE:
The Importance, Standards and Ethics of Modern Journalism

To most of you here, James M. Minifie is, I suppose, just a name, perhaps a symbol... perhaps a picture on the wall.

To me, though, James M. Minifie—or Don Minifie as he was known to his friends—was a friend, a colleague, a mentor, and a man passionately dedicated to improving the quality of journalism. He was a man of intense emotions, and his overwhelming desire—in fact, demand, of himself and his colleagues—was accuracy in reporting. I recall time and time again he'd bitterly complain about errors of fact in copy. As a Washington correspondent of the CBC, and before that for the *New York Herald Tribune*, he spent hours at Congressional Committee hearings, press conferences, watching demonstrations, talking endlessly to sources in and out of government, in embassies, at the State Department, Pentagon and White House and Senate, trying to get the story right.

Don Minifie fully endorsed the comment of Joseph Pulitzer who once said he had three words of advice for journalists: "accuracy, accuracy and accuracy."

In partnership with his striving for accuracy was Don Minifie's endless curiosity about people, about issues, about the impact and repercussion of events. Seeing a press release, hearing a speech, seeing a wire service story, was really just the beginning.

His demand for accuracy, propelled by his curiosity, gave Don Minifie a great many scoops and exclusives as well as professional respect, whether he was covering the Spanish Civil War, Harry Truman, Dwight Eisenhower, John Kennedy, the Black Revolution in the U.S., or the Vietnam War.

That demanding, meticulous, striving search for accuracy and his never-ending curiosity were central characteristics of Don Minifie. He had one other dominating characteristic and that was enthusiasm.

I've never met anyone who so enjoyed, who was so thoroughly excited by, enthused by, and loved being a journalist than did James M. Minifie.

It always has struck me that those three qualities of his—an implacable demand for accuracy, an insatiable curiosity and an irrepressible joy in being a journalist—are the qualities the very best journalists must have. And they are qualities that bring me to the theme of my comments today—my comments entitled, "Cleopatra, Harlots and Glue."

Now you may not think those three have much in common but they do indeed; they all relate one way or another to the importance of, the ethics of, the standards of, modern journalism.

IMPORTANCE

First let me take the "glue" part of my title: I profoundly believe journalism is the glue that holds together our democratic society. We stake everything on a rational dialogue of an informed public and on an awareness of public concerns by our political leadership. Only journalism can reach the mass of the people to provide information they must have for that rational dialogue. And only journalism can, in effect, send messages back and forth between the masses and the politicians, between the governed and the governing.

So without journalism you simply can't have a viable democratic state. It is, as I've said, the necessary glue that holds us together. But two factors challenge the effectiveness of that journalistic role.

EXTERNAL CHALLENGE

First, the Cleopatra syndrome. If you remember your Shakespeare, when the messenger arrives and advises Cleopatra that Marc Anthony has married Octavia, Cleopatra's anger at the news is taken out on the messenger. She calls him an "infectious pestilence," and suggests he be "whipped by wire," "stewed in brine" and "smart in lingering pickle," be scalped and finally killed. Obviously she was upset with the news and blamed the messenger.

Ending her tirade, Cleopatra says, "Though it be honest, it is never good to bring bad news." In saying that, she was echoing what Sophocles said a few centuries earlier: "None love the messenger who brings bad news." That's the essence of the Cleopatra Syndrome: if you don't like the message, blame the Messenger. And that's exactly what many of society's leaders are doing today: when they don't like the message they blame the media. And they try to change the message, to distort reality so that the public will buy their arguments and not those of their political, social or economic adversaries. A few—and only a few—are quite prepared to lie and cheat to try to persuade the public of their point of view. A great many others may be less blatant rascals in their effort to distort reality for their own benefit, but are equally dangerous in their attempts to have their point of view dominate over all others. Their attempts range from delicate forms of bribery to powerful appeals to patriotism, from threats of legal action or public denunciation, to privileged, but dangerously conditioned private access to the highest decision-makers.

But despite Cleopatra, despite contemporary attempts to manipulate the media, journalists must vigilantly, constantly strive to present a fair reflection of reality even if that reality is sometimes unpleasant. And that reality includes airing widely, and sometimes wildly, differing points of view. I believe journalism serves democracy best when it does this because in a democracy there always must be freedom for the thought you hate.

So the "Cleopatra Syndrome" is the critical external factor challenging journalism's fundamental role in helping to make democracy work.

INTERNAL CHALLENGE

The second critical factor is internal. It is credibility. Our credibility is the central pillar of the media's strength. Without it, we have nothing.

Perhaps the harshest criticism of journalism came about half a century ago from the British Prime Minister, Stanley Baldwin. He was attacking some of the more virulent forms of yellow journalism in Fleet Street which had plagued him. He told the House of Commons that some journalists enjoy "power without responsibility . . . the prerogative of the harlot throughout the ages." That Baldwin accusation still stings today as some in journalism continue to ignore their responsibility to journalistic professionalism and to our democratic society by pandering to the lowest common denominator with trash journalism . . . lazy, shallow, sensationalized, simplistic and too often inaccurate journalism. That, in abbreviated form, is my thesis and perhaps explains the title of my lecture: that journalism is the glue of our democratic society; that in carrying out our responsibility to society to help hold it together, journalism is challenged by the external threat of the Cleopatra Syndrome, the attempt to distort reality by those who don't like reality; and that journalism is challenged internally by the quality of our credibility . . . our fairness, our honesty, our accuracy—our ability to combat effectively the accusation of being harlots with power but no responsibility.

GLUE

Let me explore the first proposition that journalism is the glue that holds together a democratic society. In the first place, I should say this is a relatively new phenomenon that has evolved as democracy itself has evolved. Indeed, only in this century has this really developed with the transfer of political power from the classes to the masses, and especially since the arrival of television news 30 years ago. A real, participatory democracy can't survive without free, independent and professionally and socially responsible journalism. Only through an independent and responsible journalism can the citizens of a democracy know what's going on, who's saying what, and what the background and implications are of the issues being debated, events occurring and actions taken. As we move through the 1980s, it's clear that issues and events are moving so quickly and becoming so complicated, things are so inter-related, that there, in fact, seem to be no clear-cut solutions to anything any more, just trade-offs. So our need to know what's being traded off for what gains and what losses, becomes more critical than ever.

AGENT FOR THE PUBLIC

In our increasingly complex society, the media constitute the only way the mass of the people can find out what's going on, can communicate with each other, and can communicate with their government and through which their government can communicate with them.

In essence, modern government in a democratic society is becoming more and more government by public words rather than government by private deeds as it used to be. This, in turn, increases the importance of journalism in a democracy as, in effect, an agent of the public. That's our "glue" role between the governed and the governing: to inform, to explain, to background, to look to the future, to stimulate interest in public affairs, to review various points of view on issues, actions and events, to reflect social co-operation as well as social confrontation. If we don't perform that role with utmost professional and social responsibility acting as an agent for the public, then we not only fail as journalists, we fatally undermine our democratic society itself.

I was reading somewhat wistfully the other day a book on the history of the BBC which records a perhaps more journalistically leisurely day. In one instance the anchor-person on the BBC main radio news went on the air saying: "Good evening. This is Good Friday. There is no news. Good night." With so much happening these days, that kind of a newscast is improbable today. Winston Churchill once said, "History is just one damn thing after another." And that applies to journalism too, since, essentially, journalism is history on the run ... a first draft of the historical record.

HISTORY
May I, for a few moments, look back at history—at the evolution of our practices, ethics and standards in journalism.

Journalism goes back to the earliest days of Rome, if not before, and ever since there have been arguments about objectivity, balance, fairness and accuracy. I suppose the earliest record of that argument may have been at the trial of Jesus Christ when Pontius Pilate raised the question: "What is truth?"

Mass media emerged very much later, in the 1400s. And as soon as the printing press was invented, Church and State censorship scrambled to control the media. But the technology of mass communication, mass printing—as developed by Johannes Gutenburg and his presses—began to undermine the authoritarianism of Church and State. Soon the spread of printed material simply swamped the ability of government to censor everything before it was printed.

So governments were forced to resort to punishing editors after publication, not before.

It was John Milton's objections to prior restraint on publishing in England which laid the cornerstone for the eventual freedom of the press. He argued as early as 1644 for what he called the "free marketplace of ideas." He felt if all ideas were freely published, the best ones would win the most public support. An editor's total freedom, he argued, was the prerequisite for an effective democracy. This eventually led to the very opposite of authoritarianism—to a libertarian laissez-faire theory of the media.

The assumption was that the citizen could and would read all available journalism, absorb all political points of view, sort out the good ideas from the bad, and come to his or her own conclusions.

This perhaps excessively optimistic view of the citizen and the media was pursued in the United States a bit later by Thomas Jefferson. He said: "Were it left to me to decide whether we should have a government without newspapers or newspapers without a government, I should not hesitate a moment to prefer the latter"—that is, newspapers without government.

I should quickly point out, however, Jefferson said that before he became President of the United States. He had, I believe, a rather different point of view once in government in the White House. But obviously the media were becoming important. For instance, Napoleon said, "I fear three newspapers more than a thousand bayonets." And, of course, in England there was Edmund Burke's comment when the right to publish Parliamentary debates was granted. He looked up at the Press Gallery in the House of Commons saying: "Yonder sits the Fourth Estate, more important than them all."

Important the Fourth Estate was then, but it quickly grew even more so. In the nineteenth century, most of the press was a "party press" bought and paid for by political parties. So it was necessary, but probably impossible, for a citizen to read all the papers to get a full perspective.

Then along came the news agencies—the wire services such as Reuters and Associated Press—providing news to newspapers of all political stripes. That forced a political neutrality in the wire service reports and, in turn, began to force newspapers into a rough form of political balance and fairness.

Then, too, advertising came along. Publishers found they could survive on advertising revenue instead of political party subsidy.

So the arrival of advertising and the news agencies played a key role in the evolution of a free and independent mass media, almost as fundamental as the philosophical arguments of Milton and the printing presses of Gutenburg.

TELEVISION

The next big explosion in news dissemination was, of course, radio and television, and for the last 30 years, especially television.

Television is without doubt the most dramatic and most effective means of mass communication the world has ever seen, the most powerful instrument of journalism in history. Survey after survey shows most people find out what's happening in the world from television. And most people, according to the surveys, put more belief in what they see on television news than what they read in the papers. The recent Kent Royal Commission on newspapers has reiterated that.

I saw a survey a while back which vividly reaffirms that, for me, rather worrisome reality. The survey asked people which would they believe if they saw conflicting stories on the CBC's *National* and in their local newspapers. By something like a five to one margin, they said *The National*. Now for me, that not only is worrisome, it's downright frightening. As good as I think *The National* is, I know it's not five times more reliable than the newspapers. I know that for anyone to be well informed they must read the papers, magazines, books and listen to radio as well as watch the television news.

But it is a reality that, like it or not, television has become the most believable and central source of news for most Canadians. And, because it has such a huge platform, television journalism has the heaviest responsibility in its news programs to be more than just a circus, a show, an entertainment mélange of bubble gum news and trivialized glances at important issues and events. The bigger the platform, the bigger the responsibility.

Let's remember, though, there are limits on the capacity of each part of the media. Television, for example, cannot deal in as much detail in explaining ideas and abstractions as newspapers and magazines can. TV is more impressionistic, more emotional, more visceral, while the printed word is more structured, more intellectual. That wise old Saskatchewanian, Graham Spry, once said: "Information is the prime, integrating factor creating, nourishing, adjusting and sustaining a society."

MANIPULATING THE MEDIA

And it is precisely because the media are the glue in our society, providing that life-sustaining information, that society's leaders try to manipulate the media. That's why elites try to have their own political, social and economic messages dominate the news rather than somebody else's. It's why political parties alternately woo and castigate the media. They want to shape our reporting to their objective. And their objective, of course, is to win elections, not necessarily to be fair or honest or sometimes even accurate in what they say and do.

Politicians and governments know full well there are no solutions to problems any more, as I mentioned earlier, only trade-offs, and they seek to mask their trade-offs. George Bernard Shaw once said, "A government that robs Peter to pay Paul can always depend on the support of Paul." But if it wants to stay in office, it also had better make sure there are more Pauls than Peters.

Prime Ministers, Presidents, all political leaders, view managing the media as a vital precondition to their domination of the Legislature, the public, and the whole political process. It's the same manipulating story in business, labour, or any field where someone is trying to persuade the public that their ideas or products are the best. They try to sell their ideas or products in the most glowing terms, emphasizing good points, ignoring bad points, and all too often economizing on truth.

But stripped of the glowing protective colouration of public relations, what governments, politicians, business, labour and social activists of all kinds want is to have the media reflect their own self image—in itself, a natural desire. They prefer a sympathetic and sometimes sycophantic media, not an assertively independent media.

I was chatting about this at lunch not long ago with an old colleague of mine, Morley Safer, who is a correspondent on the CBS program *60 Minutes*. Morley used to be a CBC correspondent and before he joined *60 Minutes* he was in Vietnam for CBS. In fact, he probably was the best broadcast journalist in Vietnam, more vividly and effectively reflecting the real issues of that war than anyone else. So much so, that President Lyndon Johnson tried to have him fired because, Johnson said, "he's a communist." When repeatedly assured that Safer was a Canadian, not a communist, Johnson replied that, well, anyway, he knew something was wrong with him.

The trouble, of course, was that like Cleopatra, President Johnson simply did not want to hear the harsh truth. He did not want to hear the reality of Vietnam because it profoundly differed from his perception and led people to question what he was doing.

ADVERTISERS

I mentioned earlier that advertising played a key role about 100 years or more ago, in freeing publishers from the straitjacket of political subsidy and control. That was a major step toward freedom of the media. Advertisers, of course, sell their products with shimmering promises and smiling optimism, although sometimes taking excessive liberty with truth.

Occasionally they go further. Sometimes in evaluating a product the media will find there is less in it than meets the eye. And this can lead to shrill, vituperative threats from the product-maker damning the media as biased, unfair and anti-business. I certainly know the CBC has had some of that reaction to consumer programs such as the very popular *Marketplace* or other programs examining advertising claims.

But there is a more insidious danger when advertisers demand a happier news environment in which to place their ads. For instance, a couple of months ago, John Craig Eaton, Chairman of Eaton's stores and one of the most powerful advertisers in Canada, warned in a Toronto speech that newspapers must provide what he called a more positive content or else, he said, advertisers would stop putting ads in the papers.

Although Mr. Eaton agreed newspapers should report gloomy economic news, fires and crime, the newspaper environment itself, he said, should find new ways to project what he called "good vibes." "It must be balanced equally," he said, "with positive, stimulating and exciting content . . . you must create more good vibes than bad."

I can appreciate his desire and his perspective, but for journalists, and taken on the face of it, that is a prescription for journalistic disaster. C.P. Scott, Editor and owner of the *Manchester Guardian,* said some 60 years ago, "A newspaper has two sides to it. It is a business like any other and has to pay in the material sense in order to live. But it is much more than a business: it is an institution; it reflects and influences the life of the whole community . . . its primary office is the gathering of news. At the peril of its soul, it must see that the supply is not tainted." To deliberately set out to "taint" the news with more "good vibes than bad" too easily becomes a prescription for "happy talk" news. Certainly the media should and must look for stories that reflect the community as a whole and not just the noisier elements. That is part of having a professionally and socially responsible journalism. But to threaten the media with economic reprisals if there are not more "good vibes than bad" reported comes perilously close to those who demand a media subservient to political masters.

FREEDOM

Freedom of the media—freedom for an assertively independent media which reports "good vibes" or bad as reality demands—is the price of democracy. It is a necessity for a mature, well-informed electorate. It's a simple fact that those in authority, whether in the public or private sectors, must be able to cope with a sometimes cantankerous media, sometimes obstinate media, so that the country as a whole can preserve the greater values of freedom of expression and the right of people to know.

That freedom, incidentally, doesn't exist very widely in the world. Today, according to the International Press Institute in London, only about 20 countries actually have what we know as a free media. The demand to provide "good vibes" in a political sense exists in all dictatorships whether communist or fascist, in most of the so-called "Third World," in the Middle East, South America and Asia.

The leaders of these countries view the media as an instrument of the State. They demand and they get "good vibes" because, in their dictatorial judgment, that will help improve society. Much of that philosophy is propelling a current and dangerous UNESCO drive to harness all the world's media to a "New World Information Order" that would restrict media freedom. Basically, UNESCO wants to improve reporting on developments in the Third World—in itself a good idea. But UNESCO's remedy is to use the media to promote Third World objectives, all clothed in language professing protection of the citizens and greater understanding. In fact, the UNESCO declaration is a bit breath-taking in its scope. Indicative of the approach, it's known as the "UNESCO Declaration on Fundamental Principles Concerning the Contribution of the Mass Media to Strengthening Peace and International Understanding, the Promotion of Human Rights, and to Countering Racialism, Apartheid, and Incitement to War."

That's quite a mouthful of international do-goodery, but it simply means the media must be an instrument of the State. I think the media can do much more good for society by devoting the news pages to being an assertively independent, fair witness to reality without any externally-imposed political or economic straitjacket.

JOURNALISTS, NOT ENTERTAINERS

Criticism of the media today comes from governments and organizations all too often not so much because of a lack of accuracy, but in a dissatisfaction with the nature of the messages we deliver.

While some politicians, businessmen and labour leaders may want to kill the messenger for delivering "bad vibes" and negative messages, journalists have to remember that we are not entertainers. We're not here to entertain or please politicians, businessmen or labour leaders. We're not singers, dancers, jugglers or actors seeking audience applause. Our basic job is not necessarily to please anybody, I suppose, except Diogenes with his lamp.

Therefore, so long as we in journalism are doing our proper, professionally and socially responsible job as agents for the public, there will and there in fact should be a continuing love-hate relationship . . . often tempestuous, sometimes ferocious, but a never-ending conflict between the media and the news-makers.

Let's remember our jobs are simply quite different. The news-makers are trying to sell something—an idea or a product. The media are trying to reflect reality; not only one person's or party's idea, or one company's product, but all ideas and products that have relevance and importance to society.

CREDIBILITY

There is, however, another side to all this. There are those who feel the most formidable threat to consistently responsible journalism comes not so much from the external pressures of politicians, bureaucrats, businessmen, labour and social activists, trying to manipulate the news, but from the media themselves. And I share some of that apprehension.

Certainly, our job must be to enlarge public understanding of uncomfortable problems, and I quite understand how that gets some people riled up. But in doing our job, in getting some people riled up, our effectiveness boils down to one word: credibility. As I said at the very beginning, without credibility we've got nothing.

And this is the heart of what I wanted to say today. I wanted to say it, though, within the context of the critical importance of the media to society and of all the pressures on the media to distort and to manipulate news.

The heart and soul of our business is our credibility. We get that credibility, and the respect and the power that go with it, only by being a socially and professionally responsible agent for the public. Reporters, editors, producers, and all of us in journalism and the organizations we work for, do have power—immense power—because it is only through us that the public at large knows what's happening, how, where, when and why. So the public, as well as the news-makers, have a right to expect a proper journalistic job. That means reporting the news accurately, fairly, thoroughly, comprehensively and in a balanced manner.

In some ways journalists have to have the same attitude to news as an employee of a bank has to money that isn't theirs. We're handling it on behalf of other people, so it cannot be converted to our own use. If we do, it's embezzlement. Reporters cannot try to change people's minds or confirm their beliefs. We must give untainted news so the public can make up its own mind. We can report apparent abuse, but not crusade for its abolition; we can call attention to what seems to be law-breaking, but not advocate prosecution; report a demonstration, but not take sides. In other words, don't embezzle the news.

Reporters simply report; we do not approve or disapprove. We're not a bunch of little moral thermometers. There are, of course, those journalists who do comment, who do advocate, who do approve or disapprove, but they are opinion columnists and commentators and editorial writers. That's a separate and necessary journalistic function, but quite different from news reporting about which I am primarily concerned. What is critical is never to confuse or contaminate fact with opinion within news stories—to always clearly separate what's news and what is opinion.

There is a certain contemporary distemper about our reportage. Some of it is self-serving by would-be news manipulators but some is from our clients—from the people we really work for, the public. Since, I believe, we are accountable to the public, we'd better listen to the concerns of the public and we'd better examine ourselves.

And, in examining ourselves, let me say first and unequivocally that I think the media today are more honest, more comprehensive, fairer, better overall, than ever before in journalistic history. But it's not good enough—not good enough because journalism's role today is more important than it has ever been to our democratic society. Thus we must narrow even more the differences between our professed ideals and our daily practice.

So let's look at ourselves.

"SHOWBIZ" NEWS

Perhaps the most worrying cancer on journalism today is the idea that the news business is show business.

It sure as hell is not.

There is a role for "show biz" in news, but it is supplementary to the basic function. In news, the important must always take precedence over the merely interesting. Of course, a journalist must make certain the important is written and produced in as interesting, attractive and understandable a way as possible, without trivializing or distorting the story. That's especially true for television journalism where pacing and snappy production values are needed because of TV's more transitory character.

But the function of all these techniques is to enhance understanding of the facts, not to overwhelm them. Too often today some news organizations and reporters give priority to theatricality over substance. That's a particular danger for television and tabloids which too often surrender to their susceptibility to trash journalism in a frantic search for greater ratings and readership. When "show biz" takes over news, a totally different set of priorities result. The emphasis is on entertaining, not on informing and enlightening. Sometimes I think it would be a good idea to take some of the glamour out of the news business and thereby lessen the dangerous infiltration of "show-biz."

A HOT PROFESSION

Journalism today is a "hot profession." It has graduated from the raffish irresponsibility of the fedora and trench coat days of the *Front Page* to the zealous crusading of the post-Watergate era. But the over-glamorizing of investigative reportage—of the valid work of Woodward and Bernstein or Seymour Hersh—has too often led to journalistic irresponsibility.

I am an ardent supporter of investigative reportage. It can be journalism at its finest when done with thoroughness, painstaking accuracy, honesty and fairness. But serious problems have arisen. Too many people try quickie investigative journalism on the cheap. It's not cheap; it's damn expensive, time-consuming, often frustrating and always laborious.

But because of their hurry for the glamour of investigative journalism some organizations and some reporters don't want to pay the price. For some reporters, under pressure from editors for a scoop, under their own ambition pressures for instant fame, promotion and money, they simply commit journalistic felony. In their self-indulgence, they embezzle at the bank of journalistic credibility by unscrupulous or careless or lazy reporting.

You're all familiar with the tragedy of Janet Cooke of the *Washington Post*, a talented young reporter who fabricated a story brilliant enough to win, temporarily, a Pulitzer Prize. Or the gifted Donald Ramsay of the *Toronto Sun* who this summer had a dramatic scoop about a Cabinet member in Ottawa using his position to make a fortune in the stock market. But it just was not true. They faked their stories. They ruined their own careers. They betrayed all journalists.

All the abject apologies of the *Toronto Sun* or the *Washington Post* cannot make up the harm done not only to their own credibility, but to the credibility of journalism as a whole. These examples are warnings for journalists against letting ambition get in the way of integrity.

"NEW JOURNALISM"

The glamour of "Deep Throat" and his secrets has been particularly seductive to young, ambitious reporters attracted to something called the "new journalism." For me, that's an arrogant, pretentious and contemptuous term reflecting a style that seems to put more weight on assertion than on evidence—that puts a premium on impressionistic and cynical reporting rather than on the plodding, detail work of truly investigative reportage. It makes a story more exciting, more dramatic, more high profile, but it's a trap—a trap for the reporter and for the paper or station he or she works for. Sooner or later, the reporter taking this ethically loose career path gets caught, as witness Janet Cooke in Washington or Donald Ramsay in Toronto.

Important and valuable as investigative journalism is, we need to be wary of a crusading penchant for righting perceived wrongs. This, too, can be part of what some call the "new journalism." Now, of course, there's nothing wrong at all about righting wrongs, about seeking justice. And if you want to do that, go into politics, or be a social activist of one kind or another, or be a columnist or commentator or an editorial writer. But don't be a reporter. Part of a reporter's job is indeed to expose abuse of power, but it's not to prosecute or convict.

OBJECTIVITY

There is a great deal of talk about the need of objectivity in journalism. I happen to think objectivity is impossible to achieve because we are all products of our background and environment, with various points of view. But what must be done is to continually strive for objectivity—to put aside as much as humanly possible our prejudices, the most passionate likes and dislikes of political leaders especially, and strive to come as close to objectivity as we can. In other words, I suppose, simply to be fair. And I prefer the word "fair" to "objective."

In speaking of fairness, that also means equality of fairness. It is easier to be fair to a big man than to a small man. It is easier to be fair to someone who can hit you back. It is easier to be fair to someone you like. By fairness, I mean giving justice to all—big and little, the likeable and the unlikeable.

There is another word that comes into play in discussing the role of the media and that is "adversary." There are those who say there must be an "adversary relationship" between the media and the politicians and the government. I simply don't agree. I think that's hairy-chested, poisonous machismo—a breast-beating search for self importance. And these days more journalists are ruined by self-importance than by liquor—which, in itself, is saying something. If the word "adversary" means enemy or to oppose as it does in most dictionaries I've seen, then that's the job of the official opposition, not the media. The media's job is to inform, to enlighten, to investigate, to reflect and reveal what some in power might rather not see exposed to the public. But that's different from assuming the role of an adversary.

CYNICISM

Cynicism is yet another word that applies too often these days to some reporters. I believe news people must develop a healthy skepticism, but must stop short of cynicism. Skepticism is necessary for an enquiring mind; cynicism is a malign prejudgment. It may be that the cynicism we see today is a reaction to seeing too many authorities talking high principles and using low practices, seeking to manipulate the news. Perhaps Senator Keith Davey was right when he said that for many idealistic young journalists the newsrooms of Canada are "boneyards of broken dreams."

But I hope he's wrong. Sure, there are rascals and ne'er-do-wells in politics or business or labour and probably in journalism too for that matter—but they don't reflect the majority of politicians or businessmen or labour leaders. Therefore it is unfair and unprofessional for a reporter to take the cynic's view into his work.

RIGHT TO KNOW

Finally, there is the major ethical problem of when the public's right to know conflicts with the equally fundamental right in a democracy of privacy and a fair trial. Conflict it certainly does. Unhappily, there is no clear-cut formula for when the right to know overrides the right to privacy, except that it does so, in my judgment, rarely.

If evidence of abuse of power is uncovered, past personal history of the public official is important and relevant in evaluating his or her current public duties. But these, and perhaps a few other circumstances, must be exceptions to a general rule that the right of privacy is generally supreme. The media have no divine right to recklessly, lasciviously prowl through the private lives of citizens on journalistic "fishing expeditions."

Every time the conflict arises between the right to know and the right to privacy, reporters and editors have to ask themselves seriously: is the story important, relevant, and fair? It's a judgment call, but one based on the highest sense of journalistic professionalism, not on prurient curiosity intended to titillate.

MIRROR

Let's remember too, the media are not simply spectators at the issues and events of our time. We are—let's admit it—participants, because we in the media identify and choose what we consider are the significant trends, issues and events, and set others aside. The media hold a mirror up to society but we do so selectively. We have to recognize the very raising of the mirror will change the character of the event or issue by intensifying it or glamourizing it or denigrating it. So we must be as sure as we can that we are giving a fair reflection of reality and truth when we raise that mirror.

We're not giving truth a fair chance if we are adversaries, if we sensationalize, if we're lazy or careless or unscrupulous, if we're "show biz," if we're shallow—simplistically looking only for good guys and bad guys. Too many in the media today do not look deeply enough for the significant nuances and subtleties of complex situations.

All these ethical and practical frailties exist today among reporters and editors—less, as I said before, than ever, but they're still there and need to be sharply diminished if we in journalism are to live up to our social and professional responsibilities. I am not sure precisely how to do that, except by emphasizing and re-emphasizing within our newsrooms the fundamental ethics and standards essential to a professionally and socially responsible journalism. And that's also a responsibility for the newspapers, networks, stations and magazines for which we work.

THE ORGANIZATION

The reporter has a responsibility to be fair, accurate and thorough. So does the news organization, and it must spell out its policies and practices. It must regularly articulate its standards to reporters and editors and to the public. It must let the public measure its practices against its policies to be sure the latter are being lived up to. Sometimes this is done individually by newspapers with their own "ombudsman." Sometimes it is done through Press Councils. Radio and television have responsibilities to the Canadian Radio-television and Telecommunications Commission, the government regulatory agency, and some work closely with their communities. But clearly not enough is being done, not enough news organizations take this part of their role seriously. Some are just lazy. A few feel the public has no right to stick its nose into their business. I, for one, think the public has that right, since we are responsible to the public as its "agent"—as the link between the mass of people and our political, social and economic leaders.

It is the responsibility of news organizations also to provide overall balance and comprehensiveness in coverage. And to be impartial in news stories. That means having the widest possible range of views expressed and taking into account the weight of opinion holding those views. The greater emphasis obviously goes to views that are held by more people. But the challenging of the establishment and of accepted orthodoxies must be reported, too, since an important function of the media is to alert society to change.

TELEVISION CHALLENGE

Television organizations have particular problems. Even more than newspapers, magazines and radio, the pressures of time and space force a worrisome compression in television newscasts. There must be longer TV newscasts and more news programs exploring issues, events and personalities.

One difficulty with television is that while it has all the opportunities of its impact and believability, it also has all the temptations of tabloid journalism. Often in TV, we communicate lots of basic information but make too little effort to communicate knowledge. There is a profound difference between the two.

I'm glad to say the CBC is clearly leading the way in trying to provide both information and knowledge, with its new news and current affairs programming. *The National* is moving into prime time at 10:00 p.m., immediately followed by *The Journal,* a program examining in some detail, the central issues, events and people of the day. What we need is more of this kind of comprehensive background programming at both the network and local levels. It's the only way we can properly function as agents for the public in providing information and knowledge on what is happening and why.

You can measure the quality of any journalistic organization by the effort it puts into seeking to avoid the temptations of unprofessionalism that I've outlined. Some try harder than others. Some succeed better than others. What's important is for the organizations and individual reporters and editors to recognize the temptations and take action to try to eliminate them.

ORGANIZATIONS

Let me sum up in capsule form the standards, and ethical responsibilities both for the individual journalist and for the news organization itself, as I see them.

For news organizations there should be:

- A written code of policies and standards;
- An internal process for the regular articulation, application and monitoring of those policies and standards;
- Availability of the code to the public so it can measure policies against practices;
- Greater responsiveness to public criticism;
- A process of redress for errors or unfairness;
- A clear separation between opinion journalism and factual reportage;
- A clear priority for the important over the interesting but trivial;
- Better hiring practices;
- Improved training both at the beginning and during staff careers;
- More specialized reporters to provide explanation and enlightenment on significant events and issues at home and abroad;
- No overvaluation of the argumentative and undervaluation of the reasoned;
- Examination of the quiet achievement as well as the splashy success;
- Readiness to withstand the pressures of the news manipulators whether they be advertisers, politicians, labour leaders or social activists;

- An underlying philosophy that the heart and soul of the news business is its credibility.

INDIVIDUALS

The responsibilities of individual journalists include the following:

- Remember you are an agent of the public serving as the link between the governed and the governing;
- Put aside your own prejudices in doing stories and strive to be objective, and certainly be fair;
- Reporters are not crusaders. They are producers of fact, not opinion;
- Do not embellish, fabricate or shrink reality even in small ways such as illustrative but fictional quotes;
- You're not an adversary, only an observer;
- Do not sensationalize;
- Be accurate, thorough, balanced, comprehensive and fair;
- Do not let ambition overcome your integrity;
- Hear the soft-spoken as well as the loud-spoken;
- Be skeptical, but not cynical;
- Invade a person's privacy with extreme care and only if it's important and relevant.

I've spent a good many years in radio, television, wire services and newspaper newsrooms. Of course I know practice does not always measure up to good intentions. It likely never will, given the constraints of time, space, and human frailty. But what is important is that we: have those good intentions and guidelines; articulate those policies, standards and ethics; monitor and review them; make the public aware of them; and come as close as humanly possible to achieving them.

I can think of no occupation that performs a higher public service than serving the public's desire, and need, to know. Especially so, in this "age of anxiety." The very survival of democracy itself depends on how well the journalist performs that service.

The best guarantee of performing well is a steady accumulation of standards, and by studying the best in journalism. The very best role model I can think of is the man after whom this lecture is named—James M. Minifie. As I said at the very beginning, he brought to his work the qualities essential today for anyone reaching for a successful journalistic career: an implacable demand for accuracy and fairness; an insatiable curiosity; and joy in being a journalist.

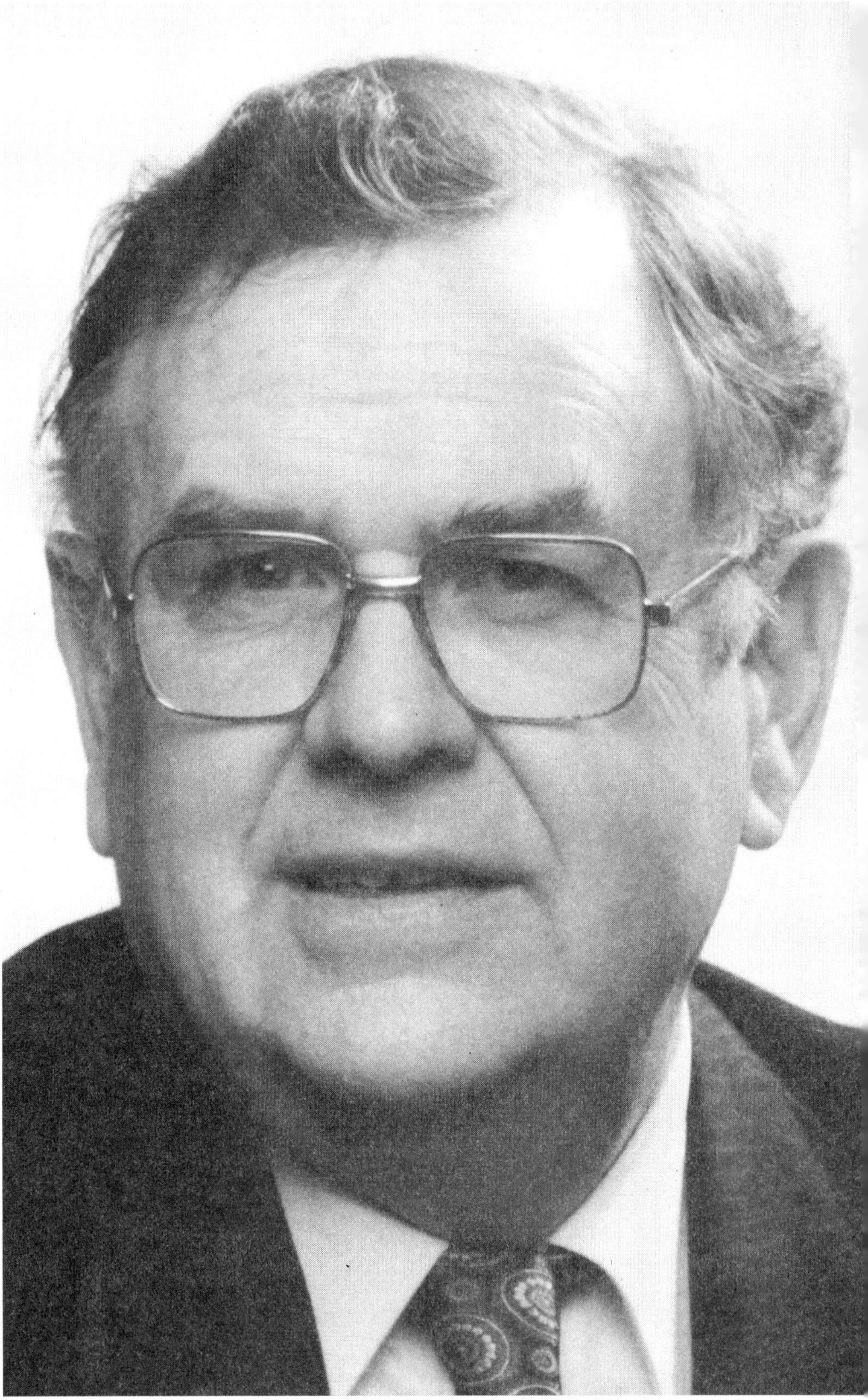

–1982–

CLARK DAVEY

Clark W. Davey graduated from the first degree course in Journalism in Canada at the University of Western Ontario in 1948. He served *The Globe and Mail* as Parliamentary Correspondent from 1956 to 1960 and as Managing Editor from 1963 to 1978. He was the Publisher of the *Vancouver Sun* from 1978 to 1983, the *Montreal Gazette* from 1983 to 1989 and the *Ottawa Citizen* from 1989 to 1992. He is a past chairman and executive secretary of the Michener Awards Foundation, and the 2009 recipient of the Michener Lifetime Achievement Award for public service journalism. Davey is also a past president and chairman of the Canadian Press and past chairman of the Canadian Managing Editors Conference.

1982 | CLARK DAVEY

BACK TO BASICS:
The Enemy is Us

It perhaps should not need saying but I am flattered to be here as the first representative of the print media to give this lecture in honour of James M. Minifie, known to me and his other colleagues in journalism, both print and electronic, as Don.

I'm not sure exactly when I met him but it was in the period loosely referred to as the Diefenbaker years, years when being a national political correspondent was perhaps no less hectic than it is now but in a considerably different way. I recall flying into Regina late on the night of June 10, 1957, with prime minister-elect Diefenbaker. The national media accompanying him on that flight consisted of only three print reporters, from each of the Toronto newspapers. The Canadian Press reporter had gone home exhausted a day or three before, and as chairman of CP I'm almost ashamed to say that our national news gathering agency didn't like Mr. Diefenbaker's chances enough to staff him on election night.

There were no representatives of the electronic media, not even the CBC, aboard and we had to fly to Regina rather than Saskatoon in order to get access to the national network. Shades of the crystal radio era.

Don Minifie's contribution to a whole generation of us who were trying to grow up journalistically in those simpler times was to demonstrate by shining example that it was possible to be both a good—not just good but outstanding—practitioner of our craft and a gentleman to boot. A good many members of our fraternity today would be the better for following that example. I am sure Don would have been thrilled to have his name associated with this university and with its school of journalism.

Perhaps I might be permitted a word or two on the subject of journalism education itself. As most of you must be aware, this was a disastrous year for those in the 1982 graduating class who were seeking permanent work in daily print journalism. Caught as we were at what we hope was the bottom of the economic saucer, editors across the country were forced to turn away scores of young journalists who had demonstrated by their newsroom performance their right to a job.

THE YOUNG ACTIVISTS
I know there was no more difficult day in a series not exactly noted for its joyfulness when Bruce Larsen, our managing editor, and I decided we could keep none of our summer group, not even the top three whom we knew had the talent and the discipline to make an instant contribution to improving the quality of our newspaper. Some of the people turned away will never find their way back and that, in a sense, is almost more tragic for us than for them.

I don't believe that same situation is likely to happen again, and I hope it doesn't blunt the desire so many bright young Canadians have to work for a better society through their involvement with the media. One of the most encouraging developments of the last two or three years was the return of the young activist journalist, bent on changing the world rather than, as had been the case through the latter part of the seventies, trying to find a safe job in an increasingly competitive world.

We in the media—and I would specifically and importantly include the Newspaper Guild in this embrace—have an obligation to work out a system which in future summers of economic malaise would permit us to offer more than pious hope to a substantially increased number of these very bright, very dedicated journalists.

As the good ladies on the CBC *Journal* have found, there's a considerable professional danger in following Knowlton Nash in anything. Knowlton's speech last year on this same occasion touched so many of the important issues of modern journalism in Canada and dealt with them so well that I cast about for months seeking an original theme. Suffice it to say that I didn't find one. I suspect that speakers who follow me to this podium in years to come will be forced to build on one or all of the chords Knowlton played last year.

Ron Robbins and I had talked about the need for a return to the basics, for a renewed emphasis on accuracy almost as a goal in itself, a goal which seemed to have been obscured in the rush to investigative journalism or to personal journalism—the journalism of the me generation—even disco journalism. And I still love the definition of that last one—disco journalism is journalism for people who have to move their hips while they read.

FULL OF ITSELF

I had been thinking—in fits and starts as most of us do about such long-range projects as preparing a lecture—about accuracy, when I was brought up short by a powerfully articulate speech on the shortcomings of the media. It was in May in San Francisco at the annual meeting of the American Newspaper Publishers Association. The speaker was Kurt M. Luedtke, former executive editor of the *Detroit Free Press* and writer of the screenplay for *Absence of Malice,* not every newspaperman's favourite film of the last 12 months. I was prepared to dislike him.

Only minutes earlier James K. Batten, president of Knight Ridder Newspapers Inc., had set the tone for Mr. Luedtke by stating that, "Newspapers too often come off as arrogant, insensitive, self-righteous, sloppy with the facts, and probably too powerful. The truth is a lot of the public don't much like us or trust us. Some of that antagonism, of course, goes with the territory. But we are facing something much more serious than that these days."

Well, as I said, that set the tone for Mr. Luedtke. Here in brief excerpts is the flavour and some of the substance of what he had to say:

"How many of you believe that the public is really capable of making important decisions for this society?

"OK. Then let me ask you this: Are you willing to put your definition of the role of the press to a popular vote? Will you let your readers decide how useful you really are? Will you let the public determine the extent of your rights and privileges?

"Because if you won't, what do we do to protect ourselves against an institution grown so powerful and become so undisciplined that we are defenceless against your ability to affect our lives?

"On your discretionary judgments hang reputations and careers, jail sentences and stock prices, Broadway shows and water rates. You are the mechanism of reward and punishment, the arbiter of right and wrong, the roving eye of daily judgment.

"You no longer shape public opinion, you have supplanted it. There are good men and women who will not stand for office, concerned that you will find their flaws or invent them. Many people who have dealt with you wish that they had not. You are capricious and unpredictable. You are fearsome and you are feared because there is never any way to know whether this time you will be fair and accurate or whether you will not. And there is virtually nothing we can do about it.

"We have bred a whole generation of newspaper people who without apparent difficulty hold simultaneously in their heads the notions that they are armed with a mandate from the public and are accountable to no one save you. You ride whichever horse suits you in the situation until eventually you are persuaded that whatever you choose to do with your newspaper is somehow done in the service of the nation. The press is full of itself these days, and frequently, it is simply full of it.

"There is no such thing as the public's right to know.

"You made that up, taking care not to specify what it was that the public had a right to know. The public knows whatever you choose to tell it, no more, no less. If the public did have a right to know, it would then have something to say about what it is you choose to call news.

"The publication of a newspaper is in itself a pretentious act: it should come with a daily apology. We are met instead with your firm insistence that you must be uncontrolled so that you can perform—unbidden—an essential public service which is so essential that the people for whom it is being performed must not be allowed to control it. Such thinking must inevitably lead to arrogance and it has.

"But your continued claims to special privilege and your vigorous refusal to acknowledge that you do a difficult job imperfectly require that we measure your performance against a much higher standard. It is then clear that while you may be good and useful, you're not that good and useful. You're asking for more than you're entitled to.

"Your shortcomings would be more tolerable if we had a sense that you were willing to listen, but you do not suffer your critics gladly and surely not with humility.

"Your dismissal of your critics is not very subtle, but it is certainly efficient. The silence which results may be soothing, but it is easily mistaken for approval. It is a personal opinion of mine that reporters really don't realize how inaccurate they are simply because they assume, as I must say I would, that a story is correct until someone complains. Left out of that equation are all of those who don't want to make waves, or who are afraid of offending you, or who don't know how, or who cool down and don't bother, or who are brushed off by whomever answers the phone. Call your city desk anonymously some time and see if you like the feeling."

But for all that, Mr. Luedtke gives us a passing grade, grudgingly perhaps, but a passing grade. To wit:

"By a reasonable standard, the American daily print press turns in a performance that is simply competent. It is highly motivated, usually well-intentioned, frequently accurate, occasionally useful. And every now and then, when it combines with the moral indignation for which it is notorious a correct perception of what it is that's really relevant to those it swears to serve, it is a prime mover in the betterment of the society. I'd give it a 'B' and vote to keep it."

Why have I quoted Luedtke at such length? Because simply a lot of what he had to say struck a responsive chord somewhere deep in my own conscience. A working lifetime spent in daily newspapers—the last 20 years in positions which made me a lightning rod for some of the public's most serious complaints—led me to the realization that what Mr. Luedtke and many other critics less well-informed have to say is all too often true.

He had a lot to say, as well, about relevance or, as applied to newspapers, irrelevance, but that's another subject, perhaps for next year's speaker. If we're not prepared to deal with the related problems of credibility and of accountability then our relevance will be, in fact, irrelevant. They're not new problems but they haven't gone away. I'm not even sure they've diminished.

ACCURACY FIRST

One of the big stories of the last 20 years has been the rise of consumerism and the response of the media in reporting the public's demand for better products. From time to time the questioning gaze of organized consumerism has been turned on the media. Each time, it seems to me, the questions have been tougher, more probing. And our responses, I submit, have not kept pace. There's a lull, at the moment, as the public's attention has been diverted by our economic troubles. But I can guarantee that the same public which wants safer cars and a cleaner environment also wants better newspapers. The questions will come again, sharper, more demanding of answers. We will have to be more ready with them than we have been.

Let's start with the question of accuracy. After all there's simply no substitute for being right. One of the hazards of becoming a senior editor or indeed a publisher is that it exposes you to public reporting, to being reported. After my first few skirmishes in the press—sometimes in the very columns for which I was responsible—I began to think I had a communication problem; that I was thinking one thing and saying another. That I was comparing the reports of what I had said with what I thought I had said, a defence I had used often enough first as a reporter and then as an editor having to answer the complaints of other public people who felt they had been skewered by my own reporting or that of one of the reporters for whose work I was accountable. Finally, it dawned on me. The problem was not in my communication prowess but in the reporting skills of some very good reporters.

That's a humbling experience. I have long since learned not to give myself a privilege no other speaker or source has at any paper—that privilege of checking and, if necessary, correcting, a story in which I am a direct participant.

A friend, Roger Tatarian, vice-president and editor of United Press International before leaving to become professor of journalism at California State University, has recounted similar experiences. "And I was to discover," he wrote earlier this year, "that my experience was hardly unique. In fact I have yet to meet an editor, print or electronic, who will not admit in private that he or she, too, has undergone similar trauma—often at the hands of his own staff."

My own experiences have been soul-searing to the point where more often than not I am prepared to accept as fact, until otherwise demonstrated, the complaints of an aroused speaker or source who doesn't like what he has read in my newspaper about his speech or his statement. It has made me more ready than some of the editors in my newsroom would like me to be, to harken to the words of Mr. Luedtke and critics like him.

Roger Tatarian resolved to do something about it in his own small way, a way which underlines not so much the importance of being right but the difficulty in getting there. You can tell reporters, he said, time and time again, that in reporting even the simple words of people, far more is involved than getting a few key quotes: that emphasis, juxtaposition, nuance and other difficult-to-define factors are involved, and that a story can be technically correct in specific detail but still be a bad story if attention is not paid to all the ingredients.

Working on the thesis that no one knows context better than a speaker, Roger turns every one of his intermediate reporting students into a speaker. Every student is required to make a speech from a written text.

Others in the class take notes (no tape recorders) and turn the written stories over to the speaker. The speaker checks quotes and facts against the text, which only he has, and then reports his findings at the next session of the class. Without exception, the speakers are shaken by what their friends and classmates have done to them. In marking up the stories, they are fairly ruthless in pointing out what they hadn't said that way, or hadn't said at all, and chances are better than even that the lead angle will reflect what they regarded as a trivial portion of their speeches. In their verbal reports to the class as a whole, however, the speakers pull their punches, perhaps in fear of lynching. They begin almost invariably by saying that "a lot" of the stories are "pretty good."

Does that mean, you ask, that "a lot" of the stories are ready to be published without a single editing mark? Well, no, not really. How many, then, can be published as is?

A HUMBLING EXPERIENCE

Well, maybe a couple. Like some stories of their professional colleagues, these student stories often fail on minor detail: a wrong age, middle initial, or even a non-crucial date or percentage. But the speaker will spot them, and so will others familiar with the subject, and the reaction is the inevitable one: "If that happens in stories I know something about, what is happening in stories I know nothing about?" What indeed?

Those are questions every reporter and every editor should ask himself or herself every day of his or her working life. It is a humbling experience and not just for the student reporter but for hardened old publishers, one which has encouraged in me a strongly felt need for a return to accuracy—the most basic attribute of the kind of reporting we all want to be able to defend. And, as I've said, it has made me immensely more sensitive to the complaints I must field as a matter of course in my daily work.

I usually come away from such encounters more concerned than ever about fairness—that handmaiden of accuracy. It is one thing to define accuracy even if you admit that truth in journalism is in the eye of the reader or the ear of the listener, and it is quite another to decide what constitutes fairness.

In this regard we face a whole series of self-imposed hurdles: headlines, which we think, often mistakenly I believe, are necessary to increase sales or Nielsen rating points, doctored pictures, anonymous sources (after all, we should be in the business of trying to reveal not protect our sources), and stories without credit of origin.

Of all the complaints made against print journalism, the charge of sensational, inaccurate, unfair headlines is perhaps the easiest to relate to and to sustain. And until there's a much stronger commitment in our business to produce better headlines we're going to stand convicted by an increasingly sophisticated reading public.

One protection some members of our craft have been able to raise against the charges of inaccuracy and unfairness is the almost daily recital of mistakes made and corrections listed. It's one of the healthiest developments in print journalism. Our electronic cousins have lagged far behind and produce a correction usually only when faced with a libel action. I cannot be persuaded they make fewer mistakes than we in print do but they seldom produce the kind of correction that has become almost routine in many Canadian newspapers.

Don't get me wrong. Our performance is far from ideal. Corrections too often don't admit to the original error, don't produce the simple statement: We were wrong when we said such and such. As a result, some corrections leave readers wondering what in the devil that was all about. I was raised in a generation of newspaper people—and there are one or two similar generations behind me—who believed that a story became sacrosanct once it had been printed and that an admission of error, even a small one, was a confession of weakness. We cannot expect oncoming generations of reporters and editors to become converts to this holy cause until we make sure that all our senior editors embrace and propagate the faith. It is easier to deal with a fairness doctrine once you're prepared to admit fallibility. Mind you, as I said somewhat earlier, there isn't any substitute for getting it right the first time.

It has been a long time since I worked on a small daily—and those days long ago were some of the most satisfying of my professional life—but I sense that the related problems of accuracy and fairness are more apparent on major dailies than they are on the smaller ones. In smaller cities and towns reporters and editors and, yes, publishers are much closer to their communities. They know that a mistake can still result in a disgruntled reader or source turning up to thump the editor's desk or to shake a fist under a reporter's nose on the street. In the competitive atmosphere that pervades big daily newsrooms, it seems to me that some young reporters strive more to get their stories on the front page or even into the paper than they do to get them right.

THE UNHEARD MAJORITY

I raised this question with some of our summer staff as they were leaving and they agreed that in an operation as large as ours there's a feeling—usually unspoken—that the paper will defend its reporters regardless of error and that, in fact, sources are reluctant to complain about any but the most serious errors for fear of alienating the reporter, the editors or the organization. That's an unhealthy situation and I'm convinced that it's not unique to us.

Newspapers traditionally have seen themselves as having two roles: holding a mirror up to society and acting as the cutting edge of change by preparing society, through information leadership, for reform. All of us should be worried that our mirror is not wide enough, that there are too many blind spots, that the direction of change is not necessarily the direction in which perhaps a majority of our readers—and certainly a majority of our non-readers—believes society should be moving.

Another major problem we have in the fairness/credibility area—and this is something of a hobby horse of mine—is the fact that the newspaper business attracts and employs journalists who are largely liberal. By that I mean consistently somewhere left of centre, and not large 'L' Liberal. They can't and don't reflect the range of our readership. On a great many social issues of the day, more than half our readership supports what I would describe as small 'c' conservative positions. Who in the media speaks to them or for them? Precious few reporters or columnists, editors or editorial writers. We should make it a priority to search out spokespersons for this group and give them their say.

We have also allowed ourselves to be increasingly manipulated by small, vocal groups on both ends of the political and social spectrum and have failed to reach out to the usually unorganized mass who hold the middle ground. If we can't find better ways of doing just that, we can hardly expect to be believed or supported by people who honestly feel we have nothing to say to them.

In recent years we in the print business have adopted with varying degrees of success a number of other safeguards aimed at protecting the intertwined basics of accuracy and fairness. We've given readers much greater rights of access through expanded letters pages.

Some of us have appointed ombudsmen, although I must confess that I've known only one truly effective ombudsman. Charles Steib had been the managing editor of the *Washington Star* and was hired by the *Washington Post* on a five-year, no-cut contract. The moment he felt his total independence was being interfered with by *Post* editors he was free to take his entire five-year salary and walk away.

Credibility and accountability are at the root of the problems we are having with the federal government and have more to do than many of us realize with the fact that the faceless lawyers we never get to confront are hard at work in Ottawa drafting a Newspaper Act.

One of the traps we stumbled into when the Kent Commission made its report was that we spent so much time and effort and, yes, anger reacting to the ludicrous suggestions in the report, that we didn't pay enough attention to what the report had to say about accountability and credibility, about our inability to persuade a substantial number of people, some of whom sit around the cabinet table in Ottawa, not of our good intentions in terms of answering charges of inaccuracy or unfairness, but of our ability to carry those good intentions through to the satisfaction of some of our most articulate critics. And, as a result, we're likely to get a Newspaper Act which, by mandating a national advisory council to act as some sort of super press council, will be seen to be poking the Pinocchio-like nose of government into the newsrooms of the nation. To a very considerable degree we brought that unwanted plague down upon ourselves.

THE ENEMY IS US

After lengthy internal debate in a small committee a statement of principles was adopted by the Canadian Daily Newspaper Publishers Association's annual meeting in April, 1977. It's a relatively short document and I want to read it to you. It sums up, as well as any one document can, what I consider to be the basics of the craft in which I labour. Like many such declarations it opens with what almost amounts to a disclaimer but then moves quickly to the heart of the matter:

I. ETHICS

Newspapers have individual codes of ethics and this declaration of principles is intended to complement them in their healthy diversity. As individual believers in free speech they have a duty to maintain standards of conduct in conformance with their own goals.

II. FREEDOM OF THE PRESS

Freedom of the press is an exercise of the common right to freedom of speech. It is the right to inform, to discuss, to advocate, to dissent. The Press claims no freedom that is not the right of every person. Truth emerges from free discussion and free reporting and both are essential to foster and preserve a democratic society.

III. RESPONSIBILITY

The newspaper has responsibilities to its readers, its shareholders, its employees and its advertisers. But the operation of a newspaper is in effect a public trust, no less binding because it is not formally conferred, and its overriding responsibility is to the society which protects and provides its freedom.

IV. ACCURACY AND FAIRNESS

The newspaper keeps faith with its readers by presenting the news comprehensively, accurately and fairly, and by acknowledging mistakes promptly.

Fairness requires a balanced presentation of the relevant facts in a news report, and of all substantial opinions in a matter of controversy. It precludes distortion of meaning by over or under-emphasis, by placing facts or quotations out of context, or by headlines not warranted by the text. When statements are made that injure the reputation of an individual or group, those affected should be given the earliest opportunity to reply.

Fairness requires that in the reporting of news, the right of every person to a fair trial should be respected.

Fairness also requires that sources of information should be identified except when there is a clear and pressing reason to protect their anonymity. Except in rare circumstances, reporters should not conceal their own identity. Newspapers and their staffs should not induce people to commit illegal or improper acts. Sound practice makes a clear distinction for the reader between news reports and expressions of opinion.

V. INDEPENDENCE

The newspaper should hold itself free of any obligation save that of fidelity to the public good. It should pay the costs incurred in gathering and publishing news. Conflicts of interest, and the appearance of conflicts of interest, must be avoided. Outside interests that could affect, or appear to affect, the newspaper's freedom to report the news impartially should be avoided.

VI. PRIVACY

Every person has a right to privacy. There are inevitable conflicts between the right to privacy and the public good or the right to know about the conduct of public affairs. Each case should be judged in the light of common sense and humanity.

VII. ACCESS

The newspaper is a forum for the free interchange of information and opinion. It should provide for the expression in its columns of disparate and conflicting views. It should give expression to the interests of minorities as well as majorities, and of the less powerful elements in society.

Those principles, worked out after much negotiation, are easy enough now to state. But like most such simple statements they're deceptively difficult to accomplish. I would not want anything I have said tonight to suggest that the responsibility, the accountability for our problems rests anywhere other than with the publishers and senior editors of Canadian newspapers. We owe that responsibility to our public, to our craft, to our staffs and to ourselves. We have to become much more demanding of our staffs, less tolerant of error, less accepting of unfairness. Walt Kelly, that genius of the comic strips who created Pogo back in the late Forties, said it all for me when he put these words in Pogo's mouth: "We have met the enemy and he is us."

And that's really the core of my message. In the never ending fight for accuracy and fairness, the real enemy is us. If we remember that and do something about it we can restore to journalism the basic strengths that will again be our best protection and the public's best protection against the government intervention that neither we nor the public want or can afford.

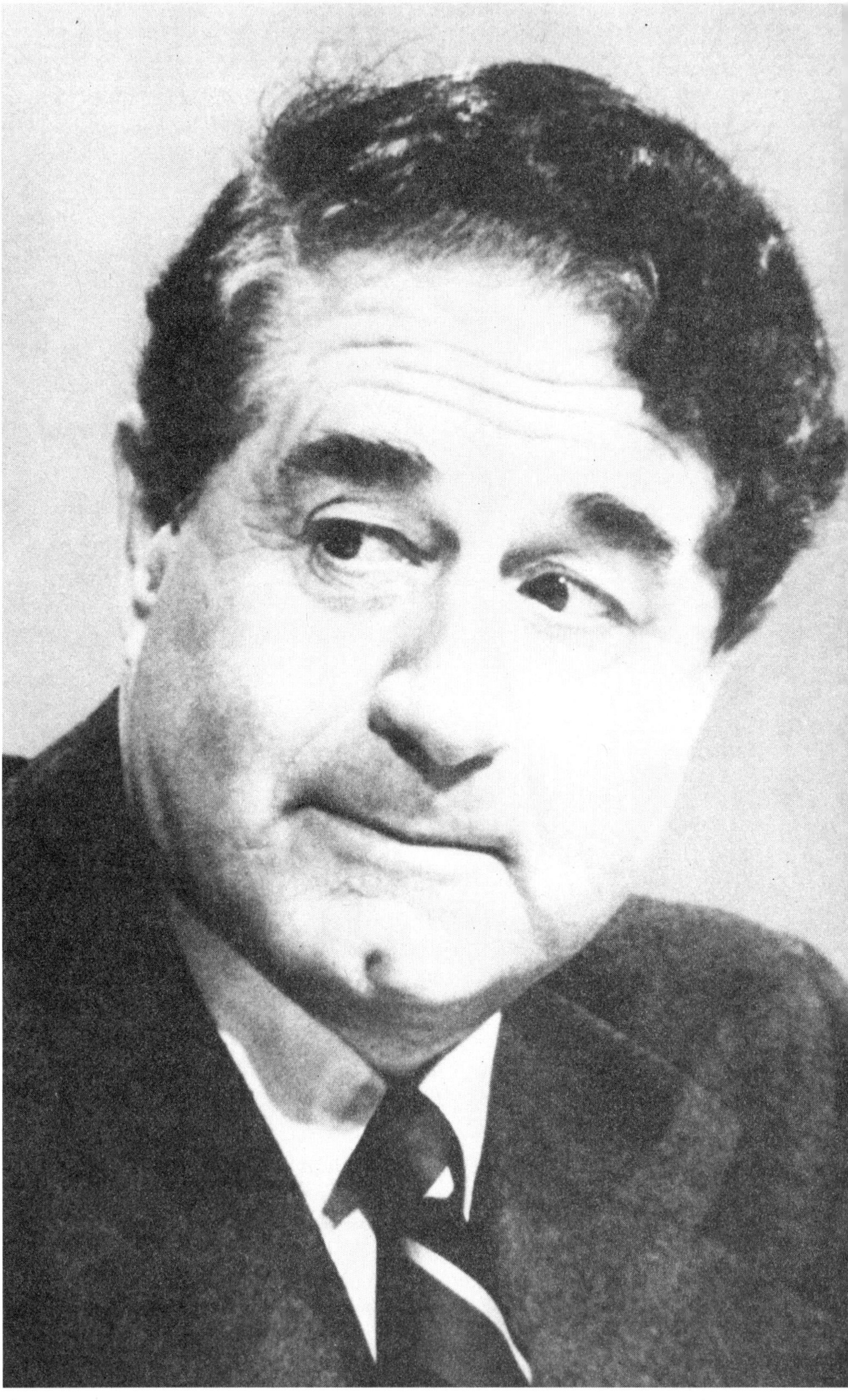

—1983—
WILLIAM STEVENSON

A reporter, foreign correspondent, documentary maker and best-selling author, Stevenson's varied career included interviews with India's legendary leader Nehru, Trotsky's assassin, General Gehlen (Hitler's expert on the Soviet Union, who became the first post-war chief of German intelligence), and Ho Chi Minh. Stevenson was one of the first Western journalists based in communist China. In his career, he covered Hong Kong, Laos, Cambodia, Vietnam, India, Taiwan, Japan, Nepal, Pakistan, Afghanistan, Malaysia, Thailand, Indonesia, Ethiopia, Somalia, Belgian Congo, Urundi-Burundi, Zanzibar, and Tanzania as well as the Middle East. He authored several books, including the best-selling *Man Called Intrepid,* published in 13 languages and made into both a film and television mini-series. *Ninety Minutes at Entebbe* was serialized in major newspapers worldwide and made into a film, starring Elizabeth Taylor.

1983 | WILLIAM STEVENSON

PHANTOM LOVERS, SECRECY AND THE RIGHT TO KNOW:
The Modern Journalistic Experience, Its Perils and Opportunities

It is a great honour to deliver the annual James M. Minifie lecture.

Television has revolutionized the ways in which we get our news. A pioneer in the Canadian field was Ron Robbins, for so long in the forefront of televising foreign news. A pioneer, too, was Don Minifie, the name by which most of us knew him. These men, like myself, have lived through an extraordinary period.

Public broadcasting first burgeoned in Manitoba, long before it became a part of life in Britain as the BBC, or in the United States as PBS. The idea then was that broadcasting had a great power for good—or evil. It seemed to many wise men that the best guarantee of objectivity was to place public broadcasting in the hands of a national committee, answering to government. Today, we see the hazards in this apparent solution. Government control of the media is one short step away from government financing of a public broadcasting corporation.

We still have a tendency to suppose that technical advances and the involvement of government agencies are necessarily all good. When news can be presented electronically before our eyes, even as it happens, it seems at first that government interference and censorship must be impossible to impose. But the greatest manipulator of news was Adolf Hitler. He said the bigger the lie, the more people will believe it. The 'Big Lie' was put over by Hitler primarily by his use of modern technology, by the use of film, by special lighting effects, and by the sound of his own voice, greatly amplified.

The fact that news can be transmitted so very fast is not, of itself, either good or bad. It is how we make use of the technology that matters.

Unfortunately, we've become complacent about this. In previous centuries, journalists had to fight constantly against government censorship, and official interference in the flow of information. No literate citizen in a political democracy was in any doubt that his freedoms depended upon that free flow of information. The term 'the Press' became embedded in the public mind. The freedom of the Press was jealously guarded.

The modern term is 'the media'. Somehow it softens the issue. It conjures up magical ideas about high technology that will somehow protect us against dictators. I'd prefer to stick to the old term—the Press. I'm far from downgrading the importance of other forms of communication when I stick to this terminology. I simply believe 'freedom of the press' has become too important a battle cry. It is part of civilization's history. The rest of the media recognizes the old battle flag of the free press is still valid, and must lead the rest.

Democratic society is founded upon precedent, and the precedents upon which press freedom rests today are much too precious to throw away.

Both Don Minifie and Sir William Stephenson contributed to the freedom of the press, and also to secret intelligence, in wartime. Stephenson you know as Intrepid, the master spy from Winnipeg who helped establish General "Wild Bill" Donovan's Office of Strategic Services (OSS), the forerunner of today's Central Intelligence Agency (CIA). Minifie, in a less well known role, was a member of OSS operations.

We shall see later how these two men resolved an apparent conflict between freedom of the press and the wartime requirements of secrecy.

AUTHORITY VS FREEDOM

Those in authority frequently see themselves as experts in what the public should know. This is true of governments, political parties, the presidents of large business corporations—and especially it is true of military leaders.

The job of a writer or journalist is to get through the secrecy. A reporter goes after facts. Sometimes, a writer conveys those facts more effectively by the use of imagination. When the Russian writer Alexander Solzhenitsyn wrote about conditions in a Siberian prison camp, he gave us a sense of the reality without necessarily providing statistics. He wrote: "In a totalitarian state, you must assume that the facts and the statistics are all lies. . . ."

It's easy to see the truth of this, when we talk about a dictatorship. Whether it is Stalin or Hitler, the dictator is recognized as committed to presenting as pretty a picture as possible of his regime. But the distortions are not so easily identified within our own society. The struggle between press freedom and secretive authority has been going on for hundreds of years.

Today, it's much more complex than it has ever been. We hear many more justifications for secrecy. A government will tell us that, in the interests of national security, this or that information is secret. But experience shows that the more often a government invokes national security, the more likely it is that the government is concerned about the security of its own position. The more a bureaucracy professes to be in love with the idea of informing all the people all the time, the more likely it is that the same bureaucracy is covering up facts about its own incompetence, its own waste, its own failures.

Nearly 40 years ago, a Russian intelligence officer defected in Canada. He was Igor Gouzenko. He was interrogated and his disclosures led to the uncovering of Soviet spies in Canada and the United States. Some of his testimony was made public enough that we discovered the existence of the so-called atom spies. The secrets of the atom bomb, developed here, had been betrayed to the U.S.S.R.

But Gouzenko also brought with him the details of how Moscow's intelligence agencies operated, and how they subverted Canadians and Americans in public service. He described the existence of Soviet double agents, now known as 'moles.'

Gouzenko was debriefed by security men who, back in those days, were totally concealed from public scrutiny. In consequence, the most important part of his testimony was never acted upon. Soviet moles at the top of Western intelligence services suppressed Gouzenko's attempt to expose them.

I have some personal knowledge of the situation because I have just completed an investigation of the Gouzenko case. Today, it is clear Gouzenko's real value was deliberately destroyed. The Liberal Party in power in Canada in 1945–46 was more concerned about protecting its position than it was about protecting the public— or so-called national security. Gouzenko pointed to the existence of the notorious traitor Kim Philby, who at the time was chief of the anti-Soviet section of the British Secret Intelligence Service. If Gouzenko had been given a public hearing, if the authorities had acted on his disclosures, there would have been few if any of the spy scandals that have now become commonplace, from Philby to Anthony Blunt, to the latest self-confessed American traitor, Michael Whitney.

Here was a case of the guardians of secrecy proclaiming that they were keeping the secrets in defense of democracy. In fact, they kept the secrets to protect themselves.

Whenever an institution or a government tries to impose secrecy, the public has a right to know why. There are times, obviously, when secrecy seems necessary. But in the modern world, secrecy as a part of national defence needs to be challenged.

During the Korean War, the decision was taken by United Nations forces under General MacArthur to drive into North Korea. Obviously, you would say, it was a clear case for imposing the most strict secrecy. However, there was then working in the British Embassy in Washington a Russian spy, Guy Burgess. He knew the MacArthur plan. He told Moscow. The Russians told Peking. And the Chinese ambushed MacArthur's troops, with heavy loss of life. We have only discovered how this happened in the last few weeks, through the confession of an American mole.

All too often, a military blunder is hushed-up by the use of secrecy. The more a man waves the flag, and huffs and puffs about the national importance of some military decision, the more likely it is that he has something to hide. Dr. Johnson wrote that "patriotism is the last refuge of the scoundrel." War correspondents, down through the ages, have had their patriotism called into question because, in fact, they were doing their patriotic duty in exposing the incompetence of a military leader.

THE PHANTOM LOVERS

Indeed, what becomes clear is that those who profess to love freedom are often the very opponents of that freedom. They go to war in defence of freedom, but suffocate freedom in the process of going to war. They join that army of politicians who turn into phantom lovers. What they claim to love, they secretly fear, or hate, or simply cannot understand.

George Orwell foresaw this, when he wrote *1984* and other political novels. Nineteen eighty-four is next year. We shall be hearing a great deal about George Orwell with the arrival of this ominous date. Orwell saw the development of Newspeak, in which words meant the opposite of what they seem to mean. Peace is war in the language of the tyrant. Freedom is slavery. All people are equal but some are more equal than others, he wryly commented in *Animal Farm*. And phantom lovers turn out to be destroyers of the very things they claim to love.

In James M. Minifie's day, the work of a reporter required him to cut through this verbal camouflage. Minifie was very good at this. He belonged to George Orwell's generation. During the Second World War, however, as I said earlier, he also served with American intelligence services. For a time, he had to suspend his instincts as a journalist. But he never forgot that his prime duty was to dig out information, and to disseminate that information without fear or favour.

He understood that intelligence and information are the same thing. A democracy survives on information, which in wartime sometimes reaches us as secret-intelligence. And Minifie knew how frequently the dull-witted and the incompetents conceal their real ignorance by stamping *secret* on information that was of little value to the enemy.

INTELLIGENCE, INFORMATION AND INTREPID

The blend of intelligence and information was explained by the wartime chief of our coordinated intelligence services, Sir William Stephenson, "Intrepid." Intrepid spoke only twice in public on this subject. Once, before the war, he made an appeal for the West to see through Hitler's propaganda and the Nazi claims that they were not planning global warfare. The second time, he spoke to Canadian publishers in the mid-1950s about the need to see through Soviet Russia's use of words like *peace* and *people's democracy*.

Intrepid's theme was that democracy is blind without information. And the best information came from freedom of the press. A good, lively, alert body of reporters in the media could be relied on to dig out the truth, dig out the facts, and help to keep the democracies on their toes.

This was the view of a pragmatic businessman who survived, in peacetime, by competing fiercely and effectively within the system of free enterprise. And it is this that differentiates the great practitioners of secret-intelligence from the bureaucrats who make a career of secrecy, whose jobs and promotion and pension depend upon secrecy. Intrepid's Chief of Special Operations, General Gubbins, once told me that as a professional soldier he realized that the most effective agents, saboteurs and guerilla warfare experts came from civilian life. They were street fighters in the peacetime world of free enterprise. The professionals, by contrast, were totally unfit for the ruthless world of cloak and dagger.

1983 | WILLIAM STEVENSON

BUREAUCRATIC SECRETS

Bureaucratic secrecy is the enemy of us all. It helped bury the truth about the great traitors of our time, like Philby. It makes a cult of secrecy, so that when truly urgent military matters of secrecy are at stake, no distinction is made.

Let me give you an example. The so-called balance of terror that prevents the big nuclear powers from launching a war is based on a complex system of missiles and calculations made by commercial contractors. One such contractor is based on the American west coast at a site called Space Park. The security around Space Park used to be a blanket security, so that everyone going in and out was supposedly prevented from giving away secrets. But an awful lot of those workers knew nothing of importance. The security system was a token routine. Eventually, a very young man was given a job as a clerk. He did nothing very important but he did it in the heart of the system, where he was able to see communications of utmost secrecy. So he began taking these secrets out of Space Park in his briefcase, and selling them to the Russians. He betrayed such a wealth of secrets that the most advanced surveillance system was rendered useless. As a result, the Soviets were kept fully informed about the West's defense against their missiles, and they were able—if they wished—to blind us on the eve of a missile attack.

How did this lowly clerk get the secrets out of Space Park? He was regularly sent to the neighbourhood liquor store to smuggle in booze for parties. This was so common, the security guards always assumed that this lowly clerk concealed in his briefcase booze, not secrets. Security, you see, had become a matter of habit—and since it was all laid out in bureaucratic terms, no single individual took responsibility. Nobody was going to spoil the fun of the regular office parties by questioning the gofer, the clerk who was told "go-for" coffee, "go-for" whisky and gin, and who was told by the Soviets—go for the West's most intimate secrets.

Now, when the young man was caught, the security authorities' first thought was this: How to keep it from their own public? The contractors did not want to lose their huge defence contracts by being exposed as incompetent in the protection of secrets. So, in the end, when reporters should have been performing a public service by reporting to the public a scandalous failure in security, they were stopped from doing so—on the grounds of national security.

Today, more governments than ever practice bureaucratic secrecy. Surveys show a sharp decline in freedom of the press, and a very sharp increase in the number of countries exercising some form of media control. These countries have lately combined in a mass assault on the Western tradition of press freedoms. They are Third World countries which, through the United Nations, propose that each country should—in effect—decide what news can be published on its own affairs. This proposition comes in the guise of national interest! The argument is that the great international news organizations—agencies like Associated Press or Reuters—or broadcasting organizations like Canada's CBC, fail to reflect the aspirations of the people inside these less developed nations. On the face of it, a fair complaint. But look closer.

Behind this move are those phantom lovers of free speech, the Soviet Union, Communist China, and the East European countries. To them, truth is whatever the Party leadership decides is true.

Their slavish respect for authority has obtained for them a doubtful honour. The United Nations recently announced, without any visible sign of embarrassment, that the best reporting of UN affairs is that of the Communist bloc. The Western media are accused of making "grossly inaccurate charges" that the UN is an inefficient and swollen bureaucracy. This UN report is the work of UN information officials. Obviously, they are protecting their own jobs, their own "swollen bureaucracy."

But how can the UN defend this? How can it seriously praise the Communist news media, all totally under party control? The answer is quite simple. The UN today is dominated by the Third World. We, the West, pay the best part of the bill for keeping the UN alive. But in the past 30 years, the influence of the Third World has grown spectacularly, until today these countries represent eight of ten votes . . . that is, 123 Third World countries have 78 *per cent* of the UN voice.

So what this remarkable UN report tells us, when it gives such high marks to the Communist controlled media, is that eight out of ten governments *not including the Soviet Bloc and China* actually believe in a controlled press.

INDIA'S PRESS "FREEDOM"

This gross contradiction between the professed aims of the United Nations and the reality can be observed in greater detail if we examine any one of these "Third World" countries. Most claim to be non-aligned—Cuba, for example, where jail and execution await anyone who disseminates a report not officially approved. Cuba, in fact, reflects the dictatorial attitude of its mentor, the U.S.S.R. What about other countries like India, touted as the world's largest democracy?

When I first worked in India, the rest of the world had to listen to the moralizing of India's leaders about freedom of the press. But today they express love for freedom of speech, except when it affects their own interests. Then, they suppress whatever they can.

The first Prime Minister of India, Nehru, handed down the leadership to his daughter, Indira Gandhi, a phantom lover of press freedom. Once, discussing India's affairs with her, I realized she was describing the kind of India she wished existed, and not the real India.

I was making a TV documentary. I wanted to film in the Prime Minister's backyard during a religious holiday. Mrs. Gandhi agreed I should station two cameramen on the roof of the residence. Nobody had ever before filmed or photographed this scene. It seemed like a coup, of sorts. Unfortunately, I forgot a golden rule in journalism: When you've got what you want, get out. Instead, I lingered and somehow Mrs. Gandhi started talking about a book highly critical of India. I said the book was written with a genuine affection for India. I also said it was foolish of the Indian government to ban the book.

Mrs. Gandhi declared the book was not banned. It was simply not possible to buy it in any bookshop, that was all. Well, I said, if you stop a book from entering the country, you ban it. No, she said, India never censored or banned anything. It was a silly argument. Of course, I lost it. Mrs. Gandhi was the voice of authority. I lost a lot more. Mrs. Gandhi also cancelled the next day's arrangements for filming Nehru in his own backyard. So much for the present Prime Minister of India's love of free speech.

"IMPROVED" REPORTING

The self-righteousness of those who want to gag the press is often overwhelming. When the Egyptians got rid of King Farouk, I was in Cairo. The first revolutionary leader, General Naguib, was overthrown by another revolutionary, Nasser. I managed to track down the deposed general. He gave me the identity of the man in charge of Arab propaganda against the Jews in Israel. He was a Nazi war criminal. He worked in Nasser's Ministry of Guidance and Public Enlightenment. He had been Number Two to Dr. Goebbels, Hitler's chief of propaganda. He was disguised under an Arab name. Then I ran down the Nazi himself. He was so surprised, he confessed the whole story of his escape from Allied prison camps, and his recruitment by Arab zealots.

I brought along a witness of this Nazi war criminal's confession. I was expelled from Egypt the same day. But the man who dispatched my cables was thrown in jail, where he died.

Yet Egypt at the time led the Afro-Asian movement to "improve" the West's reporting of their affairs. Improve meant, of course, suppress. That was the purpose of the Ministry of Guidance and Public Enlightenment. When a government uses such portentous language, you can bet it is really talking about misguiding the public and suppressing the enlightenment.

All governments regard the free press as biased when it is critical, and enlightened when it is supportive. Here in Canada, politicians and bureaucrats tell us they love freedom while they propose at the same time to interfere with the structure of our news services *for our own* good. The ruling Liberals make outrageous suggestions for improving the freedom of the press with legislation that really amounts to control. They would like to see a kind of print equivalent of the CBC, while they see the CBC as an agency of the government.

POLITICS AND THE CBC

Orders are not handed out to the CBC, telling it how to handle TV and radio programs, nor what to put on them. And, after you have lived in the United States a while, believe me, you appreciate the very fine programming done by the CBC, especially on radio. But this is Canada, not America. And Canadians have every right to be concerned when it seems the ruling party regards the CBC as a political instrument. The Liberal influence is subtle, for the most part. In theory, of course, the CBC is insulated from political influence by its constitution. In practice, those who are appointed to run the CBC know very well they are political appointees. And all the way down through the system, there is an unspoken awareness that life will go much more easily if, in news and public affairs, the producer or reporter is objective—objective that is, in the Liberal sense of the word.

However, in the Canadian media, as in the media almost everywhere, professionalism asserts itself. We have seen the CBC investigate, for example, the pervasive nature of Soviet intelligence operations on this continent. We have seen the CBC investigate the so-called October Crisis, when the federal government suddenly perceived a state of emergency, and Canadians in Quebec woke up to discover the army had taken over.

These programs were the result of dogged persistence on the part of individual reporters and producers. I do not say, however, that they did themselves much good with the top brass.

Anything that reflects badly on the present federal government is unlikely to win a CBC journalist any good marks or promotion. Some time ago, after I got back here from the Soviet Union, a documentary on Khrushchev was slated for CBC prime-time television. The documentary was based on Khrushchev's own memoirs. I was curious to see it, because Khrushchev's memoirs were no longer popular. Khrushchev was no longer popular. The Russians had gone back to their old admiration for Stalin.

The Khrushchev documentary was to be shown on a Sunday evening. It was heavily promoted, right up until the preceding Friday. Then, suddenly, without warning or explanation, it was taken off the air. When asked why, the explanation given was that NBC and *Time* magazine, jointly responsible for the show, had insisted on editing it in a certain way that met with the disapproval of CBC's top brass.

However, much later still, I learned from a Soviet diplomat a very different story. The Russian explained that his ambassador in Ottawa had talked to the Canadian prime minister, Mr. Trudeau, on Saturday. The Soviet ambassador had told Mr. Trudeau that Moscow took a dim view of the documentary and would regard it as an unfriendly act if it were to be shown on CBC, that well-known arm of the Canadian government. So, literally overnight, the show was taken off the air. Now, if we'd been honest and if the CBC had said this resulted from a Soviet protest, Canadians would at least know the circumstances. But instead, a lie was told. And I think the fact that a lie was thought necessary is, in itself, condemnation.

Another example. I worked for some time in Africa. Quite recently, I went back to Tanzania to help with a TV documentary about the failure of Canadian aid. We were told officially by the Canadian government there were no examples of badly planned aid. My partner, Monika Jensen, the producer, found forklift trucks, rotting on the dockside. When Monika asked the Canadian aid officials about this, they denied the trucks were there. They said the trucks were not rusting, nor inappropriate to the climate, nor had they simply broken down. The trucks were taken away because the Tanzanians did not know how to look after them. So Monika filmed several hundred Canadian forklift trucks rotting behind some old warehouses. The trucks were in terrible condition. Some carried big signs saying they were out of action.

Then we interviewed the head of the Canadian International Development Agency (CIDA), who happened to be making a royal progress, from Ottawa, through Africa. His officials had told him we couldn't find those broken down trucks. So he said, on camera, there were none. He said this, in fact, on the same roll of film recording those non-existent trucks. Later, in Ottawa, we confronted the CIDA director again. This time, he claimed all the relevant documents were confidential. National security would be hurt, the national interest would suffer, if any documents were turned over to us. Yet the only thing those documents showed (because, of course, we got them anyhow) was that the taxpayer was being ripped off, not by the Tanzanians, but by people either handling the aid, or awarded contracts in connection with that aid.

It is not often you catch officials out in a blatant lie to such effect. In this case, it happened because even in a dictatorship like Tanzania, we found people with a belief in the importance of telling the public the facts. It was these Tanzanians who showed us where those useless forklift trucks had been concealed.

DEFENDERS OF PRESS FREEDOM

Press freedom around the world often seems to be in retreat. But there is something about the tradecraft of the reporter that instills in him, or her, a sense of public duty. Reporters are rebellious by nature. In countries where the press is controlled, a surprising number of professional reporters manage to survive. In Indonesia, for example, which is one of the world's largest, wealthiest, and least understood countries, there was a bad time when President Sukarno governed with an iron hand. He was a phantom lover of a free press. He reserved for himself the right to define the word 'freedom'. Editors who disagreed with his definition were put in jail. The country had achieved that Third World dream of creating its own news agency and controlling its own newspapers. The result was a tame press, a government mouthpiece. But when Sukarno was overthrown, independent editors and the reporters were still there. They'd had a tough time. They'd had to decide if, by going to jail, they would surrender any chance of keeping the public informed. Some stayed out of jail by trimming their sails, and once in a while managed to report the truth. Others drew attention to the true state of affairs by the very fact of going to jail.

I was in Indonesia when the first rebellions began against Dictator Sukarno. A number of Western correspondents were able to give moral support to Indonesian journalists during the bad time. We smuggled books and small luxuries into the jails, we helped families, and above all, we kept reminding the government in power that it could not liquidate the offending journalists. We were witnesses, outside the government's control. It was an important lesson in how Western press institutions can keep hope alive. Later, in the mid-1960s, President Sukarno became almost totally controlled by Communist China, so far as foreign policy was concerned. At that time, the Chinese were in their most aggressively Maoist mood. They had been defeated in Malaysia by direct confrontation with the British. Now, they influenced President Sukarno to declare a war of confrontation against Malaysia, which had become independent from British rule.

The Malaysians needed help, but they did not want the British back. So they asked the Commonwealth to help fight this new war. All Commonwealth troops from 1965 to 1967 fought under the newly independent Malaysian flag. In reality, most of the troops were British, and many were from the crack (and highly secret) Special Air Services. Finally, against all odds, Malaysia won. It was a tiny country compared with Indonesia but it won without controlling the press and without imposing the restrictions of personal freedom that usually go with war. I was involved on the sidelines, because as a correspondent I knew many of the rebel leaders. When it was all over, Malaysia returned to normal and the Malaysians took responsibility again for their own defence.

PUBLIC DUTIES VS. FREEDOM OF THE PRESS
Now, the question is this. At what point does a reporter have to say: there's some higher public duty that requires for a while suspending, voluntarily, certain of the freedoms that took so long to win?

The answer is not as easy as it might first appear. After the Malaysian war, a very senior British military officer wrote that publicity was actively discouraged in connection with that outstandingly successful campaign. It was outstanding. The campaign was won at the same time the war in Vietnam was being lost. Yet the two wars were next door to one another. One was fought with almost no publicity. The other war, in Vietnam, was fought almost entirely—on the American side—with publicity.

The British brigadier's argument was this. The public in the West had developed a repugnance to war. This made the moral cost of military action increasingly difficult to bear for any democratic government. In Europe, he said, public hostility made it almost impossible to mobilize for war. He blamed the press for undermining the public resolve. Therefore, he thought it best, whenever possible, to keep the public in the dark. The war in Malaysia was won by drawing as little attention to it as possible. The war in Vietnam was lost because the American public knew everything, and finally withdrew support.

What is the reporter's responsibility in such situations? You can't explain to the British brigadier that this is the end of the twentieth century, and he mustn't regard the public as nincompoops. The reporter's job is simply to get at the facts and then publish them as best he can.

But suppose he gets hold of facts that hurt the national interest? First, he has to make sure they really are facts. For the reporter in Vietnam, this became difficult. He was overwhelmed with different bureaucratic versions of what was going on. In Malaysia, he was in some difficulty finding out if there was a war going on at all, since it was waged deep in the jungle and in remote parts of Borneo, and concealed in secrecy.

In practice, the British brigadier was confusing publicity and government handouts with the exercise of initiative by the press. In the Malaysian war, reporters simply went out and got hold of whatever facts they could. They researched and wrote their own stories. The result was a low-key account of a long slogging match.

In Vietnam, the reporters were constantly awash in a flood of information. They tried to check their facts, but found different bureaucracies had different axes to grind. Vietnam became a horrible example of what happens when the government, and the military, try to perform the function of the reporter.

SECURITY VS. THE RIGHT TO KNOW

This still doesn't help us resolve the dilemma of secrecy, national security, and the public's right to know. So much of this debate takes place in Orwell's language of Newspeak, where words have opposite meanings.

When dictators and would-be dictators who now rule the larger part of mankind talk about secrecy, they do not mean national security, they mean their own security. I found, working in countries like China and Russia, it was always possible to endanger the life of those I interviewed because in such countries, a traitor is anyone who tells foreigners the simplest (but still secret) facts of everyday life that reflected badly on the ruling elite. Does this mean a reporter must avoid asking questions in case he puts his informant in jeopardy? I don't believe so. Secrecy deserves to be penetrated. The men who keep such secrets profess to be in love with their country's honour and security. In reality, they are perpetuating their own class of rulers.

In the West, very little is treated as secret. In wartime, reporters usually follow a kind of honour system. They carry the burden of deciding if they might imperil lives by disclosing certain facts. But there is a very wide gulf between war and peace, and in peacetime, the rule of thumb should be that a reporter never listens to anything off-the-record. Too many politicians and bureaucrats use this as a device to silence the reporter. Off-the-record they tell you something that if you found out, and published, might damage them. So, never listen to anything off-the-record. After that, as a reporter, what you find out is hardly likely to be secret. If the reporter finds the facts by legitimate investigation, so can anyone else.

The other side of all this, of course, is the media's ownership.

If the media, or a broadcasting network, is in the hands of businessmen with profit as their only motive, then the reporter obviously has a problem. In my experience, owners and publishers do not interfere in news coverage and are respectful of editorial opinion. It is public institutions like the CBC that become targets for those who wish to put across their own propaganda. Newsrooms are recognized as the nerve centres through which public opinion can be manipulated. In a way, this is a back-handed tribute to the effectiveness of a free press. It is perceived as exercising more influence than propaganda agencies. For this reason, any democratic society must be constantly concerned about the condition of its news services. Are they professional? Are they employing reporters who understand their jobs? Are they free from pressures exercised by one group or another?

The answers to those questions will not be found in any government-inspired commission of inquiry into the press. You all know the commission I have in mind. Such inquisitions remind me of the RCMP raid on the office of the *Toronto Sun*. The Mounties were looking for a letter said to contain a security leak. After many hours, they gave up. The letter was lying in a desk drawer of the editor-in—chief, but his desk and all the drawers were just stuffed to overflowing with papers. As one of the reporters wrote later, the Mounties couldn't find anything in all that mess, but they might have lost a Mountie.

In the secret world, security agencies use the phrase: 'need to know'. It means that secrets are kept within the circle of those who need to know. This is in direct conflict with the democratic view that the public has a right to know. When the Mounties search a newspaper office, they symbolize the conflict. And they get in a mess.

In a democracy, the press is always a mess. It defies organizing. It defeats the would-be suppressors. That is its strength. The press remains free by the very fact of its being untidy, always in flux, always irritating the lovers of order and convention—and by always insisting upon the public's right to know.

New technology may seem, at first sight, to advance the public's cause. But how the public handles the news is what matters and defines the kind of society we are—untidy, rebellious, impossible to discipline in the way so many political leaders would like to discipline us, and mostly a mess.

Winston Churchill once said, about democracy, that it was messy, inefficient—and the best political system we'd got.

The same can be said about a free press. It is no respecter of phantom lovers. It looks behind the professions of love of freedom. And anyone who tries to intimidate it is in danger of getting lost in the mess.

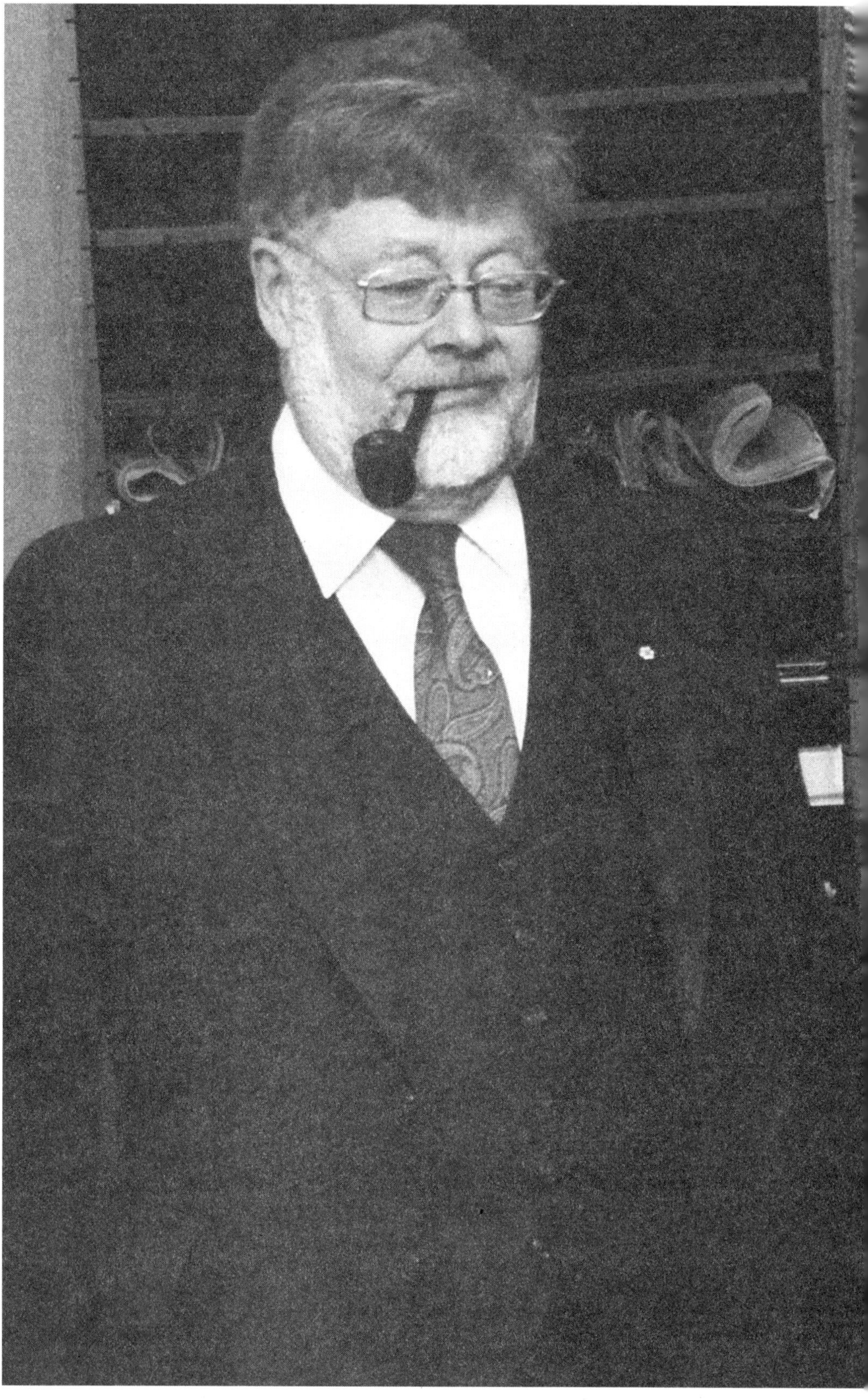

−1984−

CHARLES LYNCH

Charles Burchill Lynch was a journalist and author of eight books. Lynch was appointed Vancouver bureau chief of the British United Press in 1940 after writing for the *Saint John Citizen*, the *Saint John Telegraph-Journal* and the Canadian Press. The next year, he became a divisional manager in Toronto. In 1943, he joined the Reuters News Agency as a war correspondent. On D-Day, he was one of a few Canadian reporters to accompany troops ashore. After the War, Lynch reported on the Nuremberg War Trials. Reuters next stationed Lynch in Brazil and New York City. In 1956, he became the CBC's United Nations correspondent. In 1958, Lynch accepted the post of Ottawa Bureau Chief for Southam News. By 1960 he was Chief of Southam. Lynch's historic two-month trip to communist China resulted in his first of eight books. *China, One Fourth of the World* was a Canadian best-seller. From 1970 to 1974—while still acting as Southam News Chief—Lynch co-hosted the CBC television program *Encounter*. In 1977, Lynch was named to the Order of Canada. In 1981 he was inducted into the Canadian News Hall of Fame and in 1998, the Charles Lynch Award was established in his honour by the National Press Club of Canada. It recognizes outstanding coverage of national issues.

1984 | CHARLES LYNCH

HOW CELEBRITY CORRUPTS JOURNALISTS, AND OTHER TALL TALES

James M. Minifie was the conscience of Canada in Washington, the conscience of our relations with the United States. He was a pioneer in the idea that we should be independent. He wrote his famous book, *Peacemaker or Powder Monkey*, in which he urged that we ease back on our alliance with the United States. He was a foe of the CIA, of Joe McCarthy, Richard Nixon, and I think in his latter years he became almost obsessed by the thought that he was being pursued by agents of those agencies.

I'm not sure his suspicions were misplaced. He almost had a persecution complex about it at the end, after he had his stroke.

But he was, at the height of his powers, a Canadian expatriate who spent most of his journalistic career abroad. He came home without ever coming home. He re-established his Canadian identity from Washington. The CBC ran special programs of James M. Minifie's Washington and took you on tours with Minifie as the guide.

He was Canada's idea of what was going on in Washington, and he was the main communicator of what was happening there. He was equally at ease with radio as he had been with print. I don't think he ever really came to terms with television in quite the same way. He was very proud of his prairie heritage, like Matt Halton, who used to boast about his background in rural Alberta.

He became one of our first celebrity electronic journalists, and I'm going to talk a bit about the joys and perils of celebrity. He packed halls from coast to coast when he made his lecture tours. He and I used to vie for the biggest audience on the Canadian Club circuit, and I think he always won.

He and Matt Halton were our most distinctive foreign correspondents. They were our first foreign correspondents. Both were trained in print. Both had a taste for the exotic and the flamboyant, with a touch of the theatre. When they were famous, hardly anybody else in media was.

The stories about Minifie that I remember best are covering the election campaign of 1963. He used to despair, as I would, at Lester Pearson's invariable habit of taking a "hot hall," an audience that had been warmed up by the local speakers, the introductory speakers, and then cooling it out by making a flat speech. And Pearson did that more times than I could count.

Fond as we were of him, we used to despair of him, and finally there was a meeting in Moncton in that '63 campaign and Louis Robichaud, the premier of New Brunswick, had warmed up the audience in a fantastic fashion, and he had them screaming, and Pearson got up and we waited for him to fall flat, and he didn't. He made a short speech, he made a punchy speech, and it was terrific. Everybody went home happy, and as I was walking back to the hotel with Minifie I said, "Don, that's the best I ever heard Pearson," and Don said, "Ya, I think he smells pussy." And he did. He felt that he was going to win. He had long years in opposition and then he won that election. That was the best speech I ever heard Pearson make.

On that same visit to the Maritimes, Minifie did a memorable broadcast. He was sitting in the front of a fishing dory, and the camera shot him including the front part of the fishing dory. It was rocking back and forth with the sea in the background, and what they didn't know was that we had the dory propped on a piece of wood, and I was at the other end pumping it up and down. That is what you call the introduction of a bit of show biz into journalism.

FAME OFTEN CORRUPTS

Since what I call "the Minifie Era," celebrity journalism has thrived in Canada and it's corrupted many of the things that it has touched. It wasn't new with electronic journalism and with Don Minifie and his colleagues in the CBC. We had it before with Gordon Sinclair, who was both a celebrity and a journalist, and with Greg Clark, who was a great storyteller. Both these men were supreme showmen. Gordon Sinclair still is. And then there was Ross Munro, who was celebrated but who was no showman at all. His coverage of the Second World War made him a national hero.

The celebrity journalists of the last 25 years have included, besides Don Minifie, Norman DePoe, Ron Collister, Tom Gould, Bruce Phillips and Knowlton Nash, who inaugurated this series of lectures—all of whom I submit were splendid reporters and good writers, better before they became famous than they were after.

And there were the continuing print celebrities heavily influenced by television: Allan Fotheringham, Richard Gwyn, and to some extent myself, which is why I'm standing here making a speech rather than covering them, as we used to do.

The principle hazard of celebrity journalism is attracting more attention than the people being reported on. Being sought out and flattered by people who may want a mention, but have no tidings to impart.

How many times did I see Don Minifie come into an election hall and attract more attention from the audience than the person who was there to campaign? The celebrity journalist winds up being smothered in fluff by people who say how great it is to see them or, in Don's case, they have even less hair than they thought, or their jowls are wrong or their whiskers, I don't like them. But they don't have anything to tell you about what you came to report on. It's like Fred Friendly of NBC once said, "You get pecked to death by ducks."

Celebrity journalism, on the other hand, has tremendous advantages for those of us who practice it. It means big bucks, which come with big ratings, leading in many cases to big egos. Some say big influence comes with it, and I'm not sure about that. The danger is that the care and feeding of a national reputation takes over from the business of reporting on the story itself, and that's addictive. Like taking dope.

NEGATIVISM PERSISTS

A persistent theme of today's journalism, particularly the commentary journalism, the personal journalism, the signed column, or the commentary on television or the anchor people from television, is negativism. The public, I'm sure, is aware of this. We ourselves are aware of it, and we don't seem to shake it. It's true that bad news is the best news and that negative comment sells better than positive praise. The definition of news in my book goes back to the back fence of the neighbourhood, and bad news, a piece of dirt, will spread through the neighbourhood a lot faster than a piece of good news about anybody in that neighbourhood.

If you magnify that and project it onto the larger screen, you get the reason why so much of the news you see is bad news in our media. The business of attacking a piece of government policy is more compelling to the reader in our minds than a piece of praise. This is particularly true in Canada, when you hardly ever read a commentary about a piece of government policy, be it provincial or federal, that is positive, or that is supportive of the policy. You will see that most often we take a negative view, we find out what's wrong with that policy and deal with that in a very gripping way.

Sometimes personal journalism has become so pervasive that the paper will run the column that comments on a government policy without ever having run a news story telling the people what the policy is. I have had letters from readers saying, "That was a brilliant piece of critique that you did, but what was the policy that you were attacking?" The danger there is that the column has its set place in the paper and the story about the thing that you were writing about may not have made the paper. I call this negativism, the 'Gordon Sinclair factor,' because he made millions doing just that. Being the great iconoclast and being the great outrager.

We had a program called *This Hour Has Seven Days* in the earlier days in television, and it was the most successful, in terms of audience, public affairs programs in the history of Canadian television. But it dealt in shock, and that meant that each week it had to shock a little more than it had the week before and finally it self-destructed, by being so shocking and so hard and so tough and so independent that it could not be sustained. The authorities of the time killed it, and it is still very controversial, that killing. But the fact is that the program never did a positive piece in support, or in explanation of, a government program.

This is why my colleague, Allan Fotheringham, is so popular. If he ever writes a nice piece about anything he will be dead. Every knock is a buck. We all do it, because it's easier than the positive and it does contain that shock factor.

THE POSITIVE IS NOT REWARDED
I wrote a positive piece... once in my life. I supported Trudeau's constitutional proposal, the patriation of the constitution and the insertion of the Charter of Rights. I had wearied of covering endless federal/provincial conferences at which they argued over how to get the constitution home from Westminster, and I despaired of going to my grave covering these conferences because they never got anywhere. They'd work out formulae and we learned them and we wrote about them and suddenly the formula failed so I said somebody should just go ahead and do it.

Trudeau said, "I'm going to go ahead and do it. If I can't get agreement I'll do it anyway and we'll reckon the cost afterwards." And I said, "Hurrah!" and went out in support of it and made speeches.

A memorable speech I made in support of it early in the constitution debate was to the Calgary Chamber of Commerce, and the minute I declared I was there to support and explain Trudeau's constitutional proposal, a roar of protest came from the audience. It was a black tie audience. It was their big affair of the year. And the ladies in long gowns were standing up, and at the end they were on the tables shaking their fists in protest at what I was saying—that this was something that was long overdue and should happen.

And at the end I remember the president gave a rebuttal to my ridiculous thesis and got a standing ovation. The people stood up and cheered him. All through that I was criticized by my colleagues who said, "There you go, you sold out. You are preaching for a senate call. You're doing all sorts of things." Peer pressure of a very heavy kind was there—the few times when we do write positively, our colleagues turn on us.

That's a trite reason for not writing. But you'll see less positive journalism in Canadian media than you'll see in the media in the United States or in Britain or in any other country. It's not unusual for people like us to be seen and heard saying, "The President has made a proposal. Maybe it makes some sense."

You'll not see that very often in our media, either in the columns or in the editorial pages.

OTTAWA POLITICS BORING?
In 30 years in Ottawa the thing I have heard the most often from editors is that we are giving them too much politics from Ottawa. The most deadening factor in any news story, they say, in papers across the country, is the Ottawa dateline at the top. People turn away from news on that account. Canadians outside of

Ottawa use Ottawa as a dirty word; it's a pejorative word. A word that they say with scorn and suspicion and yet it's the centre of our national politics.

We used to be known as a well-run country, where little interesting ever happened. Nobody has said that about us for the last 25 years—neither that we are well-run, nor that little interesting ever happens.

We in the media try to jazz things up by emphasizing personalities and oddities. We tap the entertainment factor which was implanted by television and has been aped by the accent on packaging in newspapers. Those same papers that used to claim hours of the readers' time now have to settle for minutes. The stuff that is in those news columns, around all those ads that pay the bills, has to arrest the reader. It has to make the reader stop and shake his or her head and pause for a read.

The best that can be said is that print makes the audience work harder than television. People who pick up a newspaper are doing something more tangible than people who turn on their television sets. Their minds have to be turned on and they have to be receptive to verbal images rather than pictures. In 25 years working in print and dabbling in television at the same time, I can testify that scarcely a single audience comment on television has had to do with anything I said. Every audience comment from the newspaper column, by contrast, has dealt with something I wrote, either pro or con.

The TV comments are about the jowls or the hair or the teeth or the fidgeting or nose-rubbing. The producer of the television program says, "You were great," and you will say to him, "Well, what did you like about it?" and he'll say, "You didn't swivel around in your chair. You didn't pick your nose." And I'd say, "Well, what did you think of what I said?" "Well," he'd say, "I didn't pay any attention to that, I was too busy."

When people comment about something, they are inclined to remember it. Now celebrity journalism has hazards beyond the mere corruption of professional standards.

The public is a very fickle mistress. They say on Fleet Street that you don't win a reputation, you lease one, and that the reputation can disappear as quickly as it came. Everybody in show business knows that. That's why the care and feeding of show business reputations—those celebrity reputations you read about in *People* magazine and the host of magazines that exist to dine out on celebrity—they require armies of flacks and hucksters. They sustain the images of celebrity. It is their job to promote their clients.

Celebrity journalists in the United States do that. They all have agents and they all have promoting departments, either in the networks for which they work, or they hire them individually. Agents make sure that the celebrity product is kept front and centre, and marketed. We haven't yet come to that here in Canada, but I predict that we will.

JOURNALISM—STILL NOT A PROFESSION

When I started out 48 years ago in newspapering, my pay was $7 per week. The people who are starting out in journalism make considerably more than that now. Journalism is still not a profession. We have no standards of admission, we have no codes of conduct and we don't operate the way the higher professions do, but we do have working conditions and take-home pay. It makes it a career that people can come into and aspire to stay in for the whole of their working lives.

The celebrity journalist can be snuffed out, and in print today there is no place across the street to take your stuff. There are the Sun papers, which have grown up in Toronto and Edmonton and Calgary, but they don't provide much of a market for political commentary. They are the 'T' and 'B' newspapers—the tits and bums papers for people who can't read—and they are very successful, God bless them. They create a market for journalism, but it certainly isn't the kind of market that the established papers used to create. The stars cannot take their audience with them when they go because they have no place to go. Nobody is going to stop buying a newspaper because a favourite columnist has gone. There is no other newspaper for them to buy. So there is no job security.

We have always been, in the end, beholden to the proprietors for our jobs, even though some of us have been blessed with proprietors who would never dream of telling us what to write, and what not to. In all the 26 years that I have been with the Southam Company, nobody has ever given me a directive of that kind or ever said that I shouldn't have written anything.

They may not publish it. There is no compulsion on them to do that. There is no compulsion on any paper to run the column on a day-to-day basis, and many of them are quite selective about it. But they don't issue directives.

However, I know, and that publisher knows, because that publisher is a hired gun, that in chain journalism there aren't any proprietor-publishers anymore. They are all hired by the proprietors of the chains. They know who hired them and they know that the job security isn't there. None of us have contracts, none of us have assured employment, and while they don't crack the whip, you are aware of this uncertainty and this insecurity. We can be fearless in print about everything except our own business, where our inhibitions show. And if you haven't noticed that in the coverage of all the controversy about chain journalism in this country, you haven't been paying attention.

Does anybody pretend that the CBC's fine documentary and investigative shows are as fearless about the CBC itself, which is a nation state within itself? Are as fearless about dealing with that as they are, say about dealing with Canadair, and whether the Challenger can fly or not? Or whether Pierre Trudeau should go or not? Or whether John Turner should be the next prime minister or not?

The fearlessness tends to be moderated when we deal with our own field, which is a very big field in terms of the public's interest. Does anybody imagine that myself and Allan Fotheringham and others of our splendid stable of Southam News writers, called the Cadillac of news services, that we were as outspoken about companies like Southam as we are about people and parties that govern the country, or about the educational institutions, or whether the Liberal monopoly on federal power should be broken at last?

What we boast about—our independence—is open to the criticism that we get crotch-bound when we are dealing with our own business. Is it in the public interest that so few people own so many newspapers in this country? We had a royal commission on that subject, which was commented upon in a very limited way by people like myself, and that was followed by a court case which the government lost trying to restrict the expansion of the chains; and the cabinet minister who tried to introduce the Newspaper Act was destroyed by the reaction of the proprietors in the statements they issued and by the editorials that were written.

The problem of minimal ownership of so many newspapers remains.

They are good newspapers. They are probably better newspapers than they were when they were independently owned, but the question of whether a few people, because they have the money to buy and operate newspapers, should own that much of the media in the country remains unsolved.

Because of the failure of the government intrusion (which we all deplored), there is nothing to stop the Thomson Company from buying the Southam Company and owning virtually all the newspapers in this country. This would result in more concentration of ownership in Canada than exists in any other country in the world.

CHAINS EXIST ELSEWHERE

Chain journalism is not a strictly Canadian problem. It exists in the United States and it exists in almost all the countries in Europe. Our boast about our independence is open to the criticism, that while we are celebrity journalists who are supposed to comment fearlessly, we are on ego trips that have little to do with the public good or the welfare of the citizens. I have had dialogues on this subject with my *confreres* from the communist countries, particularly the Soviet Union and the People's Republic of China, and have said, "How can you make yourselves tools of the apparatus? You are intelligent people. How can you stomach the fact that you are not free to express yourself?" And they said, "How can you stomach the fact that you operate the way you do? Do you operate in a way that makes your country easier to govern? Do you aid and abet the process of governance in your country or do you impede it?"

And I said, "Well, I've got the right. I can get up and I can say whatever I like about the prime minister, and I do." And they say, "To what end do you do that? How does the public benefit from the things you say and do? Can you prove that the public is better off?"

In the end, the argument was inconclusive. I went away not having convinced my *confreres* in those countries that our kind of freedom or the kind of journalism that I practice is at all more useful to the general weal than the kind that they do.

DOES PRESS FREEDOM AID UNITY?
Certainly we have freedom in this country, but has it helped to save the union? I said I supported government on one occasion. There were two. The other was during the national unity crisis.

At the time of the election of the Parti Québécois government in Quebec and the Quebec referendum, I lacked 'objectivity'. I was in favour of the preservation of the union and said so. Some of my colleagues were critical. They said, "You are not being at all objective here. You are supporting one side of the argument."

And I said, "Yes I am, and the reason I'm doing that is because the framework within which I operate with my freedom is the national framework. If the country breaks apart, the first thing that will happen, I'm sure from the evidence of other countries, is that authoritarian governments will be set up in the remnants. Certainly an independent Quebec will not be tolerant of freedom of expression to the extent of opposing the new nation of Quebec. The freedom to countenance political parties that advocate the overthrow of the union as we've known it, notably the government of Quebec, and whether this freedom is beneficial to the continuing of what was one of the most successful national experiments in the world, I think is open to question."

JOURNALISM HAS IMPROVED
Now having said as much as I have said critical of my own business (and I don't use the word profession because we are not, though we would be if we had more practitioners who were as learned and as aggressive in terms of what they believed as Don Minifie was), I have to concede that the practice of journalism has improved in Canada.

The papers are better than they used to be. Now that's more a comment on how bad they used to be than it is on the excellence of papers today.

Businesses and politicians can't buy coverage the way they used to. Within my memory, the reporters in Ottawa were paid or were given gifts at the end of the year by the government of the day. Very much more recently, up until following the Second World War, this same practice was followed in the press gallery in Quebec. It was taken for granted that newspapermen could be bought and we had freebies of all kinds. We travelled freely around the country on passes. We did all sorts of things. The same was true of journalism in Britain. They used to have a limerick: "You cannot hope to buy nor twist, thank God, the British journalist. Seeing, unbribed, what he will do, there isn't any reason to."

News is not as easy to suppress as it used to be, and journalists are not for sale to advertisers or power-brokers as they used to be. The bribes that I speak of existed in all parts of the country, and they were there to slant the news, and a lot of the papers that created the competition of those days were actually owned by the political parties. When Jimmy Gardiner dominated the politics of Saskatchewan, he dominated the newspapers of this province as well. And for years after the CCF came to power in this province, it never received anything like a fair shake in the news columns in the papers of the province.

This wasn't peculiar to Saskatchewan, but that was a conspicuous example, and today I think it's fair to say that that party probably does receive a fair shake in the coverage the papers carry. Now, I don't think there is any paper in the country that has supported the NDP editorially, but at least in the news columns the policies of the party are presented, and that didn't used to be the case. In my native New Brunswick, when I was a young reporter, we treated visiting CCF emissaries from Saskatchewan like communist agents. We looked at them as people who came from another planet and who were there for some sinister reason. And they got no press coverage at all. I was assigned to cover the almost surreptitious events that they attended and held, and turned in my reports for the benefit of the proprietors of the newspaper, who never put a word of it in their news columns.

When the Mackenzie-Papineau battalion sailed from St. John, New Brunswick, for the Spanish Civil War, I went and met the train. There were 900 men on that train who sailed for Spain. I wrote 10 columns of the news. I interviewed them all and wrote about the whole thing, not a line of which ever appeared in the local paper. Not one line. The whole thing was for the benefit of the proprietors.

That, I don't think, could happen today. It's better now, in that sense, and we also don't write puffs for advertising. You don't see things in the news columns disguised as news that really isn't news, at least not to the extent that you used to. So that degree of morality in our business is better. I hope it will continue to get better. Provided the Thomsons don't buy Southam. And remember that the Thomsons own the Hudson's Bay Company, and all kinds of other enterprises. The questions recently put forward by the government were whether it was healthy for conglomerates to own newspapers or whether it's right for large advertisers to own them.

As I remind you again, that argument was held and was never settled. It was just dropped because it was thought to be too hot to handle by the government of the day.

MONOPOLY PAPERS HEALTHY

Now that there are monopoly papers in virtually every city, the newspaper is a big, healthy business. It is, in some cases, the biggest business in town. It occupies tremendous new buildings, and this engine of public opinion is a source of pride to the proprietors, alongside the growth of the radio stations and the television stations.

The Kent Royal Commission on Newspapers sought, among other things (and it went too far in some ways), to give working journalists independence from the proprietors: to make the editor a separate person from the proprietor; independent of him and more connected with the community. That aspect of the report was laughed to scorn.

The feeling is now firmly entrenched in our business that there must never be any government intervention, that we have successfully beaten them back and that freedom is secure. And yet those of us who work in the news business know that the biggest news service in the country is the CBC. You have a monument to it here in Regina and they have news bureaus all across the country. The CBC spends more money on the collection of news abroad than anybody else in the country, even Southam which spends $3,000,000 a year on our news service. This is peanuts compared to what the CBC spends. That whole CBC news operation is financed entirely by money voted by Parliament. We have to scratch our heads and ask, "Well, is that tainted news? Is it so horrible to have government money used to subsidize the biggest news service in the country? Is the CBC the agent of government? Has it been corrupted by the fact that it has public money in it?"

The fact of the matter is that the CBC leans over backwards to prove that it isn't the handmaiden of government, that they operate freely and independently. They claim to be the most independent vendors of news in the whole country. Indeed, the negativism that I have spoken of is more pronounced in CBC news coverage than it is in CTV's or in the newspapers.'

LEFT WITH A RIDDLE

If you watch CBC programs, like the CBC news and *The Journal,* you will know what I mean. They use that as an instrument of criticism, more than as an instrument of praise. So we are left with this riddle of how to safeguard your right to independent news and views, uninfluenced either by government or by huge conglomerates.

Well, I have posed more questions than I answered. Some of the questions that I raised don't have an answer, and if I gave you a pat answer I would be fooling you. But I hope I have disturbed you a little bit. Minifie would have liked that.

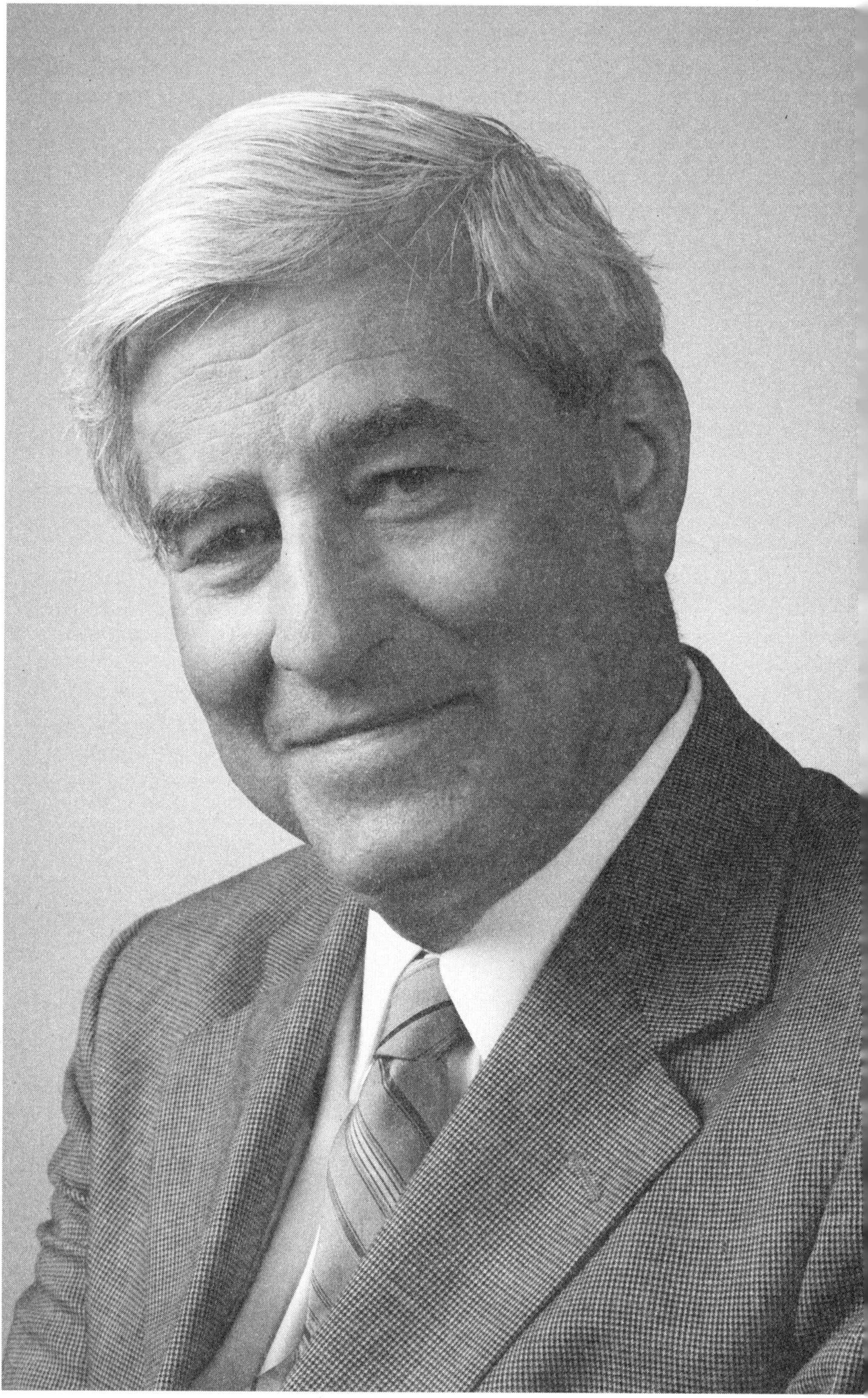

—1985—

JOE SCHLESINGER

For four decades Joe Schlesinger has reported for CBC Television News from every corner of the world. He has covered wars from Vietnam to the Persian Gulf. He has also served the CBC as its Chief Political Correspondent in Ottawa, executive producer of *The National*, and head of CBC TV News. As a foreign correspondent, Schlesinger was posted in Hong Kong, Paris, Washington, and Berlin. Schlesinger's 1990 memoirs, *Time Zones*, was a best-seller. *The Power of Good*, a film he wrote and narrated, won an International Emmy award in 2002. The film deals with the exploits of Sir Nicholas Winton, an Englishman who saved more than 600 children from the Nazis—Joe among them—by organizing *Kindertransports* that took them from Prague to Britain in 1939. Schlesinger has won four Gemini awards, the John Drainie award for distinguished contribution to Canadian broadcasting, a Hot Doc award for documentary writing, and a Lifetime Achievement Award from the Canadian Journalism Foundation. In 1994, he was named a member of the Order of Canada.

1985 | JOE SCHLESINGER

JOURNALISM:
It's Not Minding Falling Off an Elephant

You may not know it but you are here for a celebration. It's 30 years this month since I got a job as a reporter at the Vancouver *Province*. I had dabbled in journalism before then, but this was it, the big break, and I've been at it ever since.

Now, when I say this is a celebration, I don't so much mean celebrating that 30th anniversary of mine. What I am here for, what I want to do today is to celebrate the glorious business of being a journalist. I can think of no better place for such a celebration than the forum of the James M. Minifie Memorial Lecture here at the University of Regina.

I knew Don Minifie only casually. He was leaving the CBC just as I was coming in. But we did have a few things in common. I came to the CBC as he had done: from Europe by way of the *New York Herald Tribune*. And now, as I approach the age he was when I met him, I, too, have pulled back somewhat from knocking around the world ceaselessly to ensconce myself, as Don did a generation earlier, in the comfort of the CBC's Washington bureau.

I have studied the Minifie lectures given by those who preceded me on this podium. My predecessors haven't left me much manoeuvering room. Between them, they pretty well covered many of the most important problems and pitfalls of journalism. They spoke eloquently of the duty of journalists to be fair, accurate, aggressive in the search of truth, and, above all, not to succumb to the sin news people are most frequently charged with these days—arrogance. To all of these things, Don Minifie would have said: Amen.

JOY OF JOURNALISM

But I did find one aspect of journalism that these distinguished gentlemen left all but untouched in their lectures—the joy of being a journalist. To that sentiment, from all I know of the man, Don would have tipped his hat and raised his glass.

Never mind all the obstacles we face in this business. Never mind that so many of the jobs in journalism are badly paid. Never mind that so much of the work can be drearily routine. Never mind the ethical conundrums and political problems that face journalists today. Never mind that much of society regards us as somewhere between a nuisance and a modern-day equivalent of the black plague. For a moment, let us indulge ourselves in our own private secret, the secret we fear to shout from the rooftops lest we be condemned as hedonists, dilettantes, bums and clowns, the secret knowledge that journalism is above all . . . fun.

I know that some of you may say that it's all very well for me to talk about journalism being fun when I seem to spend my time gallivanting all over the world. All I can say is that I have done just about every job there is in journalism and that I've enjoyed them all. I've worked on newspapers, for news agencies, on radio and television. I worked night shifts for years on end. I've been a reporter, rewrite man, wire service slotman, newspaper editor, TV producer and executive. I've written editorials, magazine pieces and newspaper columns. I've even sold advertising space and set type. Just about the only editorial job I haven't done is draw cartoons. And after 30 years I can still say that doing these jobs—any of them or all of them—beats working for a living.

MANY SATISFACTIONS

There are many satisfactions in journalism: chasing a story and nailing it down, getting it first and telling it right, chipping away at a story that has been mangled into incoherence until it shines with clarity, making up a front page that tells it all as it should be told; or honing the pictures and pruning the words until you get that special magic that television can bring to journalism. But for me the two greatest pleasures of being a journalist ultimately have little to do with the finished product or how it's perceived by readers, watchers or listeners—or, for that matter, how it's received by editors.

First and foremost, there is the joy of just learning—not of learning in the usual formal sense—but of being constantly bombarded with information on just about every subject under the sun, of being able to wander through fields of ideas and forests of events, of always being confronted with something new and fresh. The curiosity of journalists, usually more roving than probing, may be the intellectual equivalent of joy-riding. But what a job and what a ride. And then there is the delight of words—of fiddling with phrases, polishing paragraphs, refining ideas, of composing and combining, of matching words with pictures, of searching painfully for just the right word and the elation of finding it, the pleasure of trying to capture a mood, a milieu, a sound or a rhythm on paper and then lifting it off that paper to make it sing.

It isn't great literature, it may not be profound, but good journalistic prose is clear, robust, entertaining, informative, useful and, thank goodness, even mildly remunerative for its practitioners.

FOREIGN CORRESPONDENT

But enough of that. What I am here for more specifically today is to talk about the craft at which Don Minifie and I spent most of our professional lives—the craft of being a foreign correspondent. It's nice work if you can get it. But it has its price. Dislocation for one. Travelling in exotic places, roughing it in dangerous and unpleasant places, never really knowing where you'll be tomorrow may be all very nice and well when you are young. In fact, it is exhilarating. But when you do it year after year, decade after decade, it takes its toll. Not only on the correspondent but on his family, if he still is lucky enough to have one.

This is where I get to the elephant in the title of this lecture—*Journalism: It's Not Minding Falling Off An Elephant*. I have to tell you first that it's fun riding an elephant. It's like trading in a stinkpot of a motorboat for a sailboat. It's a soothing, contemplative way to travel.

My elephant story happened in Cambodia in the spring of 1972. The army of Marshal Lon Nol, supported by the U.S., was fighting the Khmer Rouge. And though Lon Nol's forces had all sorts of firepower supplied by the Americans, they were doing badly and, of course, eventually lost to the Khmer Rouge, who fought with much more primitive weapons. I ran across a Cambodian army colonel who had formed an elephant patrol. His reasoning was that, in the area of jungle and rice paddies where he operated, American mechanized equipment was more of a hindrance than a help.

ELEPHANTS MORE SENSE

Elephants made more sense to him. In the jungle, they could go where jeeps and armoured personnel carriers couldn't. And when an elephant crossed a rice-paddy it didn't churn up the fields and destroy the crops the way the tank tracks of the American armoured personnel carriers did.

It was obviously a dilly of a story. Not just nice pictures but a political story.

The colonel wasn't really trying to prove that elephants were the secret weapon to victory. He was just protesting the way his superiors were submitting to American dictates on how to fight the war. His argument was that making farmers mad by destroying their crops and shooting up their villages with artillery and air strikes was a sure recipe for defeat. To him, elephants were more light-footed than modern technology. And, fortunately for me, he was right.

We sat on wooden platforms on top of the elephants, two men per elephant. The soldier who was with me sat there, relaxed, with his legs crossed, cradling his automatic rifle. I tried to do the same. We were crossing some rice paddies. To retain the water when they are flooded, paddies are separated by low dikes. Our elephant stepped up on one of those dikes. I was sitting there so studiously casual that when the elephant stepped down on the other side of the dike, I slid right off that platform, down the elephant's forehead, past his trunk and down into the paddy.

The elephant must have been as surprised as I was. Yet even as I looked up at him from the ground—and an elephant, believe me, is pretty huge when he is right on top of you—he shifted his poised foreleg to miss my head by what I remember as inches. If that had been a motorized personnel carrier I am sure I wouldn't be here today.

I got up, bruised but otherwise unhurt. And, even as the Cambodian soldiers were still snickering at my exhibition of round-eye incompetence and clumsiness, I got right back on top of that elephant—not very elegantly maybe, but I got right back on—and off we went again.

WHAT DOES IT MEAN

Getting back on top of the elephant as often as it takes, that's what being a foreign correspondent is all about.

There comes a time in each correspondent's life when he feels he's fallen off one elephant too many. He doesn't ever want to see an elephant again. And he certainly doesn't need another one of those bouts of dysentery that somehow always seem to come with elephant territory. He is sure he knows all he will ever need to know about elephants and that, when the next elephant story or crisis comes along, he will be perfectly capable of pontificating knowledgeably about elephants without even leaving his desk.

But it just doesn't work that way. The very thing that makes covering the world so exciting—the constant change—also makes it imperative for a foreign correspondent to keep going, to keep travelling, and to resist the temptation of turning in his air travel card for a set of pontificator's laurels. Once you stop, you become, at best, a teller of old tales and at worst a bore who passes off half-baked history as news. You might as well settle down to write your memoirs to give yourself something to snooze over in your old age.

Now, since this is an academic forum, I had better get down to some definitions if I want to avoid getting an F. What we need to define here is what I mean by a foreign correspondent.

There are all sorts of foreign correspondents, just as there are all sorts of reporters, editors and producers. We don't license people in our business, thank God, to allow them to pin these labels on themselves, but it does create confusion.

At its simplest, a foreign correspondent is someone who furnishes reports of one kind or another to a journalistic organization in another country. Most of the time—but not necessarily always—he or she even gets paid for it.

I have known quite a few people who did just enough of this that they could call themselves something other than what they were really doing, which was mostly nothing. I have even known a few who got themselves accredited as foreign correspondents just because it brought them one perk or another: a tax reduction, maybe, access to hard currency, or just an enrichment of their social lives.

RIP AND READ

A much more common phenomenon, though, is the rip and write or rip and read artist—the foreign correspondent who never actually covers a story. He simply reads the papers and wire service reports or uses footage from the local telly for a quickie rewrite job. A correspondent can't always be everywhere, so we all do this on some stories some of the time. But if you do it often enough, there will be nothing you can bring to your stories that couldn't just as well have been supplied by a rewrite man at the home office.

Some of the rip, write and read artists are that way simply because they are bad and lazy reporters, or, really, no reporters at all. But there are others who do it, not because they want to, but because that's what is required of them. They are where they are, they do what they do—for the dateline.

They get sent to places such as London or Washington to give their organization the cachet of having a London or Washington bureau. But their employers, having spent the money to set up the bureau, are not interested in spending more to have their correspondents waste their time actually chasing stories or, heaven forbid, piling up huge travel bills. It costs a lot of money to send people out to ride elephants. It's cheaper having them sit in the bureau writing about elephants.

Of course, travel, of itself, is not necessarily enlightening. There are other news organizations, notably the U.S. television networks, which employ journalists to do nothing but ride elephants. They are known in the business as firemen. They fly from crisis to crisis and from war to war. Their main qualification is their "have typewriter, will travel" eagerness and their capacity to adapt and survive. They are the bang-bang artists, the cannon fodder of journalism. They are not usually expected to think too much about the meaning of what they witness.

MINIFIE AN EXAMPLE

But there is another group of foreign correspondents. These correspondents have done their share of the quick and dirty rewrite jobs, their share of covering wars, firefights and riots. But they're not just paparazzi of the pen. They've seen enough, travelled enough, read enough, learned enough to have some idea of what the world and our part in it are all about. They can make connections between what they witnessed in one place and what they saw in another, between what happened a decade or 20 years ago and what's occurring now, between developments in Canada and parallel events elsewhere. Don Minfie was such a foreign correspondent. But to tell you the truth, Canada has had very few like him. It's not that we lack talented journalists. We have had plenty of them. Why, we even export them.

But being a foreign correspondent is not really considered as a serious career in this country. Oh, to have been a foreign correspondent for a little while is great. To have worked a year or two in London is Canadian journalism's counterpart of the international jet-set credential of having attended one of those snooty girl's finishing schools in Switzerland. It's the fast lane to advancement to high places.

But as a career, well, being a foreign correspondent is considered somewhat un-Canadian. In Britain, in the U.S., in France, it may be an honourable calling and an interesting and useful way of spending one's life. In Canada, being out of the country too long makes you suspect of just wanting to stay out of the cold, or, to put it in French, of having become *dépaysé,* of having lost touch with Canada.

Mind you, there is a way in the foreign correspondent business of having your cake and eating it, too. If you think you can't quite afford to waste a year or two in such a frivolous manner, don't despair: you can always spend a week in Beirut and maybe another in San Salvador. It'll look great on your resume to be able to say you covered the Middle East and Central American wars. And don't think I'm kidding; it's been done.

One tour of duty abroad, maybe two at most, that's all right. But if it's any more, you could be missing the boat. To get ahead these days, go to Parliament Hill, young man and young woman, or, better still, take a course in information management systems.

Don't get me wrong, I know there are plenty of people out there—and all but surely in this room, too—who would love to be foreign correspondents. But it's a long way from the wish to the reality.

PITFALLS

The first pitfall is that by the time journalists have acquired enough experience at home to go abroad and work on their own, they may be making too much money or be too comfortably established to start all over again. And many of those who try it fall by the wayside. Some cannot adapt to foreign ways and foreign languages. For others, it's the disruption to their family life. Many who did very well under the direction of a city editor or some other such direct goad, don't have the self-starting capabilities it takes to work on your own halfway around the world. And there are the simple things: health, food, the plumbing, and the hours. There is nothing more demoralizing than to have people in Canada calling you consistently at 3 a.m. your time, only to start out meaningless conversations with the question: "What time is it at your end?"

And good health is essential. In fact, the main qualification for being a foreign correspondent is to have a cast iron stomach. There is nothing that paralyzes the will and the brain quite as much as a good bout of dysentery.

But above all, it's not letting things get you down. I know of several correspondents who got so preoccupied with petty problems, such as not being able to get the plumbing fixed, that they never got around to doing their job properly.

Now, lest you accuse me of sounding negative, let me say right here and now—just in case you didn't get the message earlier—that I am extremely happy as a foreign correspondent and can't think of anything else I would rather do. Let me also add that I am concerned by the shortage of qualified people willing and able to do the job year in and year out. It may be good for me not to have the competition of too many people with extensive experience in foreign news reporting running around, but it's not good for Canadian journalism and, what's more important, it's not good for Canada.

MORE NEEDED

We need more and better foreign correspondents. We also need to utilize their experience more after they get back. There are too many former foreign correspondents sitting around newsrooms whose experience abroad rarely, if ever, gets tapped. We need these people not so much to boost the circulation of newspapers or the ratings of broadcasting outlets—we need them for the good of Canada. We keep ignoring that we are a nation that depends for its living on foreign trade and how dependent this makes us on the rest of the world. Other countries as heavily involved in foreign trade as we are—Australia and Sweden, for example—have far more foreign correspondents than we do. They realize that they need them to keep themselves informed about the world in which they are trying to squeeze out a living. That doesn't just mean economic news or political news that directly affects trade. It means everything from social trends to culture to fashion.

We don't seem to feel the need because we live in the shadow of the u.s. The North American community to which we belong is so large that its sheer mass creates in Canadians, at least in English Canadians, a sense of self-sufficiency and security that breeds a certain smugness and insensitivity to others.

Then there is the ease and convenience with which we can get our news from American sources. Why, in English Canada, we don't even have to waste our money translating the stuff!

CANADIAN EYES

But quite aside from the fact that the u.s. has interests in most of the news spots of the world that differ from ours, there is also the problem that we cannot afford to be quite as cavalier towards other countries, as ignorant about them and as insensitive to their needs and feelings as a superpower can. There are countries out there that would not tolerate from us the kind of behavior, whether justified or unjustified, that they may have to take on the chin from the Americans.

That's why it is so important to get our news of the world through Canadian eyes. The most important thing a Canadian foreign correspondent does is to explain how what's going on in the world affects Canada, to demystify foreign affairs, to give Canadians information that allows them to cope with this fast-changing world of ours.

But covering foreign news, riding those elephants, is expensive. And you can't blame Canadian news executives too much for being somewhat reticent about spending more money on foreign coverage when world news isn't exactly boffo box office in this country.

But there is some good news on the foreign coverage front. After Canada's preoccupation with domestic news in the late seventies and early eighties—because of the threat of separatism, the constitutional crises, the upsurge of nationalism, and various political and economic crises—there is now a renewed interest in foreign news. That interest has brought with it more money. In the past couple of years, there has been a notable expansion of bureaus and correspondents in Africa and Washington, all of it in the print media.

I hope this expansion is the harbinger of a long-term turnaround. But I remain skeptical. It's not cynicism, you understand. It's experience. I've seen this sort of thing before.

When I started writing a column on foreign affairs, a news syndicate manager warned me not to expect too much. "Advice to the lovelorn, a column on how to lose weight, that I can sell," he said. "But there aren't too many editors out there willing to give space—never mind money—to a foreign affairs column."

But it doesn't matter. For all the talking I've just done about the importance of what my colleagues and I do, I am happy to confess that I would do it even if it weren't important. In fact, if you promise not to tell my employers, I might even confide to you—completely off the record, of course—that I would do it even if they didn't pay me at all.

You see, being a foreign correspondent, riding that journalistic elephant is not just fun—once you've done it long enough, you can't stop. It can throw you, it can trample you, and you'll still get back up again asking for more. I know I will and that I wouldn't have it any other way. Neither did Don Minifie. And that's why we are here today, why we still remember him.

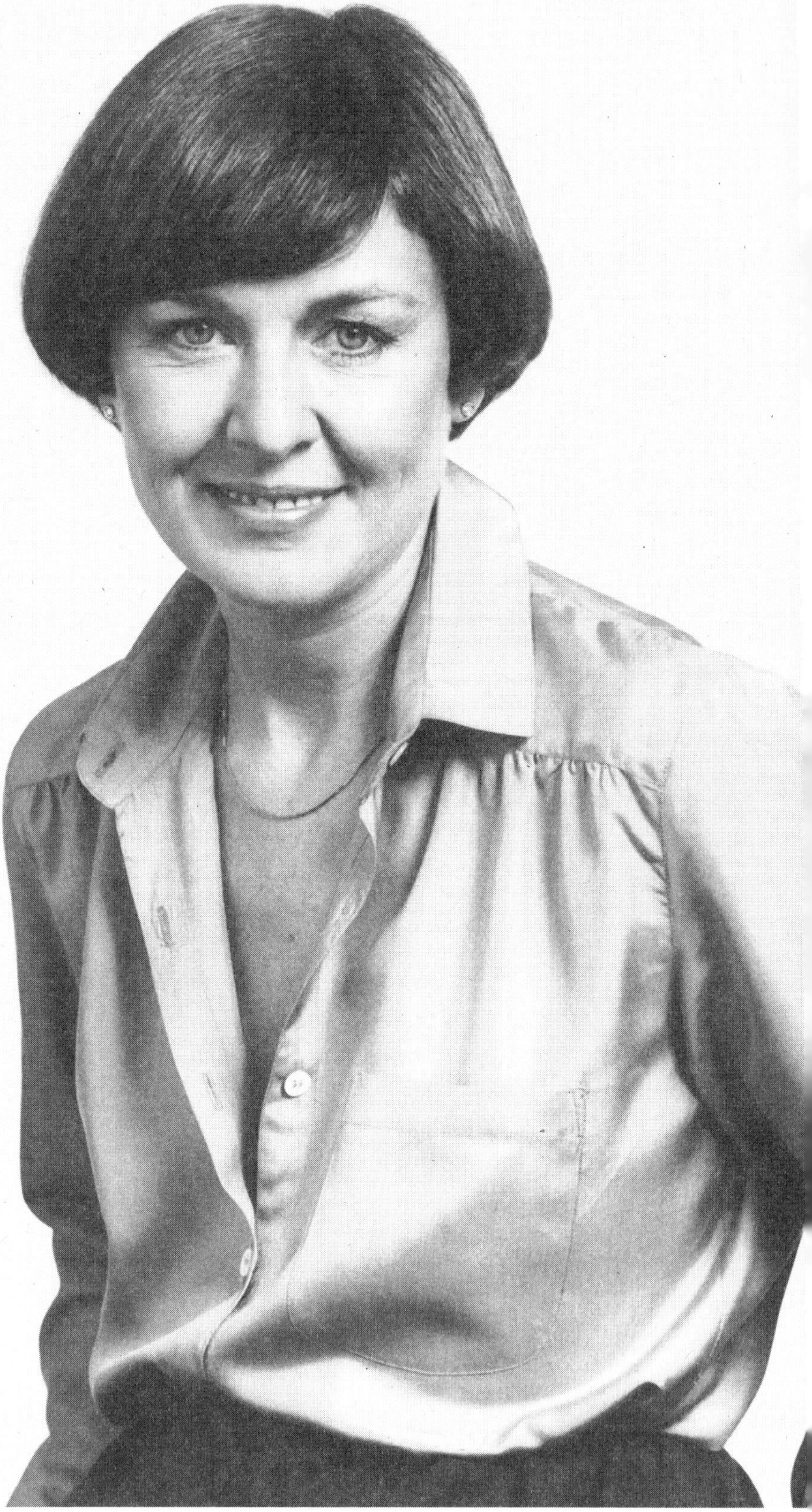

–1986–

HELEN HUTCHINSON

Helen Hutchinson began her career in radio, hosting programs such as the CBC's *Paperback Reader* and the public affairs program *Matinee*. She was also a contributing host for *This Country in the Morning*. Her move into television also saw her lead the way for women into sports reporting. In 1968, she debuted as a commentator on *Sportsview*. She later conducted interviews for *Hockey Night in Canada*. Hutchison went on to host *Women Now* and *Helen Hutchison*. She also spent many seasons as a host and reporter for CTV's flagship investigative program, *W5*. She won the 1975 ACTRA Award for Best Television Public Affairs Broadcaster in Canada.

1986 | HELEN HUTCHINSON

IMAGES, SELF-IMAGES, AND THE LONG STRING

'm very pleased to be here tonight. I'm always happy to head west, because I am a westerner. It's a fact I must constantly reinforce with some of my eastern colleagues, who are cursed with the unshakeable conviction that Canada ends somewhere between Bloor Street and Eglinton Avenue in Toronto. When pressed, they may concede that it might extend as far as Brampton, Ontario, the home town of Bill Davis.

I'm particularly honoured to be the first woman asked to give the James M. Minifie Memorial Lecture.

I'm always a little surprised to see myself described as a journalist. Back in the fifties, when I was an undergraduate at the University of British Columbia, I was privileged to win the B.C. Women's Press Club Scholarship. I admit that I accepted it a little sheepishly, because, at the time, I had no intention whatever of becoming a journalist. I had my sights set on becoming a professor of literature-a teacher. My chief competitor for that scholarship was a young woman who did intend to pursue a career in journalism. She went on to become a splendid journalist, although that's probably not how you know her today. Her name is the Honourable Pat Carney, Energy Minister.

Rather than journalist, the description I use is broadcaster. I like that word better because I think it describes more accurately what we're supposed to be doing, and that's scattering information—which is, in fact, teaching.

SELF-IMAGES

I know that most of us don't consciously regard ourselves as teachers, but think of what it is we're doing. We come into your homes, electronically, to tell you about what's happening around the world, or down the block. We tell you about other people, and, by doing that, we tell you about yourself. We're creating images and self-images, and if that's not teaching, I don't know what is.

Speaking of self-images, I'd like to go back to the word "broadcaster." A lot of my younger colleagues tell me it's an old fashioned term and it probably is. The 1921 *Oxford English Dictionary* defines broadcast as meaning "to disseminate audible matter from a wireless transmitting station." The scattering, as of seed, definition goes back to 1767. Man has been broadcasting for a long time.

My younger colleagues say I should call myself something else, but I'll tell you why I won't. Back in the days when I worked in radio I knew a woman who tried a variation on the theme. She was a freelancer who worked mainly for the northern service of the CBC. One day, the enumerator arrived at her door and asked her to state her occupation. She was a proud woman, proud of both her race and her profession. She said that she was an "Indian Broadcaster."

That was back in the sixties when computers were just coming into use and none of us knew how to talk to them. A few weeks later, my friend burst into my office in a laughing fit. On her way to work she'd stopped to read the voters' list tacked to the telephone pole, and found her computerized occupation: "Indian Broad."

So you see why I don't embellish.

Whether broadcaster, journalist, whatever term you choose, the role is the same: to put events into context, to try to make some sense out of all the information with which we're bombarded, *before* we scatter it.

But, because we've glided into an age of technology that celebrates immediacy, that encourages glibness and discourages thoughtful reflection, too often we find ourselves seduced by the race to be first.

In the old days the ace reporter raced to the scene—which had to be within a cab's ride—gathered the information, phoned it back to the desk, and within a couple of hours folks were reading the latest scoop.

Not so anymore.

The day after the space shuttle disaster, one Toronto newspaper columnist berated the CBC for staying with scheduled programming for 22 minutes before switching to the American feed. In the same column, he quoted top news people from both CTV and Global, each man insisting that his operation was first to put the tragic event on the air.

In the area of hard news, yes, I can understand the need for haste, but even in the area of current affairs television, as opposed to news, there is this need to be first with the obvious. Perhaps it's merely human nature, but whatever it is, it bothers me.

OBJECTIVITY BE DAMNED

Here's a glimpse into a hypothetical current affairs program story meeting. Someone pipes up—remember, this is hypothetical—"Why don't we do a piece on sliced bread?" At least three people will jump in with, *"the fifth estate* did that two years ago." What does that have to do with anything?

No matter who has done a story on any subject, when the next person tackles it, it's going to come out differently. And thank heaven for that, or the poets and novelists and playwrights would have packed it in centuries ago.

The fact is that each of us carries around his own intellectual and emotional sieve through which all information is strained. Each of us edits his or her own life.

As broadcasters, one of our jobs is to edit other people's lives. As viewers, we need to remember, even when we're watching 30-second news clips, that someone has edited them according to his or her own lights.

Objectivity be damned. There's no such thing. What we, as journalists, broadcasters, teachers, need to do is learn to use the big string. This is a remarkably useful notion I learned from the most memorable teacher I ever had, Roy

Daniells, who was then head of the English department at the University of British Columbia.

He urged us to look at all human achievement, from the beginning of time to the present—and the present grows with each day—as beads on a string.

The string is the continuum of time. Everything goes into the string: Shakespeare's sonnets, the industrial revolution, the invention of the safety pin, the breaking of the four-minute mile. In short, the whole shooting match.

Some beads are larger than others, but they're all there on the string. Nothing exists in isolation. When you look at an event or achievement in this way, when you sit back and contemplate that big string, it's much easier to get the perspective in place and to decide how each new bead fits in with the others. The idea is stunning in its simplicity.

It's becoming familiar and then staying familiar with the big string that takes a lot of work on our part.

You can't teach if you don't learn.

A classic example of rushing to be first and failing to consult the big string: The Geneva Summit last November. For days, the summit made headlines and led the newscasts all over the western world. For days, we were subjected to seemingly endless reports on every external detail—even down to the wardrobes of the wives of the two leaders. Every word that was uttered publicly was dutifully duplicated hundreds of times over, then played and replayed on equally endless newscasts.

What do you remember out of all that coverage? The most lasting impression I have is one of all the reporters—2,100 of them—pushing and shoving to get a better shot of the two principals. The point is unless it's put into some sort of context, an event even as potentially momentous as the Geneva Summit drowns in a sea of trivia. Off go the reporters, racing to the next big event, anxious to compile more faces which, if not threaded onto the big string, are quickly dumped into the dustbin of history. We're left with nothing more than an exercise in futility.

WOMEN IN JOURNALISM

When I accepted the invitation to speak here tonight, I discovered that I was in some pretty fast company. The five men who've preceded me at this podium—Knowlton Nash, Clark Davey, Bill Stevenson, Charlie Lynch and Joe Schlesinger—have spoken to you about most of the issues important to journalists, from the joy of journalism, to the importance of being responsible, accurate, aggressive and ever mindful of the role of the journalist as a disseminator of news, not the object of it.

But there is one important issue which none of my distinguished colleagues has touched on in their lectures, probably because they are all men. I'm speaking, of course, about the role of women in the profession. It's an issue of interest, and concern, to me, and one that I know is important to a number of you as well.

I'm not going to apologize for raising this issue. I'm aware that about half of you here tonight are men, and your interest in the subject of women in journalism is less than that of the women in the audience. Hang in. I think you'll find that what I have to say is interesting and pertinent to you as well.

Here we go with images and self-images again. When I was a small child I was a radio addict. My parents worried about my health because I preferred, even at the tender age of four, to listen to the radio rather than go out to play.

Thinking about this the other day, I tried to conjure up my earliest impressions of women, as I knew them from radio. These are my earliest impressions: I remember Big Sister, Our Gal Sunday, Young Widder Brown and Ma Perkins. I remember Kate Smith, Judy Canova, and Evelyn and Her Magic Violin. My earliest recollections of women on Canadian radio are of Kathleen Stokes at the organ—the boys in the Happy Gang occasionally let her speak a few words—and Just Mary.

So, you see, women have always been there, as long as they were silly, sang, sobbed, showed motherly concern, told stories to children, or played the organ.

My earliest memory of female intelligence at work is the agile adolescent mind of Ruthie Duskin on *The Quiz Kids,* as she consistently drubbed poor smart Joel. I never missed that program. I remember Ruthie so vividly, I think now, because I identified with her. She wasn't sobbing or singing. She was being smart, and being praised for being smart. And, so I identified with Ruthie Duskin, but I don't remember wondering at the time why it was okay for a kid to be so smart on the radio, when all the grown-up ladies either sang or sobbed or were silly and occasionally talked very seriously about recipes or how to get the puke out of baby's bib.

By and large, I was being told things by men.

Men told me the news, told me about the records they played, even told me to "scoot" at the end of the children's broadcast, which came on after I'd learned all about feeder cattle and rape seed.

I don't think I need to spell it out to you. I think you know why, to this day, I remember Ruthie Duskin's name.

As I grew, radio was always there. And, still, as the years went on, it was men telling me about my world. Where were the intelligent women, I asked myself. Where did all the Ruthies go when they grew up? Did they simply shun the world of broadcasting, or—oh sinister thought—did the world of broadcasting shun them?

THE BIG STRING

An illustration: When Anne Francis attempted to break into broadcasting in 1941—that was at CKY in Winnipeg—the station manager told her she was simply a society woman with a bright idea. The idea was a backgrounder in simple language so that children could understand why the grownups were so uptight during the war.

Well, you know where Anne's broadcasts took her: Eventually all the way to the chairmanship of the Royal Commission on the Status of Women in Canada. Some society woman. Some bright idea.

At this point, many of you are probably saying to yourselves: but that's ancient history. It's not like that anymore. There are women in almost every aspect of the broadcasting business.

And you're right. There are women writers, editors, producers, directors and researchers. There are women newsreaders, reporters, interviewers and hosts.

What I'm trying to do here is put an historical bead on the big string, because I truly believe that had it not been for Anne Francis, a.k.a. Florence Bird, and her Royal Commission, I wouldn't have been able to rhyme off that list.

Sure we've come a long way. Mainly by ourselves and out of necessity. And after that, because the uncomfortable necessity was duly pointed out to the boys at head office.

Once again, back to the project-image and self-image. I don't think, and this is something men don't think about at all because they've never had to, that our mainstream of information should be filtered through one set of conditioned responses—those of white, middle class males. Yes, each of them filters information a little differently from the other, but as culturally conditioned males, each shares a peculiar bias, revulsion, fear perhaps.

I'll give you an example. It wasn't so long ago that social issues such as contraception, divorce, incest, pre-menstrual tension, menopause, wife-beating and rape were not considered "important" enough to warrant investigation and exposure on prime-time television, or *any* television. Those, among many other subjects, were considered to be "women's issues."

I'm not here to indulge in cheap psychology, but all of you know that almost every male born and raised in the western world carries within him a deep, almost primal fear of, and revulsion toward, the workings of the female body. So, to a man, it makes much more sense to do a story on a decrepit ex-boxer reliving past glories while he rots in a flophouse than it does to do one on the latest medical research on menopause. Men may have wanted to know that their wives might develop the debilitating condition known as osteoporosis, but until recently, the networks weren't going to tell them.

TEN YEARS AGO

Let's go back in time again. It's, say, 10 years ago, and we're in the middle of a current affairs program editorial meeting anywhere in Canada. Question: Why don't we do a piece on contraception? Answer: That's women's stuff. Why else did science give us the pill? Question: Well, what about divorce? Answer: Maybe you've got something there. Just look at how many poor guys are put through the financial wringer. Question: Why not look at incest, its incidence and effects? Answer: Ugh! Are you kidding? Only half-wit hillbillies do things like that. Question: Pre-menstrual tension? Answer: To begin with, there's no such thing, and even if there were, who'd be interested except a bunch of female hypochondriacs? Question: Well, then, why not a story on wife-beating? Answer: Look, our male viewers are not moronic brutes. Question: Rape? Answer: Sure, it happens. But what could we say about it that hasn't already been said? And besides, a lot of women are just asking for it.

Okay, I exaggerated slightly. But if that isn't fear talking, I don't know what is. You think I'm making this up? I'm not a creative writer. I've heard variations on all those and many other subjects all too often over the years. And all of you heard what the illustrious members of the House of Commons thought about wife-beating just last year.

The good news is that today, it's generally accepted that these subjects—issues, if you will—are important. Not just to women—who, in any event make up over 50 percent of the population and, therefore, the viewing public—but to men as well. It's now accepted that these are human issues which, one way or another, affect us all. Yet, even 10 years ago, you would never have known it if you tuned in to prime-time current affairs television. Are the men who control current affairs programming—and make no mistake, the people with the power are almost all men—suddenly more enlightened? Yes, they are, because we've damned well forced them to be. We, and you. Public response is the big barometer.

The visible influx of women into broadcasting over the past 10 years has changed the viewing public's perception of the role of women. It's now perfectly acceptable to most people to listen to a woman read the news, for instance. We, as broadcasters, used to be told that the female voice carried no authority, which was a charming way of saying that since you lot don't sound like Lorne Greene, nobody's going to believe you.

We were told that, speaking technically, the female voice had too much top and not enough bottom. That was the voice. Never heard that about the body.

I'm not talking about the days of the crystal set.

I'm willing to bet that some of you remember the uproar across the country in the late sixties when some intrepid soul at the CBC decided that a woman staff announcer should read news on radio. The announcer in question had, and still has, one of the most arresting female speaking-voices I've ever heard: deep, rich, smooth. It was all right for her to announce music programs and the like, but read the news!

I've never been able to find out whether the biggest stink was raised by the listening public or by the otherwise all-male announce staff itself. It makes no matter. The offending female voice was removed from the news. The reason given to the press was that her speech, though beautifully modulated, had a shade too much of an English accent, which was unacceptable to Canadian ears. Bah! Humbug! The time just wasn't right.

Because I travel so much for *W5*, I have the opportunity of watching local newscasts all over the country and throughout the United States. I guess you could call it one of my hobbies. Morley Safer paints pictures of his hotel rooms and I watch local newscasts.

Almost without exception, the news desk is manned—or should I say occupied—by two people: one man, one woman, both attractive. Gone are the weather girls who, not so long ago, were used primarily to decorate the set. The reporters in the field seem to be split about 60 to 40, with the extra 20 percent on the women's side. I don't know why this is. I don't know whether it's good or bad. I merely observe it.

SELF-IMAGE AGAIN
What *is* good is that young women can now look at their television sets and see themselves. There's that old devil self-image again.

Another one of my away-from-home hobbies is to read the crawl, the credits, after news and current affairs shows. That's where you really see the women at work. Read *W5*'s crawl some Sunday and you'll see what I mean. You'll also notice that the top jobs, the jobs with the power, are held by men, but that without the women, we couldn't put the show on the air. I'm not carping. CTV is actually an enlightened network compared to the CBC when it comes to opportunities for women. I'm just observing.

The reason I bring this up is that this year, as in every year since at least 1980, roughly 65 percent of the graduates of journalism schools in this country will be women. I certainly don't mean to imply that all of them will want to work in television, but I do think that figure reflects an optimism among young women today that broadcasting, unlike many other professions, offer women unlimited opportunities for advancement.

For work: possibly. For advancement: not as likely. Not as likely unless they can see 20 years down the road. The reason is as plain as the nose on your face. Men have been there longer than women have.

I don't have any statistics to back up my observation, but I do think that broadcasting is no longer the rapidly-expanding business it was during the sixties and seventies. The market is pretty well saturated. You have to remember, too, that a lot of us have been there for quite a while and have no intention of quitting because we're having too much fun. At the same time, the pressure to hire and promote women has eased off. There is a sense—even among broadcast executives—that equality has been achieved. After all, *W5* has a female co-host, and has had for years. CBC *Midday* and *the fifth estate* both have women co-hosts, and *The Journal* made headlines when it went on air four years ago with two women anchors. The fact that that was news tells us something about how far we have yet to go. Even the viewing public became uncharacteristically silly at the time, writing snide letters to the editor about Barbara's clothing and Mary Lou Finlay's eye make-up. Had they been two men, the letters—if there were any at all—would have dealt with content, not form; with substance, not image.

The truth is, women entering broadcast journalism today are going to have a tougher time of it, in many respects, than I did when I started over 20 years ago. When I began, it was a small shop, in relative terms. Everybody knew everybody else and we all changed and grew as the business changed and grew.

COMPETITION STIFF

The closer you get to the top, you'll find that everybody still knows everybody else, because we're still that same tattered band of irregulars. So women are still going to have to work harder to prove themselves because the competition for jobs is much stiffer. There are simply more people vying for a limited number of positions, which means fewer breaks for women. But that's all right because, to quote the late Charlotte Whitton, former mayor of Ottawa: "Whatever women do they must do twice as well as men to be thought half so good . . . Luckily, it's not difficult." It's not difficult, but there is a quirky risk involved.

While I was still on *Canada AM* I did a series of interviews with women in so called male professions. The stunner came when a woman surgeon—and you have to admit, there aren't many of them—told me how proud she used to be during her residency when the older surgeons praised her for handling complicated surgery just like a man. It took her about a year to figure out that was no compliment. It was condescension mixed with surprise.

So I worry sometimes when I sit in my hotel room watching all those women field reporters scurrying across the face of North America.

I worry that they will be seduced into trying to fit themselves into the male stereotype after fighting so hard to struggle out of the female version. You know what I mean: big boys are tough and aggressive, big boys don't go soft, big boys don't show fear and, of course, big boys don't cry. It's a foolish myth, but it's still alive.

POINT TAKEN

I fell into that trap once myself, at least once that I remember. I sat in a studio for many years and in a studio it's easy just to be yourself. It's very much like having a dinner party and welcoming guests into your own home. The studio is home, and they all come to visit you. It's a controlled environment, and you're in control. Out in the field, the story is quite different.

One morning in March, 1981, I was lying in bed with a dreadful head cold, contemplating whether or not to call in sick. The office beat me to it. The message was that I was on the four o'clock flight to Naples. There had been an earthquake in the mountains.

Three flight connections and a day and a half later, I hooked up with the crew. When we finally reached the site, it was like nothing I had ever seen in its awfulness. There was total confusion, mess and filth. People who had lost everything—their homes, their belongings, their families—were stunned, powerless to help themselves, sleeping 25 and 30 to a tent, the tents precariously upright on a sea of mud and human excrement.

Mountains of medical supplies, clothing and food sat rotting in the tainted mud and the rain. We were there for three days, but we, at least, could make the long drive back to Naples at night.

I can't count the number of times I was in tears during those three days. But when the time came for me to talk to the camera, I bravely fought them back and said what I had to say. After the piece went to air, one of our cameramen took me aside and said, "You were on the verge of tears a couple of times. Why didn't you just let go and cry? It would have been much more effective." He was right. I had been trying to be a good soldier, just like a man, when I should have simply been me. Point taken. Lesson learned.

Since I started in broadcasting 24 years ago, I've worked on so many radio and television shows that I can't even remember the names of them all. Looking back now, it's all kind of a blur, the same kind of blur as everybody's school days. We all remember that we were in grade six once, but we can't remember exactly what we did or what we were learning.

One of the important things I *do* remember learning is that if you want a nine-to-five job with weekends and holidays off, find another business. Another important thing I've learned is that most people are extraordinarily generous—with their time, their thoughts, their feelings—and not just when they're trying to flog a book.

For instance: In 1969 I was host of *Matinee* on CBC radio and just starting to work in television. One afternoon I did a half-hour live radio interview with Peter Ustinov, and was scheduled to tape a 20 minute interview for television immediately after.

As we were walking across the parking lot to the television building, I said that had been a terrific half-hour of radio, and perhaps we could just do it all over again for the cameras. Ustinov looked down at me—I come approximately to his waist—and replied, "I never repeat myself."

I felt like a nit.

Now, here's where we get to the generosity part. I remember this as though it were last week. I started the interview by asking a nitlike dumb question: "How did you begin?" Before I could complete the asinine question, he leaped in with, "As a baby." He then went on to carry the entire interview for 20 minutes, even doing his racing car and squeaking door sound effects, which he has always vowed he will never do on television. That's the generosity of the first rate. The second rate will never display such magnanimity, which is one of the ways we can spot them.

THE ORDINARY PERSON
Then there's the generosity of the ordinary person. When I sat in a studio, the people and their stories came to me. With *W5* the process is reversed. I go to them. More accurately, we invade. We've filmed a woman having a face-lift and a man having bypass surgery, and they let us do it. We've interviewed on film, victims of child abuse, victims of rape, women who've been beaten and the husbands who beat them. We've filmed winners and losers and a lot in between.

One of the most extraordinary sensations is that of picking up the phone in Toronto, calling a complete stranger halfway across the country for an appointment to come to his office or factory or home—maybe all three—and being granted that access. I can't think of another profession which is willingly given the right to step into another person's life.

The story that comes most readily to mind is one I did last fall for the hour-long special *W5* did on AIDS. We contacted a man in Fort St. John, B.C., who had lost his wife to AIDS only three months earlier. She was the victim of a blood transfusion.

He and his two young children were still in mourning, but he didn't hesitate to invite us to come and see him. He opened his home to us and he encouraged the other people in town to open their doors to us as well, to share the shock, grief and fear the community had felt when AIDS claimed one of its own.

He went through the pain all over again with us because he hoped that his experience would help others.

We were privileged because we were broadcasters. With that kind of privilege comes responsibility. And we must never lose sight of that.

James M. Minifie, the man in whose honour we are all here tonight understood the journalist's responsibility to the public. His reports set the standards for the day in accuracy and clarity.

Hugh Keenleyside wrote of Minifie: "Even after he 'retired' to Victoria . . . Don Minifie maintained his active interest in national and international affairs. His occasional broadcasts were fascinating in their recollection of events past and in the relation of those events to the recurring crises of an increasingly complex and dangerous world.

"This was a man whose restless and incisive mind illumined, for us all, the weaknesses and the cruelties, the foibles and the humours, the virtues and the values, of our baffling human existence."

Don Minifie knew about the big string. From what I remember of his broadcasts from Washington, he *used* the big string every day to sift through the trivial that appears important, and the important that appears trivial.

And that, ladies and gentlemen, is what broadcasting is all about.

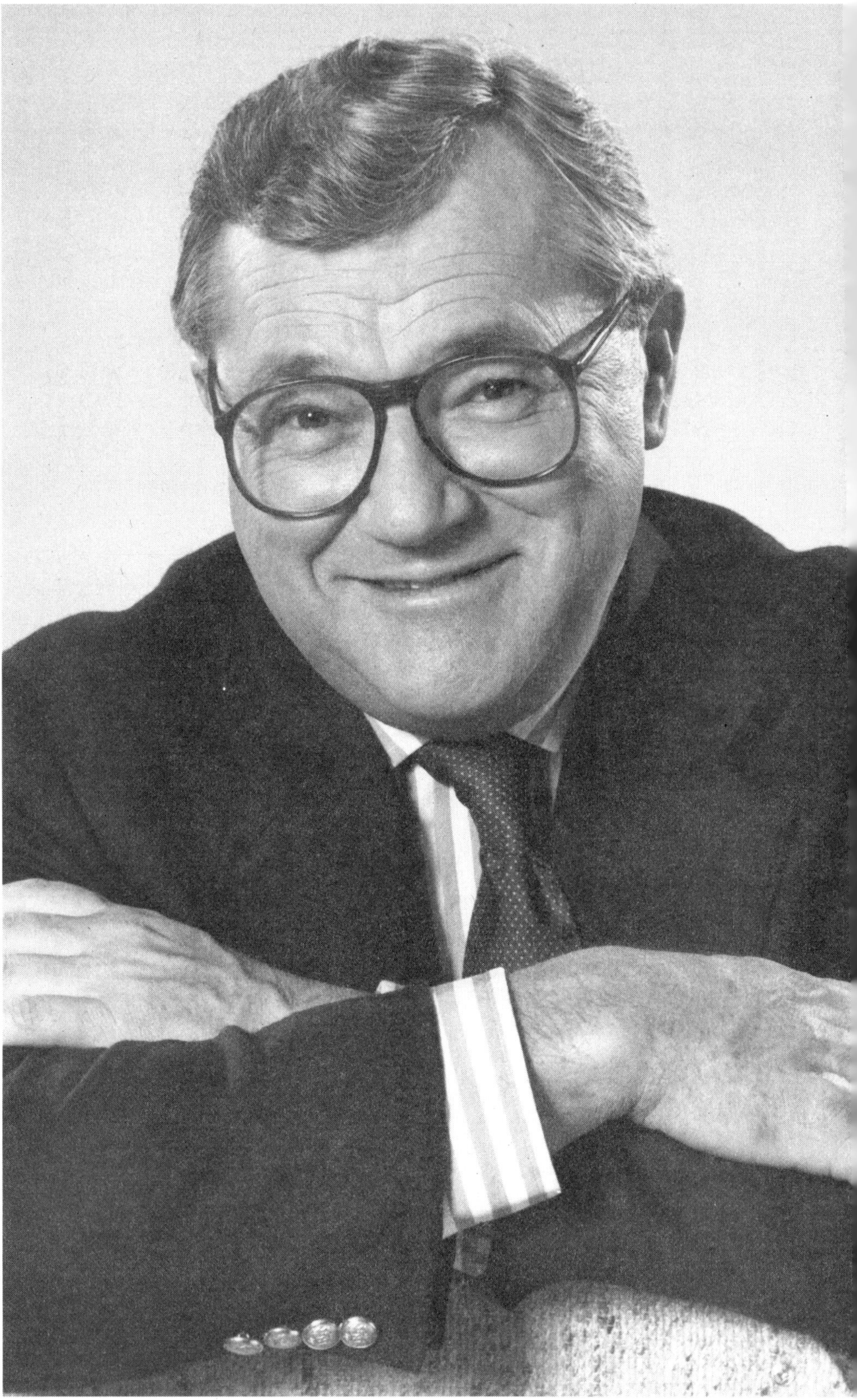

—1987—

ALLAN FOTHERINGHAM

Allan Fotheringham's columns have appeared for over 30 years—in the *Vancouver Sun*, *The Financial Post*, *The Globe and Mail* and in Southam and Sun Media papers across Canada. He has published six books. He has traveled in over eighty countries, reporting from the former Soviet Union, China and Africa. Fotheringham was a columnist in Washington for five years, covering the Reagan and Bush administrations and has traveled extensively in the United States, missing only four states. Fotheringham wrote for *Maclean's Magazine* for 27 years. He was a ten-year panelist on the famous Canadian television show, *Front Page Challenge*. Fotheringham has received the Southam Fellowship in Journalism, the National Magazine Award for Humour, the National Newspaper Award for column-writing, the Bruce Hutchison Lifetime Achievement Award and was inducted into the Canadian News Hall of Fame in 1992.

1987 | ALAN FOTHERINGHAM

MUTUAL IGNORANCE:
Canada and the United States

I must confess to you at the outset that I am here under somewhat false pretences, because I am not a speaker, I am a writer, and in circumstances like this I feel rather like Zsa Zsa Gabor's sixth husband: I know what to do but I'm not sure I can make it interesting.

But I am, as you know, from British California. It is also known as Bennett Columbia, the home of the Socreds and the Sasquatches. The Sasquatches are the ones with the big feet.

British Columbia is a unique political entity. It certainly is unique in Canada, perhaps unique anywhere in the world, because you know we had a premier, "Wacky Bennett," who ran the province for 20 years. Then, after a short interregnum with Dave Barrett, his son, "Mini Wack," took over. I used to be a friend of Bill Bennett and I used to play tennis with Bill Bennett and I used to drink with Bill Bennett, so people would always ask me legitimate questions, such as whether he was simply a chip off the old block? Was he merely a clone? And I would say that in fact he wasn't and Bill Bennett was very much his own man. As an example, I would always tell them that whenever Bill Bennett went over from Vancouver to Victoria to the legislature he took the ferry. His father used to walk.

Of course, we now have a new premier, "Bill Vanderslap"—"Premier Moonbeam." Do you know why Bill Vander Zalm wears wooden shoes? To keep the woodpeckers away from his head.

Things are not very good economically in British Columbia. The drop in the world prices for resources hasn't helped. I was in Vancouver a couple of weeks ago in the bar of my hotel and this guy was moaning to the bartender. He said, "Look, I am in the furniture business and I am going to lose my ass." There was a girl sitting down the bar and she said, "Look buster, I'm in the ass business and I'm going to lose my furniture."

However, it's nice to be here. I have just come from Washington, where I live. Sondra Gotlieb wanted to be here tonight but she had a previous engagement at Madison Square Gardens.

The London *Sunday Times,* each week, runs in its colour magazine a "careers" page—to guide young people who are confused about their future. Each week features a different profession, or trade. The "black art of journalism"—as Kipling called it—was the subject several years ago. *The Times* enlisted one of its star reporters, Philip Knightley. He has just published a superb book, *The Second Oldest Profession: The Spy as Bureaucrat, Patriot, Fantasist and Whore,* on the idiocy of the spy industry—to explain journalism to the unwashed.

"The only requirements to be a successful journalist," he wrote, "are rat-like cunning, a plausible manner and a rudimentary command of the English language. The last requirement is least."

This is the best description of the black art I have ever seen. The rat-like cunning is necessary so one can deal with all the devious politicians and businessmen and other authorities who devote their life to concealing the truth from the public. The plausible manner is necessary—the proper disguise of clothing and clean fingernails—to insinuate oneself among the rats and non-rats so as to gather the information they don't want gathered. The tentative grasp of the English language is only needed to get your purple prose past the editors. Editors, as someone once explained, are the guys who separate the wheat from the chaff—and then print the chaff.

Following on my commendation of rat-like cunning, I started my career in journalism as a thief. The locale—this was about 1938 or so—was the post office in downtown Hearne, Saskatchewan, some 40 miles south from where I stand. Hearne, naturally, is named after one of the great explorers of Western Canada, Samuel Hearne. People from Hearne are called "Hearne." In fact, the town was so small we couldn't afford a village idiot—everyone had to take turns. I later moved from Saskatchewan to British Columbia and this improved the IQ of both provinces.

I digress. My mother was the post-mistress and the post office was in our home, shaded by the only tree in Hearne at that time. My brother, my two sisters and myself were the only children in the town. The mail slots in the post office had their open ends facing into what would be our living room. Each day, I would steal a Regina *Leader-Post* from the slot of some unsuspecting subscriber, carefully take it out of its wrapper, spread it on the floor, peruse the sport pages and then carefully tuck it back into the uncreased wrapper and return it to the mail slot. The rat-like cunning has never left me.

I am honoured to be asked to deliver the Seventh Annual James M. Minifie Memorial Lecture because, as Minifie proved, all the great ones come from Saskatchewan.

As proof, I submit the fact that we went to a one-room schoolhouse three miles from Hearne. Twelve grades, one room. There were only two of us in grade one, in grade two, grade three. My buddy's name was Kenny Newans, who is now the sports director of a major Calgary television station. So, out of the Depression, out of that tiny town and surrounding farms, the two schoolmates have ended up—one making a good living out of the spoken word, the other making a good living out of the written word. Must be something in that old-time religion after all.

LINKED TO OTHER LECTURERS

I'm also honoured to be the Minifie lecturer this year because I have so many links with my distinguished predecessors. The second Minifie lecturer, Clark

Davey, was my last publisher at the *Vancouver Sun*. The fourth Minifie lecturer was Charlie Lynch, an incorrigible man who was my columning mate at Southam News in Ottawa. We both shipped columns from Disneyland-on-the-Rideau to the 15 Southam papers stretching from Montreal to Vancouver and, inevitably perhaps, one paper printed my column—calling Trudeau a moron—under Lynch's byline and printed Lynch's column—calling Trudeau a genius—under my byline. Charlie therefore suggested that henceforth we share a mutual byline: Fynch and Lotheringham.

The sixth Minifie lecturer was Helen Hutchinson, who used to be my girlfriend 150 years ago at the University of British Columbia, and still is a close buddy. The fifth Minifie lecturer was Joe Schlesinger, the man who got me into this terrible business.

Schlesinger is so bright that within a year of fleeing Czechoslovakia he was editor of the University of British Columbia's celebrated campus newspaper, *The Ubyssey*, which is the best journalism school in Canada. It has produced such as Earle Birney, Pierre Berton, Ron Haggart, Helen Hutchinson, Pat Carney, and somebody called John Turner.

I was a lowly sports columnist and Schlesinger asked me to run in the democratic election in which incumbent editors would choose his successor. I said there was no chance, since the obvious favourite, an abstemious son of the manse, had stayed on at university for years as a graduate student waiting for this chance. Joe told me not to worry. He stuffed the ballot box and I won. Rat-like cunning.

It's clear, as you can see, that the sponsors of this fine series, once having creamed the crop, have now started to reach down to the dregs as successors.

When I tell this story in press clubs around the world, with Schlesinger present, he is slightly embarrassed, but he does not deny it. In a mild attempt to get even, he merely says, "And he's writing basically the same sports column he wrote in those days—only the names are changed."

This is meant as an insult, but I do not take it as such. Journalism is nowhere near as complicated as many people think—mainly those inside journalism. I started at the *Vancouver Sun* in 1954, the day after my final exam, while the sports editor for whom I had worked nights for three years was suing me for some campus satire about him.

My reservations about journalism were based on its low pay—I could always make more in the summer as a logger or steelworker—and I vowed not to start a penny below $50 a week, after taking a few weeks off for a deserved brain transplant. When the legendary *Sun* managing editor Hal Straight finished his interview, he asked me how much I wanted. Stupidly, I said, "Am I worth $50 a week?" "At the moment," he replied, "You're not worth a goddam cent. Forty-five bucks. Report Monday 7 a.m. Goodbye." And then put me to work for the sports editor who was suing me.

DON'T SECOND-GUESS THE EDITORS

As a fuzzy-cheeked neophyte, I used to repair at quitting time every day, 3:00 in the afternoon, with the senior reporters to the beer parlour of the Lotus Hotel on Pender Street, across from the Sun Tower. I would sit, puzzled, as they explained what had really gone on in the background of the stories they had been covering. They just assumed, in those more formal days, that they couldn't get the down and dirty, the real stuff, past the editors.

Those sessions in the Lotus beer parlor have been the secret of my alleged success in journalism. All I have ever tried to do is print the stuff that the rest of the guys talk about over beer. Schlesinger, in essence, was right. The only things that have changed are the names.

This forms the basis for my first rule of journalism: Don't censor yourself. So many reporters think "they won't print that." The rule is: Hand it in. If anyone is going to be a censor, make the editor the guy who kills it. Don't censor yourself.

Since those days in the beer parlor I've traveled through 67 countries. I've chased Bobby Kennedy just before he was killed, had sugar put in my gas tank in Selma, Alabama, pursued Pierre Trudeau from Venice to Rome to Norway, not to mention the unknown wastes of Alberta, and tried the unfathomable of unravelling Ronald Reagan's mind. I've been through Poland by scooter, Russia by Volkswagen, China by jet, Africa by plastic, and best of all I've done it on someone else's money.

People always ask me if I've always been in journalism. I reply that it's the only thing I can do; I'm a one-talent guy. Otherwise I'd have to get a job.

THE SECRET: LISTEN

Second lesson of journalism: the greatest shortage in the world today is not of White House aides who tell the truth, not of card-carrying heterosexuals, not of food banks, but of listeners. Listeners are the most scarce commodity in the world. Most people do not listen. They are merely waiting for a break in the conversation to implode their own pressing views. When you are telling them about your aunt's appendectomy, they are not listening; they are simply waiting for an opening to dazzle you about the broken ankle they once suffered.

Bartenders make their living, not by mixing highballs, but from wiping the bar while listening to patrons who explain why their wives don't understand them. Everyone in life thinks that, basically, they are misunderstood. If only they could explain their case, everything would fall into place. This goes all the way up the ladder, from cleaning woman to cabinet minister.

You'd be amazed at the people in very high places who—if you just nod, mutter a lot and express astonishment with a lot of raised eyebrows about their inner turmoil—will blurt out their life's inner secrets. A soft shoulder for someone to cry on is the greatest weapon a journalist has.

It is why, essentially, I am against all the modern aids that have turned journalism into an electronic mailbox. Tape recorders have made politicians more honest; they can't lie anymore, claiming "misquote." But they make reporters lazy. They don't listen anymore, relying on a mechanical backup which really should be their brains.

I am so old-fashioned that I think newspapers were better before telephones were invented. Then, reporters actually had to go out of the office and talk to people.

This is, admittedly, a prejudice projected by a curmudgeon who has the advantage of being a columnist.

But I honestly think the basic rules apply to a reporter as well. The best definition of a columnist is a good reporter who has strong views. The best columnists are those who are never in the office. Drew Pearson, the famous American syndicated columnist, was once in the library of a small Kansas town, searching through the files. A woman, spotting him, asked him if he wasn't the celebrated Washington columnist. He allowed as to how he was. Well then why, she queried, was such a wealthy and renowned columnist out here doing his own research? "Madam," Drew Pearson replied, "I prefer to make my own mistakes."

ALL JOURNALISM IS INVESTIGATIVE

I am always slightly amused—as Drew Pearson would have been—at the new fad term "investigative reporting." This, in the current terms, is what my Oxford dictionary defines as tautology, which is defined as "saying the same thing twice over in different words." All true reporting, surely, should be investigative reporting.

There is now even such a thing as a Centre for Investigative Journalism in Canada and its guiding force, or inspiration, is a good friend of mine who is possibly the finest reporter in this country. His name is John Sawatsky. When I was a columnist at the *Vancouver Sun,* John Sawatsky was at Simon Fraser University, sleeping in a Volkswagen van stationed in the campus parking lot.

He arrived in my office one day and said he would like to do research for me. I explained that I then had the finest researcher in the world, Marilyn Stusiak, and couldn't afford a second one. Oh, he didn't want any money, he explained. He would come down at nights and weekends and work for nothing—just so he could learn something. (This was at a time when the Newspaper Guild was negotiating—and winning—a demand that every reporter on the paper be given a holiday on his birthday.) I knew right then that John Sawatsky would be one of our major figures in journalism. He now writes books full-time and has broken most of the stories about the RCMP undercover work and our intelligence services. In one book, he paid me the highest compliment I have ever had, dedicating it to his old mentor who—went his quote—"taught me that journalism is more than a job."

He gave up his reporting job that paid some $50,000 in Ottawa to pursue his books and, he explained to me one day, that old Volks van still sits on his father's farm in Abbotsford, British Columbia. If the money runs out, he can always go back and sleep in it. There is a journalist.

I don't want to bore you with too many strictures about journalism but, since this is the Minifie Lecture, I guess that's what I am here for. Advice.

I learned something long ago from my wise publisher at the *Vancouver Sun*, Stuart Keate. He told me, over our third martini, that a journalist really can't have any friends but other journalists. Too true. Sad, but true. Eventually, when you befriend one prime minister—as I modestly admit I have done—you run up against the fact that you have to talk about his warts. It don't work. When you become social friends of an ambassador in Washington, or a governor-general in Ottawa, there almost inevitably comes a time when the facts you have to report rub up against the friendship. It's a lousy job, but someone has to do it. My old publisher was right. That's why they invent press clubs.

There are three other lessons I will give all you people out there in this audience who are just dying to become journalists, and devote your livers to the cause of truth and democracy.

BROAD EDUCATION NEEDED

The first one is to get a good broad education. Political science, economics, philosophy—the lot. I don't even think a future journalist should take English at university. If you are not already devouring five books a week in your spare time, you shouldn't be in the trade. You can't write unless you read. That's a given. Read, read, read. It doesn't even matter if you read some junk along with the good stuff. A steady diet of *People* magazine will not guarantee you the Pulitzer Prize, but the sports pages never hurt anyone. As a matter of fact, they usually contain the most graceful—and almost the only witty—writing in any newspaper.

The second rule is to travel. You can't be a journalist unless you travel. There is only one value in travel.

It gives you perspective. You can't understand your own country until you see other countries. Distance gives you perspective. The reason I know Canada is the best country in the world is because I've seen all the other ones.

The third rule of journalism is not to get married until you are 30. Because you can't do the two above unless you obey the third.

If you do all these things—and stay out of the clutches of the public relations and advertising industry—you may then be able to set out to do something about the Canadian ignorance of the United States. Actually I don't mind the mutual ignorance that now characterizes the relationship between the Excited States of America and The Great White Waste of Time (as one Fleet Street paper calls us).

US IGNORANCE IS USEFUL

I think the American ignorance of Canada is a useful buffer, a cocoon that protects us. The Canadian ignorance of the United States is another matter. If you're a mouse in bed with an elephant, you'd better know everything possible about elephants—especially as to when they become sexually excited.

Canadians have to get to know Americans better simply to protect ourselves. Precisely because the Americans, in these ridiculous free trade negotiations, are talking about putting cultural issues on the bargaining table. The country that exports Vanna White and *Wheel of Fortune* is now eyeing our broadcasting system, our publishing industry. Have you ever heard anything so ridiculous? The Washington negotiators are now hinting that our medicare system is an unfair subsidy. This, from the only advanced country in the world that still doesn't have medicare. Bismarck introduced medicare to Germany in 1897 and here we have the richest nation in the history of what we laughingly call civilization still, in 1987, without a government medicare program.

The Canadian ignorance of how American society works was illustrated by the sudden flap in Ottawa over the shakes and shingles affair and the softwood lumber fiasco.

WHO'S COVERING THE YANKS?

Canadians do not take seriously their coverage of the United States. Here is the Number One power in the world, with a communications industry and financial clout that dominates us and owns so much of our industry. Who explains it to Canadians? The Canadian Broadcasting Corporation has one English-language television reporter, my old friend Joe Schlesinger, to cover the entire United States. The CBC has one English-language radio reporter, Hal Jones, to cover the entire United States.

Canadian newspapers have no reporters stationed in the South, on the Pacific Coast, in the Midwest; nowhere outside Washington and New York. My newspaper group, Southam, has just opened a new bureau in Moscow. *The Globe and Mail* is going to open a bureau in New Delhi. But the Sleeping Giant to the south of us (which one of us is the Sleeping Giant, really?) goes relatively unreported through Canadian eyes.

Those of us in the news business have complained for years of how Canadians used to get their world news filtered through American eyes. American news services filled our papers. American newscasts brought us news of Vietnam and Lebanon interpreted by American eyes.

That problem is getting better. Southam News now has reporters in London, Moscow, Malta, Zimbabwe, Hong Kong, Costa Rica as well as Washington and all across Canada. *The Globe* now has reporters in Moscow, London, Africa, Central America, Tokyo and Beijing. Great! But who's covering the Yanks? We are so smug. We read so many copies of *People* magazine that we think we know the country. We don't.

This is my plan, you see. I don't care if they don't know anything about us. But I think we should know everything about them. Burrow into their soft underbelly. That's the only thing the mouse can do when dealing with the elephant.

The American ignorance does not bother me. When I would get worried was if the United States did take a sudden interest in Canada. Because I think of all those countries that have attracted American attention. I think of Chile. I think of Vietnam. I think of Iran. I think of Lebanon. I think of poor little Grenada. I think of Libya. And, I think of Nicaragua. And so I say: let's keep that ignorance flying.

Don Minifie, as James M. Minifie's friends called him, was the first Canadian journalist to popularize the unheard-of-thing of a Canadian delivering news from Washington with a distinctly non-American view—i.e., a Canadian view. Knowlton Nash, who is now such a household face, was his protege and made his reputation on what he learned from Minifie in Washington.

Minifie was ornery and independent and that is the type of reporter who changes history. We will note that columnists don't overthrow governments. Reporters do. We will note that it was two unknown night police reporters, Bob Woodward and Carl Bernstein, who uncovered the evidence that brought down that certified crook, Richard Nixon. It wasn't Congress. It wasn't the CIA or the FBI. It was two young reporters.

It was an obscure little paper in Lebanon that broke the news that has destroyed the credibility of the most popular president in American history, and has completely shattered the Reagan government. And it is reporters in Ottawa—not the Opposition parties—who have uncovered the scandals that have so damaged the image of the Mulroney government.

Don Minifie would have been proud to have witnessed it all. Because he was one who recognized that journalism, indeed, "is more than a job." And that's why I'm honoured tonight to be asked to deliver the James M. Minifie Lecture. I thank you.

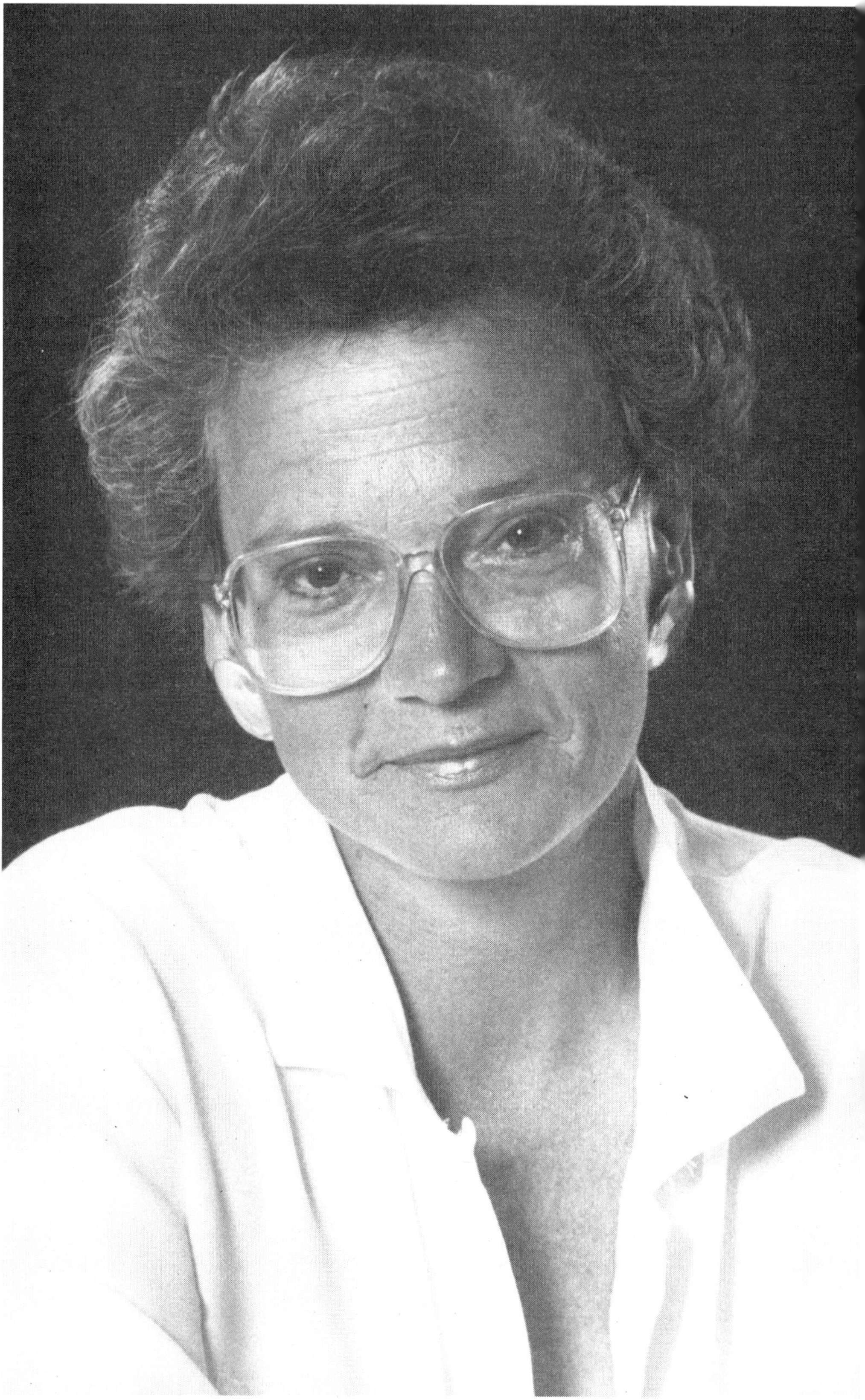

—1988—
ANN MEDINA

Ann Medina is originally from New York City. She was a Producer for NBC and then Network Correspondent for ABC News before marrying a Canadian in 1975. She then became CBC's Senior Foreign Correspondent, doing topical documentaries in the Mid-East and throughout the world. In 1983 and 1984, she was the Beirut Bureau Chief for CBC. Her reports aired regularly on BBC and PBS and won numerous awards including an Emmy. She also moderated three Federal Election Debates. Currently, she hosts History Television's *History on Film* and *Fact and Film*. Medina is Past Chair of the Academy of Canadian Cinema and Television, Past Chair of the Cultural Industries Council of Ontario, and has served on numerous boards. She has also served on the Advisory Board for Canada's Minister of Foreign Affairs. She has received five honorary degrees.

1988 | ANN MEDINA

FUDDY-DUDDY JOURNALISM:
I'd Rather not Rather

CBS News President Howard Stringer called it "Aggressive Journalism." Dan Rather called it "part of a reporter's job: trying to ask honest questions and trying to be persistent about answers."

Nevertheless it was Rather and not US Vice President George Bush who was on the cover of *Time* magazine. It was Rather who became as much a part of the story as Bush's answers or non-answers to questions relating to the Iran-Contra Affair. And, finally, it was Rather's style of questioning that was debated, not the questions themselves.

Let me begin by saying the questions should be asked. They were important. And I congratulate CBS for trying to get the answers. But, what went wrong was that Dan Rather "Star" did the interview instead of Dan Rather "Reporter." Rather revealed his belief that the answers to his questions were critically important to the country. He lost his detachment.

The Rather case is not unique though perhaps it's an exaggerated symptom of some of the problems creeping into television news—namely the reporter as star and crusader and how that relates to Mr. and Mrs. Smith's watching. We're not talking here of government officials or company presidents, but about the people who think *Broadcast News* presents an accurate picture of our business; the people who wonder if Barbara Frum is asking her own questions, or if someone is really giving her the questions through her ear telex; the people who ask me whether I write my own scripts when I report; the people who call a reporter to complain about the accuracy of an item and are told: "They're to blame," pointing to editors or even a committee of producers and researchers; the people who feel that more and more reporters are crusaders, reporting in order to further some cause.

Now, one can say that we're being questioned because people don't like what they hear on the news. Certainly that's true in too many cases, but the concerns can't be answered by only pointing to the fact that people want to shoot the messenger when the news is bad. Something else is at work here. That something else is simply that people today are confused as to who is doing the reporting—or to put it another way, they're confused as to who should be held accountable for the truth or falsity of reports and how. That's the problem that concerns me here today, and I think it's a problem that we in television news ought to be addressing.

32 PERCENT DON'T BELIEVE TV NEWS
Are we loosing public trust in our search for "stars" or in our concern and worry about events taking place around us? A 1987 Gallup Poll found that 32 percent

of Americans feel that television news is not believable. Ouch! And maybe they're not all crazy.

Consider the case of General Westmoreland vs. CBS Reports. At the time of the broadcast, Mike Wallace was credited with being the chief correspondent. It was a tough program and Wallace figured prominently throughout: in the interviews, the narration, and on camera. He certainly looked as if he were the chief correspondent.

However, once the suit was filed look what happened. Mr. Wallace suddenly was transformed into a "Narrator," and the producer of the item, with the researcher, were brought in to answer the questions of accuracy and content.

Now I don't want to digress here into what the appropriate role of an item producer is. I've been one and have usually worked with one in most of the items I've done for CBC. Suffice it to say, the producer obviously does have a role in the content that varies from program to program and from individual to individual. The producer has a role, but so does the reporter or the correspondent, and that is what I want to concentrate on.

Very simply, a narrator is not a reporter and is not seen to be one. When Wallace's title was changed, so did his accountability. It was no longer his job to be accurate. That now became the job of the producer.

During the trial, Barbara Walters interviewed Wallace for her very glossy and well publicized network program. At one point she asked Wallace how he did his interviews and he went into a long song and dance about the meetings he had with the producer and the discussions they had about focus and structure, etc. He very definitely left the impression that the process was a collaborative one.

Then, however, Barbara produced a list of some 30 or 40 questions that had been prepared by the producer, and pointed out that some 90 percent or so of the questions Wallace had asked in the broadcast were lifted verbatim from that list. Wallace then congratulated her, and called her point a "gotcha."

In fact, however, Wallace must have been grinning inside. Yes, he was being seen as a front, a mouthpiece, but that was still better than being seen as someone who was being challenged in the courts for the accuracy of his reporting.

REPORTER OR FRONT PERSON?

It was all very subtle. Slowly the role that Wallace played in the program became reduced from champion of the anti-Vietnam movement and hard hitting reporter to "Star" or "Narrator" who asks the questions that someone else thinks up and reads the script that someone else writes. Thanks to the Westmoreland case, the truth snuck out. There are stars, and they don't report in what I'm going to call the old fuddy-duddy sense.

Is it any wonder then, that the public is skeptical or suspicious? Is it any wonder that I'm asked, for example, whether I write the scripts I voice on *The Journal*? Suspicion spreads. It's contagious. And the role of the reporter has suffered.

Now, maybe there are some who say, who cares?

After all, someone, in this case CBS News, was held accountable for the facts ... and that, certainly, is what matters most. Certainly it matters, but it doesn't erase the fact that the public is recognizing that little tricks are being played on it. People who call themselves reporters really aren't. Or, to take another example, programs that appear to be live are really pre-taped. Or, reporters who appear to be reporting from a specific country really aren't there. And I could go on. We can't play around with trust. If you cut a corner here and cut a corner there, the square disappears.

What I call fuddy-duddy journalism is really very straightforward: That reporters remain as reporters and don't become fronts ... or mini-anchors in the field who, like the anchors, read someone else's scripts and aren't held accountable for the content. They are reporters in the old-fashioned sense—where they go out on a story, ask some questions, witness events, listen to people make statements and then write it up. If they're right and it's a good story, they've done a good job. If they're wrong, they've goofed, and should say so. The test is always accountability. There's no mystery or great philosophy behind it. That's simply what reporting has been about.

But, maybe, that's not what reporting is becoming and this notion of reporters as mini-anchors is not as far-fetched as it might seem. Let me give you some examples: There is a trend in the States to use stars on the big stories. "Big Footing" it's called. The normal beat reporters go out, as do producers and crews. They bring in the facts, and observations and tape, and then the "Star" reporter, in a sense collates the material. He or she summarizes it, often staying in an office while the other people go out into the field.

ACCOUNTABILITY

Now there may be some cases where time and the number of locations require a reporter to include the findings of others. I accept that. But we have to distinguish between that kind of a case and one where a "Star" flies into a situation he hasn't seen, and does the report based entirely on the observations of others. It's easy to conceptually slide from the one to the other, but it is qualitatively different.

I recall, at *The Journal,* there was a time when reporters were doing short items to set-up interviews and then one of the bigger "Name" reporters would be asked to voice it. Well, some of us objected, saying we were sounding as if we had seen such and such or talked to so and so when in fact we had not. We would voice the item, but only if the in-studio introduction specified that we were narrating or voicing the item and not reporting it.

Take another example. Often on weekly magazine programs, in Canada and in the US, the reporters can't physically do what I and others have done on *The*

Journal. They simply don't have the time. So, in some cases, a producer does most of the putting together of the story including the writing of the script.

There's nothing wrong with this, anymore than there was anything wrong with Mike Wallace fronting the report on Westmoreland. The point is, we shouldn't try and fool the public. When people are reporting, call them reporters. When people aren't reporting, call them narrators. When people aren't being held accountable for the facts, then they aren't reporting.

Here some people will say: "But Sam or Sally really is a journalist, so they still bring their journalistic skills to an item that they haven't had the time to research and put together. They still are functioning as a kind of filter for the information. They are reporters so what's wrong with calling them that?"

What's wrong with it is they aren't reporters on that specific item and, once again, the test is accountability. Last year, I narrated an hour-long documentary on the "War Correspondents." I didn't collect the facts, or structure the program, even though it was a topic that I knew a lot about. Whatever journalistic skills I may or may not have, I still was not responsible for the content. Yes, I cared about the script, and even made some changes, but that is different from accountability.

So far in Canada, we have not adopted the 'Star System' of reporting to the extent that the networks have in the United States. And here, I'm speaking for both the public and private networks.

Part of the reason is simply one of money. In an ironic twist, I'm sometimes glad that we don't have the dollars to send in a "Star" reporter to big foot, or to hire producers and five crews on a story. On *The Journal*, where there are producers, they may often be in charge for financial and internal reasons, but it is the reporter who is right or wrong on the facts. They are on the story every day. They see, and they listen, and they watch. It is their eyes and ears that guide the viewer along. And they write the script.

We still have real fuddy-duddy reporters who are sent into the field to find the stories rather than being told by a desk hundreds or even thousands of kilometres away what the story is. So, we are not as far along as the US in the commercialism of television news. News organizations aren't in the business to make money, and editorial desks, the ratings book, and sweeps week don't determine where and what the stories are . . . yet.

Finally, I want to touch upon a second problem in reporting—one that haunts us in disturbing ways when we cover famine or terrorism, and that's the degree to which we should use our reporting to affect the world around us.

POOR DAN RATHER

Let's go back to Dan Rather and his persistent—to put it mildly—questioning. There's no doubt in my mind that he felt quite strongly about the importance of the Contra issue and Bush's possible involvement in it. I, too, feel quite strongly about it—that the funding of the Contras under North's leadership poses a very serious threat to how we view a democracy, and could undermine not only the reputation of the U.S. but the principles of constitutional and electoral systems. I care, and Rather cares. But what do we do when we are interviewing, in Rather's words, as part of a reporter's job? If we aren't getting the answers we think the public needs—or if we don't see changes that we think are necessarily taking place—what do we do?

Last year a former Canadian journalist was quoted in a magazine article about her saying that journalism was very frustrating: She complained that she couldn't make a difference herself, but instead had to be "dependent on striking a chord in someone else" who might, in turn, make a difference.

Certainly a lot of people may get into reporting with the idea of changing attitudes or events, but today, I want to point to the dangers of such a view. I call it "reporting in order to"—in order to save lives, or in order to stop corruption, or in order to bring about peace in a region. These goals sound very lofty. Surely, one might say, no one could question a reporter with those kinds of concerns. Well, I do. Too often those who report in order to end up playing God.

Take an apparent clear-cut case. The coverage of famine. In our reporting, should we want to save lives?

Well, what happens when we learn, for example, that many officials in a country are pocketing money intended for famine relief. Do we report it, or not?

If we do, it can be argued, additional lives might be lost because such a story might discourage future aid and, thus, lead to more people starving. On the other hand, one might claim that publishing such a story might lead to international pressures and criticism that would stop such practices and thus increase the aid getting through to those who need it, and thus save lives. Which position do we take?

Do we suppress the story out of fear that aid would be cut-back, or do we publish it?

Well, I want to claim that no one has a crystal ball that will tell us with certainty what will happen if we do x or y, and furthermore, if we begin to doctor or change our reporting on the basis of what we believe, we are indeed playing God and setting ourselves up as censors for the good of the world as we see it.

We should not play God. We should not look into a crystal ball. We should publish the story even if we think it might end up costing lives.

That may sound very cold, even arrogant.

Certainly it ought to spark some debate in some journalism classes here, but I think it must be the case if we are to retain our integrity as journalists.

Remember Vietnam. At that time the U.S. government said that the news media shouldn't report that the US was doing poorly because that would only bolster the morale of the North Vietnamese, and thus prolong the war, and thus cost more American lives.

Well, the government pressured the Networks, and, as you know, they complied. The government argument certainly seemed persuasive. It placed the possible guilt for American deaths squarely on the shoulders of the media.

On the other hand, one could argue that accurate reporting might stir up protest against the war and thus, shorten it and save lives.

In the end, as you know, the networks did begin covering the war as they saw it, and finally, pressure did build to pull out.

IT'S NOT OUR JOB TO START A PROTEST

The point is, however, the networks shouldn't not report, or report accurately "in order to." They are playing God if they decide how to cover a story on the basis of how it will be received, either by the enemy or by the American public.

It isn't our job to stir up protest against what we feel is wrong. It's our job to be fuddy-duddy journalists and, once again, report what we see, what we hear, what we can touch and what we know. As individuals we may want to pressure and protest and cry out and change attitudes—whether it's war, abortion, famine or governments. As individuals we may want to do that, but that isn't our job as reporters.

Now having said all that there may be a few cases where we just feel in our gut that we know a story will result in someone's death. In that very rare case, I probably would suppress it and I cite the case of Terry Waite as an illustration. I wouldn't have done a story about the charge he was receiving CIA funds for the hostage-takers while he was still in Beirut. But that is a rare case, and exceptions such as that don't justify our changing our whole way of reporting.

As individuals we can want to achieve a whole range of wonderful goals. But, as journalists, we must let others decide how or even whether they will work towards peace or against corruption.

In conclusion, I must say I've probably been unfair to poor Dan Rather who has certainly done some superb journalism in the past. But I guess I look at the United States and I worry that I see our future. Already the public—and the government—worry that we editorialize too much as reporters. People sometimes doubt that we write our reports or that we really have seen what we say we have.

I know that we're not a star-studded group of puppets nor are we left-wingers or right-wingers in our reporting. *Broadcast News* did not describe the reality of television news. But we must make sure that the public knows it too.

The temptations to play a part in the controversies of our time, and to be effective communicators can slowly change the role of journalism. We do play a part and should try to communicate effectively, but the temptation to do more can easily lure us to editorializing and stargazing. I don't want that to happen—and to stop it, we must recognize it when we begin to see it happening.

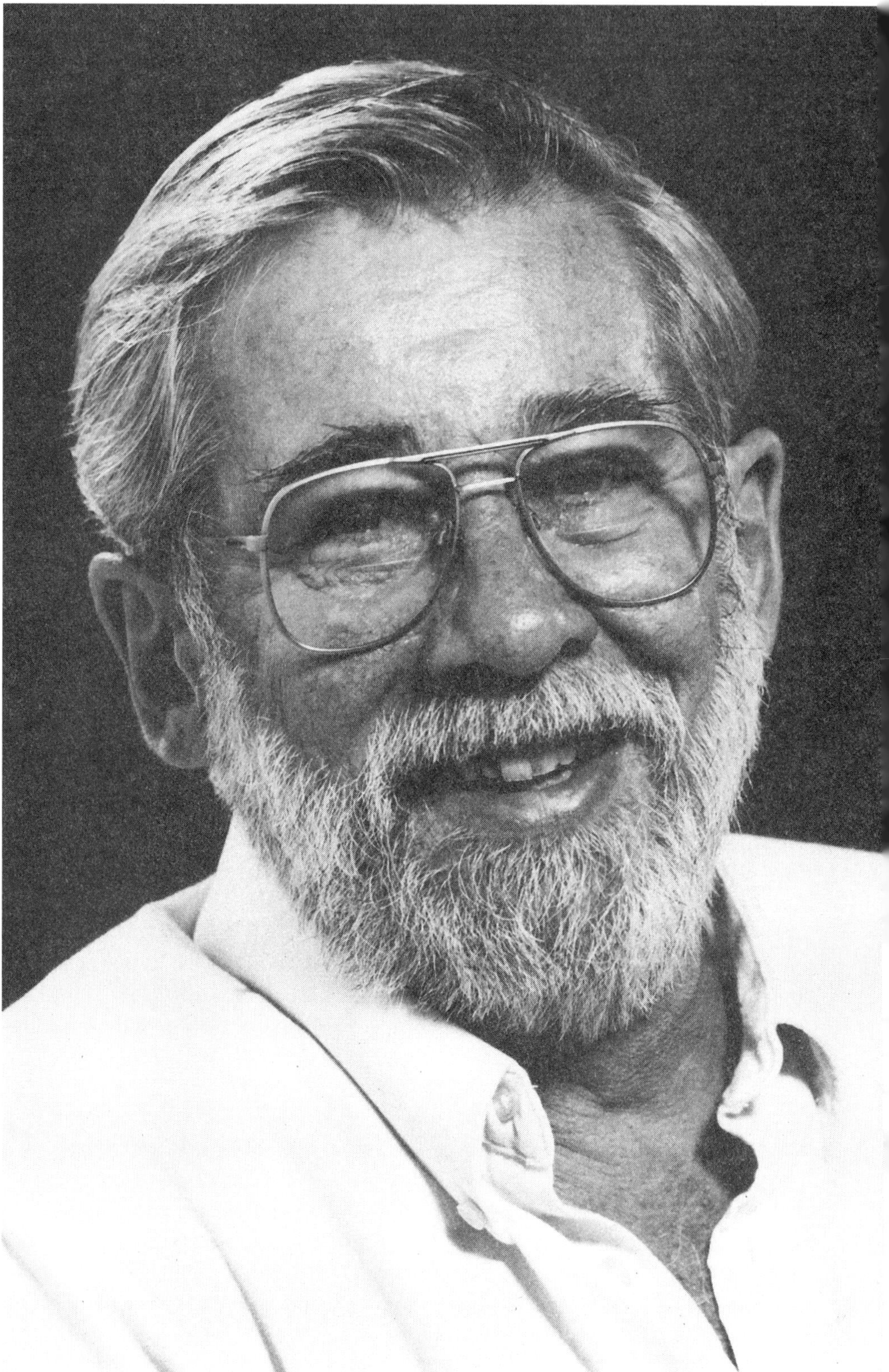

−1989−

PETER GZOWSKI

Peter Gzowski was a popular writer, reporter and broadcaster who wrote 18 books. He is most famous as host of the radio show *Morningside* on CBC. Conducting 27,000 interviews as its host, Gzowski was both a household name and an icon of Canadian cultural nationalism. Gzowski also hosted television shows, and wrote for newspapers and *Maclean's* magazine. For his contributions to Canadian culture and identity, he was awarded 11 honorary degrees. While in school Gzowski edited the student newspaper. He also worked at the *Timmins Daily Press*, became city editor of the *Moose Jaw Times-Herald*. At 28 he became the youngest-ever managing editor of *Maclean's*. From 1976 to 1978 Gzowski also hosted *90 Minutes Live* on CBC Television. Over his career, Gzowski received three ACTRA Awards, an International Peabody Award for broadcasting and was named an Officer of the Order of Canada and promoted in 1998 to Companion. The Peter Gzowski Foundation for Literacy was founded by the federal government in honour of Gzowski's work in promoting literacy in Canada. Georgina Public Libraries in Ontario also renamed their Sutton Branch the Peter Gzowski Branch.

WHAT I KNOW NOW THAT I DIDN'T KNOW IN THE DAYS WHEN I KNEW EVERYTHING...

First of all, thank you not only for the words of introduction, but for inviting me to take part in this remarkable series of lectures. I feel as if I were being handed a baton this evening, carried so impressively from the starting blocks in 1981 by Knowlton Nash, and taken a little bit farther—if sometimes in different directions—by those who have followed: some of the most distinguished exemplars this country has evolved of the people who are, in James M. Minifie's phrase, "the quarrymen of history," or, as I'm sure the coiner of the phrase himself would have amended it in the late eighties, the quarrymen and women.

I am different from the majority of the quarriers who have preceded me here in at least two ways. One is that in spite of my age, I never had the pleasure of knowing personally the man so many other lecturers here have remembered fondly as "Don" Minifie. I knew his work, and admired it. But, I confess with some regret, it was only in doing some preparatory reading for this evening that I came in contact with the grace of his prose, the breadth of his knowledge and the strength of his dedication to our craft. Reading about him, as I say, I wish I'd known him and I envy those of my contemporaries who did, just as I know there are and will be others who will envy me the chance I did have to work with such other giants as Ralph Allen, Blair Fraser or Norman Depoe, all of whose paths, among others, I was lucky enough to cross, and in all of whose footsteps I aspire to tread.

If for no other reason, then, may I begin these remarks by saluting this university and the people who have helped it to assemble the repository this series of lectures has become, and for fostering the very important sense of continuum that our craft so badly needs. If there is one thing that I know now that I did not know back in the days when I knew everything, it is how wise were the people I had access to then, and how important it is to carry the torch they passed to us. There are many mornings when I face difficult decisions when I wish, for example, that I could talk to Ralph Allen, who has been dead now for 20 years. When he was around, I realize now, I thought I knew too many answers. Now, I know I'm still learning the questions. I share the thought with Lloyd Barber, "It's amazing how, as I get older, how much smarter my father gets."

The other principal difference between me and almost all the people who have stood here before me is that I have spent nearly all of my working life in Canada, whereas they, or many of them, have roamed the world, their trench coat pockets jammed with the notes and observations of, as Knowlton Nash puts it, history on the run. In the year when I didn't graduate from the University of Toronto—I chose to edit what was then an undergraduate daily instead of attending lectures—and when all of my friends were going to Paris and London and Zagreb, I went to Moose Jaw, Saskatchewan, to be the youngest (and least-qualified) city editor in Canada. "Where is River Street anyway?" (I had to buy some horn-rimmed glasses to make myself look both like Clark Kent and old enough to run the paper.) In the years since, I've made London a couple of times—most notably in the 1960s, when the *Toronto Star* pulled the rug out from under the weekly magazine I'd been editing and I went to England to drown my sorrows (not an especially good condition to look for work in, I assure you) but never Zagreb, and the only Paris I've been to is in Ontario, on the Nith River, just downstream from where Wayne Gretzky's grandmother used to live.

I say this with no sense of braggadocio—not that being Canadian, I would know how to brag if I wanted to. Canadians don't brag. When Lester Pearson won the Nobel Peace Prize in 1957 for preventing World War Three, he said "Gee, thanks." When Paul Henderson scored his famous goal in September of 1972, he thanked his teammates and, a few years later, joined the Christian ministry, at least partly out of gratitude. When, on *Morningside* (the CBC radio program I host), I told Robertson Davies that a few days earlier, Anthony Burgess had suggested that he, Davies, be given the Nobel Prize for literature Davies said, "Goodness gracious, I'm sure I don't deserve it."

NOT BAD, EH?
A Canadian invented the telephone, although the Americans have claimed him, as they claimed Lorne Greene, the Shakespearean actor, voice of doom, cowboy patriarch and dog-food salesman. Two Canadians discovered insulin. Other Canadians invented Pablum, the variable pitch propeller, the vacuum radio tube, the photo-finish camera, the snowmobile, five-pin bowling, the green garbage bag, basketball (though we are not tall enough to beat the people who stole it), Marquis wheat, Social Credit, the slap-shot, the Bloody Caesar and Trivial Pursuit. And, as I learned the other night when I offered a similar list in Victoria, we also invented the zipper . . . but I learned that because I went through a similar list and when I was talking to someone from the crowd later on, having stood in front of them, he said, "You forgot the zipper." Which is why I asked for a lectern this evening. While I wasn't present at any of the inventors' moments of triumph, I am reasonably certain that where a Greek would have said "Eureka!" or an American "Hot damn!," a Canadian would say only, "Not bad, eh?"

"Not bad, eh?" could well be our national motto. Instead, of course, it is *"a mari usque ad mare"*—from sea to sea. But as we can tell even from here in land-locked Saskatchewan, this lovely land reaches not just two oceans but three—from sea unto sea unto sea—a *mari usque ad mare* et cetera.

Still, I suppose, two out of three is . . . well, not bad, eh? And at least it is not bragging.

And so, no, when I say the decision I made to choose Moose Jaw, instead of the London bureau of the Canadian Press, set a course for me that I have followed ever since—though I still haven't been, as I say, to Zagreb, I've been to Aklavik seven times, and, even as I speak to you, have just completed a swing that has taken me from Tofino on the west coast of Vancouver Island, eastward through the Rockies and the foothills and this morning to here, in what I have described as the most Canadian of all provinces, broadcasting as I go. When I say that, I am not bragging; I am, rather, pointing out only that the beat I have chosen to cover—Canada, as opposed to some of the more exotic corners of the world—can be a satisfying and rewarding one too, and explaining why, as I offer some of the suggestions that occur to me as I hold the baton, I will not be dropping my experiences with any of the world leaders whose names adorn some of the earlier Minifie addresses. I don't mind saying, however (even if it does smack of bragging) that I know Wayne Gretzky personally, and I have danced with Karen Kain.

That said, may I point out how deeply I share the concerns about my craft that echo through the first eight Minifie lectures: concerns about accuracy and fairness, about accountability, about the increasingly difficult relationship—far too often an unnecessarily antagonistic one—between the people who make the news and the people who report it, and, perhaps most of all, about the television-based phenomenon of turning reporters (or, perhaps, "anchorpersons" who are all too often not reporters at all) into celebrities and the news they bring into entertainment—the trivialization of what all of us who have given these addresses have all done, however differently, to make our livings.

On the matter of accuracy and fairness, Clark Davey, then the publisher of the *Vancouver Sun* (he is at the Montreal *Gazette* now), speaking here in 1982, quoted a friend of his who had left the practice of journalism to teach it in the United States, and who had, he told Davey, introduced into one of his classes the following exercise. First, each of his students would make a speech, from a text. Then, the other students, working only from the notes they have taken during the speech—no tape recorders—would turn in a written report on what they say they heard. Without exception, Clark Davey's friend reported, the speakers were shaken by the variance between what they had said and what their classmates had reported they had said. This is a dramatic and useful demonstration—I am not sure how many of Davey's friend's students would remember it when they began covering speeches for money and I would recommend it to any teacher. But, were I to teach journalism, knowing now some things I didn't know when I began to practice it, I would go further. In one of my first classes, I would assign each student the task, first of chatting briefly with the student on his or her left—by briefly I mean an hour or so—and then, based upon that interview, of writing a brief profile. I wouldn't have these assignments read to the class. Instead, I'd just have each student read the next day what the person on his or her right had written about him or her. I don't think I could change the world with this little exercise. But as someone whose career—which began as writing about other people (and who still thinks of himself as a reporter who works on the radio)—involves being written about, I am convinced that those of us who have dashed off some glibly clever sentences in sketches of people we scarcely know have no idea of how wrong we can be, or how simple-minded, or how much harm that glibness and simplicity of mind can do not only to our subjects but to the higher cause we serve, or ought to serve, which is the truth.

CUT THE "BON MOTS"

On the subject of glib and fancy writing, I am reminded of something Ralph Allen used to say at *Maclean's,* back in the days when that was a magazine written by people who had seen what they were reporting on—as opposed to its state now, when nearly everything is rewritten at a desk by people who have done no more than read the files of those who've actually witnessed the events they're describing. "If you're going to cut something," Ralph would say, "start with the writing you're most proud of." You'd be surprised how often that works; the more you're impressed with your own cleverness, I think it's fair to say, the higher the chances you're writing balderdash.

And if I can just slip in another observation by another hero of mine that seems to apply to some of the things I find distasteful about, for instance, magazines written by people who've stayed at home, may I cite the great A.J. Liebling, who, although he was an American (he wrote for the *New Yorker* from about 1940 until his death in the early 1960s), ought to be on the curriculum of every journalism school everywhere. Liebling said once that a reporter is someone who goes somewhere and tells you what's going on; an observer is someone who goes somewhere and tells you what's going on and what it means, and an expert is someone who doesn't go anywhere and tells you what everything means. (Which is at least better than a definition I heard once in the north, which was that an expert is some bastard from the south with slides.) But it troubles me that more and more of the information we are being asked to sort our way through every day is delivered by people who, if they are qualified at all, are more "experts" than reporters, or who so see themselves. Since this series of lectures not only honours the name of a man who was first and foremost a reporter but has been given so far almost exclusively by people who earned their credentials as reporters, I thought it appropriate to note this evening what the basis of our craft really is, which is reporting. And I cannot help but say that though a lot of good things have happened to the craft I practise while I've been in it, I rue the decline of reportage.

Have you ever noticed this about the way people read newspapers? (It's actually an observation that would be dramatized by the experiments in teaching journalism that Clark Davey's friend and I would like to institute.) Let's say the reader is a doctor. She'll read the medical news first and shake her head about how misinformed the reporter is. But then she'll turn to, say, the sports page and read the 'inside' account of a hockey game and lap up every word as absolute truth—or the account of a political meeting or a trade deal or a speech given at the University of Regina. But if the reader is an athlete, who played in the hockey game, he'll wonder if the same reporter whose words the doctor lapped up was at the same event at all. But he, in turn, will turn to the medical news and read it as gospel along, of course, with the politics and the trade and speech last night at the university. I'm sure you've had the same experience yourself, as a reader: The more you know about an occasion or a situation, the less accurate you will find the way it's been covered. But as you turn to the coverage about the areas in which you are less well-informed, you will forget the skepticism whose justification you have just seen so splendidly illustrated. Or, if you do remember it, you will join the increasing numbers of people who are concerned about the way the information they need in their lives is being delivered to them.

In making this point—and it may be worth noting that the first person who drew my attention to the fact that our willingness to accept a story's accuracy is often a function of our distance from the event was Beland Honderich, now the chairman of the *Toronto Star*—I do not mean to throw mud indiscriminately at all journalists. I am, after all, not the Spiro Agnew of the 1980s, but a journalist myself and proud of it. Nor do I belong to the community of grey-bearded curmudgeons who say the old days were the better days. (I can't help noting that in Victoria last weekend, when I made a pilgrimage to the house of yet another one of my professional heroes, Bruce Hutchison, and sat sipping coffee in front of a crackling fire and the warmth of his wisdom. I said something about the old days, when, as a fledgling copy editor at *Maclean's*, I used to handle the impeccable prose which he sent in on little three-quarter sheets of newspaper copy paper. Bruce said, "How old are you Peter?" and when I told him my age he said, "I'm 87 and I've got a son older than you." Since he still writes every day and feels good about things, I don't think I'm yet ready to carry the banner that proclaims universal decline.

JOURNALISM IS LIKE HOCKEY

When I compare the journalists I learned under, in fact, or those of my own contemporaries who have risen to positions of power, when I compare them with the people who are coming out of journalism schools now or standing in line to take over the jobs we will inevitably step aside from if, that is, you can convince us to let go—my mind turns inevitably to hockey. I don't know if you know that they have been doing some work in Ottawa on some old hockey films, and using technology to compare, for instance, the way Howie Morenz used to skate with the way Paul Coffey skates, or the speed of the game in the golden days of, say, Howe and Richard, with the speed of it now. But you know what? Howie Morenz was the greatest player of his day and for his funeral, when he died of a broken heart after a broken leg ended his career, the Montreal Forum was jammed to capacity (the biggest public funeral in Canada until John Diefenbaker's). But Howie Morenz fell down a lot.

I'm not kidding. You can see it on the films. Just as you can see, by adjusting the speed of old films to match them with new ones, that the heroes of the old six-team National Hockey League—the league that guys of my vintage and older will tell you was the greatest hockey ever played—skated more awkwardly, shot with less power, checked with less force and, except perhaps for stick-handling (which they learned on ponds, where it should be learned) played with less skill than the players of today's much maligned 21-team league. (Except perhaps for the Toronto Maple Leafs, who don't count). And why not? The players of today are better trained as kids, better nourished (and therefore bigger and stronger), better equipped and better coached. Furthermore, as hockey has drawn from a steadily bigger pool, with the Canadian reservoir expanded to include Americans and Europeans, it has had, inevitably, a larger number of potential Morenzes, Howes, Richards, Orrs, Gretzkys and, yes, Lemieuxs to draw upon. (One more digression, since I'm talking about hockey: Did you see that wonderful all-star game on Tuesday night? And did it occur to you, as it did to me, that they don't put the goons on all-star teams, and if the NHL could just get rid forever of the players who can do nothing more than hold, slash, fight, or sit on people, we could watch hockey of that kind—the game of joy—played all season long?)

The parallels to journalism from the changes in hockey are profound. (I was going to say except for the goons until I started to think about what is happening to daytime television recently. It is, to be sure, a marginal form of journalism at best, but it has taken some of the techniques of real information programming to present an almost overwhelming torrent of lesbian nuns, children of incest, racial confrontation, male strippers and other forms of human activity, if that's indeed what it is, previously confined to the tabloids you see in supermarkets. Of course, nobody admits to reading them, but they have circulations in the uncounted millions.) But in real journalism, surely, the analogy of the improved level of hockey holds.

Unless, I'm wrong, for instance, only one of the people who have preceded me here—Clark Davey again, who was one of the first students groomed by the University of Western Ontario Journalism School—ever actually studied journalism. The rest of us, Nash, Charlie Lynch, Joe Schlesinger, Ann Medina, etc., all learned on the job. My own biography is fairly typical: a little of this, a little of that—some time on Thomson papers that rapidly threw me into positions I wasn't qualified for, just because the people who were moving on and, luckily for me, a chance to work, in a then much-smaller community of professionals, with the very best people around, before the bad habits I had been teaching myself at Thomson (or which had been passed on to me by people who had long since given up hope of making their craft any better) had time to take hold of me completely. But in all the years I have been doing what I do, the only classrooms I've had have been in were beer parlors or on re-write desks, or in the solitude of my own company over a typewriter while I've tried to absorb the lessons of the editors—tyrants all, whose rigid standards I came only later to understand and respect—the comments that they had scribbled all over the raw genius of my original prose. In formal terms, in fact (tonight being a kind of case in point), I've actually talked more about journalism than I've had it talked to me. And, as the roster of previous speakers here shows, among my contemporaries, I'm more the rule than the exception.

By contrast, the people who are applying now for the jobs we started with are consummate professionals. My own daughter, as I wrote in the book I published last year, is now working her way up through the early stages of a career in CBC radio—which could, of course, lead on many other paths. Partly handicapped by her curious last name—nearly everyone who thought of hiring her realized they'd be accused of favouritism—she had a very difficult time getting started, and, as I chose to go to Timmins, Ontario, to break in, she set out for radio in St John's, Newfoundland. She's 29 now, very bright and, at last, doing very well. It sometimes discourages her to realize that when I was her age—a phrase with which I have taken an oath never to begin a conversation with one of my children—I was the managing editor of *Maclean's*. (Neither one of us bother to remember that the year after that, when I was 30, I was out on my ear—albeit through my own choice.) But there is a very great difference between the situation that surrounded me and the one that now surrounds her. I fell into a time when the job choices were so limited in professional journalism in this country. There was no television, to take the most obvious illustration, and *Maclean's*, bless its heart, was virtually the only national outlet we could aspire to—that very few people even thought of starting at the bottom of the ladder.

As well, the trade (I still think it's presumptuous to call what we do for a living a "profession") has learned to take itself seriously. So that not only is my daughter, who has an arts degree from a university (which I, as I say, don't), and a degree in journalism, which I don't (from Ryerson in Toronto), better trained as a young current affairs radio producer than I was when I was the boy wonder of Canada's national magazine, she, like a young man trying to crack the line-up of the Edmonton Oilers, is surrounded by a wave of contemporaries who are equally well trained. (Whether, like the hockey players, they're also better nourished, I'm not prepared to comment on—nor am I sure it would make any difference (though it does seem to me young reporters of today drink less than we used to. Heaven knows they couldn't drink more.) But, with their educations, their knowledge of and access to computers and information retrieval and other technological advances that I don't understand, I'm sure they're better equipped. And, to fill in the last remaining corner of my analogy, it's certainly true that today's newspapers and magazines and radio and television stations draw on a larger talent pool than those of my day did. For Europeans and Americans in this case, simply substitute women.

MAJOR CHANGES IN NEWSROOMS

The three biggest changes I see from my day when I walk into any newsroom of the 1980s are (1) nobody smokes, (2) there's no noise—since everyone's composing on whispering word processors and doing their homework plugging into some giant data-bank I don't understand, and (3) (certainly the most important when I look at the future of our trade) about half the desks are occupied by women. Each time I go into a newsroom, in fact, the desks they occupy seem to symbolize more power. We are still a long way short of where we ought to be. I spoke to a conference of Canadian managing editors a couple of years ago and noticed not only that they were all about my age—that they learned their business on the desks of their own *Moose Jaw Times-Heralds* and *Timmins Daily Presses*—but they were all male. (I noticed that they nearly all wore ties with diagonal stripes sloping in the same direction, too, but I didn't know what to make of it.) That's wrong, but if I went back even this year there would be at least two exceptions and, I'm sure if I went back a few years from now (if what I see among the rising stars of this craft is true), we will be much, much closer to equality. At CBC radio, in fact, I have already—and to my delight, I hasten to add—been in a position of working for a woman executive producer who reported to a woman deputy head of current affairs who reported to a woman vice president of the CBC. Now this may be one of the reasons CBC Radio is regarded as one of the most enlightened media in this country, which is, I think, not bad eh? and is certainly a long way from the days at the *Timmins Daily Press,* when the only woman on staff covered weddings and teas, or at *Maclean's,* where very early in my career I was promoted to copy editor, over the heads of two women assistants who had been there longer than I had, made much less money, and nevertheless held my hand long enough to teach me how to do the job either one of them could have done better than I did.

Two stories, if I may, about my early days as a reporter. If nothing else they may serve to remind us all how truly bad we really were a generation ago, and to relieve the tone of unremitting solemnity that even as this year's Minifie Lecturer I have a hard time sustaining.

1989 | PETER GZOWSKI

One is about my award-winning career as a news photographer, the other about the beginning and end of my adventures as a critic. They both took place in Timmins, before I went back to university. I was 19, a two-way man (a phrase we could say in those days because it meant you could take photographs and wrote stories), and was on duty one weekend all by myself when there was a forest fire in the neighbourhood. It was really bad so I thought I'd go and take a picture, so I jumped in the red *Timmins Daily Press* photo-journalist's truck and I drove out to the perimeter of the forest fire with my 4×5 Speed Graphic camera in my hands, and I'm going to get myself a photograph. So I wandered around the end of this fire and I saw this perfectly symmetrical tree, and on a nearby tree I saw a sign that said "Help Prevent Forest Fires," so I went and took the sign off that tree and put it on the symmetrical tree. Then I saw another one that said something about "don't smoke." I can't remember all that it said. I took it off and I put the two signs on the symmetrical tree. The fire is raging and coming at me all the time and I'm standing there ready: I've got the perfect tree framed in my camera and every damn tree in the forest was catching fire except my perfectly symmetrical tree, and I don't know how close you've been to a forest fire but they're warm, and this was really hot, but I was too young to be smart enough to care, but it was hot and actually later I looked and the paint on the truck I was driving had brown blisters. And I'm standing looking at this damn tree and it would not catch, and finally I did it: I brought a branch of another tree and made a torch, and I set a perfectly symmetrical fire to my perfectly symmetrical tree. Canadian Press News Photo of the Month, October, 1955.

And then there's my career as the music critic of the *Timmins Daily Press*. This is not a heavy assignment because in those days you got about four concerts a year. My device for covering them was I was dating this piano teacher in town and she was terrific: she would tell me all the appropriate Italian words and she would help me through the concerts. She taught piano and her father played the piano at the Empire Hotel, and so one night the *Jeunesses Musicales* concert was on and I got the menu for it beforehand, and we went to get relaxed at the Empire Hotel to hear her dad play the piano and I took the program for the concert and I asked her about it, because when you're writing this kind of review you must never be critical, never too severe, so I'd be mild and say they played a little too Largo and I'd write this down on the program before we went. Well, one thing led to another, and the jazz player at the Empire was better than the *Jeunesses Musicales*, so I never went to the concert. But I had all these terrific notes, so I went back to the office of the *Timmins Daily Press* and typed up this review, not too critical and handed it in to the city desk and went home. The next morning I was sitting in the back of the newsroom, and the phone rang, and thank the Lord I answered it, because the call was, "Could you tell me why last night's Jeunesses Musicales concert was cancelled?" That review was never published.

DEEP RESERVATIONS

Having made these confessions, and having poured such praise on the young journalists of today, let me quickly add that I also have some deep reservations about what I see around me. The most important, goes back to what I was saying about "experts"—or would-be experts.

Years ago, if you had asked me to make predictions about the wave of journalists who would come after me, I would not have said they would come from journalism schools. I would have thought, by now, we would have had people trained in the law writing about law, doctors writing about medicine, political scientists about politics and so on. It just seemed to me the way things would have to go in an increasingly complex and sophisticated world (one fact about science that sticks in my mind is that when Einstein wrote down $E=mc^2$ there were only four or five people in the world who would understand him and yet now you can't begin undergraduate physics without getting at least its central idea). In that world, the fourth estate would simply have to reach into the other estates and root out people who were trained in their elements. When we found a scientist who—like David Suzuki when he first discovered radio and television—would be more interested in spreading the word about what other people were doing than in following the pursuit of knowledge for its own sake, it would be easier to teach that scientist the essentials of our craft (how to type, what -30- means, and that the only real way to learn to write is by writing) than to teach those of us who knew how to type the essentials of science. But the exception of David Suzuki only proves the rule. It hasn't worked out that way.

We have, as a trade, become so engrossed in our own practices that we are in danger of losing sight of what those practices are really for, which is to spread the news about what other people are doing. The experts we are producing are experts about nothing at all except perhaps being experts—just as a whole class of celebrities in the United States (we have not quite reached that stage here) are famous largely for being well-known. Much of that development, I'm sure, has been inevitable. If we're going to get more and more of our news from television, where, after all, someone has to read it to us, we are going to learn to recognize the person who does the reading. So, through exposure alone, the people who read the news have become stars—just as, to my own continued amazement and frequent chagrin, I've become more widely known through what I do on radio than a pure reporter ever ought to be. The deliverers, in other words, become the source of our knowledge.

But what, when you come to think of it, do the deliverers know? Though many of them, in this country at least—Knowlton Nash is a splendid example and so, of course, is his successor, Peter Mansbridge—started out as people who found things out for a living and then told other people what they were, in nearly every case, when they become "anchors" (there's a word, eh?) all they ever find out for themselves is what the real reporters—"over to you, Mike"—tell them. And far too many of the rest of us, I fear, feel we have to compete with them. We have to be experts, too. We have to be certain, judgmental, quick and simple. But the world is not quick or simple. The world is intricate and profound. And when we say things with the kind of certainty that experts are called upon to deliver—and most especially when we say them to people who (as we often do not) know more about what we're supposed to be talking about than we know— they think we're not as smart as we think we are.

And if I had to live up to the billing I gave myself for this lecture—"What I know now that I didn't know back in the days when I knew everything"—I think I'd say that too: We're not as smart as we think we are. We are the scribes, you know, not the governors; our function is to report what other people do. In fulfilling that function, of course, we have a right—even a duty—to pursue the truth as ruthlessly as we can, and from time to time the necessary ruthlessness of our task will ruffle some feathers and step on some toes. So be it. But the only person in the end who can pass judgment on the people and the subjects we write or broadcast about ought to be the reader or listener or viewer. That's his job, or hers, and ours is only to make available what information we can to make his (or hers) easier. At its highest, I think, doing journalism well is the ultimate act of democracy, in that it is based on the premise that an informed populace, a people aware of the facts, will act for their common good. At its meanest, doing journalism arrogantly is a denial of that same principle, for to publish or broadcast your own judgment—not your arguments based on the facts you have marshalled, but your own judgment—is to assume for yourself the role that properly belongs to the people.

ADMITTING MISTAKES

If I can pursue this line of thought just one paragraph more—though I warn you my paragraphs are often equivalent to the "word" in "and now for a word from our sponsor"—I want to add to it a thought about the unwillingness of the press and the broadcast media to admit their own errors. I don't know why this should be, although of course, in the days when I knew everything I knew also that I never made mistakes. (I remember, too, sending snotty letters back to readers of *Maclean's* who wrote to say our type was too small, and note that only now, a quarter of a century later, do I realize they were right unless, of course, the type is shrinking.) If anything, I think, a willingness to say you're wrong when you are—provided, that is you don't have to do it too often—strengthens the signal you send about your own credibility, just as the rare times when a politician will actually say, "I got that wrong" or even "I spoke too soon," makes him seem not only more human but more honest. (I think, for instance, of Ross Thatcher—the real Thatcher of Saskatchewan politics, whom I covered as a young reporter in

Moose Jaw, facing down people who dogged him from meeting to meeting when he had crossed the floor from the CCF to the Liberals, yelling "traitor" and "turncoat" at him, and Ross, cigar clenched in his teeth, staring bull-dog-like right back at them, and saying simply "I changed my mind.")

I've made that point about politicians before. But speaking from within a trade that is at least as unwilling as its subjects to admit to error, it's hard to be convincing. *The Globe and Mail*, to its credit, has taken in recent years to running a department called "Our Mistake," and I notice that other papers are following suit. But have you ever noticed that department is seldom about the mistake at all? It's really about the correction. They almost never tell you how they messed up, only that so and so, wrongly identified yesterday, is really the president of the teachers' union or whatever. Why don't they say what they said in the first place?

Late last year, as it happens, I had some first-hand experience with what occurs when someone gets something wrong about you. It started with a business column on *Morningside* during the election campaign. The column was on not long after the Liberals had shot up in the polls, and the stock market had taken a nosedive, apparently in response. In my role as host, I asked three columnists—a journalist, a stockbroker and financial analyst—what they made of the market-drop. Somewhat to my surprise, I received in return not their usual rational analyses of what had happened but a very strong—and unanimous—set of arguments that the business community was right: free trade would be a disaster for Canada.

Although my own views on that matter were, like many of my views, mixed (instinctively, I confess, I opposed free trade, but I thought the attempts at logical discussion were equally outrageous on both sides), I tried (still acting as host), to provide some balance. Without giving you every detail of the conversation that followed, I can report that it was heated, although we were friends when it ended. The next day, a columnist in St. John's, Newfoundland, used it as the basis for a bitter attack on me, something he has, of course, every right to do. Except that in this case, he (1) put some words in my mouth (and in direct quotation marks) that I had not said and (2) tried to "prove" his point by saying he had also seen me on *The Journal's* television debate on free trade, working the corner of the opponents, as they say in boxing, and, indeed, whispering encouragement into Bob White's ear. Well, not only had I not attended that TV debate—we were planning our own, as it happens, a three-hour program, of which I'm particularly proud, in which we hired a couple of the country's top courtroom lawyers and used the technique of witnesses, expert testimony and cross-examination to look at the whole matter—I hadn't even seen it on TV.

These were, as you may remember, parlous times for CBC radio hosts. Dale Goldhawk, my colleague and the host of *Cross-Country Check-Up*, was under ferocious attack—an attack launched, by the way, by Charles Lynch, one of my predecessors here—not for anything he'd said on the radio but for what he was, which was president of ACTRA, a union that had been outspoken in its opposition to free trade. Dale, in fairness, had also occasionally been the union's spokesman on the matter. But since what was threatening his job was not the exercise of a bias in his role as host but the lesser offence of being potentially perceived as being biased, the accusation in the paper in St. John's was, to say the least, troublesome to me. I took some action.

In the end—and, again, to be fair—the Newfoundland columnist did the honourable thing. "I was wrong," he wrote in his column, "and I apologize." But what bothered me about this issue, and the reason I have gone into it in some detail here, is what lengths I had to go to get him to do so. Finally, in fact, I wrote that apology myself, and had my lawyer send it to him with an ominous kind of "or else" letter. Whatever I thought of my critic as a reporter, I would have thought more of him as a gentleman and, much more important, would have been more inclined to believe anything else I read in his column in the future—if, at the first indication that he'd blown it he'd simply stepped forward and said the magic words himself: "I was wrong."

This self-righteous outrage, I should remind you, comes from someone who has just confessed to writing a review of a concert he didn't quite attend.

What has happened in the interim to make me change my mind? Well, for one thing, as you may have noticed, I've kicked around a bit myself. The suggestion I made earlier about beginning a course in journalism and having to read something written about yourself by someone who barely knows you was based on some pretty bitter experience. It was perhaps especially bitter in my own case because the biggest bloodbath I took was over one of my brief careers in television, and since what people write about you on television tends to be not about your work but about your very being, it was an indelible and useful lesson. I think, too, that having achieved a kind of undeserved early success based more, as I tried to indicate earlier, on the times I lived in than on my skills—gave me an inflated sense of my own importance. When I lost that sense myself—and I spent a long time in the wilderness when the phone didn't ring—I may well have developed an acute ability to detect it in others and to distrust it. Now, having had a very lucky chance to return to the job I now hold and start again, I am grateful where I once was cocky. Having been able to travel so widely in this country, I have come to realize that the sense of diffidence I take to be so central to its character, is one—even if you have to learn it the hard way—that does no harm in the practice of my chosen craft.

I, now, too, note the length to which I have gone on such a single theme, much of it based on my own observations of matters raised by previous Minifie lecturers. When Sat Kumar first invited me to join you this year, and I began to run over in my mind what I might say, a lot of subjects and ideas ran through my mind. But I decided the most satisfying one to start with would be to try to carry the baton a little farther. Now, I see that I've used up almost all of my time here—and perhaps all of your patience—although I look forward to a little session to follow, of conversation between you and me, the Q and A as we call it.

Before we do that, and on the grounds it may strike some response among people who will follow me here, may I just throw some other ideas at you in short-hand, and hope they will spark either your interest or your concern.

IDEAS FOR NEXT TIME
I would have liked to talk, for instance, about what I have come to call the wave theory of news. This is a hypothesis that says that the modem journalist has come to function as a watcher from the shore, gazing out on the rolling ocean of current events and trying to spot the individual waves as they take shape in the distance. When he (forgive me the masculine pronoun just once) does see one coming he cries an alert, and all his colleagues on the beach join in the observation, so that each wave, once spotted, is followed relentlessly to the shore: AIDS, for example, free trade, the ozone layer and the greenhouse effect, violence in hockey, pornography, abortion . . . pick your wave, from my own all-time favourite non-story of the 1980s, killer bees, to this week's (or this month's) special, the deficit.

The trouble with seeing stories as waves from the shore, is that waves break when they hit land; they roll in a crescendo over the reefs and, when they hit the shore, disperse, never to be seen from the shore again. Thus, of course, AIDS; where is it this year? Free trade: having read 10,000 stories and watched 10,000 broadcasts on how it might affect all our lives—all of them based on those unerringly accurate forecasters, the economists—may I ask where are the stories now that we've got it? The greenhouse effect? What greenhouse effect? Wasn't anyone in Saskatchewan 10 days ago? Either all the stories we have been reading have been wrong or this incredibly aberrant winter is yet another symptom of the way we've messed up the atmosphere—and either way, if the wave hadn't broken, it would be a story. And so on and so on. With the exception of the killer bees—a wave I fear (or hope) will be offshore forever—everything comes, taking its turn, and everything goes away. Now they've spotted the deficit which in real terms, surely is neither better nor worse than it was two years ago or, for that matter at the height of the election campaign, when our attention was focussed on the free trade wave. Meanwhile, to take just one example, the language crunch in Quebec this winter, which I for one take to be as serious a crisis as this country has faced in recent times, has, for all intents, disappeared from our view.

The wave theory: the fashionableness of issues. No wonder, I suppose in a world that now gets so much of its news totally out of any context whatever, that absorbs so much of its information in a form that Neil Postman, the smartest man now writing about the media, calls "and now . . . this," every 40 seconds.

In the same vein, I would like to have talked about the steady trivialization of the news, the gradual but ineluctable transformation of the dispensing of information into the production of entertainment. As a symbol, I would have started with a supper-hour television program I watched in Toronto last week, in which the sportscaster came on at about the 15-minute mark to tell us that the Maple Leafs had played the Blackhawks last night at the etc, etc, and that later on he would be back to give us the score. What occurred to me, as I watched him, was that in the time he had done his own promotion he could have given us not only the outcome but the names of the people who'd scored the goals. He wasn't a journalist at all, I thought, if journalists are people who find out what you want to know for you and tell you about it. He was a show-biz figure whose only purpose in appearing early in the program was to tease you into staying with it longer.

I might have talked, too, about the latest sensation of the newspaper business, *USA Today*—which isn't far from a broadsheet national version of the tabloids that have sprung up in so many Canadian cities recently. Almost everything in it, from the four-coloured weather map, to the short, short stories (and now . . . this), to the titillating picture of scantily clad models, makes it television in print.

And I probably would have concluded with a note about something I saw this week as I huddled in a hotel room during *Morningside*'s trip across the West. It was on *Entertainment Tonight*—another symptom in itself, since it too uses the guise of information to dispense froth. It was a report on the making of a video on the models who were to wear the swimsuits for *Sports Illustrated*'s 25th annual swimwear edition. And I would have said that I remember when *Sports Illustrated* was launched, an attempt to bring literate writing to the world of the jocks; now it is noted mostly as a place to see sexy pictures of young women—the swimwear edition outsells everything else the magazine does. But not only that, it has become a video. And not only that, they're making television programs about a video, about a magazine. And not only that, I'm up here talking about it . . . oh, dear. Before I came here I watched a TV news show, just 6:30 tonight. It reported to be about fashion in lingerie as set by the movies, but if watched carefully you realized that it was just an excuse to show me Susan Sarandon, Madonna and a whole lot of other women whose names I didn't know, in their skinnies.

There are other subjects, too, I'd like to have pursued. Some comments I have about the way the media have come to concentrate so much on death, pestilence and destruction, for instance, are in the book I published last fall, and some are not.

CURIOSITY IS VITAL

I want to make one more point about something I know now that I didn't know back in the days when I knew everything. It's about curiosity. When I was younger and smarter I used to think the business I was setting out on was all about techniques: tricks of the trade, anecdotal leads, smart questions, editing devices, source books, hot phone numbers—all the things the people graduating from schools such as this have learned before they start in the business (or should have) and which all the people of my time picked up (or should have) along the way. Now, at last, though I don't know all the tricks (I learn new ones every day), my arsenal is pretty complete. But the closer it comes to completion, the more I realize how unimportant it is compared to the essential ingredient of curiosity. If you follow your own nose, if you pursue the questions you genuinely want to know the answers to, rather than those you feel you ought to want to know the answers to, you will be the best journalist you can be.

And, if I can direct this last remark to the students at this school, if you will set out on a course of trying to do that, and keep trying all the way, and stick to your goals of truth and fairness and accuracy, you will have a very rich and rewarding life indeed.

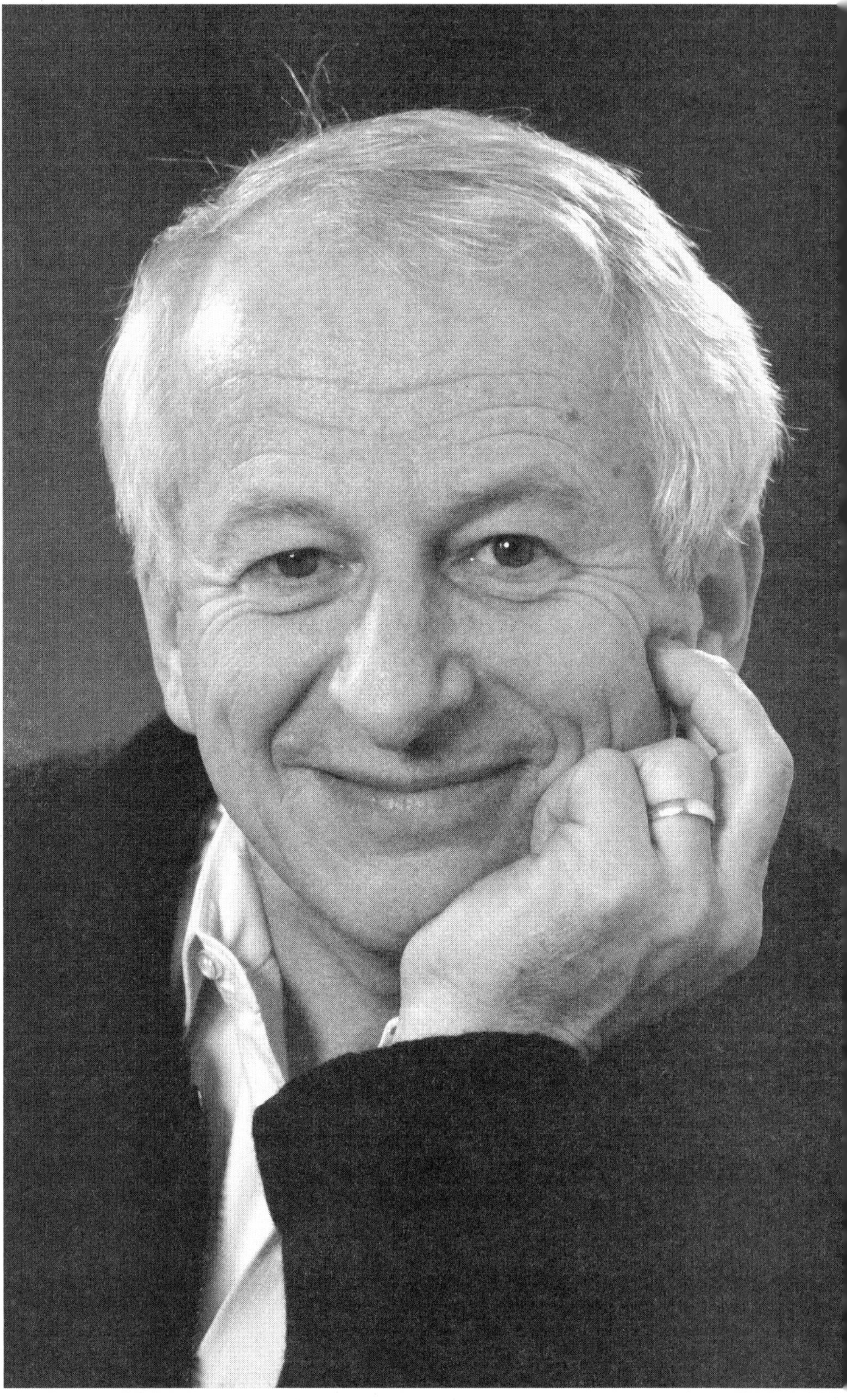

–1990–
PATRICK WATSON

Patrick Watson is a writer, producer, director, actor, television host, and interviewer. He wrote, produced and directed *The Undersea World of Jacques Cousteau*. He co-founded the best-known Canadian series *This Hour Has Seven Days*. He directed the ambitious *Heritage Minutes* series, dramatizations of moments from Canada's past. Watson's many awards include two Emmies, three ACTRA awards, two Canadian Film Awards, the Canada 125 Medal, and the Queen's Jubilee Medal. He was named an officer of the Order of Canada in 1981 and promoted to Companion in 2002. Watson was co-producer of the CBC's first current affairs television magazine series, *Close Up*, produced and directed the National Affairs series *INQUIRY*, and was the first North American producer ever to film in The People's Republic of China, creating the documentary classic *The 700 Million*. In 1975, he was named Best Television Journalist of the Year for *The Last Nazi*, his 90-minute documentary with Hitler's architect and Armaments Minister, Albert Speer. In 1989, the international co-production television series *The Struggle for Democracy*, which he created and hosted, won best documentary of the year in both languages: the Gemini and Gemeaux awards. As host and interviewer, his programs have also included *The Watson Report, The Canadian Establishment, Flight, The Passionate Affair, Lawyers, Live .from Lincoln Centre,* and *The Fifty-First State*. He was Chairman of the Canadian Broadcasting Corporation from 1989 to 1994.

1990 | PATRICK WATSON

THE GREAT CANADIAN IDENTITY MYSTERY

I am very happy to be back in Saskatchewan. I never lose the opportunity when I come here to claim a kind of parenthood in the province, because my mother was born in Moose Jaw. Whether it is for that reason or not, every time I come to this province I find the most enormous hospitality and warm welcome. It makes a body feel very good to be here.

I went to Moose Jaw a few years ago to explore a bit of that city, to find out what it was that my mother had been born in. She had moved back to Ontario at the age of two but also wondered about the city, and went back in her early twenties to teach in Moose Jaw. I was invited by a group of teachers to come and talk to them, and went and did that, and had a schmooze around the city. I felt a little sentimental and thought about my mother a great deal. When I was leaving the hotel after a couple of days, a Moose Jaw chambermaid who had been watching me closely as I came and went in the hotel, was waiting for me outside my room with an autograph book thrust out before me. As I approached her she withdrew the autograph book a little bit and she said, "Before I ask you to sign this, can I ask you a very personal question?" I said, "Yes," and she said, "Are you a born-again Christian just like me?" I said, "Well, I'm a Christian, maybe not exactly like you." And she said, "Oh well, it doesn't matter. I always watch you on *Man Alive* anyway."

So I had to consider some value issues here about compassion versus truth and as I was writing "Roy," she said quietly, "I never miss one of your programs."

On another occasion I was in Calgary. Calgary gives you a different kind of welcome than Regina. It does me anyway. One of the great welcomes I got in Calgary was when the Canadian Petroleum Association asked me to talk on the subject of why there is so much warfare between the media and the oil men. I prepared a very thorough examination of that question and it was a dinner meeting, with about 800 people in a huge hall. It's the only time in my speaking career, which is a long one, that more than once during the speech people called up from the floor, "Bullshit, Watson." I think it was meant in a friendly way. But what I wanted to say about the welcome was that before I even began my speech, we had the dinner. The soup was about to be brought out, and they asked the senior rabbi of Calgary to do the invocation. He said, "Lord, please call down thy blessing upon those who are in need, and those who are oppressed and those who are suffering and those who are especially in need of thy grace, especially our guest who is an easterner."

Also in Calgary, I was waiting in the lobby of the Calgary Inn for some friends to come down for dinner one night and they were a bit late. I was eyeing the elevator, when down the hall on my right, in the direction of the bar, there came absolutely the thinnest human being I have ever seen in my life: A female human being, adult, but literally about "that" thin. She was wearing one of those polished white leather cowboy suits that squeaks when you walk, with a flat-brimmed polished leather white cowboy hat with a little fringe around it. And as she came in front of me, she kind of did a swirl and she said, "Uh huh," and I thought, "I don't remember this person." She said, "What are you doing in Calgary?" I said, "I am here on business," looking anxiously, eagerly I may say, at the elevators, hoping that the door would open and my friends would come and rescue me. And she said, "You wait right here. My old man is in the bar with my kid. Wait until he knows you are here." Off she went down the hall and before my friends came out of the elevator she reappeared from the direction of the bar, dragging a reluctant guy with one of those mustaches and a black leather cowboy suit—he was pretty thin too—and one of those hats. He was dragging by the hand a very reluctant kid, a fat kid. The kid was wearing a black and white cowboy suit too. She looked at her husband and she said, "You see, I told you: Laurier La Pierre."

After that, I got famous and it didn't happen again for a long time. But one of the culture shocks that I am going through now, as chairman of the CBC instead of being an independent producer (and there are many of them), is not being able to be on television anymore. It has its rewards and it has its liabilities as well. Just the other night my wife and I were sitting in an Indian restaurant in Toronto and I saw a man whispering to his companion and looking over at me and presently he came over (and really this one still continues to puzzle me, and I think it will you too). He pointed and said, "Normie Patterson, eh?" I said, "Nope." He said, "Well I guess I got the name wrong but you are on *Front Page Challenge*, eh?" "No." "C'mon, c'mon," he said, "I work at the CBC."

I was telling someone at CBC Toronto about that a couple of days later and he said, "Maybe at the end of your tenure as chairman you will be old enough to be on the *Front Page Challenge* panel." It was Larry Zolf, and Larry said, "By then it will be okay because they will be producing the show out of an oxygen tent."

Another part of the culture shock entailed in my present job is that I have to get used to using the word "we" in a news sense. Now I have to come home and say to my wife about the CBC, "Guess what we did today, dear," whereas I am used to coming home and saying, "Guess what those bastards did today, dear." So that takes a certain amount of reorientation. People are asking me a great deal these days, "Now that you are the Chairman of the Board and Mr. Veilleux is the President and Chief Executive Officer, how do you divide up the work?" and I say, "Well, why don't you take a look at what the press says?" One day the press will do an article on the restructuring and re-organization of the administration and management of the CBC and say, "Veilleux is streamlining CBC management for the 1990s," and then in the entertainment pages of the same newspaper there will be an article saying, "CBC sitcom is so bad even CBC staff don't laugh," and buried in the article will be, "Patrick Watson must be losing his touch." So that is the difference between what the two of us do.

Actually it is a very good partnership and he and I discuss very closely the development of policies and strategies for the CBC. One of the things we are most concerned about is to make it a more open organization; both open to our public, our audiences, but also an open organization in terms of relationships between staff, management, and producers, between producers and producers and managers and managers. Mr. Veilleux said to me one day a little while ago, "How do you think this is working, Patrick, I mean the openness motif?" and I said, "Girard, I think it is fabulous." I said, "You know, before we came here CBC employees were stabbing each other in the back. Now they are doing it in the front."

EXPLAINING THE TITLE

When I was asked to come here some months ago, I was asked for a title. I am certainly glad I didn't yield to my temptation to do what I was working on: "Why the Berlin Wall will never come down." In order to fudge it, I said, "Let's tell them we will do something about the Canadian Identity," and that is the reason for the title you will have seen on the poster. But it does have something to do with some thoughts I have had about examining the Canadian identity through our humour as well as through our institutions.

By the way, I meant to mention that one of the benefits of my preparing for my new appointment was that during the negotiation period, after the Prime Minister asked me to consider taking the job on, I had a chance for the first time to get to know Mr. Mulroney a little bit. He had been a figure whom I had met in broadcasting studios a couple of times but I didn't know him at all. We had to sit down and talk about some things in very close quarters and in a very man-to-man way. I discovered to my great astonishment that Brian Mulroney and I have a number of characteristics in common.

Tremendous modesty to begin with, exquisite taste in shoes. He uses his less for walking on water than I do, but he is probably going to be the only Prime Minister of Canada to walk on the waters of Meech Lake with 60 pairs of Gucci shoes all at one time.

One of the things that also surprised me to hear him say in our conversations was that despite his public posture of disdain and contempt for his predecessor, Mr. Trudeau, he had in fact some very fruitful conversations with Mr. Trudeau during the transition period and he learned a great deal.

I said, "What kind of stuff did you learn, Brian?" He said, "Well, you know, I am very concerned about how to pick good staff, good surroundings, good lieutenants, and I asked Pierre how he does it, and he said, 'Well it's simple. I look for intelligence and the way I test for intelligence is to throw out a brain teaser very quick to somebody I want to try out. I'll give you an example.' And he called out, 'Is Chrétien still waiting for me in the outer office? Ask him to come in please.' Chrétien came in and Pierre said to him, 'Jean, I know a man who is your father's son but is not your brother: Who is it?' Chrétien said, 'Easy boss, it's me.' Trudeau said, 'See.' Mulroney said, "That's wonderful." So when he was putting together his team and trying them out, at one point he called in Crosbie and he said, 'John, I know a man who is your father's son but is not your brother: Who is it?' And Crosbie said, 'Brian, I would like a bit of time to think about that one. Can I get back?' "Any time, John, just take your time." Crosbie whips into his office, picks up the phone and calls Mazankowski and says, 'Don, I know we have had some bad blood sometimes, but you have to help me out on this one quick. The boss wants an answer right away. Now listen, here is the question: I know a man who is your father's son but is not your brother: Who is it?' Mazankowski says, 'Easy, it's me.' 'Whew,' says Crosbie. So he goes back in, knocks on the door and the Prime Minister says, 'Come in.' 'Boss I got it.' Mulroney says, "Alright, John, let's hear the answer." Crosbie says, 'Brian it's easy, it's Mazankowski,'" and the Prime Minister says, "John, you are so stupid: it's Jean Chrétien."

In thinking about the way in which jokes reflect what we do in this country, and what the nature of our character is, I often come back to conversations I had with my late friend Marshall McLuhan who believed jokes were the real indicator of what is going on in this society. Marshall would say things like, "Behind every joke there lies a grievance." "Behind every joke there lies an insight into social conflict." Marshall loved jokes. He loved you to bring him jokes and he loved to retell them and Marshall's favourite Newfie joke, which he would tell at the drop of a hat, was the following.

There was a Newfoundlander sitting on a bench in the sun at Gander Airport having a cup of tea and watching the airplanes come and go, when a corporate jet came in from Texas to refuel before going across the pond. And a big guy in a Stetson and cowboy boots got out of this gleaming airplane. He went into the terminal while the bowsers were doing the fueling, picked up a cup of coffee and came out and sat down on the bench beside the Newfoundlander. The Newfoundlander said, "Well, son, that is a hell of a nice airplane. What kind of business are you in?" The Texan said, "Friend, I am a farmer." And the Newfoundlander said, "Well now ain't that a son-of-a-bitch of a coincidence? I'm a farmer too. Now tell me, how big is your farm?" The Texan said, "My friend, I get into my car in the morning and start to drive across my spread and come sundown I still haven't got to the other side." And the Newfoundlander said, "Now there is the second damn coincidence: I used to have a car like that."

Another story that has been going around that reveals something about us that I like is the one about the cannibals who captured three people, a Frenchman, an American and a Canadian. They lined them all up for the ceremony and the chief of the cannibal group came forward and said, "Now, boys, I want you to understand that what we are about to do is not done with malice. We have real respect for you. We are going to eat you with pride and even affection, and as a token of that we would like you to have a last wish. We can fulfill almost anything you want. We are a wealthy tribe. You have seen the Mercedes-Benz and the jet over on the strip, so, anything special that you want." So the Frenchman said, "Well, uh, I would like to have a wonderful last meal with some Dom Perignon, *canard a l'orange, petit fois gras,* and then I would like to make love to a beautiful woman." And the Chief said, "No problem at all. I'm happy to arrange that for you." He turned to the Canadian and said, "What would you like to do?" I believe the Canadian was an Ottawa mandarin. In any case the Canadian said, "Well, I would like you to get the whole tribe together because I would like to make a speech, and I would like to make a speech about how, in our great country that stretches from sea to sea, with all the cultural differences and conflicts that we have, we have been able to resolve most of those conflicts in a humane way and we have developed an entrepreneurial spirit and kept the sense of adventure in the frontier that our American friends have but they have developed more violence than we have." And the chief of the cannibals said, "You can make that speech, brother, no problem. I would be glad to gather the folks for you to make it." And then he turned to the American and said, "And you sir, what is your last wish?" And the American said, "Eat me before he starts."

[Mr. Watson then played segments from two CBC comedy shows.]

HUMOUR REFLECTS EXPERIENCE
I believe the identity of any nation comes from the experiences it shares and that the culture of any nation is the expression of the sharing of those experiences. The fact that we have sat here together and laughed at some stories, and some bits of television and some bits of radio, laughed at humour that would be largely cryptic to anybody who was not intimately familiar with Canada and the fabric of Canadian life, is an illustration of what I mean by that shared experience defining a nation. We are a nation which has gone through so many laborious exercises asking ourselves what it is we are all about. The best way, I believe, we can find out what we are all about is to continue to express to each other what we do, and to share our experiences through humour, through drama, through journalism, through travel, through visiting. And perhaps we could profitably spend a little less time than we now do worrying about what the identity is, and a little more time sharing it and enjoying it and celebrating it and getting into it.

So the only point that I wanted to make by bringing the stories I told and bringing those two broadcasting artifacts with me, was that we do have an immensely rich shared experience which is opaque to people who haven't been in it. Oh, sure, some of the jokes you have heard are funny jokes whether or not you know the references, but they are not rich jokes until you know what the references are. Because these are things we are dealing with and living together with day by day as a nation and that is what a culture is.

It sounds like a banal idea or a simple idea. But it is something important to be reiterated at a time when, for example, people are telling the CBC that it has a special responsibility for the culture of this country. They then set out sometimes to define the culture that the CBC is supposed to purvey in a way that excludes a number of the common and ordinary activities that we share and that make up our character as a nation, in favour of those more dressed up activities that have to do with classical music and serious theatre and the ballet and the other things that many people often put a capital-C for Culture on. And while I think those arts are an extremely important part of what we do together as a cultural nation, it is really the day-by-day living we do together, the things that we have to fight over, the things that we have to compete for space with, the things that produce our jokes, that are, to me, the quintessential part of the Canadian life.

A GREAT PRODUCER AND A GREAT QUESTION

As I take a look at what we in the Canadian Broadcasting Corporation must do over the next five years of my tenancy of this job, and the next 10 years of this decade, I find myself thinking that we have crossed into a new era in human affairs in which the demands upon those of us who have power in media have changed substantially.

I was trained in part by a very distinguished, extraordinary and imaginative television producer named Ross McLean. He invented the first-ever television current affairs magazine. He asked me to work with him as an associate producer on *Close Up* back in 1957. It was fascinating to be present at the development of a form: the idea that a print-form magazine could be transformed into television. It is a form which has now become the bread-and-butter of television journalism all over the world, at least all over the industrial world, the western world.

Ross McLean—who was a bumptious, difficult, sometimes outrageous, very controversial, humorous guy, a huge ego (it takes one to know one), a tremendously inventive director, a great discoverer of talent, a very ambitious guy—brought together a small group of younger producers and would-be producers, to bring *Close Up* into being. When we would bring Ross a program idea for consideration, he would listen to the budgetary implications and the story line and what was entailed in time and equipment and travel to make it, and what the content of the piece would be. After having asked his questions and gone around the room to get a response from everybody else within the small team, he had one final question which you had to be able to answer effectively or you did not get to do the program segment, and that question was, "How does this serve the audience?" You got to be prepared after a while to expect that question and to be ready to answer it, but the first few times it was a bit of a shock because you got excited about doing a satirical piece on Bluenosers in Nova Scotia or a controversial piece on government scandal or God knows what, and you were thinking about expressing what you had discovered and expressing it in the most compelling and entertaining, pointed way you could and Ross would say, "You have to tell me how it is going to serve the audience."

One of the most important lessons that I learned from my association with that man was that service is what we in the public broadcasting system are all about. We are not there to get an audience, but to serve an audience.

Most broadcasting in North America is designed to get an audience. It is designed to get an audience, wrapped up in packages which can then be delivered to advertisers: "Here is 500,000, here is one million, here is five million."

Advertiser writes a cheque and says, "Thanks very much, glad that you delivered us the audience." Most broadcasting uses audiences. Audiences are there as fodder for most broadcasting.

The public broadcaster has a different mission. The public broadcaster must constantly ask, "How do we serve the audience?" Because that is what we are there for. If the programs we are doing do not serve the audience, they shouldn't be done. It will sometimes be extremely difficult, intricate, complex, time-consuming, to analyze what constitutes service and what not, but ultimately that is a question, Ross McLean's question, that has to be answered if we are to justify what we do as public broadcasters. This is a formulation that people in the public broadcasting game can respond to: That is what we do, and that is what's different about what we do.

You will find, by the way, very many private broadcasters who say, "That is what we would like to do and we try to do a good deal of that." But that is not their central mandate. The private broadcasters' central mandate is to provide a return on investment to shareholders and that means delivering audiences to advertisers.

SERVICE IS MEDIA MANDATE

I am beginning to feel, as I look at the 90s and on into the next millennium, that the concept of service must not be left only to the public broadcasters. I am beginning to feel that we who have power in the media, who publish books and newspapers, who produce and broadcast television programs and radio programs, who sell records and tapes, who do theatre, who make movies are guardians, are stewards of a trust.

It isn't just the public broadcasters. The power is so immense: to change attitudes, to create attitudes, the power to bring a vision of reality into the homes of people all over the world, this is a vision the vividness of which has to be responded to with emotion and understanding or the struggle to understand. Those of us who have that power, have stewardship over something that can spell the survival or the destruction of this planet. If we are to use that power only to exploit audiences, in order to satisfy advertisers or to satisfy box offices or to satisfy investors, then we have betrayed that trust.

I am going to be asking my colleagues in media over these next few years to consider that proposition very seriously. Not because I want them to commit an act of charity and start being nice to people but because I believe the time has come when people in all kinds of industries formerly considered cynical places to work, like the advertising business, are ready to listen to the idea, and in fact are already listening to the idea and thinking about the idea, that the world has indeed become too small for us to fool around with it anymore.

We have become a family of brothers and sisters living on the same planet who have responsibility to each other. I have a feeling, historically speaking, that we—the human race—have gone through a kind of experimental period in which you could try out any kind of wild idea and it didn't matter very much because there was always room for the wreckage to fall. There was room to throwaway the garbage. There was room to try again. But it was kind of like adolescence, where you could take all kinds of chances because your parents would always be there to bail you out. But the parents in this case were the plenitude of the planet, the forgiving nature of the atmosphere, the forgiving nature of the space that we dwelt in. And that space is no longer forgiving. We can't trifle with it anymore. We do have the power to destroy each other so easily, and not just with nuclear weapons which we seem to be getting a bit of a handle on.

The other factor is the shrinking globe, the fact that we are now rubbing shoulders with each other in both a metaphorical and a real sense. We are becoming aware of each other in a way that we never did before, through, to a very large extent, television. Many of us are also becoming wealthy enough to travel. As a result, people from various parts of the world are seeing each other up close in a way we didn't before. This has presented those of us in the media with an opportunity to take stock of a new possibility, a possibility of saying to people who were once driven only by the bottom line, that we must expand the concept of that bottom line to include the survival of the human race.

TALENT WASTED ON VIOLENCE

I am appalled, personally, at the amount of brilliant craft that goes into the representation of human experience, the most significant part of which is blowing other people away with pounds of explosives. It just seems to me to be such a sad commentary that we have developed such tremendous capacity to communicate and to be witty and to express love and compassion and intrigue and curiosity and all of the things that we can express through our media and we spend so much time in that expression and so much of our resources with the celebration of death. We do it not because like Shakespeare in *Macbeth* or *Titus Andronicus,* we are puzzled and perplexed by death, but because we know jolts per minute will bring them into the box office. That is what I mean by exploitation.

As I talk about violence in media here, I am not calling for a moratorium on violence in media. I am not suggesting that there should be censorship of violence in media. I think that would be worse than having to put up with it. What I am saying is if you look at the representation of human activity and you find that it is being used only to provide the jolts that will keep people coming into a box office and not to investigate our life together, it doesn't matter what the subject matter is, if that is what it is being used for, then it is exploitation. We have come to the point that we can't afford to do that anymore, and anyone who goes to his grave a rich film producer or a rich television magnate or a rich publisher, having made that wealth only by using the power that we have to exploit, will go to his or her grave having not really lived a life that is worth being remembered.

JAMES M. MINIFIE: A FINE PROFESSIONAL

As I draw to a close I want to say a couple of words about Don Minifie. Ron Robbins (founder of this school of journalism) has referred to his skill and his human qualities and his scholarship, all of which were tremendous. I had the great pleasure of briefly, on several occasions, working with Don. I remember him with great affection as a generous minded, gentlemanly, scholarly professional from whom, in the short acquaintance that I had with him, I learned a great deal. He was a man with a great sense of humour, and a wonderful twinkle.

The last time I was with Don Minifie, in his house in Georgetown, was shortly after the death of John F. Kennedy. We were talking about what that meant to the world, and Don had some very trenchant things to say. But I remember, most vividly of all, the humorous twist he put on it at the end. He went up to the window and he sort of peered out. By now it was getting dark in Georgetown and he said, "You know, Patrick, you know what I think I am going to miss the most, you know what we are all going to miss the most, especially here in Georgetown?" He said, "Seeing that long black limousine snake through the streets of Georgetown, and we would say to ourselves, there is Kennedy off to another tryst."

I am often introduced as a journalist, and we are here to celebrate a journalist and here because of the work of the School of Journalism, a distinguished one. But I am always a tiny bit uneasy when people refer to me as a journalist. I often ask them to put quotation marks around it. Or when people say, "What do you do?" and I am moved to boast, I say I am a journalist. I used to put it on my passport although it gets you into a lot of difficulty in some countries. When you present a passport that says "journalist" you may be taken into a small room and asked a lot of questions for a very long time and then thrown out of the country. That has happened to me too. Now I put on my passport "Chairman." That is neat.

But the reason I say I am a little uneasy being called a journalist is that I have never been in aspects of that craft where many of my colleagues have been. I have never been a newspaper reporter, for example. I think that I recognize a wide-ranging cast of journalists, I am not sure that when I look at myself I say, "He is one of them." Joe Schlesinger is a journalist. There is no question about that. Anthony Sampson is a journalist. Ann Medina is a journalist. Trina McQueen is a journalist. I sometimes think that what I have been in my life is a kind of non-fiction entertainer, using realities, using film, the film camera, the documentary—to communicate. With the camera and the microphone I have had a lot of fun with experience—sometimes to weep, sometimes to grieve, sometimes to explore complicated fields of emotional response to reality that don't have much to do with celebration. But I think primarily I've tried to celebrate the fact of being alive and aware and having this extraordinary thing that we human beings are given, this capacity to communicate with all the various forms that we have, the capacity to sing. And so I guess I will go through the rest of my professional life, especially now that I am a chairman, wondering if I really ever was a journalist.

But I must add there is no doubt in my mind about Don Minifie: James M. Minifie was one of the finest, and you do me great honour to ask me to come here and speak in his name.

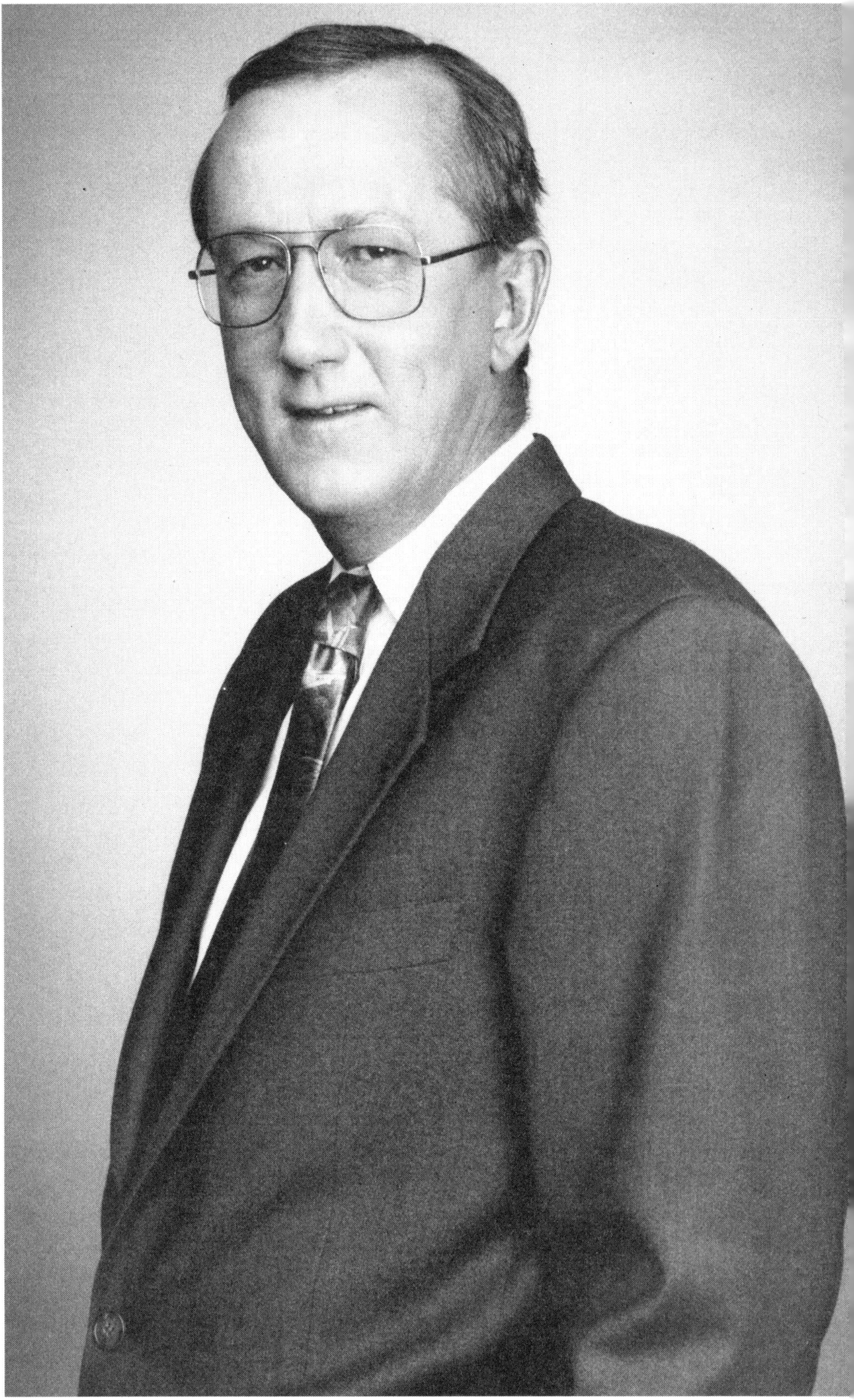

—1991—

ERIC MALLING

A controversial television journalist from Swift Current, Saskatchewan, Malling was a hard-hitting contrarian and investigative reporter who was the host of CBC's *the fifth estate* from 1976 to 1990. In 1978, his one-hour documentary on the illegal export of artillery shells from Canada to apartheid South Africa created a public outcry. Similarly, the Federal Minister responsible for Fisheries, John Fraser, was forced to resign after Malling uncovered Fraser had bowed to corporate pressure, overruling his own health inspectors to allow the sale of tainted tuna. In 1990, he moved to CTV to host *W5 with Eric Malling*. Malling won six ACTRA Awards, three Gordon Sinclair awards for excellence in broadcast journalism and a Gemini Award.

1991 | ERIC MALLING

RECIPES FOR SACRED COW

It's intimidating to give a talk in the name of such a prestigious journalist as James M. Minifie. In the early days of this lecture, they chose people who knew Minifie, and I am reviving that tradition.

As a kid, I knew his name from the radio. I couldn't help know him, because every time he came on the radio, my father would sit me down and make me listen and ask me if I knew he was from around Vanguard, south of Swift Current. I remember thinking that once, twice, 10 times was probably enough for me to get the point, but I realize now that my father had to keep reminding me (or himself), because it was an important connection from Swift Current to the big world. He was so proud that Minifie was from here. I guess I was proud too, but a little confused at the beginning.

When I grew up, we didn't get television until I was in grade seven or eight, so we listened to the radio, CBK from Regina and CHAB from Moose Jaw. I remember as a kid, the big thrill driving down old Number 1 highway on the way to the animal park or Johnson's Dairy in Moose Jaw. Along the way, I used to see the transmitter. That is where the radio came from, and it had this little white building under it. I could never understand how they could get the band, Howdy Doody, Pally Pascoe and Cy Knight's Mailbag into that little building.

The world eventually became somewhat less confusing, and one day I even met the legend—the connection between Swift Current and the big world. I was introduced to James M. Minifie when I was about eight or 10 years old in the old curling rink in Swift Current. He was very easy to pick out He was the one who wore a suit and didn't have a white forehead or a cap on.

I think the country is in a real state of paralysis, and not just on national unity, but in finding solutions to all manner of problems, not least of which are the environment and the economy. The world is changing terribly quickly. I think we're falling behind. The Japanese say that were it not for borrowing to keep up appearances, Canada would be a Third World country.

I grew up believing Saskatchewan was the bread basket of the world. Now France produces more wheat than all of Canada. We face difficult prices, a real shakedown, and I think the media is doing a lousy job getting us ready for it. I think we've been too simplistic, too negative, and too eager to be used—first by business and politicians for their agenda, and now by interest groups for their agendas, which are often narrow and the product of zealots and gripers. The media have let single issue organizations control us at a time when we need perspective and compromise and trade-offs more than ever before. The fundamental tenet of most interest groups is "no compromise."

So let me talk a little bit about television. It's something I know a little bit about. My friend Val Sears (visiting Max Bell Professor at the School of Journalism and Communications) has his view of TV news. He says, "If I ever get so old and feeble that I need someone to read me the evening paper, I'll hire a nurse." But the fact is that only half the households in North America still take an evening paper, or any kind of paper, and the polls show, sometimes to my horror, that they believe most of what they see on the tube.

I think television is tremendously important. That's not to say the people who work in television are important, but the technology itself is so potent. Consider a politician who goes on *Canada AM,* or Pam Wallin's *Question Period,* or *The Journal.* That's a bigger audience then they'd get in their entire lives making speeches in the House of Commons or back in the riding. These programs, and of course the national newscasts and talk radio, are the real forums for debate in the country. The House of Commons revolves around Question Period, but that is just an expensive casting hall where the players audition for a spot on the news that night for the real debate.

The problem is that television, because of its reach, has all this power, but very little in the way of brains. Politicians may think there's a great conspiracy against them whenever they're in power, but the fact is we are not organized enough to conspire against anyone. We select news by habit, by instinct, by routine, and most of all by access. Is it a story we can get, can shoot? Will someone talk?

And guess who is always available to talk? People with a gripe, people who will make a nuisance out of themselves or want to sell something, be they in politics, business, or on the street. We've let a variety of interest groups, within and without the system, set the agenda, and frequently it's not an agenda that serves the public.

In simplest terms, who's most likely to make the evening news? Will it be an important politician with a "no comment" on something that's not so important anyway, or a public realm muse in Halifax who has found a way to deliver some program better and cheaper? Next in the lineup? Will it be 100 protesters out in front of Parliament, or a university professor who really has something to say about how things work or how we can do things better? You know the answer.

It's an age where news is dominated by routine political games, and staged events by interest groups; be they the anti-abortionists, the environmental crusaders, or the folks who'll impede anything that in any way infringes on their particular neighbourhood.

Part of the problem in television is the tyranny of pictures. Politicians and protests are easy to shoot. Thinking is not. A plane does a belly landing in Denver. It'll be on every newscast although no one is even injured. Hundreds die every day because we don't require airbags in cars, but it's not news.

And I think there's a deeper reason. We have gone overboard in the notion that it's the media's job to criticize, to be the real opposition to whomever is in power. Coming from one who's done a fair bit of criticizing himself, this might sound strange, but I think we now have to pay a lot more attention to offering some better solutions as well.

It's said of reporters that we are either at your feet or at your throat, and it's true. Not so long ago the press was at the feet of anyone with power. Reporters were like stenographers, paraphrasing whatever they were given. I remember covering the legislature here for the *Leader Post*. Every MLA got a story about each speech, and all about the same length, whether he or she had anything to say or not.

It was a tame press. Watergate, Woodward and Bernstein, are generally thought to have changed all that. Suddenly there were more kids in journalism school than jobs in journalism, all out to, if not take out an American president, at least get a company president. It's been called "Watergate envy." Actually, in Canada it was not Woodward and Bernstein. It was Val Sears who said during one of the Diefenbaker campaigns, "To work gentlemen. We have a government to overthrow." It became famous and it's what led Val to believe that he was a legend in his own mind.

I hesitate saying it in these parts, but John Diefenbaker used to lie now and then, or as they'd say in Parliamentary lingo, he was "economical with the truth." When he said that Krushchev had banged his shoe on the podium at the UN because of his (Diefenbaker's) speech, Val pointed out that the events were months apart. The prime minister was a liar, and that was significant in the middle of an election campaign.

And Tony Westell, who runs that other school of journalism in Ottawa, took to writing frontpage stories with what Diefenbaker said in quotes, and the truth in brackets. It was brave and intelligent. It showed that just because someone important says something, that doesn't mean it's true.

In the years that followed, reporters did become tougher, more independent, critical, but then it started to flip. Instead of being routinely obsequious toward the powerful, some of us became routinely contemptuous. Instead of cheerleaders, many became naysayers. From boosterism, the attitude turned so that for some, only critical reporting could be quality reporting. Some of the so-called investigative stories, or the term I prefer, original stories, were important.

In this country, I was proud of the story we did on Canadair, a $2 billion boondoggle. It was the largest business loss in Canadian history, and the government had never admitted it to Parliament. In this province, we did a story some years ago on Pioneer Trust. There was a lot more to its collapse than bad luck. The government had much to answer for, and coincidentally, the company president and chairman quit the next day.

Those were stories we originated, stories we could prove. They didn't come from whatever interest group was stuffing the mailbox with press releases or parading on Parliament Hill. Ever since the thalidomide tragedy and the infamous Love Canal, the environmentalists, to take one example, have found easy ways to use the media to take over the agenda.

A couple of years ago, *60 Minutes* did a big so-called exposé on Alar, which is a herbicide used in apple orchards. Kids were going to get cancer. Suddenly, people were afraid to pour their apple juice down the sink to get rid of it because it might contaminate the ground water.

The Journal ran a whole program on Alar. The U.S. government banned it. Everyone was hysterical except the man who developed the test for carcinogens in the first place, the test that shows whether something is harmful by exposing it to bacteria on a slide instead of killing 10,000 rats. Environmentalists, not to say rats, had been ecstatic and he was their hero. His name is Bruce Ames, of the University of California in Berkeley.

I went to talk to Ames and learned that Alar might indeed cause cancer, but the cancer risk of eating an apple a day that had been sprayed with Alar was exactly the same as drinking one bottle of beer every two years, or eating a mushroom from the health food store every couple of years, or a peanut-butter sandwich. The apple a day would obviously do any kid a lot more good than whatever theoretical risk there was from the spray.

But the environmentalists had whipped up *60 Minutes,* which had whipped up the public. The ban, which extended beyond apples, would cost North Americans $2 billion a year in lost product and higher prices.

From the Food and Drug Administration's own worst-case figures, it'll cost $6 billion to prevent one cancer. Balance that against food worth $6 billion, and ask how much good that would do for public health. When I put this to the environmental group which had won such a triumph, they didn't dispute the figures. They simply argued that any risk at all was unacceptable, and any man-made substance added to the environment was bad.

By that reasoning, we shouldn't be worried about Alar. Let's ban the automobile. It's a far greater risk. Now we have asbestos, another cause for the protest groups and reporters who are hungry for the big scare story, the big expose. Asbestos does cause cancer; mostly in old people who have worked with it unprotected all their lives and are also heavy smokers.

But suddenly it's "killer asbestos." Protesters surround a school with asbestos around a few pipes. It's on the evening news and next thing we know, Ontario and other provinces are spending hundreds of millions of dollars to tear apart public buildings. And in the US, they're spending $3 billion a year to get rid of asbestos in buildings, although a lot of the tests show there's more of it outside than inside. It's in the ground and in the air. It's a natural mineral.

What do we get for all the billions? Well, according to Harvard, the risk from asbestos in school buildings is one-third that from being hit by lightning or being killed in a hurricane. Chances of expiring from smoking are 22,000 times higher. Killed in a car crash? Sixteen hundred times higher. But you don't hear that in most of the stories.

Asbestos was in the news in Toronto last year after they closed the student pub at York University because someone found a pipe wrapped with asbestos in one of the storage rooms. Safety hazard. Close it down. I can only speculate how much safer the students were when the pub reopened and they got back to fights in the parking lot and mayhem on the highway. But the lesson is that once the environmentalists and the media call out "cancer," common sense goes out the window.

"We can't afford to be too careful," is the line. But we have to make choices, and it's hard to make wise ones when a few zealots spoon-feed lazy reporters who get the public hysterical and push quivering politicians to bad decisions. We're being used.

This year, we've had the spectacle of the environmentalists dragging out school children and forcing McDonald's to replace styrofoam with paper packaging. It was a good story for slow Saturdays, but completely ignored the science which shows now that paper is far more of an environmental nuisance than the plastic.

If we want to save the environment and save lives efficiently, let's use the Alar or asbestos money to convince people to quit smoking and improve their diets. Put air bags into cars. And instead of pulling the asbestos from the schools, let's have better lunches, safer school buses, and hire more teachers so the kids will do better and have less temptation to get into drugs.

We must make smart choices, but people don't know who or what to believe anymore. In our zeal for criticism, we've convinced them to revile all politicians, ignore bureaucrats, and, of course, distrust anyone in business or even science. It leaves the special interest groups, be they amateurs parading with their placards, or the paid lobbyists and publicists, whose main skill is manipulating media with emotional, dramatic stories or pictures that are just too good to resist.

Political parties have certainly become irrelevant in the debate about social and economic change. Part of that is their own fault, but as well, we in the media become impatient with complicated, sometimes messy, brokerage politics. Enter the single-issue interest group, with simple emotional causes and a flair for the dramatic. We just couldn't resist. We helped create these monsters, and now they're eating us alive. They've taken over much of the agenda, and what they offer is simplistic responses to complex problems, unbending dogma when trade-off and compromise are needed more than ever.

If you want a platform, why run for Parliament? Hook up with Greenpeace or David Suzuki. And if you want power, forget becoming a deputy minister.

You should go to work for one of the lobbying firms that are a real political cancer in both Ottawa and the provincial capitals these days. It seems that every defeated politician, ex-bureaucrat and many of the political hangers-on have declared themselves consultants. They're all five-percenters, all promising access to power and sometimes the media.

It's tacky. It makes us look like a corrupt little kingdom running on baksheesh. But it's up to Parliament to control that racket. My concern is how the media get used quite openly, publicly and often stupidly by the true-believers who are supposedly without motive.

I interviewed a very wise professor at the University of Toronto earlier this year. Like Bruce Ames in California, he had been a founder of the environmental movement and hero of it. Phillip Jones was one of the originals in Pollution Probe. He started the Institute of Environmental Studies at the University of Toronto, and most important, he had a key role in getting phosphates out of soap.

But Jones has split with the environmental leaders now and gone to Australia. He says his old allies have begun to view their use of the media to create public hysteria as an end in itself. "Eco-terrorists" he calls them, dependent on scaring the dickens out of people by telling them that everything is dangerous, so they'll keep sending money. They have their own vested interests, and some have turned into the ecological equivalent of TV preachers.

Most important, they're often preventing practical solutions to environmental problems by demanding perfection, by bringing out the placards and with them the cameras anytime anyone proposes doing anything, even something to help clean up.

Take PCBs. Canada developed the technology to burn them that's being used around the world, but can't be used here because the protestors claim, without evidence, that it can't be done safely. The media rushes to report it, and of course there's never a story about PCBs without calling them "deadly PCBs" or "PCBs linked to cancer." But there's just no evidence of this. I'm not anxious to mix them into my orange juice, but the danger, according to scientists, is overstated.

So we get the nonsense a couple of years ago of a truck leaking some PCBs across Northern Ontario, and the whole national media is out there talking about tearing up the Trans-Canada so people won't get cancer driving over it.

Two summers ago we had the further nonsense of the "death ship" taking "dreaded PCBs" to Europe where they were to be destroyed by methods developed, ironically, here in Canada. Our incineration technology is used all over the world, but not here at home because the environmentalists don't like it. They're philosophically opposed. But next, the environmentalists created a furor, and the ship came back to Baie Comeau, where the only serious PCB danger was from protestors being run over by police cars. Today we pile the PCBs in barrels. We store them and guard them. And because we get uncontrolled fires, that is dangerous.

It's the same with tires, and the same with garbage in the big cities. The only crisis is the paralysis and fear among politicians cowed by media which have allowed themselves to be used by special interest groups to whip up phony fears. Prof. Jones talks about microchemophobia. Soon we'll be able to detect a single molecule of something in Lake Ontario. Does that make it a health threat? Of course not, but if one environmental zealot calls a press conference, you can bet the reporters will be out.

This isn't investigative reporting. This isn't being a public watchdog. It's being a stooge for people who often know more about writing press releases than they do about science. The process goes something like this. Interest groups use the media to dramatize an issue. Pollsters measure emotional response as opposed to considered views. Politicians react, and it suddenly becomes conventional wisdom, so the people back on the protest line can say, "See, I told you so."

It's a closed circle, often bereft of common sense, but we play our part in it because we're just such suckers for the scare story, the dramatic headline, and sometimes too lazy to get the perspective that would distinguish between significant and trivial.

And it goes way beyond the environment. Look at the GST. I went to New Zealand last year, and saw how the tax works there. There's much to be said for a consumption tax, although our government certainly botched its implementation here. One thing we all know is that with more than half of federal income tax now going just to pay interest on the debt, we have to do something.

But instead of much real examination of the tax, or the worse one that it replaced, almost all the coverage at the end of the year was about whatever protest group decided to go to a mall and say, "We don't like it." Then the GST became the "dreaded GST," and as it was with PCBs, I think we in the media turned grousing into conventional wisdom, that the GST is bad, because it was easier to cover the special interest groups than deal with a difficult issue.

I interviewed Saskatchewan Senator Davey Steuart earlier this year, seeking his reflections on retirement. Davey has always been my favourite politician, and although he is a Liberal, it doesn't infringe on my objectivity anyway because, near as I can figure over all the years, Davey has been devoid of any political philosophy. I have no reason to feel compromised. Davey, who's been pretty good at taking the lumps over the years, complains that these days the media have gone overboard on trivial criticism.

He makes a good point. We're providing two dollars worth of service for a buck-and-a-half of tax. Everyone wants more, and it's easier to get attention demanding new programs than it is talking about how we'll pay for them.

As you'd expect from a politician, Steuart also claims we're getting too picky about private lives. He objects to the furor after *The Ottawa Citizen* revealed that the former, unlamented defense minister, Bob Coates, had gone to a sleazy nightclub in Germany. Maybe he's right. Who cares? There are a lot of reasons Coates should have resigned—bad taste for a start—but was his nocturnal rambling really such a big deal, a security threat, or are we making too much of stupidity?

Don't discount stupidity. We spend a whole lot of time trying to nail politicians for corruption.

An MP's brother-in-law is selling pencils to the government. But in my experience, corruption as the cause of our problems fades almost to oblivion compared to obvious lethargy, cowardice and stupidity.

Davey Steuart also wonders why John Fraser should have to quit over a few cans of rancid tuna.

There I draw the line, but I must point out that I never hounded Fraser from office. I didn't even harass him. Basically I asked only one important question: whether he thought this should be a story about fish or integrity. From then on, he started interviewing himself. Always a mistake. He asked himself some really good questions. It was the answers that got him in trouble.

If the environmentalists are the true masters at manipulating media, natives in Canada are not far behind. Oka was an event last summer because television came. If a group of Mohawks had sat down on a golf course for a few weeks without cameras, no one would have cared. Here was a group of radicals who had been accused of intimidation and terrorism by the elected leadership of the reserve. Suddenly they were directing the national and international media.

It was a true media event, the purest form.

Our presence made it a story. Although I rarely agree with Ted Byfield of *Alberta Report,* I think he is right on this. He says that if it is only news because we are there, we must ask ourselves twice about whether we should go.

Another of the staged media events this past summer was the visit of Archbishop Desmond Tutu from South Africa. He went to a reserve called Osnaburgh up in Northern Ontario. The national media was in tow, and all reported basically the same story.

They said that Tutu compared Canada's treatment of natives to the plight of blacks in South Africa and that, on this reserve, people were getting sick because they had to drink polluted water. A cardboard shack was on the tour, and by implication this was typical of living conditions. And finally, sacred burial grounds were going to be flooded by Ontario Hydro.

It was on CBC, CTV, in *The Globe and Mail* and the *Toronto Star.* The only problem is, none of it was true, as I found out back on the reserve a few months later. Is Canada like South Africa? It's not worth spending a lot of time on that. No one is forced by law to live on a reserve. No one is prevented from going to school, from voting. Natives are not a source of cheap labor. We have horrendous problems with the standard of living of natives in Canada, but it is not a deliberate policy.

Programs may be misguided, badly handled, but a great deal is spent to try and improve the lot of natives in Canada.

The bad water? Tax money had been used to buy a brand new water truck for almost $50,000, and that much again was provided to operate it. But the band, in a year, never got around to starting the truck up. Is this South Africa?

Living in shacks? Well, lots of new housing has been built, but 80 of the dwellings have been torched over the past 10 years. Is that the fault of a government that thinks like South Africa's? The old lady who lived in the shack shown everywhere had actually moved into a brand new Panabode-type log house right next door by the time Tutu and the cameras arrived, but no mention of that. I frankly don't know how some of the cameramen got the camera angles to shoot the shack without getting the house in the shot.

Flooding burial grounds? Ontario Hydro has no plans to raise the water levels, ever, and couldn't if it wanted to. So none of it was true. And what's wrong with that?

First, it's bad journalism. But second, it helps no one. Lord knows there are problems on reserves in this country, but we need generosity and practical workable solutions to solve them. Misrepresenting the efforts to help, and ignoring what went wrong, is just as destructive as some of the environmental lies. It focuses our attention on the wrong things, and takes our energy away from practical solutions to real problems.

Single-issue interest groups will always try to push their narrow point of view, but it's up to media to ask if it's true, if it's relevant, if it's in perspective. That's our job, and we don't do it very well or very often. The first rule of journalism should be to try to get the other side, and try to tell the whole story. And I'd go beyond that. I think in this country there's a real hunger for new ideas, for practical ways we can do things better, instead of griping on the one hand, and moralizing on the other.

This leads me to another staple of bad television journalism. Call it the "whine of the week."

These are the emotional encounters which are so often billed as "gripping" or "compelling." Give me a break. It's a strange phenomenon. People will come on the trashy talk shows and confess things they'd never tell their neighbours. They reveal intimate details of the most hideous personal traumas. They form societies. (Personally, I don't like talk about sex in public. Actually, being from Saskatchewan, I don't like talking about sex at all.) But even with most of the network magazine shows, plight and disease are staple fare, heart-rending stories about hard luck cases.

I think it's important to show plight if you can use that to change something, but not just for the sake of putting people through the emotional wringer. There's nothing compelling about reporters milking misery. As important as it is to make people feel, we also have to help them think. We already know there will always be some homeless, some disabled, some abused, some trapped in welfare, some discriminated against for their race or sex. Canadians are not heartless, and on a good day at least, not completely cynical, but they look for practical ways to make things better instead of just endless emotional wallowing.

People don't believe us in the media anymore, when we employ sweeping indictments and hyperbolic language to describe disputes or difficulties. The words roll out: "racism, sexism, genocide, crisis, catastrophe, disaster." I'm tired of budget problems at the school board being described as yet another "crisis." War is a crisis; the school board has problems.

There's another change. People are more realistic these days. They know the government is not like Dorothy from Oz, who can dance along the Yellow Brick Road and make everything okay. Furthermore, with a lot of the so called exposes, the teacher or civil servant or small business person knows you can't simply blame everything on the awful "them," because we are all now "them."

Every viewer is an insider in some area, and when they see stories about their area of expertise, they see reporters revealed time after time as the ones who don't understand how things get done. So they don't believe us on other things. We've been too simplistic, too naive. We don't put enough effort into finding out how things really work, so we can go on and explore ways to make them work better.

His timing was wrong, but had he been speaking today, Spiro Agnew might have hit a chord when he complained about the "nattering nabobs of negativism." In those days, along with Agnew's own corruption, reporters were dealing with civil rights, the Vietnam war, Watergate, environmental indifference, and corporate irresponsibility. These were great issues, but relentless investigative reporting changed a lot of things.

In a way, we won. Across the spectrum, activists and an activist media changed history and changed forever the way we are governed. Imagine today, blatant racism practised by public agencies. Imagine politicians flaunting corruption. Imagine companies with open contempt for the environment. Imagine a war where the government brazenly lies about tactics. It's a long way from a perfect world, but we've all demanded and won much more accountability from powerful institutions.

Now much of the time, government is running scared. It's traumatized by fear of making a mistake that will expose it as being unfair, negligent, uncaring. If anything, we might have overkill. Hand in hand with interest groups, we've terrified them so much they're incapable of taking a risk, even making a decision.

Today, more than 10 years later, we're using all the big guns appropriate for exposing abuse of power, when more often than not the problem today is a power vacuum. That's why even the simplest decision has to go through endless studies and commissions and hearings, all orchestrated by lawyers and consultants and government-funded objectors. Ontario set out to build a toxic waste disposal plant back in the early eighties. It was supposed to be urgent, but the hearings are still going on.

They've cost more than the whole plant was supposed to cost in the first place. It's another example of environmentalists preventing environmental solutions. In the meantime, dozens of lawyers are on their third BMW, and have put their kids through private school with the proceeds.

We in the media are part of the problem, because we've been nattering about trivial things. Parts per billion is no Love Canal. Bob Coates is no Richard Nixon. Times have changed. In our determination to blow the lid off this or that, we end up nit-picking. We're like lawyers, perish the thought, who look at something and ask, "How many legal issues can I find here?" We all should be asking instead, "What's really wrong here, and what can we do about it?"

Borden Spears, a great newspaperman from the *Toronto Star,* defined our job as preparing people for change. That makes a lot of sense. Historically, the media have failed woefully to report the ideas and trends which are ultimately far more important than most events, or pseudo-events like the latest vacuous political non-statement, or another threat from some crusader who's probably funded by the government anyway. Looking back, who covered Karl Marx sitting in the London Museum? Who covered the development of the work on the first birth control pills, the things that have truly changed our lives? Those are hard stories to get, but I think we have to look for them.

We had a tremendous response to a little idea story a few weeks ago. It was about running cars on natural gas. There was a time, a few years ago, that for the money we were spending in a single year to subsidize oil companies, we could have converted fleet vehicles, taxis, police cars and delivery vans to natural gas and never had to import oil again. It's clean, cheap, plentiful and ours.

We can do more with practical ideas, more on things like natural gas, which is a lot more useful as a story than covering press conferences given by the people who think it's sinful to drive at all, or an indulgence to keep warm in winter. Let's find out why a particular Indian reserve works well, instead of reporting yet another threat of violence if some native politician doesn't get his or her way in Ottawa.

It's the journalist's role to create interest, to take the dull specialist who knows something about how things work, and make it into something people want to know about. New ideas. Today, while the communist world is being forced to examine all of its assumptions and daring to destroy its own ideology, politics here seems brain dead. Apart from *Doonesbury,* most of the popular media here are as predictable as *Pravda,* or as *Pravda* used to be.

In the search for new ideas and things that work, we must speak the unspeakable, even if it seems like heresy in today's polite television climate. Bilingualism, regional development, multiculturalism, universality, affirmative action, the green movement, native sovereignty. Great ideas perhaps, these sacred cows. But do they work? (Wherever a reporter hears "sacred cow," the mind should turn to 600 pounds of pot roast.)

I reject the elite notion of some "enlightened" reporters that ordinary readers and viewers have to be protected from critical consideration of righteous principles, lest they turn overnight into flaming radicals or frothing rednecks. Canadians are fixers. Our only destiny is to hope. Most of us believe that given enough time, and a trip to Canadian Tire, we could fix the damn thing just as well as the expert. We are practical, and give short shrift to moralizing and lofty rhetoric. It's because most of us have had the pipes freeze in winter, and outside precious Toronto, it's a personal disgrace to have to call a plumber for a plugged sink or a tow truck to boost your car.

I think it's time we see more in the media that reflects that attitude. We have a lot of problems, and we'd better come up with ideas for ways to do things better or we're going to end up a Third World country. It happened to Argentina, and it happened quickly.

On *W5*, we're at least trying to spend a lot less time on posturing and griping, focusing instead on effectiveness. In the sixties and seventies, everyone was protesting, "No way." In the eighties, it was, "What's in it for me?" I think in the nineties, people will be worried about getting poor, and asking, "But does it work?"

It's up to all of us in the media to cut the mindless criticism, ignore the simplistic zealots, layoff predictable plight, and give short shrift to those politicians or business people who have nothing new or significant to say.

Val Sears was probably right when he said almost 30 years ago that we had a government to defeat. If he said it today, I suspect no one would pay much attention, because that's what we're obsessed with most days anyway. We're so used to putting everything through the political filter, with all its trivial bickering, that we often lose sight of the real challenge, which is exploring ways to make this country work, regardless often of its governments.

The country needs leadership these days, and we can do our part by paying attention to the people, from whatever walk of life, who are talking about things that are smart and have ideas about how they can make them work. It's time for a new attitude.

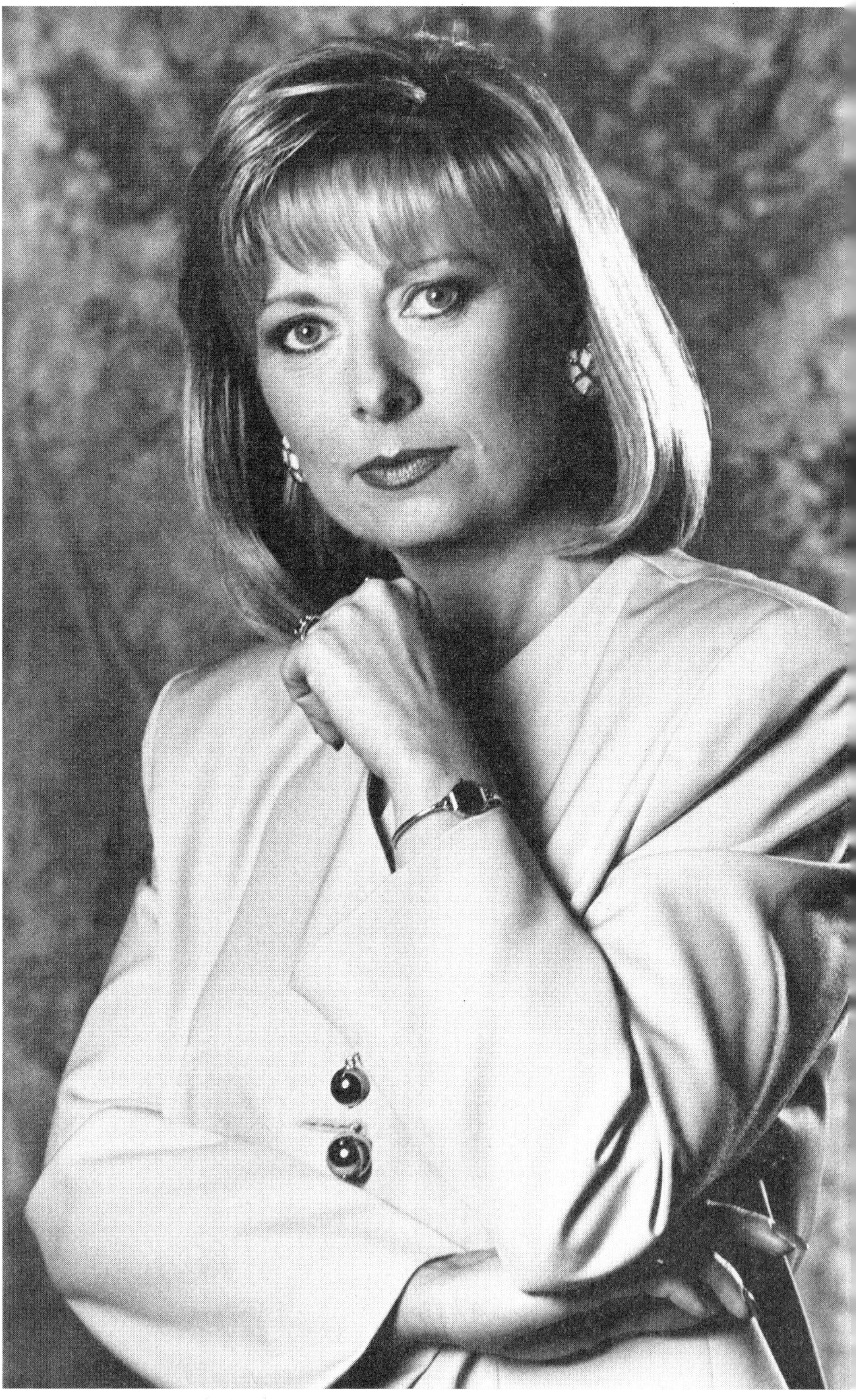

−1992−
PAMELA WALLIN

A graduate of the University of Saskatchewan (Regina Campus), Wallin has worked for CBC Radio, the *Toronto Star,* and became host of *Canada AM* in 1981. In 1985, CTV named her their Ottawa Bureau Chief. From 1992 to 1995, she co-hosted *The Prime Time News* on CBC, later hosting *Pamela Wallin Live* on CBC Newsworld. Wallin has also published two books, *Since You Asked* and *Speaking of Success.* Pamela was Consul General of Canada in New York from 2002 to 2006. In 2008, Wallin was appointed to the Senate of Canada, where she sits as a Conservative. Wallin is the Chancellor of the University of Guelph and serves on several corporate boards, including CTVglobemedia; Gluskin Sheff & Associates; Oilsands Quest; and Porter Airlines.

1992 | PAMELA WALLIN

REFLECTIONS ON TELEVISION:
The Other Side of the Screen

As I walked in tonight I recalled that this is the room in which I sat as a first-year student in one of those chairs looking at some professor on this stage. I wondered whether I'd ever figure any of it all out and what I'd be when I grew up anyway.

Well, at least I know a little bit about the latter point. I'm not sure what I know about the former.

This was my school when we were still fighting about the name and its independence. It's nice to have a mother who is an alumna and a cousin who is an honours student. So it's nice to see the tradition going on. And it is an honour as well to present this 12th annual lecture in the name of a most respected journalist. Sometimes in our business we bemoan the fact that our collective professional and institutional memory is shamefully lacking. And we long for the perspective that the James Minifies of the world brought to journalism.

This series of lectures, in Don Minifie's name, helps change that. Young journalists can hear the perspectives of those with a few stories under their belts. And we can re-discover the fine journalistic tradition—and the fine journalists—Saskatchewan has produced.

Don Minifie's work may have cost him his eyesight, at least in part, but never his insight. And his ability to capture the prairies is compelling. For many, myself included, Saskatchewan is a reference point, it's a touchstone—and it's a spiritual home as much as it is a birthplace.

There are millions of words and succinct phrases that one could summon about the art and craft of journalism. There are still more about my chosen medium, television. Most have been said before and few are novel. Still, you will not be spared them all. I will repeat some tonight and I will re-invent some others because I hope it will help set the stage for our discussion about television and about how we will communicate with and understand each other in the future.

KNOWLEDGE INCREASING AT AWESOME SPEED

But, if there is only one thing that you remember from my remarks tonight, please let it be the following from Janice Moyer, the president of the Information Technology Association of Canada: "The total of all knowledge gained throughout history up to and including 1991 is just one percent of all the information that will be available to us in the year 2050!"

Just think about it: In 50 short years, we will know more—a hundred times more—than all that we have discovered and learned over the past centuries and all of that information which now fills every library shelf and every microchip in the world. It's nothing short of staggering. And for those of you who have chosen journalism, it will be your task to understand, explain, translate and synthesize some of that information for others.

It is an enormous and daunting responsibility and one with which I grapple every day. But regardless of your chosen field, we are all a part of the information age, and the valuable commodities in this information economy are knowledge and brain-skills.

Knowledge is that crucial skill that allows you to add value to products—we can no longer just take from the ground or the water or the mines or the forests. We have to figure out smarter ways to make things and to improve existing things and technologies and to improve even our ideas. And we are going to have to keep on learning—for a lifetime—just to keep up.

I grew up with the notion that with a university degree in hand I would knock on some lucky employer's door and offer my skills and my enthusiasm—and he would respond with a paycheque, a pension plan and the offer of security.

JOURNALISTS FACE MANY CHALLENGES
Well, it didn't quite work out that way and it won't for you either. Today's graduates will likely face 10 job changes in their working lifetime, and all of them will involve learning new skills. But crucial—and common to all of them—will be that ability to absorb, process and use new information. Today, 15 percent—and some say that's a low estimate—some say 30 percent—of our high school graduates are functionally illiterate. You simply won't survive if you are in that category, and now is the time to start thinking about how to find and secure your place in an information economy.

And again for those of you who have chosen journalism—chosen to be a spectator of, or a commentator on life—that will not shield you from the realities of it.

Technology is changing rapidly, and the information overload means you must be more discerning and understand more history so that you can offer context and insight. If you do not have the skills to distill the essence of what goes on around you, you will become obsolete—like yesterday's Underwood typewriter that belongs to the journalism of another era.

IMPACT OF TV INCREASING
Twenty-five years ago, most people read the newspaper. Today, they watch television. Its immediacy, its vivid images and the technology make it relevant and readily accessible. Ninety-eight percent of homes have a TV—most have two. Even in remote villages in Central America, and I have been in some, where there's no running water and no electricity, you can see this blue flicker of battery-operated TVs reflecting through the thatched walls.

Today more than 80 percent of North Americans cite television as their primary, if not exclusive, source of information about the world around them. Most people now form opinions about everything from which shampoo to buy to whether or not the Gulf War was necessary based on what they see and hear on TV. Therefore, it goes without saying that both *what* you watch and *how* you watch it is important to understand.

We, as individuals, have opinions on a full range of issues with which we have no direct experience or knowledge. And for many, those opinions, which may well influence how you vote or where you live or how you work, are based on information and beliefs that you glean from your television screen, and I don't just mean newscasts. Lifestyles, relationships and values are all influenced by what we watch.

TV is a powerful force and one that should be respected and admired but also analyzed.

First, a little admiration. Back in 1962 then President of NBC News talked about this new force that was altering our world: "For centuries," Robert Sarnoff said, "man has dreamed of a universal language to bridge the linguistic gaps between nations. Man will find this true universal language in television because it combines the incomparable eloquence of the moving image—instantly transmitted—with the flexibility of ready adaptation to all tongues. It speaks to all nations, and in a world where millions are still illiterate, it speaks as clearly to all people."

Pretty heady stuff. And maybe today, it might even seem just a little naive. But some fundamental questions remain, that each of us must try to answer: Television may well speak to all people, but what does it say? And to what end will we use this compelling, eloquent and provocative language?

At this moment, nearly one-third of the world's population in more that 150 countries are sitting in front of millions of television sets, many of them watching exactly the same program. For example, CNN is now available in 90 countries around the world. So TV has tapped into the things that we have in common, regardless of geography or colour. And in some cases it has actually created common denominators for us. TV has become an international social connector. It has made "their" problems "our" problems and concerns, politically, environmentally and socially.

TV has "intruded" into almost every facet of our lives and it does, to some extent, blur the boundaries between what is news, what is public relations and what is entertainment. You all know the phrases: infomercials, newzak, infotainment. In short, what we're really talking about here is that TV often blurs the line between reality and unreality.

So tonight I want to engage you in a discussion about the role of television—about the journalism it creates—but more importantly, about all the pressures, and influences and expectations that shape both TV and our relationship to it.

BLEAK FUTURE FOR NETWORKS

First, let me talk about dollars and cents, because television, as a business, is in the midst of some very dramatic changes. The economics of television in the 1990s are pretty bleak—the recession has cut advertising revenues; budgets and reporting staffs have been pared. And the fragmentation of the market has given both viewers and advertisers so many choices that networks cannot command the price they once did from advertising.

So what does that mean? It means that network television will likely not survive in the form that we had come to know it in the 80s. The three big American networks—ABC, CBS and NBC—just 15 years ago claimed 9 out every 10 people who were watching television at any one time. Today they have lost one-third of their viewers to the cable options and of course advertising revenues have fallen in direct proportion.

The reason is pretty simple: In 1976, the average home had seven channels to choose from. Now each viewer has an average (and this is in North America) of 33 channel choices. Cable is in 60 percent of all homes. And with a dish, you can have as many as 150 channels to choose from! That's a competitive business and it's not surprising that economics is changing what we do. A second important factor that is influencing TV is the growing level of public awareness about what we do and therefore the growing level of public criticism about what we do. Now in fairness, let me say that all forms of journalism are coming under increased scrutiny these days—and so they should.

But television, it seems, is an industry that many people love to hate. I am forever picking up a newspaper or a magazine to read that TV is to blame for yet another one of society's ills. Most people believe that violence on TV encourages and perhaps even causes crime and that programs depicting nudity or sex encourage immorality. And many people look at the staggering levels of illiteracy in our country and say it's all the result of too much time spent in front of the tube.

Just on that latter point, it is true that in 1991 only two out of every five North American households actually purchased a book—and the single largest group of buyers is over 65. But can television be the only culprit? Families, schools and individuals themselves must bear some responsibility. And of course when it comes to politics, everyone—from the politician to the voter—lays some of the blame for the mess we're in at our doorstep.

There is some, but very little, concrete evidence of a direct cause-and-effect relationship between, for example, political reporting and the quality of our politicians and the decisions they make. There is no doubt, however, that the pressures of instant and visual communication demand a more shrewd, articulate and quick-witted candidate. And, as Minifie himself noted, "The fact of being observed modifies the phenomenon under observation."

But I am amazed when a politician or a viewer says: "Why did you show so-and-so fumbling that football or making that stupid remark?" I can only respond that we do not create the news in a Hollywood special effects suite. If we show you a politician saying or doing something dumb, then that's because he or she was doing or saying something dumb in clear view of our cameras. Now, of course there is an editorial process and we do make choices about what we air, but politicians make choices too. And to choose public life, for better or worse, means a life that is open to scrutiny and evaluation and television cameras.

But I'm digressing. Back to the topic of sin and TV's alleged incitement of it. No doubt there is some truth in many of the accusations that I have just discussed. And I stand here tonight not so much to defend those sins, but to join forces with you and to recruit you in the cause of making television better and smarter, and in making all of us wiser and more critical users of it. After all, television is viewer-driven and the public too must accept some responsibility for what is on the screen and how much of it any one of us chooses to consume.

Ratings are the lifeblood of commercial TV. The viewers reward or punish networks by watching them and by buying the products advertised in the commercials that seem to be slotted with annoying frequency into the news or dramas or game shows. So the viewer wields a powerful force and influence and that power should not be underestimated or subjected to any less scrutiny than that of the TV programmers or the on-air presenters.

Let me cite one positive example of how this works. Straight demographics already are beginning to command change. Our population is aging, so women over the age of 29 are no longer being tossed off the screens at the first sign of a wrinkle or a grey hair and that's good news for me. But let me not leave a false impression—I think there is still a long way for the women in this business to go because there is no doubt that for women our "shelf life" is shorter than that of our male counterparts. In other words, it seems our "best before" expiry date always comes up first!

But there is another side to the ratings game. TV is responsiveness, and the overwhelming popularity of *Geraldo* or *A Current Affair* or the soaps that perpetuate myths and stereotypes about all of us sends very strong signals to the programmers as to what the viewing public wants! It's the old chicken-and-egg argument: Do we give the viewers what they demand or do they simply choose among the options we offer? Well, of course, the answer is, both. That means we, as broadcasters, do have a responsibility to provide a menu that includes some nourishing, healthy and substantive entrees.

We do and we try to—and no one knows better than those of us inside just how difficult that is in recessionary times with the fiscal squeeze, and the fragmented market that gives you so many more entertaining and sometimes even titillating choices. But your power is growing far beyond the simple flick of the channel changers. VCRs and pay-per-view television are giving the viewing public a new kind of choice. You can sit before a menu of programs and order up *à la carte* what you want on your screen and at what time. With this "video on demand," the viewer is more and more able to design a personalized program day.

And I'm sure you've all heard the phrase "interactive TV." It's already in use now and that will give you even more power. You can, for example, watch replays, on command, while your neighbour next door does not. During the hockey game you can watch from whatever angle you want. Interactive TV also means the viewer can create or should we say, re-create, a newscast to suit his or her own taste. During a newscast, for example, you can edit the reports, view longer or shorter versions, skip past some and watch the stories in the order that you prefer. In other words, you can determine your own intake of information, and that takes away the power and editorial control that now rests with editors and producers and programmers. It puts power in your hands to be exercised with the assistance of your trusty channel changer.

TV NEWS FACES TOUGH FUTURE

Because of all of this—new technology, the financial factors I mentioned, and the audience demand that we create for all these varieties of choices—there is now, I believe, in this country, a very uncertain future for news, current affairs and documentary television. I say this because, apart from publicly subsidized television (and even there, too), TV news is being treated increasingly as a business where the bottom line counts for as much as the public service that we provide.

The special role of journalism, *as one of the guardians of democracy,* is under some threat. And this must be a concern to more than just those of us inside the profession. The author of a book called *Three Blind Mice*, US business writer Ken Auletta, predicts that two of the three major U.S. television networks will probably soon be out of the "news business" altogether, because they can no longer afford to do it.

Coverage of major political events both in the US and at home is diminishing because the networks cannot afford to lose the money they do, when they pre-empt prime time dramas or sitcoms for things like political debates or budgets or first ministers meetings on the future of our country.

But there is also another nineties style challenge to the future of this industry—some new and powerful forces affecting both what I do and what you watch. Television is "under siege" in the sense that we are becoming the front line in the battle over ethics and between special interests in this country. In the first place, we are becoming a society dominated by special-interest politics. Our fledgling Charter of Rights has encouraged both individuals and groups to "fight for their rights" and to seek confirmation for them from the courts. And, of course, each then wants its access to the TV screens so that its particular issues and priorities are aired and reflected.

Secondly, in our ever-shrinking global media village, we are still and perhaps more than ever, struggling with fundamental issues like right and wrong, good and bad, fairness and privacy, and even the right to die and the right to life. Our society is confronting an increasing number of these moral dilemmas. Since many of us live, vicariously, through television and because we spend nearly seven hours a day in front of our sets we base most of our opinions on what we see on TV—and on how the Cosby family or Roseanne or Murphy Brown deals with all these problems. We have come to expect that our dilemmas will be debated on television, and somehow resolved on TV.

VIEWERS GET MAD AT TV

Predictably, people get mad at their TV sets, when the people on TV don't have all the right answers or have answers they don't like. Viewers get angry at those of us who work on TV. There is a bit of the "shoot the messenger" syndrome at play.

The constitutional debate is the perfect example. Everybody complains of constitutional fatigue "Quit talking about it and just solve it," says the public. But they don't want the politicians to go behind closed doors, where these things are likely to be settled. Furthermore they no longer trust the politicians—whether they're behind closed doors or in front of open ones! So they want public participation and they want debate. And then when we in the media cover this debate, and explain all the intricacies of the Triple E or the division of powers or what asymmetry means, then the public cries "circuit overload!" And for us—who are the link between the governed and the governing—we can't seem to win for losing.

We expect TV to entertain, to inform, to enlighten, and now we are asking it to replace all those traditional forms of social interaction and some of the traditional forums for public debate which have become a little discredited or are simply not accessible to a vast majority of people. Parliament, for example, has failed to modernize enough to tackle some of the really fundamental and very controversial issues of the day that seem to be of the greatest interest to people. And while television can be many things, it cannot be a substitute for social or political action. So when I talk about the battle over ethics I mean much more than just how we, as journalists, conduct ourselves in the pursuit of stories, or how we decide what you view. We're all grappling with some pretty dramatic change. Television, which is a mirror of our society, is also trying to cope with all these changing values.

The greed of the eighties is supposedly gone, exchanged for a more pragmatic approach to life. Climbing the corporate ladder, and dressing for success has been replaced to some extent—and in part due to the recession—by cocooning and a return to traditional values. The baby boomers—now the bulk of the viewing audience—are in search of quality of life and, because they now spend more time at home in front of the tube, their demands on it are increasing.

This whole idea is raised in a book called *The Unreality Industry*. The authors argue that we are so connected in this age of "information proliferation" that any act, anywhere, can potentially affect any other event. We are overwhelmed by this all-too-complex reality, and we tend to want to escape into entertainment. People demand programs that become a substitute for the real debate surrounding all the complicated issues. On the sitcoms and the soaps, of course, there's always a happy ending miraculously at 29 minutes after the hour, but when it comes to news—to real life—there is seldom a neat and tidy resolution.

The pre-occupying nature of television is enough to make all of us uneasy. I am, by virtue of some training right here and a lot of curiosity, a "psychologist" so the relationships between people and process intrigue me. That counts for my love of politics, but the relationship between people and technology, particularly when the technology like television has a very real and human face, is also fascinating.

VIEWER AND TV ARE SYMBIOTIC

The relationship between the viewer and television is a symbiotic one and it's worth a look. There's no doubt that, through TV, we are bombarded with images—and many of them negative—and they all seem to reflect the pain of the victim—the victim of recession or of war or of change, or of famine. And sometimes we end up feeling overwhelmed. We no longer know how we really think or how we feel or how best to respond to all the conflicting demands and pressures that are on us. And the television images just keep washing relentlessly over us, and we slowly become a little bit more desensitized.

But still, we are drawn to it. Each image must be more evocative than the last. Starving babies or bloody corpses hardly even catch our attention because "we've seen that all before." The response of some is to simply turn off the TV, as if that will make it go away. The response of others is to demand more good news so that we feel better. But the response should not be this kind of censorship.

Quite the contrary. Because television does reflect and mirror our society it is, therefore, perhaps one of the most powerful educational tools that we have. It is urgent that the medium be understood and that the viewers, be they child or adult, become critical spectators and informed consumers.

A little earlier, I said it was important not only to discuss *what* we watch and *why* we watch what we do, but also *how* we watch TV. As much as it is the task of those of us who are presenters and reporters to help explain the world around us to our viewers, it is perhaps even more important that we begin to explain the filters through which the viewer sees that world. I am one of those filters. And so are you. And the responsibilities for both of us are very real. In the television industry we are entrusted with one of the country's most important resources—the national airwaves. And we have direct access to perhaps the greatest resource of all—the hearts and the heads of the people of Canada.

IS TV CHANGING THE BRAIN?

Our responsibilities—both yours and mine—are enormous because I believe the very future of the next generation is at stake. Their minds and their thinking will be shaped in large measure by what and who they see on TV and by the circumstances under which they do their viewing.

I mean this quite literally. In a new book called *Endangered Minds: Why Our Children Don't Think,* author Jane Healey suggests that we are actually rearing a generation with very different brains. She suggests there is a radical change in the way humans are processing information and that could have some pretty profound effects on our society. She cites many reasons for this—the education system, the unstable and changing family patterns, lifestyle and of course, the electronic media.

Scientists describe the child's brain as "plastic" and believe that what children see or do every day actually changes their brains both functionally and structurally. When you think that, by the age of seven, a child's brain has attained 90 percent of its weight for life, the viewing habits acquired and the programs consumed during that period are crucial. Moreover, the television viewing that goes on between the ages of three and seven is the least regulated by the parent or the caregiver—and the least monitored of all viewing. The TV series as an electronic baby-sitter.

The average child will have witnessed some 8,000 murders and more than 100,000 acts of violence by the time he or she finishes elementary school. By the age of 16, the average American child will have seen some 200,000 violent acts on TV, including some 33,000 murders. Healy says the problem with TV and video games and life in the modern electronic environment is that children are always being externally stimulated. The child is always being "visually jolted." We get into the habit of ignoring language, waiting instead for some visual cue or auditory gimmick.

That leaves little time to reflect or even to talk to themselves in their own heads. TV, she argues, can rob children of the chance to develop their own mental pictures and the kind of visual imagery that helps in solving math and science problems later on. Compared to other countries like Japan and Germany our math and science skills are already appallingly inadequate. Unless something is done, we can never hope to find that competitive advantage to maintain the standard of living that we have come to enjoy in this country. There are a million and a half unemployed people in Canada and there are 600,000 jobs that are empty because we don't have people who are qualified enough to fill them.

There is some excellent Canadian research on the same topic done by Tannis MacBeth Williams. She discovered that television viewing can reduce persistence for problem solving, and can provoke a dramatic increase in verbal and physical aggressiveness and in sex-role stereotyping. While it's very, very difficult to measure, researchers also suggest there is actually a decrease in creativity.

TV AS BABYSITTER

There are some other fascinating studies on the effect and impact of TV on the minds of our children. Consider this if you will—babies as young as 14 months old are actually capable of "watching" TV. Furthermore, they understand what they see and they learn from it—and that's more than we can claim, some nights! A recent study done at the University of Washington shows that children under the age of two years can perform a relatively complicated task by simply mimicking what they see on a television screen. They can, for example, take apart a toy they have never seen before by watching a demonstration of how to do it on TV. And what is truly amazing about this process is that they can translate the two-dimensional image that a flat TV screen projects and relate that to their three-dimensional world.

These days babies are exposed to about two hours of TV a day—so the potential for learning is significant. Kids between the ages of two and five watch about four hours a day. And then the serious viewing sets in. Most young kids in Canada are watching between 30 and 50 hours of television a week and that may not include the increased viewing that has occurred because of the VCR revolution.

Most Canadian homes, as I've said, now have at least two televisions and the average family spends about seven hours a day watching TV (or at least it's turned on, though they may not admit they are watching it). That's roughly the same amount of time that you spend at the office or in your bed sleeping. With the help of computer projections, experts claim a normal North American will spend over the course of his or her lifetime: 24.5 years sleeping; 13.5 years at work and at school; 3 years eating; 3 years reading; nearly two years in the bath; and a year on the phone.

AND YOU WILL SPEND NEARLY 12 YEARS OF YOUR LIFE WATCHING TV!

My point, a little overstated with all these statistics, is that television is having a profound influence on our lives and it is incumbent upon all of us—as parents or keepers of the on/off switch—to ensure that viewing is done judiciously, with purpose, and in an informed manner. That is not to say that watching TV purely for entertainment is not a wholesome and legitimate activity—it most certainly is. And of course it helps pay my salary! But we must pay attention to the need to be "television literate" and to foster "critical spectatorship."

TV VIEWERS MUST BE CRITICAL

Many others take this proposition very seriously—people like advertisers, for example. Let me cite one other case in the United States. In exchange for access to school students, a Tennessee marketing company has given schools free TVs, free VCRs, even free satellite dishes. The company is test marketing a 100-minute newscast designed specifically for kids. And the real motive behind all of this philanthropy is that the newscast, like most others, comes complete with a two-minute commercial break.

Why? It's because North American children have about $5 billion in spending money at their disposal each year and they directly influence buying decisions involving another $50 billion. Today's child watches between 30,000 and 40,000 commercials on TV each year, and given the increasing number of households with single or working parents, children are at earlier and earlier ages becoming the designated shopper.

This raises some very interesting questions: Are we allowing the exploitation of a captive young audience by bribing financially strapped schools? Or, if this actually promotes discussion and helps create a more conscientious and discerning consumer, are we in fact encouraging real education? These are some of the dilemmas we must think about in a world of television.

US PRESIDENT "USES" TV

Understanding how politicians and their handlers use this medium is important too. In deciding whether to go to war, George Bush used you. He used all of us. Behavioral experts, psychologists, strategists, TV doctors, pollsters all huddled for hours in rooms with banks of TV monitors. They studied the President's public pronouncements and they monitored focus groups—people like you and me—measuring not just words or opinions but involuntary responses. They measured heart rate and brain waves to see whether the prospect of war excited them or scared them or made them angry. In one such test, the heart rate of the test population sitting in a room doubled at the prospect of "teaching Saddam Hussein a lesson." References to the flag, patriotism and "America standing tall" evoked the same positive responses. In the end, of course, we know what happened. The US and her allies, including Canada, kicked up a Desert Storm. Television technology is a powerful tool.

BROADCASTERS CONFRONT DILEMMAS

These are the kind of ethical and moral dilemmas that we, as broadcast journalists, confront and wrestle with a dozen times a day. What is the impact of our product? Who will be affected by this story and in what way? Is there a vested interest on the part of those telling me the story that may cloud the facts or even change them? Whether you are the producer or the consumer of these "products" or the parents of the consumers of all of this, these are pretty important questions.

Television is, by all objective accounts, now the pre-eminent form of communication in our world. And most people get most of their information from the television screen. In 1991 a US study (*America's Watching: Public Attitudes Toward Television,* co-sponsored by the National Association of Broadcasters and the Network Television Association and carried out by Roper) found that during preparation for the ground war against Iraq, a record 81 percent of Americans were getting their information from television. Television's primacy has been substantiated since testing was started in 1961. What's really amazing these days is that Americans are now at the point that they believe that television is the more credible and the most believable when it comes to all other forms of communication and sources of information.

This holds true in Canada as well. The latest poll done by Environics shows that 73 percent of Canadians cite TV as their primary source of both international and national news. Compare that with a mere 16 percent who cite newspapers, and eight percent who cite radio. In fact, since 1986, when the last Environics study was done, there has been a marked increase in those in the ages 25–34 who cite television as their primary source. Even those with university degrees—who used to favour newspapers—are now turning in greater and greater numbers to TV. Ninety-eight percent of the population watches television in any average week and that's why it is so important that we understand our relationship as viewer and producer.

How we watch TV is as important as the amount or perhaps sometimes even the content of what we watch.

Initially, television was a spectator sport: passive viewers consumed a prepackaged product, usually in a pretty docile environment in their own home. But life is a lot more hectic these days. Television is not only more common but TV sets are much more strategically located throughout the house and the workplace than ever before. And, more importantly, someone with a perverse sense of humour invented the remote control. All that has not only enabled us to actually watch more TV but it has allowed us to be exposed to more ideas in less time.

See if you can recognize yourselves in this profile of a typical Canadian TV viewer: Nearly half of all TV viewers are doing something else while watching TV—eating, dishes, laundry, fighting with the kids or the spouse—in fact some of you are actually reading when you're watching TV. At some point during every half hour of viewing you'll get up and walk out of the room while still claiming that you are watching the program. One-third of you never make it to the end of a program that you start watching. And more than half of you watch at least two programs—often more—at once. The channel changer and the seemingly endless variety that cable and pay-TV now provide is the stuff of nightmares for broadcast journalists such as myself: If you don't like my voice, my hair or the news I bring—*zap*—I'm history.

EXPERTS FEAR ZAP-HAPPINESS
In fact, all this zap-happiness, and that is exactly what the experts call it, is predictably a very costly concern to programmers and advertisers. Initial studies suggest that zappers can cut the audience and hence the advertising rates for prime time commercials by as much as 10 percent. And no wonder. Even light zappers change channels once every 20 minutes and nearly half of all viewers fall into that category. In fact, more than a third of all viewers change channels at least twice every six minutes. Heavy zappers change channels more than twice every two minutes and can, in one viewing day, change the channel 1,000 times. All of this shows that TV has become very much a participatory sport. And this forces us—to some extent—to alter what we offer you because we are vying for your attention, and as these numbers attest, your attention span is getting pretty short.

Keeping your attention and still imparting necessary but sometimes tedious facts, can be pretty difficult, to say the least. It means we sometimes have to keep facts to a minimum. We aim instead to leave impressions and general understandings, and all the while we try to wow you with a little razzle dazzle with all our modem electronic wizardry, so you don't change the channel. But the incredible shrinking attention span also tends to focus attention, not just on this technology, but on personality and on looks, and we hope this is not at the expense of journalistic credentials.

I told one story to the journalism students earlier today about an urgent phone call I'd received from a woman on two consecutive days, regarding the program. Finally, I thought I'd better phone her back: This could be the most important story of my career and I've missed it. And I phoned Mrs. Smith and she says, "Oh, Pamela, thank you very much for calling back. I just have to tell you, I hate your eye shadow."

TRUTH-TELLING TAKES TWO
In the words of Edward R. Murrow it takes two people to tell the truth—one to speak it, and the other to hear it. Our world is complicated and becoming more so every day. And we in TV deal in the whole notion of simplification, so it's very difficult sometimes to sort out what's true. In TV news, we are the first to concede that the 90-second news story is not the best vehicle for in-depth explanations of all the difficult issues that we face in this country. It's true we do stand guilty of trivializing and of using clichés. We often celebrate notoriety while letting achievement pass unnoted, and we may even be accessories after-the-fact to the crime of enticing and then using the best one-liner of the day as a substitute for meaningful critique. Let me add though, in our defense, that a

critic's impatience or a politician's willingness to respond less than thoughtfully or for reasons of expediency for the cameras is no excuse for ill-conceived political decisions by our leaders.

Minifie, of course, wrote about this. Discussing the problems we face in covering politics these days, he referred to the "mantle of invincibility." The politician needs to believe he or she is invincible, and such self-assurance ensures victory and triumph. But, eventually, it also prevents the politician from withdrawing after his or her usefulness is over. And these are some of the dilemmas that are very hard to deal with in our business.

Despite all the motives that are attributed to us, we seldom deliberately set out to uncover human flaws or scandals just for the sake of creating pain or embarrassment or defeat. That being said, let me confess that there is no better justice or deterrent than catching the once virtuous politician blushing and confessing to sins that he or she so readily denounced when it was the other guy getting caught. In this business of journalism, we look for contradictions and for incompetence and that sometimes leads us to discover the aforementioned.

But I'll challenge anybody who would question our legitimate curiosity to explain how knowing less about issues or those who lead us can make us better able to make choices or judgments about those same politicians or policies.

JUST A JOB? OR A MISSION?

Although the public does not really consider journalism a profession motivated by the pursuit of the common good, some of us would beg to differ. For me, this is part mission, and part job. And in many cases, it is certainly more a passion than just a profession. We are, as one colleague once described us, the "writers of the rough draft of what will, in some small way, become part of our collective history." And the task is no less, for those of us who make our living in the world that our critics call light, bright and trite.

We are all still, however, grappling with some very basic questions that have perplexed journalists for decades. We have come a long way from the days when Pierre Elliott Trudeau declared that the state had no business in the bedrooms of the nations. But we still have not answered the question: Does the press? And if not the bedrooms, what about the boardrooms? As we head into the nineties we are still, it seems, debating the basics like censorship and the age-old conflict between the right to know and need not to tell.

In this search for something more satisfactory, what role will the journalist play? What is the role for our television industry? And what role is there for you the viewer, the voter, and the consumer? Who will decide if we are fair and balanced and unbiased? And who will decide if you are?

As a profession, I believe we are a little vulnerable because we have not initiated the debate about the changing role of journalism and our changing role in society. In the words of one of TV's modern messiahs, Ted Koppel, "There is no culture in the world as obsessed as ours with immediacy. In our journalism, the trivial displaces the momentous, because we tend to measure the importance of events by how recently they happened. We have become so obsessed with facts that we may have lost all touch with the truth."

Finding truth is difficult, and so too is separating it from propaganda, from cynicism, from bias, and from manipulation. It makes it harder and harder to practice Murrow's basic rule: that it takes two to tell the truth.

Television is about people interacting. TV leaves an impression, TV is nuance—the sweaty brow, the shifting eyes, a tiny, wry smile—all this speaks volumes. And we all bring our own biases to this relationship.

So I stand here tonight to ask you—perhaps plead with you—to participate with more than just your channel changers in this world.

Do change the things you do not like, take a stand, exercise your voice and your franchise and also please take your viewership seriously. Don't just stand on the sidelines and shoot the messenger if you don't like the nightly news and the fact that we have to tell you the world is not exactly a bed of roses. I say this to you because only your high standards can help ensure ours. Again the words of Edward R. Murrow, one of the high priests of journalism: "To be persuasive, we must be believable. To be believable, we must be credible. And to be credible, we must be truthful." I think that's good advice regardless of which side of the screen you're on.

Thank you.

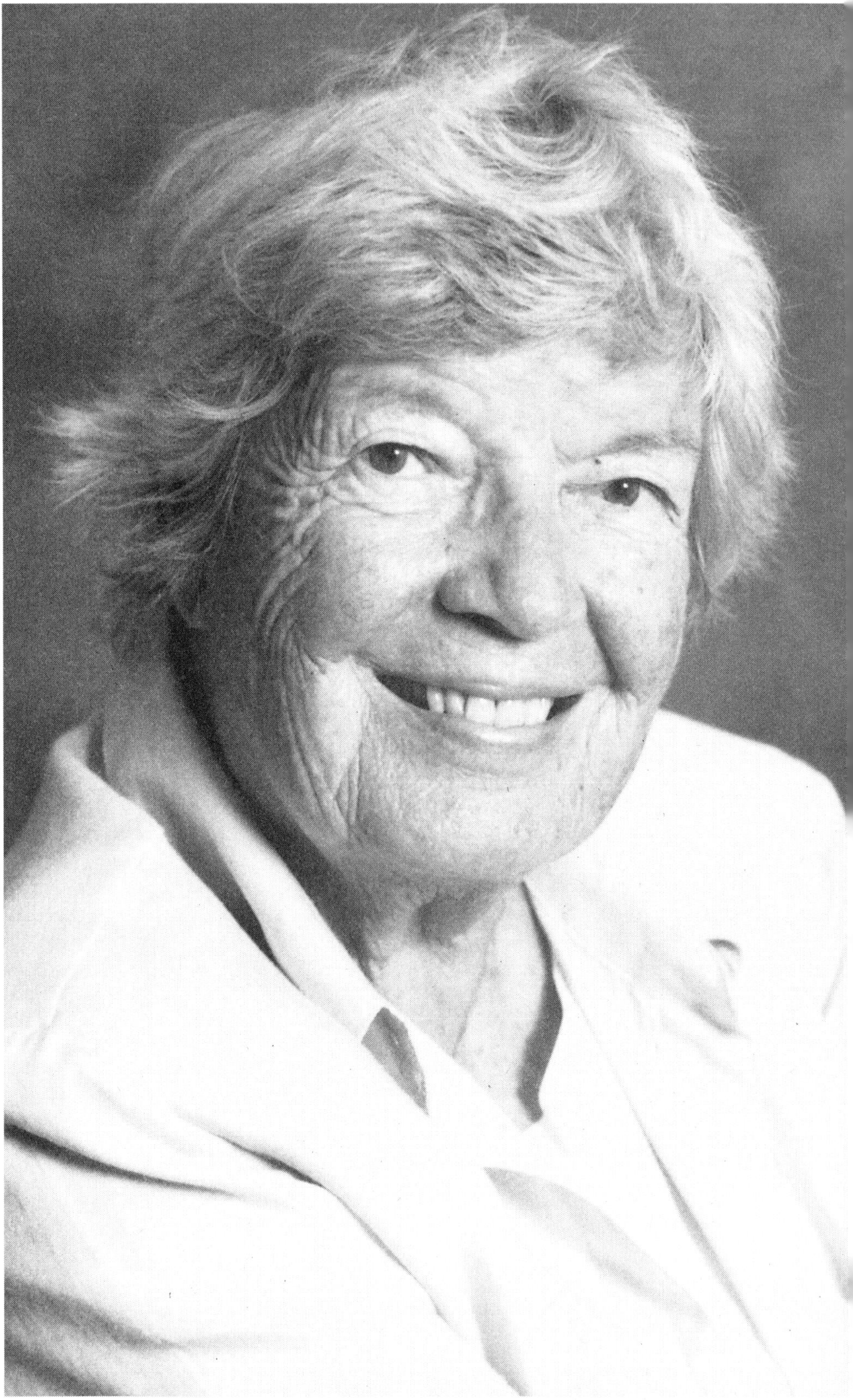

−1993−

JUNE CALLWOOD

Journalist, author and social activist, June Callwood challenged conventional wisdom from the day she dropped out of school, where she was editor of the school paper, to work for the *Brantford Expositor*. In 1942, she joined *The Globe and Mail*. She continued to use her own surname after she married because *The Globe and Mail* of that time did not employ married women. Callwood published widely as a freelance journalist, authoring books and magazine features and ghost-writing many auto-biographies. On television, she hosted the series *In Touch* on CBC Television from 1975 to 1978. She also hosted two series, *National Treasure* and *Caregiving with June Callwood,* for Vision TV. Callwood's career was marked by an abiding commitment to journalism's classical concerns with democratic participation and the public interest. She was most concerned to give voice to the voiceless, particularly on issues important to women and children. To advance the basis for democratic freedoms and a more equal, caring community, she helped launch over 50 Canadian social action organizations, including youth and women's hostels. She founded Casey House, a Toronto AIDS hospice, PEN Canada—to protect persecuted journalist's freedom of expression, the Canadian Civil Liberties Association and Feminists Against Censorship. She was named to the Order of Canada in 1978, promoted to Officer in 1985 and Companion in 2000. June Callwood Way in the Toronto neighbourhood of Queen Street East and Broadview Avenue is named in her honour, as is a Toronto park. A professorship in social justice was also established at Victoria College, University of Toronto, to mark her contributions. An atheist throughout her life, Callwood stated in her last interview that she still did not believe in God nor an afterlife. Instead, she believed in kindness.

1993 | JUNE CALLWOOD

THE JOURNALIST AS ADVOCATE

I read all the other James M. Minifie lectures with great envy for how articulate all of my predecessors were. I noticed that almost all of them began, in order to ingratiate themselves with the audience, by saying they were from the West. This was supposed to take off the curse. Well, I lived in Regina—so there!

I came here in 1939. My father had enlisted the day after Canada entered the war. He was here when that happened, so we moved out here to be with him until he was sent overseas. I absolutely rejoiced in Regina for one year while I went to Central Collegiate.

I remember one night crossing that little park that was between the Drake Hotel and the Hotel Saskatchewan. It was one of those sparkling nights, and the snow was like diamonds. I'd never seen anything like it. It squeaked when I walked on it, and I had frost on my eyelashes. I thought I was in an enchanted place.

We came to Regina in a bus, which was the cheapest way. There was no Canadian highway, so you came through Chicago to get from Ontario to Saskatchewan. We crossed the Canadian border near dawn. I looked out and saw a sign saying it was King's Highway No. 1. The road wasn't paved, and on either side was nothing but brown dust and deserted farm houses and tumbleweed. I thought, "Why didn't I know about this?"

I didn't discover the answer until recently, when I was helping Floyd Chalmers, who was editor of the *Financial Post* at the time, with his autobiography. He said that it was an effort of the magazines and newspapers during the Depression not to write too much bad news, because it would maybe prolong the dip in the economy, and that if you just told people good news, we'd get out of the Depression faster.

That brings me directly to my subject: The journalist as advocate. It's customary that the fortunate and honoured person chosen to give this annual lecture has to pick a title. You get a phone call, months in advance. You're asked, "What are you going to talk about?" Most of my distinguished predecessors did very well with this task, especially Peter Gzowski, who titled his sprightly address, "What I know now that I didn't know in the days when I knew everything." A wonderful title. But the title that I chose, rather hastily, was, "The journalist as advocate." I'm stuck with it, and so are you.

Later, after I chose the title, I encountered Knowlton Nash, the splendid occupant this year of the Max Bell Chair. The encounter was not entirely unexpected, because it took place in his living room. I told him my proposed title and he reflected a moment. "I'm opposed to advocacy journalism," he said in that deceptively mild manner of his. Knowlton Nash, as you must all have learned by now, is a tiger on matters of principle and professionalism. And then, noting my dismay and remembering that for part of my career I've been a columnist, he added tactfully, "Except for columnists, of course."

But I plan this evening to commit a heresy. It is my view that all journalists are advocates and they should, indeed, extend themselves to recognize that factor in themselves and their craft, and deal honourably with it.

Let me cite an example drawn from my more than 50 years as a journalist. About 40 years ago, I was ghost-writing for a very prominent woman who had a great deal to say that was progressive and stimulating about the lives of women, but she didn't have time herself to write. The articles appeared under her name, but I did them. It's a line of work which is not highly regarded, but it pays.

I chose from comments that she'd made over a one- or two-hour interview, and then I would throw in anecdotes of my own if she didn't have enough of hers. We had a nice, amicable understanding about that. I kept all the notebooks. I've kept all my notebooks all my life. And what's clear, when I read them when there was talk of bringing her book out in another edition, was that she was trying to have me write that same-sex love affairs are not different in any important respect from heterosexual love affairs.

These observations are in my notebook, and all of the notebooks where I interviewed her, but they never made it to the printed page, because I was shocked. I didn't think she should have such an opinion, although the fact that she was a lesbian was quite plain to see. To put my decision in the context of this address, I was an advocate for heterosexuality, and I was not open to a challenge.

All journalists take that kind of baggage with them on every assignment. The mind makes adjustments based on aspirations, blindness, emotional fragility, information, upbringing, fatigue and a degree of calculation directed at personal advancement which usually is masked as pragmatism.

When I moved from Ontario to Regina in 1939 I was 15 years old. (If you're slow in addition, I'm now 68.) I had been a dismal flop socially in Kitchener, which is the city we lived in. So I determined I was going to make a new start in this new city. And as a signal to myself that I was newly minted and now adorable, I gave myself an adorable new name. I told everyone my name was Toby. My mother was astonished. Within weeks of my arrival in Regina, however, Toby Callwood was as dismal a flop socially as June Callwood had been. I discovered to my dismay that I had brought myself along on the journey.

Journalism school may give you a new name—"journalist"—but it can't create a new person. You will still have to deal with the gaps in reading, the flaws in understanding, and the flash-points in your nature. Those quirks may be invisible to an outsider in the work you produce, but they most emphatically alter everything you write.

As observations go, that one isn't all that profound, but the current efforts of management to sanitize the private lives of media employees give rise to doubts that editors and producers appreciate the importance of human development in the acquisition of professional skill. Journalists are forbidden, on pain of losing their jobs, to enter into any community activity that carries a taint of advocacy or even a decent level of concern for the quality of life of one's neighbours.

Publishers and owners of radio and TV stations are not held to such a standard, of course, as Gerry Sperling points out in the *Prairie Dog* (Aren't you lucky to have an alternative press. I hope you're all supporting it). In an article about the myth of objectivity, he points out that reporters are supposed to avoid conflicts of interest, but the proprietors can be directors of powerful corporations which have a very serious interest in controlling the news and discouraging inquiry.

Journalists, like judges, are not supposed to join an environmental group, or a food bank organization, or a protest against racism. This is done to insure that prejudice and bias do not creep into their stories.

This pious camouflage may succeed in lulling subscribers, but simultaneously it assures that the journalist will have a marked lack of familiarity with the topic. Isolating journalists in the newsroom is supposed to result in a public perception that the journalist is completely impartial, which is palpable hogwash. As E.B. White, the great essayist once wrote it the *New Yorker*, and I may be paraphrasing, but I think I've got it, "All writing is slanted. A writer cannot be perpendicular, but can aspire to be upright."

Whether they are barred from joining community organizations or not, journalists do have strong views about conservation and hunger and racism and child care. The patent sophistry of the embargo on public commitment to a cause results not in purer reporting, but in reporters with a poorer context in which to adjust their perspective, a narrowed band of experience, a dearth of first-hand information about the community in which they live, not to mention a list of sources that reflects yesterday's views.

A journalist I know surreptitiously became a volunteer tutor in an illiteracy program. From this clandestine beginning, she helped some mothers on welfare organize a self-help group. Her editor doesn't know about this, of course, because that same editor once fired a reporter for similar activities, but the consequence of her personal involvement is that when she writes about poverty, she makes points and sees nuances that are beyond the ken of reporters who are circumspect enough to confine their extra-curricular activities to complaining about the publisher.

Would the media authorities have reporters covering the Pope's visit stop observing their religions? Would they want reporters covering labour disputes to resign from the guild? Would they assign black journalists only to stories that did not involve race relations? Such restrictions on reporters are unthinkable, but the eighties saw a rise in efforts to prevent journalists from enjoying the rights of citizenship in a democratic country—the right of free speech, the right of free assembly, the right to protest against injustice—and in that burst of sanctimonious wrong-headedness, weakened the ties that journalists have with their communities if writers are to be relevant.

Last week, I attended a bail hearing for Guy Paul Morin, who was first acquitted of murder by a jury and then mysteriously back in court again before another jury, and he was convicted. Kirk Makin was covering the hearing for *The Globe and Mail*. Kirk Makin is author of the book about Guy Paul Morin, and he makes it crystal clear in that book that he believes that Guy Paul is innocent. *The Globe*, wisely, knows that Kirk Makin, who is a superb reporter, need not be barred from covering this story because he has partisan views, and they're well known. In fact, his superior background means that he is the best person for the assignment. His accounts of the lawyers' arguments were devoid of bias, but demonstrated a thorough grasp of the significance of the points that were made, and they were a clear gain for the reader, which is surely the point.

An able journalist vigorously involved in housing for homeless women, for example, may well be exactly the right person to cover the inquest of a woman who froze to death when living in an abandoned truck, which is something that really did happen in Toronto. Just as an able sports writer who plays tennis may be the best one to send to Wimbledon (my husband, in short).

Editors should celebrate multifaceted experience outside the newsroom instead of vigorously discouraging it. I wonder at the sinister purpose behind discouraging writers from being involved in their community. The result of the restrictions on community involvement often is that the journalist's experience, being limited, exactly matches that of publishers and proprietors: that is, it's isolated and rarefied.

The group to whom journalists can be compared is the judiciary, which similarly is supposed to remain aloof from the maddening throng. The result, as we have seen all too well, is that judges for the most part are insensitive, obtuse, arrogant anachronisms. Like generals, they're always one war behind.

Newsrooms are almost always restless places where egos suffer agonies of bruising, and ambition can sourly fester. The ferment of nasty internecine bitterness used to be offset somewhat by the bonding that goes with a shared cause, when reporters think of something larger in the scheme of things than any individual petulance. There is a unifying force. Rancor fades when journalists see their jobs in good part as a mission, a scared responsibility. Morley Callaghan once said to me, "Do you know what is wrong with you?" I gave this good thought. I had many options. But he went right on and said, "You're a thirties idealist. You think things can be fixed."

So did we all, all the journalists who came with idealism into the profession, and who still do. Journalism was seen then, and often is still seen today, as a way to contribute to the public good. It was associated with a zeal to expose corruption, to remedy wrongs, to attack untruth and humbug, to achieve justice for the downtrodden. We used words like "downtrodden" then. The newsroom was a thrilling place where good things could happen. Working journalists still feel great pride and exhilaration when the paper behaves well, and goes after the rascals.

An element of probity is the distinguishing feature of Canadian journalism to a much greater extent than journalism in either the United States or Great Britain. For almost two centuries, journalism has been a home for altruism in this country, a haven for optimists, the headquarters for those who thought that society was far from fair for all and not at all perfect, but journalists could remedy some of the imperfections by keeping their wits about them and refusing to be intimidated or lazy.

The satisfaction in being a journalist came not from the salaries, which used to be abominable (and still aren't wonderful), or a sense of personal importance, since bylines were infrequent, but from contributing to something wonderful like an attitudinal change in your community, or occasionally participating in the spectacular toppling of a dishonest person. Reporters knew their communities, and no one thought it odd or unseemly that they should. Would reporters, embedded in their communities, have missed the Mount Cashel story?

I am, of course, in accord with the criticism of journalism schools that was contained in a University of Oregon report which suggested that courses in journalism should be better connected to courses in political science and other social science disciplines. Sometimes, a generation or so ago, I admit, identification with news sources went too far. Until very recently, journalists covering the legislature, for example, were drinking buddies of politicians and tended to be very protective of their friends. This ill-advised kind of chumminess reached its zenith in the forties at *The Globe and Mail* when I was there, when Charlie Oliver, who covered the police beat, turned in a story describing a robbery that would take place later that night. He explained he wanted to go home early, so he was filing it in advance. True story.

Recent efforts to deny journalists the full privileges of citizenship have unhealthy consequences for journalists, for the media, and for the country. Albert Camus wrote that it is natural for a state to behave badly. That's just what states do when they can get away with it, and they will do so unless their citizens rise in opposition. Freedom, he said, cannot rely for its growth on governments. It is not in their interests to promote freedom. Advocacy can only come from the grassroots, and the expression of that advocacy is journalism.

If journalists are not permitted to associate with grassroots organizations, much is lost. Early warning signals are not seen and, for instance, when a riot erupts, reporters come unprepared to interpret cause except by building on guess and projection. How many times have we seen that early reports are "sensationalized," a word that really means the reporter hadn't the haziest idea what was really going on, and therefore concentrated on the bloodshed. Only days later do we hear from community leaders protesting that the media missed the point, but by that time public interest has moved on.

This poverty of background is nowhere more evident than in the way our media cover stories relating to prison experience. The public has no way of understanding that releasing prisoners before the end of their sentences means that they'll be supervised tightly during the critical period of adjustment to life outside the walls, because few reporters know that. The public doesn't know that the longer a person stays in jail, the more dangerous that person is likely to become, and the reason the public lacks understanding of this singular truth is because journalists know little about our penal system.

Prisons are brutalizing places where men and women rot. A handful of dangerous people probably should be locked up forever, but in most cases the quicker we can get offenders out of prisons, the better and safer it will be for society. You won't find that perspective in the media. Reporters don't know prisoners, they don't visit prisons except on guided, orchestrated tours, and they aren't allowed to join organizations which take an interest in prison conditions. The result is a badly skewed view of institutions which cost the Canadian public billions of dollars and do much more harm than good. The distance between journalists and the realities of prison nourishes the public's tendency to believe in simplistic, punitive solutions to complex social ills. Shallow journalism supports a penal system that shames us all.

Journalists are supposed to *find* the story. More often, they're satisfied to *get* the story, which is different. They use their eyes, they use their ears, but the depth is not there. Lacking comprehension of the issues behind the activity they are examining, they become impressionists. If heads of newsrooms were allowed to encourage participation in the community and regular communication with people who toil on the front lines, professionalism would only be enhanced, and there would be a reduction of the disasters that are caused when journalism reflects partial truths, misunderstanding and prejudice.

The challenge to that line of argument, of course, is that journalism is fact finding. A trained journalist can get to the heart of any matter. This undoubtedly is true if the journalist is covering a Rotary luncheon, but it's not necessarily so if the journalist is reporting on, say, people recovering from incest. The public in the latter case is served up a platter of talking heads, whether it's print journalism or radio or television. There's an expert (usually someone self-appointed as such) who says this, then the incest survivor says that, then a group leader says that, and all of it's topped off with a poignant lead about the woman having sad eyes, or the man.

That's skim-milk journalism. It covers the story, but it doesn't move the reader from the superficial into perspective, engagement, information, concern.

When journalists are fettered by the denial of participation, the questions they ask, however neutral and sensitive, can only result in simplified answers. The information obtained is one-dimensional, not because the report is unintelligent, or unsympathetic or untrained—conditions which almost never occur anymore—but because the reporter simply doesn't know enough about the community's stress points and the history of the issue to ask better questions.

Consider, by way of illustration, that a neighbour is working on the engine of a car. This happens usually on Sunday afternoons in fine weather. The jaws of the car open and the neighbour's head disappears. A child says, "What are you doing?" and the neighbour says, "I am fixing my car." You stroll over and you say, "What are you doing?" and the neighbour says, "There is something wrong with the carburetor." The teenager on your street, who is a trained mechanic, says, "What are you doing?" and the neighbour tells the teenager exactly what the problem is, and in considerable detail.

Wherever journalists have free rein to examine injustice at close hand, they become a threat to the status quo. It is significant that despotic regimes always deal with opposition by silencing journalists. Journalists familiar with local conditions understand the protest. Perceiving the wrongs, their consciences are engaged. They go to work. They report the realities that contradict the state's propaganda. Moving on the streets and in backroom meeting places, they learn where injustices lie and they're in a position, if they dare, if they can find an outlet, to tell the world the truth.

When authorities are up to mischief or evil, they naturally are reluctant to have this process occur. Those in power can lop off the heads of journalists, symbolically, or with a death squad. Unrest drops to a sullen, invisible twitch. Worldwide, journalists are among the first people to be assassinated for their beliefs. In the past 10 years, writes Nick Fillmore in that excellent publication, *Content*, more than 300 journalists have been killed or have disappeared. In one informed estimate, there were 1,100 attacks on reporters in 100 countries last year alone. Despotic governments, like media owners in this country, prefer journalists who don't get involved.

John Stuart Mill, in his classic *On Liberty*, observed, "The peculiar evil of silencing the expression of an opinion is that it is robbing the human race." This remains true even when the opinion goes against the facts, or sensibilities, or reason. When the richness of colliding views is not permitted by the thought police, we are all the losers. Democracy cannot flourish when opinions, however annoying, vexatious, insulting and wrong-headed, are smothered by powerful interests on the left or the right, when euphemisms and blandness are more important than lucidity and reality.

In this country, we accomplish a high level of censorship and suppression in the name of sanctimonious political correctness, which I find ultimately patronizing and degrading. Another pernicious force these days, however, is libel chill. Libel laws are used everywhere to protect powerful interests and assist them in stripping the economy to its bones, unencumbered by critics.

Arguably, the Reichmanns were able to continue their high-rolling business practices because journalists could not do their jobs without risking financial ruin for both themselves and their publishers. Elaine Dewar's book on the Reichmanns was never written because of libel chill. Would banks have been so free, disastrously free, with lines of credit to Olympia & York if she'd been able to write her book? *Globe and Mail* award-winning Kimberley Noble's proposed book on the Hees empire, which is now tottering, may never appear, and for the same reason—libel intimidation. We may not execute writers in this country, but libel laws make it possible for powerful people to execute writing.

In all countries, journalists are on the forefront of social change. That's the nature of the beast. In Canada, journalists are descended from a long line of dissenters who knew their communities and spoke out fiercely against inequity and iniquity. Indeed, this country's history would be very different if journalists had not been brave. They were almost the single voice of opposition in a new nation where authority was concentrated in the hands of a comfortable few.

The earliest warning cry from Quebec came in 1803 when a newspaper, *Le Canadien,* appeared with the motto, "Our Language, Our Institutions, Our Laws." The editors, Mssrs Bidard, Blanchet and Taschereau, promptly found themselves in prison and were held there without trial—which is the quintessential Canadian response to troublemakers. I remind you that more recent reprise happened in 1970 with the War Measures Act.

In 1835, Joseph Howe, who was editor of the *Nova Scotian* at the time and a fighter for democracy, stood in a courtroom in Halifax, facing judges who wished to jail him because he questioned their fairness. A few years after that, William Lyon Mackenzie's presses were destroyed and thrown into Toronto's harbour because he didn't like Upper Canada's Family Compact. In the end, as you know, he made a significant contribution to the development of responsible government in Canada. And a nut who changed his name to Amor De Cosmos ran a newspaper in Vancouver and brought British Columbia into Canada (well, sort of brought it into Canada).

And let us celebrate Bob Edwards, who ran the *Calgary Eye-Opener.* The front page of that historic, irregular Calgary paper featured pictures of CPR derailments and collisions. The captions under them were usually, "Sample of everyday train wreck." Once he ran a picture of R.B. Bennett, later prime minister of Canada, but then he was CPR's lawyer, and the caption was, "Another CPR wreck."

The sheer drudgery involved in good journalism continues to make improvements, big and small, whenever reporters are given the time and the support to do their jobs. This calling, journalism, is truth-finding, and it demands the highest ethical standard. And sometimes, on glorious days, it gets it. Often the gains are very quiet. There's a shift in public understanding of an issue. It doesn't make a sound, but the tilt becomes solid ground. Take, for example, the movements now to address the problems of violence in families, which 10 years ago got great laughs in the House of Commons.

John Hersey wrote that a journalist, in any effort to render truth, has three responsibilities: to the reader, to her or his own conscience, and to the human subjects under examination. I would add that the journalist's job is to rock the boat a little, to be liberated enough from conventional thinking to entertain a shred of doubt, a grain of skepticism, a touch of anarchy, a wisp of hope, and to present the public with the comprehensive and comprehensible facts, as fairly as it can be done.

Here is Thomas Jefferson's famous epigram: "Were it left to me to decide whether we should have a government without newspapers, or newspapers without a government, I should not hesitate a moment to prefer the latter." That said, what is the point of a press, or any of the media, if the reporter is lashed to the masthead? (Good little picture there.) John Gregory Dunne observed, "There are no good stories. Only the singer really matters—seldom the song. What a writer brings to any story is an attitude, an attitude usually defined by the wound stripes of life." An attitude, I submit, shaped as well by a vigorous engagement with the life of the city, the country, that lies beyond the press box and the parliamentary gallery.

We live in a time of deepening and widening poverty, of desperation, of isolation, of racism, violence and suffering. Journalists must place themselves in the thick of it and do their level best to help this country understand what's happening, and find the will to take better care of one another.

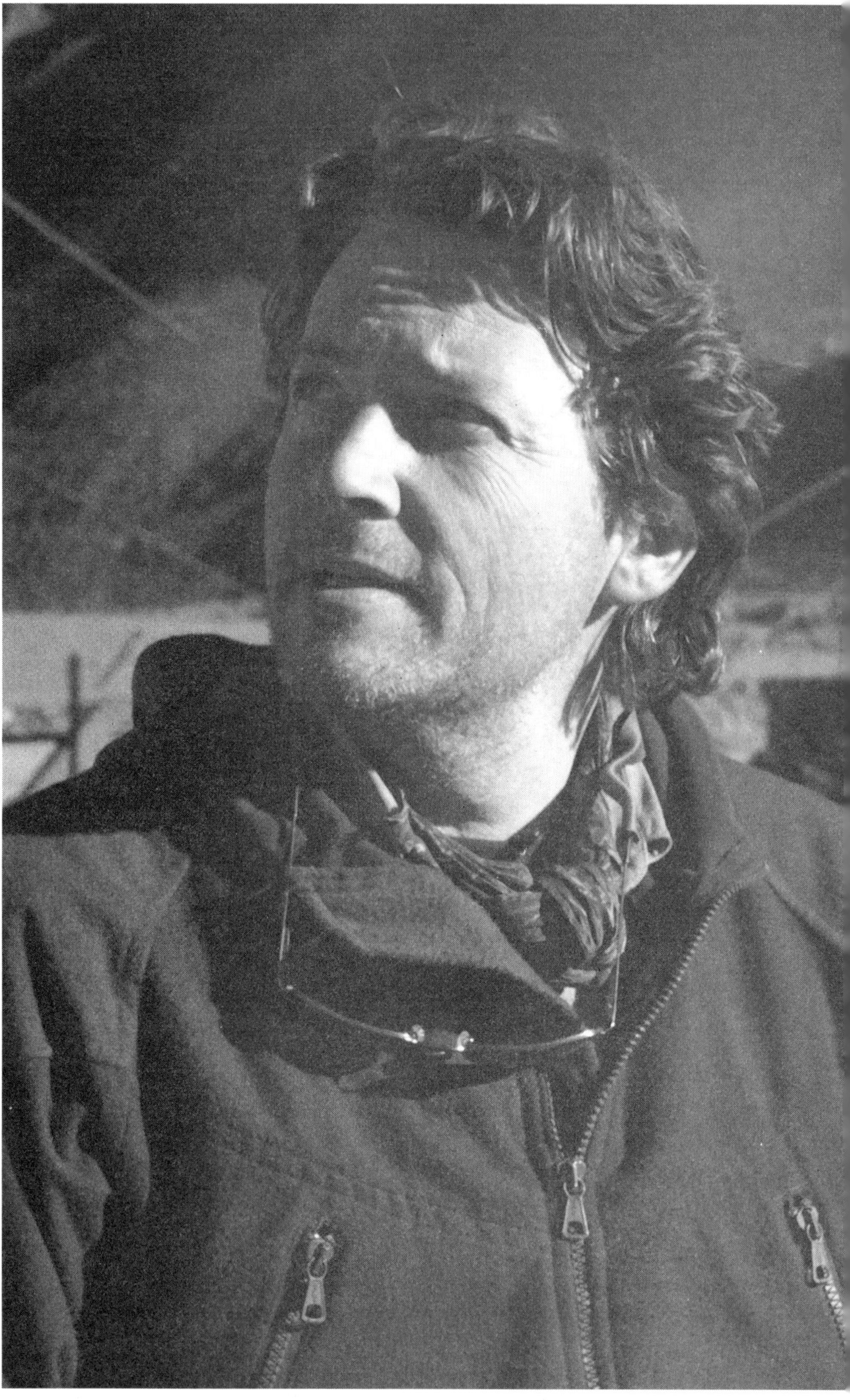

–1994–

ARTHUR KENT

Arthur Kent has specialized in international affairs, filming his first documentary in Afghanistan in 1980 and continuing to file reports at skyreporter.com. In 1989, Kent won two Emmy Awards for NBC's coverage of the Tiananmen Square massacre and the Romanian uprising. His documentary *Afghanistan: Captives of the Warlords* was broadcast by PBS three months prior to the terrorist attacks of September 11, 2001. After 9/11, the program was re-telecast in the US and Canada.

1994 | ARTHUR KENT

CAN PROFESSIONAL JOURNALISTS SURVIVE CORPORATE AUTHORITARIANISM?

It's very good to be here, of course, to deliver the James M. Minifie Memorial Lecture. To me, the concept of delivering a lecture is rather unusual. I don't see myself as a lecturer, but as a reporter. I have some interesting things to report this evening and to tell you. It is of course a huge honour to speak in the shadow of such an accomplished journalist and someone whom I listened to as I was growing older, before I realized that I wanted to be a reporter.

Last autumn when I was invited to deliver this lecture, I was asked for a title. Since I was engaged in very, very, vigorous litigation with my former employers, I suggested "Can Professional Journalists Survive Corporate Authoritarianism?"

Well, I am here tonight to tell you that the answer to that question is "Yes, yes, yes!" How do I know that? Let me count the ways and we'll be here all night, I assure you.

PRAIRIE ROOTS

It's great to be home, in western Canada, particularly here in Regina. In this city, more than 100 years ago, my grandfather, James "Jim" Kent, was working as a teamster at the railhead of the Canadian Pacific Railway, hauling supplies from the end of the railway as it was being constructed to the next location. One night in his camp he witnessed the Northwest Mounted Police bringing in one Louis Riel and served him water from his canteen.

James Kent went on to Lacombe, Alberta, where he built a homestead with his bare hands and an axe. He raised a family: six girls, two boys. One of those boys, Clyde, was killed in the First World War at Passchendaele Ridge. The second son, Parker, was my father.

Parker Kent became a reporter. In the 1930s, he worked for the *Calgary Herald* and was singled out and shouted down by a fiery "Bible" Bill Aberhart, Premier of Alberta—blasting the *Herald* for its anti-Social Credit dogma. And he went to Europe on an exchange program in the late thirties. Touring Germany in 1937 he encountered Adolph Hitler at a diplomatic reception in Berlin and found him to be a very unremarkable man, whose plans, of course, disturbed him deeply, contrasting markedly with the appearance of this diminutive, terrible personality. Parker Kent served in England in World War II with the Canadian Army. There he married my mother, Nursing Sister Aileen Fears, herself a 1st Lieutenant in the Canadian Army, and they returned to Canada and raised five children, with my father, Parker Kent, writing for many, many years with the Southam newspaper chain and carrying out a very successful career as an influential columnist.

Now, why do I bring up all this family history, all this tradition? Because it has been an essential guide to me and to my family: Susan, who is an accomplished literary editor, has worked editing books around the world, now works in Toronto, and is one of the best freelance book editors in the country; my sister Adele Kent, who a few weeks ago was sworn in as Madame Justice Kent of the Alberta Court of Queen's Bench in Edmonton; my youngest sister, Norma, who you know from *Newsworld*, great anchor, great reporter and doggedly determined to show that it is in fact the Kent *women* who have all the brains in the family; my brother, Peter, who is undoubtedly, in my opinion, the most naturally gifted broadcast journalist I've had the pleasure of working with and following in the business.

Part of our family's history and tradition was my father's way of drawing our attention to his business. He explained that he wrote columns and editorials—opinion pieces, he always told us, based on fact. If you want to impress someone and make a definitive argument, he said, you must present the facts *truly*, in such a way as to be indomitable. He also drew our attention to the work of great journalists whom we were hearing, seeing and reading. People like James M. Minifie, Walter Cronkite, Charles Lynch, Joe Schlesinger, Laurier LaPierre, John Chancellor, David Brinkley, Derek Utley and others, some of whom I've had the honour to work with later on in my career.

To me, as a young man and as a young reporter, and even now, when I watch his work, Minifie's work was, and is, steeped with authority. Recently, an edition of *Newsmagazine,* CBC's great news program of the early decades of the corporation, was shown on News World. This *Newsmagazine* was from 1958, I believe, hosted by the great Norman DePoe. It was a live program in 1958 from Los Angeles covering the visit of Nikita Khrushchev, the Soviet General Secretary. It was marvelous to watch this half hour show, done live, patched together, city-by-city, using film shot in previous days and live camera positions and Norman Depoe seeming to simply create paragraphs without the aid of a script, though perhaps with the aid of regular refreshment. I remember a lesson there for all journalists: Norman DePoe had to remark as the aircraft carrying Khrushchev pulled up into the Los Angeles airport and there was the figure of Nikita Khrushchev, fresh from his shoe-heel banging incident at the United Nations, coming out and DePoe pointed out, "Look at him, he knows where the television cameras are and he's playing to the cameras." There he was, Nikita Khrushchev, from another society, almost in those terms, technologically another planet. Within days of his arrival in North America, as a good politician, he knew how to play the cameras, he knew how to draw their attention and he knew how to direct their attention as well. It was an enormously successful trip for him, irrespective of his behaviour. And there in the middle of *Newsmagazine* is James M. Minifie, in Washington, live on a "hot switch." Not easy to do in 1958. (Let me tell you, it's not that smooth right now; it gives all of us butterflies to know we are coming up on a hot remote.) There was Minifie adding a gracious, reserved brand of reflection, and dignity, to analysis. And to me, those qualities, born of knowledge and experience, and ethical standards—that's what makes authority. That's why Minifie had authority.

POWER IS NOT AUTHORITY

I think older journalists who I have worked with—Chancellor, Utley, people who've spent 40, 30 years at our craft and trade, still plying it, and those of us who are attempting to survive in the nineties, at a mid-point in our career, can see that there is a lot of confusion over authority in broadcasting today. Especially, in my view, at the top of some broadcasting companies, where raw power is misrepresented as authority.

The evidence, I believe, shows that however much broadcast managers and owners might crave it, maneuver for it, scheme and plot to obtain it, power alone does not constitute authority, and never will. But it does often lead to abuse of authority—one definition, I suppose, a pure definition, of pure "authoritarianism."

While I was preparing to speak to you tonight, of course I had to turn to Webster's Dictionary, and it's very instructive. The English language is a wonderfully illuminating medium of expression.

The dictionary says that authoritarianism is "an unquestioning obedience to authority, rather than individual freedom of judgment and action." That of course is, to me, the most precise definition of the antithesis of journalism—authoritarianism.

The destructive thing, in broadcasting, and in print, is that seldom does authoritarianism breed benevolent, talented, capable dictators. When I was young, I learned early that if you find yourself a readily inspired dictator of an editor, you'll go far. Listen to what he says—he'll drive you into the ground, but you'll produce great work. I've been looking, and looking, and looking. I've had the pleasure to work under some terrific editors at CBC, at CJOH in Ottawa, at CTV, at the *Observer* newspaper in London, a few other places I've passed through, and at NBC News. Terrific editors, people who inspired me to go beyond the call of duty, which, as experienced journalists will tell you, is the daily bread of a real reporter. You cannot work eight hours a day, though that's all they'll pay you for, if you're lucky. It is a 24-hour, seven-day-a-week occupation. But authoritarianism? No, you're not going to find a capable dictator. In fact the history of journalism, like politics, shows that authoritarianism is almost always manifested by stupidity and failure.

PAYROLL CUTS FAIL

One clear example of that, and not just in journalism, is North American corporate budget tightening, financial control. Recently, for instance, Robert Reich, the U.S. Labor Secretary, gave a really illuminating address on this topic. He said a recent study of 531 (mostly large) companies, found that although three-quarters of the companies had cut their payrolls, most of those companies reported that the cuts had failed to achieve their expected results. Of the companies surveyed, earnings increased for just 46 percent of them. Less than half of the companies experienced a rise in profit or revenue. While 58 percent expected higher productivity, only 34 percent experienced it. While 61 percent sought to improve customer service, only 33 percent concluded that they had achieved it.

Another excellent example, in last week's *New York Times*, involved the Gibson guitar factory—something that is very dear to all of us who ever became entranced with rock music, the medium of wild expression of the latter half of the twentieth century. The Gibson guitar factory was built on the strength of their original Les Paul guitar, which became the standard for jazz and rock groups in the fifties and sixties, when people wanted guitars; and anything that looked like an electric guitar sold and sold and sold. But, in 1972, the Gibson guitar company sort of reached its zenith, after an Ecuadorian company, with interests in concrete and beer, acquired control of this stringed instrument maker. Sounds strange? Yes. And what did the experts say? Corporate bean counters from thousands of miles away started dictating to the sales department that the old stuff was stale, and that they needed new, new, new. That, says a guitar retailer in New York City, led to all kinds of stupid design changes. Sound familiar? Well, the quality began to slip, the company went into the toilet, and it was saved, just in 1986, by a man named Henry Juscovitz. And he went back to the original, the Les Paul guitar, one of the most famous instruments of popular music in this century. And they went back to basics. What did he do? Well, he had to layoff some workers. Where did he start? Management. He let all of the management team go. Then they went back and they examined the original sound pickups that the first electric Gibson guitars used. And they replicated the original sound. And of course everybody wanted that original sound. And now you've got Chet Atkins, B.B. King, Steve Miller, Jim Hall, Eric Johnson, Albert King and Joe Pass, among others, out there hailing the rebirth of Gibson guitar. And they are making mandolins, and guitars—and money, money, money.

Now, what possibly could guitar-makers and broadcasters have in common? Well, lots. You just have to look at one of my previous bandstands, NBC News.

A big part of the reason that I and Mr. Andrew Lack, the current president of NBC News, were able to patch up our differences this week, was that he and I found ourselves, in recent months, strumming the same tune on our Gibsons, about his predecessor, Michael Gartner. It was a re-worked version of "Michael Row the Boat Ashore."

It was reworked, because Michael had rowed the boat of NBC News straight out to sea, and he nearly sank it there.

1994 | ARTHUR KENT

NBC FORSOOK FOREIGN NEWS

NBC News president Andrew Lack was quoted as recently as August by Ken Auletta, of the *New Yorker* magazine, stating: "Gartner did nothing for foreign news." (Oh boy, what an understatement.) And now Mr. Lack, Gartner's successor at NBC News, finds himself struggling to redress the lack of resources overseas, and wasting a lot of time, and money, settling past, totally unnecessary disputes like my own. And I must congratulate him and commend him for having the courage to bridge this 18 months of needless, fruitless, contentious litigation to get on with work. And I've pledged my support to help him do that.

Now, could Mr. Gartner have reached shore, paddling way out there at sea, if he'd adhered to NBC's great traditions and practices? If he had listened to his journalists? Of course he could have done.

But, the principal lesson of the downfall of corporate authoritarians is that corporations, and corporate management, in the nineties, cannot be expected and relied upon to protect and encourage the heritage and ethics and excellence of great news companies. Only journalists can do that. Only thinking human beings can be expected to do that, and that we must do. That is why we are here tonight. I believe that is why this institution exists. The School of Journalism and Communications here at the University of Regina is a place where knowledge and experience and theories are pooled and developed, so that in the future, we can have a thinking population which is given real information, real analysis and a basis for forming an understanding on how their family, their town, their city *and* their society should develop and should cope with the pressures of the outside world. So my message to young journalists here, particularly students of this School who are here tonight, listening to this, is that when the midgets of bad management accuse you of being "passionate" and "irrational" and "difficult," remember those great names of the past, gather up the facts and stand up for your rights and beliefs. And if you have to, Give Them Hell!

My experience of the past few days is that it is good for management, too. I think the most meaningful congratulations I have had in the past 48 hours have come from broadcast news managers, many of whom realized at the time what *really* had happened in my dispute with NBC management. Now, of course, they see in graphic detail just how excessive, just how unnecessary, just how misguided, and yes, just how stupid those authoritarian acts were.

I am reminded, thankfully, that there is always room for humour in any battle—we had a lot of great laughs in this past one. And I can tell you there is a lot of graveyard humour that keeps us going on the road when we're reporting, no matter how desperate the battle. I remember a year ago when I was in Olovo, Bosnia, a beautiful spa town founded by the Romans, a beautiful mountain setting, houses set among the hills. But now, sadly, as it's situated only 50 miles north of Sarajevo, Olovo is a place of destruction and bloodshed and terror. I was there photographing the Bosnian Serb artillery bombardment of civilian portions of the town, with refugee families hunkered down in cellars and basements. But my friend and translator, Slavco, a Croat journalist who came from the nearby town of Vares where he had built a home-made television station and was broadcasting "TV Vares" even as the war closed in behind him, asked me as we ran from the basement of the Serb church down the hill in the middle of a bombardment, "Say, Kent, don't leave here without promising to send me back some movies on videotape that I can broadcast on my TV station." And I looked around Olovo, at the steaming, smoking wreckage of the homes, the graveyards in front of the school, the terrified faces looking behind shattered glass, and I said "Slavco, whatever kind of movies would you expect me to send to you to broadcast here?" And he looked at me and he said. "Well, we could use a little comedy!" Sadly, Slavco—a Croat—was guiding me to Fadil, the captain in charge of Muslim forces in Olovo. Since my visit there, of course, the Bosnian, Muslim and Croat communities fell into the most horrible kind of genocidal attacks on each other's civilian populations. Vares was overrun by Muslim units, but I feel that Slavco must have survived. Hopefully he put his television station underground. Hopefully he will get a chance to go back, now there has been a rapprochement between the Croats and Muslims, and people like Slavco certainly will be engines of repairing the damage between those two communities. And I'll bring him his videos, I'll bring him anything he asks.

SOME TV IS WORTHLESS

The continuing horror of Bosnia, and the risks that journalists, that colleagues of ours, are taking to cover that war, bring home to me and other journalists, who come back from the war to North America, the remoteness of it all. The gulf between the reality of events overseas and the programming we see on US television. This is not the distance of an ocean but the distance of a universe. It strikes us how ludicrous and irrelevant is most of the television product currently served up in the guise of news here in North America.

John Carman, that excellent columnist for the *San Francisco Chronicle*, recently put all of this in perspective just by listing a few dubious moments in broadcasting, in just one week in November of last year:

- On *The Maury Povich Show,* porn star Marilyn Chambers taught viewers how to make their own sex movies at home.
- *A Current Affair* screened a rock video called "Snake Skin Voodoo Man," starring Joey Buttafuoco, his wife Mary Jo, and an Amy Fisher look-alike. The video is "like the final chapter in a cartoon," Mary Jo told reporter Steve Dunleavy.

- *American Journal* profiled a Florida man who held his wife hostage after he saw her picture on the jacket cover of a porn video.
- *Inside Edition* aired a three-part interview with "Son of Sam" killer David Berkowitz.
- *A Current Affair,* at it again, same week, flew a squabbling couple to a deserted island in the Caribbean so they could try to patch up their marriage. After thinking it over on the island, Brian and SuAnn Wade decided to go through with their divorce but to stay together anyway.
- And, yes, Heidi Fleiss showed off her new line of sleepwear on CNN's *Showbiz Today.*

That's one week in November, on television, in North America.

Now, I know there are good journalists like Jim Morea at CNN's entertainment bureau in Los Angeles, trying to make the entertainment beat meaningful every day. I can't argue with that, who can? One of my friends, Bob Gilmarten, a terrific journalist who stood on points of principle at *Dateline NBC,* and yes, is no longer there, he's at *American Journal.* Bob's a great reporter and I know that he is not likely soon to be doing pieces about wives held hostage after being found on the covers of porn videos. I mean, everybody likes a good spicy yarn every now and then. I remember growing up with stories such as Gerda Munsinger, the Manson Killings, Richard Speck, the killer of several nurses in Detroit—there was a man who terrified me for an entire summer. I learned about those killings, I think, the first night of the Stampede in Calgary, when I was entering my teens. And I remember listening to the radio and trying to imagine the terror in that house, as that maniac broke in and killed those student nurses one by one. But I also recall that there was balance in our craft at that time. The scandals and pot-boiling exposes were like a tasty dessert after a main course of real, hard news, delivered with intelligence and wit by people like Minifie.

What's happened now is turning that tradition on its head. This tabloid tendency has consumed the news agenda. So stories like Tonya Harding, with limited importance to society (interest, yes, and some appeal regarding greed and sport) mushroom into immense sagas that distract us all from everything else that's going on in the world, in our country, and in our communities. But editors and journalists don't have to let the agenda be set by the lurid fascinations and speculations of the supermarket-style, so-called tabloid magazine shows. The nightly news broadcasts, the serious electronic journalism each evening: did they have to chase Tonya Harding to that extent? Apparently so.

It brings real sadness to the hearts of those of us who've worked overseas, and have watched good people being killed in the pursuit of our craft, to see the entire spotlight taken up by pirouetting, scheming people on skates. It doesn't make sense. It doesn't make sense to me, and I know it doesn't make sense to you. Although it makes sense in the ratings books, what also makes sense is to keep balance in the news. And that is what we are talking about now. How can we expect North Americans, distracted and dazed and, in the final analysis, misinformed by this vapid nonsense, to have any time or any capacity to absorb the complexities of Bosnia, and the other stories going on around in the world that can really, one day, affect their communities, their lives, their families? If the Balkan War rages out of control, how many troops will the United Nations have to scramble to eastern Europe, next year, or two years or three years from now? The Canadian forces are already taxed having as many peace-keepers in the field as they do. If Canada is called upon even to make a modest contribution of another 10,000 or 20,000 men overseas, that means conscription, from towns and cities like Saskatoon and Regina. And that's one reason that you don't spend every night sitting down watching the latest on Nancy Kerrigan in Disneyland. That's why before you turn on Mickey Mouse you want to see at least five or ten minutes of news and analysis of the history of the world that day that may effect you and the people you love.

This kind of pollution—and that's not too strong a word—of journalism is something that deserves to be resisted, to be fought, and to be overcome, no matter what kind of authoritarian leaderships try to force good journalists into that kind of programming, into that kind of empty, blind alley of sickening distraction.

I am fortunate, now, to be working at the CBC. And I'll take issue with Louise Lore, my excellent executive producer, and ask her what she means, suggesting I'm not going to stay? How silly! Is she ushering me to the door? That's not what she told me yesterday and it's certainly not what I told her. I consider myself fortunate, first of all to be working in Canada, where we have a very strong tradition of training journalists, at institutions like this. And I know the managers and editors of good newspapers and television systems in the United States agree with me: Canada is an excellent training ground for good journalists, and good journalism. We have training structures here that are superior to that of the United States. And many young American students and journalists ask old war horses like myself as we travel around "Gee, how'd you get started, how did you get to this level?" And we explain the various steps. But will we have these opportunities in future? Only if we all fight against the kind of authoritarianism that changes programming, that closes down institutions, that chokes investment by communities in universities, such as this one.

Bad corporate management is delighted when it hears about journalism schools being closed down. "Oh boy, good news—30 less troublesome priests next year. I can pull them out of high school, train them, brainwash them, and get them onto Heidi Fleiss faster than you can say 'negligee.'" Good corporate broadcast managers despair at the thought of universities like this one ever having to decrease their enrolment, ever having to cut back their programs, because they know that in the pursuit of real commercial news broadcasting, you need real commercial news broadcasters and writers and newspaper journalists and magazine writers, and that is what this battle is all about.

And the battle, let me tell you, continues. At the CBC (which is not a perfect world) I hear many people in management debating as they try to chart a future for the corporation, now that the CBC is free of the pressures that are exerted by the kinds of public figures who 100 years ago might have suggested rolling up the Canadian Pacific railway and selling it for parts. Who needs the CBC? Why, in an electronic world, should a country bother having a national broadcaster, concerned with national culture? Of course it's essential. And at the CBC, I find management people, particularly hands-on journalist-managers, who are interested in fostering the kind of heritage and tradition that Mr. Minifie stood for, and still stands for today.

MAFIA TEACH MORALITY

To us—our team at NBC News Rome, soon to be reunited, in one way or another—resisting sleaze was as natural as it was imperative. We had a great object lesson swirling on around us in the Italian state between the years 1989 and 1992. It was the war against the Mafia. We covered the story, occasionally, whenever we could get back home to our base from the Gulf War, from Eastern Europe, from some other armpit we'd been sent to for this week's disaster. But God bless those times. When I turn on the television set today, I just don't see the same degree of attention and effort and vigour being taken by the big American networks to cover those stories. And we here in Canada have to be proud that the CBC, and yes CTV, Global and local stations, are still maintaining an interest in foreign news reporting, even against the pressures, the economic pressures and political pressures that have been brought to bear.

But to us, when we got back to Rome, the story to cover was the Mafia because the octopus had wrapped its tentacles around the state. As one of our sources, one of the leading academics in Italy under the Mafia, told us, one part of the state is working *against* the Mafia, the police and so on, while another part of the state, the politicians at the top, are working *with* the Mafia. And we got to know a fascinating man, Giovanni Falcone, a judge, Italy's chief Mafia investigator. Giovanni and his wife, also a magistrate, became a team consumed with trying to nail the leaders of the Sicilian Mafia, in particular, and to find the leadership and the methods of control the leadership exerted on the Italian state. Falcone became fascinated, from a young age, with the strange codes of conduct that protected this authoritarian criminal leadership, such as the "code of silence"—*Omerta*—and "truth among thieves." Falcone's work caused him to put his own values and those of the Italian state to the test. He wrote: "knowing and working with these *Mafiosi* has profoundly affected my attitudes towards people, and even my beliefs."

"I have learnt that whatever happens, you have to behave decently—to show real respect for what you believe in and not just make meaningless gestures. This harmony between one's beliefs and one's actions is crucial to our physical and mental well-being. I have learnt that every compromise—every betrayal, every time you fail to face up to something—provokes a feeling of guilt, a disturbance of the soul, an unpleasant sensation of loss and discomfort with oneself. Just as the categorical imperative of the Mafia is 'to tell the truth,' this has become a cardinal principle of my personal ethics, at least as far as the really important relationships in my life are concerned. However strange it may seem, the Mafia has taught me a lesson in morality."

He was driven to despair to learn that lesson, because he could not count on the state authorities above him not to betray his evidence and frustrate his efforts to undo the crime families of southern Italy. They not only taught him a lesson in morality, of course. They killed Giovanni Falcone and his young wife. They blew them up in the spring of 1992. Two months later they killed his partner, Paolo Borsellino. It was in many ways the outrage of all Italians to these killings and of world authorities associated with the Mafia-hunt in that country and abroad, that accelerated the search, that built further pressure on the investigations of Judge Antonio Di Pietro in Milan and other parts of Italy. They are now well on the way to busting the Mafia in its present form, at least as it was constituted in 1992.

To us, that was a terrific object lesson in staying true to your beliefs. And although we kid around a lot on the road, and we fight, we argue, among the foreign reporting corps, there's a great feeling of camaraderie and common purpose. And as our companies began to strip us down, as our corporate managements began to steal friends by way of layoffs and resources by way of budget cutting, we began to make bonds with one another. Our former rivals at ABC and CBS became our brothers-in-arms because they were facing the same adversity, all in the name of viewers being able to see more about Lorena Bobbitt and Tonya Harding and the Long Island Lolita and Heidi Fleiss and Waco and all those wonderful, momentous events that have so much to do with the futures of your families and communities.

NBC DEAL OFFERS HOPE

It has been a terrible time for us, but personally I have great hope. Many of us realized something special this week, when we proved that we could reach a dignified acknowledgement of past wrongs and correct them, without hysteria, and go on. And I think, I would hope, that there's been a reopening of a channel of communication for this reporter and that management. I don't hope to part the Red Sea of tabloid television, but I would hope to somehow influence their thinking to see a few more foreign crews traveling next year. It would truly be a failure if I could not achieve some kind of amelioration, at least in the sphere of my own work, and within CBC as well, to help tell Canadians that it is time to get on the telephone and phone Ottawa, and tell them "Get off the CBC's back."

If the CBC is ever going to reform itself and stay healthy, it must do it with intelligent debate within the corporation, and from without. Those who've worked with the CBC before—outstanding Canadian broadcasters such as Mr. LaPierre, who have very pointed opinions, and very firm, creative thoughts on how the CBC should develop—should be involved in that debate, and you should be involved in that debate too. But for heaven's sake, don't tolerate people telling you that it's time to close down a television station in Regina or another town, or that it's time to close the Moscow Bureau of CBC, which offered, during the coup last autumn, due to the efforts of Don Murray and his colleagues, the only full-time, real-time live broadcasts of the coup to viewers in North America, aside from CNN. The three big commercial networks in the United States wouldn't interrupt their movies to show the terrible bloodshed outside the television station in Moscow. The CBC shone there. The CBC news tradition shone there, just through the weight of the collective consciousness of all the journalists who have had the honour to follow Mr. Minifie and who inhabit the CBC at so many different levels, and who represent a lot of healthy resistance to unhealthy suggestions from the top and outside.

In wrapping up I would like to end on a positive note. I think there's hope as long as we all keep striving and as long as the public keeps tuning in to programs that matter. Have dessert: dessert is going to be there for a long time, I can promise you. But please let people know, for the sake of the students who are trying to get into the business through institutions like this and for the sake of people like myself who are still trying to get on the air with expensive and difficult foreign pieces, please let the managers of our broadcasting companies in Canada know that you want a decent *steak* every now and then—that you need some protein, as well as the sugar and the spice at the end of the meal.

And, we'll do what we can to continue doing good programming.

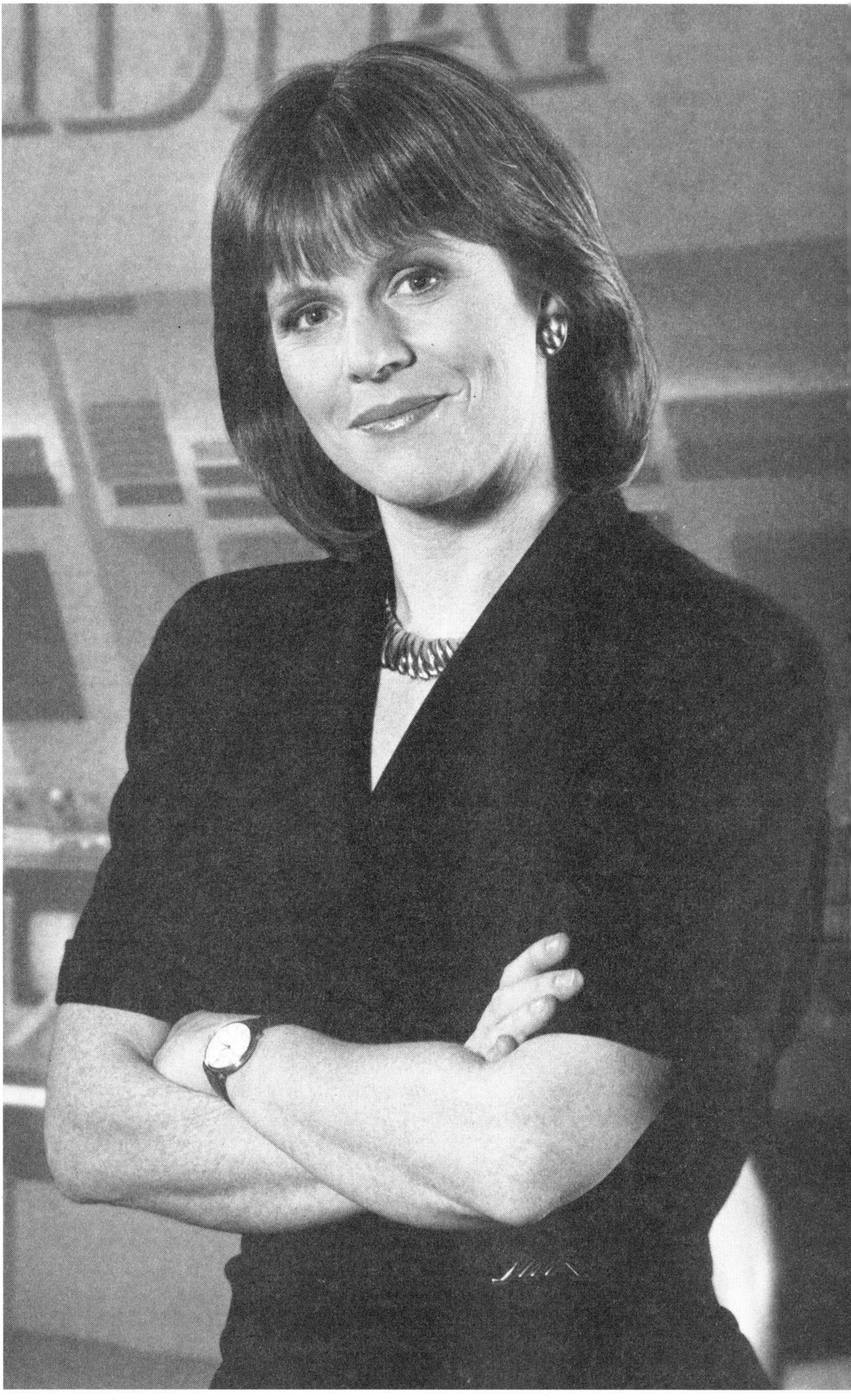

−1995−
VALERIE PRINGLE

Valerie Pringle is a graduate of Radio and Television Arts at Ryerson. She hosted daily news and current affairs programs on CFRB Radio in Toronto, CBC-TV's *MIDDAY* and CTV's *Canada AM* from 1980 to 2001. She has hosted and produced documentaries and series for CBC, CTV, Discovery and Vision. She is actively involved in many not for profit boards, including The Trans-Canada Trail and the Centre for Addiction and Mental Health. She was named to the Order of Canada in 2006.

1995 | VALERIE PRINGLE

THE RING OF TRUTH:
The Trials and Tribulations of Interviewing

I'm thrilled to be here. I never make speeches. I don't travel and do this. I've got three children and a job and so I always weasel out of it somehow. When I was invited, I was so impressed to be asked, I was so honoured, that I couldn't say no. I looked at the list of people who had spoken before me and thought I don't measure up really, but if they are asking me then I must go. And I was also thrilled reading about James Minifie because, to be perfectly honest, I didn't really know very much about Don Minifie. And, reading his curriculum vitae, especially when I saw it juxtaposed in the program next to mine, I felt really truly not worthy. What a wonderful man! What a career! So I'm thrilled to be here to deliver this lecture in his memory and in his honour.

I'm speaking tonight about what I do for a living, which is interviewing. I've been doing a daily news and current affairs program for 14 years now: four years on radio on CFRB Radio in Toronto (some of you might have missed that there were some fine interviews though), and for the last 10 years on national television—eight with *MIDDAY* and two with *Canada AM*.

Edward Price Bell is a name you might not be familiar with: he was with the *Chicago Daily News* a long time ago. He was an interesting character; he interviewed such people as Mussolini, Mackenzie King and the Grand Wizard of the Ku Klux Klan. He wrote back in 1929 that in his view the purpose of all great interviews is to "unlock the lips of wisdom—and make the sphinx of judgment speak." It's pretty impressive, not a bad description. When I read it I thought, "Gee I talk more to the sphincter than the sphinx." But, the point is well taken. The job of the interviewer is to make lips move, make people talk and to focus them, and engage them, and challenge them, and coax them (and Connie Chung might say trick them) and compel them to tell you (and therefore your listeners, who it's all about anyway) stories, information, plans, feelings, ideas, policies, and to bear witness. And, sometimes it works.

One of the best descriptions I ever heard of what an interview is looking for, came from Barbara Frum, when I interviewed her on the tenth anniversary of *The Journal*. It was just a few months before she died. She told me she was constantly listening for what she described as the ring of truth. Words that were so real, or so surprising, or so human and so unfiltered that you just knew, you could physically feel right away that they were true. So I guess, the ultimate task of the interviewer is not only to make the sphinx of judgment speak but speak the truth.

It was also interesting when I got this little pamphlet about the speech tonight, with the title "The Ring of Truth." I thought I was much more clever than I realized. I saw a little *double entendre* there that I hadn't intended, because I started to see that ring as a physical thing, which is how you often feel as an interviewer too. It's almost an impenetrable circle, sort of a cipher or a mystery. One of my favorite Robert Frost poems is just a little couplet that goes: "We dance round in a ring and suppose, and the secret sits in the middle and knows."

I often feel that when I'm interviewing I'm dancing around in that ring and I can't get at it. So, I'm dancing and trying to listen for the ring of truth. Those are the great moments. And that's what you're looking for.

Unfortunately, those are the good times. Most of the interviews that you seem to do are about selling. You know, they're about selling politics and personalities or records or reputations, or something. And very often as an interviewer you feel like you're part of some nightmare Arthur Murray dance routine. You ask A, they answer B. Cha cha cha. It's over. Thank you very much. It's been a pleasure to meet you. It's about as interesting as an infomercial (I know, I've done millions of interviews like that). But when there is honesty, when there is intelligence, when there's an element of surprise in the questions and in the responses, then the interview takes off. And that's when it's fascinating listening.

Tonight I'm going to give you a little bit of history about interviewing, things you might not have known. You know, it didn't start with Barbara Walters! I'm going to tell you about the different types of interviews and how Brian Mulroney is different from Madonna. And, I'm going to give you some tips, the keys to successful interviewing as I see them, so you can go and take my job—although I'm sure none of you would want to do that.

HISTORY

The *Oxford English Dictionary* puts the origin of the word "interview" as a journalistic term in 1869: that's the first record of it. There's still some debate as to who to credit for creating the interview. There is one guy, Horace Greeley from the *New York Tribune*, who interviewed Brigham Young, the founder of the Mormon Church, back in August 1859. There's another fellow, James Gordon Bennett, Sr. of the *New York Herald*, who first interviewed American President Martin Van Buren.

In its early days, there was a fair bit of debate about the quality of this new form of journalism. It's described very well in a book called *The Penguin Book of Interviews*. On the one hand, it was argued in the contemporary press that the interview was something really stunning, that it managed to grip the reader because it conveyed this illusion of intimacy with celebrities and people who are witnesses to momentous events. (It's the same today.) Purists, on the other hand, saw interviews as (and these are their words) toadyism and flunkeyism. This was 130 years before Arsenio! They knew it then.

Interviewing was viewed as an American invention and art form for a long time. Even after European journalists had taken it up, they thought of it as something really American. They owned it for a long time. There was a wonderful quote from A.J. Liebling, who said, "There is almost no circumstance under which an American doesn't like to be interviewed, an observation which I have had a chance to verify in cracks in the Tunisian rocks under mortar fire. We are an articulate people, pleased by attention, and covetous of being singled out." And someone else wrote "America is the interviewer's paradise. Where else is a murderer's best friend his interviewer?" This is so true! But it does seem to me that, after doing many, many interviews, Americans make great subjects—in fact, they are generally better than Canadians, except for Newfoundlanders, who are the best storytellers. In the early days all interviews were done from memory. They didn't even really take notes: it was thought unseemly. Obviously, there was no tape recorder. There's a great story about Joseph Stalin reviewing a transcript of an interview done by Eugene Lyons of United Press in 1931. He actually scribbled on a corner of the transcript "more or less correct, J. Stalin." You can only hope you got it correct. I guess Eugene Lyons wouldn't have been around long if he hadn't.

One interesting thing, and the women of the School of Journalism might be interested in this, is that the interview was an early aspect of journalism where women could compete equally with men. In the 1890s, a woman named Elizabeth Banks wrote that interviewing was "the most pleasant, interesting and edifying branch of journalistic work that can be taken up by a woman, because it throws her into contact with the great, the extraordinary and the interesting people of the world," and that women make "much better interviewers because they were usually more tactful, quicker, more apt at observing and taking into account the little things in life." Huh.

I've done lots of interviews that are complete dogs in my years, countless stinkers during which the guest contributed nothing, so I really got a hoot out of an interview which was done with American President Ulysses S. Grant back in 1874. The reporter said: "Your Excellency, I have come to ask you, if the inquiry be deemed pertinent, what your views are on the third-term question." President Grant said: "I have nothing to say on the subject." The reporter said: "Well, I thought as the subject occupies a large share of the public attention . . ." Grant: "I have nothing to say on the subject." The reporter: "At least, I might be pardoned for asking you in case . . ." Grant: "I have nothing to say on the subject." The reporter: "I was merely wishing to say that in case you had good reasons for not wishing to comment . . ." Grant: "I have nothing to say on the subject." The reporter: "I trust, Your Excellency, that this subject will not be deemed an intrusion?" Grant: "I have nothing to say on the subject." The reporter: "At least nothing could have been further . . ." Grant: "I have nothing to say on the subject." The reporter: "Your Excellency, I am, in any event, glad that I have had the pleasure of . . ." Grant: "I have nothing to say on the subject." The reporter: "Good morning." Grant: "I have nothing to say on the subject."

What a nightmare! I'm trying to imagine what Eric Malling would have done with him.

TYPES OF INTERVIEW

This brings me quite neatly to the next part of this address which is on the different types of interviews, and the number one category (I hope there are not too many here)—politicians! As that poor intrepid reporter in 1874 discovered, interviewing politicians is difficult. You know, very little is straightforward—they can't/won't/don't tell you very much. I can honestly say I don't think I've seen more than a handful of interviews with serving politicians, in the past two decades, that have had a ring of truth to them. Think of Gzowski a week ago with the Prime Minister, listening to this barrage of statistics and qualifications and explanations. This is difficult.

What makes it more difficult now is the politicians are so media trained that the obvious difficulties they have, and I understand that, in giving straight answers all the time, are exacerbated by this seemingly media friendly appearance of answering the questions, and being open and amenable to them. The result is even more frustrating than that President Grant interview. You've all heard it a million times: "Mr./Ms. So-and-so, is health care in this country being dismantled?" "Well, that's a very interesting question, and I think it's very important for all Canadians to know and understand . . . blah blah blah . . ." The answer is prepared by the communications advisor, carefully strategized. So the interviewer then thinks, "Oh, I'd better look tough, I'd better look in control, I'd better look like I realize he's getting away with murder": "You haven't answered my question." The politician knows enough to go for the audience sympathy against some bullying, rude, obnoxious, overbearing host, and says, "Please let me finish my thought, my sentence (it'll just take me 5 or 10 minutes or so, how long is this live interview going?)" So they kill the time and so it goes. A dialogue of the deaf. And even if it was lively or contentious, what we call in the trade "more heat than light," and was good TV, you didn't learn anything.

I am still waiting to see what the next stage in the evolution of the dialogue between the press and politicians will be. I think we've stalled at a highly distrustful plateau, and have been there for quite a while.

The approach of British TV journalists to interviewing politicians was, "Why are these lying bastards lying to me?" That's how they went into every interview. I thought I was not nearly that cynical, but I must say that when it comes to the art or joy of interviewing, I would take almost any other category of person. Luckily, there are a few exceptions to this rule. One is the day they resign: *there* is a window of opportunity. You get a chance for a real answer. And sometimes, politicians will surprise you. I remember talking to Kim Campbell, when she was Justice Minister, about the abortion law that she was introducing. There had been comments by doctors who were concerned about being charged under the new law. I was presenting the litany of complaints to her and she said, "Well, I don't care if it passes or not," which was stunning. I mean ministers never say this. It was her bill. She said, "I'm pro-choice. I've crafted this bill as best I can to accommodate both sides. It may be an unsatisfactory compromise for both sides." (Which it was: It didn't pass. There's still no law.) But that was a stunning glimpse. Another case I remember distinctly was talking to Lucien Bouchard about being a politician, and being a boss and running the party, and he said, "I've discovered I can't work under other people. I couldn't even work under my 'friend' [Brian Mulroney]." The veil came down.

I think journalists love the idea that they're going to trip up a politician. (And we get research notes from producers, and they're generally younger than I am, and it's a riot to read them. In the last month I've had research notes that have exhorted me to make one minister cry and to really trip up another, and I don't think this is about to happen.) I always think of Charlie Brown and the football—he's running, misses it, and winds up flat on his back just one more time. I think you probably end up like that more often than not. Even people far more effective than I am at interviewing politicians (and I would say there are many), mine tons and tons of manure for just a few flecks of gold. I guess, really, one of the most golden moments to me is Prime Minister Mulroney's "roll of the dice" line about Meech Lake. That line was just so revealing. It had a stunning ring of truth about it. They're rare, but that is what you're aiming for, with politicians.

STARS ARE DIFFICULT
After politicians, the most frustrating people ever to talk to are big movie stars. It's interesting to see these very famous people develop an amalgam of themselves; one description of it is a co-mingling of image and personality, or "impersonality"—which is understandable. It's a defence against the relentless attention they receive and the invasion on their privacy. It's also often a very clever marketing strategy. But you probably haven't heard many moments with a ring of truth from Madonna or Tom Cruise. I mean the ring of truth they sort of subscribe to would be the Robert Frost variety where they're hiding in the middle, if they're there at all. This is also exacerbated by the fact that most people, including myself, who interview celebrities ask really stupid, soft, sucky, questions: "What do you want to do? Was this role a challenge? Isn't that interesting? Was it a stretch? Are you like this character?" You don't ask them questions that challenge them, or push them along, and who cares about their politics anyway. So this makes it tough.

But in fact, the very, very worst part about interviewing movie stars is having to deal with the self-important, officious, rude, horrible public relations people they surround themselves with. They act like they're coordinating the Gulf War, rather than a movie junket. Just for an example—and this isn't the worst by any stretch—I was interviewing Mariah Carey not long ago. She walked into the room, and it was like the scene with the Cowardly Lion in the *Wizard of Oz*. She came in after me, of course: they always do. But she had someone there fluffing her hair; there was another person literally straightening the bows on her knee-high lace-up boots; there was another person plucking the fluff off her angora pop-top; and another person who made sure we shot her from the right angle with the right light. This was after being kept waiting for half an hour. Yet we felt lucky, because two of the crews who had been sitting there with us had been cancelled, because she was tired. Of course, in the face of all that, she could afford to be charming and she was. She was delightful, but there were all these dragons around her.

Celebrities a little further down the food chain are easier to deal with. There are lots of famous people, artists, who are wonderful to talk to, but these *Vanity Fair* covers are a problem.

My final observation on interviewing celebrities is that the biggest thrill comes from talking to people who were your heroes when you were a kid. That gap between big and little never narrows. In fact, the people I have been most in awe of talking to are Captain Kangaroo, Lucille Ball, Julie Andrews (I couldn't believe it when I sat with Julie Andrews) and James Taylor (which was fairly recently, I was so shy I could barely look up, but I just loved that man for so long). They are a much bigger deal to me than a Jimmy Carter or Jodie Foster: someone who's big when you're big, is more a meeting of equals. Childhood heroes are huge. But, I guess, Robin Williams was the best of all.

THE "GOOD TALKERS"

The next category of interviews form a kind of amalgam. It's all the authors, "experts," journalists, academics. They're called "good talkers" (if you go to story meetings you hear that a lot: "Is he a good talker?" "Yes, he's a pretty good talker." "A really good talker." "Not a good talker." "A 0 to 10 good talker."). And they usually have lots to talk about. The trick is to elicit what they have to say—their best stories and examples and anecdotes—and try not to make it go on too long (with the greatest of respect).

"ORDINARY PEOPLE"

All three of these categories are interview professionals. What makes the final category distinctive, to me, is that they're not. We have different names for them: "civilians"; "ordinary people"; "normal people." These are people who, by virtue of being witness to, or a participant in, some great event, come to the attention of the great gaping maw of the media. Sometimes they're selected solely for their ability to represent the views of the average person. This is something the media discovered fairly recently, after the Charlottetown Accord. We decided the elites were out. We'd go and get all these "normal people" and put them in town halls and on panels and let them into the discussion and see what they thought.

The fact is, I love interviewing those people most because they're fresh territory—virgins, unspoiled, un-glib. There are so many more opportunities to be surprised and moved. Now, this doesn't happen always. The flip side is they can be disasters, because they're terrified, or because they're not used to this. You talk to these people who are sort of glassy-eyed, and their hands are trembling and they have a stress rash moving up their throats, and they can't talk. Oh great, oh good, we got a live one here. Can't get a sentence out. However, when it works, you know, those moments have enormous power, more power I think than anything else.

I was just thinking back over the last couple of months, about interviews I've done. I was thinking about Ken Jessop, quietly and in a very heartfelt way saying "I'm sorry" to the Morins, who were sitting there with him, whose son (Guy Paul) had been wrongly accused of killing his sister. I thought about Janet Connors, who's a wonderful woman, in Nova Scotia. She and her husband Randy both contracted the AIDS virus. He was a hemophiliac, through bad blood. After her husband's funeral, she was saying that she now had full-blown AIDS as well. She asked people to look at her, saying "I am the face of AIDS. I'm somebody's mother and I'm somebody's daughter. This is what we look like." Even this morning there was a woman called Yvonne Young on the program, whose brother, Donzel Young, was killed in prison. She was telling a story this morning. This woman, never having been on TV, with this amazing quiet dignity, told the story of getting home on Monday night and listening to her answering machine. She heard a message from her brother saying, "I woke up this morning thinking of you my sister, pray for me." She listened to it and thought, "That's nice" and erased. She heard five hours later that he was dead and wanted that tape back and wanted his voice back and wanted that moment back. I mean, she told that story so well your eyes would sting. And those are the moments through all the clutter of chatter on TV and radio talk that touch you and inform you and make it worthwhile.

TIPS

I'm going to give you the first commandment of interviewing. This is hardly worth the price of the trip to Regina, because it's so obvious. But, the first trick is to *listen*. And, it sounds so obvious, but I can't tell you how hard it is. I'll just illustrate this with a story. I remember so well a day that Bill Cameron, a former co-host of mine and one of the best interviewers in this country, came up to me and said he'd just finished filling in for Barbara Frum on *The Journal*. He said, "I listened to everything my guest said." And you think, "Here's this guy, I mean he's doing *The Journal*, shouldn't he be able to listen?" But it's just an illustration of how hard it is. *The Journal* is a scary show, you know it has scary music, scary producers, scary guests, scary everything. To be able to be confident and comfortable enough to control the questions, know where you're going, have your line of thought worked out, a bit of a strategy, but to then be able to relax, to see what comes at you and play with that and move it along, or ignore it or say, "What do you mean by that?" That requires lots of practice and experience. Needless to say, it is the key to a good interview.

Apart from listening, preparation is obviously critical. You've got to read, you've got to research and you've got to think. What do you want to know from this person? What does your audience want to know from or about this person? You think about what might provoke them, what might get a story, what might release them, what might unlock those lips of wisdom?

Good questions are obviously important, but they're not critical. It's my view that it is as much *how* you ask the question as *what* you ask. I've had a lot of experience with this. A *rococo* statement (one of my specialties), or a gesture, or a noise, or just a "hm" often will get as good a response as some perfectly parsed question. There are some exceptions to this. One is Margaret Thatcher. Before I interviewed her—talk about *The Journal* being scary—I did five hours of preparation for a 15-minute interview. I watched a documentary, I read her book and I did something I rarely do, which is write out questions verbatim. I thought long and hard about what to say because she's one of these people, like Clyde Wells, who'll start picking your question apart. They'll start correcting your quote or your misapprehension, or your punctuation, and that's just a waste of an interview. That's not giving you anything in an answer—it may give you a small glimpse into a character, but probably nothing you don't already know.

Silence is a really important and seldom-used interviewing tool. It is also one that takes a very long time to learn. A sound vacuum worries people. People are uncomfortable with it, they want something to happen. Unfortunately, very often in an interview, when there is silence, the interviewer, thinking it's their job, will leap in, with an answer, or another question. However, if you can force yourself to resist the temptation to fill that awkward silence, then maybe your guest will.

It is a very clever thing to try and do. You get surprising results, if you try and think of it like a chess game and just wait, wait that extra beat or two. Make sure the person is absolutely finished. Even if they thought they were finished, they might then give just one more thing. It is a very, very useful thing to do.

Some people prefer dead straight interviews, where the interviewer is just the straight man—an interviewing machine, unobtrusive. I, personally, as a viewer and a participant, like something to rub up against, between the interviewer and interviewee. It is obviously more important to hear what the interviewee has to say. You're there to hear their story, or their explanation, or their experience. But I still like a full blown person in that interviewer's chair. I find much more often you'll get a surprise that way: you're less likely to see some Arthur Murray thing that you've seen many times before.

Peter Gzowski, another one of your distinguished Minifie Lecturers, had a really interesting analogy. He likens an interview to a canoe trip, which is the classic Canadian analogy. He says the interviewer is in the stem steering, or it goes nowhere. And this is completely true. If the guest won't talk, the interview will not work. It's a disaster. Often the interviewer thinks it's their fault.

I'll tell you the exact moment when I snapped. I was interviewing Holly Hunter, the actress, about the movie *The Piano*, which I loved. So, I'd seen the movie, I spent half an hour or so reading clippings and going through things and making notes, and I interviewed her on one of those days when she was doing one of these interview junket things. I came in the room, sat down, we tried schmoozing, cappuccino, this and that. I ask questions that I obviously think are reasonable questions that are worthy of consideration and time and she just couldn't be bothered. I kept going. There was a crew there, people who've gone to trouble, and the people back at the station are expecting an interview with Holly Hunter. But at that moment, I decided I'm too old for this. You know, "I may be your 30th interview honey, but you're my 10,000th. And I've put enough time and effort into this that you can play along. This is a *quid pro quo*." So the next time, I'm stopping it. It hasn't happened yet, but I can't wait to say to someone "Well, we are clearly wasting each other's time." And it will happen. In fact I'm almost looking forward to it.

Interviewers have their own style or tricks of the trade (or tricks, just plain tricks). One of the things I'm a firm believer in is the warm up. This isn't the same for all interviews. I used to see Barbara Frum sitting with people before they started talking, just looking down at her notes. This was what she did, that's how she was comfortable and how she approached it.

Maybe it's these live interviews or the short time I have mostly, but I'm determined to make *sure,* as best I can, that this guest, who's sitting across from me will perform, talk, play, paddle, so this canoe goes somewhere other than in circles. And, depending on what I feel is required, I will cajole, calm, bully, tease, stage-manage, turn handsprings, sometimes in 60 seconds which is maybe all I have before a conversation starts to try and lay the groundwork for this interview. Energize the person, make them think that five minutes is critically important and they can't warm-up into it because of course it's over just before they get going. Too bad, I've seen that happen too many times. So I really do maybe come on strong. Sometimes people take an immediate dislike to me. But, it's a risk I'm willing to take for the benefits the rest of the time.

There's also an element of seduction to interviews. The intense eye contact of an interview is duplicated only in a very heavy-duty flirtation. You do find yourself staring into someone's eyes with that "you're the most fascinating person I've ever met." Sometimes afterwards, you think, "Oh, what was I thinking?" Sometimes you're faking it and I'm not telling you when. But lots of time, I mean really, if you're gazing into the eyes of someone like Joni Mitchell or Pete Townsend or Gloria Steinhem, Dr. Spock, Lucien Bouchard, it is very easy to be caught up in these people and eye contact obviously is critical. Does it matter if you like the person or they like you? No. I mean sometimes I think it is actually better if something's going on. Again, this is the idea of something to rub up against, particularly if it's a personality interview. I don't know if you remember the interview that Barbara Frum did with Margaret Thatcher. But, sparks flew, it was uncomfortable to watch, but it was so fascinating to look at both of them and how they were handling the situation.

So, to sum up, the advice on interviewing is: preparation; big warm up; what you ask and how you ask it; using silence to get more; and, above all, *listen*.

CONCLUSION

As an acknowledged journalistic form, interviewing is about as old as Canada, said that reference in the *Oxford English Dictionary* of 1869. Print interviews obviously have their niche, their strengths, but they have been superseded, like many other aspects of journalism, by the electronic media, radio and television—particularly television. It is interesting to think that our most vivid impressions of our contemporaries come from interviews. Most of the information we receive now in our lives comes from one person asking questions of another person. So, what people say, how they say it, how they handle a question, really determines, to a very large extent, our opinions of them and whatever it is they represent. So, this confers substantial power on the interviewer, and we take it seriously, whether you are a tough, aggressive interviewer like Jack Webster or Mike Wallace, or an affable, tell-me-more type like Peter Gzowski.

I don't know if people feel they are over-interviewed. There's an advent now of cable television and satellites and endless signal clutter, all-news, all-talk, all-interview, all-talking-head TV. Sometimes it seems like: a) either everyone in the world has been interviewed; or b) the same people are being interviewed everywhere. And the question arises: Is it just sickening? I mean is the currency debased by all these endless chat shows and interviews? Do you immediately think "Oh, Shut Up" when you see a couple of talking heads on TV? And I think the fact is, *no*, which is pretty interesting. When there's a compelling guest (and you don't even have to know who it is), how often have you been not even paying attention and you just start to listen. You start to watch even though you don't even know who that is? You know if you've got an interesting guest, with someone steering the conversation along, when it is surprising, or challenging or honest, you listen. The fact is, in the history of the world I don't think we have found anything much more interesting than a good conversation with a fascinating person. That hasn't changed. The technology to broadcast it has, but the fundamentals of conversation have not.

I mentioned Charlie Brown and the football earlier. You know that cartoon—he's always there, taking another shot at it, ending up flat on his back. Or, one of my favourite lines is from Wilbur the pig in *Charlotte's Web*, which gives you an indication of my intellectual capacity. One of the lines from that book is "Wilbur ran again to the top of the manure pile, full of energy and hope." And I feel like that quite often. I think interviewing is like that. It's unpredictable, because it involves other people. So hope springs eternal. You never know, though. You never know what you are going to hear, and what you are going to be able to get out of somebody. So that's what keeps you going and that's what makes it such a privilege to be able to do what I do and to be part of the conversation.

Thank you very much.

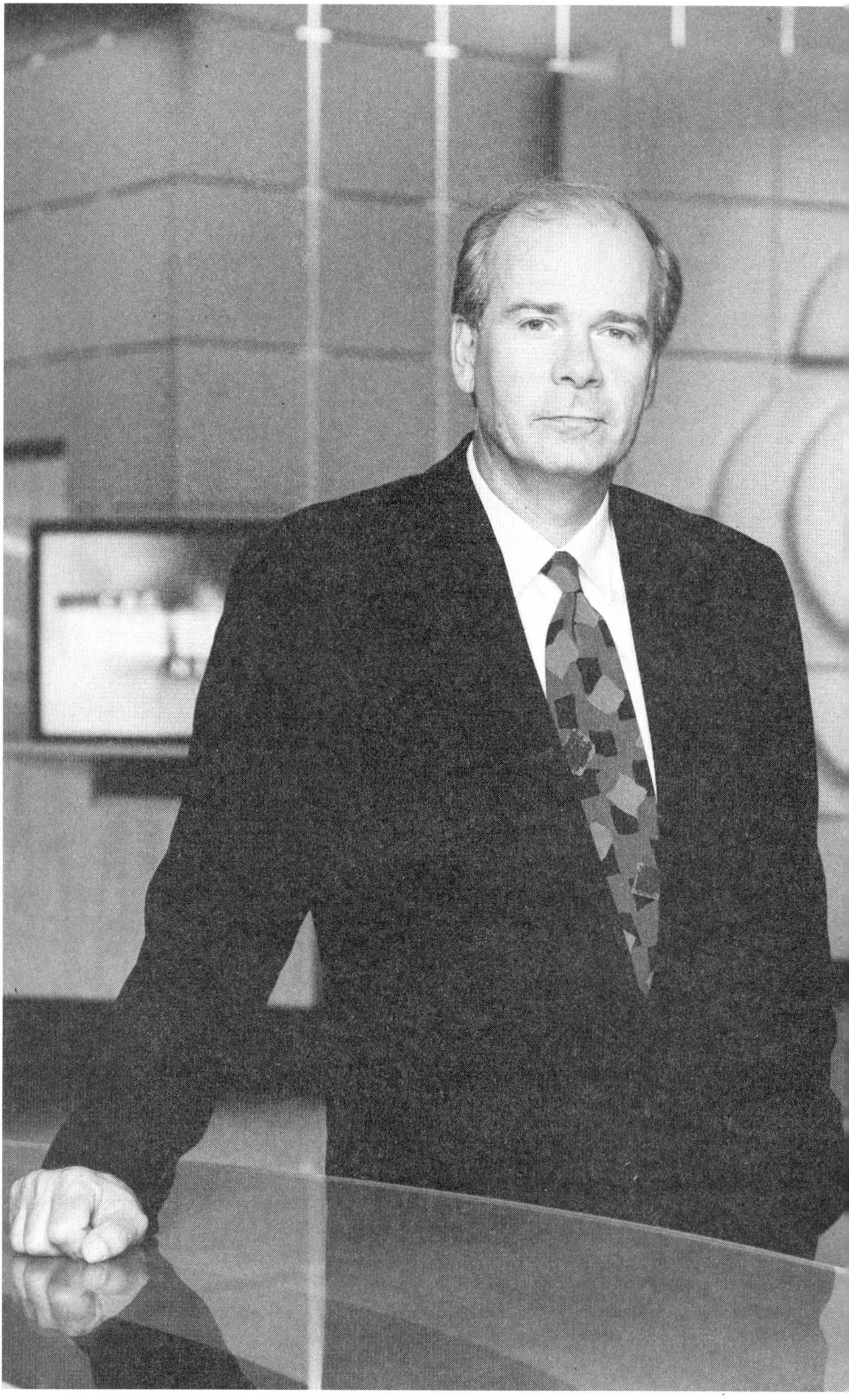

—1996—
PETER MANSBRIDGE

Since 1988, Peter Mansbridge has been the Chief Correspondent of CBC News and anchor of its flagship nightly news program, *The National*. He anchors all CBC News specials and hosts CBC Newsworld's *Mansbridge: One on One*. In 40 years with CBC News, Mansbridge has provided comprehensive coverage of the most significant stories in Canada and around the world. Mansbridge has received 12 Gemini Awards for excellence in broadcast journalism, and six honorary degrees. In 2008 Mansbridge was named an Officer of the Order of Canada.

1996 | PETER MANSBRIDGE

CANADA WITHOUT CBC NEWS:
A Win or a Loss?

It's not that I haven't given lectures or speeches before this one. In fact I've spoken in dozens of cities, in all 10 provinces of this country over the past 15 years. I've spoken at universities, colleges, service club luncheons, and various association dinners. I've spoken to small groups of 15 or 20, and I've spoken to larger groups, in the thousands.

But I've never spoken, and that's why I find this experience humbling, I've never spoken at a gathering that is in memory of a person who means so much to me.

I never met James M. Minifie, but I feel like I knew him. I grew up with him. His voice, his name, his thoughts were a part of my childhood. In fact it's hard to imagine any Canadian who grew up in the 1950s or 1960s, who had access to a radio or to a television, who wouldn't say the same thing.

I grew up in a family where listening to the major CBC Radio newscast in the morning was not an option. It was a required part of the daily routine. It was as important as orange juice and cereal. And that meant you heard James M. Minifie almost every morning, and it was from him that you learned about the major issues facing the world. The Cuban Missile Crisis . . . the Kennedy Assassination . . . the Vietnam War. I can still hear his distinctive voice . . . I can still remember his solid journalism . . . and I will never forget his trademark sign off.

In some ways he was Canada's Edward R. Murrow and it bothers me that so many young Canadian journalists know the Edward R. Murrow name before they know Minifie's. So while I'm humbled to give my thoughts on journalism in a lecture bearing his name, I at the same time applaud the University for keeping the Minifie name, the ideas, his values, alive so future generations of Canadian journalists will know their heritage as well as they know their southern neighbours'.

That is a point I can't make strongly enough. It is a passion for me. And it is something that concerns me greatly. And perhaps that's why I've picked the title you've seen for my comments this evening: Canada Without CBC News: A Win or a Loss?

There will be no mystery to you what I think the answer is to that question. My hope here tonight is to ensure that your answer is the same as mine. I'm not here to enter a debate with federal politicians who want to cut the CBC. That's not my job, or my role. I'm not here to enter into a debate with some of Canada's private broadcasters who feel there's no need for a CBC. I may get into that argument, but that's not why I'm here. And I'm not here to defend the status quo. Because I don't always believe in the status quo.

I am here to challenge you to try to imagine a Canada without the CBC, and specifically without CBC news. What kind of a Canada would we have? What kind of Canadian journalism would we have? And is that the kind of Canada that you want, or the kind of Canadian journalism that you want?

Let me make one thing clear before I go any further, because I don't want there to be any misunderstanding about the remarks that follow. I have an enormous amount of respect for the journalists who work in other news organizations in this country, especially in my field of television news. There is no doubt that CTV News—various organizations within CTV, like BBS [Baton Broadcasting System] here in Saskatchewan—is a respected news organization, with solid journalists. I've worked with many of the CTV people over the years. In fact, many of the CTV and BBS people began their careers in television journalism with the CBC. And the same goes for Canwest Global . . . a news organization that works very hard and has my respect. Now, having said that, I want to talk about the CBC's role, its place, its need in this country.

I see the CBC as one of a dwindling number of national institutions that help define this country. We've lost a few over the past decade . . . some have gone with a fight, others have gone with a whimper. All have taken with them a little of how we define ourselves as a country and as Canadians. There are those who now argue that the CBC should be sent to pasture as well.

Some reorganizing of national institutions should be expected in the life of any country . . . the old order giving way to new ideas and new institutions. But there's no sign on the horizon that I see, of a new national cultural organization to replace the CBC. And for those, like myself, who worry that Canadian culture is becoming even more of a minority culture in its own land than it ever was, that would be a travesty.

From the beginning of this country, Sir John A. Macdonald was looking for ways that the country could bind itself together from east to west. Without those bindings, our first Prime Minister argued, a pull from south of the border would make a north-south binding inevitable.

And while Sir John A. was a lot of things, even he couldn't have foreseen the birth of a binding institution that would link Canadians from east to west electronically—first by radio waves, and then later by television signals as well.

The CBC was founded to serve that purpose, and that is still its aim, still its mandate, still its continuing goal. A lot of other networks have joined the business over the years in both radio and in television. And because of that some people feel it's time to cut the public broadcasting ties. After all they do cost you a billion dollars a year. Cut those ties and allow the marketplace to be governed exclusively by the private broadcasters. That would lead to a Canada without the CBC and again, that's my challenge to you this evening. Imagine that country.

James M. Minifie left the CBC in 1968. As it happens, I first began working for the CBC in that same year, part time. I joined full time a year later, in 1969.

1996 | PETER MANSBRIDGE

THE GOOD OLD DAYS?

I think it's worth remembering a few things about the CBC of that era, the late 60s, because many of our present-day critics, in backing up their argument that it's time to get rid of the CBC, say things like, "The CBC isn't what it used to be. If it was as good as it used to be then it would have more support now." Interesting points. Are they correct?

Let me give you a sense of the CBC Television's prime time schedule (when I say prime time I'm talking about the evening hours), in the year that James M. Minifie left the CBC. It might help answer the question . . . has the public broadcaster improved in its efforts to define the country, or has it lost ground?

What were some of the most popular programs on the CBC—Canada's public broadcaster in its so-called Golden Era—in 1968? The number one show: *Bonanza*; number two: *Ed Sullivan*; number three: *Rowan and Martin's Laugh-in*; number four: *Red Skelton*. What is common about all those programs is that they're all American.

And the list of US produced shows on the CBC TV Schedule in the sixties went on—*Bill Cosby*, *Green Acres*, *Walt Disney*. CBC Radio was a lot different back then as well. For starters, it had commercials and lots of them. A couple of the most listened to CBC Radio programs that year—The World Series and the Frazier-Ellis World Heavyweight Boxing Championship. That was before the Blue Jays and the Expos.

Of course, it was a different time. Most Canadians didn't have access to those American shows because it was before the explosion of satellites and cable. But that's not really the point. The point is that three decades ago this country's national public broadcaster was airing a lot more American programming in prime time than it was airing Canadian programs.

What was Canadian (and there was Canadian programming then) was great: *This Hour Has Seven Days*, *Tommy Hunter*, *Front Page Challenge*, *Juliette*, to name just a few.

But taking a hard look back to the "Golden Era" does help keep some things in context—in particular it tells you that the CBC has been marching in the right direction in terms of Canadianizing its schedule and therefore in its attempts to fulfill its obligation of reflecting this country to its citizens.

Yes, we still run American programming. But our reason now is different than it was 30 years ago. Then we ran American programming. As I said, for most Canadians, they couldn't see it any other way and so there was a certain obligation to run it. Today we run it for advertising revenue. That's a sorry sign of the times.

But make no doubt, the pendulum has swung, most of the programming that tops the list of most watched CBC television shows now are not American. They are Canadian. Names like the *Royal Canadian Air Farce*, *This Hour Has 22 Minutes*, *Hockey Night in Canada*, *North of 60*, *Rita MacNeil*, CBC *Sunday Night*

Movies and *Road to Avonlea*—programs that cut across the mosaic of Canadian arts and entertainment and drama.

THE MANDATE REMAINS: NEWS & CURRENT AFFAIRS

The heart of CBC's TV schedule and mandate, and among its most watched productions, remains the same today as in Minifie's time—programming that relates to news and current affairs. Whether on radio or on television, Canadians can find no other organization in this country which affords so much time, and specifically so much prime time, to Canadian programming that informs and enlightens on the issues of the day.

Consider for a moment just some of what the public broadcaster's journalists present in prime time in a normal week, while our competitors either replay or in some cases ape American entertainment programming. We're running *the fifth estate, Venture, Witness, The Health Show, Undercurrents, Marketplace, The Nature of Things, Man Alive*. It's an honour for me to share a stage with Roy Bonisteel, the man who made that program a household name. Those are all names that have become familiar to Canadians. They are names that represent areas of Canadian life that are reflected to Canadians, almost without exception, exclusively on the CBC.

And if you'll excuse me for a moment I'd like to isolate one program, and argue why it is truly distinctive and without equal in this country. And that is the one at which I work—*The National*. There is no other national network in this country, or on this continent for that matter, that devotes any part of its daily prime time schedule to news and current affairs. Only the CBC does. For an hour, every night. But what's more important is what is done with that hour. What Canadians see in that hour. What Canadians learn in that hour. What they see about their country and their world in that hour. And what they wouldn't see or wouldn't learn in that hour if it didn't exist, or if the organization that produces that hour didn't exist.

For starters, *The National* is produced by Canadians for Canadians. It uses, almost exclusively, items researched, edited, written, reported and produced by Canadians. This is not a program littered with American network reports lifted off American-based and produced programs. We pride ourselves with that distinction and we consider it very, very important. We think Canadians want their news reported from a Canadian perspective, not an American one. This is especially true when it comes to major international news.

I invite you to watch us, and any of our Canadian competitors, on any night of the week. Count the number of reports *The National* takes from an American network. I'd be surprised if you saw more than one a month, and then only a story that covered a fire, a flood, a crash. You won't see a major international story with political or diplomatic overtones reported on our newscast by anyone other than a Canadian correspondent.

At the same time, please watch our competitors. When I do, on some nights I see three or four reports from American networks on what purports to be a Canadian newscast, considered by the CRTC to be Canadian content, on a Canadian network. I'm enraged when CBC critics watch our Don Murray on the ground in Sarajevo covering Bosnia, and then watch an American report narrated from London about events in Sarajevo on another Canadian network and then conclude that the two newscasts are the same. They are wrong. They do us and they do Canadians a disservice when they make that claim.

Is the litmus test of a television newscast in this country how well one records and plays back stories from other networks? Or is the test how well you use your own resources to tell stories from across your country and around the world?

None of this is an attack or a criticism of American journalism nor should it be seen that way. Instead it's a reflection of the fact that American journalists, quite correctly, report on international events in a way that reflects American values, American concerns, and those are values and concerns that are not always shared, as we well know, by Canadians.

THE NATIONAL: MORE THAN NEWS

But there's more than just the news of the day on *The National*. In the great tradition of *The Journal*, but updated to reflect a new generation, *The National Magazine* is bringing into Canadian homes journalism not seen anywhere else. Where else in the past few months could Canadians see things like:

- Our series *What Kind of Canada?:* a regular exchange of ideas, debates and conversations about where the country is going and why. This series has gone to the heart of the very issue that confronts us all: "Who are we?" This is not an inconsequential time in the history of our country. Where else do you see these debates on our national television landscape?
- A behind-the-scenes documentary like *The Managers,* where we went behind the closed doors of a major Canadian hospital facing cuts. We watched how the decisions were made, who made them, who was affected. While other networks may mention cuts, we went behind the headlines and showed the real economic and human story. We devoted resources and time to tell a story that all Canadians are experiencing directly or indirectly: the pain of laying off, or of being laid off. We told the story through the people involved on both sides.
- When Robertson Davies died, where else could Canadians gather together to celebrate his work, and explore what he left this country. It was a celebration of our culture.
- Another documentary, *Where it Hurts,* profiled the people who lived in a poor neighbourhood of a major Canadian city and let them tell

their stories of what it's like to live on the edge. It wasn't patronizing. It wasn't a story told by a reporter. It was *cinema verité*, and it gave a voice to people often marginalized by society, and worse, people often marginalized by the media.
- Just two weeks ago, CBC aired *The Cape Breton Town Hall*. This was a program about a region where the jobs have left with the coal. It was remarkable for two reasons. Canadians from across the country could learn the dilemma facing those living in the communities across Cape Breton. But they could also learn that we're all in this together—the crisis in Cape Breton is a national issue. We let Cape Bretoners talk to each other that night and hundreds of thousands of Canadians listened in and learned more about their country.
- Laurie Brown's documentary, last week, on fathers and sons and hockey. What could have been more Canadian, but less discussed on television? Told through the experiences of ordinary and not-so-ordinary Canadians, this program plumbed the depths of the very personal relationship between a father and son; and how in so many cases, in this country, that relationship was built on early mornings and backyard hockey. This was so good, and so Canadian, that the Hockey Hall of Fame has asked for its own copy to have on continuous display at their building.

I could go on. In fact I could go on for a long time offering examples of what we do that no one else in this country does on a national scale. I won't. In fact I rarely do this kind of CBC boosting speech. The people at CBC headquarters used to beg me to go out on the road and talk about all the wonderful things we do, but I've always refused and opted instead to take journalistic issues and tackle them on the road in my speeches. And sometimes those speeches aren't entirely flattering to my work. I can and have been critical, at times very critical, of the work we do as well.

So why this? Well let me be blunt. I understand criticism. I welcome criticism. The CBC has become a better organization by learning from its informed critics. However, I'm tired of listening to ill informed, mean spirited people tell whomever will listen that the CBC is a waste of money and that it does nothing for Canada. On that, they're wrong. And they shouldn't be allowed to sound off without being challenged.

For too long, too many of us who work at the CBC have been too silent about our contribution in helping define this country. I don't mean we should be entering debates about federal budgets or political platforms or revenue raising possibilities for public broadcasting. That would be inappropriate. However, surely it is appropriate for us to defend our work, our existence and our role.

When I hear someone argue that the Canadian television landscape would be no different without the CBC, I'm appalled. That person either has a personal or professional agenda in trying to make that argument or they're simply ignorant of what it is we at the national public broadcaster offer the Canadian public.

When CTV is running *ER, America's Funniest Home Videos, Cybill* or any of the dozens of other American programs it runs in prime time, what exactly is that telling you about your country? When Canwest Global is running *NYPD Blue, Seinfeld, X-Files* or any of its dozens of other American programs, what exactly is that telling you about this country?

MORE PROOF: AWARDS SHOWS

Look at the awards programs that run on Canadian networks. The privates run the Grammys, we run the Junos. They run the Emmys, we run the Geminis. They run the Oscars, we run the Genies. Yes, they get much bigger audiences, but that simply speaks to the overwhelming influence of American culture in our society. Canada's private television networks aren't just innocent bystanders of that happening.

How does broadcasting American awards programs—and I haven't mentioned all the others from the People's Choice Awards, to the American Country Music Awards—on a Canadian network contribute to the development of Canadian talent? How are Canadians to appreciate what we grow at home if our best are denied recognition? We often lament that Canadians have to leave for the United States before we notice them. Surely part of the reason they do so is that on all but one regular English-language television network in this country, prime time homage is paid only to American talent.

If these armchair critics want to be asking questions like, "Why do we need the CBC?" they should ask that. We should answer it. Maybe they should also be asking, "Why do we need CTV and Global, we already have access to American networks?" And if the answer is "Who cares, they don't use public money," well that answer isn't totally correct. Obviously no network depends on the public purse in any way like the CBC does. But, the private networks do some Canadian programming beyond news, and in most cases that programming is supported by Telefilm dollars, and those are your dollars. It's also useful to remember that even the private networks are using public airwaves.

But then, as I said earlier, I'm not here to dump on the privates... They're in existence to make money for their shareholders and if they're convinced that the only way they can make money is to run almost exclusively American programming, or make Canadian programming helped by your tax dollars that often has more of an American feel than a Canadian feel so they can sell it outside Canada, well that is their business.

But it's not our business. Our business is to work for our shareholders and deliver to our shareholders, you the Canadian taxpayer, the Canadian public, a channel devoted to Canadian interests. To offer Canadians an insight into their country that no one else does and no one else can.

CANADIANS VALUE CBC

In spite of what you may hear, most Canadians do recognize the value of the CBC. I won't quote from CBC research—you'd be correct to wonder about just how impartial that might be. Instead let me quote from one of the country's leading public opinion surveyors, the Angus Reid Group. Last summer Reid conducted an extensive survey into Canadian perspectives on the news media.

About CBC television news, Reid concluded—and these are his words not mine—that Canadians "rate the public network as far more believable than private networks or US networks."

It's not just polls, surveys and studies that bear out that point. One of the largest television audiences in this country in the past 25 years happened last October 30. It was referendum day in Quebec. Quebecers made their choice on a ballot. Millions of other Canadians made their choice—how to watch the results—by choosing a network, and as often happens every time there's a major news event in this country the decision was an overwhelming one. The CBC crushed its opposition that night—all of its opposition. All of its opposition combined.

I remember two other recent events where Canadians chose the CBC, but on those occasions the decision was even easier because there was little or no competition. It's debatable whether there should have been competition, but it's not debatable whether the CBC, the public broadcaster, should have been broadcasting.

The first was June, 1994. It was the 50th Anniversary of D-Day; the day allied troops hit the beaches in Normandy. We broadcast live from a small town in France called Saint-Aubin-sur-Mer. A town where thousands of young Canadians, many from this city, had hit the beaches half a century before, a town where too many of those young Canadians took their last breath, sacrificing themselves to liberate people they had never met from the worst evil this world has ever seen.

The ceremonies were moving reminders of our proud past. No other network covered the story the way we did—hours and hours of live coverage. One network chose instead to pick up NBC coverage from Omaha beach—that's where the Americans landed. Do I need to express how depressing that is?

The second example was May of last year. The 50th Anniversary of VE-Day, the day the war ended. We looked for a way to remind Canadians who could remember and teach Canadians who did not know, just how much this country did in the Second World War. How so many Europeans still remember, still teach their children about something that we don't teach ours. Teach them about the Canadians who came to save their country, and about how so many thousands, 42,000, died doing just that.

So we chose to go to Holland. And we brought Canadians the single most emotional day of television that I've ever been part of. Hundreds of thousands of Dutch lined the streets of a community called Apeldorn to cheer, and to hug, and to touch, and to kiss, to hail, to honour—to worship would not be too strong a word—Canadian veterans who had liberated Holland 50 years ago. It was a day you could be so proud to be a Canadian. And you could be there because of CBC News.

If you watched it, then among other things, you saw the daughters of a Canadian soldier who was killed in Holland in 1945. These two women had never been to their father's grave before. They told us what seeing the grave meant to them. They told us what was in their hearts when they saw Dutch children laying flowers at their father's grave. They told us it brought them peace to understand that they grew up as children without a father because he had sacrificed his life for other children.

We broadcast live more than 35 hours of VE-Day ceremonies over four days. It was public broadcasting at its best. There was not a commercial minute. No other Canadian network was on the air with this story. No other network broke into their morning fare of American games and tabloid talk or afternoon American soaps to tell that story. If the CBC hadn't told that story who would? Nine million Canadians learned something that weekend about their past. That's how many Canadians chose to dial into that coverage. They also learned something not just about our past, but about why there's a need in this country for a national public broadcaster.

We should be able to make that argument at the CBC every day with everything we do. If we can't, then that's when there'll be an argument to close the CBC down. That's when I'd have trouble standing here arguing anything different.

As far as I'm concerned we are delivering on the argument for the CBC, now more than ever. When this fall arrives, in spite of the budget cuts, the corporation will be more committed to that goal than at any other time in its history. CBC Television will go 100 percent non-American in its fall prime time agenda. I say, it's about time. Now let's start working on the rest of the schedule!

So, am I proud to be a part of the CBC, and especially CBC News? With every fibre of my being.

Do I think the CBC is perfect? No. Not all our shows win awards. Some of our shows should never win awards!

We are the people who fixed what wasn't broken when we moved *The National* from 10 o'clock to 9 o'clock, changed the name and the format. It was a stupid, bone-headed move and quite rightly it cost us a great deal of public support.

We're the people who air too much (two months) of professional playoff hockey, making people quite rightly question our commitment to journalism. No other network on this continent, private or public, treats its flagship broadcast with such disdain.

WHAT WOULD MINIFIE THINK?
In conclusion let me tell you that, after I was asked to deliver this lecture, I began to wonder. What would James M. Minifie think of CBC News today?

Well, I'm sure he'd be amazed about some of the things we have accomplished: CBC news bureaus inside the country from sea to sea to sea; foreign correspondents not only in Washington, London and Paris as we had in his day, but also now in Moscow, Beijing, Johannesburg, Jerusalem, New Delhi and Mexico City. We have a 24-hour news channel. We have a second 24-hour news channel beaming the Canadian view on news to international destinations.

And I'm sure that James M. Minifie would be astonished at the quality of the people at CBC News today. The days of the hard-boiled men smoking and drinking their way through lives in journalism are long gone. Today's journalists simply don't have time for that—not that they wouldn't want to—but the incredible advancement of technology has meant air time is the deadline, and you can feed live into the newscast from almost anywhere in the country and the world.

As for the correspondents of this day, I'd be happy to match our group of men and women who cover the foreign beats with those of past years. I'm sure James M. Minifie would have no trouble at all calling people like David Halton, Anna Maria Tremonti, Don Murray, Paul Workman, Ann MacMillan, Patrick Brown and Liz Palmer "colleagues." They perform their jobs in an increasingly difficult environment with courage, dedication and excellence.

So, yes, I think James M. Minifie would look at today's CBC News and declare that it is worthy of the legacy he left us. And believe me, most of us are acutely aware of that legacy. What James M. Minifie, Matthew Halton, Norman Depoe, Knowlton Nash, and Joe Schlesinger have passed on to the next generation is not taken lightly. They lit the torch of CBC News, they raised its reputation to the highest levels. We'll be damned before we falter.

Thank you.

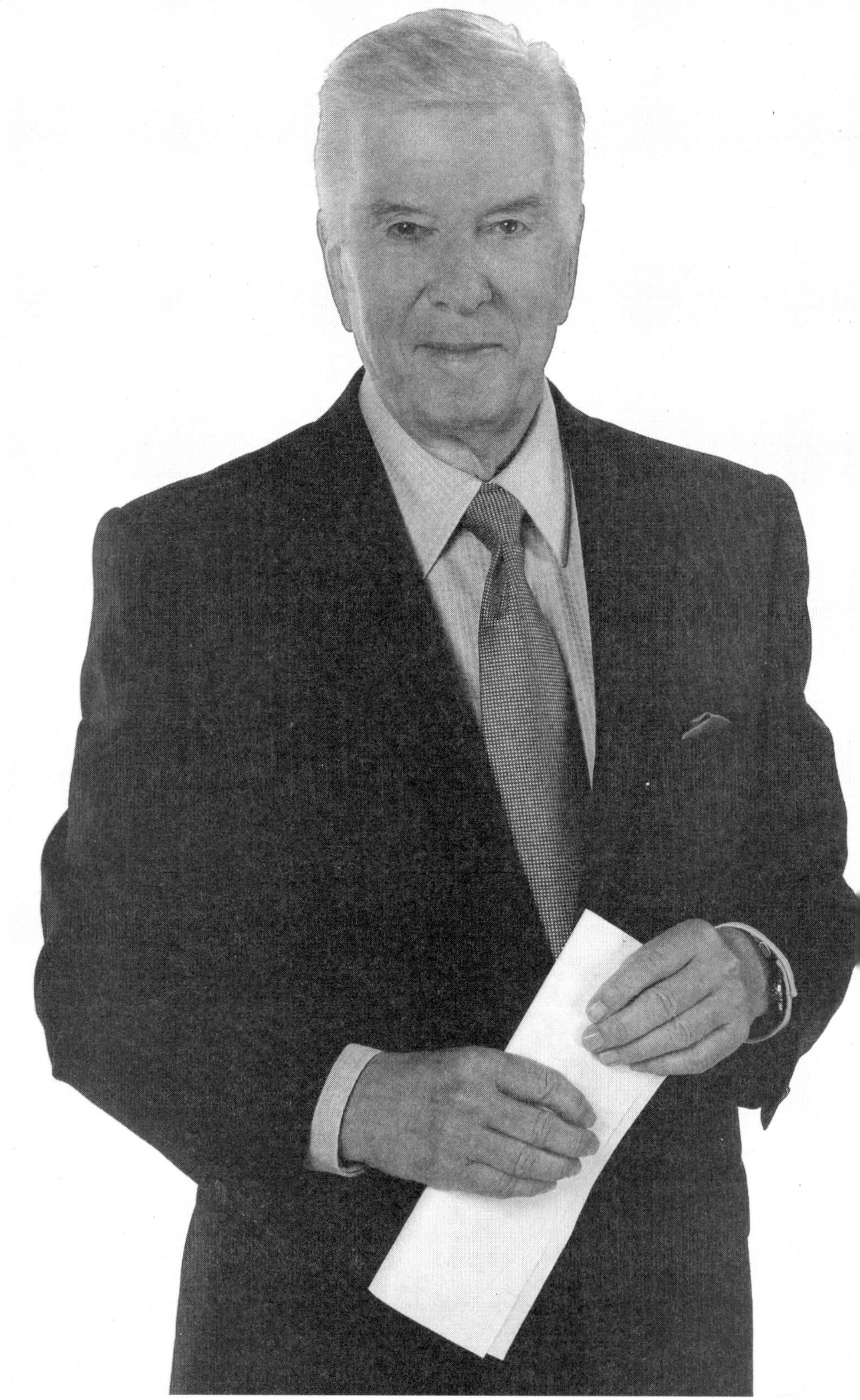

—1997—
LLOYD ROBERTSON

Broadcasting for more than 50 years, Robertson anchored CBC's national news program from 1970 to 1976. He joined CTV in 1976 as Chief Anchor and Senior Editor of CTV News, hosting *CTV News with Lloyd Robertson*. In 2007, Robertson was the first journalist inducted into Canada's Walk of Fame. Robertson also hosts CTV's awarding-winning investigative news series *W5*. In 1998, Robertson became a Member of the Order of Canada. Also among Robertson's honours are three Gemini Awards, the Radio Television News Directors' Association (RTNDA) President's Award and an honorary degree from Royal Roads University in Victoria.

1997 | LLOYD ROBERTSON

NEWS MEDIA IN THE NEXT MILLENNIUM:
Outrunning the Bear

I am delighted to be back in Saskatchewan for the beginning of spring. I also enjoy coming to Saskatchewan because so many broadcasters and journalists came from here. Pamela Wallin from Wadena (she even has a street named after her there), Allan Fotheringham, of course, from Hearne, Saskatchewan, and innumerable broadcasters who have came out of places like Moose Jaw, North Battleford, Prince Albert, Saskatoon and of course Regina, so I feel I'm coming back to a community that I know very well.

As Robbie (Ron Robbins, founding director of the School of Journalism and Communications) noted in his introduction, I was here for the opening of the school 17 years ago. The thing about Robbie that I remember most is that his eyebrows move all the time, and they are very thick. The thick glasses and the thick eyebrows. When he used to look at me through the control room in the studio when he was producing a broadcast, they would scare the living daylights out of me.

He mentioned the first computerized election broadcast. Robbie gave me a piece of information which I've never forgotten as a broadcaster about the use of computers, and I'm sure it applies to any of you who use a computer on a daily basis. "Don't let them run you, you must run them." I have never forgotten that, and it helped in terms of my many years in broadcasting because we are constantly confronted with technology; it unfolds before us all the time, advanced, yet again, from the year before. So I have been able to overcome, I think, the hump, in terms of letting it control me, by simply remembering Robbie's phrase, "don't let it run you."

Some of you out there are looking and saying "He is shorter than I thought he was." "I thought he was fatter." My young people here from the Journalism School, I addressed them this afternoon and I'm about to give them a piece of advice that Robbie gave me years ago: if you are coming into the electronic journalism field (some will go into print, some will go into broadcast), grow some skin, you are going to need it. The things people say to you. For example, I hear over and over again "Who is doing the news tonight?" That's the favourite. Now, I'm not kidding about this. I was in Venice, about 15 years ago, and my wife and I were going under a bridge on a canal and a Canadian yelled from the bridge, "Who is doing the news tonight?" You really have to get used to it. The other thing about it, I heard someone say to me this afternoon, "I've never heard you make a mistake." Ha! I think he watches the other guy. I recall my two greatest errors. The first was in 1967, when Lyndon Johnson was stepping away from running again for the Presidency in 1968, and he was making a "plea for peace" as we called it. He had asked for network time and received it, so that night we described it as a "plea for peace" in the copy, but I left out the critical letter L when I read it. It was kind of an embarrassing moment. And, of course, there was the night that I was at CTV and I had been there for about a year and was feeling very comfortable and I said "Goodnight for CBC News." Harvey Kirk, who was a wonderful colleague of mine for eight years, turned around to me and said "What did you say?" and I said "I finally did it." It really is a wonderful life and I can't think of anything else that I would have rather been doing these last 45 years.

TRIBUTE TO "DON" MINIFIE

I'll begin by briefly paying tribute to the man for whom this lecture series is named, James M. Minifie, and I want to acknowledge that some members of the Minifie family are in the audience tonight and I'm delighted to have met you and to share this evening with you. James M. Minifie was far advanced in his career when we first met and I recall always coming away enriched from our brief encounters. They were sometimes chance meetings in the hallway or in the parking lot and occasionally they happened after one of our on-air talkbacks when he had come up from Washington to do a "special" here at home.

Minifie was the consummate gentleman journalist. Apart from his insatiable curiosity and irrepressible wit he had a boundless enthusiasm for his life and his work. He always had time to stop and talk or just gossip; he was always ready to share his insights and opinions on John F. Kennedy, Lyndon Johnson or Richard Nixon. Near the end of his career he became deeply concerned about American power falling into the wrong hands and about the extended and, in his mind, menacing reach of the FBI and the CIA. Some of those concerns were legitimate and were laid bare for all to see with the Watergate era and the fall of Richard Nixon.

What did he teach me about becoming a better broadcast journalist? Most of all it was about communication and about being yourself. He was a masterful communicator on both radio and television. Canadians seemed to know instinctively that here was someone who knew what he was talking about and cared deeply about his subject. He worked hard to get to the essence of a story while holding a deep respect for the facts. I was to learn from him that the most important part about growing up in journalism is to keep learning, keep growing intellectually, be open to new ideas, read as much as you can and continue to develop your knowledge base. And when you are out in front of your audience be the best of what you have become.

Minifie, of course, was in radio and around television before we had all the bells and whistles and electronic aids we have today. He was to a large extent a one-man band; getting the story, putting it together and then delivering it on air. He would be amused indeed to see that our industry has now come full circle; heading back to a time when one reporter would be out there (today, camera on shoulder) getting the story, editing and narrating it and making sure it gets to air. Yes, the one-man bands are in vogue again and this new era brings us to an exciting, perhaps even a frightening new stage of electronic journalism that will test our skill levels and our collective will to hold to the standards we treasure. Newspapers are changing hands and revising formats as they continue to try to carve out their own special place in an ever expanding news universe. While television is my area of expertise and the bulk of my remarks will be geared to the changes on the tube, newspapers have been making adjustments to realities for several years and TV news people can probably learn from print that finding your own niche in the market and holding to your plan can help assure the survival of an enterprise. All of which brings me to my title: News Media in the Next Millennium: Outrunning the Bear.

Several years ago colleagues of mine began using the phrase "feeding the bear" which related to the unrelenting demand television places on its full-time high-profile correspondents and producers. There was a time when you only had to worry about one, or at the most, two files a day for a main national news show and perhaps an early syndication feed. The major news program was probably 15 or 20 minutes in length. We would have to cram in all the news we could, all the things we thought would be of interest or importance to people in a strictly limited period of time. All that changed during the late-sixties and early-seventies when stations and networks saw an increasing public demand for news and managers began to see the glow of gold at the end of the information rainbow. News departments sprouted by the dozen and expanded and every new station that came on the air committed itself to full and complete coverage of its area. Executives in both private and publicly funded operations saw that news departments could be the anchor for the entire station or network, giving identity and credibility to their organizations. The bear suddenly got hungrier.

Along with a more highly educated populace had come an increasing demand for more information. Information became a singularly important commodity and it wasn't limited only to the traditional news of the day, that is the normal run of political stories and natural disasters. People appeared to have a craving for all levels of information; whether it was business, medical, environment or social affairs, the need to know became important. Knowledge was power. The much vaunted "Information Age" was upon us. While newspapers struggled to remain relevant by updating their formats, the bulk of responsibility for filling the information demand fell to television. It was the new kid on the block and had captured the public imagination to an extent that all other media were swamped.

There has been some leveling of the playing field since that time but generally television remains the dominant media force today. Marketing and sales departments which had formerly regarded news as a bothersome impediment to their scheduling of sitcoms and game shows, came to understand the value of giving pre-eminence to news. It added credibility to the entire medium and the stunning impact of television's live-event news coverage was there for all to see with the Kennedy assassination, the landing of men on the moon and the various dramatic moments that became part of vivid history when cameras were present during convention and election broadcasts in both Canada and the United States.

RATINGS RULE

Alas, news programming was to become ratings-driven just like everything else. News directors soon found themselves facing marketing analysts telling them who among their on-air personalities had gained audience acceptance and who hadn't, which of the stories on a given evening had caused jolts or bumps in the ratings and which had caused people to turn elsewhere. We all had to adjust to this new reality or learn to do something else and we also knew it would be important for those of us in front-window positions in the industry to try to uphold the basic values we had learned over the years from James M. Minifie, Edward R. Murrow, Walter Lippman, Norman DePoe, Walter Cronkite and the other luminaries of our times in both print and electronic journalism. It often meant reminding corporate executives, sometimes at our peril, that news was special. Programs disseminating public information had to be treated differently from the fantasy hours that dominated so much of television.

At the beginning of this period it was customary to pine for the good old days—to the time when managers paid less attention to news and we were allowed to languish in comfortable backwaters well out of the limelight of the show business of television. But most of us also realized it was more fun working in a branch of the medium people were paying attention to, as opposed to operating on the fringes.

What we were to discover, if we hadn't already known, was that television is an intensely personal medium; the public came to identify with the anchors and the senior correspondents of news programs with an often fierce and abiding loyalty. Those of us who were fortunate in gaining the public's trust then had an added responsibility in making sure we didn't abuse that trust.

Of course this period also brought front and centre a whole new group of Harry Hairspray and Mary Makeup types whose first concerns were cosmetics rather than content and a few of them are still around. I came across a 21-year-old copy of a national magazine the other day and there on the cover was a drawing of someone with face and hair very much like my own. The title of the piece was "The Pretty Face Problems of TV News." It takes a long time to get roughed up and earn your spurs in this business but I know I'm not just a pretty face anymore.

There is general agreement that the golden age for those of us working in TV news was the seventies and early-eighties. News departments had money to spend, and competition was limited to a handful of networks and a small group of local stations in communities across Canada and in the United States. We didn't have to think twice about sending reporters off to cover stories anywhere in the world. Now, of course, we are all tuned in to the bottom line and we must all bow to the siren song of downsizing, rationalizing—whatever you choose to call it. And we even have some experts forecasting our demise.

Alvin Toffler, the futurist, author of *The Third Wave* and one of the early headliners in the prediction business, forecast in a speech in 1994 that networks would become "a faint forgotten blip in the image archives of tomorrow." He said they would be replaced by the personal computer, which would bring in satellite television. The format would be digital and the system called "Invideo." There would be vast program options and the individual viewer would be his or her own producer, using a computer to put together programs of personal interest and writing their own news lineups—all of this material would be pulled down from the satellites. But TV industry experts who were there for Toffler's speech were cool to his vision. They said it can and probably will come to pass but only as one option. As Richard Parker says in his book "Mixed Signals," the telephone has been around for a long time, but only 60 percent of the earth's inhabitants have ever made a phone call. And half the world has no electricity. Another respected North American TV writer, Les Brown, said "My own reaction to Toffler's speech is that it was good theatre but questionable fortune telling. Futurists tend to be more at home with technology than human nature and it struck me that Toffler doesn't understand the dynamics of broadcast television at all." Parker and Brown know the medium and believe that broadcasters with expertise in journalism and communications will still be the purveyors of choice for most people. But even as we take comfort in that optimism we can see that technology is dramatically changing our industry and plunging us into uncharted waters.

There are now more than 2,000 satellites in orbit with 125 devoted to television relay. CNN International (as opposed to CNN US) is a decade old. Its signal can reach 200 countries and five billion people. It has been joined by BBC's World Television Service, broadcasting to four continents, and by MTV's European, Latin American and Asian efforts. In the United States there are two CNN services—the general service news channel and "Headline News." There are all-news regional channels in New York and other centres. We also have MSNBC, the all-news marriage between NBC and Microsoft. And there's "Fox," owned by international media czar Rupert Murdoch, both as an added fourth mainstream network and with its own all-news channel. Many of these services are already available in Canada as well as CBC all-news through "Newsworld" and soon the CTV news headline service. And this is only a partial list of the services available throughout the world.

Yes, the bear is getting hungrier and so ravenous that there is no longer any point in trying to keep him fed. In the next millennium we'll have to learn to outrun him.

Can we do it? And at what cost? As all of these services fight for a piece of the action, will the day come when national newscasts fade into pale imitations of shows like *Hard Copy* and will the phrase "If it bleeds it leads" (a tired maxim with which our critics love to hammer us unfairly) become the mantra for news line-up editors everywhere?

I'm prepared to say "definitely not" and go even further in saying we are turning the corner. It's becoming clear the national newscasts have already won the battle over the tabloid programs as audiences differentiate between information and titillation. True enough, we have perked up our formats to make our shows more watchable and there has been some trimming of the sails to accommodate more features and lifestyle pieces, but the national news programs can still be counted on to deliver, first of all, the major stories of the day in a comprehensive manner—and they are doing that.

We work in a visual medium and none of us should have to apologize for making effective use of our most powerful instrument—the television picture. But good editors and reporters know that "effective" in this case also means "discriminating." We must be aware of public tastes and trends and know how our separate programs are positioned in the audience's perception. If we bow too readily to what can be seen as prurient interest or sensationalism we sin against ourselves. Please understand, I'm not talking here about particular local news shows that have fallen over the edge and decided to go with a mix of crime, sex and stranded cat stories and have decided mistakenly, I think, that's what the audience craves.

MUST REMEMBER FUNDAMENTALS

Wide-ranging discussions over what should go into a program mix are a daily diet in most major television newsrooms in the country. We understand we are the guardians of a process put in place by the pioneers mentioned earlier, and while the constantly expanding demands of the medium force us to adjust to hold our audiences we must never lose track of the fundamentals things like getting it right, being fair and respecting experienced judgment and the boundaries of good taste. Yes, our critics will continue to excoriate us, some of them in shallow and uninformed manner, but all media have to understand we are regarded as a major power centre in these times and criticism simply comes with the territory. We should be among the first to encourage it and we should also be among the first to have answers at the ready for our myriad mistakes and fumbles.

While the CBC is now experiencing the agony of cutbacks, those of us in private television know all about it. We have been getting our wings clipped economically since the glory days of TV when money seemed to be growing on trees and there were budgets for all manner of ventures. We have pretty well concluded the good times will have to fade into a distant memory. The new universe will enforce that reality as we all compete for a piece of the same advertising pie. With CBC now running commercials right up in the body of its newscast we are presented with an even more competitive environment. Of course, the CBC reserves the right to seek revenue wherever it thinks it can find it, but up until now News had escaped the internal corporate pressures to squeeze in more advertising. But I'm not here to engage the argument whether CBC should be running commercials in *The National*, only to acknowledge the reality they are there. Will these commercials corrupt CBC News in some manner? I doubt it. As one who has worked for both national networks, public and private, I am often asked about the different pressures that come to bear on journalistic practices within the separate systems. Even though the question came before CBC was accepting commercials in the newscast the answer is still relevant, mainly because of the basic difference between the public and private networks. CBC is overwhelmingly funded from the public purse, from an annual government grant—CTV is totally funded through advertising. So is the pressure from advertisers on CTV News greater than the pressure from politicians on the CBC? The answer is an unequivocal "no."

Pressure from advertisers in Canada is almost benign compared to the pressure from politicians.

I have great admiration for my journalistic colleagues at CBC when they fearlessly challenge politicians or government officials regarding matters of public record. It is quite possible their questions or reports will evoke an angry phone call from a cabinet minister to a CBC official the next day. But CBC newspeople can be counted on to treasure their independence from politicians, even though their institution is ultimately answerable to Parliament, just as our CTV newspeople can be expected to show independence from Procter and Gamble or General Motors, even though we are ultimately answerable to our shareholders, and our managers must attract advertising dollars just to stay in business. As journalists we must always try to follow our own code of ethics as we attempt to assure a free press functions without pressure from the special interests.

AUDIENCE SOMETIMES UNSYMPATHETIC
And the future will not be without its challenges from a more vigilant public. Giant media conglomerates will come under increasing scrutiny and sometimes the public interest may tend to get lost in legal battles between the media organizations and the corporate entity their journalists may be investigating. Take the case of Food Lion versus the ABC network in the United States. In a striking and costly decision in January of this year a jury in North Carolina ordered ABC

to pay Food Lion more than $5.5 million in punitive damages over an undercover investigative report on the program *Prime Time Live*. The interesting point here is that the supermarket chain did not sue for libel or legally contest the accuracy of the broadcast which alleged unsanitary food handling practices like bleaching and doctoring spoiled fish and meat for resale at some Food Lion stores. Instead, the jury found ABC guilty of fraud and trespassing for the way its two producers lied to get jobs as Food Lion clerks and then shot footage with miniature cameras hidden in hairpieces. Hidden microphones and cameras are a grand old tradition of investigative journalism. But the jury was concerned ABC had gone too far by committing fraud in lying to Food Lion executives to get jobs. In a pitiful defence of itself Food Lion pointed to lost business and lay-offs resulting from the ABC item, as though those effects were supposed to excuse the supermarket for its abominable practices. But it based its strongest complaint on fraud and trespassing.

Journalism history is rich with examples of news people going undercover to expose horror stories. We can go all the way back to 1887 when Nellie Bly, a pioneer in the art of investigative subterfuge, feigned insanity to gain entry to New York City's Asylum. Her expose on the brutal treatment of patients spurred reforms in the system. There are those in journalism who object to this style. They call it "stunt" journalism and believe it has more to do with self promotion than uncovering the story. But what the critics miss is the heart of the matter. While ABC may have overstepped the boundaries, especially in allowing their people to lie to get the jobs, the public interest was ultimately served by exposing the seamy practices of the supermarket owners and in the final analysis the truth and only the truth should have reigned supreme.

The reason it didn't may be due to something else that turned up in the analysis of this case: a transparent hostility to the media from the jury panel. When a whole community gets burned with job losses and bad publicity as a result of the actions of a few reporters and producers, a negative response is quite natural. It is the responsibility of the media organizations involved to explain their actions and while the justification of digging out the truth may be obvious, wide sections of the public are clearly uneasy at the methods employed. Many have come to view media, especially television, as arrogant and uncaring. In the hurly-burly and highly competitive world of digging out stories for daily journalism it will be hard to correct the impression. The media can't expect to be universally loved and that would be wrong anyway. All we can hope for, and try to get, is a reasonable level of respect for those organizations trying to do the job properly.

Ultimately, it is choice in the new and hotly competitive universe that gives viewers the power anyway. The worst punishment for perpetrators of schlock or devious practices is to be tuned out and turned off or, in print, designated to the recycling bin.

The real concern among Canadians about the approaching proliferation of channels and satellites is a cultural one. In spite of our ability to compete on an artistic level, is there a danger we will simply be swamped and lose our sense of unique Canadian identity? This question of uniqueness has already been addressed in Europe where the onslaught of American news and entertainment programming is making considerable inroads. "Do these ventures represent a major step towards the global village?" asks media giant and one-time Prime Minister of Italy Silvio Berlusconi. He responds with an unqualified "*No.*" In the sense that events can be seen by people around the world at the same time the concept of the Global Village is valid. But as for bringing us together as a world community, no way. All these services are competing with one another and many, like the Playboy or Golf channels, are aiming at particular audiences. Berlusconi contends that once people have surfed all the alternatives they will come back to search for reflections of themselves and will continue to see the world from their own national perspectives. As Christina Ockrent, a Paris TV anchor, says, "To me, CNN is a US channel with a global vocation but which sees the world through an American prism." She believes, as do plenty of others, that audiences will continue to identify with their own.

The American television writer Les Brown thinks all of this means national network news will be around for a very long time because it has a singular purpose that matters to people. He says what is important to anchors and editors is also important to the viewer and he sees "the anchor and the reporter as having a much longer future than was expected even a few years ago."

People want their news from people who talk the way they do, and have the same outlook. Canadians want their news from Canadians, Americans from Americans and so on. This gives the national networks an affinity with their audience. Our context is Canadian and it mirrors the way we think and talk—eh?

Even in the explosion of television channels and all the spinoffs of technology on the way to the new millennium, it is still the essential human dimension that can be expected to prevail. People talking to people, telling stories, bringing a shared sense of community to all parts of the country. That's the kind of world it will continue to be.

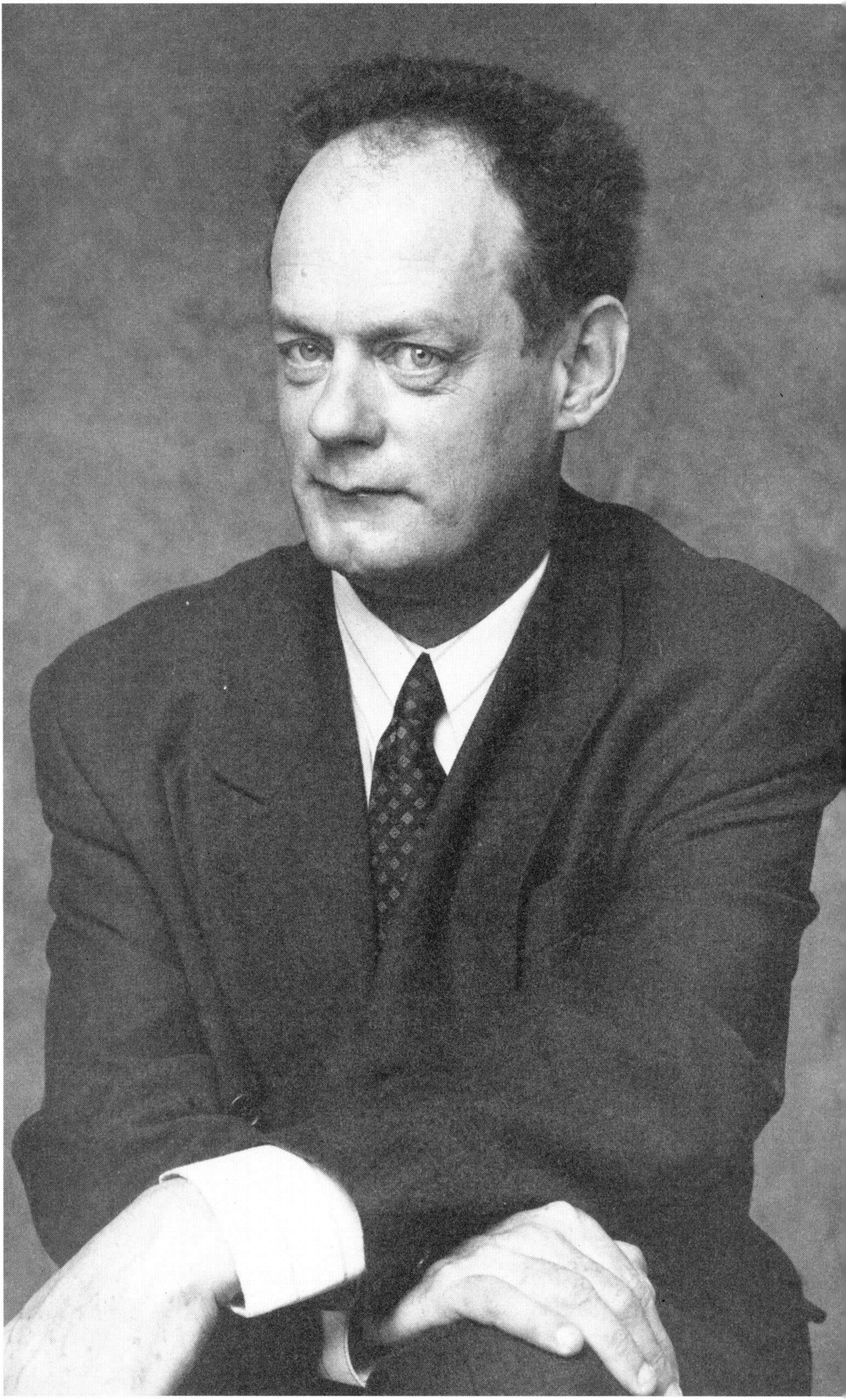

–1998–

REX MURPHY

A Rhodes Scholar, Rex Murphy ran twice for office in Newfoundland provincial elections—once as a Liberal, once as a Tory—and lost both times. Now the longest running host of Canada's national radio call-in show, *Cross Country Checkup*, Rex Murphy also contributes weekly political commentary to CBC TV's *The National*. Murphy does documentaries, writes book reviews, and a weekly column for *The Globe and Mail*. A collection of his columns, reviews and commentaries has been published in two books: *Points of View* and *Canada and Other Matters of Opinion*.

CRIES AND WHISPERS:
Late Twentieth Century Journalism

The contours of American public life offer much to the spectator, rather less to the participant. When it was revealed, for example, that on the very day Mr. Clinton accepted his party's nomination for President, his chief campaign advisor, and the author of the "family values" platform, Dick Morris, was amusing himself sucking the toes of a rented companion, America was not shocked.

But my favourite moment out of the US recently has nothing at all to do with the spate of goatishness at the White House from Mr. Morris to Monica Lewinsky. Oprah Winfrey, the Scourge of Mad Cow Disease, recently offered on her daytime show on the subject, that she would never eat hamburger again. Beef has civil rights in the US, which is probably good news to Rush Limbaugh. A group of demented Texas ranchers hauled Ms. Winfrey to court for libelling the byproducts. It's a strange country where people will go to court to protect the reputation of a chuck roast, and yet suffer a President who stands accused of more impalements than Buffy the Vampire Slayer.

We Canadians sometimes tepidly bemoan that our public life does not live up to the soap opera rigors of our American cousins, and to some degree, it is true that we do not. But we have our moments. I do not think there is a Paula Jones moment in Mr. Chrétien's career, but this does not mean that 1600 Pennsylvania Avenue has all the drama. When Aline Chrétien warded off the intruder at 24 Sussex Drive, by wielding a soapstone Eskimo carving, the episode had charm. This is true whether we regard the incident as an episode in art appreciation, or as a parable of home security—sleep lightly and carry a big knickknack.

When the separatist delegation protested Canadian flags at Nagano—the presence of the Maple Leaf in the Land of the Rising Sun—it was more than an unnerving distraction to Quebec athletes. It was difficult to fight the conclusion that they wasted the marijuana test on the snowboarder. Not that Ross Rebagliati's fable of second-hand passive pot did not have its own subtle, almost Clintonesque, insouciance.

And then there is the Speaker of the House of Commons. I have never understood why the House umpire is called the Speaker, since of course the Speaker is the only party in that subsidized Tower of Babel not allowed to participate in debate. The recent confounding by Mr. Parent, as between New Brunswick and Cuba, Frank McKenna and Fidel Castro, dazzles the mind—the Speaker may have been fatigued, though that is usually Mr. Castro's failing.

On occasions such as this, which combine a measure of ceremony and, at least for the speaker, a sense of heightened address, it is difficult to dispose of the temptation to advance upon "the large topics of our day." When I consider the venue, the School of Journalism, when I consider those who have spoken in this place before, when I consider the gentleman and journalist in whose memory these talks have been instituted, the temptation is, if I may borrow a subdued metaphor from the breakfast cereal makers, enriched and fortified. Then too, the delicious beckonings of vanity, and vanity is, I may tell you, every journalist's chosen aphrodisiac and a veritable Spanish fly for those in the broadcast trade, rather customize the inclination.

When Bryan Olney first advanced upon me, these thoughts were ripe in my mind. What to speak of? That was the question. *Civilization and its Discontents* offered itself as seemly and spacious, but then, the dreadful and prurient Sigmund Freud has already claimed that wide territory for his own clammy purposes. *The Decline and Fall of the West* had, you will agree, a certain roominess, but settling upon this as a title would open me, I quickly understood, to charges of poaching upon Spengler, or what is worse, an overt fascination with Preston Manning and Ralph Klein. *Culture and Anarchy?* True Matthew Arnold, the William Bennett of the last century, had done a nice op-ed under this banner. *Culture and Anarchy*—but then, why travel all the way to Regina, merely to rattle on about Toronto?

Instead, I have elected to do something of a survey—if I were more confident I would call it a diagnosis—of one of our national emotions. I am going to speak of the "curious" phenomenon of Jean Charest, and that extemporaneous impulse which, with some intensity, visited the country when the prospect of Mr. Charest unhitching himself from the rocket-sled of the national Tory leadership, and returning to the well-mortared trenches of Quebec politics to duel with Mr. Bouchard, became the country's "lead item" a few weeks back.

The question I have posed, and hope to shadow with an answer, has actually very little to do with Mr. Charest, and very much to do with us. Mr. Charest and his eventual fortunes in the Stygian morasses of separatist politics will be determined by time, and is best left to time for its dissection. The national emotions I hope to sketch have been with us very long, and will continue to abide. They are at the centre of how we see ourselves and our future as a Canadian community.

I think, taking not too chauvinist a view, we can be fairly pleased with our situation here. One definition of Canada from which I would be willing to take comfort is a place which didn't give birth to Jerry Springer; and further, a place where sexual mischiefs and alleged sexual mischiefs of the nation's executive don't—as yet—constitute 98 percent of public discourse. It seems to me, beggar's choice though it may be, that as between the Neverendum and the saga of Monica and Paula and Bill and Katherine, we Canadians have gotten off lucky. We may think lowly of our House of Commons now and then, but even at its worst, it will not be confused with the set of *Three's Company*.

Tracking the intricacies and realignments, redrawing the map of the political landscape, in the event of a Charest change, is a manoeuvre of considerable delicacy and finesse, comparable to unravelling a ball of cold spaghetti, and not nearly as nutritious. So many questions grow out of that move. What will be its effect on the futures of Ralph Klein and Preston Manning for example? In the words of the famous cartoon beagle Snoopy—"the theological implications alone are staggering." But I am going to bypass speculations in these misty, though inviting, atmospheres.

Rather I'd like to examine that boomlet of recent weeks and put things somewhat in scale. The drive to capture Charest for the Quebec Liberals has not been a tidal wave, nor has it been a trickle. As an emotional phenomenon I place it midway between that ancient, careless exuberance the nation (out of homage to the Beatles, I suspect) christened Trudeaumania, and what happens (for this part of the comparison, I should declare, I'm relying entirely on hearsay) when someone buys a new houseplant. It's certainly not an hysterical overreaction, nor is it the low Zen buzz that comes with a trip to Garden Centre and camouflaging the coffee table.

Quite a number of people, inside Quebec and outside, have a reasonably profound response to the idea of Mr. Charest taking on the role of federalist champion in Quebec; and rather than here assessing whether or not Mr. Charest will or will not live up to the expectations of the people who urge him to that role, I'd like to look at why, because it is unusual people have found themselves so engaged in the question in the first place. Standing back for a minute, it's a trifle astonishing that the citizens say, of Saskatchewan or New Brunswick, or British Columbia, have declared any interest at all in who will assume the leadership of the Quebec Liberal Party. The political parties of most Canadian provinces, when they are in opposition, are not madly charismatic institutions. I remember being in the backrooms of the Liberal Party of Newfoundland when Clyde Wells was in Opposition. It was like being clerk of the vestry on a slow day. It had all the glamour of being the third leg in a sack race.

And it should be noted that in ordinary times, were the leader of a national party to be the subject of massive speculation, on whether he was to step down as a national leader to enter a contest to become a provincial leader, I think the psychotherapists would be calling for a public holiday in appreciation of all the extra work going their way. But this is Quebec and, of course, politically speaking, things are never normal in Quebec, and as for normal times, politically speaking again, we haven't seen 'normal times' in this country for 30 years.

I suggest that the Charest phenomenon has much less to do with Jean Charest, than it does with us. And by us, here I mean all those citizens of this country, in Quebec and out, who are "reasonably contented" with its shape, its manner, and its ways.

Please note, in this one particular, how I have chosen to phrase the sentiment. Not jubilant, nor rhapsodic, nor riven with the spasms of ecstasy—but reasonably contented; not agitated by monstrous distresses beyond the reach of correction, nor stricken by uncontrollable or unaccountable injustices which we are coerced to endure, but reasonably contented. In any moderate scale of things, and on any moderate scale of measurement, this is a reasonable country, reasonably structured, and reasonably (I am thinking of its institutions) governed.

So the "us" here is all those Canadians who are reasonably contented. And I have said that the Charest phenomenon speaks more to us, and of us, than it does to any assessment of him. I am not seeking any diminishment of Jean Charest when I say this. Yet the force and scale of public sentiment that has been magnetized by the possibility of Mr. Charest switching parties and jobs has at least as much to do with an enduring and central Canadian dilemma as it has, in fact, to do with him.

The enduring and central Canadian dilemma is of course separatism. Journalistic myth has it that Canadians are tired of hearing about separatism. Or at least that is the myth of a thousand "morning meetings" in editorial offices and broadcast conference rooms around this country on any given day. And it is fodder for columnists and pundits from Bonavista to Vancouver Island. Your school of Journalism could add to its already achieved luster by establishing a prize, make it an annual thing, for the best column or commentary—while I think of it, you might want to trawl among the open line hosts too—huffing in the best populist accents on the theme: We're Sick of All This Quebec Business. It has a fractionally more elegant variation under the banner: Let's Put This Separatist Nonsense Behind Us and Get On With the Business of Running the Country. This is intellectual catnip for the opinion mongers. There's a journalistic cottage industry in the small art of telling Canadians, in print or on air, that they are bored with this question, why they are bored with it, that they will remain bored with it, and that they should be bored with it. I do not know why it should be so but the opinion pieces themselves, which shunt this narcotizing freight, are among the most excitable products of the late twentieth century Canadian journalistic mind. Writing these tedious bulletins evidently chews up quite a lot of oxygen. I defy the diagnosis. I scorn it and reject it. And in my softer moments I pity its sad and febrile messengers.

The great anatomizers of human sentiment in the Western tradition are the nineteenth century novelists. The regal overlords in this domain of analysis and commentary are George Eliot and Jane Austen. And while it's a bit like commandeering a pair of howitzers to dislodge a mouse, I summon their example to say they would have been tipped into apoplexy over the confusion of categories inherent in the journalistic payload under discussion here. Never confound exasperation with boredom. A considerable depth of frustration may manifest itself, have the same outward signs, as tedium, lack of response, but it shields and houses a very different emotion.

On the separation issue many, very many, Canadians feel "outside the box." We all recognize the supreme importance of the debate to the citizens of the province, where it is at the utmost and absolute centre. And we are also commendably sensitive that a debate, *intra fratres,* within the Quebec community has many prominent features, that are, the phrase sounds harsh, none of our business. The thought of our "interference" of our "intrusion" in the debate makes many Canadians recoil. English Canada, that bland phantom, very properly keeps its nose out of French Canada's business. But these categories won't do either, neither of them. And in a very operative sense what is going on within Quebec, what has been going on for three decades, while it is in its most emphatic manifestation, a discussion within Quebec, among Quebecers—has always had, and most critically, continues to have, consequences of the highest import to all citizens outside that province.

We are all of us incorporated in the consequences of the separation debate, because an alteration of a fundamental kind—a new statehood—of the province of Quebec, is inevitably, ineluctably, an alteration of a fundamental kind for the citizens in the remainder of the country. If separation wins, we're going to change too. Where we live, ironically, will probably be the site for a much more visible, more tangible set of consequences than in the house of separation itself.

Knowing this instinctively, or at the level or articulation, feeling the anxieties that attend the realization, sensing something profound and undesirable always around the corner—yet simultaneously abiding by the tacit understanding, living the tact of non interference—most Canadians, I believe, suffer an immense sense of impotence; they are spectators at a play that is not a play; they are an audience in their own national drama; they are profoundly outside the central exchanges and calculations of their own futures or destiny. People object to being witnesses of a process in which they feel they should, in some way, be agents. It is this equivocation in the role that citizens outside Quebec have been asked to sustain—you're involved, but you're not involved; you should speak out, but maybe it's better you didn't; of course the future of the country is your business, but the referendum is Quebec's business—it is this equivocation, this mixture of contradictory impulses, that feeds those difficult and strained responses to the dreaded "Quebec question," and makes it the monster that for many it really is. Why ask me what I think, if really, in the end, I can't *do* anything.

When it impinges on questions of country, politics is an emotional business. The response of Canadians, who are not separatists, to the enduring threat of Canadian dissolution is a confederation (I am being metaphorical here) of disparate and often conflicting emotions. Respect, alarm, concern, anger, frustration, high-mindedness and impatience. At various times, depending on the state of the crisis, one or other of these emotions predominates. Three days before the last referendum, before Brian Tobin made himself the travel agent for all those Canadians outside Quebec who saw the ship of state heading for the Falls, it was alarm. Referendum over, hair-splitting win for the No side, and it's a mix of anger and relief. No referendum immediately on the horizon and generally it's displayed unease, weariness, and that state of perpetual low level exasperation and resentment. It's that mode of resentment we feel when we are vaguely summoned to expend energies on matters we feel either should have been settled already, or that we have dealt with so often before that expending further energy seems pointless, futile and (if we're being honest) in some way demeaning.

Canadians have more mood swings on separatism than Hamlet has soliloquies. I must indulge a brief digression. It doesn't help that every now and then some Senator who's not living on the Costa del Sol or paving Mexico with loonies, says ex-Cabinet Minister Pat Carney, emerges from the sleep of the flushly retired partisan, to announce, say, that British Columbia is going separatist too. A separatist threat, led by the Senate. Now there's a counter-revolution. We really are going to have to schedule more bingo games for the Senate, or insist that after bed-count there are to be no press releases. We've done this dance now for over 30 years. And in that tormented interim the collective response outside Quebec has wilted, and in some cases, petrified into a reluctant hostility.

We are a country that, by comparison with others, is remarkably spared a Big Headline history. After watching Ken Burns' documentary on the American Civil War, I recall thinking, aside from how well the series was done, how lucky Burns was to have at his disposal, so to speak, such a tale.

It *was* a Civil War—the bloodiest and most terrifyingly intense of all conflicts. It was a conflict with an unambiguous moral centre: the issue of slavery. It was the issue, in other words of whether it was right, or just, that one set of human beings should own another set, to use, abuse, torment and dispose in any manner whatsoever, purely on the basis of skin color. It had great citizens and generals. Grant and Lee would not be out of place in an Homeric epic. There was the ferociously eloquent black leader, Frederick Douglass. And there were those moments—so many of those moments—of high courage, individual transcendence, of pity and glory, that resonate right at the heart of human memory and regard. Finally, of course, there was Abraham Lincoln, a shepherd of his people in a time of great trial; surely the most gifted and spiritually resourceful of all those who have occupied the White House, of all those that is, who regarded it as something other than a convenience store for the slaking of decaying appetites, and a gyroscope for the amusement of spin doctors. There was an idea at the centre of this conflict, the nature of America. There was a great moral cause, slavery, constituting its present incarnation. And there was a full human being,

Abraham Lincoln, to articulate its costs, navigate its terrors, and celebrate the dead. Idea, cause and leader. The proportions of a gratifying symmetry.

I raise this here not because I feel any diminishment because our story does not share the heroic and crowded proportions of the American one. It would take a dementia superior even to mine to envy another country its civil war. I present it rather because it is the central event in the fashioning of our neighbour nation, and as a massive illustration. It is an illustration of the kinds of circumstances and the types of issues that justify the conflict they aroused. There was in the American story, in other words, an issue, the future of the nation, and a cause, that of slavery, which was proportionate to the actions, and the conflict, which determined that America continue.

This is not true in our, the Canadian, case. The separatist project is hollow at its centre. It lacks the proportion of cause to effect. What is the "occasion" that justifies so massive a response as the dismantling of a functioning, harmonious, and civil country? Where is the grievance in Quebec that is so central, so profound, and so injurious, to the pride and functioning of that province and its people—that matches, that justifies the utter removal of that province from the country of which it is a founding member?

Simple enough to assert, if you're not a Quebecker, some might rejoin. Well, just to demonstrate it's not merely idle assertion, let's test the case. Can any of us imagine, or speculate upon circumstances which might justify the threat to separate or justify the objective of doing so? Well, yes. Very easily.

Civic injury or civic impediment to any group or province for one thing. If there were in the Canadian constitution, or in practice, restrictions on the democratic franchise for French-speaking citizens of Quebec, and only on them, then the idea of separation would very easily be justified. Let us, for argument's sake, imagine a circumstance in which such citizens were by statute or custom, barred from holding the office of Prime Minister. Now I realize that the prime ministership is only one office in the federal government, but there are times, though not as many as I'd like to see lately, when it can be very important. It can actually have a sway in what the country does, and how it thinks of itself.

If there were a law that said, for example, no citizen from Saskatchewan could be prime minister, then I can easily see Roy Romanow saying: "Hey, that's not right, and we're not going to take it. Change the rule or we're leaving." And he'd be right. The same would be right for Quebec. But if the experience of the last 30 years is anything to go by, why in fact, we have something of an opposite rule. The rule in Canadian politics is, more or less, if a Prime Minister from a province other than Quebec is elected—then there must be some mistake. And it'll be fixed very, very shortly. And please allow me to say that pointing this out does not constitute Quebec-bashing or many of its myriad variations. I do this as neutrally as the case allows.

The most recent testing of this laudable understanding came from the infallible Tories, when they rejected Jean Charest, who is from Quebec, in favour of Kim Campbell, who is from British Columbia, as leader. The other prize moment came from the equally infallible Liberals, when for a brief spasm, they opted for John Turner, who is from Toronto but ran in B.C., instead of Jean Chrétien, who is from Quebec. This blurt into the unknown was quickly corrected by the electorate when they chose, to all our unfathomable delight, Brian Mulroney, who is from Quebec.

Well not everyone can be Prime Minister. So maybe this test is too narrow. I could easily see a province or a territory which felt that over time it could not significantly have a reasonable influence on the nation's destiny, that was perpetually confined to the piccolo section of the orchestra, while others monopolized the brass and drums, saying "this isn't good enough. We're going to start an all piccolo band." So if, politically, Quebeckers could make no headway in the nation's councils, if they were on the periphery of the nation's councils, and this was understood to be perpetual demotion, then—once again—yes I could understand the issues of pride and influence which might work to a justifiable ambition of separatism.

But what is the case? There is, to the contrary, an arrangement, conventional rather than legal, by which Quebecers own a portion of the federal cabinet. Far from being discriminated against, they are discriminated in favour. There is an affirmative action program in place, from the PM's office on down, which works to ensure the enduring weight of Quebec voices in the highest chambers of our national deliberations. To argue, as separatists argue, some exclusionary understanding, is, on a quite strict understanding of the term, perverse.

What other grounds could there be? In the case of Quebec, the ineluctable territory of division has to be language. If Canada's national government, or the Canadian people, held as a policy that the French language was in some measure inferior, or withheld its operation in clearly public circumstances, or had an English-only policy of immigration, on something so vital to identity and culture as language, I can see all Quebec and Quebeckers speaking: "this will not do. You cannot insult or diminish our living language and pretend this is a Confederation." They would choose to separate, and they would be right.

But what is the case in reality? Far from shunning or degrading the fact of French speaking, this country has made itself, quite properly, in sensitive response to this most sensitive area, officially bilingual. Far from seeking to give offence on language, it has gone through the great upheaval, not without political costs, of bilingualism. And it has gone further than that. It has silently, and I suspect with very little relish, looked upon the opposite practice in Quebec (where English, by law, has strictly subordinate status) with controlled understanding. Even against the prevailing absurdities of language cops and the silly imperialism of petty language bureaucrats.

In the raw commodity of political power, and in the far more profound arena of linguistic respect, this country, Canada, has a vigorous record. There has been a profound accommodation in Canada towards the sensitivities of Quebec. And one of the principal reasons why so many of us have tired of the Quebec debate, grown exasperated by it, turns on the relentless mischief by which these acts of accommodation are mischaracterized, not given their due, or contemptuously ignored.

The line of the separatists is that Quebec cannot pursue its destiny in Canada, that there are vast impediments of policy and deficits of respect. This is Mr. Bouchard's humiliation aria—which makes it incompatible with the self-respect of Quebeckers to remain in this country. My point is, this isn't just wrong: it's absolutely upside down.

This is also what I mean when I argue that separatism is hollow at its centre; that it has no occasion to justify the magnitude of the separatist response. The real grievances, the substantial humiliations, the structured subordination that was once part of Quebec life within Quebec have had their day; they have passed with the generations. The day of the French Canadian speaking English to the sales clerk at Eatons in downtown Montreal has gone the way of whalebone corsets and the wish to wear them. Today's corset is ideological, the anachronism of a separatist movement without a separatist cause.

Widespread, deep and intractable malice or animosity, directed towards one particular section of the country by the rest, could also justify a vigorous separation movement. This is so far from being the case with Quebec as not to be worth expansion.

From Expo 67 to the present day, everyone rejoices in the achievements of Quebec and Quebeckers; where I work, in Toronto, many people gladly wear their sense of envy at what they perceive as the greater artistic and creative vibrancy of the neighbour province. Montreal, before it was pitted by the unnecessary separatist wars, was the glory of Canadian cities. It was a mark of sophisticated one-up-manship—unipersonship, if there are any sensitive gender monitors present—to yearn for the cosmopolitan glamour of Montreal, over the delights of grey Toronto back in the dim nights when I was a student. Yuppies before they knew they were yuppies, and trend slaves everywhere, pined for Montreal as if it were the BMW of cities.

This is the second source of Canadians' resonant dissatisfaction with separatist politics. The abiding sensation that the cause is larger than the occasion of the cause; that the remedy sought is too extravagant for the dispute in question; that the large rhetoric is a stand-in for a real purpose. The differences don't oblige the size of the quarrel. The equation that is the separatist argument doesn't fit the actual picture on the page.

There is a third. And then I will have done with this business and this tax upon your courtesy and patience. This third is the easiest of all. Canadians are galled by how the game has been played, and how it is being played. Caesar began his fabled Commentaries with what became in time the greatest cliché. All Gaul is divided into three parts. Caesar's Gaul and mine are different. Canadian gall over the mechanics and conventions of the national struggle is divided into three parts as well.

1. There is the insane unfairness of a Referendum that only becomes significant and has consequence when the answer is "Yes." A Referendum is an extraordinary instrument of democratic consultation. It's called to resolve the otherwise irresolvable, decide something truly momentous, and expedite a departure from the moral consensus. It is not a carnival show pop gun when for a dime you can shoot at the dummy until it falls down. No once. No twice. No a thousand times. It doesn't count. Yes, once, and it's game over. I don't know how we got into this absurd rigging of the crap shoot; well, I do, so do you. But I won't detain on it. The process is fundamentally wrong. That bothers everybody.

   We, the outsiders, those who are to be the collateral recipients of its result, are asked to acquiesce in the "democratic process" when the result is what the separatists like. The Quebec people will have spoken. No one likes a stacked deck. And no one likes a mechanism that pretends to be about choice and has only one preset result that counts.

2. Then there is the question. Whole swamps have been cleared as hazardous to human health that were not as murky as the last two referendum questions. Those questions were so congested with ambiguity and avoidance that if separation to the separatists is the sun of Quebec's destiny then these questions were its total eclipse. A straightforward answer required some humiliation of the intellect before it could be contemplated. If we agree Quebec has the right to separate, and that Quebeckers have the right, predominantly, to choose, then surely it is not nitpickery to insist on a clear question and a clear answer. This, too, bothers a lot of people. And it's outside the orbit of their control or influence.

3. The final aspect goes also to the heart. The most vigorous, the most impassioned partisans of the cause are the shepherds of the vote itself. Not only do they write the question, determine the percentages necessary for victory, run the propaganda, and predetermine what is acceptable from anybody else. They are also the ones in charge at the polls. I still get shivers at the result last time. Keep in mind the James Bondian devices and desires of Jacques Parizeau had they won and

the slim 60,000 votes that separated win and lose, Canada or No Canada, and the relief from the Canadian perspective that the country squeaked through obscured the interference and manipulation that was widely reported in many of the so called "English" ridings. If we are to put the country up on the ever-rotating wheel until the separatists get the answer they want, then mere dignity demands a neutral captain at the roulette table.

I began this by promising to un-riddle at least one dimension of the extraordinary public response to the idea of Jean Charest translating himself from the federal to the provincial scene, and from the Conservative to the Liberal party. The key to that response lies in all that I have said to now.

The Charest candidacy, outside Quebec, is almost instinctively seized upon as somehow conferring a voice and a presence to all those Canadians who resent that the terms and conditions of our national debate effectively reduce them to spectators, hand-wringers and diminished citizens. The vacuum of powerful leadership nationally on this question, the temporizing stance of the federal government, the insistence that the debate is framed as an exclusively Quebec decision, the relentless experiencing of deep and anxious frustration every time the Quebec question reaches crisis—as it will again—has long awakened an appetite for such a presence, such a voice.

Charest is seen, wrongly alas, as a proxy presence for all Canadians. This perception is more hope than substance, more wish than fact. As the central debate of our time is now framed and constituted, as the conventions surrounding that debate have evolved in the last 30 years, and the last 10 in particular, it is *de facto*, a Quebec debate.

We are disenfranchised from the central deliberation of our time and of our country.

The Charest candidacy, more to the point—our response to it, is the clearest, most vigorous and most emblematic instance to date of Canadians outside Quebec attempting to achieve some purchase, some measure of significant interplay, on the fundamental question of the country.

Mr. Charest is, as I have said and implied throughout this little waltz, viewed—even if not consciously so—both as a proxy representative, and as a channel, for that current of mixed emotions and frustrations Canadians harbour whenever they turn their minds, reluctantly but profoundly, to the concern of national unity. On the most basic plane, Canadians want a chance to have their say on what they perceive as the structured unfairness of the way this issue of separation has been framed, and the conventions that have evolved for its resolution and management.

If they could speak through a single voice they would say to Mr. Bouchard, "You do not pursue equity through a fundamentally iniquitous process. You do not claim monopoly jurisdiction on a process that fundamentally means as much to another mass of people that are outside the immediate arena of debate. You cannot rest the cry for the dignity of independence on the strange mathematics of separatism referenda in which "No" represents an invitation infinitely available and one "Yes" is foreclosure for eternity. The cause must bear some proportion to the reality. The historical and social dishevelment that will follow a real break-up is so far beyond the scale of disagreements being addressed, and the scale of real difference within Quebec that will ensue as to make the separatist project absurd and irresponsible. You cannot weave ambiguity and equivocation into the very fabric of the question. And finally they would say, "There is never any right moment to talk of these things."

It is—and I acknowledge it—the most tiring of all topics. We Canadians can never find a moment to speak of them that seems somehow correct, appropriate and in tune. We are always calculating the response that other people may have if we say what we have been thinking . . . always in a benign sense, always willing in a Canadian fashion, capitulating to the overwhelming imperatives of tact, in advance, before we join the debate.

Well, in my view, this moment is too sensitive . . . this moment is premature . . . this moment is too late . . . and this moment, well, perhaps we shouldn't. We always vacillate.

I have chosen my moment: The moment of the Minifie Lecture, in a part of the country that is politically and intellectually one of the seed grounds of all Canada, to present these impressions. What there was of presumption in my choice of forum, please weigh with my acknowledgement of the honour of your invitation, my delight in your company and the vitality of your welcome.

The message that surrounds the nature of this country and the channeling of the emotions of all of the people outside the Quebec arena, where they will find their proper place, their functioning and their effective exercise, is the predominant political factor of our time. And, it is certainly the most profound set of journalistic materials that are available.

I thank all of you for inviting me here. I don't get out much . . . and I enjoyed tonight!

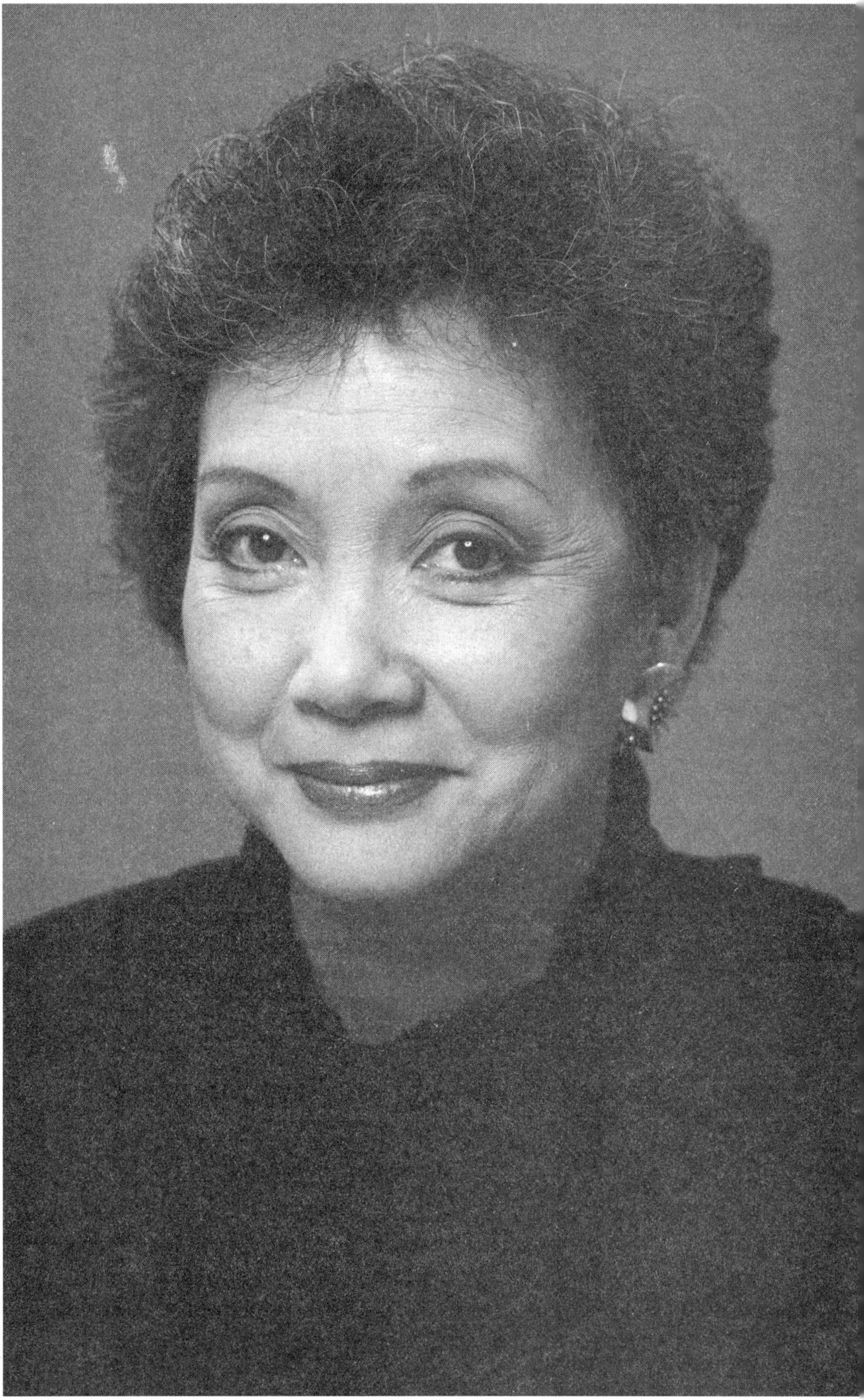

–1999–

ADRIENNE CLARKSON

Clarkson worked for the Canadian Broadcasting Corporation for nearly 20 years, hosting more than 3,500 television programs. As co-host of *Take 30*—an afternoon variety show—she was one of the first members of a visible minority to rise to prominence on Canadian television. She remained with *Take 30* for a decade, while also contributing to *Maclean's* and *Chatelaine* magazines. From 1975 to 1983, Clarkson hosted CBCs's new investigative program, *the fifth estate* where she earned several ACTRA Awards. She received a Gemini Award and a Gémeaux Award (the equivalent of a Gemini for French productions) as host and executive producer of the arts show, *Adrienne Clarkson Presents*. She hosted for four years. She was the 1995 recipient of the Donald Brittain Award, a special award given every year for the best social/political documentary program. Clarkson's career in journalism led to her appointment as Agent General for Ontario in France, to the position of President and Publisher of McClelland and Stewart, and to appointments to the Order of Canada and as Governal General of Canada from 1999 to 2005. She is the author of three books.

1999 | ADRIENNE CLARKSON

THE ART OF THE ONCE-OVER

I was very excited when Roy invited me to become the lecturer in honour of James M. Minifie for this year because I admire James M. Minifie. I entered the CBC at a time when his presence was, shall we say, enormous. But I knew him from before that time.

The reason I knew of him is that, and this is my suggestion to you for a future James M. Minifie lecturer, I was at university with David Halton.

The David Halton you all know as our news correspondent is currently in Washington and has been for some time, which was what James M. Minifie did. But David Halton is also the son of the great, great CBC war correspondent, Matthew Halton.

The voice of Matthew Halton on the radio! Even as I was a tiny child I always remember hearing, "This is Matthew Halton from Ortona! This is Matthew Halton from liberated Paris! This is Matthew Halton!" And when David came back to Canada to university—Matthew Halton died tragically quite young and David was brought up in England—he was surrounded not only by the aura of the fact that he had gone to a public, i.e., private, school in Britain, which was really different for us who came out of collegiates and high schools; but he also was the son of Matthew Halton, who many of us could remember vaguely, or certainly our parents did. And he was very closely linked to the person he called "Don Minifie."

Later, when we went to Paris at the same time as post-graduate students David and I had a kind of, what shall I say, a competitive relationship. David was already working as a stringer for the CBC, which in those days was a hallowed place, a cathedral-like place that you never thought you could ever enter. It was a place filled with people like James M. Minifie, with the ghosts of people like Matthew Halton. And would you ever have been allowed in!

Well, David Halton, age 21, was already doing things in Paris for it. And I'll never forget what David said to me one day. He said, "You know if you meet me tomorrow afternoon at the Cafe Clooney, I might take you to an interview that Don has set up for me with Rex."

And I said, "Rex who?"

And he said, "Rex Harrison, of course."

And I said, "Really, you'd take me along?"

And he said, "Maybe, if you turn up there at three o'clock."

So I was there at 2:30. I brought some books, I drank some coffee, I waited, I waited, I waited. David never came. About 5:30 I got back to my residence, and I called him and left him an angry little message. The next day he phoned me and he said, "It wasn't yesterday, it was the day before yesterday." And I just had the feeling that somehow I was being cut out of all of this. Anyway, David went on immediately to join the CBC in the news department.

I had no idea that I would ever join the CBC, but James M. Minifie was a figure to me. And when I eventually did join the CBC, which was about three years later, I would glimpse him around the hallways. He was to me an august figure. He was somebody who was not only a correspondent in Washington, and somebody who you heard and saw. He was somebody who wrote, who wrote books. He wrote *Who's Your Fat Friend;* he wrote *Peacemaker or Powder Monkey*, which had quite a huge success. I was just looking it up at the library the other day and it went through five or six printings in 1960. These are essays which I looked at recently preparing for this encounter here in Regina. These essays are of the highest quality, the best research, and the most profound kind of understanding, not only of international affairs, but particularly of where Canada should be and where Canada had a place in the world.

I think Minifie got that from his roots here in Saskatchewan. He was the child of English immigrants, as you all know. Brought up on a farm at Vanguard, he went overseas when he was sixteen and fought for two and a half years in the First World War, which certainly at that age and in that war must have been the defining experience of his life. He went on to further studies and became a Rhodes Scholar from Saskatchewan. He then joined an American outfit as a reporter before coming back to the CBC. So he brought with him a lot of knowledge and a lot of learning. Looking at his character was the kind of thing that inspired me to talk to you tonight about what I think the art of journalism really is.

I ironically called it "The Once Over" because Cyril Connolly, the writer whose essays I admired the most when I was first reading essays of a certain kind of quality, said that. He said it also to me at an interview I did with him in England because I asked him what exactly he had meant by it because it always intrigued me. He did both journalism and literature, and he said, "The art of journalism is the art of writing something that only needs to be read once. The art of literature is the art of writing something that must be read more than once." I used to think for many years that he meant journalism was superficial, but he didn't mean that, and I confirmed it with him when I interviewed him just before his death. What he meant was that the art of journalism is the art of bringing to the surface something that you can understand and see and seize immediately. But that seizing of it immediately did not mean it was superficial. It meant that it was explained; it meant that you could understand it; it meant that it reached out for understanding.

I think that's what Minifie was able to do. I think that he was able to do that "once over" in a way which was profound, interesting, and added to our knowledge of ourselves as Canadians, our knowledge of ourselves in the world. If you read his essays now, of course, they're out of date because everything that is current affairs is out of date. His attitude towards NATO is not out of date; his attitude towards NORAD is not out of date. He had a curious attitude towards Canada as being a kind of possible Switzerland, a neutral kind of country, which I guess he thought was the way in which we could behave *vis à vis* the giant to the south of us. I would like to know what he thinks now. I would like to ask him now what he thinks considering where we have gone down the road with the neighbour to the south, which was not nearly as dominant at the time he was writing thirty to thirty-eight years ago, as it is now.

Looking at Minifie as a journalist, you get the character. The man who was formed by the First World War. The man who was educated on two continents, who continued to educate himself, who was a person who had suffered, who lost an eye. You had a person who obviously continued to educate himself in every possible way. You had a person who was enormously productive in what he did, and all that is the model for what a good journalist ought to be.

I think that it's very important when we look at someone like Minifie to compare what's happening today to what was happening when he was here. After all, he went through two World Wars, one as a participant and the other as a reporter. We don't have that kind of thing. We don't do that anymore. Yet communications are faster, everything is happening, we are more and more addicted to news, and all of that. But what does it mean for us? And how do we form ourselves as people who wish to purvey an understanding of what's happening around us? It doesn't matter whether it's in a very tiny particular way: in our town, in our community, in our little neighbourhood, in our neighbourhood association, in our province, in our country. How do we prepare ourselves for that? And how do we prepare ourselves to really understand what is going on because understanding is the root of it.

I'm not so sure that we ever get at something called "truth." And I think that people like to think that they are getting at truth. It helps them as a goal. But I'm not sure we get at it because there are many things that make it impossible to know "what is truth?"

You must always ask yourself as a journalist who will benefit. That is one of the important things when you're looking for what the story is. Who is going to benefit from this particular conflict or thing between these people? Sometimes you don't have to even ask yourself the question. I did a story on *the fifth estate* years ago in which there was a strike against a medical clinic at the Lakehead, Thunder Bay. The doctors had locked out their nurses, and the doctors had taken to doing things like swinging baseball bats at their nurses. It doesn't take a lot of intuition or knowledge to think that those doctors weren't good guys. That's your starting point, then. You have to figure out why they behaved in that way, and why they felt—not only did they behave in that way—why they felt they had the right to behave in that way.

And standing in your position looking at this story or at any story is you, the reporter, the journalist, the person who is going to give the story. And in television that's a particularly complex thing because we work very collaboratively, something people don't quite understand. In fact, television looks in a way so easy. It brings an enormous amount of easy fame to people. I think that is truly one of the crosses that sincere and intelligent people have to bear. It brings such quick fame and that is not really what it is all about. It is easier to deal with being just a by-line than being a constant face which is glorified because it is famous. That is really not why you do it; and, in fact, it can get in the way. The real story is what you are giving and taking from the story as well as how you have developed in order to be worthy of looking at the story.

I think there is not enough thought given to the fact that in order to be able to look at stories of any kind you have to know a lot of stories. You have to have a very, very good education. Yes, of course, you can learn on the job, there is no question of that. You can pick up any amount of knowledge doing stories, following people about, doing apprentice-type work. But the way in which you can almost jump-start it is by having a really good education and by reading an enormous amount. That I would say has to be in the liberal arts—and I make my pitch for this all the time—which is the Humanities, Philosophy, History, English. I leave out Political Science and Economics. That is something you can learn very quickly. Political Science is a kind of illegitimate son of History. It is not a science and it is frequently not political. History is the thing that tells you about politics. The study of history is what really tells you about how world events happened. The study of literature, whatever language it happens to be in, gives you what is really the condensed thought in poetry, drama, prose, and fiction of the distillation of people's lives.

Then there are other things, of course, like music and the visual arts, which I think also feed the person. If you have a great education anybody can teach you. I could teach you in three months how to put together a television show if I know you've had a terrific education. I could send you out on a story, know that you could do the research, know that you could come back with the research. You might not be able to put the images together. We could work on that together. When I'm working with younger people that is what I look for. Do they know anything? If they know nothing I can't help them. I have to send them away till they want to know something. They have to want to know it, and they have to reach out for knowing it. So basically curiosity is the thing that I look for always in a person who is going to work with me. They have to have enormous amounts of curiosity and want to know how everything works.

I'm sure that's what Minifie had when you read everything he wrote about because he sometimes writes little bits of gossip, too, and gives wonderful stories out of school about Churchill and Roosevelt and so on. You have to have an understanding and a curiosity that operates at all levels. That kind of knowledge knows it will never have bounds no matter what kind of degrees an institution is going to give you: a B.A., an M.A., a Ph.D., a license in this or that. That has nothing to do with anything. It's the motion of the mind. It's the ability to go to a stack in the library and find things that tell you what has been thought about. And with that kind of information you gradually become a person. Now you don't become any person. You don't become somebody else. You aren't going to become James M. Minifie. You are going to become yourself, hopefully, with the aid of that knowledge.

And if your curiosity leads you to be a journalist, to be somebody who wants to find the story or wants to ask the question—which is what the interviewer does under a spotlight on television—if you want to be that kind of person, you aren't trained the way a lawyer is trained. Those of you who are lawyers know that you don't ask in court any question to which you don't know the answer already. The interviewer's job is quite different from that. I think of the interviewer's questions as really being part of the curiosity. Like a black wood stove which I have at my cottage in Georgian Bay. If you put a little cube of ice on it, the rivulets run in different directions. You have to follow them, see where they run. It is the same with questions. And when you follow questions, that's a good interview.

When you interview somebody you don't have a list of eight questions. It doesn't matter whether they're the most famous person in the world or a simple person trying to get through some kind of conflict with their local school, for instance. It doesn't matter who you are talking to, in that sense, you have to follow them where they're going.

Out of that, and especially under pressure of time, I'm giving you here my biggest secret: you ask the question three times and you will get the answer. Roy knows this already because all good interviewers do. There's almost no human being in the world who can resist being asked something three times. You don't have to ask it in the same sentence in the same way. You can say, "Is there torture in Iran?"

He says, "I don't like the question."

And you say, "I know it's an unpleasant question, but is there torture in Iran?"

He says, "I don't want to discuss anything that has to do with torture in Iran."

You say, "Well, let me just ask you a last time, is there secret police who do torture in Iran?"

And he gets very excited at this point and says, "Don't talk to me about torture, we don't have to torture people in Iran. We are as sophisticated as you are in the western countries with getting information out of people."

That takes a kind of patience. It also takes staying your ground. It also means maybe you don't know the answer. Maybe he is going to surprise you. Maybe he's going to say, "Other people do it and I wish they wouldn't." I mean there's all sorts of possibilities. He could have said, "I don't control my secret police. My family does it. I don't really do it." But you really hit the jackpot with what he says, what he did say. And it is a kind of jackpot because you actually in your heart of hearts know that that's the answer from the research you've done. And you've done a lot of research before that. That's where the curiosity will take you.

The other thing that you have to have as a journalist is the willingness to be totally and utterly humiliated. An education helps you with this, although your character will also have to come into play, and a number of other experiences can help you. Now people think that is not something that should happen to anybody, but any good journalist knows that that has happened to them on any number of occasions. They may just have hidden it a little bit, or they may have just covered up a little. But the ability to be humiliated is the ability, actually, on the other side of the coin, to be humble and face the knowledge that you gain. Even when a great story plays itself out in front of you and you know you've got it, you have to be certain that you really do. And it's not ever with that whole sense of triumph.

I can tell when I'm reading good stories, good investigative stories, or I've seen them. It's where the turning point is in the story, where the person has become really desperate and then has become sure. This comes with a certain kind of knowledge, the sense of self that will allow you to get through a humiliating process of not getting the story, or thinking you're not getting it, or having people turn you down. This also comes with the sense that you really have the knowledge to back yourself up and can go to another avenue if things don't work. Now how do you develop that? You can't develop it by bravado and by pretending that you're better than anybody else anyway so it really doesn't matter. That's not really what it is. You can't do it even if you have tremendous self-confidence and self-esteem and supportive family and all those sorts of things that Academy Award winners thank the families for. You don't get it that way. You've got to get it yourself by certain kinds of experiences.

The knowledge experience is one of them—learning things, coming up against wonderful ideas which challenge you. The second one is, of course, travel, which many young people I know love to do. They love to get their backpacks and off they go to Indonesia, Thailand, who knows. Usually now it's become like a lifestyle because it takes more than two or three months which was all we were allowed when I was growing up before we had to get out and earn a living somehow. But now, you know, people are taking more time; and I, for one, am not upset by that. We can't give them jobs anyway so they might as well travel. We were all in a rush. Everybody rushed out of my graduating class to go to a three-month course at Ontario College of Education so that they could immediately go and teach high school. There was such a need for high school teachers at that point. But I resisted this because I felt I had other things I wanted to do. One of them was to go to Paris because David Halton was going to be there and would maybe take me to an interview with Rex Harrison.

Travel is a very important part of education for younger people because it gets you out of your context, because you're cut off from everybody who knows you and could care about you. If you throw yourself into it in a good way you will learn an enormous amount provided that you also add a new language. I'm very demanding on this. If somebody comes to me and says that they really want to take a year and do something, I suggest that they do it in a country where they will have to learn the language because that also helps with the humiliation process. Learning a new language as an adult is the most humiliating thing that can possibly happen to you short of being rejected by somebody you love.

Going to a European country to learn a language is certainly a humiliating experience. Some people say, "Oh, I couldn't possibly do it, you know, go to France. They're so mean to you. You try to speak their language and they're so mean to you—they won't help." So what? What skin is it off your nose if they're so mean to you? Other people love you. You have other people in your life. You're going to have other people in your life. So who cares if for three months people look at you with your little maple leaf on your knapsack and because they don't understand your French or your German say to you in broken English, "What do you want?" What does it do to you? Nothing, so humiliate yourself.

Not only that, it's not a matter of learning a language for the sake of learning a language. The point is that it does something for your character if you learn it well enough. And I refuse to believe people who say to me that they tried and they could not possibly learn a foreign language, not ever. There they are, children of Dutch immigrants or Ukrainian immigrants, and they can't learn another language. I cannot believe that. Anybody can learn a language if they have to eat, if they have to travel or read a railway schedule.

The point about learning somebody else's language is that you go into another culture's mindset. And you can't do that without doing the language. Now it's not possible to learn, you know, maybe ten languages, or whatever; but, if you apply yourself, and keep applying yourself, you will be able to learn two or three. I think that's important because we are now in a world in which if you go to Europe you will meet people. You're young, you are going to meet people who speak three and four world languages. You can go to Fontainbleau, or you can go to graduate work in Germany, or you can go to the Scandinavias, which is the worst example because they all speak five.

And, if you go to these other countries which up until now only spoke their own, they are now all speaking three and four languages. So you are not going to compete. You are not going to be part of this world where people can move easily and fluently back from French to English to German to Spanish. It's a world which you need to know if you're going to be part of it and able to observe it.

If you are going to be able! That's where the world has changed since the world of the Minifies and the Morrows, really. I think that the world has become the kind of place in which languages have become extremely important. In our country with the amount of French immersion schooling that we have, that we didn't have when I was growing up, we are able at least to give a head start to a lot of kids to learn the second language. I'm involved with a group that is going to have a conference in about three weeks. We've chosen six hundred kids from across metropolitan Toronto who are in French immersion. The reason why we've done this, and are setting up a foundation to do it, is that we want to give them three days of talking to people who have done something because they speak French but are not Francophone. Although provincial governments often put money into French immersion, we felt that once the kids came out of school they had no idea what they were going to do with it. It was a clever little trick like taking an extra math course. But it's not about that. It's about what you can really do with it.

And language is part of our country. We are the only country in the world except for Mauritius to be bilingual in two world languages. The other bilingual countries have one major world language and the other is not a world language: Belgium—French and Flemish; South Africa—English and Afrikaans. Mauritius and Canada are the only ones. We are very fortunate because that second language is a world language. It gives us a leg up in almost everything, and we should be taking advantage of that at every point.

When I was Agent General in France I used to have kids streaming through who'd come to Paris because they thought it would be fun and would stay for three months and do something. I was very happy that I persuaded three different young people at that point to stay for two or three years. One of them did a Faculty of Law degree in French after having done law in Toronto. Two others did doctoral studies in Art History because they learned their French after three months and applied their French and got a degree. I think that's terrific to be able to do that. They were able to take that time at that age and still come home at the age of twenty-four, twenty-five and start doing what they wanted to do. A couple of them are now making films, actually.

But in all of this where is the self? See, when I'm reading Minifie I have the sense that Minifie knows I know who Minifie is, that Minifie is addressing me when I'm reading those essays. There is a persona there. And I think that's something that we don't understand because there is a "plasticization" that happens with a lot of television nowadays, which I think is very regrettable. And I hope that our own network will continue to try and fight against it.

The plasticization really is the sense that if you can read from a teleprompter in two minutes, and blink enough so that people don't know you're doing it, then you can get away with that and are somehow doing something real. I guess one of the advantages of growing up in television in an age when there weren't teleprompters is that you didn't do that. You went into a studio at a certain hour, you had one dress rehearsal or two dress rehearsals on a daily show, and then you half-memorized the script and ad libbed the rest. And, if you forgot something, so what! You had tomorrow to go on to. It was really not that important.

Nowadays, of course, that's not the real thing. It's got to be always absolutely word perfect. Everything is "click-click," like that. I think there may be a reaction to that, and I hope there would be. I'd like to see the CBC go back to doing more live programs where there are chances for flubs and where things don't go right. Even when it goes all across the country. You know, people make mistakes! I don't think that's a big deal. I think we're getting much too concerned with making things look as though they're magical or come from another planet or are part of the *Star Trek* set. It's not a good thing.

The person who is the journalist, who is going to delve for the story, who is going to make the judgment: that's what it's all about. Ultimately, that's where the problem with the truth comes in, to go back to that. The person who is going to make the judgment is you. And what kind of person is that person? Who are you? I think if you can't begin to figure that out, and realize that it is going to be that life long journey, you're going to have real trouble keeping up a career as a good journalist, real trouble. There is going to be so much input you're going to be deluged with stuff, with information. And, if you want to be cheap and lazy, it's the easiest thing in the world to be a cheap and lazy journalist. I read stories everyday, and I can go through them with highlighters and say, "Well who else did you talk to? Why did you just talk to the lawyer for that guy? Why didn't you check on who that lawyer is?" All that sort of thing. I can see how cheaply done so much of it is.

When we were at *the fifth estate* we never went to a story, worked on a story even, or started to roll any film on a story, until we had done research for at least three or four or five months. Sometimes years went into files if they were very—some of them were very—sensitive files. One of them only came to trial this year. I mean there were files on that at *the fifth estate* for 20 years! When we went to story meetings about what we were going to be doing in the next month or six weeks or two months or that season, we'd classify what the stories were and how much more we needed to know about them. We challenged each other an enormous amount. The reporters never worked together. We fought a lot, but we always respected each other.

Let me come back to the person who is the journalist who is making that judgment: unless you really have the feeling that you can be a full person, you are not going to get to the story. Now there are certain investigative journalists who I think of, and I have worked with them in the past, who are certifiable nut bars. And the reason why they are good investigative journalists is that they are obsessed. They get onto a story and they can't give it up. It's like seeing a terrier going for something and dragging it around the room even though it weighs five times more than he does—and going at it, and going at it, and going at it. That kind of person is a real person. He may be a nut bar, but he's a real person. And luckily in public broadcasting we were always able to accommodate eccentricity and madness in the personality. Not everybody is a nice person. Some people are unfaithful to their wives and drink and are terribly needy—and they become President of the United States! Other people become journalists.

When I went into the CBC in the sixties there was a whole culture of male-natural journalism which I think is over now. These guys drank a lot. I just remember being told stories by a friend of mine who became my producer on *Take 30*, a female who came out to Saskatchewan at the time Medicare was being introduced. These were hilarious stories about the reporters who were on the story. They were getting the story, yes, but it was taking a while. Finally, Knowlton Nash came out and shaped them all up and dried them all out. And they all worked and their stories were great. But it was never unforgivable, anything that happened like that. We've become much more puritanical in our view!

Also, it's a much less male atmosphere and that's all to the good because formally that kind of male atmosphere I don't think bred the right sort of things. There were some great journalists, I'm not denying that. But I think that the introduction of women into that whole stream has been enormously helpful. Women have curiosity in a different way.

If there is something that is important for a young person to know about I would always set them to reading Plato, and particularly that treatise in which Socrates says to one of his inquirers, "The unexamined life is not worth living." And the unexamined life is not just your own life, it is the unexamined life of everything around you. If you don't examine that, if you don't look at it so carefully with everything that you are, then you really don't deserve it. You don't deserve to be in that role. I think you have to ask yourself that question all the time when you are doing something as privileged as presenting a story, and it's a good story. How are you going to present it? You also have to ask if you are really worthy of it.

I'm talking here about a certain kind of moral centre. It isn't fashionable to talk about these things. Somehow people don't want to think that there is some kind of judgment going on always in the person. I was brought up in such a way and had an education that makes me have to ask those questions. Without those questions I wouldn't want to do it. I'm not interested in interviewing famous people or asking people how often they've had their face lifted. It just isn't interesting to me: that's not what I consider to be worthwhile. If other people want to do it that's fine, and if they have a huge audience that's fine, too. If people want to sell ads for that at $800,000 for 30 seconds that's their business. I just hope the CBC never does it.

It's really not about that. It's about whether or not you see the story. And I don't mean by that that you judge like you're God or some kind of big deal or other. But you've got to at some point weigh out the story. Whose side tells the story better? If they tell the story better are they telling something approaching the truth? Can you get at it another way? You're bringing yourself to bear on this one all of the time. Without it you really have nothing.

I'm getting at a certain kind of authenticity in yourself. Without that authenticity you don't get anywhere and you can see it immediately. It's amazing how much we are really animals without knowing it because we try to believe that we are not. Although, we are coming back to that realization that we really can smell and sniff people out. I've often marvelled at the fact of that. Even in social situations, you know, you'll be with six or seven people for dinner, maybe you've organized the dinner, and these six or seven people don't know each other. And the next day a couple of them call to thank you for the dinner, and one of them says, "You know, that couple don't get along do they?" And they never said a cross word to each other. They were perfect to each other, but the other people felt it.

We don't give enough to our intuitions, and that's the other thing that has to be honed. If you have an education and are able to reach for authenticity, and if you are able to have a depth of knowledge in academic kinds of things as well, then you can work the intuition in a way that it isn't all about "what I feel"— you know, "I feel good about this, I feel bad about it." It's not about that. It's using all of these things in a way that has balance, and you can only get at them if you use them all together. Every time I ever started a story or started on research I would always look over a desk with lots of papers and say to myself, "What actually is going on? What am I being told in this information and in these research notes?" And I'd put that in the back of my head for when I would actually do the story or start the interviews.

Sometimes they were really, really tough to do. The Olympic story in Montreal was something we spent three months on in the coldest winter that Montreal has had. It was awful. I don't think I was at my best for most of it because it was so difficult for me to get my head around the fact that the people that I was interviewing were actually crooked: that they were dishonest; that they were taking public money; that they were really criminals. It was really hard for all of us. Brian McKenna was my producer on that. And we were pretty sure, but we kept saying to each other at dinners at night, "Can it really be true? Can it really be true that they are completely and utterly dishonest?" Eventually, yes, they were. You wouldn't have had 30 cranes hanging out there not doing anything but being paid for by us, the tax payers, but mostly by Montreal, without it being dishonest. The evidence was there, but it had to come in such a way that we could process it.

And that processing is through you as a journalist, as the person with authenticity. That's what you should work for. I'm not saying that you get there, but you must work for it. You have to have balances, too, in the way you look at it. I've worked with journalists who are avenging angels, and they are not the most attractive people in the world. There has to be some sort of balance. And, no, you can't forgive people for spending public money and lying about it, of course not. But you do have to look at a whole situation.

I'll always remember one of the books that really marked me as a youth was *Darkness at Noon* by Arthur Koestler. It's about how communism failed a man, how the religion of communism failed a man, and what happens to him. The thing that I always remember in the book comes from Dostoevsky, and the torture and everything that the man goes through in the book is set off by this. It is the idea "man, man, you cannot live without pity." I think that this must be in the background of all that knowledge and all that excellence you can bring through your understandings, your education with the persona, and the personality that you can develop through the understanding of other cultures.

You cannot live a life as a journalist without some kind of compassion. That doesn't mean that you're a bleeding heart or that you forgive horrendous deeds. It means that your understanding has reached a certain point where you meet the story at a certain level and are able to give this to other people so that their comprehension will reach it. We know always the horrible stories: murders, serial killings, all of that sort of thing. If in the reporting of this you can never get to a point where the general audience can look at it, then you have failed as a journalist.

The great Japanese filmmaker Akira Kurosawa said something in his autobiography that I've never forgotten: "The artist never averts his eyes." I would say this is also true for the journalist. You look at everything. In that look there must be everything brought to it that you have become, that you have reached out for, that you have been taught because so much of life comes to you through teaching. And in that you must never forget that you cannot live without pity.

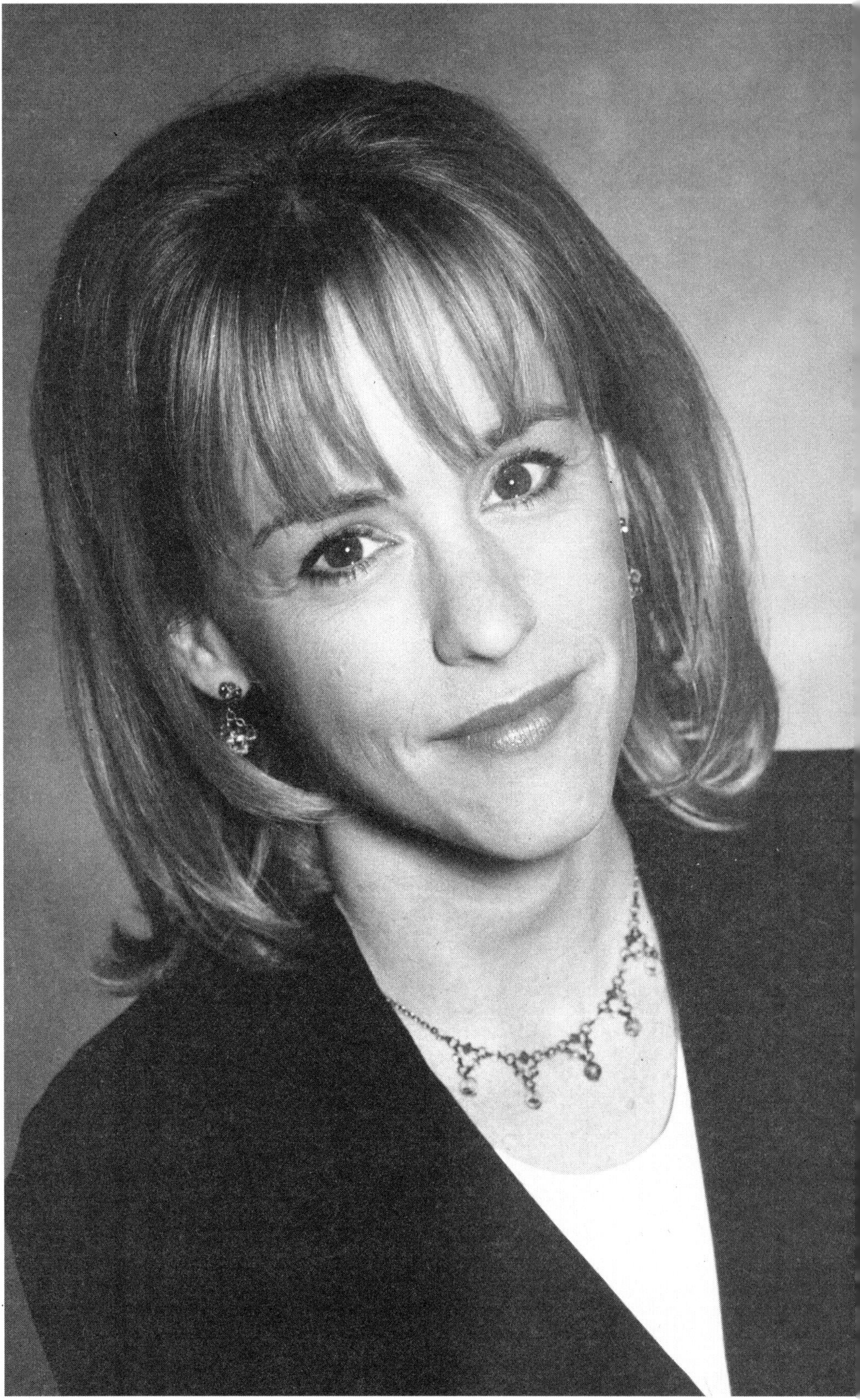

−2000−

WENDY MESLEY

Wendy Mesley is the host of CBC Television's acclaimed consumer program *Marketplace*. Previously, she was the host of the Gemini Award-winning *Undercurrents*. The winner of three Gemini Awards and a John Drainie Award for Distinguished Contribution to Broadcasting, Mesley began her television career in 1979 in Quebec, covering some of the most fascinating politicians of our time, from Pierre Trudeau to René Lévesque. During the late-eighties, she was posted in Ottawa as a parliamentary correspondent, reporting on external affairs, free trade negotiations and the constitution. In 1990, Mesley began anchoring, for many years as host of *Sunday Report*. Today she co-hosts CBC's *Test the Nation* and is a regular contributor, and back-up anchor, for the public broadcaster's flagship nightly newscast, *The National*.

2001 | WENDY MESLEY

MY LIFE AS A DINOSAUR

"My life as a dinosaur"—that's kind of a strange name for a speech. It came up because of a deadline, not mine. It was the deadline of the person making up the posters for tonight's speech. "Just give me the title," he said. "I don't need to know what you're going to say."

Good thing! I didn't have a clue. I'd been really busy on *Undercurrents,* and the speech, my deadline, was months away. But I had to give him something, so I thought, "What matters to me? What do I want to talk about?" And I realized I wanted to tell you about my love of journalism—the old-fashioned kind.

I don't know where you stand, whether you're like me and see journalism almost as a calling, or maybe you look at journalism as just an interesting, perhaps glamorous or—ha!—a well-paying job.

Maybe you won't think I'm a dinosaur, but I know many Canadians would think that many of my old notions about journalism are hideously out of date, and that I am a relic. Well, I am a relic, a dinosaur, hideously out of date and proud of it.

In fact, I want to make the case that journalism is a proud calling—not necessarily that we all deserve to be trusted and respected, but that it is possible, and it's definitely worth striving for.

I was a journalism student once, back in the Dark Ages, before the Internet, before zines, almost before cable television. My first job in the business was while I was in high school, answering phones at CHUM radio in Toronto. And there was some guy there with this idea of taping rock musicians and putting their songs on television. "What a dumb idea," I thought. "Who'd watch that?" He went on to produce MuchMusic.

I was just as quick in college. I took the journalism program at Ryerson. I thought it was pretty easy, even though I was working at other radio jobs on the side. But then, in third year, I failed my advanced reporting class. It turned out a deadline really was a deadline. I left Ryerson with 31 out of 32 credits, and no degree.

It took me 10 years of agreeing to speak at any function at Ryerson before the head of the department finally told me I could appeal my grade. My mother feels much better knowing that if this gig ever dries up, I could always . . . what? What exactly does one do with a degree in journalism? No one's ever asked me if I had a degree. The degree itself may not matter. What matters is the exposure to ideas. But what ideas?

A couple of weeks ago I had a scary encounter. At a staff party I got to chatting with a journalism student from Ryerson who'd worked briefly as an intern at *Undercurrents.* I asked what she was studying in her last semester. "Television writing, documentaries, and I'm taking an elective in public relations," she said.

Public relations? I was appalled. Why was public relations worth a credit in a journalism course? When I was a student—here comes that dinosaur theme—public relations types were hacks, somewhere lower on the evolutionary chain than even engineers or business students. (Good thing my husband, the marketing M.B.A., is not here.)

The student said it was kind of weird that her investigative journalism teacher would rant on about the message track and other manipulative PR behaviour, and then an hour later, down the hall, her PR teacher would talk about how journalists and PR people are all working toward the same end communicating, enlightening; that we are natural partners.

Well, yes, some of us do seem to have become partners. We are either so lazy, so overworked, or so blind that we take their statistics, their polls, their videos, their experts, their stories, and put them in our newspapers and on our airwaves. But we shouldn't, because our mandates are not the same.

Public relations is about selling—selling a person, a product, a company, a political party, or even a cause. It could be selling something good or worthy, but it's still selling, and that's not journalism.

Good journalism is about doing your homework, asking questions that lead a little closer to the truth, and giving all sides a chance to make their case. PR people work hard. Some of them even write better than some journalists, but when you're selling something, another side to the story can be counter-productive.

Public relations people are often the ones who stand between us and the story we're trying to tell, or at least our version of the story they want us to tell. It's their job to manipulate us. Before they give us an interview with the CEO or politician or celebrity we're after, they make sure we're going to make their clients look good.

And if they suspect your story might be critical, their job is to indoctrinate you. If that doesn't work, they simply block access. A really good flack can stall you for weeks, all the while pretending to be helpful. I'm not saying it's not a skill. It's just not journalism.

The public's regard for journalists has sunk so low that it's hard to say what I'm about to say without making people laugh, but here goes.

I believe public relations is the art of making people believe what you want them to believe. Good journalism is the art of telling people what you honestly believe to be fair and true. It is about clarity of expression, not spin and obfuscation.

Ten years ago, I would never have ranted on like this about the evils of PR, but two things have changed.

First, I used to cover politicians, and they could deny you access only for so long. You could file an access to information request, and you could stake them out. Their offices were, after all, on public property. Now I spend most of my time covering corporate behaviour. Their PR commandos make the politicians look like neophytes.

And second, I'm not sure the public cares much now when the media complain about the spin, the stalls, and the other techniques used to keep us at bay. Many people would just as soon give the benefit of the doubt to the people we're covering.

Even the journalism student I mentioned is not sure what to believe in these days. She argued that journalists are selling a product, too, that they or their employers want to sell magazines or sell ads or even just make a name for themselves.

She's right, of course. Every day there is more pressure on journalists to write the stories that are an easy sell—anything with a celebrity in it, anything with gossip, anything about cool stuff, or that old standby, anything about sex.

But—and it's a big but—few journalists would argue that these stories are serious journalism. This is what the network bosses and newspaper barons use to attract people. But it is not what we aspire to. At least it's not what we dinosaurs aspire to.

We've all noticed how a number of twenty-somethings have made names for themselves with chatty columns or commentaries. I'm sure they consider themselves to be journalists.

But I have a lot more time for another group of twenty-somethings who are making names for themselves in the old-fashioned way, by stirring up shit—not by writing about their date with a gigolo, but by taking the powerful to task, by doing a lot of homework, asking hard questions, and dealing with issues that really matter, by making their readers or viewers think about something beyond the way they look, who's boinking whom, or how much money they make.

Here comes the dinosaur again. To me, good journalism really is about old fashioned values, like courage—the courage to go against the flow, to ask the questions no one else is asking. It sure won't make you popular with the powers that be, and maybe not even with your colleagues, but you'll probably be a lot prouder of your contribution, because that's what it is.

That's what makes journalism more than just a job. You have a contribution to make, and you can make a difference.

Okay, dinosaur rant number whatever—a trend I call the new narcissism. The latest trend in journalism says there's no such thing as objectivity, that you might as well just tell people your personal opinions on every controversy so that they know where you're coming from when they read or hear your story.

Well I don't mean to be rude, but who cares? Wouldn't you rather hear the opinions of the people involved, people who have spent their lives thinking about or living with the issue? Everybody has opinions, and my family and friends really care about mine, but why should anyone else?

As a journalist, I'm there by proxy, as a monitor. It's my job to tell people what happened as truthfully and fairly as I possibly can and let them decide for themselves what they think. It's called living in a democracy, taking on responsibilities as a citizen, trying to contribute to the public good.

One of the first stories we did on *Undercurrents,* five or six years ago, was about how *Adbusters* magazine, the culture jammers, were trying to force the CBC to run their car ads. Now these ads weren't selling cars. They were denouncing them, or at least our addiction to them.

During the interview, the editor said something that really struck me—that the goal of television is to deliver an audience to the advertisers. I was shocked. I'd always thought it was about delivering fine programs. But, of course, he was right. The CBC, because it's partially subsidized by the taxpayers, is less beholden to the ratings race, but it, too, feels the pressure.

My illusions about programming, that content mattered more than the commercials, were shattered a couple of years ago when *Undercurrents* was cancelled. The CBC was facing budget cuts something had to go—and we were the new kids on the block, the most expendable. But the executive producer and I decided to find a way to keep it alive. We'd had all kinds of people approach us about how they loved the show, that if we ever wanted to take it to another network do call, if we ever needed this or that corporate sponsor, call this number.

Well, we made all the calls, did all the lunches, and it soon became very clear that the only way we'd get someone to pay for our show would be for me to wear a sandwich board advertising all our sponsors, and to change our stories so that they became much chirpier. "Wow, have you seen this new technology? This cool new product? Isn't Bell an amazing company?"

At some point during this process the CBC, which, of course, we'd been lobbying, too, found a way to keep us. We never told them we'd come to realize that no one else would let us tell the stories we wanted to tell.

In the fall, we'll start with our sixth season. At the beginning, I used to worry we'd run out of story ideas. Well, with the explosion of new media issues, and the ever-increasing sophistication and deviousness of the PR, advertising and marketing worlds, I think we have years of stories to tell.

The problem for us now is getting people to talk. Funny, the better known we become, the harder it is to get people to return our phone calls. It seems there is a penalty for refusing to play the PR game, and guess who are the hardest people to get to talk? The people who are paid to communicate. As one PR guy I know told us, in good PR, the agents should always be invisible.

Marketers never want to talk about how they get people to buy something. It would expose the whole game. Take a story we did this year on the marketing of shyness. A drug had just been approved to help people suffering from social phobia, and just imagine how many pills you could sell if you get everybody who's shy to seek help.

It took some doing, but after months of a slowly building campaign, you ended up with huge headlines and even a couple of magazine covers that touted there was now a cure for shyness. We thought it was a great story, but could we get any of the participants to talk about it? The American Psychiatric Association, the drug company, and the drug company's PR firm all gave us the runaround. None of them gave us an interview.

We did another story this year about the marketing of Tylenol. Seems to be a theme here. I guess the link is that pharmaceuticals are growing so fast there they often push the limits with their advertising and public relations. Anyway, the Tylenol story was about a drug company commissioning a poll that just happened to make their product look good and their competitor's product look bad.

Well, I hate to say this, but even though the drug company's name was mentioned in small print at the bottom of a press release, a lot of media took the story and ran with it as news, without mentioning that the drug company had commissioned the poll. Again, we couldn't get the drug company, or their public relations firm to talk to us. I was reduced to chasing some poor guy around his building with a blow-up of his press release telling the media to call for more information.

It's not just the corporations and their PR people who give us a hard time. In all of these stories, we have a hell of a time getting journalists to talk about their roles, too. I guess they feel a lot more comfortable putting other people's feet to the fire than feeling the heat themselves.

Talk about honesty in journalism! Talk about courage! Have the courage to ask hard questions, and for God's sake, have the courage to answer them, too.

We did a story a couple of years ago about journalists on the speech circuit. There are a dozen or so high-profile journalists who make more money giving speeches than at their day jobs. There were two reasons we wanted to tell this story. First, we wanted to see if there were any conflicts between who they were taking money from and the stories they wrote. Second, we thought our audience would find it interesting just how big a market this was.

Journalists, back in dinosaur times, used to be very middle-class. They did not make a lot of money and they did not hobnob with the powerful. In other words, they were not insiders. For the most part they weren't very different from the people who watched or read their work. Lately, that's begun to change, and the increasing presence and reliance of journalists on this speech and talk show circuit is a major factor.

Anyway, we tried to get these journalists to talk to us about their gigs, about what they charged and who they talked to. Almost all of them refused. Jeffrey Simpson, *The Globe and Mail* columnist, bless him, gave us an interview, but because he was virtually the only one who let us ask hard questions, he probably came off looking more guilty than those who refused to comment.

If Jeff had hired a PR consultant, the advice would have been, "Don't talk to *Undercurrents.*" But Jeff is an honourable guy. He told me, "How can you ask other people to be accountable, and then refuse yourself?" Exactly.

Every journalist likes to think of himself or herself as an independent thinker, someone who does not follow the pack, someone who cannot be fed a story. Yet nowhere is it harder to break from the pack than in political reporting.

I was a parliamentary correspondent for CBC National News for several years. I covered Meech Lake, the GST debate, and free trade, and I was part of the pack. It was hard not to be. There were so many things to cover—the news conferences, question period, the scrums—that there wasn't much time left over to dig up something different.

The only way to stay sane was to act like a pit bull in the scrums, to refuse to accept the pat answers, and get in a hard question. But it was hard. On big issues, before the politician even got to us, they had been through umpteen levels of spin. We all knew that much of it was, if not obfuscation, then thin gruel. But day in, day out, we all went back to scarf at the trough.

Last week, during the mini-mutiny in the Liberal party, there was a real breath of fresh air. It had been revealed the night before that Paul Martin's supporters had had a secret meeting to discuss ways of giving Chrétien a little push. Martin first tried to tell reporters he hadn't known about the meeting. When that didn't work, he said the meeting was only to reassure his supporters that despite all the rumours, he would not be leaving politics to go run the International Monetary Fund.

That's when Bob Fife, a great old hound of a reporter, decided to break scrum etiquette. The unwritten rules say you can ask all the hard questions you like, but you can't laugh in their face. When Martin said the meeting was all about the IMF, Fife said, "You don't actually expect us to believe that, do you?" To me, it was like a burst of music from the heavens, a real moment live before the cameras. But I'm sure it was a blip.

I've talked a lot about old-fashioned values—the need to tell stories that matter, not just titillate, the need to ask hard questions even if that means you'll never get a job at Time Warner or be the most popular girl on the Hill. I personally believe that stirring up shit about things that matter is the best way to get a good job and influence people. I've also talked about my fears about what we cover, what we think is newsworthy.

But mostly, I want to leave the message that a job in journalism is the best job you could ever have.

Where else can you get paid to meet interesting people, never stop learning, and make a contribution to your community? We're very lucky to be journalists, and we should treat the craft with respect. And if we do, maybe the public will respect us a little more.

The justification for putting a lot of the sensational/celebrity/gossipy stories out is that "that's what people want." Well, if that's true, why do they hold us in such contempt? That contempt is dangerous. It plays into the hands of all the forces who try to use us to manipulate the public. Controlling the message means controlling us, and their techniques are becoming increasingly sophisticated.

I don't think the average person has a clue what a constant battle it's become. We are besieged by the powerful, and by the firms they've hired to bombard us. We are flooded with their "handy dandy just add water and it's news" press packages and lured by their friendly sounding corporate-journalistic associations meant to make us all best buds, all the better to plant their stories on us.

Then there's always the silent threat. We'll be cut off if we don't play the game their way. It often means you won't get your calls returned, won't get tipped off on breaking stories, won't get invited to all the parties.

Even when you do try to take them on, to ask questions or tell stories they may not like, they keep finding new ways to wriggle out. It's long been seen as bad form to be quoted saying "no comment," so the latest weaselly escape method is to refuse an interview, but issue a statement. That way, they can say they responded, without having to answer any hard questions.

The saddest thing is that increasingly they're getting away with it. The world has changed. Everything is about selling, and good journalists don't further the cause of consumption. There are now a lot more jobs and a lot more money in PR. No wonder some of the newest recruits to journalism are dreaming about jobs in public relations. Those people are in demand.

Journalists get in the way.

Dinosaurs like me think we should get in the way more often, before we become extinct.

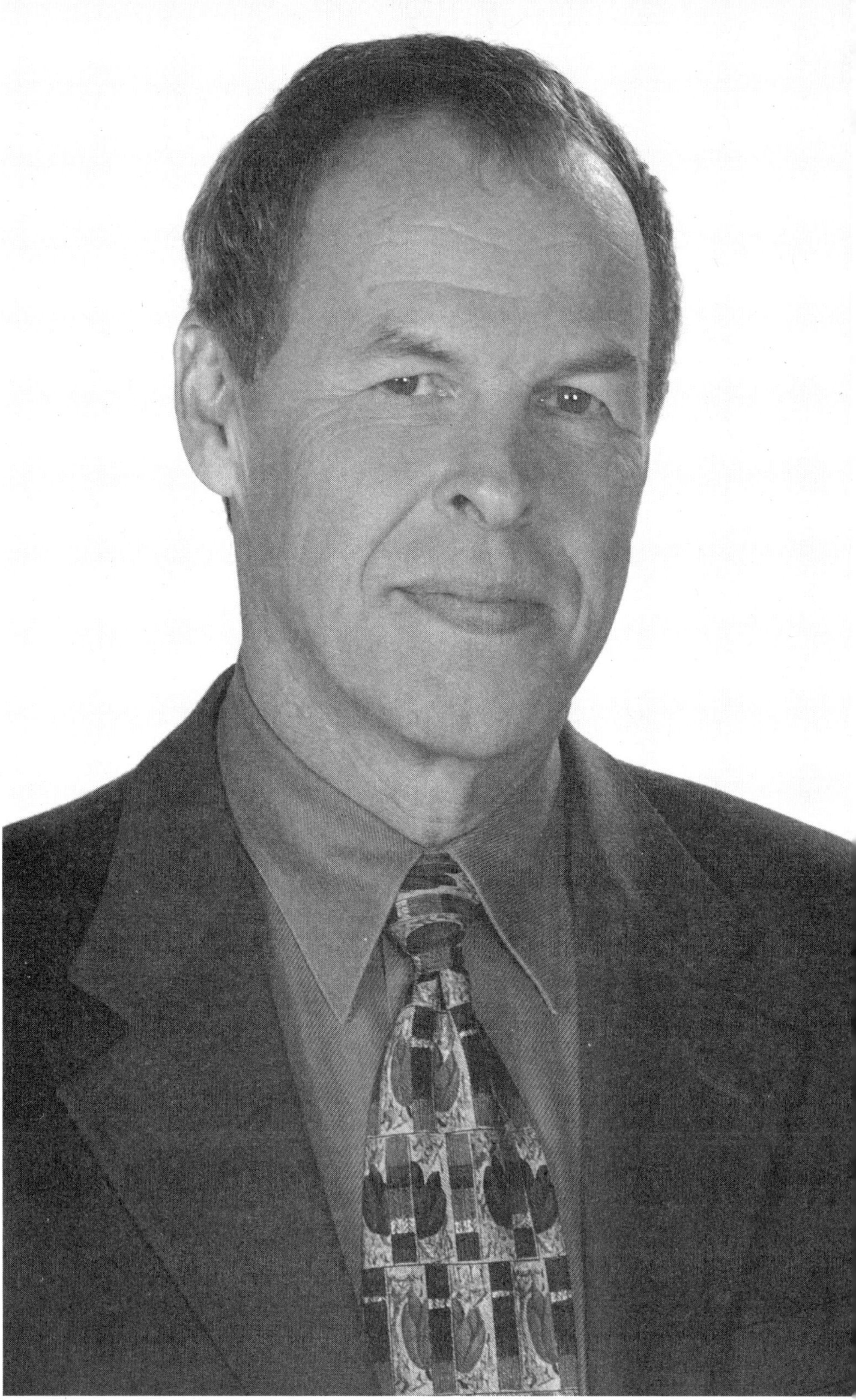

—2001—
LINDEN MACINTYRE

Since 1990, Linden MacIntyre has been the co-host of *the fifth estate,* CBC's flagship investigative program. Before that, he worked as a reporter for *The Chronicle Herald* and *The Mail Star,* of Halifax. He spent most of that time as parliamentary correspondent in Ottawa. He was also a reporter for the *Financial Times,* also on Parliament Hill. He spent three seasons hosting a regional current affairs program called *The MacIntyre File* before going to work as a producer-journalist for CBC's national current affairs program, *The Journal.* He was assigned to documentary reporting in various parts of the world, including the Middle East, Central America and the USSR. For two seasons, MacIntyre was host and national editor for *Sunday Morning* on CBC Radio. MacIntyre is the author of four books, and several award-winning documentaries for the PBS program *Frontline.* He's won nine Gemini Awards, an International Emmy, several Anik Awards, and the Michener Award for meritorious public service in journalism. On November 10, 2009, he was named the 2009 winner of the Scotiabank Giller Prize for his novel *The Bishop's Man.*

THE SIXTH ESTATE

A few months ago I was shooting a story in Saskatchewan and it required an interview with a provincial cabinet minister for symmetry and balance. The story raised a number of questions about the administration of justice, and we wanted to hear how a responsible politician might reply to the questions.

I don't know what other media call such interviews, but *the fifth estate* has been around for a long time; ever since the mid-seventies. We call these sessions "accountability interviews." It's a phrase that originated in a time when people, individually, felt more influential than we do today. It was a time, characterized by higher public expectations and a lot of personal confidence.

People really thought that politicians were accountable, that commercial corporations and trade unions actually feared the wrath of their shareholders and the public. And most people believed that the mass media spoke for them, worked for them, represented their interest, which was what gave the media its power.

The story for which I wanted some accountability was about a large family from the Saskatoon area. I won't bother you with the sordid details, other than to say, that a group of people, mostly members of one family, were wrongly accused, investigated and charged with serious crimes. People in the justice system eventually discovered that the charges were mostly based on twisted fantasies, but they refused to acknowledge it. A whole lot of completely innocent people found themselves, years later, still under a horrible cloud.

People in powerful positions of public trust, people on the public payroll, made decisions that ruined the lives of innocent members of the public. The media has a public function. The CBC, as a matter, of fact, is a public-service broadcaster.

I'm an old-fashioned journalist. I believe that when we become aware of a situation like that, it is our responsibility to find out how and why it happened. And it is the duty of the people who made the decisions that caused it to tell us.

I confess that I have, over time, come to feel awkward about the public's right to expect accountability from people in positions of public trust and influence. People in the media, like members of the public at large, have developed doubts about our legitimacy as representatives of the public interest. Over the years, there have been profound changes in the mass media, the structure of ownership, the technology, the content.

One of the most frequent complaints about the media is about the amount of bad news that finds its way into the content, and it's a fair observation. I'm told that there was an editor at the *Baltimore Sun* who used to keep handy a photocopy of a good news front page, just to send out to readers who complained about all the bad news. It happened to be the front page from April 15, 1912, when the headline read: "All Titanic Passengers are Safe; Transferred to Lifeboats at Sea."

The mass media emerged originally as a vehicle for conveying all kinds of news and opinion, good and bad, about the lives of ordinary people, and communities, and about the performance of people entrusted with power. It still has that purpose, but I would argue that the delivery of unbiased information has become, at best, a secondary function of the communications industry.

One can argue about how well the mass media ever performed as a delivery system for information, or whether the media as a business ever really existed to speak for the public. It is significant that journals and journalists who have emerged as strong public voices stand out in history as heroic exceptions. This would suggest that most journalists practise the craft without any particular sense of public duty.

Journalism for many, I can unhappily report, is a vehicle for personal ambition at best, and a means of ego inflation at worst. But I believe that no matter how imperfectly they may serve the ideal of public service, people in the media have always seen themselves collectively as performing a necessary function in a free society.

And so, when my colleagues and I were preparing a story which raised serious questions about the Saskatchewan justice system, we felt a responsibility to put those questions to somebody in a position of public responsibility, and we genuinely believed that some responsible person should answer them.

The government of Saskatchewan disagreed. Here's what we were told privately: aspects of the case were still before the courts. Nobody in government or the justice system can discuss matters that are before the courts. They will not even discuss why, nearly a decade after this particular case was seen to be largely without merit, it is still before the courts, and they will not publicly discuss why they will not discuss it.

That was the reasonable part of their position. But there was more. A spokesperson of the government of Saskatchewan presented us with the following syllogism: "According to the traditions of journalism and the journalistic policy guidelines of the CBC, all stories must be fair and balanced. There are two sides to every story. To be fair and balanced, every story must include both sides. We cannot and will not tell you our side. Therefore you do not have a story."

I am not making this up.

And so I got up very early one morning in Saskatoon and started the drive to Regina with a TV crew. It was our intention to inflict a moment of accountability on the government of your province.

I've been in journalism for nearly 37 years. There has not been a single day in that period of time, and we're talking about 13,500 days, when someone hasn't paid me for committing journalism. I'm still not certain how it all started, but at some point in my impressionable youth I became enamoured of belonging to a profession that was called "the fourth estate," a public entity that Edmund Burke held to be of more importance than any of the other three estates—commons, nobility and clergy.

For a young person growing up in what would now be classified as social and economic poverty, it was a seductive notion, to become as important as the priests and politicians, bankers and lawyers, without working as hard as they did to acquire the credentials of importance. It became irresistible. I joined the fourth estate without certificates or ceremony.

Time and the advance of technology have grafted onto the fourth estate a fifth estate, a description that acknowledges the development of an electronic medium, which has in many ways eclipsed the older print-based service. Radio and television achieved influence and credibility in just a few decades. People like James M. Minifie and Matthew Halton and J. Frank Willis, with their distinctive and authoritative voices, gave radio broadcasting credibility as a medium of journalism.

It was probably inevitable that one day someone would actually name a television program *the fifth estate*. It was much less inevitable that I would one day end up working for it, but I did, almost 11 years ago.

the fifth estate is a journalistic community within the CBC that has now been in existence for nearly 30 years. Any institution that has survived for nearly 30 years develops a certain culture, and I'm happy to say that the culture at *the fifth estate* retains remnants and a certain character that is resonant of attitudes that were more prevalent in the early and mid-seventies than they are now. I'm referring to the perception of the media as an influential public service.

the fifth estate, in the spirit of the sixties and seventies, believes that people in position of public trust are accountable to the public, whether or not they want to be.

The phrase "public accountability" has a quaint ring to it these days. It's almost naive in its presumptions. It presumes that I, on behalf of the general public, still have a right to ask someone who is in a position of public trust and influence, to explain behaviour or decisions that have had an impact on other people's lives.

But it has become an awkward phrase because most people in positions of public trust and influence no longer feel accountable to me or to anybody else, except perhaps to each other.

This is a dangerous development, for no matter how imperfectly they functioned, the mass media have traditionally provided a forum for the relatively free exchange of information and a place where the public can demand that people in positions of power and trust explain themselves. The media, through the practice of journalism, should be a kind of free-for-all to surprise and test the powerful with honest questions about how they do their jobs.

But last fall, when we were badgering the Saskatchewan justice department for answers to questions about how individuals performed their duties in one particular case, we were told that if we persisted, they'd consider laying criminal charges—against us!

I've made the drive between Saskatoon and Regina a number of times in my life and I never cease to be affected by the perspective it gives me. My reaction to this landscape is not unlike my reaction to the ocean. It gets me up close to the notion of infinity in a way I seldom can in more cluttered places.

I become aware of absolutes, and I remember driving southward that morning last fall watching the sunset fire to the eastern sky and realizing in a deep way why people who work on land like this, like people who spend their lives on oceans, become rather stubborn. And why, even if the idea of public accountability has become archaic and old fashioned in most places, maybe, in Saskatchewan it still has a little bit of currency.

I've discovered that powerful people hate surprises. Surprises bring out the worst in powerful people. Surprises bring out their basic insecurities.

Try to set up an interview with somebody of importance, and the first thing they want to know is what questions you're going to ask. What's the story really about? They hate spontaneity because people who exercise power, always in the service of noble ends, sometimes use means that lesser people might find less than noble. So they like to talk about ends, but rarely about means.

A politician is always much happier talking about a new highway than about the messy expropriations that went into making space for it. Its part human nature to want to celebrate achievement without dwelling on the often-sordid or cruel details that brought the achievement about. Where abuses of power occur, it is always in the means to the ends, the part of the process that usually unfolds in privacy or secrecy.

Power is like the iceberg. We never see the part that sinks the ship.

A large number of journalists, starting in the early-seventies, developed an aggressive new attitude toward power and secrecy and a style that is frequently called "investigative" journalism. It is proactive and provocative toward authority and it abandoned some of the old-fashioned notions of objectivity.

Traditionally, reporters took a literal view of what objectivity means. For most, it meant keeping your own personality and opinions out of the work, which is a fairly commendable ideal. But it is impractical, and it is fundamentally dishonest to pretend that any mortal can report events without exercising judgement, and that human judgement can be free of subjectivity.

I'm reminded of a story from my friend, a former potash miner who worked in Saskatchewan during the seventies. He was on a train once and he overheard a young person remark to an older one, presumably a school teacher, that "Saskatchewan has black sheep."

He'd been looking out the train window and saw a black sheep standing in a field. The teacher looked at the sheep and pronounced that it is always important to state only that which we know objectively, therefore the student should have said, "There is a black sheep in Saskatchewan."

My friend the potash miner, who was on his way home to Cape Breton, couldn't resist butting in with the comment: "If that's the case, he should have said that there's a sheep in Saskatchewan that is black on one side."

A thinker named Erich Fromm, writing in 1966, came up with a new definition of objectivity and a lot of reporters embraced it. Objectivity in journalism, he said, cannot be scientific objectivity, which implies detachment and an absence of interest and concern.

He asked a crucial question: "How can one penetrate the veiled surface of things to their causes and relationships if one does not have an interest that is vital and sufficiently impelling for so laborious a task?"

In other words, it is necessary to get close to your subject if you hope to get close to the truth.

And so, on a lovely autumn morning in October of the year 2000, I was heading for Regina to inflict a moment of accountability upon an unsuspecting public official, the Saskatchewan Minister of Justice, a man of intelligence and decency and ambition named Chris Axworthy.

We had spent weeks badgering his office with requests for a formal interview and, in response, got journalism lessons, and lectures about fairness and accuracy and ethics, and eventually threats from people who work for him.

We timed our arrival in Regina to coincide with the beginning of a weekly cabinet meeting. I wanted to introduce myself to Mr. Axworthy as he arrived at the meeting and politely ask the questions that I believe he was obliged to answer, and to at least give him a chance to present his reasons for not answering them.

Even though I have been in this business for 37 years, 25 of them on television, I am not widely known. I am not a Mansbridge or Murphy or Mesley. I'm not exceptionally smart and I'm far from lovely. I'll never be famous. However, just to be on the safe side, I decided to make myself inconspicuous as we arrived at the legislature building here in Regina. The camera crew and producer went in first. I waited outside.

I was thinking about an unkind remark once attributed to Dalton Camp, that Jean Chrétien looks like the driver of a getaway car. That's what I felt like, hanging around outside the Legislature.

Over the years I have learned to expect zoo-like confusion around media events like cabinet meetings. The "scrum" used to be a rugby term. It now describes the most common kind of encounter between the public media and politicians. It is also just about the only opportunity reporters get any more to extract comments out of politicians that have not been pre-scripted to eliminate any possibility of surprise.

I expected the usual scrum outside the Premier's office where the cabinet meetings take place. When I eventually skulked up there to meet Mr. Axworthy, I was surprised to find that the scrum would consist of me and two local reporters, one a television reporter/cameraman, the other a radio reporter, both from CBC.

Obviously we had lots to talk about, and as we stood chatting at the door the cabinet ministers normally entered through, waiting for Mr. Axworthy to arrive, somebody spotted him slipping through a different door. I just caught a glimpse of him and while I can't swear to it, I'm certain that he was smiling.

A colleague of mine attributes these moments, and various other snafus that inevitably arise in the course of preparing our stories, to the work of a vague entity that exists in most institutions called "the department of program prevention."

I'll go a step further. My friend was being sarcastic. I believe program prevention has become a very real factor in the world of communications. I've spoken about the fourth estate and the fifth. I believe there is now a sixth estate. It is a marshalling of professional skills, bureaucratic resources and a great deal of money, all dedicated to managing and blunting the exercise of accountability by the fourth and fifth estates.

The primary objective of the sixth estate is to remove all spontaneity, and therefore the possibility of surprise, from any encounter between a journalist and a government or corporation decision-maker. The sixth estate draws its skills from journalism, the law, and advertising. Its mandate is to filter the flow of public information to remove anything detrimental to the interests of important and powerful people, and to amplify anything that will enhance those same interests.

And I can tell you it is having a frightening effect on relations between members of the public and the people who represent our interests in positions of power and responsibility. The sixth estate have created a wall between the people and their public servants, both in the private and public sectors, and on both sides of that wall we can see a developing spirit of distrust and outright hostility.

I'm not talking about public relations here. I've always had a genuine respect for people who work in public relations. They have a crucial and difficult job to do, if they chose to do it honestly. They are responsible for crafting corporate communications in a fashion that will serve the corporate interest and the truth at the same time—sometimes two objectives that are difficult to reconcile.

But they also should serve as advocates for the public interest within the corporation, a responsibility which, if carried out with too much zeal, will lead to a rather short career. But I've known admirable PR practitioners who made it their personal mission to try. Unfortunately, in many corporations and in most government agencies and departments, the responsibility for public relations has been taken over by the forces of the sixth estate.

The sixth estate exists to manipulate thought and taste, how people vote and how people spend their money. It is an occupation in which truth is defined according to the potential effect of any given piece of information. If the information is good for the client it is true. If it's bad for the client it is a lie and it must be suppressed.

The sixth estate is a product of a siege mentality in the corporate sector, and when I use the word "corporate" I use it in the broadest sense, a corporation being any large group with a common set of exclusive interests. Those interests are usually pursued in the absence of any ethically based sense of public responsibility.

The sixth estate is a mercenary function that is dedicated to the service of particular corporate and political interests to the exclusion of any others.

Many years ago, when I was a young reporter, it was considered entirely appropriate and part of the job to visit or telephone specific people in politics and business and the public service and ask questions. And it was considered to be safe and proper for ministers and public servants and corporate executives to answer them.

We formed mutually respectful relationships with important people and they were based on a common sense of obligation to the public. You had their home phone numbers. They were always on call. Their spouses knew who you were.

I remember my first day on the job in May, 1964. I was told to call the Premier of Nova Scotia for a comment on something of significance at the time. I did. I misquoted him and he called me back, gave me hell. It was a good journalism lesson and we got along fine after that.

Some years later I recall an editor asking me to get a comment from K.C. Irving, who was at the time, I think, the fifth or sixth-richest man in the world. I called the company switchboard and asked, for his office. He answered his own phone. We talked.

Today, in order to reach a person with the answers to questions we have to spend all our energy and time arguing with experts in communications, about our right to ask the questions. In our Orwellian world, being a communications expert usually means they're good at suppressing questions and controlling answers. At the end of the exercise we get nothing, or a performance that we don't entirely trust.

The Scottish philosopher David Hume once offered an insight which might explain the emergence of this dark presence in the realm of public communications. He wrote that "as force is always on the side of the governed, the governors have nothing to support them but opinion. It is therefore upon opinion that government is founded."

Think about it. The people are the source of power. To control power, it is necessary to control popular opinions. Opinion is best managed, in a democracy, by subtle manipulation. The mass media affects public opinion, so the mass media must be manipulated.

One of the great public journalists of out time, an American named I. F. Stone, famously commented that "every government is run by liars, and nothing they say should be believed." I always thought that this was a bit extreme, but listen to some other quotes from recent history.

Sissela Bok, a British author who wrote a book called *Lying, Moral Choice in Public and Private Life*, found that many people seem to believe "that a certain amount of illusion is needed in order for public servants to be effective. Every government has to deceive people to some extent to lead them."

Jody Powell, the former press secretary to President Jimmy Carter, observes in a book he wrote: "From the first day the first reporter asked the first tough question of a government official, there has been a debate about whether government has the right to lie. It does. In certain circumstances, government not only has the right but the positive obligation to lie."

And another, from the political leader who best represents the mood of the eighties and early nineties, Margaret Thatcher: "You don't tell deliberate lies, but sometimes you have to be evasive."

Not quite so recently, no less a moralist than the illustrious St. Augustine seemed to agree: "There are two kinds of lie that are not grievously sinful . . . when we lie either in joking or for the sake of our neighbour's good." With that ethical insight, Augustine cleared the way for the creation, many centuries later, of a medium called the sixth estate.

The emergence in public discourse of manipulation and even telling lies as a legitimate means to the ends of governance wouldn't be so worrying if the mass media and the profession of journalism were in a position to restrain the self-interested enthusiasm and distortions of the sixth estate.

But it is my perception that while the need for skeptical and disinterested journalism has never been greater, the illusion that journalism is flourishing has never been more misleading.

The communications experts in the sixth estate really don't have much to worry about from the lesser estates of journalism. There has seldom been less incentive for, and fewer resources dedicated to, genuine unbiased inquiry aimed at generating an accessible and comprehensible flow of information to the public.

Communications media now function within vast conglomerates of commercial enterprise and impenetrable financial imperatives. ABC/Disney, NBC/General Electric, CNN/Time Warner, CTV/*The Globe and Mail*/BCE, The National Post/Hollinger/Canwest/Global/Southam, and God knows what else. It is no longer clear who controls the priorities of the mass media. And we can no longer assume that journalism is a priority for the owners of the tools of journalism, the cameras and presses and satellites and Internet servers.

I believe that while many people working in the media still see themselves as a part of public service, most media institutions most commonly function for purely commercial ends, for entertainment and marketing. The objective delivery of information—what we call journalism—is now a marginal and sometimes subversive concept to many of the people who own the media.

To make matters worse, a lot of people in positions of public trust, and in the general public, no longer believe that the mass media represent the public interest except where the public interest coincides with the particular interests of the media owners, shareholders and advertisers. I get the feeling that we have evolved to the point where, in the minds of most people, the mass media is no more a public service than the liquor industry.

It's futile to expect any near-term attempt by the mass media to help correct this situation. There's an illusion of journalistic affluence and influence that's fed by a proliferation of specialty channels for television, the constant babble of commercial radio, fat newspapers full of slick advertising and self-promotion, the vast and chaotic Internet.

But the structure and ownership of the media are now so driven by the corporate imperatives of cost-cutting to maximize profits that the resources available to unbiased journalism are being downsized to insignificance. If you doubt this, visit your local newsrooms, including the CBC, which has become a hybrid of public and private enterprise philosophies. Everywhere in journalism today there is emerging a widget mentality, a preoccupation with productivity and/or profits.

The result is what seems to be an ever-decreasing number of journalists who have the time or the energy to look beyond what's being shoved in front of them—material usually crafted by the sixth estate. And sometimes there aren't even people available to take the handouts. I'm told that the government of Saskatchewan recently called a press conference to announce an infrastructure program worth more than $100 million. Two networks, Global and CTV, didn't have anybody available to send.

The decline in proactive independent journalism leads inevitably to a decline in credibility of the news media.

The loss of credibility becomes part of the general trivialization of culture, and helps to accelerate the loss of trust, in all conventional institutions. Journalists are probably as truthful now as they ever were. There just aren't enough of them, and there certainly aren't enough who are in a position to independently chase stories and surmount the considerable obstacles that are being put in front of them by powerful interests, including, at times, their own bosses.

There's another problem affecting the credibility of the media. I don't think people believe in the existence of truth the way they once did. I believe this fact is reflected in a loss of faith in a large number of professions and institutions. Politicians, doctors and lawyers, teachers, the clergy and journalists no longer acquire, with their professional credentials, and their certificates, a cloak of credibility.

In fact, there is popular subscription to the opposite view, that in circumstances that involve our personal or corporate interests, we use our public advantages for private enrichment, that when self-interest is involved, we're all liars. Which, if true now, probably always was, but it *seems* more accurate now.

I find it significant that there is now a noticeable movement in the United States toward what they are calling civic journalism, or public journalism. Its aim is to create a media with the primary purpose of helping people to function as citizens rather than consumers. Its commitment is to give people the information they need for making sensible decisions in a democratic society.

It is, according to one mission statement, an effort to reconnect with the real concerns that viewers and readers have about the things in their lives they care most about. It seeks to reconnect, not in a way that panders, but in a way that treats people as citizens with the responsibilities of self-government, rather than as consumers to whom goods and services are sold.

This is a principled attempt to revive the ethical ideals that, as far as I know, originally legitimized the institutions of journalism. I admire the instincts behind the movement, but inasmuch as the media mirrors society, it might be a mistake to think that the way to start fixing society is to reinvent the media.

The media is a reflection of reality. Trying to make it a reflection of the good intentions and the ideals of earnestly moral citizens is, I would argue, just as dangerous as trying to make it a reflection of liars and thieves and pornographers. I would suggest to the people behind civic journalism that if you don't like what you see in the media, start fixing the society the media reflects.

I applaud these initiatives in civic journalism, but I remain a little bit skeptical. Maybe my skepticism is based on the fact that we have had civic journalism in this country for more than 67 years, ever since a national broadcasting act mandated the Canadian Radio Broadcasting Commission to take over the broadcasting arm of the CNR.

Up until very recently, governments, with our approval, had been vigorously weakening the national public broadcaster by forcing it to rely to an ever-increasing extent on commercial advertising revenues for survival. In Ontario and Alberta, we've witnessed similar assaults on provincially owned networks.

Federally and provincially, Conservative and Liberal governments have attempted to marginalize public broadcasters and, I would suggest, civic journalism, into irrelevance, to the great satisfaction of the private sector—including, shamefully, the private broadcasting industry. I'm happy to report that they have failed. But maybe not for long.

This, I believe, is part of a broader vision for the country, a general devolution of power from the public sector to private enterprise.

I'm not complaining about what has happened to the CBC in the past 16 years. I am, however, alarmed as a citizen because I think the diminished commitment of this society to public broadcasting is an indication of a diminished Canadian commitment to the health of public institutions in general.

Contemporary politicians like to boast that they've withdrawn from the business of doing business, but they are still very much in the business of creating business for the business sector. And this represents a diminished commitment to the whole ethos of community life, the ethos that has justified and enriched this particular community that we call Canada for nearly two and a half centuries. Many of the deliberations and decisions that led to this state of affairs have occurred in secret, because of a lack of attention by journalists, because of obfuscation by the sixth estate. We like to think that in the wired world with its search engines and universal access there are no more secrets.

There is a new goddess of truth named Google, and she's at the beck and call of everybody. Ask her anything and seconds later she will have an answer.

But it is a well-established fact that there are two equally effective ways to hide the truth. You either conceal it behind a thick wall of secrecy, or you bury it in a lot of distracting and largely unimportant detail.

People who use power love secrecy. This is not always because of malevolent intent on their part. It's just that work is easier when you don't have a lot of people looking over your shoulder and second guessing every move. People who exercise power, like all of us, believe in their own fundamental decency and the integrity of the ends they are trying to achieve. What harm can there be in a little secrecy when the agent is decent and the end is good?

But the unlovely child of secrecy is propaganda, a process which justifies untruth for the common good. And, of course, untruth spawns more secrecy.

Almost 200 years ago, Jeremy Bentham told us about the danger of secrecy in the justice system: "In the darkness of secrecy, sinister interest and evil in every shape, have full swing. Only in proportion as publicity has place can any of the checks, applicable to judicial injustice, operate. Where there is no publicity there is no justice. It is the keenest spur to exertion and the surest of all guards against improbity. It keeps the judge, himself, while judging, under trial. The security of securities is publicity."

During the last decades of the second millennium, we saw a collapse of public confidence in government. I believe it was directly related to the increase in official secrecy and the haze of confusion manufactured by spin doctors in the sixth estate.

We see the effects in the ongoing decline in the prestige of public institutions. We should not be surprised by the recent phenomenon of an irritable and unbelieving news media. We should not be surprised by the parallel increase in public cynicism and despair about the quality of political leadership and media reporting.

I think most responsible people know that secrecy merely nourishes suspicion, ultimately breeding paranoia and cynicism, which create volatility in purchasing and voting patterns. This should be most alarming to the people who are manufacturing the secrecy and the distortions for the purpose of controlling the market and the electorate.

But the response has not been to make the exercise of power more transparent. It has been to create illusions of transparency and accountability by the skillful manipulation of words and images, the creation of a peculiar kind of light that leaves us in the dark.

I want to leave you on a hopeful note. My visit last fall had a relatively happy ending. After it became obvious that the justice minister had outfoxed us, I gave a short form of this speech to a young woman who worked for the then-Premier, Roy Romanow. She actually listened and then she made her own little speech.

It was about how a lot of people in position of public responsibility and vulnerability have valid reasons not to trust journalists. She agreed with some of my points. I agreed with some of hers. We agreed to disagree on the rest. Then I told her that I'd be extremely grateful if she could somehow convey a message to either the Premier or his Minister of Justice.

My message was that we intended to wait outside that office, at both doors, until either the Minister came out or hell froze over, whichever came first. She said she'd try.

About two hours later, Mr. Axworthy emerged. I had half a dozen or so questions. He had a single answer. His answer was that it wouldn't be appropriate to answer.

But the beauty of the answer was that it was delivered personally—and I say without sarcasm—honestly, and directly to the public. Whether or not we liked his answer is an issue for another day.

The point of the exercise was public dialogue, and we achieved it, in spite of the sixth estate.

Dialogue is always less than perfect, but it beats the alternative, which is alienation and often, violence.

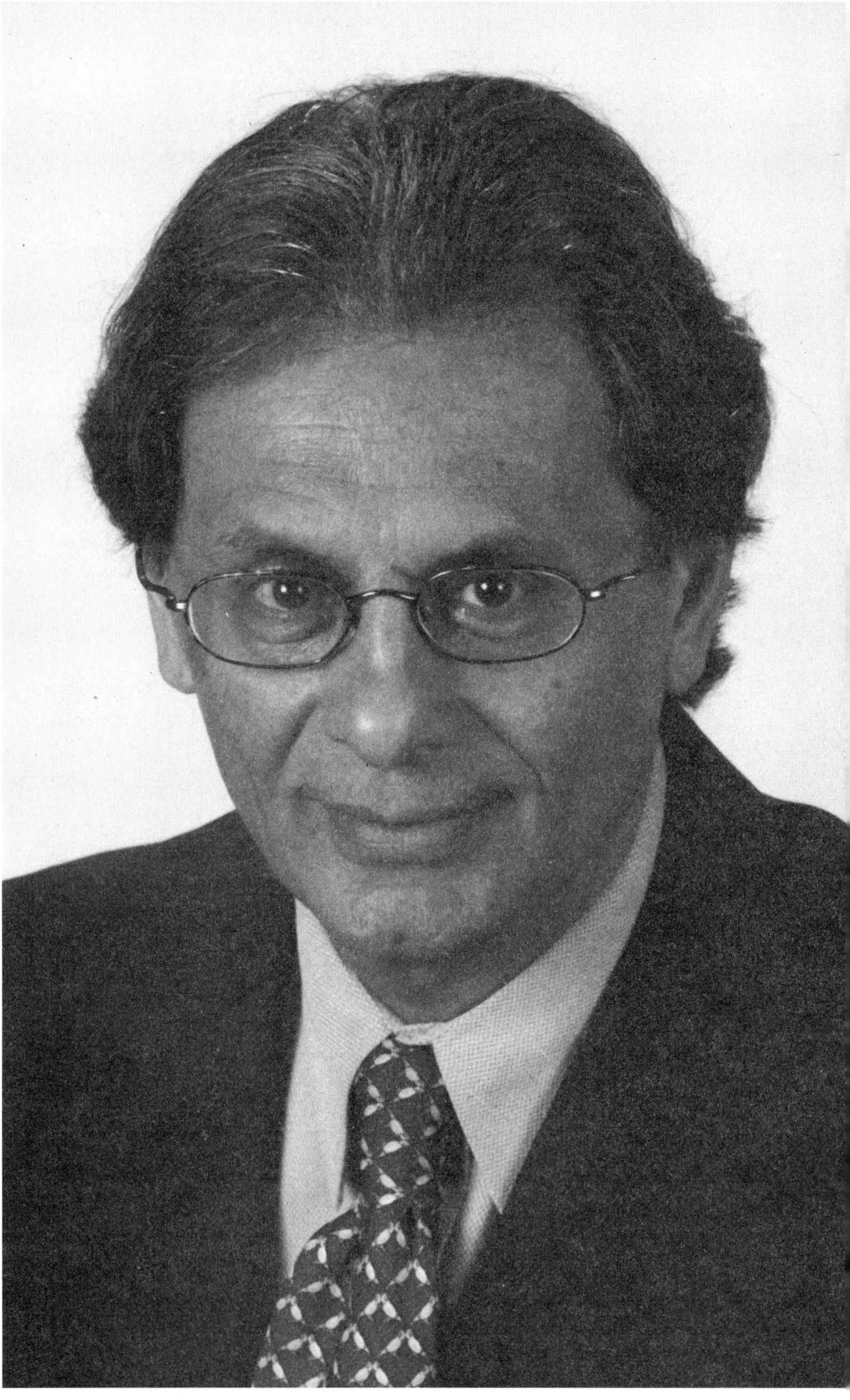

—2002—
HAROON SIDDIQUI

Haroon Siddiqui is a columnist for the *Toronto Star*, Canada's largest newspaper. He is a former editorial page editor, national editor, news editor and foreign affairs analyst. Earlier he was managing editor of the *Brandon Sun*. He has travelled to 40 countries and covered, among other events, the Soviet invasion of Afghanistan, the Iranian revolution, the Iran-Iraq War and, lately, the emergence of India as an economic and regional power. He is a member of both the Order of Canada and the Order of Ontario. A former president of PEN Canada—which protects writers around the world who have been persecuted, imprisoned or exiled for exercising their freedom of expression—he is a director of International PEN.

ARE CANADIAN MEDIA LIVING UP TO THEIR MISSION?

I am happy to be in the land of James Minifie and John Diefenbaker and Tommy Douglas, at least two of whom I had the privilege of covering in the late-sixties and early-seventies.

I will talk about the four Cs of Canadian journalism: Corporatization, Concentration, Convergence, and Creeping Censorship. I will follow that with the sociological shortcomings of the media, as I see them, especially post-September 11. But first, I will make a few statements of the obvious, to clarify the confusions that often clutter debate on the media.

1. Media are a business, except for the CBC, which I support wholeheartedly. Warts and all, it's our only non-profit and national media that truly connects Canadians from coast to coast to coast, and also the nether-reaches of rural Canada. Had there been a print version of the CBC, I would have supported that, too.
2. Media are a business but, equally obviously, they are more than the business of, say, manufacturing soap or widgets. The media, being in the business of news and opinion, play a crucial role in the functioning of democracy. Indeed, they proudly proclaim just such a role. However, they tend to be dodgy about the concomitant responsibilities that may come with such a lofty turf.
3. As a business, media must make money. At their most reductive, then, media deliver audiences to advertisers. This economic dynamic was well grasped long ago by Canadian communications guru, Dallas Smythe, of Regina.
4. If advertisers are the chief source of revenue, it is but human that some of them would be tempted to penalize the medium that may bite the hand that feeds it. The smaller the medium, and the more economically vulnerable it is, the higher the chances of it succumbing, subtly or overtly, to advertiser pressure. The bigger and the more economically stable the medium, the more likely it is to be more editorially independent—if it is so inclined, i.e., if the owner is so inclined.

With the owners' right to own the press also comes the guardianship of the freedom of the press. Some exercise it well, others not. The smarter ones make the argument to advertisers that the best way to sell their products is to place their ads in the media that have the higher credibility which, of course, can only come by safeguarding the media's editorial independence and by practising journalism fairly and fearlessly.

5. Advertisers are not the only ones with the potential to circumscribe our freedom. Media being a business, they are not in the business of offending their clients to the point of driving them away. Stated another way, they cannot get too far out of sync with majority tastes and values—cultural, social and political. Media can, and do, nudge public opinion to the right or the left, but slowly. There's an internal debate between catering to the lowest common denominator or aiming for the highest common factor. Some follow public opinion, even pander to prejudices, and others lead public opinion, even at the risk of angering those who may not want to hear the truth.
6. No survey of the lay of the journalistic land is complete without, of course, noting that the notion of journalistic objectivity has been oversold. Journalism is subjective by definition. We do not provide the minutes of last night's city council meeting but its essence; hopefully, a fair representation of what transpired there—or at any event that we cover. What is left out of a story, what is emphasized, in what tone, where the story is placed, on page one or page 35, with what size headline, are all subjective judgements, based on something called news value. There are, of course, guidelines on what constitutes news. But, in the end, they reflect the biases, prejudices and preferences of the editors, who reflect the values of the owner.

All this is not as scandalously new as we might think. It has always been so, dating back to Confederation, when we had Grit newspapers and Tory newspapers, and they wore their biases on their sleeves. In the decades since, the Thomsons, the Irvings, the Bassetts, the Southams, the Siftons, the Honderichs have never really hid their favourite hobbyhorses.

So, what is new? Where are the media falling short, and why?

Concentration of ownership, combined with the economics of newspapers, gave us one-newspaper towns. The phenomenon pre-dates Conrad Black and Izzy Asper. But there was an ethos that if you ran the only show in town, you had an extra obligation to reflect the diversity of opinion. And most papers tried, and succeeded in varying degrees. However, this ethos is dying, if not already dead in some markets.

The attempt at fairness and balance was facilitated by publishers and publishing empires that, for the most part, had a hands-off approach to the editorial content of their papers.

However, this clearly changed when Conrad Black bought the Southam chain. He owned 58 of 105 dailies in Canada, the highest level of concentration in Canada, in fact, in the western world. He was also ideologically driven, something of which he made no secret. He was also fairly intimately involved with the content of his newspaper, as he was fully entitled to be.

To the complainers, he had a rejoinder: that, after years of domination of soft-liberal thinking, what he colourfully called "the virtual monopoly of the soft left," he was injecting some right-wing balance into the media.

The rejoinder to his rejoinder was this: the small-l liberal media bias at least reflected the general small-l liberal values of the sixties, seventies and eighties, whereas what Black's papers reflected was his own very narrow vision, which was, arguably, out of sync with the majority of Canadians. Whereas he thought of the Liberal government of Jean Chrétien as the chief curse of the land, Canadians elected that government to an unprecedented three straight majorities. Canadians also did not agree with his pathology of running down Canada and looking up to Britain and also the United States.

Canadians also did not agree with his, and Barbara Amiel's, view of the world: that the only good foreigners were Americans, Britons and perhaps some Europeans; and that the rest, especially those from the Third World, were irredeemable. His domestic priorities—corporate and personal tax cuts; snipping the social safety net; privatizing parts of medicare; etc.—were also not in keeping with the priorities of a majority of Canadians, according to public opinion polls.

Again, Conrad Black was entitled to his views, but the point remained: in one-newspaper towns, where he was the owner, his readers had no choice but to put up with his vision.

Black had another argument for critics of concentration of ownership, one that has now been picked up by his successors at *The National Post* and Southam, the Aspers: given the proliferation of media outlets, the wide choice of radio and TV stations in most cities, and the advent of the Internet, there really is no danger posed by concentration of ownership.

It is a slick argument, except it has no relevance to newspapers, i.e., the lack of diverse voices in them, especially under an ideologically driven owner. The same point applies, even more forcefully, to the Aspers, as we shall see.

But, it must be recorded here that with the sale of Southam newspapers to the Aspers, diversity of ownership has actually increased, at least for daily newspapers. The Aspers own only 27 dailies, and Black now only 10. The fear of the late 1990s that we may end up with just one or two owners of all major newspapers has, in fact, dissipated. Ownership of dailies is more fragmented. New buyers are on the horizon. FP Canadian Newspapers, formed to buy the *Winnipeg Free Press* and the *Brandon Sun*, is looking to buy more. So is David Black of Black Press. So is Horizon, the company that owns papers in Thunder Bay, Lethbridge, Medicine Hat, Kelowna, and Penticton. Michael Sifton who bought 18 papers from Conrad Black last year is looking to buy more. There are more buyers than newspapers for sale. This is a healthy development.

Yet, there is a reason for concern regarding Canwest, when you consider that it also owns 120 community newspapers plus, of course, a national TV network. I read the other day that Canwest, in effect, owns 60 percent of newspapers and TV.

The Aspers are also keen to cut down the CBC, complaining of its "subsidy." I presume none of their TV stations runs any film or documentary or program subsidized directly by Telefilm or other government agencies, or indirectly subsidized by tax write-offs!

Whereas private ownership may live with smaller profits, in order to produce a good journalistic product, a market-driven newspaper is obligated to provide decent returns for investors.

Shareholder-driven newsrooms are generally smaller newsrooms. They have fewer resources to cover their communities well. They rely more and more on easy institutional coverage, and less and less on investigative journalism. It's easier and cheaper to take dictation from politicians, or record their poses, than probe their performance. Slowly, the initiative is handed from the newsroom to the other side: to politicians holding scrums, corporations arranging media kits and press conferences, demonstrators holding phony protests. Some of it may be real news but most of it is manufactured news. If Noam Chomsky was concerned about manufacturing consent, we should be concerned about journalistic gullibility to manufactured dissent.

Not all of this is attributable to corporatization, by any means, but much of it is.

Despite all the hype surrounding convergence, the jury is still out on it. First, buyers pay hugely inflated prices to achieve it. Then, they start nickel-and-diming the companies they have bought. The savings are also overstated. The benefits of convergence are the opportunities for cross-promotions and cross-platform selling of advertising. But the question remains: At what cost? One answer is provided by the market. Canwest stock went down after the purchase of *The Post* and the Southam chain.

Between convergence and concentration, five companies now own most major newspapers and TV stations: Canwest, Bell-Globe Media, Quebecor, Rogers and Torstar Corp.

A question poses itself: Which is the bigger threat? Concentration or convergence? Whatever the answer, there is certainly no will in Ottawa, perhaps rightly so, to undo what has already happened. On convergence, there's a half-hearted attempt by the Canadian Radio-television Telecommunication Commission to build a firewall between TV and newspaper newsrooms in case of common ownership. But it is, I am afraid, the wrong way to go, for it can compromise editorial independence. In the long run, it may also be unenforceable.

Conrad Black's *National Post* appeared as an unapologetic right-wing newspaper, not just in editorial and opinions but also in its news columns. But that didn't really matter much in Toronto, because it was the fourth newspaper in that market. In many ways, it was a welcome foil to the liberal *Toronto Star*. But, as I said earlier, people in other cities with views different from Black's had trouble being heard, at least beyond letters to the editors.

With the advent of the Aspers, the situation has worsened. They decreed that editorials written in their head office—on such issues as property rights, Triple-E Senate, military spending or the Israeli-Palestinian conflict—must run in all their 14 big city papers. Among those who did not like it was Stephen Kimber, a columnist for the Asper-owned *Halifax Daily News* and director of journalism at King's College. His column was killed. He quit in protest. When another columnist, Stephanie Domet, did not like the treatment meted out to him and wrote a column on Kimber, it got canned. She quit, too.

When Peter Worthington of *The Sun* chain wrote against all this, his column got canned from the Asper-owned *Windsor Star*. "They are trying to eliminate another point of view in other papers," he said.

Among those protesting were the Canadian Association of Journalists, Quebec Federation of Professional Journalists, Canadian University Press, PEN Canada and the National Conference of Editorial Writers of North America, as well as 55 writers at the Aspers' Montreal *Gazette* who withheld their bylines.

Another Halifax columnist, Peter March, professor of philosophy at St. Mary's University, got canned, he said, because he had written columns critical of Israel.

Doug Cuthand compared the plight of Palestinians to that of Aboriginals here. His column in the *Leader-Post* and *The StarPhoenix* was killed, the first to meet such a fate in 10 years.

All this is chilling.

Over at *The Gazette* in Montreal, veteran reporter Bill Marsden was quoted as saying this of his new bosses: "They do not want any criticism of Israel. We do not run in our newspaper op-ed pieces that express criticism of Israel and what it is doing."

There is an irony here. Canwest media are often critical, rightly so, of undemocratic Arabs who practise censorship against democratic Israel. Yet here we are in Canada witnessing creeping censorship against the Arabs.

The Aspers have argued they have a right to their views. But that was never the real issue. Rather, it was their censorship of other views, either because of a head office directive or, worse, because editors are second-guessing their bosses and exercising self-censorship.

To sum up the four Cs then. One ventures to say that in the domain of the Aspers, all the four Cs have come together. This is unprecedented.

I want to move now from these structural and economic dynamics to the sociological shortcomings of the media, as I see them.

Besides the age-old ill of the media that they are conflict-driven, that they are incapable of conveying the love and harmony that reigns in our blessed land,

and that journalists are usually the last people to discover a social trend, there are new challenges posed by Canada's multiculturalism and pluralism that our media are failing to tackle.

Despite the declarative demands of the Broadcast Act and CRTC guidelines, that broadcasters must reflect the multicultural reality of Canada, neither the private broadcasters nor even the CBC reflect our growing diversity. They and our newspapers are slow to catch on to our demography. This is bad journalism.

The point is best made here in the prairies, the cradle of original mass migration and multiculturalism. Canada today has more immigrants than the United States. One in ten Americans are immigrants. But one in five Canadians is an immigrant. In fact, that's the 1996 Census data. The new census taken last year, the results of which we will begin to see this year, may show that one in four Canadians is an immigrant. Yet you would not know that from our media. A mindless anti-immigrant narrative continues to dominate their content.

There are an estimated 4.5 million visible minorities in Canada. That's more than the combined population of Atlantic Canada, and more than the population of every province except Ontario, Quebec and British Columbia. Toronto's population is 54 percent immigrant, and 51 percent non-white. In Vancouver, 45 percent are immigrant and perhaps 40 percent non-white.

Yet these visible minorities are invisible in the media. When they do make an appearance, it is only when they are in trouble. The media narrative on them remains implacably hostile, not unlike the coverage by men of women's issues in the seventies or eighties, or even worse.

Visible minorities come across not as us but they, foreigners or aliens who happen to be living among us. They are stereotyped and clichéd according to their place of origin. They are rarely shown outside of the context of their exotic ethnicity. Their troubles are highlighted, their achievements under-recorded, or rarely recorded. They are rarely portrayed as "normal" Canadians.

Two York University professors, Carol Tator and Frances Henry, who have analyzed the media extensively, have accused my profession of practicing subtle racism: "The media do not take an overt or explicitly racist stance. They publish report after report in which derogatory cultural characteristics are highlighted."

Henry, who did a stint as chair of Diversity Studies at Ryerson School of Journalism, analyzed 2,622 articles in *The Globe,* the *Star* and *The Sun* over a four-month period. She saw a "major discourse which unjustly stereotyped Vietnamese and blacks, especially Jamaican, as criminals and problem people."

How so? By over-reporting their criminality; by identifying blacks twice as often as whites in crime stories, even though blacks do not commit crimes at double the rate of the national norm; and by racializing immigration and refugee stories.

An even bigger study, done by Scot Wortley, University of Toronto criminologist, came to similar conclusions from an analysis of an even bigger sample, nearly 8,000 stories and photographs.

Even the original inhabitants of our land, our First Nations, do not make it to our mainstream media, except when they fit the stereotype and our neo-conservative newspapers can heap some more abuse on them.

The Aboriginal population of Saskatchewan is 10 percent, half of whom live in urban areas. Yet when I looked at a whole week's worth of *The Leader-Post* recently, the only photograph of an Aboriginal was Grand Chief Ted Moses of the Cree in Quebec, signing a hydro deal with Premier Bernard Landry. But no Saskatchewan First Nation person was allowed to enter the domain of *The Leader-Post*. This is shameful. There's no other way to say it.

Some media people, and not just in Saskatchewan, rationalize such near-absence of coverage of Aboriginal issues by pointing to the socio-economic problems of our First Nations and that highlighting those opens them to charges of racism, which they then blame on so-called political correctness. This is a curious admission: that they do not know how to do their job of covering society, with all its successes and failures.

No discussion of the media today would be complete without a comment on post-September 11 journalism in Canada, especially since most of what comes flooding into Canada from CNN and other American media is not journalism but jingoism.

As Canadians, we felt the pain of our neighbours and walked with them in their bereavement. But many Canadian journalists have forgotten that we are not Americans. Some of our journalists have been swept away by patriotism, American patriotism.

There is a new kind of colonialism abroad in the land. One hundred years ago, Canadians were expected to be totally loyal to England, without question. Post-September 11, we are being told to be totally loyal to America, without asking any questions. But, as James Minifie would have said, Canadians have a right to their perspective, which, in fact, can be helpful to the United States. Criticism of American foreign policy ought not to be confused with anti-Americanism. To do so is to give in to a new kind of McCarthyism.

There has also been a spillover into the Canadian media of the American demonization of Arabs and Muslims and Islam, because all 19 deranged suicide hijackers happened to be Arabs and Muslims. It is as though we have not learned much from history.

On May 22, 1944, this is what Anne Frank wrote in her diary: "What one Christian does is his own responsibility, what one Jew does reflects on all Jews."

Ordinary Muslims are no more responsible for 9/11 than Japanese Canadians or Japanese Americans were for Pearl Harbour! They are no more responsible than Canadian and American Germanic people were for the Nazis. As the Canadian Race Relations Foundation has reminded us, terrorists come in all colours and religions. Yet Canadian media have fallen into the American trap of putting relentless pressure on Muslims to go on proving their anti-terrorist credentials, even though all leading Canadian Muslim organizations have condemned terrorism, repeatedly.

No wonder the backlash against Muslim Canadians has been palpable and hate crimes have shot up dramatically, as police statistics show.

In this age of much misunderstanding between civilizations, Canada is uniquely placed to advance inter-cultural, inter-continental and most particularly, inter-religious dialogue and understanding, both at home and abroad. Yet our media have done little more than be a poor echo chamber of America.

I consider myself an incurably optimistic Canadian. As one who has seen much of the world, I have said very confidently that, our shortcomings notwithstanding, Canada is as close to heaven on earth as it gets. We are successfully managing the melding of virtually every culture, religion, ethnicity and language under the broad canopy of Canada. Ours is an experiment in heterogeneity the like of which has never been attempted in the history of humanity. We are the first truly post-modern nation of the twenty-first century.

It's too bad our media do not have the smarts to reflect our collective greatness and glory.

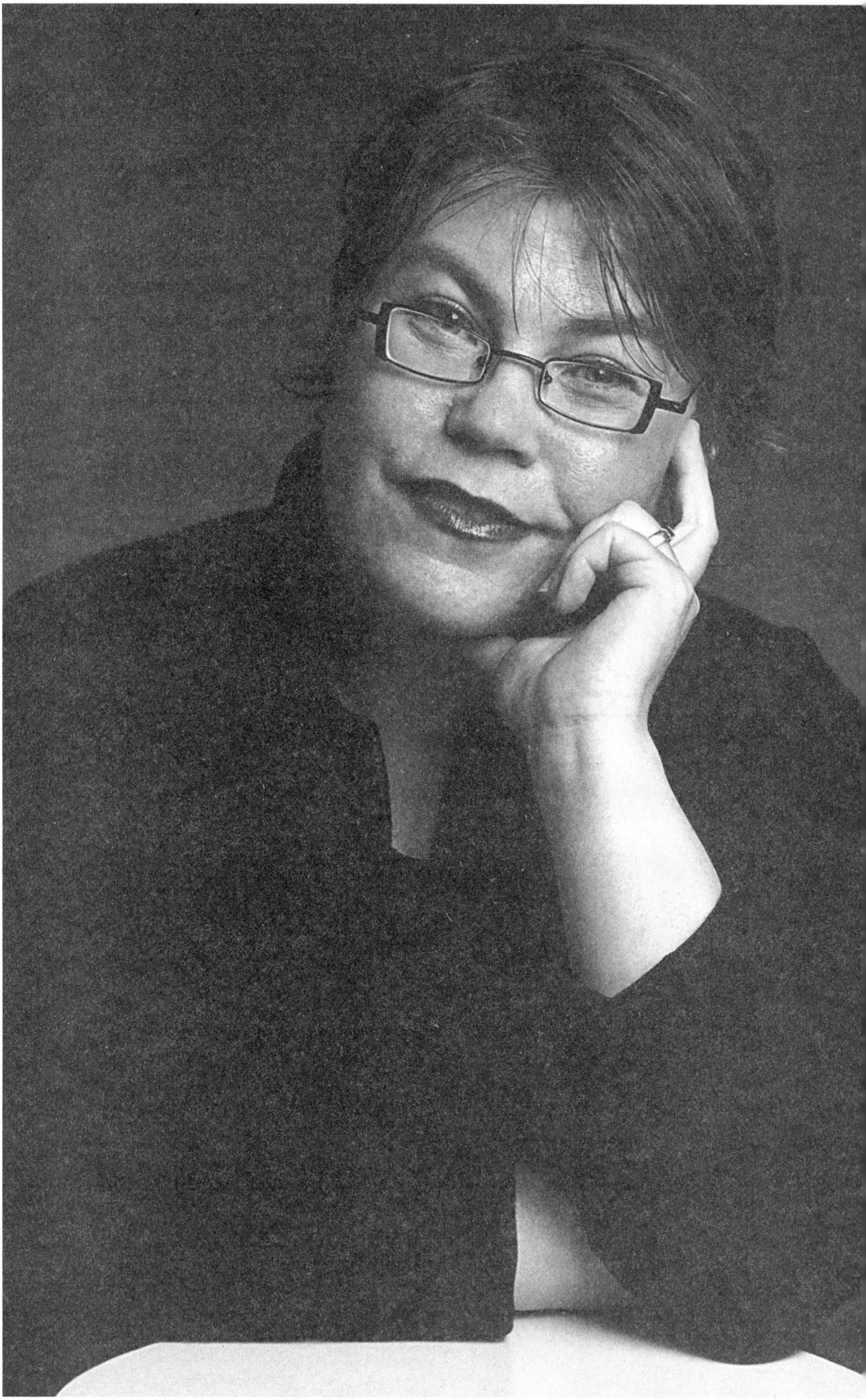

—2003—

ALANNA MITCHELL

In 2000, Alanna Mitchell was named the best environmental reporter in the world by the World Conservation Union and Reuters Foundation. Ms. Mitchell grew up in Regina and studied at the University of Regina and the University of Toronto. She worked for three years as a business journalist at *The Financial Post*, covering real estate and banking. In 1990, she joined *The Globe and Mail*. Four years later she set up a news bureau for *The Globe and Mail* in Calgary, later serving as Calgary bureau chief. She returned to Toronto in 2000 to become the newspaper's first Earth Sciences Reporter. Ms. Mitchell left *The Globe and Mail* in late 2004 to write science books. Her latest, *Sea Sick: The Global Ocean in Crisis* is an international best-seller.

KYOTO:
The Real Goods on Climate Change

First, let me say how very pleased I am to be back here in my home town, at the university where I first really knew the intense joy of letting my mind soar, letting it be governed by curiosity, by the certainty that intellectual thirst was going to be necessary to my life. That knowledge has sustained me ever since, no matter where I've travelled, no matter what I've done. And I'm grateful for it.

My curiosity has led me on a bit of a wild ride over the past few years and before I get to our main topic tonight—the Kyoto Protocol and climate change—let me fill you in a bit on where I've been and what I've learned, and why I care about climate change.

Two years ago I was in the Amazonian rain forest of South America in Suriname, the former Dutch Guyana, looking for a Harpy eagle. Harpy eagles are huge, the biggest eagles in the world and they are incredibly rare. You can live in the jungle for years and never see one. That's because the habitat they need to live is disappearing incredibly fast, mostly cut down by loggers.

I was with one of the most wonderful scientists I have ever met, Russ Mittermeier, a specialist in monkeys and lemurs. Russ had heard that there was a Harpy off some remote little tributary of the Amazon and he was determined to see it. I was there living with him in the jungle for about a week writing a story for *The Globe and Mail*.

So we set off in a little dugout canoe, quite a leaky one if the truth were known, no life jackets. If we fell in, the river was full of piranhas. If we made it to shore, the undergrowth was full of Bushmaster snakes. Those are the ones that sever human limbs in a single bite. Of course, the mosquitoes carried malaria. So I'm sitting in this little dugout, looking at the tropical forest crowding in around us. Vibrant, chaotic, alive, unfathomably complex. One of the few remaining great swaths of pristine tropical rainforest. The Amerindian guide in front of me is hacking away at the vines with his machete, making a passage for us.

Finally we get near to where this Harpy is supposed to be. Russ turns to me and says: "Oh, ya, they eat humans, especially women about your size. And they don't give you much warning. If this one wants you she'll just dive bomb into the forest canopy and pick you off. So if you see her move at all, crouch down in the dugout and hold your arms over the back of your neck like this . . ."

We saw the Harpy, in the end, and she was gorgeous. She was particularly ferocious that day because she was guarding her young while her mate was off looking for little humans or big monkeys for lunch. She spotted us but didn't swoop.

Three years ago, I was in Madagascar, where the forest cover has almost disappeared and the red earth gets washed away into the ocean because there's so little plant cover left. There's only about 10 percent of the forest left, and it's not all in a contiguous stretch, but instead, is broken up along the eastern coast of the island in little bits. So it's still possible to find chaotic, complex forests in Madagascar like the one I was in Suriname, but it's a heck of a lot harder.

Because so much of the forest cover is gone, Madagascar is more threatened with mass extinction of its species right now than any other part of the planet. It's a sight you don't forget once you've seen it. Prince Philip, husband of our present Queen and honorary patron of the World Wildlife Fund, once said flying over Madagascar is like looking at a large animal bleeding into the sea.

But of all the devastation to the land and animals that is so evident in Madagascar, it's the fate of the children that got me thinking the hardest. I was in a little village on the very southern tip of Madagascar—Evatraha—and the children were big-bellied from starvation and parasites. Their curly black hair had blonde streaks from malnutrition. There, too, the mosquitoes carried malaria. And cholera had killed 15,000 Malagasy already that year. The eyes of those children keep me up at night to this day.

And they are what keep me interested in climate change. Because I've seen how bad some of the worst ecological devastation is already, before the effects of climate change have really kicked in. And it's clear to me that as the effects intensify over the coming century, those Malagasy children are going to suffer even more. And that terrific, whole, rare rainforest with its Harpies and Bushmaster snakes and liana vines and even its piranhas may not survive at all.

I have to be frank with you. At the beginning, I didn't know what the heck to think about the science of climate change. I still remember muddling through some of the views on this, not really knowing where to go for good information. Not knowing whether this was some sort of scam.

Five or six years ago, my newspaper was still run by an editor-in-chief who didn't believe in climate change, and we very, very rarely wrote about it on pain of excommunication. So about a month after he left the paper, I got a sly note from one of my colleagues who had read an off-hand comment in *Rolling Stone* magazine about the fact that the Northwest Passage might eventually be open for shipping, because of climate change, and maybe I should look at this.

I remember tracking down all sorts of reputable scientists at good universities and government agencies—because that's how I believe in doing journalistic research—getting them to point me to peer-reviewed, scientific literature, looking for both the case for and the case against.

Finally, I found Andrew Weaver, a climate scientist at the University of Victoria. He was somewhere in the United States, at an airport, catching a plane to yet another meeting. I could hear the tiredness in his voice as he started to explain what scientists know about climate change and the human hand in it.

I said to him: is this stuff real? And he said he was getting damn tired of the question. The science on climate change is so clear, he said, that the CBC, which used to book him for talk shows and panel discussions, wasn't doing it any more because the producers couldn't find anyone credible on the other side, and unless they could have two sides to a story they wouldn't run it.

So here's this top-notch climate scientist—I've gotten to know him better since and he's brilliant—telling me that the knowledge about climate change is now such a given in the scientific community that there aren't two credible sides any more. In the scientific community debunking climate change is akin to believing the earth isn't round but flat.

I've done a lot more reading and interviewing since then about climate change. I've been to the High Arctic in January and seen the open expanses of water where there should be permanent ice. I've seen the graves sinking into the ground where the permafrost is melting.

Scientists have done a great deal more research, too. Let me just list a few of the findings a group of over 1,000 scientists came up with in the most recent report of the Intergovernmental Panel on Climate Change, a gathering of the most eminent climate scientists organized by the United Nations. (Ask yourself next time you take a pharmaceutical or a herbal remedy whether that kind of scientific rigour has been brought to bear examining it.)

This is from the "Summary for Policymakers" of the synthesis report of the 2001 assessment of the Intergovernmental Panel on Climate Change, approved at its 18th plenary in Wembley, UK in September 2001.

- The Earth's climate system has demonstrably changed on both global and regional scales since the pre-industrial era, with some of these changes attributable to human activities.
- There is new and stronger evidence that most of the warming observed over the last 50 years is attributable to human activities. (Natural effects would have caused cooling, so they are being offset and reversed by human activities.)
- Observed changes in regional climate have affected many physical and biological systems and there are preliminary indications that social and economic systems have been affected.
- Concentrations of CO_2 in 2100 will be anywhere from 540 parts per million by volume to 970 ppmv compared to 368 ppmv in 2000 or 280 ppmv before 1750. Temperatures will rise 1.4° to 5.8° C, without precedent in at least 10,000 years, based on paleoclimate data. It's not known what effect 970 ppmv would have on life.

- The higher the concentrations, the greater the likelihood of extreme weather events like flood, droughts, cyclones.
- High concentrations of carbon dioxide gas in the atmosphere "could set in motion large-scale, high-impact, non-linear and potentially abrupt changes in physical and biological systems over the coming decades to millennia . . ." including maybe the abrupt and possibly irreversible change in the flow of heated ocean water to the high latitudes of Europe. Ice sheets will lose mass and the planet will continue to react to climate warming for thousands of years after climate has been stabilized.
- Thresholds are poorly understood when it comes to ecology, but if we cross them, change could become irreversible
- Cutting down on greenhouse gas emissions could delay or reduce effects of climate change.

Of all of this, the thing that worries me the most is the possibility for non-linear changes, or things that don't proceed in a nice, orderly pattern. It strikes me as much more likely that the changes will be geometric, as in the coming cascade of extinctions. I think of the metaphor used by the Stanford scientist Paul Ehrlich. He said that if you're flying in a jumbo jet, you can lose some rivets that hold the plane together, but at some point, losing one more rivet will crash the plane.

So, as I sorted through all this, I had to ask myself, what is the debate about climate change—and the Kyoto Protocol, which is a baby step towards the reductions in emissions that have to happen to avert the worst effects—*really* about? I concluded that it's not about the science. That's just an alibi. It's about denial, in the best psychological tradition. It's about a threat to a value system. It is about the legends society tells itself. It is quintessentially human.

Follow me, if you will, back to England under Queen Victoria, because that's where I went to understand all this. This was part of my research project at Oxford last year where I was a visiting scholar at Green College as a fellow of the Reuters Foundation. Back to Charles Darwin as he was putting together his twin theories of evolution and natural selection.

He was horrified when he came to the conclusion that species evolved. He was a naturalist, trained in the Church of England, promised to the church as a curate. Like most people of his day, he believed that creation had happened in one glorious burst, at the hand of God and that it had ended there. All the species on the face of the Earth after God had finished were still there and always would be. This was called the fixity of the species. There could be no such thing as extinction or the adaptation of species to their surroundings. Some of the first dinosaur bones were just being dug up around that time and scientists were tying themselves into pretzels trying to account for them.

The theory of the fixity of the species was so entrenched that Darwin himself was in denial about his new theories even as he developed them. He sat on his theories for a generation—try getting away with that today!—and published them only because another naturalist, Alfred Russel Wallace, had come to a similar theory in the Malay archipelago. The two officially published together in 1858, 23 years after Darwin set foot on Galapagos during his world travels. *The Origin of Species* came out in 1859, nearly 150 years ago.

Darwin told a friend that it was like "confessing a murder" to piece the theory together. He began to refer to himself as a "Devil's chaplain." He became a recluse, refusing to debate his theory in public. Instead, the brilliant scientist Thomas Henry Huxley did the debates and orchestrated a positive scientific review of the theories.

Still, it was a ferocious debate. It's hard to understand today because we're not immersed in the same set of beliefs. The legend of our day is quite different. But back in the Victorian era, little of it was about Darwin's science. Instead, it was about Christianity, about man's place in the domain of God. God had deliberately made humans just the way they were, and had created all other creatures to serve him, the thinking went. The Bible's stories about Adam and Eve, the fall, original sin, atonement and redemption were critical pieces of the Christian belief. If these events were fictitious, how could the concepts hold? Worse, rather than being the centrepiece of God's beneficent creation—His best work, created in His image—men and women were a come-by-chance species created by the ruthless forces of nature. It was unbearable. It demanded banishing the cherished belief that men and women had a special destiny, that humans were the centre of the universe. That all this, everything, was here just for us.

The resistance ran high and low. The Roman Catholic *Dublin Review* published around the time the *Origin* came out summed up the establishment view: "The salvation of man is a far higher object than the progress of science: and we have no hesitation in maintaining that if in the judgment of the Church the promulgation of any scientific truth was more likely to hinder man's salvation than to promote it, she would not only be justified in her efforts to suppress it, but it would be her bounden duty to do her utmost to suppress it."

The low-brow mass-market periodical *Family Herald* put it this way in its issue of May 20, 1871: "Society must fall to pieces if Darwinism be true." As for academics, some who supported Darwin, including Oxford geometry professor Baden Powell, were accused of heresy and some prosecuted.

It brings to mind the persecution of Galileo, who argued in 1632 against the fixity of the Earth by saying that our planet revolves around the sun. He was tried and found guilty by the probity of the Inquisition and sentenced to life in prison. The church banned his book "as an example for others to abstain from delinquencies of this sort."

Back to Darwin. Despite the debate, by about 1870, 11 years after the *Origin* was published, the debate over evolution was largely settled among the educated men and women of the western world simply because it explained things they saw before their own eyes. There were, and are some skeptics still in academia and in the public. But by and large Darwin's theories have been the mainstream for more than a century. An industry of Darwin research has arisen, thousands of volumes. I spent three months in the Bodleian Library and the Radcliffe Science Library in Oxford trying to plough through them all. I swear, there are scholars today who can list all of Darwin's burps.

By the end of his own life, Darwin was redeemed. The Devil's chaplain was buried in a state funeral on April 26, 1882 at Westminster Abbey, the ultimate sign of honour for a British citizen. The choir wore white and sang of resurrection. This was nothing short of a beatification for the most celebrated scientist of the Victorian age.

The Roman Catholic church finally embraced evolution too, on October 23, 1986. Our current Pope wrote in an encyclical that the science supporting it is now too strong to deny. I note that society has not fallen to pieces despite the fact that Darwin's ideas have held sway, that people still believe fervently in the teachings of the Bible, that Christianity continues to be a strong and vibrant faith system in the modern world.

What was really going on in Darwin's day was a battle that took place on the level of metaphor. It was not about true or false. It was not about good science or bad. It was about good versus evil, dressed in the clothing of science. I believe that only when the church shifted on its pegs enough to accommodate Darwin's theories did the theories get widespread acceptance. Evolution and natural selection had to fit into the orthodoxy of the day—Christian belief—in order to take hold.

I'm thinking of a quote from H.H. Milman, in *The History of Latin Christianity*, 1855: "History to be true must condescend to speak the language of legend; the belief of the times is part of the record of the times; and though there may occur what may baffle its more calm and searching philosophy, it must not disdain that which was the primal, almost universal motive of human life."

It all brings me back to the debate over climate change. At stake now is a different orthodoxy than in Darwin's day. This is not about how humans came to be. It's about how much humans can use before the resources of the planet run out. It's not the fixity of the species, as in Darwin's day, or the fixity of the Earth, as in Galileo's, but the fixity of ecosystems that is at stake here. We buy into the myth that the planet is inexhaustible. It's all here for us and we can't possibly use it all up. We must keep growing, keep doing better, keep improving our standard of living. When was the last time you heard a first-world leader talk with pride about the fact that the economy was growing at 0 percent? In our world, we demand more and more. This is not a theological belief system, but an economic one. That's the legend that underpins the debate over Kyoto.

And, as in Darwin's day, the debate is about symbols, not about science. It pits good against evil, stacking an old economic orthodoxy that is toxic to the global environment against the idea of a new system that could be environmentally benign.

Look at US President George W. Bush. One of his first acts on gaining office in January 2001 was to withdraw from the Kyoto Protocol, even though the US had agreed to it in 1997. He called for a team of American scientists to look at the climate change issue and see if there was anything to it. The chair of the IPCC at the time was Robert Watson, an American who is a key member of the World Bank. But Bush said that the science was unproven and that the Kyoto targets really wouldn't cut down emissions much anyway, so why ratify? (That part makes me laugh. The US was one of the main forces behind lowering the targets of the protocol before it could be adopted internationally, saying it couldn't be expected to do more. Now it's saying it won't ratify because it won't make enough of a difference. I've thought of using a version of that argument on my 9-year-old son, but he's too smart for it.)

I suggest that the science is merely inconvenient, not unproven. Granted, it's not unanimous. Science never is. Scientists are trained to try to figure out what the next question is, not settle for what they know already. But a month after Bush got into office, here's what a spokesman for Exxon Mobil, the most profitable corporation in history and a big donor to Bush's election campaign, had to say about climate change science: "Science is a process of enquiry," said Frank Sprow, the company's head of safety and environmental health. "I'd like the answer tomorrow afternoon, but it may be a decade before the science really gets crisp, because there's so much fundamental information that has to be worked on" (*The Guardian*, April 17, 2001).

Here's the president himself on March 30, 2001: "I will explain as clearly as I can, today and every other chance I get, that we will not do anything that harms our economy. Because first things first are the people who live in America. That's my priority. I'm worried about the economy. And the idea of placing caps on CO_2 does not make economic sense for America" (*Los Angeles Times*, March 30, 2001).

It reminds me of the message from the *Dublin Review* in Darwin's day, which said that the salvation of man is a much higher goal than the advancement of science. What these modern-day political leaders are saying is this: Science be damned. The most important thing is the uninterrupted short-term economic progress of rich countries.

I have a lot of favourite quotes from politicians and paid lobbyists—dutifully quoted throughout the Canadian press, including the *Leader-Post* which my dad clips for me—propounding on the disasters that will befall the Canadian economy if Kyoto is ratified. It's been a ferocious campaign. My all-time favourite, though, is from Mr. Anti-Kyoto himself Ralph Klein, Premier of your next-door neighbour: "Well, Jesus, you know, we'll quit breathing. If everybody quit breathing, can you imagine how much carbon dioxide we could avoid sending into the atmosphere?" (*National Post,* February 27, 2002).

I think of the *Family Herald* of 1871: Society must fall to pieces if Darwinism be true.

And then there's the infamous study put out by the Canadian Manufacturers and Exporters Association, averring that complying with Kyoto would destroy 450,000 jobs in the manufacturing sector alone, cost the economy $40 billion, double some consumer energy prices and force consumers to spend untold thousands of dollars altering their lifestyles. That study came out while I was at Oxford and it was reported even there. I checked into it when I got back to Canada. Apparently, the association phoned up its members and said: How many jobs do you think Kyoto's gonna cost you? It added them up and came up with the number of 450,000. And they call the science of climate change junk?

And the best one, repeated by your business columnist Bruce Johnstone of the *Leader-Post?* That investment will flee Canada for the US if Canada ratifies. I long to point out to people who argue this that while the US federal government has not ratified Kyoto, 20 of its states had, last time I checked, and so had 120 of the biggest cities. Some of these are setting up their own emissions trading systems. Already, the so-called anti-Kyoto US has cut back on the growth of emissions much more than the so-called pro-Kyoto Canada has. Nowhere in the world is there more and better research into technologies that would reduce emissions than in the US. That means, of course, that the US is likely to make pots of money from other countries selling new technologies on how to reduce emissions. In my book, the US attitude to Kyoto is called having your cake and eating it too. There are massive new fortunes to be made in new forms of energy and these guys know it all too well.

So why the wrenching debate over Kyoto? I wouldn't argue that it's all been duplicitous, all been a cynical bid to get more concessions for business from the taxpayer. I think provinces and businesses had some legitimate concerns about how Prime Minister Chrétien chose to handle this file.

But bearing in mind the ceaseless hue and cry from the corporate sector in the months leading up to Canada's ratification of the protocol, I would like to draw your attention to this poll, published in *The Globe* on January 23, 2003. It's a poll of 314 chief executives of Canada's most respected corporations, taken between August 6 and November 30, 2002. The question is: what do you think are the most serious issues facing Canadian businesses? This was asked during the teeth of the Kyoto debate when corporations were saying they'd all go out of business.

By far the most serious issues ranked were: globalization, taxation, productivity, education of the work force, and so on. Kyoto ranks twelfth on the list, right after concerns over NAFTA. The poll was finished in the field by November 30. Kyoto was ratified by December 11.

I want to end up by going back to Madagascar. While I was there, I interviewed some of the villagers of Evatraha, one of the most remote villages in the world. The children I saw there were some of the very poorest children in the world, wearing shreds of clothes, hand-me-downs from the developed world.

The trees around their village were mostly gone, cut down one at a time by hand for firewood. The hills were barren because they had been so thoroughly depleted by slash and burn agriculture. Yet the villagers of Evatraha couldn't see that they were harming the trees. They believed that trees had their own magic of regeneration, not controlled by humans. They said to me: If we keep walking we will always find another tree.

It would be easy to feel superior to those Malagasy villagers. We in the first world can look at aerial photographs of the forests of Madagascar over time and tell the people: more than 90 percent of your trees are gone and they are disappearing far faster than nature can replenish them. But I think that we here in the sophisticated, educated West are in thrall to pretty much the same legend of society as the Malagasy. We, too, believe in the inexhaustibility of the Earth's resources. We believe that the trees, the oil, the cod off the coast of Newfoundland, are here just for us. That if we drive species to extinction, we can clone them. That we can never irreparably damage the chemical exchange systems of the atmosphere by putting too much carbon dioxide into it. That if we go too far, we'll realize right away and human ingenuity will put it to rights.

I think the Canadian debate over the Kyoto Protocol was the ultimate proof of how we are bound by these legends. Like the Malagasy, we believe that if we keep walking, we will always find another tree; if we keep fishing, we'll catch another cod.

I want to suggest to you that we are at a special place in the history of humanity's reign on Earth. We have an opportunity not given to many ages, and that is the opportunity to rewrite the legends that tell us how society works. Darwin's age had this chance and rose—magnificently—to the occasion. In Darwin's day, though, the challenge was intellectual, really rather abstract. Today, the challenge is practical, tactile, played out in the hungry bellies and dying lemurs of Madagascar, the vanishing rain forests of the Amazon. The evidence is before us. The pressure is urgent.

And what's at stake if we don't? Some will tell you that humans are a suicidal species, bent on the destruction of the very life forces we need to survive. I'm undecided on that point. I think it's pretty clear though that the planet will survive, whether we do or not. Other life forms will eventually take over—millions of years from now—if we die out or diminish to a few million scattered over the planet from our current 6 billion. This I have faith in. As for humans? I think we have two generations to make sure the shelf life of our species is as long as possible. If we haven't figured things out by then, nature, I believe, will have her merry, ruthless way with us.

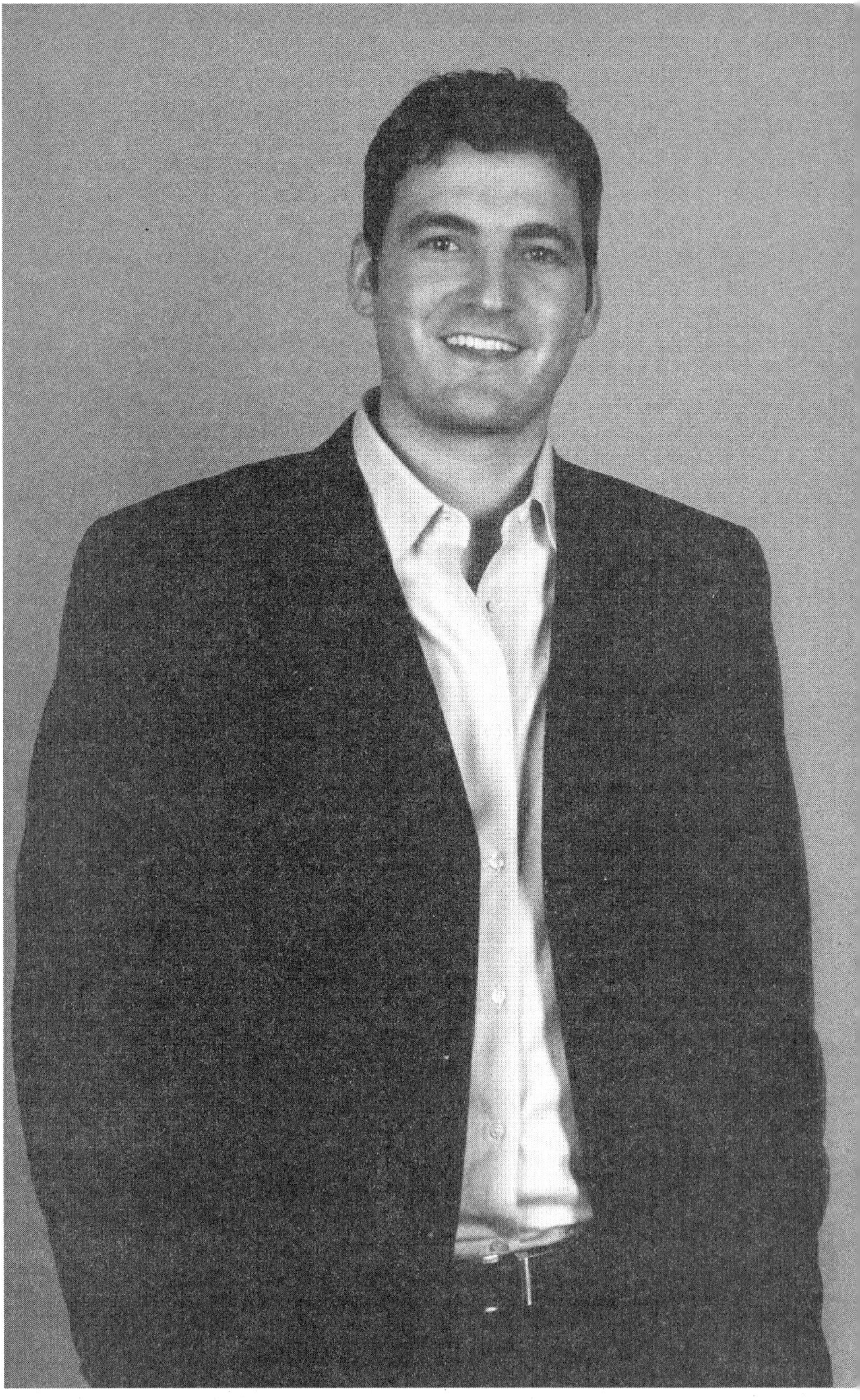

—2004—

EVAN SOLOMON

Two-time Gemini Award-winning journalist Evan Solomon is the anchor of CBC television's national flagship political show, *Power and Politics with Evan Solomon*. Solomon spent eight years as host of the Gemini Award-winning weekly news and current affairs shows *CBC News: Sunday* and *CBC News: Sunday Night*. Solomon has also anchored *Hot Type*, the CBC Newsworld show about print culture and *Future-World*, a Gemini Award-winning series on CBC Newsworld about technology and ideas. Solomon was a co-founder of *Shift Magazine*, an international award-winning magazine about technology and culture. He was the editor-in-chief from 1992 to 1999. Solomon has written several books, including best-selling *Fueling the Future: How the Battle Over Energy Will Change Everything*, and *Feeding the Future: From Fat to Famine, How to Solve the World's Food Crisis*. Solomon writes a monthly column for *The Globe and Mail* called "How They See It." He has a B.A. and an M.A. from McGill University.

2004 | EVAN SOLOMON

VALUES, MEANING, AND FEEDING THE BEAST CALLED MEDIA

It is a great honour for me to come here to deliver the Minifie Lecture this year. I want to thank everyone at the School of Journalism and the University of Regina for inviting me.

Five years ago I had a memorable encounter with the Pulitzer Prize winning writer Richard Ford. As many of you may know, Ford has written many best-selling novels such as *Independence Day* and *The Sportswriter,* and his work regularly appears in magazines like *The New Yorker.* Ford is a Mississippi man who is as at-home in the towers of New York as he is in a duck blind, hunting on the bayou. He is famed for his charm and his wit, but equally famed for his ruthless honesty and unapologetic combativeness. When a critic once panned a book of his, Ford nailed the review to a tree, blasted it with a shotgun and mailed it to the critic. That's his version of a healthy dialogue. His resonant voice trawls slowly from sentence to sentence like a heavily armed river boat, picking up speed when he decides to lean in and go for the kill, which is exactly what he did to me during one of our many encounters.

We were deep into an interview about the nature of his work. I can hardly remember the question I asked him, but it had to do with his work and the million-man march that took place in Washington-an event that had happened that week. Clearly he was not interested in associating his views on men with this event. I saw him cock his mental shotgun. "That's the dumbest question I have ever heard about my work and it's just plain wrong," he said. "Richard," I replied smoothly, "You're getting very defensive." It is an old interviewing tactic, a neat little side step that always keeps the subject answering a question and never lets you lose the advantage. He was having none of it. He leaned forward and put his face six inches from mine. "I am getting defensive because I have something to defend. What about you? What do you have to defend, Mr. Interviewer?"

And then there was silence.

That challenge cut to the very heart of my job. What do I have to defend? What is meaningful about what I do as a journalist; about what the media does in general? Because Ford's *j'accuse* was not just aimed at me, but at the news media in general. And it is imperative that the news media have an answer to the Richard Fords, those who view the news media with deep suspicion and cynicism. After all, the public holds journalists on par with lawyers and politicians as some of the least trustworthy people in our society. That is why tonight I want to speak about values, meaning, and feeding the beast called media. I want to try to offer a defence of our profession.

And it is a difficult task to undertake. The news media beast is a twenty-four-hour news cycle with an insatiable hunger for more stories. Satisfying the hunger means that any and all stories make it into the public sphere, sometimes with no good reason. For example, the media hysteria around an event like Janet Jackson's wardrobe malfunction at this year's Super Bowl put Iraq off the front page of the paper; and the recent Todd Bertuzzi hockey incident, where the Vancouver player knocked another player unconscious with a blind side hit, wiped the news of the train bombings in Spain off the front pages of most newspapers. These events only serve to enhance the notion that the news media has lost its ability to distinguish what is meaningful and what is meaningless. And, after all, that is the very job that news is supposed to do. The media, the argument goes, has lost its way and appears to be getting worse. As one colleague said to me after the Superbowl: "After the nipple, the deluge!" Well, Ford would argue the deluge is already here.

Richard Ford is hardly the first person to make this kind of critique. The most famous person to do so is probably Daniel Boorstin, the great American writer who died this past month. It's worth re-examining his work 40 years later, as it has become more relevant with time. In 1961, Boorstin published a book called *The Image: A Guide to Pseudo-events in America*. It was actually panned by critics at the time, but slowly it became recognized as a prescient and devastating critique of the news media and it is still in print and on university curricula all over the world. Boorstin argued persuasively that the 24-hour news media world is fundamentally at war with our values and what we believe is meaningful, and therefore its practices are indefensible.

Boorstin argued that the triumph of the image over reality was a matter of historical inevitability. In 1828, when Macauley called the gallery where the press sit in Parliament the "fourth estate," there was a sense that journalism had a pure mission, to keep the state of the democracy healthy by watching over the Parliament. Indeed, journalism had an almost theological calling about it. In 1866 James Partan described the job this way: "the skilled and faithful journalist recording with exactness and power the thing that has came to pass, is Providence, addressing men." Providence addressing men. In other words, like the Gospels themselves, there is something divine in the act of witnessing events and reporting them. Of course we do not need to re-examine the controversy around Mel Gibson's movie the *Passion of the Christ* to know that the Gospels themselves have been called bad journalism. The most basic study of *Bible* exegesis reveals that even such sainted men as Matthew, Luke and Mark might not have faithfully recorded the exactness of what happened, and we know this because each of them tells a slightly different tale of the events. Well, if they are not perfect journalists, how then are we to expect lesser men and women to do the job?

The conceit that journalists have some kind of corner on the truth market wore off quickly, especially as new technologies erupted in the 1800s. Boorstin points out how the technology explosion transformed the way journalism was conducted. The advent of the telegraph led to the founding of the Associated Press in 1848—the year Marx published his *Communist Manifesto*—and news became a commodity. In 1876 Alexander Graham Bell patents the telephone, and in 1884 the first roll of film appears. Four years later the Kodak No. 1 is produced and the age of the mass-produced image dawns. Edison patents the radio in 1891 and by 1898, with the United States fighting the Spanish-American war in Cuba and the Philippines, Randolph Hearst and his papers have ditched any theological notions of journalism in favour of one idea: sell the news. His famous propaganda thumping about "remember the *Maine*"—the American war ship that was sunk in Manila harbour—probably accidentally, by the way—made him a rich man and drove America into its first experiments with a new kind of imperialism. Hearst defined news not as truth or Providence but as anything that made the reader say "gee whiz."

With colour printing, photographs, cheap paper, telephones, radio, and, by the early forties, television, Boorstin argues that the technology forced journalists to abandon their discretion and to create news to fill the voids—or feed the beast. Today's problem is only an extension of the one Boorstin analyzed forty years ago, only now the beast is even hungrier.

At the root of Boorstin's thesis is an old Marxist saying: "Your ideology determines the tools you build, but once you build your tools, your tools will start to determine your ideology." In other words, technology, though created from a certain value system, will eventually start to change that value system to suit its own needs and efficiencies. Think of television, which promised to be the great tool for public education and was soon dubbed the "idiot box." Educational TV is a tiny segment of a much larger and powerful entertainment industry. Boorstin concluded that our tools of news media transformed our initial vision of journalism: that instead of reporting on events, journalists began to create them. Instead of reporting on reality, we started to make an unreality. The advent of the information age had begun. "We use our wealth, our technology and our progress to create a thicket of unreality which stands between us and the facts of life," he wrote. This thicket of unreality, he called pseudo-events.

Pseudo-events, like political conventions or debates, talk shows, or strategies like embedding media with armies, are characterized by Boorstin as being more dramatic than ordinary reality; they cost money to create, so someone has an interest in selling them as credible events and they are planned to be reassuring to the audience.

According to Boorstin, even the widely-used practice of the sit-down interview has been ruined by the corrosive effects of mass media. I pay attention to this critique because I conduct interviews every week. It could be argued that Socrates practiced the first form of the interview, but that was actually a form of dialogue. The first interview is generally said to have been conducted by Horace Greely, who interviewed the Mormon leader Brigham Young in 1859 in Salt Lake City. Greely published Young's answers verbatim in the *New York Tribune* on August 20 of that year and the form was born.

However, within ten years the public was already deeply cynical about this kind of journalism. In 1869, *The Nation* already charged that the interview was a contrivance. "The interview as presently managed is generally the joint product of some humbug of a hack politician and another humbug of a reporter." Others called it and the whole craft of journalism "a thing of ill savour in all decent nostrils."

Of course, standards have actually gone up and not even Boorstin would argue that journalism as a whole has become a thing of ill savour, but his point is still relevant. He writes: "What ails us is a nothingness. The vacuum of our experience is actually made emptier by our anxious straining with mechanical devices to fill it artificially. What is remarkable is not only that we manage to fill experience with so much emptiness, but we manage to give the emptiness such appealing variety."

Boorstin's critique, and hundreds more like his, have led to a deep cynicism about the media—as Richard Ford so poignantly illustrated. Only recently, I was on a panel discussing the role of journalists in society and a man named Hal Niedzviecki, who works in what he calls "the alternative press"—he is the founder of *Broken Pencil* magazine, which champions zines and web sites outside of the mainstream media—declared that no one trusts the media because the public knows that objective truth so often trumpeted by news people is a fiction. There is no objective truth, according to Hal, because everything is infected with an agenda. Hal argued that it is impossible to be objective and to report the facts because there is no such thing. So, he says, journalists should simply abandon their fealty to fact reporting and do what he does: honestly declare their inherent biases and market their vision of the world. Only this forthright admission of bias will, according to Hal, expose the pseudo-events, and win back the trust of the public.

I don't believe Boorstin was a cynic, nor do I think he would support the bastard children of his media critique, the people like Hal Niedzviecki who have taken his work and used it to undermine the very important work that journalism does. Boorstin was a great supporter of the notion of objective journalism, of finding the facts. Facts matter a great deal and no fancy argument for relativism, whether from the vogue schools of deconstructionists who talk about "competing discourses of reality," will change that. When covering genocide in Rwanda, the number of bodies, the fact of them, is crucial. Holocaust deniers, for example, embrace the notion of relativism when they half-heartedly admit that some Jews were killed, but not six million. The exact number is important because a dead Jew, Rwandan, Bosnian, American and Iraqi and Canadian soldier is a person with a story and our job is to do the counting. When we no longer respect that job, when we give up on the facts, the hard facts, the killings, the lying becomes easier. So the cynicism that stems from a serious critique of the media ought not lead us to throw out the whole endeavour, or the demagogues and tyrants will triumph.

That is the first defense of media. Getting the facts right. It is a hard job but it is done all the time by intellectually courageous and hard working journalists, journalists who are not in it for ratings or for advertisers who sell hair cream, but because getting the truth out is good. It is right. Because asking questions and getting answers is the ultimate expression of the triumph that is liberal democracy. So that, Richard Ford, is something to defend. To defend vigorously.

Here, too, the role of the public broadcaster ought to be mentioned and defended. I say this because a public broadcaster has a mandate from the public to be beholden only to the facts, not to be subjected to the commodification of news. To be clear of corporate or government agendas. In the face of the nothingness and amusements that pass for news, the public broadcaster is another part of the news machine that ought to be defended, and, when it fails, to be seriously critiqued. It is, to my mind, crucial to both the health of journalism and to a healthy civil society, and that is why I choose to work at the CBC.

In answering Boorstin's and Ford's critique, and in defending the craft of journalism, we ought to realize how closely intertwined the news media is with our values and our sense of what is meaningful. By values I mean the set of principles and ideas that orient our place in the world and shape our responses to new challenges, and complexities. Generally, here, in Canada, our values have been forged in the kiln of two traditions: Judeo-Christian morality and the institutions of liberal democracy. On the surface these all appear to be easily identifiable and agreeable. I would wager that everyone in this room would argue for the importance of a rule of law, freedom of speech and of the press, respect for the rights of the individual and the right to own property—all rights enshrined in our Charter. These are what we have fought to build and, since the war of 1812 these are what Canadians have died to defend. These days, with soldiers in Afghanistan and bombs going off in places like Spain, our collective values become easier to identify and stand in stark relief to those values which are so blatantly different and, at times, so blatantly aggressive.

However if our core values are the root of what binds us, they are also at the root of our deepest divisions. Issues like the War on Terrorism and how to fight it have divided us along lines of principle and value, as have debates around legalization of drugs, gay marriage and abortion.

It turns out that values are not stagnant symbols carved in stone, but rather a set of ideas in constant flux—rather like a giant flock of birds. Like a flock, our values seem to move as one unit but really it is a hive of contradictory, individual decisions and infinite numbers of small battles, a constant tugging at the perimeters that changes shape and direction of the flock but somehow maintains a powerful unity.

Actually, ornithologists have many theories about how flocks work, how many individuals can respond and communicate with each other so fluidly and rapidly and yet present such argument and chaos. One theory calls this the "hive mind"—that the group follows an invisible set of deep instructions that keeps it together even at its chaotic peaks. I would argue that the media play this exact role in our own "hive mind." That the media have become the navigation system by which our values fly. The media play a key role in how this flock moves—it is, I think, at the core of the navigation system and we communicate our values to each other through our culture. In fact, Tad Homer-Dixon, the author of *The Ingenuity Gap*, defines culture as a set of instructions that we pass on from one generation to the next about how we order and manage the world. Culture is the way we preserve our memory, our knowledge and, most importantly, our values. For Tad, all these are crucial to the preservation of what he calls a society's ingenuity—its ability to solve problems it faces. Without a healthy culture, Tad argues, societies might not be able to unleash the ingenuity required to deal with the social and technical challenges of the future.

A century ago, the chief purveyors of our culture, and by extension our values, were our institutions—our mediating structures as the sociologist Peter Berger calls them—churches and synagogues, schools and families and governments. But the well documented breakdown of these institutions, the high divorce rates, the decline in church attendance, the higher rates of illiteracy—4.5 million here in Canada—the breakdown of the family, by process of elimination, elevated the importance of media-news and entertainment. It is now the main way a civil society gets its culture or learns the instructions it needs to survive. In other words, like it or not, the media has become the chief purveyor of our value system. This is why it is imperative that we start to talk about values more.

Let's take any example. The average child will see 40,000 commercials a year just pertaining to food, mostly to fast food, which is one reason someone like Kelly Brownell, the head of the Yale School of Nutrition and author of the book *Food Fight* argues that obesity has become, such a problem. If a child eats every single meal with a parent for a full year, highly unlikely you'll agree, that is less than a thousand times a parent can give a child a message about the value of healthy eating—still 40 times less than the fast food business is hitting that child with a different message based on a different value system. In fact, most of us are hit with 3,000 commercial messages a day, telling us what to buy, what to drive, what to wear, how to grow hair on our heads and get rid of it on our chins. Neil Postman, the great media critic, once said that we are the "first society to turn information into a form of garbage."

But it's important to recognize that the age of information has not devalued news media or corrupted it, as Boorstin and Ford might argue, but rather it has forced it to find its deeper efficiency. Let me explain.

Technological change is not about one technology coming along and destroying another technology. Rather it's about a new technology forcing an old technology to discover its deeper efficiency. For example, when television penetration rates inside the home spiked in the late-forties, David Sarnoff at RCA—who was a believer in TV—thought that radio would die off. After all, TV replaced the radio in the living room. It was more efficient use of the space because it offered a kinesthetic experience—not just the ear but the eyes could be engaged. Radio was bumped out of the living room but it didn't die off. It moved to other more efficient spaces like the car. Radio drama withered away but music and talk thrived.

The same happened to the newspaper. With the advent of the TV, the radio and the Internet, the newspaper was no longer in the news business. In the early part of the last century, what was new made it into the papers. We spent millions on the morning editions and then an afternoon and then an evening edition. But now if you watch the CBC news at 10 p.m., you know exactly what will be on the front page. You don't read the newspaper to find out what has happened but to find out what the meaning of the events are. We know bombs went off in Spain because we saw the pictures on TV, and we heard about it on the Internet, instantly. What we don't know is the significance of the events, the meaning of them.

If economists are right, and abundance decreases value and scarcity increases it, then information itself is decreasing in value. We do not need *more* information; we need more meaning, more perspective. The job of the news media is no longer to sell access to information—that has no value—but to sell access to understanding, to perspective, to meaning.

The news media has to find this deeper efficiency, and the deepest efficiency now is not to give access to events—the kind of thing Boorstin was talking about—but to give perspective on events. In fact, it is the exposure of the pseudo-events, the rediscovery of the hard facts and then the ability to find resonant meaning that gives the journalist and news media value.

In the face of so much information, spin, PR and hype, wisdom, perspective and deep meaning are rising. Journalists are no longer just information gatherers but, to use the phrase from Robert Reich, Bill Clinton's one time secretary of labour, "symbolic analysts."

Does this mean that objectivity is a chimera, an ideal from the past we ought to bury? On the contrary, reporting the facts is more crucial than ever and goes hand-in-hand with putting those facts into perspective. It is this simultaneous dynamic that makes news media defensible and necessary and meaningful.

To survive in a complex world of information and competing media, journalists have to acquire new skills in order to defend the value of their craft and to be able to stand up for it. We have to avoid ideology and try to find meaning outside of pre-arranged formats. In teasing out the meaning in the morass of facts, a journalist may have to develop a poetic skill, one that Keats called "negative capability"—the ability to hold two contradictory ideas in our heads at the same time without one devaluing the other. Again, that does not mean that facts don't matter—a body is a body, a polluted river is a polluted river, a fraud is a fraud. Facts matter but our job is to give all sides of the story, all the facts, even when they seem to contradict each other. That is the nature of the world. Not to give it a false order, but rather to celebrate the negative capability.

If journalism has a purpose, it is to tell real stories about people, to dig out the hidden facts, to make sure the powerful are not getting away with corruption, and to be the watch dog. I think that is being done in many areas and I salute the process and am deeply engaged in it myself.

But perhaps there is another aspect that we ought to think about. What does media contribute to our society? It is dangerous for journalists to engage in any civic nation building, as the impulse to editorialize is the same for the good as it is for the bad. Best to avoid it altogether. Still, there must be a way to measure the value of journalism, to know if we are on the side of meaning or meaninglessness.

I think the measure is the empathy we see in society.

What is meaningful in society? We know we are failing in our jobs by one simple measure: the levels of tolerance in our society. The news media's job is to tell stories, to let people see lives that are not theirs and perspectives that they disagree with. This allows a society to build up the key social ingredient of a healthy democracy—empathy—being able to understand difference because our imaginations have been exercised. The media can do this. They can take us all to new places and tell human stories. And that breeds empathy. A society without empathy turns to civil war, when your neighbour becomes the Other and then the Other becomes the enemy. Societies with healthy dialogue, that showcase diverse voices that listen to all people, are the healthy societies. These are worth defending. And so, here again, I would tell Richard Ford that telling stories contributes to empathy. That is worth defending.

The job of the journalist is to help order the world. It is a primal urge to order the cosmos and then to order our world. The psychologist Lynn Segal wrote in her book *The Dream of Reality*: "First, we wish reality to exist independently of us so we can observe. Second, we wish reality to be discoverable, to reveal itself to us. Third, we wish these secrets to be lawful so we can predict and ultimately control reality. And fourth, we wish for certainty. We wish to know that what we have discovered about reality is true."

That is why we so insatiably consume news. It is in us, this urge to order, and that ordering is a sacred and meaningful urge and we ought to honour it and preserve it.

In my work as a journalist I see this all the time. I should say, being asked to speak here, I think of James Minifie, who stood for all that was good and great about journalism. He abided by his beliefs.

There are other ways to work for meaningfulness as well. I have just co-founded something called the Ingenuity Project, which is an attempt to gather together the best and brightest minds in the world in order to find practical solutions to problems facing the world today. This year we focused on the battle over energy and next year it will be food. Each participant has to supply ingenious ideas—not just criticism—in plain language so they are accessible to everyone. We believe profoundly that stories, if told well, can change the world. That is the goal of journalism, that is the goal I have set for myself, and that is one worth defending.

And by the way, as for Richard Ford, he asked me to send him my novel when it was done so he could review it the way I was reviewing his. I did. He gave me a wonderful comment—a blurb, as it's called—that was used on the back of the book.

It was a proud moment—defending my own work. Journalists have to consider these things personally and professionally, and take risks.

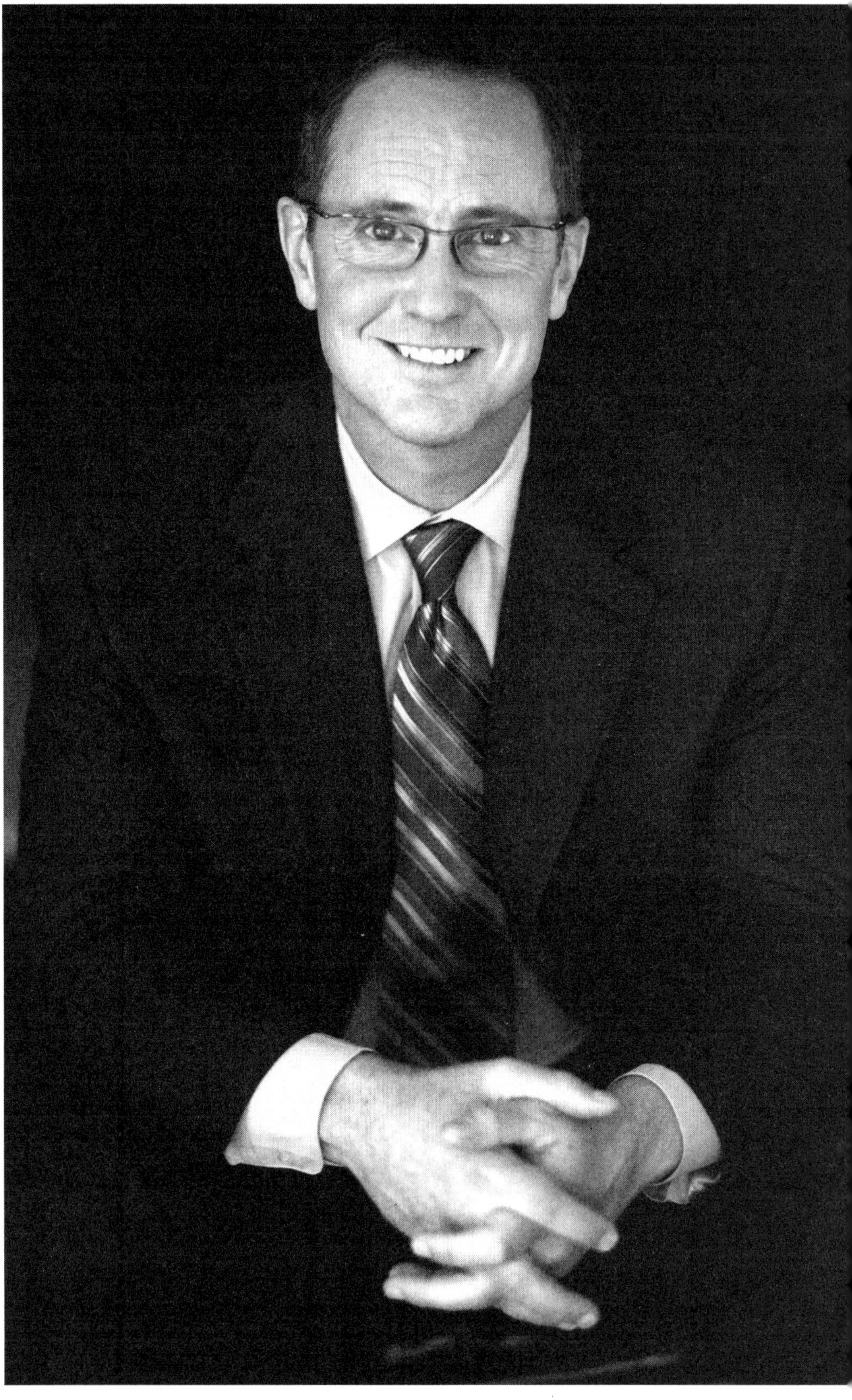

−2005−

KEVIN NEWMAN

Kevin Newman's passion for sharing stories has taken him through all three Canadian networks, and between 1994 and 2001 to ABC News in New York as co-host of *Good Morning America,* substitute anchor for *World News Tonight with Peter Jennings,* and correspondent for *Nightline.* Since September 2001 he has guided the evolution of *Global National* as its Anchor and Executive Editor. Newman has earned two Emmy Awards for his reporting and anchoring, several Gemini Awards and the distinguished Peabody Award.

IS JOURNALISM WORTH BELIEVING IN ANYMORE?

'm calling this little diatribe "Is Journalism Worth Believing in Anymore?" This is a question to which you're likely to get different answers depending on who happens to be listening. I think you know what the most common answer would be: journalists are about as well respected as lawyers in today's society.

But you are an audience with a vested interest in journalism. You either practice it, hope to practice it, or are so concerned about the state of it that you'd go out of your way to see a guy you can watch on TV in the comfort of your living rooms five days a week. Many of you, I'm told, are students of journalism.

The great value of journalism education is that it introduces the notion of accountability and critical thought into our profession. There is an unfortunate tendency in our profession to assume that we are somehow above scrutiny—that a free press must exist separate from our responsibility as citizens and that if mistakes are made they should be admitted but rarely learned from.

That's why institutions such as the school that has grown to such prominence here at the University of Regina are so vitally important. We must train our journalists to think as they react, to understand *context* when they report, and to challenge what they are told. Critical thinking is the key to everything—something that a university is particularly well suited to instill.

But the thing that makes me passionate about journalism is the fact that wisdom and perspective and context develop over a lifetime of reporting. The world is a classroom, and just about everyone we come in contact with are teachers. Let me give you an example of what I mean from the early days in my career.

Some of you may be old enough to remember the constitutional brinksmanship of the Meech Lake Accord. It was Brian Mulroney's attempt to find a new power-sharing deal in Canada acceptable enough to Quebec to get it to sign the Constitution—something a separatist government had refused to do when it was patriated to Canada. The Accord was running into trouble in many places in Canada, but particularly among rural Canadians.

I was a correspondent for CTV News in Atlantic Canada at the time. My assignment editor did what every Toronto assignment editor does—asked me to get some opinion from "real" people. To him, Maritimers meant fishermen. I ran into the same thing when I was posted in Alberta for the CBC. Find out what cattle farmers think. What—you mean there are cities on the Prairies?

Anyway, I was too green to argue at that point. I had just arrived from Toronto so the request didn't seem quite as ridiculous as it should have. So out I went with Gord Danielson, the fabulous CTV cameraman who still works in Atlantic Canada. I was full of drive and desperation, certain that any fisherman would be happy to talk with me about the Meech Lake Accord.

Gord suggested I ask the guy first before shoving a camera in his face. I couldn't really see the sense in that, but okay went along with it. Next, I went in with my in-your-face Toronto technique, demanding to know if he was for or against the Distinct Society clause—and could he please give me his opinion in 10 seconds or less as that's all the time we had. You can imagine his response.

I went back to the car with a big fat "no thanks" in my ear. Gord had a smirk on his face. He said, "just stay in the car, will you?" and up he ambled toward that poor fisherman. Gord offered him a smoke, and they talked for about half an hour. I couldn't make out what they said, but by the end of it Gord came toward me. He said, "He's agreed to do us a favour and talk to us. But don't come on so strong."

It was the single best lesson in journalism I ever got. Treat people with the respect they deserve, and if you ask them to do a favour for you, invariably, they will say "yes." In fact I can't remember any time being refused when I began an approach with "May I ask you a favour?" It is about decency and respect. I have Gord and the good sense of Maritimers to thank for teaching me that.

Those are the journalism lessons you build up over a lifetime. The ones which are painful, but can't really be taught in a classroom. Journalists have always been privileged to have this wonderful opportunity to learn the most important lessons of the trade when the formal education ends.

I would like to imagine that I am here tonight to try to give other messages of hope to the young journalists here who, to be honest, have many reasons to wonder whether they have made a terrible mistake choosing a life in journalism.

Many of you are being taught that journalism is a public service, more than a business—it is a calling. Others are growing up learning the profession from elders who instilled strict ethics and the discipline of good, sparse and descriptive words.

And then you hear no less a figure than the current Dean of traditional broadcast journalism in North America, the retired executive producer of *60 Minutes*, Don Hewitt, telling Reuters recently: "If it keeps going on this way, a grand and glorious institution, broadcast journalism as we knew it, relished it and depended on it, could all but vanish. The kind of tasteful and important journalism that made CBS, NBC and ABC News giants in the news business is, for the most part, gone, and nobody seems to give a damn."

Journalists everywhere are increasingly critical of what they see happening. The Washington-based Pew Center for Public Policy Research—and I have to rely on these American statistics as there doesn't seem to be any philanthropic organization with deep enough pockets to fund this kind of research in Canada—polled US journalists a couple of years ago. I would bet they reflected pretty closely how we might answer the same questions:

Question: "Has the distinction between reporting and commentary seriously eroded?"
69 percent of the journalists polled said *yes*.
Question: "Are news organizations moving too far into entertainment?"
74 per cent of the journalists polled said *yes*.
Question: "Are bottom line pressures hurting television news?"
53 percent of the journalists polled said *yes*.

Around the same time, a committee of journalists in the US drew up a statement of concern that 1,000 of our colleagues in the US signed. It stated "As audiences fragment and our companies diversify, there is growing debate within news organizations about our responsibilities as businesses versus our responsibilities as journalists. Many journalists feel a sense of lost purpose. There is even doubt about the meaning of news, doubt evident when serious journalistic organizations drift toward opinion, infotainment and sensation out of balance with news."

We are living in a year when some of the main titles of investigative journalism have become driven by a tabloid mentality. The new *20/20* without Barbara Walters has become the *US* magazine of TV. The new *Prime Time* is the same as the old *Dateline*—salacious. *W5* on CTV rarely tackles important issues.

In Canada we also have a degree of media concentration that is still not allowed in the US. The Republican-run broadcast regulatory agency in the United States—the FCC—recently failed in its bid to open companies to cross ownership of newspapers and broadcast outlets in the same cities, which of course is something the company I work for has plenty of. There are now only four major TV media-owners in Canada: Canwest, Bell Globe Media, CBC and CHUM. Piss one of them off and you've reduced your employment chances by 25 percent.

And the businesses that own us continue to hunt for better margins. Newsrooms were once not expected to return the same levels of profit other aspects of broadcasting delivered. Now, TV news must not just be profitable, it must be a profit centre.

We deliver 750,000 viewers across Canada every night, seven days a week. And we have a national staff of 40. That's a lot of viewers and very few employees to pay. I read in the *New Yorker* recently that CBS News, from which Dan Rather retired this week, has a yearly budget of $500 million. Ours? Slightly more than one-hundredth of that. The financial pressures, particularly in Canada, are real and a way of life in TV journalism.

So there are plenty of reasons to worry about not only broadcast journalism, and journalism as a whole, both in Canada and the United States.

And yet here we all are. I've just marked my 25th year in the profession. There are hundreds of hopefuls in this hall tonight, and a couple of people behind the cameras making a living at this. Are we crazy? Have we all sold out to fear and money? Are we all simply doing the bidding of our owners and corporate and commercial interests? I know I'm not—and neither are you if you care enough to be here tonight.

We are engaged because journalism is still the most challenging, most satisfying, most exhilarating life we can imagine. It is the most challenging because we bear so much responsibility for the kind of society we live in.

There are two rules in life I learned from Tom Bettag, the executive producer of *Nightline* at ABC News. He was perhaps the greatest editor for whom I ever worked.

One: If your job doesn't scare you, it's time to get a new job.

Two: If you don't do more than you're paid to do, you won't deserve what you get.

How many people start work each morning knowing that at 6 or 11 o'clock at night they'll be looking at their watches and saying, "Is time up already? Why are these days so short?"

How many people come to work knowing that at the end of the day, they will have a real product to show for their day's work? Knowing that every day there will be a crescendo to the day's efforts? And that if you fell off the horse that day, you can get right back on the horse the next morning?

Don't get me wrong. The mediocrity and crass commercialism, the bad journalism and cutthroat economics drive me crazy. I get frustrated. Angry. I'm a world-class worrier. I lose sleep.

And you know what? No one in this room is the first one to worry about the state of broadcast journalism.

Here's what Edward R. Murrow said to a meeting of Radio and Television News Directors in 1958: "We currently have a built-in allergy to unpleasant or disturbing information. Our mass media reflect this. But unless we get up off our fat surpluses and recognize that television in the main is being used to distract, delude, amuse and insulate us, then television and those who finance it, who look at it and those who work at it, may see a totally different picture too late."

That was 40 years ago.

If you are disillusioned by today's journalism, think it is frivolous and drifting, listen to this: "A rocket named television has lost its course. It has lost sight of what has brought it along. In the case of broadcasting, we have not only forgotten where we came from but where we are going."

That was Fred Friendly, another powerhouse at CBS News, writing in 1967.

Yes, business interests are ripping at the guts of journalism. Yes, the newsrooms of today are a fraction of the size they were when I got into the business 25 years ago. That same *New Yorker* article I mentioned reports there are now between 80 and 100 reporters working for each of the American networks. At *Global National* we have 11.

But as tight as newsroom budgets have become, there is also something wonderful happening. There is, today, a lot more opportunity for young people to add their voice to mainstream journalism.

There are more journalists writing more stories in Canada right now than at any other time in our history—much of it online. There are more stories being captured on low-cost digital video this year than all the video of the past 50 years.

Young Canadians are teaching the rest of us that we no longer have the monopoly on storytelling and history-recording. Technology is the greatest democratizing influence in our profession—the number of young people storytelling is exploding.

Where there is a real problem in our profession—I might argue it's not with the money managers, it's not with owners wanting their views reflected (as they have always tried)—it is with those of us 40 and older who are in the way of how journalism is changing.

Too many of us have become lazy in our reporting and lazy in exploring storytelling. We are not challenging authority enough anymore. We think news is what happens in committee rooms or to the rich and famous. We have relied on the same kinds of ways of telling television and radio stories for far too long. Our unions, our management, and our own fears are blocking this great buzz of freelance journalism from finding a place in mainstream media. We're threatened by it because it challenges our old order and we don't understand its power.

It is raw, uncomfortable and challenging. In that, it is probably closer to what journalism is supposed to be. Our younger journalists are creating journalism far more authentic than what older reporters are spinning out.

We need to embrace that more often and not fear it. Digital technology and the young people who understand its power are ushering in an era of renewed 'truth-seeking.'

There is a new generation anxious to use its knowledge, its own experiences, and personal biases, to seek out the truth. I don't trust anyone who claims to have found it, but a good reporter with the technology to videotape real people in real situations will at least convince me that a journey is underway to finding the truth. And I think that is what many of today's online journalists and documentary producers are supplying that mainstream media is not—a search for truth.

I'd like to share with you my own moment of epiphany on truth in reporting, as someone who has lived and worked in mainstream media his whole career—but came to realize it was becoming more about packaging stories than accurately reporting them. I was working for ABC News in New York in 2000 when John F. Kennedy, Jr. crashed his private plane off Long Island. I was ordered by *Nightline*, the program I worked for at the time, to produce eight minutes in a day on how New Yorkers were coping with the grief.

I arrived at the site ahead of the camera man and was worrying about how to fill eight minutes, when I suddenly realized exactly what was going on. Tour buses were slowing down as they passed the apartment building where the young couple had lived. People bringing flowers to add to a newly created shrine seemed fully aware that by being there, what they were doing was taking part in a television event, rather than expressing any real emotion about death. That's what I noticed and that's what I reported.

From that point forward I made it my mission to give myself the licence to say things which I felt were closer to the truth of a situation. And if I'm proud of anything we've accomplished at *Global National*, and I'm proud of a great deal, it has been in giving our reporters licence to throw away that studied neutrality of so much television journalism.

Our folks, like Mike Edgell in the Prairies, are encouraged to challenge authority, to ask the single best question when someone makes a claim to something—"How do you know that?"—and to be free to tell our viewers when spin is simply spin. We take what people say, and then go find out if it's true.

All too often in television journalism people think they're doing their job if they simply get someone else on camera to disagree or find an "expert," without ever taking the time to challenge the truth of something. We hardly ever have experts on *Global National* and we rarely let a politician on our broadcast without challenging what they say.

This lack of attention to truth seeking has cost the mainstream media a fair bit. Poll after poll shows Canadians consider journalists part of the elite in Canada. They believe we exist to defend the interests of institutions, whether it's government, big business, or big labour. This is especially costing us in terms of credibility among younger Canadians. They just don't watch national network news. They don't believe it.

The average age of a viewer of *Global National* is 53. For CBC and CTV, it's 56. And we're doing much better than our American counterparts. The average age of the viewer watching Peter Jennings is 62.

It's not, in my view, because younger viewers are getting their news from other news sources like the Web. It's because they have a very highly developed distrust of agendas. They think the mainline media buys into the agendas of corporations, in particular, and governments as well.

They are more likely to believe the uninformed opinion of some cyber-columnist on Iraq writing in Vancouver, than the reporting of someone who's actually there for the so-called "corporate media." They see non-governmental organizations like Greenpeace, or World Vision, doing more for people than our highly respected foreign aid workers.

And they think by covering Parliament so much we're missing the people who really push change in this country—the judges. Every major social change in Canada they see comes from the decision of judges: on pot, same sex marriage, abortion, and privacy rights. The politicians aren't really relevant to their agenda—which is change.

So that means that the most trusted name in news for younger viewers is Jon Stewart, and *The Daily Show*. He does more to influence the political agenda of people under 40 than any anchor or political talk show. He is neither Liberal nor Conservative, Democrat nor Republican. He told *Newsweek* magazine in October, "The point of view of this show is we're passionately opposed to bullshit."

To Mr. Stewart, and his many viewers, we in the mainstream media all too often spread the bull of others, or create our own.

Which is why truth seeking matters so much. By challenging authority—not being afraid to call someone when they're clearly covering-up or smoothing things over—we will connect with the next generation of decision makers. We've got to be tougher. We've got to not be as afraid of offending older Canadians raised on the CBC standard of even-handed journalistic balance—of never really biting back at institutions and their leaders.

We're not believed anymore by great numbers of Canadians. And that's not their fault. It's ours for not listening as attitudes changed, and suspicion grew. We took comfort in an elitist position that we don't have to change—that we'll keep doing things as we always have—and if people aren't smart enough to want to hear what we have to say, then it's their fault. Mainline journalism is supposed to connect and reflect the people. And we've got a lot of work to do to figure out how to reach the younger half of Canada who isn't listening.

Still, let me return to that Pew Center poll I mentioned at the outset of my remarks, the one that revealed we journalists are critical—very critical—of our profession.

There was one more question from that poll that you should hear.

"When you meet someone at a dinner party for the first time and tell them where you work, do you generally feel proud, or do you feel somewhat apologetic?"

Two percent of the journalists surveyed felt *both*.

Five percent of the journalists surveyed felt *somewhat apologetic*.

And 93 percent of the journalists surveyed felt *proud*.

Yes, journalism is a mess. Yes, we're in a battle. But it's a wonderful battle that has been waged by great journalists as long as anyone can remember. There are few things in life better than a fight worth fighting. And, at the end of the day, journalists are proud to have fought the good fight.

I want to close by passing on a letter to the editor I recently read in the *Columbia Journalism Review* from a television assignment editor in Los Angeles. It was addressing the issue many people in this room are confronting.

Bob Barker—no, not that one—wrote: "Remember our traditional values? I'll tell you mine. That a good reporter can make you read or listen to just about anything. They can get your attention, engage you and seduce you, and make you follow them anywhere. They can get you so interested in the way people clash with institutions that you wind up shaking your head and saying, 'Jesus Christ. Imagine that!' Our audience wants us to do our jobs as reporters. As the great filmmaker, Frank Capra, is fond of saying, 'The audience doesn't know what it wants until it sees it.'"

So to the young journalists in the room tonight, I'm here to assure you that journalism *is* still worth believing in.

The way ahead is simple, and every bit as encouraging as our most optimistic moments: Follow your nose. Find great stories. Look for and tell the truth more often. And know that broadcast journalism will survive the people who have been worrying about it for generations.

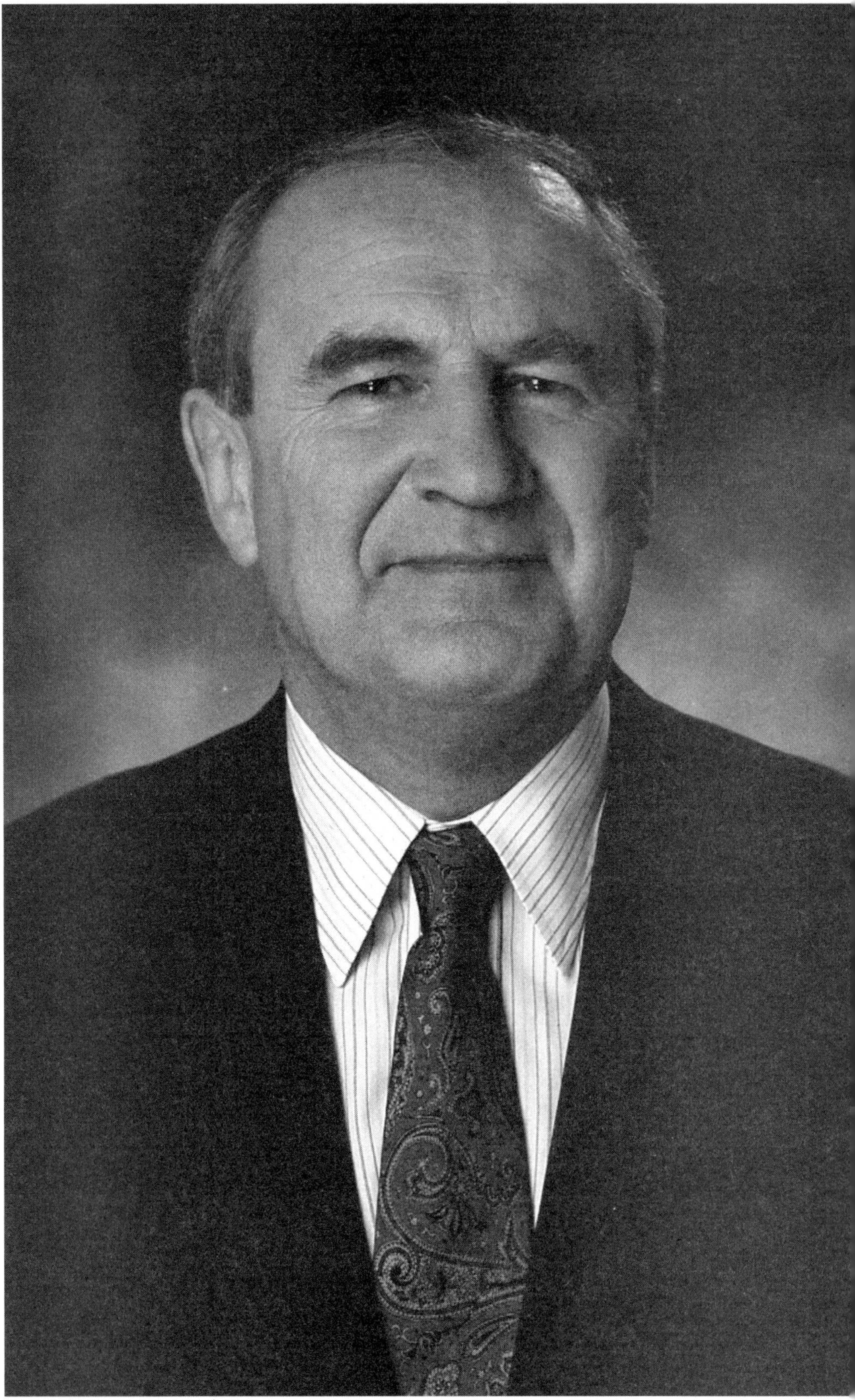

—2006—
DAVID HALTON

David Halton is an Adjunct Professor of International Relations at Carleton University and a director of the Pearson Peacekeeping Centre, Previously, he was a foreign correspondent for the CBC, posted to Paris, Moscow, London and Washington. He was also the CBC's Chief Political Correspondent in Ottawa from 1978 to 1991. On his retirement from the CBC, Halton was awarded one of the most prized Gemini Awards, the Gordon Sinclair Award for Broadcast Journalism. The award cited his "well-deserved reputation for integrity and responsibility in reporting that brings credit not only to him but also to the entire Canadian television industry."

IRAQ AND THE U.S. MEDIA:
A Tragic Failure

Not long ago, Senator Edward Kennedy said "If Congress and the American people had known the truth, America would never have gone to war in Iraq."

The assertion, I believe, is an entirely accurate one, and my theme this evening is that the US news media bear a heavy responsibility for the fact that so little of the truth did get through to the American public in the period before, during, and after the invasion. Indeed, I would argue that, to a quite extraordinary degree on this issue, US print and electronic journalists abdicated their traditional responsibility to provide critical scrutiny of government claims and actions.

Now, the phrase "tragic failure" in the title of these remarks may sound like journalistic hyperbole. But the media in any country surely has no more important a role than to examine and inform the public accurately of the reasons its men and women are being sent to war. It's an issue of particular relevance to Canada right now because of our military involvement in what, admittedly, is a very different situation in Afghanistan.

In the case of Iraq, where more than 18,000 Americans have been killed or wounded and where there have been a much higher number of Iraqi casualties, the betrayal of that responsibility has indeed contributed to tragic consequences. While one certainly cannot exclude the possibility of a good outcome in the longer term—meaning a less brutal and more democratic country than under Saddam Hussein—it is difficult to be optimistic right now about an Iraq that appears to be edging towards civil war.

While Iraq's future is unpredictable, there is no such uncertainty about several major consequences of the US-led invasion and occupation.

The war has been a propaganda coup for the cause of Islamic extremism, a boon to recruitment for terror networks, and the catalyst for a raging anti-Americanism in many parts of the world that has severely damaged Washington's influence and its credibility. This should be no cause for *Schadenfreude* here or anywhere else. Not as long as the United States—whether we like it or not—remains the "indispensable nation," to use Madeleine Albright's description, when it comes to dealing with so many global problems.

Analysis of how and why the US went to war in Iraq is well-trodden turf that I won't march on this evening. What has received surprisingly little study is the role of US media in facilitating the war. Or, to put it more provocatively, why so many American journalists went AWOL on one of the more important stories of their lifetime.

Some of the reasons are easily understood. There's a natural sense of patriotism in people when their country's soldiers are in a dangerous situation. And there is an equally natural instinct among reporters not to write or broadcast news that might demoralize troops in the field. The media critic, Eric Alterman, has aptly written that "Accuracy and accountability are never more necessary to a democracy than in war, but that is also when they are hardest to achieve." A variation of the old adage that truth is the first casualty of war.

In the US, journalists were working under added pressures. There was a public mood of lingering vulnerability after the 9/11 attacks, of super-patriotism, and to some extent of vengeful nationalism. Reporters didn't want to be seen as unpatriotic.

Add to the mix a highly popular wartime president and one can understand but not excuse the reluctance of the media to question the Bush Administration's claims and actions.

All these factors were reinforced by an elaborate government effort to sell the war and choke off dissent.

Ari Fleischer, who was the White House press secretary during most of President Bush's first term, laid down a marker early on. In response to remarks by a comedian whom he judged to be unpatriotic, Fleischer said Americans "need to watch what they say, watch what they do."

In the White House press room, where I spent a considerable amount of time over this period, there were few probing questions about the reasons for invading Iraq. Reporters rightly feared that their access to sources would be cut off if they were seen as too aggressive, hurting their usefulness to their employers. In several instances, editors at leading American dailies signaled to their staff that they didn't want aggressive reporting for fear of being cut off from inside information and leaks coming from the Administration.

The ABC correspondent Terry Moran has confessed that he "cringed at the pliancy" of the White House press corps of which he was a part. A few tough nuts who resisted the trend paid the price.

Helen Thomas, long the respected dean of White House reporters was relegated to the back row of presidential press conferences, and never recognized (until recently). In one of his rare news conferences, just before the war, Bush chose the reporters who could ask questions from a pre-selected list of those judged not likely to rock the boat.

Tom Rosenstiel, the respected director of the Project for Excellence in Journalism, has been quoted as saying "they are the most controlling, the most paranoid White House we have had in modern times."

This is an Administration that has gone to extraordinary lengths to stifle dissent and propagate its own message—and not just on Iraq.

You probably already know of the several cases of payments made to well-known journalists to write stories supporting Administration policy. And you probably know that videos purporting to be news reports—videos that use fake reporters—have been distributed by government departments to some local TV stations.

Then there's the truly bizarre case of James Guckert, which I cannot resist telling you about.

It is not easy to get press credentials for the White House but Guckert, using the alias Jeff Gannon, began appearing in the daily briefings there two and a half years ago. He worked for a Republican web site called the Talon News Service, and quickly became known for asking unusually friendly questions to the White House Press Secretary, Scott McLellan. So much so that some Democrats accused him of being a propaganda tool of Karl Rove and company. The downfall of Guckert, alias Gannon, began when he asked the ultimate softball question to George Bush himself at a presidential news conference. After falsely attributing quotes to several Democratic senators, Guckert asked this question, "Mr. President, how are you going to work with Democrats when they seem divorced from reality?"

The next day, bloggers started investigating Guckert's background. They discovered that he apparently had no previous experience as a journalist and had previously tried to market himself as a male escort. Guckert's brief career as a White House correspondent was over.

On Iraq, the Bush Administration's campaign of disinformation and spin control can only be judged a brilliant success.

Previous American governments, of course, have used deceptions to sell their decisions to go to war. One only has to think of the fabricated claims about Hanoi's attacks on US warships in the Gulf of Tonkin that Lyndon Johnson used to justify escalating the war in Vietnam.

I think it can be fairly said though that no previous US government has matched the sheer scale and consistency of the deception practiced by the Bush Administration.

I won't rehash the claims about Saddam Hussein's weapons of mass destruction—all those assertions that Iraq was six months away from producing nuclear weapons, that mushroom clouds could soon be hanging over American cities.

But I will cite one example of how even the best media outlets let themselves be used to sell the war.

When one thinks of the *New York Times*, one thinks of the "good gray lady" of American journalism, the ultimate paper of record with a world-wide reputation.

Between the winter of 2001 and the late summer of 2003, the *Times* published a stunning series of apparent scoops about Iraq's alleged weapons of mass destruction. As it turned out, the stories were also stunningly wrong.

They were mostly written by Judith Miller, one of the star reporters at the *Times* and, we learned later, they were based on leaks from neo-conservatives in the Administration and from Ahmed Chalabi, the head of the Iraqi National Congress.

On September 8, 2002, the *Times* published a story on the top right of its front page where it signals what it considers its most important news report of the day.

In the lead paragraph, Miller and her co-author wrote: "Iraq has stepped up its quest for nuclear weapons and has embarked on a worldwide hunt for materials to make an atomic bomb, Bush administration officials said today."

This, you will recall, was the aluminum tube story—the one which said Iraq was trying to buy thousands of such tubes, which US officials said were destined to build centrifuges for nuclear weapons.

The story then goes on to state this assertion as a fact.

"Mr. Hussein's dogged insistence on pursuing his nuclear ambitions, along with what defectors described in interviews as Iraq's push to improve and expand Baghdad's chemical and biological arsenals, have brought Iraq and the United States to the brink of war."

Well, largely because it appeared in the *New York Times*, the report had a huge impact, not only in selling the war to the public but in persuading Congress to pass a resolution that virtually gave Bush a blank cheque to go to war.

We have since learned more about what happened at the *New York Times* over that period. Several staff members have said that Howell Raines, then-editor of the paper, wanted to disprove Republican charges that the *Times* was a bastion of liberal bias. They said that Raines sometimes objected to articles that were critical of administration claims, and that he allowed a number of Judith Miller's stories to go into print without being adequately checked.

Listen to what Daniel Okrent, the former ombudsman at the *New York Times* said last month: "I don't think it is fair to say that Judith Miller caused the war in Iraq or that the *New York Times* did. I do think it is fair to say that general rolling over on the part of the American press allowed the war to happen."

We have to acknowledge though that there were grounds for genuine uncertainty about Iraq's weapons program until the war was over. There was far less uncertainty, if any at all, about the Bush administration's other main rationale for the war: the alleged nexus of terror between Saddam Hussein and Al Qaeda.

Vice President Cheney continued to talk of an alleged meeting in Prague between a senior Iraqi official and one of the 9/11 hijackers long after the story was discredited. Most of the time, though, officials stopped short of directly linking Iraq to 9/11 while conveying exactly that message by mentioning the two together. The campaign was so successful that at one point 72 percent of Americans believed that Saddam Hussein was personally involved in 9/11.

Many of those who didn't believe in a direct Iraq-9/11 link were nonetheless convinced by the constant claims that Saddam and Osama bin Laden were working closely together. This, I believe, was the over-arching deception that was more vital even than the WMD issue in building and holding majority public support for the war. And again, with few exceptions, it went remarkably unchallenged in the US media.

Allow me to mention a report I did for *The National* in early October, 2002, about a month after the daily drumbeat of charges had begun linking Iraq to Al Qaeda.

It wasn't particularly enterprising and merely involved the kind of basic reality checks that I am sure are taught in any good school of journalism.

I started by interviewing two former CIA experts on the Middle East. Next I talked to the former official who had been Bill Clinton's top expert on Al Qaeda in the National Security Council. Then I asked our London Bureau to interview the respected Arab journalist, Bari Atwan who had met Osama bin Laden and become a specialist on militant Islam.

From all these sources, the message was the same: that Iraq was freer of Al Qaeda penetration than just about every other Muslim country; that Osama had a long history of hatred for the secular Saddam Hussein, whom he often described as an infidel; and that any ties between Iraq and Al Qaeda were strictly marginal.

Other foreign journalists delivered similar conclusions to their readers and viewers but few, remarkably few, American reporters dared to hold their government to account for what amounted to a cynical manipulation of public opinion. The result was a badly informed citizenry that waved its soldiers to war for—let's call it what it was—a big lie. And a lie that ironically became a self-fulfilling prophecy when the US occupation began turning Iraq into a magnet for *jihadists*.

There were other falsehoods that the administration used to bolster its case that also went unchallenged by the US media. In the six months before the war, President Bush would frequently assert that invading Iraq was his last resort and was not inevitable. In fact, as we now know from the Downing Street memo and other sources, Washington had made the final decision to go to war in the summer of 2002. As tens of thousands of American troops began deploying to the Gulf in the following months, it was quickly obvious that the War was more Bush's first choice than his "last resort."

Another dubious statement was the oft-repeated claim that the United States was supported on Iraq by a vast coalition of willing nations. The US media dutifully picked up the phrase "coalition forces" when describing combat operations in Iraq that were in reality being carried out exclusively by American troops, or more occasionally by British forces. As a result, opinion polls showed that a majority of Americans believed that the US, far from being largely isolated on Iraq, enjoyed widespread global support. Americans might have come to a different conclusion if they knew that many coalition partners, such as Albania, Macedonia, Moldova and Kazahkstan, contributed mere token forces of a dozen or so soldiers. They were in Iraq as window-dressing.

It won't surprise you that the same PR machine that prepared Americans for war was also in high gear during the war itself. By and large, what Americans saw on their television screens was a sanitized version of the war. "Shock and awe" bombing at the outset, but rarely any pictures of Iraqi casualties, civilian or military. Nor would they see any dead American soldiers. Cameras were banned from Dover Air Base in Pennsylvania where the coffins come home. And, with very few exceptions, camera operators in the field were effectively deterred from showing GI's killed in action.

The practice of "embedding" reporters in military units produced some "good footage" as they say in the business. But by the admission of many of the journalists involved, it also affected their willingness to say anything critical about troops who were, after all, protecting them.

Those who broke ranks, like Jeffrey Koffman, a former CBC reporter now working for ABC News, brought down the wrath of the White House and Pentagon.

On a tour of duty in Iraq, Koffman taped an interview with a group of disgruntled US soldiers complaining about Defense Secretary Donald Rumsfeld—the ultimate taboo in the eyes of the administration.

Within 24 hours, White House officials moved to discredit the report. They passed on to a Republican blog site that quote "Koffman is not only openly gay, but"—and here's the *coup de grace*—"he is a Canadian."

In addition to intimidating dissenters, there was an elaborate effort to shape news coverage of the war. One of the more grotesque examples was the Pentagon effort to turn Private Jessica Lynch into a great American hero. You will recall how the US military trumpeted the story that Lynch was wounded in an Iraqi ambush but kept on firing until she ran out of bullets. In fact an embarrassed Private Lynch later admitted that she was only injured when her truck crashed, that she was captured without resisting, and treated well by friendly Iraqi doctors. But credulous US media lapped up the original story. And when it was finally debunked, it wasn't by any of the hundreds of American war correspondents in Iraq. It was by Mitch Potter, a *Toronto Star* correspondent, closely followed by the BBC.

Let me turn now to some disturbing wider trends in US journalism that I believe also contributed to its failure on Iraq.

In 1987 the FCC, the Federal Communications Commission, abolished the US Fairness Doctrine that had been in place for almost 40 years.

The doctrine was intended to curb political partisanship by requiring TV and radio stations to present contrasting viewpoints on controversial issues. Its abolition opened the floodgates for a phenomenal growth in talk radio and TV that emphasized high-voltage opinion over information and reasoned debate.

Enter the likes of Rush Limbaugh, who coined the phrase "feminazis" and more recently described the torture by US soldiers in Abu Ghreib as nothing more than a fraternity prank. The runaway success of Limbaugh's show spawned literally scores of imitators; many of them taking the line that the more outrageous their opinions the higher their ratings.

Almost all of the top-rated programs on both radio and cable TV were, and remain, fiercely conservative and pro-Republican.

Liberal imitators, and they are many fewer in number, invariably lag far behind in the ratings. Why?

Bill O'Reilly, the talk show king at Fox News, recently offered this explanation: "Conservative people," he said, "tend to see the world in black and white terms, good and evil. Liberals see grays. In any talk format, you have to pound home a strong point of view."

Well, no one can accuse O'Reilly of not pounding home a strong point of view. To give you some idea of where O'Reilly stands in the ideological spectrum, he once described *The Globe and Mail* as a "far left newspaper." Under the Orwellian rubric of "fair and balanced," the Fox News Channel has become virtually the house organ of the Republican party, particularly of its foreign policy hawks and its social conservatives. It has also become an immensely successful commercial operation.

For several years now, O'Reilly, and others at Fox and the conservative talk shows, have been waging a relentless and well-organized campaign against what they call the MSM—the mainstream media. They accuse organizations such as the *New York Times,* the *Washington Post,* CNN and the main TV networks of being a liberal fifth column. And in their lexicon, as you know, "liberal" has become a dirty word, synonymous with moral laxity on social issues, and treason on national security. And I can tell you from my travels around the United States in recent years, they have been highly successful in persuading many Americans that there is no such thing as objective mainstream news.

It was in this context, in the run-up to the Iraq War, that what some call "the Fox effect" kicked in. Fox News became the main cheerleader for going to war in Iraq. Its talk shows in particular were drenched in jingoism, and quick to denounce war skeptics as traitors who give comfort to the enemy.

Fox's already strong ratings began to soar, and other cable channels quickly got the message. MSNBC fired its only anti-war talk-show host, Phil Donahue, who was eventually replaced by a conservative host, Joe Scarborough.

An internal MSNBC memo at the time was reported as saying that Donahue presented a "difficult public face for NBC in a time of war—at the same time as our competitors are waving the flag at every opportunity."

It was probably at CNN though that the Fox effect was felt the most. As it was outdistanced even more in the ratings, CNN began to beat the war-drums too, accepting administration claims at face-value and giving its coverage more of a patriotic edge. Its directors realized that such programming wouldn't be acceptable to a foreign audience so, remarkably, CNN International began broadcasting a less excited, more balanced view of what was happening on the Iraq issue than viewers could watch on its domestic channels.

When the war was over, Christiane Amanpour, CNN's most distinguished foreign correspondent, delivered this *mea culpa* in a television interview.

"I think the press was muzzled," she said, "and I think the press self-muzzled. Certainly television and, perhaps, to a certain extent, my station was intimidated by the administration and its foot soldiers at Fox News. And it did, in fact, [create] a climate of fear and self-censorship in terms of the kind of broadcast work we did."

Amanpour concluded by saying that the media and the entire body politic in the US fell prey to what she called "disinformation at the highest levels."

Where, one might ask, was an Ed Murrow or a Walter Cronkite to speak truth to power during what could turnout to be a disastrous episode in modern American history?

Well, one can perhaps take some comfort from more recent trends. Mainstream US media are a litte feistier now, less inclined to parrot the government line on Iraq, and more disposed to examine it critically.

It is, of course, journalism's dirty little secret—that we tend to go easier on popular leaders and take a harder look at those who are slumping in the polls, which is certainly the case with President Bush right now. The media may also be influenced by recent polls that show that slightly over 50 percent of Americans now say that Bush deliberately distorted intelligence and misled the country into war.

As far as the Administration is concerned though, one is tempted to say as Talleyrand said of the Bourbons that "*Ils n'ont rien appris, ni rien oublié.*"

It is true that President Bush has said that there is no evidence that Saddam Hussein was involved in 9/11. But to this day he continues to talk of the prewar nexus of terror between Baghdad and Al Qaeda.

Last month he accused the media of "helping the enemy" because of reports published about illegal domestic wiretapping and the CIA's use of secret prisons abroad.

The FBI has been ordered to launch a full-scale investigation of the journalists involved, and the sources who may have leaked information to them, and officials say they will have no hesitation in hauling reporters before grand juries. Ten days ago, Bill Keller, the new executive editor of the *New York Times*, said: "It sounds like the administration is declaring war at home on the values it professes to be promoting abroad."

There is also a continuing barrage of accusations that the media is failing to report good news stories out of Iraq.

In a speech in February to the Council of Foreign Relations in New York, Defense Secretary Donald Rumsfeld took dead aim at the messenger.

He referred to the fact that the global media environment is often hostile to US policies, and that the US needs to devote far more resources and skill to public relations and public diplomacy.

Rumsfeld wasn't just referring to Al Jazeera. He was also referring to domestic media.

"Some of the most critical battles," he said, "may not be in the mountains of Afghanistan or the streets of Iraq, but in newsrooms—in places like New York, London, Cairo and elsewhere."

It was a revealing remark because it suggests that the Bush administration feels that US problems abroad are the result of a faulty media strategy rather than any flaw in the policies themselves.

Allow me to make a few final observations about the role of Canadian foreign correspondents. In terms of Iraq, I think we did a fairly good job of providing a more independent and balanced view of US war claims and actions.

Not, I hasten to add, because we were any better as journalists, but because Iraq was not Canada's war and we viewed it with a detachment not evident in most of the American reporting.

Watching our national debate unfold on Afghanistan, I am struck by the fact that the media are taking considerable pride in our troops there while devoting a fair amount of print and air time to examining the value of the mission itself. I don't see anyone in the Canadian media being called unpatriotic or a traitor because they question our new role in Kandahar.

I believe the value of having Canadian correspondents abroad is self-evident. It's important that this country sees the world through the prism of Canadian values and Canadian interests. That may sound narcissistic. But Canadian eyes and ears can often provide a dimension that you don't get from the Associated Press wire services, or from the *Daily Telegraph* or any other syndicated news service.

Alas, the numbers are not encouraging.

Canwest fields just one correspondent—a skeleton of the once great stable of foreign correspondents maintained by Southam News. Canadian Press, our national news agency, is also down to one full correspondent in Washington right now, although it has opened a temporary bureau in Afghanistan. CTV and the *Toronto Star* do a little better. But only *The Globe and Mail* can hold its head high in the print media with seven of its own foreign correspondents. CBC does well too—and so it should as a public broadcaster—with 13 correspondents abroad, and another five who broadcast for Radio-Canada.

However, numbers are meaningless without quality. And in my view, quality includes breaking loose a little more from the American news agenda, providing more of a truly global emphasis, and informing Canadians why international events are important to them without falling into the trap of parochialism.

Well, TV journalists, or in my case *former* TV journalists, are used to distilling what they think is their wisdom in short staccato bursts of about two minutes thirty seconds. Given an occasion like this one, we do tend to over-indulge ourselves.

So I will stop in my tracks at this point and give you all a chance to challenge anything I have said, and to give your views about what the media is doing well and, more important, where it is failing. Thank you.

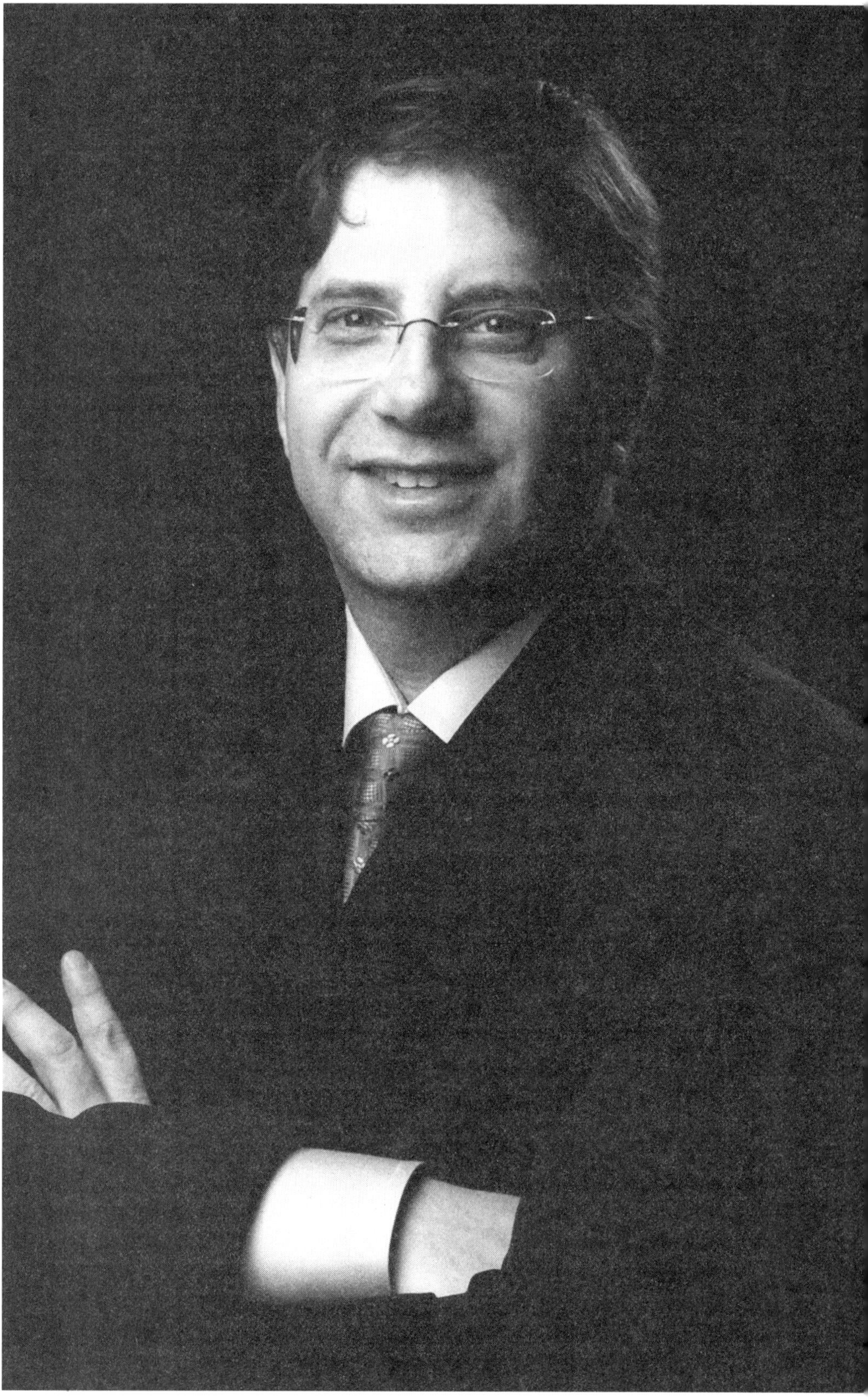

—2007—
EDWARD GREENSPON

Edward Greenspon was Editor-in-Chief of *The Globe and Mail* and globeandmail.com from 2002–09. He was the launch editor of globeandmail.com in June 2000. He began his journalism career at the *Lloydminster Times* and also worked for the Regina *Leader-Post* and the *Financial Post* before joining *The Globe* in 1986 as a business reporter specializing in media industries. He held various positions over the years, among them, European Correspondent, Deputy Managing Editor, Executive News Editor, and Ottawa Bureau Chief. In 1995 he co-authored a book, *Double Vision: The Inside Story of the Liberals in Power*, for which he shared the 1996 Douglas Purvis Award for the best public policy book. In the fall of 2001, he and pollster Darrell Bricker published *Searching for Certainty: Inside the New Canadian Mindset*. He also was co-host of CTV's *Question Period* and a regular panelist on political and media issues. Mr. Greenspon won the Hyman Soloman Award for Excellence in Public Policy Journalism in 2002 and he led *The Globe* to an unprecedented three Michener awards for public service journalism in the span of four years between 2004 and 2007.

TERROR AND THE PRESS:
The Same Old Story

Good evening, ladies and gentlemen. It is nice, as always, to be back in Regina. Especially, in the winter. I genuinely mean that. I remember my first summer here—1980. Temperatures over 40°, drought, dust, dead cows, grasshoppers and, most memorably, falling ash from the volcano at Mount St. Helen's. It was like the apocalypse. After that, I came to accept the winters.

When I moved to Toronto in the mid-1980s, I asked the landlord if there was a place to plug in the block heater on my car.

"Are you from Regina or something?" he asked.

With one year out in Edmonton for bad behaviour, I lived and worked in Regina from April 1980 until August 1984. Those were great years in my early development as a journalist. The Regina *Leader-Post* was teeming with talent and enthusiasm. Same with the CBC and Radio Canada. The journalists around this town were a work-hard, party-hard crowd. Trust me, it was a good time.

In the midst of this, a small man with a big vision named Ron Robbins founded the journalism school here at the University of Regina. He was a fascinating character and a man to whom it was impossible to say no. He had these huge eyebrows and I would always say he could browbeat anyone into anything. He also had this odd habit of calling you on the telephone, floating out the idea of *you* doing something for *him* and then, before you could react, saying "I've got to go right now" and hanging up.

He got things done, including the launching of the annual James M. Minifie Lecture. And out to Regina trooped one of the biggest names in Canadian journalism, CBC-TV anchor Knowlton Nash. No doubt after one of Ron's telephone brow-beatings. To me, it was a glorious opportunity to listen to one of the great ones at such an early stage in my career.

And so I am thrilled to be at another Minifie Lecture tonight, following in Knowlton's footsteps and hoping that out there someone will be as inspired as I was. I thank the organizers for making this prestigious forum available to me.

Not that you guys got to me quickly, mind you. First you had Pam Wallin and Arthur Kent! Valerie Pringle, and Kevin Newman! Haroon Siddiqui and Alanna Mitchell! Evan Solomon and Linden McIntyre!

This is a small country and a small profession, and I can see that you pretty well ran through the A-list before getting to me. But the fact that the university sanctions journalists at all to speak to their students and community is a very progressive act. Not everyone in the academy would necessarily accept the proposition that journalists are capable of saying anything worthwhile, let alone for 45 minutes.

Indeed, the American writer, Norman Mailer, once said: "If a person is not talented enough to be a novelist, not smart enough to be a lawyer, and his hands are too shaky to perform operations, he or she will likely become a journalist."

Winston Churchill remarked that "Journalists do occasionally stumble over the truth. But they quickly pick themselves up and carry on as if nothing happened."

Both these men were, of course, failed journalists who had to go onto other pursuits in order to save their careers.

Journalism is a highly competitive field. But one of the messages I want to leave with you tonight is the need for us, while competing furiously on stories, to co-operate on matters of fundamental principle. You hang together or you hang separately, they say.

If we can stick together on issues of press freedom or access to information, we won't have to hang at all.

One of our young reporters at *The Globe* told me a couple of weeks ago about the fallout from a story he had done. He was aghast that his colleagues in the press were critical because they thought his story went too far.

It reminded me of something that happened when I was a reporter here in Regina. It was the early autumn of 1981 and a 25-year-old father of two waiting at a red light was rammed from behind by a Trans-Am and killed. The car was going between 145 and 160 kilometres an hour. The police said they had been pursuing the car, but had discontinued their chase 15 minutes earlier as they neared the city limits.

But then a witness came forward and said that he had seen about five police cars chasing that Trans-Am seconds before the crash. He provided details about how the police had immediately whisked away the two officers in the lead chase car.

Here was a good story, but one, I am sad to say, that the local press was not keen to pursue. I had briefly filled in as a police reporter the previous year and knew how cozy the beat reporters and cops were.

I called Richard Cleroux, *The Globe and Mail*'s Prairie correspondent in Winnipeg and told him there was a good story that wasn't being covered. Richard said he couldn't get at it and suggested that I freelance it myself. My arrangements with the *Leader-Post* permitted me to freelance, and so I set out to report the story.

It so happened that the witness lived right next to the intersection where the accident took place. That's how he happened to be there. And his version was supported by a second witness who was sitting in a nearby tow truck.

When I interviewed the police, they did not so much refute the evidence, as assail the character of the witnesses, including informing me that one had a police record. When I pointed out that they didn't choose where the crash would take place but just happened to be there, the force's chief spokesman told me they were both dingbats . . . Good quote!

But the point of the story came in the reaction.

The next day was not a happy one for me at the *Leader-Post*. The police had cut off the paper's beat reporter. No overnight rap sheets, nothing. And it was my fault. I protested that *The Globe* story had nothing to do with the *Leader-Post*, but my usually supportive bosses were just a bit miffed.

In fact, the police were so angry and so trying to assert their control that they had cut off access to all the city's media. But what amazed me over the next several days was how angry my media colleagues were. And not at the police, who had behaved badly in the first place and now were acting like little babies. No, they were mad at me!

It is a lesson that sticks with me and one that is of importance today. We have to be careful to distinguish between our short-term competitive interests and our long-term interests to advance the cause of media able to perform their critical social functions, a point to which I will be returning several times tonight.

Let me just take a moment, though, to help you understand where I am coming from through a few other formative experiences.

To begin, I am one of those many journalistic children of Watergate. In the summer of 1973, I would cut class at high school and sneak home to watch the Ervin Committee's Senate Watergate hearings. I was already a veteran political junkie, having developed an addiction to political conventions and election night coverage from the time I was 10. With Watergate, I saw the tectonic interactions of the various estates of political society: the executive in the form of the President and White House; the legislature in the form of Senator Ervin's committee and a House counterpart; the judiciary in the form of Judge Sirica's crucial activism; and, of course, the fourth estate, the press, in the larger-than-life forms of Woodward and Bernstein, their confident editor, Ben Bradlee, and their courageous publisher, Katherine Graham.

I understood that the press played a critical role in society, a role that was staunchly on the side of truth—recognizing that truth often reveals itself in barely decipherable fragments and that one of the challenges of journalism is to piece these together. I learned that powerful forces would try to stand in your way and that although journalists situated themselves within the context of the public interest, that public opinion would not always be on the side of the journalist, at least not in the hurly burly of the moment.

In my third year of journalism school at Carleton University, I edited a small paper called *The Resin*. Our motley reporting staff discovered that the executive members of the residence association, which happened to be the publisher of the paper, had secretly used student funds to treat themselves to a lavish meal at an Ottawa eatery. *The Resin* withstood various threats and entreaties and shone its lantern on this fiduciary lapse. I saw how galvanized public opinion could become when journalism delivered the goods and how nasty authority could become when so exposed. *Resin* staff were subjected to ugly rumour campaigns and threatened with physical violence. About a half-dozen years later, I returned to Carleton for a residence reunion. The ill will and cold shoulder persisted.

Indeed, I sometimes think my journalism career peaked before I even graduated.

I don't want to indulge in a full career blow-by-blow here. But let me just speak of one other important juncture that colours my thinking. In the late 1980s, I was posted to Europe by *The Globe and Mail*. The timing couldn't have been more fortuitous as the people of Eastern Europe were busily prying themselves free of the iron grip of Communism. As a child of Watergate, I already possessed a healthy suspicion of authority and was happy to see one of its ugliest manifestations collapsing of its own deadweight.

I witnessed Communism both before the fall of the Berlin Wall and after. I remember one trip in March 1988 to Romania, the most miserable of the east bloc countries. I started my journey in the Transylvanian city of Oradea, where an evangelical Baptist church had become a centre of resistance to the Ceaucescu regime. I had arranged through emissaries to attend Sunday services and then meet with the pastor and some of his activists. We left the church in a car and drove in circles for about an hour to make sure we were not being followed. We then went to a so-called safe apartment and spoke in whispers so we would not be overheard by official eavesdroppers.

The next morning, I was taking photographs on the street. I was fascinated by a bedraggled one-legged man. He seemed to symbolize the missing freedoms in this police state. I took a shot of him and immediately felt the iron grip of Communism on my right forearm. A secret policeman grabbed my camera and exposed the film. I was then thrown in a paddy wagon and taken to the police station with one other person, the one-legged man.

I don't want to milk this story for more than it was worth. I was released from custody several hours later. But this visit—and many other travels through the region over the next several years—impressed upon me the painful distortions that occur in a society when fundamental freedoms including freedom of expression and its step-child, a free press, become the prerogative of the state rather than of the body politic.

Spending time in totalitarian countries naturally breeds a greater appreciation for democracy. But at home, too, we must be vigilant in protecting our freedoms. In less dramatic forms, governments either interfere with or frustrate the workings of a free press in countries such as Canada and the United States as well. And at no time do they feel more emboldened to do so as when the security of the nation is perceived to be under threat—times like now.

In the summer of 2002, I was on vacation at a lakeside resort in Ontario. I am not what you would call an early riser, an irritant to certain unreasonable family members but a natural tendency I prefer to indulge at holiday time. So it was that while everyone else went to breakfast, I slept in.

Shortly after 9:00, my youngest child burst into the room with his customary exuberance to waken me. He jumped on the bed, and froze.

"Uh, oh, it's 9:11," he said, pointing over my head. I glanced and saw the time, on the clock radio reading 9:11 a.m. For even an eight year old, those numbers were imbued with a very special meaning. A new political era had begun and with it a new dynamic in the ever-evolving relationship between the state and the press.

In the wake of September 11, 2001, a debate broke out about whether things would ever be the same again. Would 2001 go down with other hinge years of recent history, such as 1914 (the outbreak of the First World War), 1945 (the end of the Second World War), or 1989 (the end of the Cold War)?

One can argue convincingly that five plus years on, our everyday lives remain largely unaffected by the plethora of events flowing from 9/11. We go to work. We attend the theatre. We don't take the Minister of Public Safety too seriously.

Then again, if you happen to be a soldier or a Muslim-Canadian, or the head of CSIS [the Canadian Security Intelligence Service], or a cross-border shopper, your life may well have changed. Perhaps the same goes for a newspaper editor.

Several weeks ago, *The Globe and Mail* announced a joint selection of our annual Nation Builder of the Year. In this, the fifth year into the so-called War on Terror, we made what some might consider an odd coupling, Our Nation Builders were the Canadian military in the person of the heroic Sgt. Patrick Tower and that certain Muslim-Canadian for whom life will never be the same again, Maher Arar. The former, we felt, was in Afghanistan fighting for the values and rights that had been so brutally trampled upon in the case of the latter.

After the combat death in Afghanistan of his daughter, Captain Nichola Goddard, University of Calgary professor Tim Goddard said it best. With the Harper government scheming to banish any visual images of the arrival home of the caskets of our fallen soldiers, Goddard succinctly reminded the country in a eulogy that "Nichola died to protect our freedoms not to restrict them."

We didn't use to have to think this way before 9/11, particularly about the vexing issue of the appropriate balance to be struck between what Irwin Cotler has called the right to human security and the more conventional liberties that define a democratic society: freedom of expression, freedom from unreasonable search and seizure, freedom of association, etc.

Let me just take a moment to remind us of these fundamental liberties as set out in the Canadian Charter of Rights and Freedoms:

SECTION 2A)	freedom of conscience and religion;
SECTION 2B)	freedom of thought, belief, opinion, and expression, including freedom of the press and other media of communication;
SECTION 2C)	freedom of peaceful assembly:
SECTION 2D)	freedom of association;
SECTION 7)	the right to life, liberty and security of the person and the right not to be deprived thereof except in accordance with the principle of fundamental justice;
SECTION 8)	the right to be secure against unreasonable search and seizure;
SECTION 9)	the right not be arbitrarily detained or imprisoned;
SECTION 11D)	the right to be presumed innocent until proven guilty according to law in fair public hearing by an independent and impartial tribunal.

As I am sure you all know, in one of those great Canadian compromises, the first section of our Charter both guarantees the rights and freedoms that follow *and* constrains them by making them subject "to such reasonable limit prescribed by law as can be demonstrably justified in a free and democratic society."

That means that in Canada every right has its exceptions. Everything is relative. Which raises the essential question of whether we as a society are willing to accept that these freedoms should be more constrained in a time of war and terror and, if so, to what extent.

In my capacity as the editor-in-chief of *The Globe and Mail,* I am, of course, most concerned with the intersection between free press rights and "such reasonable limits" as may be placed upon them at a time when Canada has troops at risk overseas and worries about the risk of terror attacks at home.

But let me say something first about the wide application of Section 2B. It not only grants rights to people to express themselves but also, one can reasonably infer, the corollary right to be informed and thus make informed choices. To my mind, that places a positive obligation on governments, as guardians of the Charter, to ensure that information flows freely—that the public is unimpeded in its right to be informed.

Unfortunately, the tendency of government in Canada and elsewhere is to monopolize information rather than share it. We see that in the treatment of freedom of information laws, with governments becoming more and more restrictive. Exemptions are easy to declare and appeals can often take two years, generally rendering the information useless in terms of news value.

In its short time in office, the Harper government has attempted to further centralize and control public information and access to public officials. Everyone from deputy ministers to cabinet ministers have been discouraged from talking to the press. The promise of a public report by the Prime Minister's Parliamentary emissary to the Middle East was unapologetically abrogated. Long-held rules of engagement have been summarily dismissed. The attempt cooked up in the Prime Minister's Office [PMO] to restrict media access to the return of dead soldiers to CFB Trenton proved an affront even to the military, which cleared equipment from the perimeter of the base to allow photographers and cameramen unimpeded shots from outside the wire.

Then there has been a concerted effort to exercise control over who can and cannot ask questions of the Prime Minister at press conferences, the so-called List. At first, The List was said to represent an attempt by the government to bring order to the disorderly process of shouted questions. And so the Parliamentary Press Gallery offered to line up at mikes or work off a list administered by the gallery, as is done in the National Press Theatre. No go, said the PMO's communications people. Eventually, certain news organizations, including *The Globe*, *Toronto Star* and Canadian Press decided to boycott The List. Now I imagine if an orderly process is the PMO's true goal, a formulation can be easily worked out. But not one that accords the PMO communications staff the unfettered ability to select its interlocutors in public appearances and therefore the means to exclude perceived "unfriendlies" in the gallery.

The media constitute a legitimate fourth estate in society—alongside the executive, legislature and judiciary. Our legitimacy does not derive from the Constitution, but is merely confirmed by it. I've heard too many reporters and editors, in discussing the Harper government's List, declaim that we are unelected and therefore must, in the final analysis, defer to the government. I've heard journalists argue that the public isn't with us, as if we run for election rather than stand on principle.

My reply is thus: certainly the public will not be supportive if we frame this as an issue of our right to be unruly and grasping of special status. But if we place this in the context of the responsibility of a free press to provide an independent check and balance on the Prime Minister and his cabinet, people will understand. Because citizens don't like too much power to reside in too few hands and too far out of sight. They implicitly understand the danger of that.

That said, these are merely ordinary matters for ordinary times. And although even here the record is troubling, the larger question before us this evening concerns the relationship between the state and press in extraordinary times.

The playwright, Arthur Miller, once said that a good newspaper is "a nation talking to itself." Certainly, one of the functions of the media is to bring shared experience and shared understanding to a civic grouping—the raw ingredients of a cohesive, pluralistic society. This national conversation is the transmission line through which democratic discourse takes place. Some might call this Manufacturing Consent. That would be the press on its bad days. Generally, it should be called Manufacturing Debate.

But while obviously tied into the society in which it operates, the press stands apart from the formal instruments of the state—Parliament, political parties, the bureaucracy, courts, police, etc. This independence allows it to fulfill it second important function—that of a watchdog over these various agents of state power.

Generally, states are held together by some combination of consensus and coercion—the willingness of free individuals to raise a barn together and the power that resides in their institutions to imprison the malcontent who burns it down.

Arguably the highest calling of journalism is to serve as a check on the state's monopoly over coercion. In other words, we want to ensure that the government of the day, with its rented authority over the levers of coercion, is called upon to explain and justify any usages thereof whether conscripting soldiers, eavesdropping on private conversations, disrupting alleged terrorist cells, or shipping citizens off to Syrian jails.

Times of war pose special challenges to this relationship between the press and the state because the very existence of the nation and the security of its citizens may lie in peril. Opinions obviously differ as to whether we are in a time of war today—whether the war on terror constitutes real war—or whether our mission in Afghanistan has anything to do with Canadian national security. But for the sake of argument, let's say that they do.

A generally accepted principle exists in democratic states that, in times of war, the media should not put the integrity of the nation at risk. The simplest manifestation of this is the obvious fact that one does not publish troop movements or battle plans in advance, thus giving assistance to the enemy and endangering one's own troops. You don't write that D-Day is scheduled for next Tuesday or that our Enigma Machine has broken German codes, or that our defences are weak if you come up the back side of the Plains of Abraham.

Beyond that, the onus for journalists should always be on requiring a truly compelling reason *not* to publish something.

In a captivating book from the 1970s called *The First Casualty* drawn from the oft-credited quote: "in war, truth is the first casualty," author Phillip Knightley traces modern war reporting to the Crimean War of the 1850s.

There, a correspondent for *The Times* of London named William Howard Russell wrote up his eyewitness accounts without fear or favour. With the assistance of carrier pigeons, he delivered his dispatches to London on the ineptitude of the English battlefield commanders and the shortage of medicines and equipment.

For his efforts, Russell was removed from the rudimentary shelter the army had provided (call it early embedding) and was subjected to a declaration from the deputy-judge advocate that his stories constituted serious breaches of security and afforded assistance to the enemy. (I might remind you that it took 20 days for a carrier pigeon to make it to London, so the enemy was pretty well informed by then!)

The military, feeling the pressure of public opinion at home, quickly expanded its news management repertoire. It hired its own in-house journalist, a photographer, to take selectively sanitized pictures of a war going well. Military censorship followed, and it was not always exercised in a way that could be said to be demonstrably justified in a free and democratic society.

Russell's singular achievement was that he took the practice of war, previously the exclusive realm of sovereigns, statesmen and commanders, and made the public and public opinion part of the equation.

The relationship between press and government, even in wartime, has been up and down ever since, but never the same. Oftentimes, the press has been compliant or, at the very least, positioned itself within the prevailing public consensus, as was the case with the First and Second World Wars. Other times, as in the Vietnam War—a war never legally declared and therefore devoid of military censorship—the media behaved more independently. Although it should be recalled that even in Vietnam, Chomsky's "manufacturing of consent" far outweighed Spiro Agnew's "nattering nabobs of negativism" until the consensus in favour of the war among elected representatives shattered after the 1968 Tet offensive.

So how does this apply to the role of the press in the shadow lands of a war on terror? And what are we to make of our job *vis à vis* Canada's combat operations in Afghanistan?

Let me revisit explicitly the two principles I have articulated.

First, it is not within our job description to put the lives of Canadians in jeopardy.

Secondly, the fundamental freedoms that underlie Canadian society and are set out in the Charter of Rights and Freedoms do not melt away in the face of an external threat. To sacrifice democratic principles in the struggle to spread democratic principles would be absurd.

So how should an editor balance off these principles? I believe the appropriate test can be found with the US Supreme Court judgment in the landmark 1971 Pentagon Papers case. As many of you will recall, the *New York Times* obtained a secret history of US involvement in Vietnam that had been commissioned by Secretary of Defence Robert McNamara.

The Nixon administration immediately sought and was granted a temporary injunction, arguing that publication would cause "grave and irreparable danger" to American interests, a determination it maintained was the sole preserve of the executive to render. The constitutional issues at stake included whether the freedoms of the First Amendment were absolute, something we know is not so in Canada; whether the threat to national security outweighed free press guarantees; and whether publication of the Pentagon Papers even posed a national security threat.

The Supreme Court decided by 6–3 in favour of the *The Times*, putting forth a variety of reasons why such prior restraint was unacceptable. The reasoning I find most useful for our purposes was that of Justice Potter Stewart. He found that the government failed to establish that the dangers of publication "would surely result in direct, immediate and irreparable damage to our nation or its people."

Consider those words: "surely result in direct, immediate and irreparable damage to our nation or its people." Not a theoretical threat some time in the future nor an embarrassment at present nor a revelation potentially harmful to public opinion. The bar was set much higher than that.

This formulation seems to me to provide an extremely helpful test for editors confronted with the issue of how to handle sensitive stories in times of national security stress.

Some journalists might challenge such a notion on principle, invoking instead the publish-and-be-damned rule. They would argue that weighing harm represents a slippery slope into self-censorship. Perhaps. But absolutism seems to me no substitute for the exercise of editorial judgment, whether it involves the publication of obscenity or violent images or state secrets. Editors exist for no greater reason than precisely the exercise of editorial judgment.

Something along the lines of the principle I have crafted from the Pentagon Papers case guided *La Presse* reporter Jean Pelletier when he discovered in early 1980 that Canada was hiding a group of Americans in diplomatic residences in Tehran—what came to be known as the Canadian caper. Pelletier chose to sit on his story until the endangered Americans and their Canadian protectors could be safely spirited out of Iran.

Not everyone agreed with his judgment. But Pelletier argued that "you can't just simply apply your principle of publish-and-be-damned to each and every situation, regardless of circumstance."

Pelletier obviously felt that the damage of immediate publication could have been direct, immediate and possibly irreparable to the people involved. He exercised discretion in holding back his story. And his scoop held.

Likewise, after the kidnapping of Canadian aid workers in Iraq, a number of media outlets chose not to report that one of the victims, James Loney, was a homosexual. While his family members in Sault Ste. Marie were profiled in the media, no attempt was made to report on his anguished lover. In other words, the media held back from readers knowledge that it possessed. Was that right? Again, I would say that the danger to Loney far outweighed the public's interest in that particular morsel of information. Just because something may be of interest to the public does not place it within the public interest.

In contrast, a clear public interest existed in the disgraceful treatment accorded Maher Arar, citizen of Canada.

Here was an example of state actors, in a time of terror, losing their heads. *The Globe*, for one, took up the cause early, vigorously and with persistence.

The official line held that Arar and a group of other Syrian-Canadians constituted a terrorist cell. *The Globe* said "we don't care." He may have been a terrorist. But that was not our primary issue. The foundation for our coverage was the indisputable fact that he had been denied due process. And that falls outside Canadians norms.

Arar is the poster boy for what can go wrong in time of political stress. As Junius admonishes us every morning at the top of the editorial page of *The Globe and Mail*: "The subject who is truly loyal to the Chief Magistrate will neither advise nor submit to arbitrary measures."

Indeed, to me, there was a whiff of Alfred Dreyfus to Maher Arar reflecting officialdom ruled by fear rather than intelligence, and pushed along by a hint of racism.

Andrew Mitrovica has written a provocative article about the press and Arar in the January edition of *The Walrus* magazine. He decries what he calls "the sometimes inconsistent relationship between anonymous sources and Parliamentary reporters." Although he does not entirely spare *The Globe* the rod, he speaks of a great divide between the coverage of the Arar story as published by Canada's two national newspapers—*The Globe* with its persistent questions and *The National Post* either studiously ducking the obvious questions, or seemingly anxious to believe the worst of Arar. I think what Mitrovica observes in the case of *The Globe* speaks to a form of journalism that is rooted in values but seeks out truth, versus a form of journalism that is rooted in ideology and seeks out corroboration.

The trick here is to never forget that newspapers are about inquiry, not advocacy. What we did at *The Globe* was basic to journalism—in times normal or abnormal. We picked away at an unconvincing official version of events. And we kept the story alive when it might otherwise have died.

Where Mitrovica finds some fault with *The Globe*, I see an appropriate level of journalistic agnosticism.

There is little argument that in addition to being the victim of torture, Arar was also the victim of a concerted smear campaign. When the anonymous leaks began, we were among the recipients. We treated these pronouncements of government officials with skepticism, but at one point we did report allegations by Canadian and American sources that Arar had been a long-time target of a joint security investigation and that's why he had been placed on an anti-terror watch list. We felt little compunction in relying on what senior government officials were saying in part because it established a higher level of Canadian complicity than previously demonstrated.

The most famous—or what Justice O'Connor called notorious—leak appeared in the *Ottawa Citizen* on November 8, 2003. Reporter Juliet O'Neill wrote about an Arar national security dossier furnished by unnamed security sources. It contained detailed information, among other things, on his recruitment efforts for the *jihad* while studying at McGill University, his training in an Al-Qaeda camp in Afghanistan and the belief of officials that a public inquiry would "open a can of worms" that could jeopardize ongoing terror investigations. Some of these allegations were known to us earlier, but we were wary of them because: a) nobody would go on the record; b) we felt they may have been extracted under torture; and c) Arar was in jail at the time and could not defend himself. As for O'Neill, she couched her story in qualifying words such as alleged and supposed, but the weight of her article left the impression that Maher Arar was a suspicious character. (Would I have published that story? Probably, but we would have been more skeptical.)

Then on January 21, 2004, all hell broke loose as the ever clumsy RCMP raided Juliet O'Neill's house under the Security Information Act, claiming the leak threatened the very security of this delicate nation of ours.

The Mounties put the Truth Verification Section of the Behavioral Services branch on the job. Somewhere George Orwell chuckled. Both the fact of the raid and the manner in which it was carried out, breaking all the accepted protocols of press-police interactions, backfired as a highly embarrassed government and agitated Prime Minister decided to proceed with a public inquiry. Although the actions against O'Neill were extremely distressing, one can't help concluding that the torture of a Canadian citizen in a Syrian jail falls a notch below the invasion of a reporter's underwear drawer in the pecking order of official affronts.

I don't say this to be glib. I agree with *Citizen* editor Scott Anderson that the raid represented a black day for freedom in Canada. But so did Canada's role in the rendition of citizen Arar to Syria.

Ultimately, the RCMP was publicly castigated for its raid by Madame Justice Lynn Ratushny in a judgment that struck down three sections of the secrets law and affirmed the media's right to seek, obtain, and possess some government secrets. In other words, the judge found no clear and present danger that would come even close to demonstrably justifying, in a free and democratic society, the RCMP's actions in trying to turn O'Neill into an investigative arm of the state.

But one cannot leave this incident behind without discussing the implications of Juliet O'Neill's use of anonymous sources to float into the public consciousness an officially preferred version of the Arar story. Indeed, a quiet but important debate has broken out in journalistic circles about both the reliance journalists place on such sources and the proper response if these sources turn out to have peddled false or misleading information.

In his *Walrus* article, Andrew Mitrovica quotes Carleton's own Allan Thompson arguing that Arar has the right to know who orchestrated the smear campaign against him and that reporters should identify these unnamed sources.

Mitrovica returns to this theme in summing up his article, stating that journalists might want to revisit journalistic convention regarding promises of anonymity. "In Arar's case," he writes, "if anonymous sources kept an innocent man imprisoned, separated from his wife and newborn child, and tortured, and then prevented truth from emerging, all under false pretenses, then they must be ousted." While acknowledging the reasonableness of contrary views, Tony Burman, editor-in-chief of CBC news, has thrown his weight behind the burning of miscreant sources. In January, he posted a commentary on his CBC blog explaining the importance of confidential sources, but arguing that they should be exposed "if we discover they have deliberately lied."

I agree with Tony that this is fertile ground for debate. But in my view, such a course would be wrong-headed. We all have used and will in the future use confidential sources to ferret out information of interest to the public from secretive organizations. Think Watergate. Think Deep Throat. Think Daniel Leblanc's work on the sponsorship scandal.

In granting anonymity—something I admit we do with far too much ease—we need to make strenuous efforts to verify the information. We are not vending machines, but journalists. But I can tell you, having worked in Ottawa for many years that it would be impossible to serve the public interest without resorting to anonymous sources. The critical equation is not whether they are using you (that is always the case to some extent, including, we now know, with Deep Throat) but that your readers are getting the best out of the bargain.

It is quite conceivable that O'Neill's sources were scoundrels, as Mitrovica suggests. It is also possible they genuinely believed their information to be true and were misled themselves. In other words, to use Burman's prescription, do we know beyond a doubt that their inaccuracies were deliberate? It is even within the realm of possibility—although highly unlikely—that they were right in at least some of their information. After all, one of the things you learn at Carleton is how hard it is to prove a negative.

I believe that the unauthorized disclosure of confidential sources is a true slippery slope. It could well inhibit future whistleblowers (always a jittery lot). In my view, it should only be considered in the most extreme and egregious of circumstances that involve an overriding need to root out serious wrongdoing.

The better although less satisfactory approach is to confront your source, demand an explanation (you may actually learn something) and if unsatisfied, drop them from your Rolodex. Unlike Mitrovica, I cannot be persuaded that the greater good is served by exposing these sources or, indeed, that no matter how contemptible their subsequent actions, that the media leaks had any direct connection to the original matter of Arar's rendition and torture.

Let's quickly move from Arar to some of the national security debates raging in the United States, which is far more deeply engaged in waging war and anti-terror operations and where a highly ideological administration and its partisans do not hesitate to enter into battle with the so-called mainstream press.

Winston Churchill, speaking during the Second World War, declared that: "In wartime, truth is so precious that she should be attended by a bodyguard of lies." This same perspective is pervasive among conservative commentators in the United States, who blame that country's failure in Vietnam not on misplaced objectives or failed strategy but rather on the press having turned against America. Listen to one-time Nixon speechwriter, presidential candidate and media commentator Patrick Buchanan: "In Vietnam, thousands of Americans died, sacrificial victims to a suicidal construction of the First Amendment." I suspect this view is representative of many in the Bush administration.

In the past couple of years, we have seen a concerted attack aimed particularly at *The New York Times,* the most influential media outlet in the country. *The Times* like many other media companies, has been weakened both by internal scandal (the Jayson Blair fiasco) and its perceived credulity in swallowing the administration's line on weapons of mass destruction in Iraq.

But more recently, it has taken an aggressive approach in covering Bush administration actions in the war on terror. Two recent *Times* stories stand out in particular—one that disclosed the co-operation of the financial clearing house SWIFT in tracking possible terrorist transactions, and another that revealed a widespread campaign of wiretapping without resort to judicial warrants.

The wiretapping story, in particular, unleashed a torrent of criticism and even threats that *The Times* could or should be prosecuted under the Espionage Act.

Think of the position of *Times* executive editor Bill Keller, as reported in *New Yorker* magazine. At one point, he was called to the White House along with his publisher and his Washington bureau chief. President George W. Bush and his top security advisers received the group in the oval office. The President warned Keller that if *The Times* disclosed the existence of the clandestine eavesdropping program, the next time there was a terrorist attack on American soil the paper would have blood on its hands.

Now all Bush really had to do was agree to follow the procedures, as set out in a 1978 law, for obtaining warrants from such spying activity. The essence of *The Times* story was that the Administration was circumventing a special court set up for the purpose and proceeding without the necessary warrants.

I don't want to get bogged down in details. The back story here is fascinating and arguments exist that the administration did not require court approval because the eavesdropping was occurring offshore. It is also interesting that *The Times* sat on the story for a year and did not run it until after the 2004 presidential election or, perhaps more to the point, just prior to the publication of a book by one of its reporters that would have scooped the paper for which he had undertaken his investigation.

The salient point for us, though, is the kind of decision an editor is forced to make. It is not easy when the President of the United States tells you intelligence gathering will be compromised and lives put at stake. But I believe Bill Keller—ultimately—did the right thing. His bias must be on the side of publication; any arguments against would have to be powerful and persuasive. The administration's sorry record in truth telling was such that the onus upon it to produce convincing arguments, and evidence, was probably all that much greater.

Still, Keller went to great lengths to listen to the argument against publishing, agreeing as editors, as opposed to reporters, often must, to participate in off-the-record discussions with officials so they could make their case without fear it would be splashed across the front page. Indeed, in a joint op-ed piece with the editor of the *Los Angeles Times,* Keller revealed that he has withheld information that might have jeopardized efforts to protect vulnerable stockpiles of nuclear material as well as articles about ongoing counter-terrorism operations. We also know that the *LA Times* held back details of American espionage activities in Afghanistan discovered on a computer drive purchased by reporters in an Afghan bazaar and that *The Washington Post,* in revealing the existence of CIA prisons in Europe, acceded to administration requests not to name the specific countries involved.

In each of these cases the editors in question applied some version of the test we discussed earlier—whether disclosure would surely result in direct, immediate and irreparable damage to the nation or its people. They rendered their tough judgments and proceeded accordingly, in most cases reporting on the existence of controversial practices while omitting operational details.

Critics on the left don't like such collusion. Critics on the right demand to know who Bill Keller thinks he is to make these judgments. What security qualifications does he or any other editor possess to substitute their judgments of harm for those of the executive branch charged with that responsibility?

My answer would be if not Bill Keller then who? What's the better alternative? Despite living in dangerous times, we certainly don't want to live in a society where elected officials are granted the final say over the dissemination of information.

A democracy depends in the final analysis on the ability and willingness of the citizenry to exercise their rights—be it the right to dissent, the right to disseminate, the right to throw the rascals out, or the right to be informed. In the Pentagon Papers case, General Maxwell Taylor, who had been US ambassador in Vietnam, stated that a citizen's right to know is limited "to those things he needs to know to be a good citizen and discharge his functions, but not to . . . secrets that damage his government and indirectly the citizen himself."

But the Pentagon Papers' Justice Potter, while acknowledging the importance to national security of both confidentiality and secrecy, ultimately placed a higher premium on open debate and the free flow of information. "The only effective restraint upon executive policy and power in the areas of national defense and international affairs," he said, "may lie in an enlightened citizenry."

It is therefore incumbent upon those of us who work in the media to take ourselves as seriously as I think the public takes us in this function of creating the conditions for an enlightened citizenry to fulfill its responsibilities as the ultimate sovereign power in a democratic society.

We must provide our newsrooms with ample resources and expertise to practice good journalism and ensure that enough of these resources are devoted to matters of public importance. A joint Canadian Newspaper Association and Canadian Broadcasters Association poll taken a couple of years ago reported this about our audiences: 91 percent thought the role of the media was to keep Canadians informed; 86 percent thought it was to hold governments accountable; 74 percent to provide a Canadian perspective on world events. Against that, only 50 percent thought we are in business of keeping Canadians entertained.

Now I've got nothing against Britney or Posh or even, I suppose, Paris. But they are not the main reason why we in the media and newspapers in particular, exist. We exist to pursue truth and promote debate—and that means challenging the holders of power, particularly powers of coercion.

These are great times to be a journalist. The stakes are high. The issues are complex. The public is more engaged. Think back to the 2000 presidential election in the United States. The hanging chads. Bush or Gore. It didn't really make a difference. The market ruled anyway. It was all a big joke. Since then, we've had 9/11, of course, but also Enron and other scandals that wiped out the life savings of millions of people. Would anyone again treat the outcome of a presidential election with the same cavalier attitude?

It is undeniable that times of war or domestic peril render the relationship between the state and the press all the more difficult. The fact that, in this country, effective legislative oversight of the executive has largely broken down places an even greater onus on the fourth estate to hold executive power to account. Decisions about national security are probably the most important ones governments can make—injecting the nation into foreign entanglements, placing young lives at risk, tiptoeing on the line between civil liberties and public safety.

Periods of uncertainty, like these, are clearly not the time for the press to suspend its watchdog function, but rather to step up and vigorously embrace its constitutionally recognized role.

This is not the moment to be looking to write new scripts in the long and difficult relationship between press and state; but rather to re-dedicate ourselves to the principles that underline our role in society. New circumstances, yes, but as far as the press should be concerned it remains the same old story.

Thank you.

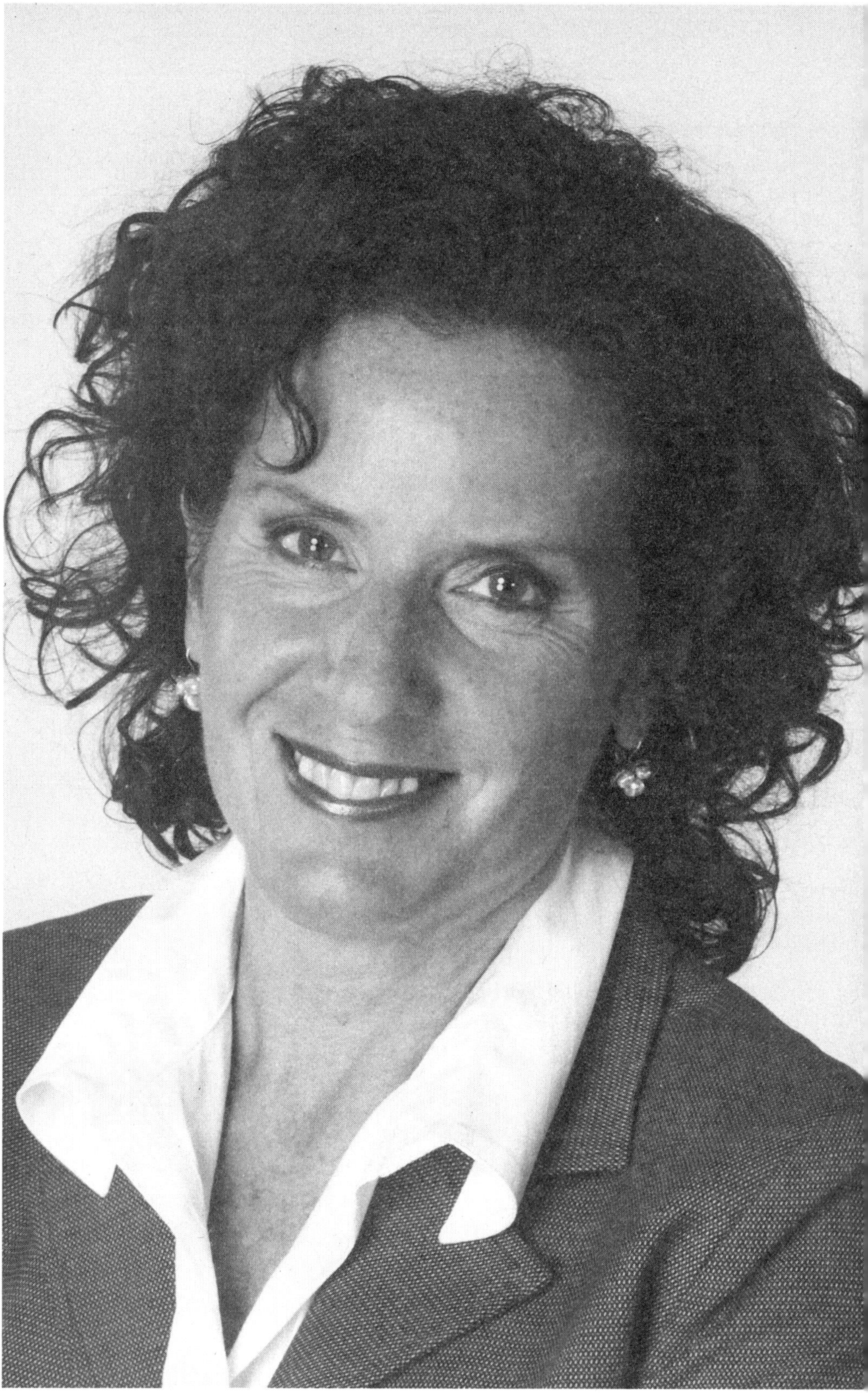

—2008—
CAROL OFF

Carol Off is host of CBC Radio's flagship current affairs program *As It Happens*. As a field reporter, she has covered conflicts in the Middle East, Haiti, and the Balkans, as well as events in the former Soviet Union, Europe, Asia, the United States and Canada. She reported the fallout from the 9/11 disasters with news features and documentaries from New York, Washington, London, Cairo and Afghanistan. She has covered Canadian military missions around the world including its latest combat operation from Kandahar. She is also the author of two best-selling books: *The Lion, the Fox and the Eagle: A Story of Generals and Justice in Yugoslavia and Rwanda*; and *The Ghosts of Medak Pocket: The Story of Canada's Secret War*, which won the Dafoe Foundation Award in 2005. Her most recent book, *Bitter Chocolate: Investigating the Dark Side of the World's Most Seductive Sweet*, chronicles the international cocoa industry. Off has won several awards, including a Gemini, two gold medals from the New York Festival of Television and the John Drainie Award for Distinguished Contribution to Broadcasting.

THE CANADIAN NARRATIVE:
Time For a Rewrite

It seemed to sneak up on us, really, this awareness that our country is at war. One day, our soldiers were peacekeepers, performing what we thought were benign and thoughtful deeds somewhere out there in the world. The next, they were in Afghanistan, fighting "the enemy." The head of the Canadian military, General Rick Hillier, told us our soldiers had to "kill scumbags." The media gave us a daily score of how many Taliban insurgents we had blown away. Canadians were left wondering when everything changed.

It's more than just our role in Afghanistan that gives people the sense that we've turned to another chapter in this country's history or that maybe we've cracked open a whole new book. The story we've read to ourselves so many times that we've memorized it—that of a wide eyed young nation of peacekeepers, earnest and caring, punching above our diplomatic weight and having some modest but important effect on international affairs; crafting a "just society" on the home front and redistributing our collective wealth from rich to poor; a conscientious people, perhaps a bit dull but nonetheless aware of the world in a way our neighbours to the south could never be—is our cherished mythology. Most of you weren't even born when that narrative was written. But you've inherited it. You breathe it in your Canadian air. But it's changing.

Al Gore noticed the change, lamenting recently in a speech that we had lost our way and the world needed for us to get it back: "There is very strong support for Canada once again providing leadership in the world, fighting above its weight class and showing moral authority to the rest of the world." Gore was complaining about the Harper government's plan to opt out of the Kyoto Climate Change Accord but the idea of Canada as a beacon of moral guidance is our international reputation, deserved or not. "That's what Canada is known for," Gore concluded.

The former US vice-president is not the only one who wonders what's come over us. Britain's celebrated environment writer George Monbiot wrote in the Canadian forward to his book *Heat* that "in the court of international opinion, Canada has been let off lightly." Monbiot painfully pokes at our time-honoured narrative. "You think of yourselves as a liberal and enlightened people," he says of our environmental record, "but you could scarcely do more to destroy the biosphere if you tried."

He goes on to say: "Thanks to the efforts of [your prime minister], Canada's global reputation is now beginning to catch up with its performance. When your government says that Canada cannot reach its Kyoto targets for green house gas emissions, it means that Canada does not intend to try . . . Having presented himself as a man who can make tough choices, your prime minister declared himself an irresolute wimp as soon as he was presented with upsetting a few industrial lobbyists or helping to save the planet."

Monbiot says this did not begin with the Conservatives: "It's true that the Liberal party made it easy for him. When Harper took office, Canadian emissions were 24 to 35 percent higher than they were in 1990 . . . They talked a better line than Harper but presided over just as much environmental destruction."

As for our economic promise: what of the just society? We think back to Pierre Elliott Trudeau. The redistribution of wealth. Take from the rich and give to the poor? Many Canadians like to believe this is what distinguishes us from the sharply divided class society of the United States. But the Canadian Centre for Policy Alternatives burst another of our mythic bubbles in a recent study. The income gap between rich and poor is the widest it's been in 30 years. The wealthiest 10 percent of Canadians earn eighty-two times what the most disadvantaged Canadians earn. That's three times the difference that existed in 1976. Both the Liberals and the Conservatives continue the tradition of taking from the advantaged and giving back to them. Tax cuts instead of income distribution has been the way we look at fairness. Our income distribution has become, for the first time, the same as that of the United States.

The hard truth is that Canada's love affair with its self-image has not been supported by reality in many years. Contrary to popular perception, we have not been a nation of peacekeepers since the last century. We now rank 52nd on the list of nations contributing soldiers to UN missions. But even the assignments we accepted over the past fifteen years were often violent and coercive, and I'm not just talking about Afghanistan. The iconic image of the Canadian in a blue beret, handing out candies to kiddies, dissolved long ago in far away places such as the Medak Pocket of Croatia in 1994, where Canadians fought with every weapon they had in order to secure a region they found had already been brutally ethnically cleansed. They possibly killed as many as 57 Croats in the battle. After they returned home, soldiers of the Princess Patricia's Canadian Light Infantry were instructed by their commanders to keep the nightmare to themselves, lest the Canadian public be faced with a reality that contradicts the more comfortable narrative.

The battle of Medak Pocket was the first occasion, for me, when I noticed this disconnect between what we do and what we think we do, who we are and who we think we are. And it also made me realize that we cannot become ourselves until we acknowledge that contradiction.

The wars in the Balkans—Croatia, Bosnia and Serbia—were not well covered by Canadian journalists even though Canadian soldiers played a pivotal role there. But we journalists failed to show up. We failed to inquire and to investigate. We missed the boat. If we had been there, the Canadian public would have been there and then, perhaps, we would have a better understanding of what we are now doing in Afghanistan.

In the summer of 1993 a battalion of the "Princess Pats" was moved into an area of Croatia known as the Medak Pocket. Croat forces had ethnically cleansed most Serbs from the region and all that was left was a small group who were unwilling or unable to relocate. The Croats began to eliminate the last remaining holdouts right under the noses of the Canadian peacekeepers.

Colonel Jim Calvin, the battle group commander, decided that he would not and could not sit by and allow the ethnic cleansing to continue, even though as peacekeepers they were required to only engage with the Croatian or Serbian military if it was in self defence.

The "Princess Pats" soldiers quickly found themselves in full combat—in fact, they fought the biggest battle Canadians had been part of since the Korean War. The "Princess Pats" killed an unknown number of Croats that day, possibly as many as fifty-seven. When the battle was over, the Canadian peacekeepers moved into the Medak Pocket to liberate the civilians there. But they found only corpses. Mutilated, murdered, robbed and annihilated. Their wells were poisoned, their houses blown up or burned down.

Back in Ottawa, the Department of National Defence was facing another crisis: the Somalia Affair. Canadian soldiers had killed two Somali youths—one of them was tortured to death. The Canadian government was engaged in a cover up. And so when Ottawa heard about the battle in Medak, the government went into damage control. As the "Princess Pats" returned home after the Medak Pocket event, they were warned to tell no one what had transpired.

Had we been doing our jobs as journalists, such a cover-up would have been impossible. But the story remained a secret, more or less, for years. Until the soldiers began to get sick. Some went blind. Others became mentally ill. Several committed suicide.

A board of inquiry conducted an investigation into all of the illnesses and concluded that the soldiers suffered a kind of post-traumatic stress disorder. The trauma of the events in Medak was compounded by the denial of those events. They could not be who they were—heroes—because Canada could not acknowledge what they did. Killing people, even in self-defence, is a violation of our self-image as peacekeepers.

I'm concerned that we are facing something similar in Afghanistan. General Rick Hiller, as ham-fisted as he might be, is telling the truth. We are at war; our soldiers are killing people, and not just the Taliban.

Canadians are ambivalent about the mission. The government of the day (the Liberals were no different) know this and attempt to put the best face on the mission. Stability. Nation-building. Peace-making. These are euphemisms for war.

An important book by an Australian social scientist called *A History of Killing* describes what happens to soldiers when they are not acknowledged. If their societies do not embrace their war efforts—celebrate them—then the anti-social act of killing—even if it's state-sanctioned killing—begins to eat away at them. I saw it happen to the soldiers who were in Medak.

Canadian soldiers sometimes kill people. They engage in combat. If we don't want this to be part of who we are, we must decide that categorically. And decide what role we want to play.

Years later when the soldiers of Medak began to tell people about their experiences, their friends and even their family members reacted with disbelief. If such a large battle had taken place, they would have read about it or heard it on the news. They didn't, so it didn't happen. The soldiers themselves began to doubt their own experience.

Those of us who have covered Afghanistan are only too aware of the spin that the government has attempted to put on our mission in South Asia. Embedded reporters have limited access to the action. When we do accompany the soldiers, all too often they express, privately, their exasperation with a mission gone wrong or ill-conceived from the beginning. The humanitarian part of the project—the nation-building of Afghanistan that was the bedrock of our commitment there—has hardly materialized. We observers fear we are in a quagmire that may take years more than Canadians will commit to, in order to dig our way out.

As for our commitment to international environmental standards, Canada as a champion of the Kyoto Accord is another myth even under the Liberals who have touted its virtues, if you can believe Jean Chrétien's former policy adviser. In a speech in London, Ontario last year, Eddie Goldenberg admitted that the previous Liberal government took on its Kyoto commitments knowing full well we would never meet them: "I am not sure that Canadian public opinion which was overwhelmingly in favour of ratifying Kyoto in the abstract—was then immediately ready for some of the concrete implementation measures that governments would have to take to address the issue of climate change," Mr. Goldenberg said.

Our involvement at the last Kyoto summit in Bali left people from around the world wondering, what had Canada become? Once the leader of the Kyoto initiative and celebrated as one of the great champions of the environment, we were all but invisible at Bali, with the exception of Environment Minister John Baird padding around in his flip-flops, ducking in and out of sessions. The new Canadian image projected around the world is that of the sprawling tar sands project in Alberta and photographer Edward Burtinsky's spectacular images of one of the biggest manufactured landscapes on the planet.

To get another picture of ourselves abroad, you only have to ask the Mayan Q'echi of Guatemala whether or not Canada is kind and decent. Since Canadian-owned Skye Resources had them evicted from mineral rich land the natives claim is theirs, our name is mud in the community of El Estor. Mining rights to the land have been disputed since 1965 when INCO obtained the nickel deposit from a violent military dictatorship in power at the time. But a few years ago, our name became well known to Indians who clung to what was left of their land rights, as they fought to stay where they had been for centuries.

But in truth, it's become unwise for travelers to sport their maple leaf decals on their back packs in many parts of the world where Canadian mining companies are flourishing—and helping to pad out our mutual fund values, I might add. We profit from these adventures. As we did in southern Sudan.

I investigated the role that Talisman Energy of Calgary played in the development of the oil fields there, where ethnic cleansing—on the part of the Sudanese military—was the precursor to fossil fuel extraction. It was only when the United States threatened to remove the company from the stock exchange that it finally backed down from production.

The truth is that Eddie Goldenberg is right. We are not ready to slow down our consumption or our extraction. Life is too good, too comfortable. We think that recycling exonerates us. That green technology will replace traditional technology and all will be corrected. Meanwhile, Canadians are among the most wasteful citizens of the planet. We have to see ourselves for what we are. Not custodians of the earth but consumers of it.

The classic Canadian story has been questionable for more than a dozen years, if the story of our generosity and caring was ever accurate in the first place. It's only now becoming obvious to observers outside of Canada like Al Gore and George Monbiot. But if the old narrative doesn't work, then what's replacing it? Are we becoming a country that projects power? That engages in war without end? That fails to live up to its environmental commitments? A society where a small minority is to enjoy the vast majority of wealth? Are we to wake up, some day soon, and look in the mirror to see a collective image we don't like: the Ugly Canadian staring back from the glass?

And most important, for you and for me, what role do we play as journalists? The place where the new narrative will be written, revised, shaped, critiqued and edited will be in our domain. Even more than the politicians, the social scientists, the pollsters, the professors, the soldiers and the students, journalists will be the ones through which the ideas will be communicated. Not just through what we quote or cover, but in what we choose to cover. In our selection of stories. In the voices we include or fail to include. In the degree to which we are even open to the idea that the country is changing. We will write the first and maybe even the final draft of the new narrative.

Have you noticed that our national media are covering United States politics more closely than Canadian these days? In part, it's our endless fascination with all things American. But it's also because something extraordinary is going on south of us. The United States appears to be re-inventing itself—again! As it has many times before. A black man and a woman are vying to lead the Democratic Party. One of them may become president. The excitement around that campaign, at least for now, is palpable.

When we cast our eyes on our own political landscape though, we feel cheated, disappointed. But we are in the same political moment. None of the old truisms work, just as they don't in the US. That may frustrate us, even scare us. But this could be a moment of our greatest inspiration. As dull as our politics might seem, so was Lester Pearson against the backdrop of the Kennedy era. Or Tommy Douglas against Franklin Delano Roosevelt. And yet look at the legacy of those two men, the Canadian self that came from the vision of those Canadian leaders. They wrote the narrative that now needs revisions and we need visionaries to do it again.

Over decades and now more than a century, it's become clear that we don't want to be a global dominatrix, a nuclear power, an economic bully, an international scoundrel. We want to be the world's nice guys, sporting the flag on our luggage, arriving at hot spots as the conciliator, respected as fair and decent partners of industry. But can we be fighting a war in Afghanistan and pursuing the idea of being an energy super-power, as Stephen Harper has told international audiences, while holding to our former self-image? Can we export our knowledge of resource extraction without exploiting others? Can we take the best of what we were and apply it to what we are becoming?

Shortly before Canada went to war in southern Afghanistan, Harper himself started to bandy about the idea that Canada was on the cusp of a new narrative, one that he planned to author. The same notion turned up among leadership candidates for the federal Liberals who argued that "the natural governing party" should be the scribe, with Michael Ignatieff insisting that he has the first draft ready to go. None disputed that the Canadian story is—in fact needs—changing. The argument is about who should shape it.

My sense is that the new narrative that's emerging is a coming of age story. A tale of lost innocence. This isn't necessarily a bad thing. Like people, nations grow up and they often go through the same pains and longings as budding adults do. As innocence is replaced with experience; it matters less what the experience is than what it is we do with the experience.

Letters and e-mails I have received from people over my years as a journalist show me that people have a striking capacity to learn and accept new things. In the 1990s, I was often surprised by sentiments from viewers or readers who thought Canada should consider having no military at all, to send only aid workers and development professionals into the foreign field. Now I find it just as intriguing to hear from people who think there is a reason to be aggressive in Afghanistan, that the only way to defeat the Taliban is to stand up to them militarily.

It's of interest that, according to the opinion polls, Canadians now accept that we must kill in certain circumstances. And even more surprising, there's an understanding that our own soldiers will die. Considering our engagement in two world wars, this should not be shocking. Yet for post-colonial Canada it has not been easy to accept. Most important, though, is the sentiment that we want to decide for ourselves what is an appropriate use of lethal force. We don't want to be lured into US interests of which we have never been more skeptical than we are now.

I don't think it's enough merely to say that we want the Canadian Forces to return to the former role of peacekeepers. Classic peacekeeping hardly exists anywhere in the world anymore. Nor can we deny what we are doing to the environment. Blaming it all on the US or the oil companies doesn't work either.

These conditions are part of our songs of experience. A lament for lost innocence, but nonetheless, the beginning of a new narrative. How will you help to tell the story? How will you engage Canadians?

In my travels, I often heard incredible stories of human suffering mixed with fear, escape and hope from ordinary people whom I interviewed. In Africa, Bosnia, Ukraine, China, Afghanistan, I have left behind people in the worst of circumstances, taking with me only their tales of woe. I often wondered why they told me these very personal narratives. Did they think I could help them? That the cavalry would arrive? That they would be saved? I rarely got that sense, even though it's what we both wished for.

I believe they were caught up in the overwhelming human need to share experiences. To communicate. And by doing so, to join with the rest of humanity in one shared experience. To add to that universal jest of God.

Canadian soldiers returning from Afghanistan carry with them experiences that are life altering. Their stories could be the raw material of the new narrative and perhaps the soldiers could even be some of the authors. They have faced the cold new reality of Canada on the world stage. Or we could cling to more comfortable, sentimental tales of what we would like to be.

Over the next two decades, the complexion of this country will change almost entirely, as we become probably the most multi-ethnic state on the planet, and so will the national narrative change. More likely, and more appropriately, the new Canadian narrative will be written by an entirely different author—by Canadians who look at themselves in the mirror and see a face of colour looking back at them. These Canadians are people who have come from places of conflict and have seen, first hand, what's required to stop aggression; they know the effects of severe environmental degradation and they know from experience what happens when globalization arrives in places where people have no rights.

Whether the established minority likes it or not, these are the people who will craft our story and define the national myth. I say pass them the paper and pen and let them begin. We have everything to gain.

And I pass the torch to a new generation of journalists. I hope that you will have the opportunity to tell peoples' stories. But I also hope that you will accept the responsibility of informing our songs of experience.

Thank you.

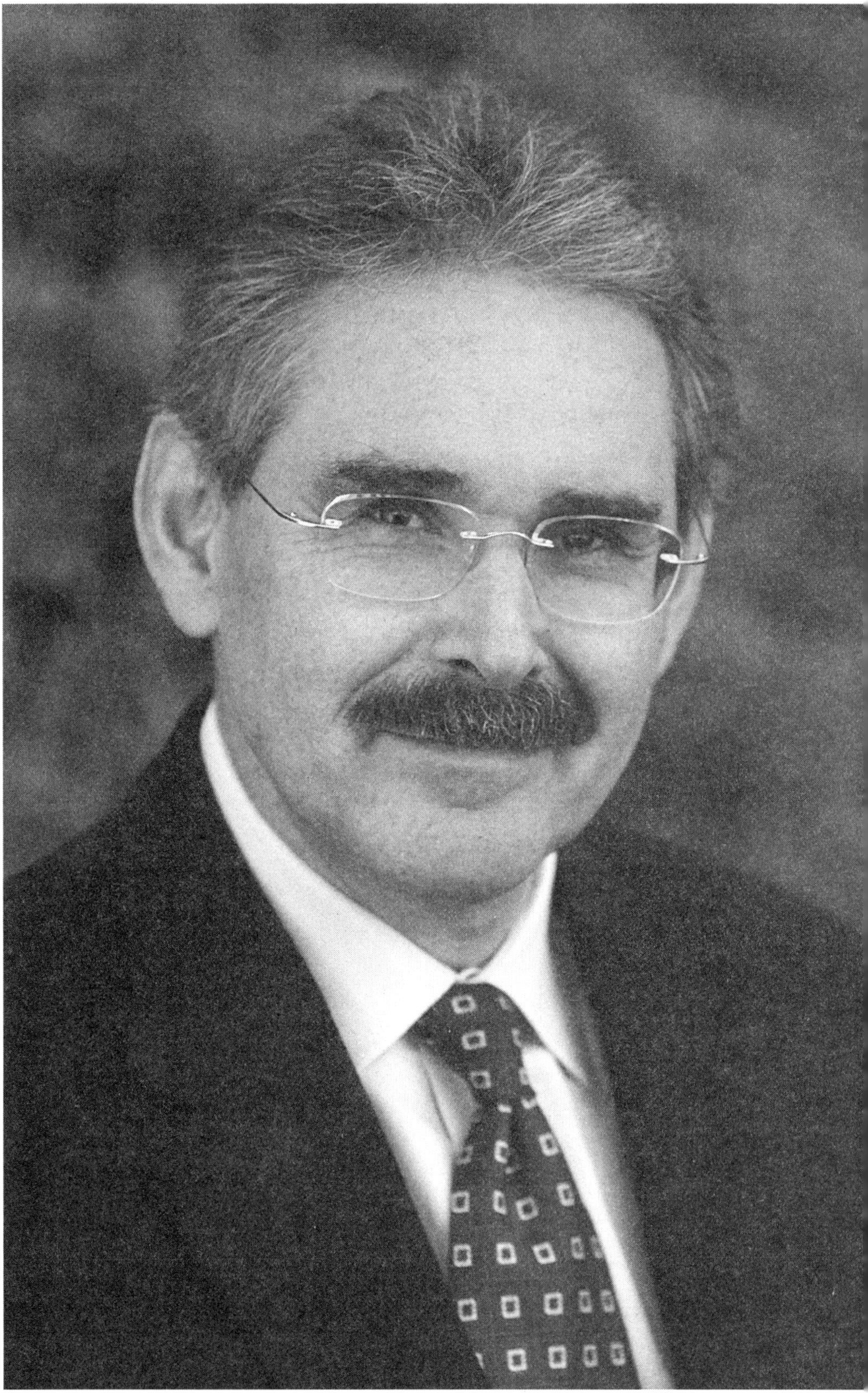

−2009−

TERRY MILEWSKI

Terry Milewski has been a correspondent with CBC News for over 30 years and has worked in over 30 countries. He began working overseas in 1982, when he covered the Israeli invasion of Lebanon, and has returned to the Middle East frequently, opening the CBC's Jerusalem Bureau in 1986. He spent eight years in the CBC's Washington bureau during the Reagan, Bush and Clinton administrations, and has also worked throughout Central America and Europe. He reported from Mumbai, India, following the November, 2009 terrorist attacks. During a varied career, Milewski has won a Gemini Award for his reporting on the 1997 APEC summit, a Webster for a documentary on the Air India bombing, and awards from the Canadian Association of Journalists and the Radio Television Digital News Association. He is married with two children and lives in West Vancouver.

THE UNSEEN MUZZLE:
How Timidity, Self-Censorship and Libel Chill Work Their Magic

It's probably fate; like James Minifie, I was raised on the slimy and sluggish River Trent in the English Midlands. He was from downriver—Burton-on-Trent; I'm from Stoke-on-Trent, upriver but, like Minifie, I came to Canada and lived on the prairies for a while before ending up, like Minifie, for a long spell as a CBC correspondent in Washington. But there the resemblance ends; he had an illustrious career. Nowadays, I'm not sure any of us has anything as grand as a "career." I sometimes quote Jim Munson, now a Senator but formerly of CTV News, who coined this immortal phrase shortly before he left CTV: "First, I had a career; then I had a job; now I have a shift."

These are words to ponder in the gloomy environment we face today.

Now this may sound like the start of yet another rant from an old-school journalist about the brutish gutter of the modern media: the collapse of standards, the brain-dead blogs and the bad grammar—don't get me started on the bad grammar. But, we're not doing that speech tonight. Nostalgia is no use because the good old days weren't that good and they're not coming back. They can't come back. The business model that drives our industry, journalism, is now skidding into history with all the grace of a gas-guzzler heading over a cliff with a sleeping drunk at the wheel.

This is why they do these Minifie Lectures: to encourage a bright new generation!

But it would seem absurd to whine about the timidity and self-censorship in our business without first whining about whether we will have a business at all. The truth is that scarcity is going to cramp our style severely in the days ahead. Obviously, you're less likely to take risks if your job's at risk. Already, our bosses can barely afford journalists to gather the news, let alone plane tickets to send them where they need to go or lawyers to defend libel suits. But the challenge of generating real, aggressive reporting on the world is not just a problem for publishers, but for citizens who want to see a well-informed and civilised world.

So we had best begin by understanding that the crisis in our industry is accelerated by, but is not a function of, the crisis in the financial markets. Revenues were in decline before the crash; Canwest Global was loaded with debt before the stock market crash of 2008; the CBC's revenues have been dropping for years. Now, we're just heading over the cliff faster—and we have to face the prospect that some cities won't have their own newspapers or TV stations. Commenting on CTV's recent decision to close a couple of stations in Ontario, Bell Globemedia spokesman Paul Sparkes said, "The traditional economic model for Canadian television is broken."

As for newspapers, the "traditional economic model" is hacking down trees, mulching them into newsprint and splattering it with ink, then hauling the result in stinking trucks to homes and boxes and corner stores. I think we know that's broken, too.

We also know that we are not living in a mere cyclical downturn, to be followed as night follows day by a corresponding upturn. This is not a temporary slump but a deconstruction of our industry. Just as GM won't scarf up billions of taxpayers' dollars and come back just like before to crank out gas-guzzling dinosaurs, the old media dinosaur is roadkill, too. The information world is going to the Internet—heck, it's gone—and it's not coming back.

So, why don't we just be bold, not timid, and move our business to the Internet?

Of course, we have already moved—but, more precisely, we have moved our product to the net without moving the business—unless you think it's a business to give away your product for free, which is what most newspapers do.

Don't kid yourself that the online ads are sufficient to pay for the content. It does not. Furthermore, putting it on the web for free means nobody needs to buy a subscription and it also allows aggregators like Google News to cash in on content for which they paid precisely nothing—and Google News is now planning ads. And giving it all away on the web leads readers to believe that content should be free. "Information wants to be free," they say. No, it doesn't. Information that's worth having wants desperately to be paid for.

So, first, we have to provide a product worth having and then we have to figure out how to get online customers to pay for it. One way to approach this might be to ask this question: does anyone here not have an iPod? You may have noticed the new feature on recent models, called Genius, which surveys your library of music to learn your tastes and then tries to sell you more songs it thinks you'll like.

Now, many people have said that the new model for journalism should be iTunes—click on Rex Murphy's rant on *The National*, pay 99¢, and away you go. But, with due respect to Rex, you might not hum along to it for weeks afterwards. Now, some sites already do fine with a subscription model: the *Wall Street Journal*, *Consumer Reports*—these are sources of high-quality, specialised information which you're not going to get anywhere else. But what about high-quality news and commentary? My own theory, for what it's worth, is that people will only fork out money for news on the Internet if the experience is as simple and as satisfying as the one which drew us to iTunes—plus, it should offer something more, like Genius. It should remember, like Amazon's Kindle reader, where you left off reading the last time. It should remember not to offer articles you've already read. It should skip all sports except the ones you follow. It should completely skip anything about Hollywood and celebrities and their crack-ups, and about golf, and any section called "home design" or "lifestyle." It should alert me to updates on stories I care about and it should know which I care about, as Genius does. And it should definitely have a full daily roundup on the latest gadgets.

So, let's say it knows that I also like to read pungent commentary by Margaret Wente and Christie Blatchford or Andrew Coyne and Don Martin—or, in the US, by Christopher Hitchens, or the big guns at the *New York Times* like Frank Rich, Tom Friedman, Paul Krugman, Maureen Dowd. Surely these are all writers who tell it like it is and command a loyal audience who just might pay them to keep writing. Notice that I didn't mention any mere news reporters because it's not clear that people will pay for us grunts who actually go and get the news as opposed to "bloviating" about it. Everybody wants to rant about the news; nobody wants to gather it.

But will customers even pay for those fancy columnists? Problem: the *New York Times* famously failed to make a go of charging for its big-name pundits with a paywall experiment called *TimeSelect*. It made $10 million a year—but the *Times* dropped it anyway, figuring it could make more money by taking down the wall and thereby generating more traffic to its site—so as to sell more ads. But the ads still aren't enough to pay for the content—so they're also interested in the subscription model. If you try the *TimesReader* version of the paper, you just might think of buying a subscription.

But that's one of the world's truly great newspapers, struggling to make all this work. Now—do you think your local paper measures up to that challenge? Let's face it, in local news, there's a problem of scale. Will there be enough readers willing to support everything the Regina *Leader-Post* does now? Perhaps not. In Vancouver, a few pathetic junkies like me will read the *National Post* and the *Vancouver Sun* and the *Province*—all Canwest papers—but for how much longer? Think of the waste. Most of all three now go in the recycle bin—because they are broadcasting, not narrowcasting—giving me all kinds of junk about golf and recipes and fashion and lifestyle and pop concerts which are for other readers, not for me. I'm sorry, that's a dead model.

So, now, newspapers and TV networks alike are moving to national sites like cbc.ca and adding local pages so that you can get a dose of local news and weather—although far less of it than you'd get in a stand-alone local product. And maybe those local products are not going to survive except as sections of a national online product. And maybe geezers like me who want to hold an actual paper and use it to mop up spills or swat bugs will just have to adjust. There's no other way if you consider the awe-inspiring growth of the Internet.

Think about the numbers recently posted by the senior VP at Google, Jonathan Rosenberg: nearly a quarter of humanity—1.4 billion people—now use the Internet, with more than 200 million new people coming online every year. Note, too, that, all over the world, people use their cell phones to get on the Internet and more Internet-enabled phones will be sold this year than personal computers. Next, think about the fact that more than three billion humans now have mobile phones—along with some loquacious commuters who can't really be considered human. So: three billion cell phones now ... and more than a billion more likely to be sold in 2009. And think about China, which has more Internet users than any other country, with nearly 300 million users; it also has more than 600 million cell phone users. The phone is becoming the poor man's computer and, if I'm doing a quick two-minute story, I will often ditch my laptop and just work on my Blackberry. Plus, I can race to a camera and have my notes on my handheld far more easily than a cumbersome laptop. And I don't have to wait a month and a half for Windows to boot up.

Of course, thanks to all this technology, everyone's a journalist now—actually, everybody's a bad journalist. Rosenberg from Google says that 120,000 new blogs are created daily—most of them with an audience of one. Over half of those new blogs are by people under the age of 19. Not that I'm saying they're narcissistic. And, in the US, Rosenberg says, nearly 40 percent of Internet users upload videos, and globally over 15 hours of video are uploaded to YouTube every minute.

What even Google can't tell you is how to create a new model where good editors and journalists can create and be rewarded for content that is more valuable than all the drivel posted on all those tedious blogs.

Bill Keller can't tell you, either—and he's the editor of the *New York Times,* which has surely one of the best news sites in the world, which Keller *says* gets an astounding 20 million unique visitors a month. By comparison, the CBC site gets about one million a month. Even so, the *Times* site does not sell nearly enough advertising to keep its superb, global reporting corps afloat.

Now all of this is only the first good reason for some timidity in our journalism: doubt and confusion about the future, even about whether there is a future, and jobs being lost at a frightening rate.

But I also said that the good old days were not something to be too nostalgic about. At the CBC, we think with good reason that we are Canada's leading source of great in-depth stories. And we inherit a great tradition, born in James Minifie's time with the famous *This Hour Has Seven Days.* That was 45 years ago, in 1964, and it was ahead of its time, with ambush interviews, and aggression, and emotion—groundbreaking journalism. But there's another side of that great tradition, of course: the show was famously cancelled after just two years, in 1966. Timidity killed it. There were demonstrations, indignant editorials, threats to resign by CBC staff and a parliamentary inquiry. But it was dead, and there have been similar bumps in the road ever since.

Some will remember the controversy about *The Valour and the Horror,* a three-part documentary aired in 1992 about World War Two, dealing not just with the valour of Canadian forces but also with the horror of the Allied bombing raids on Germany. Again, in the face of complaints by veterans, the CBC back-pedalled and apologised for the broadcast. Not our finest hour.

Another low point I know a little about was the 1997 APEC summit fiasco in Vancouver. The story was that the RCMP arrested some peaceful demonstrators who broke no law, merely because the Prime Minister's Office (PMO) did not want the sight of protest signs to embarrass his summit guests—notably the blood-soaked dictator of Indonesia, Suharto. When we reported on these political arrests, the PMO shot the messenger by accusing the reporter of being biased. Actually their spelling wasn't too hot in the PMO so, in truth, I was accused of being "bi-assed," which seemed quite rude. Anyway, instead of just answering the PMO's complaint, the CBC immediately banned me from the story on the grounds that the complaint created a "perception" of bias, even if there was no bias, so that I had to be silenced just in case. In other words, the complaint didn't have to be justified; just by complaining, the PMO got what it wanted. Of course, most people watching did conclude that there was bias at work, not on my part but, rather, on the part of the CBC's management in caving in so quickly to a political attack. And, when the CBC's Ombudsman, Marcel Pepin, finally did answer the complaint, four months later, he concluded that our coverage could not be faulted for accuracy or fairness so . . . there was a happy ending, but it was not an episode that set the standard for courage in the face of political pressure.

But this kind of thing is not exclusive to the public sector. Indeed, throughout this affair, our competitors had great fun damning the CBC for kowtowing to the Prime Minister—until Canwest did the same by firing the *Ottawa Citizen*'s publisher, Russell Mills, in 2002. Mills was sacked after his paper ran a negative story on the same Prime Minister, Jean Chrétien, in the Shawinigate affair. So, perhaps, that doesn't come under the heading of timidity; maybe it was chutzpah.

But there wasn't much chutzpah to be seen in a more recent case: the Muhammad cartoons published in Denmark in September of 2005. You remember the cartoons—or do you? If you wanted to see them for yourself—if you wanted to see what the story was about—you did not see them in *The Globe* or the Canwest papers, or on Global or CTV or the CBC. Or anywhere except the *Western Standard*, and the *Jewish Free Press* and, very briefly, a student paper in Charlottetown called the *Cadre*.

In fact, the Internet is not so squeamish—the cartoons are there on Wikipedia among other places and there are no riots about it. But, after the Danish paper *Jyllands Posten* published the cartoons and created a global furore, everyone got cold feet. CNN pixellated the cartoons; the BBC posted a detailed description of the cartoons, but no cartoons; the CBC and *The Globe* both published well-argued cases by their editors to the effect that publishing them would offend some viewers and readers for no purpose. And you might have made the same decision in view of the violent protests that occurred in the Arab world. But you'd be forgiven for wondering if it was only discretion that prevented us from offending viewers.

Of course, we happily offend them all the time: we run horrific scenes of war and death. We show pictures of people being injured and even killed—Robert Dziekanski being only the latest. And that's offensive. We have run the video of David Ahenakew railing against Jews; that's offensive. We've shown a rant by the co-founder of a terrorist organisation, Ajaib Singh Bagri of Kamloops, B.C., urging a mass murder of Hindus—and that's offensive. Reporting an artistic controversy, we showed the picture of the Virgin Mary with elephant dung on it and the crucifix immersed in urine and that's offensive. I don't think it can be denied that the difference in the case of the Muhammad cartoons was that there was an additional element: fear of violence. How to put this politely? We were, to some degree, fortified in our principled decision to avoid giving offence by raw intimidation.

I call as a witness here the incomparable Christopher Hitchens. He wrote, "I have a feeling that the decision to protect you from the images was determined this time by something as vulgar as fear." He goes on to say that, "the cowardice of the mainstream American culture was something to see," adding that, "In Canada, only two minority papers reprinted the cartoons . . . [and] were promptly taken before a sort of scrofulous bureaucratic peoples' court describing itself as the Alberta Human Rights Commission [by] the Islamic Supreme Council of Canada."

When the Imam Syed Soharwardy, the head of that Supreme Council, noted with approval that "Only a very small fraction of Canadian media decided to publish those cartoons," Hitchens responded that, "we have no choice but to conclude that Soharwardy is satisfied on the whole with the level of frightened deference to be found north of the US border. I mention this only because the level of frightened deference to be found south of that border is still far in excess of what any censor, or even self-censor, might dare to wish."

Now, you may agree with me that this was a case of timidity while also agreeing that it was justified in the quite frightening circumstances. You may have chosen, as our bosses did, not to die on that particular hill. Death threats sent the cartoonists into hiding and the actual violence was real. The Danish embassies in Syria, Lebanon and Iran were all torched. Altogether, at least 139 people were killed in protests, most due to police firing on the crowds in Nigeria, Libya, Pakistan and Afghanistan. So don't tell me you wouldn't have been thinking about that if reporters came to you, or even if Christopher Hitchens came to you, arguing that we must run these cartoons.

So—this was clearly a case of self-censorship and it can happen for the best of reasons. At other times, it's pure timidity where the threat is imaginary.

I have been in the West Bank, for instance, reporting on an act of murder by Jewish settlers in which they machine-gunned an Arab family in a car and killed a baby. At the funeral near Hebron, I heard mourners saying this was "Jewish terrorism" and I quoted them in my story. But my editors removed that line because, they said, they'd get complaints from people who objected to the phrase, even if it was quoted correctly.

And this is timidity, not bias, because it works both ways. I was back in Jerusalem after the last Lebanon war with Hezbollah. Most Israelis felt the war was botched and left them still surrounded by enemies who wanted to destroy the state of Israel. I noted that in my story—but, again, an editor wanted me to remove that line because—there might be complaints that it sounded too much as though Israelis were right to feel they're surrounded by enemies. Of course, they are surrounded by enemies, so the complaints would have been unjustified. But, in both cases, the impulse was there to avoid complaints and thereby to deliver a watered-down product to our audience.

And yet, the sky doesn't fall if we file stories which generate complaints.

On my last trip to the Middle East, we did two somewhat controversial feature stories. One was from the Gaza strip, suggesting that Hamas had its guns aimed inwards because of discontent within Gaza. We got complaints that I demonized Hamas, which had, after all, been elected. Fine; the complaints are on our site. Another story suggested that Israel will soon face a decision whether to strike Iran before the mullahs get the bomb. And again, on our site, you can see the complaints that this story was Israeli propaganda. So, whenever you touch a difficult story, you do get complaints. But the CBC, in both cases said, fine, run the stories and let them post all the complaints they want. Plus, for every complaint, there's a fan. Most unusually, we even got applause from the pro-Israeli HonestReporting.com, which more often damns the CBC.

We've also had both applause and complaints for our coverage of the deadliest terrorist attack in history until 9/11, which happened in Canada: the Air India bombing of 1985. In this case, the complaints have occasionally taken the form of death threats. My colleague, the unstoppable Kim Bolan of the *Vancouver Sun* and I have both been threatened for reporting on the terrorists who blew up Air India. But it's not the death threats that have affected us—rather, it's been the lawsuits for defamation.

A typical example is from June 2007, when we ran a documentary called, *Samosa Politics* about the pandering of Canadian politicians of all parties to Sikh extremists who claim to speak for the Sikh community in demanding a separate Sikh state. That goal is overwhelmingly rejected by Sikhs in their home state of Punjab—and one reason is that Sikhs have paid a high price, in thousands of dead, for terrorism by Sikh separatists. Yet our documentary showed how Canadian MPs from all parties stood mutely by at a Vaisakhi parade featuring posters honouring the fanatical Sikh priest from Burnaby, B.C., Talwinder Singh Parmar, who was the mastermind of the Air India bombing. And, if you think we're unduly timid, we've got nothing on politicians who zip their lips about a parade calling the worst mass-murderer in Canadian history a martyred hero. We showed politicians weaselling out of criticising the parade; we showed the Premier of Ontario dishing out public money to separatist temples with Parmar's picture on the wall; we showed how Stéphane Dion's victory in the preceding Liberal leadership convention was heavily influenced by delegates loyal to the World Sikh Organization—the WSO—which is a Sikh separatist group. We showed how the WSO is closely linked to a Punjabi-language newspaper in Ontario which ran front-page articles applauding terrorist acts by Sikhs; and we showed that the venue for Ajaib Singh Bagri's infamous call for a slaughter of Hindus was the founding convention of the World Sikh Organization, where delegates cheered him on with cries of "Hindu Dogs! Death to Them!"

Well, the WSO sued us for an eye-catching $130 million. So far, I'm glad to report, they have failed to identify a single error in the documentary. But never mind; the purpose of such a suit is not to get at the truth but to harass you, to position the WSO as somehow entitled to speak for the Sikh community and to pressure your bosses into finding some other story for you to cover. For good measure, a toxic Facebook page supporting the lawsuit sprang up, on which more death threats were uttered. One said that we should "find out where Milewski lives and put his head on a stick." Such are the people who applaud the WSO's lawsuit against the CBC.

Even so, the suit has forced the CBC to pay lawyers defending the action, and such is the chill engendered by a lawsuit that someone at the CBC immediately took our documentary off our website, in the belief that this was what you should do when sued. Of course, wiser heads quickly reversed that and, to the CBC's credit, the story remains on our site, both the original video and a more detailed written version. So libel chill does not rule the day. At Canwest, similarly, Kim Bolan has been sued by the WSO—so has Jonathan Kay of the *National Post*—and Canwest is sticking by them.

Still, the inhibiting fear of lawsuits is real enough even when you know you've got the story right. But what if that's not so clear?

That's the central question in an important case now before the Supreme Court: the *Ottawa Citizen* versus Danno Cusson. This was a case in which the *Citizen* reported correctly that, after the terrorist attacks of 9/11 Mr. Cusson, an Ontario Provincial Police officer, left his job without permission to go to New York with his dog, Ranger, to help the rescue effort. The *Citizen* said he misled the authorities there to think he was an RCMP officer with a trained dog, and they wanted him out of there. The jury found those things were true, but there were other details that were not, so the *Citizen* was ordered to pay $100,000 in damages. Then, the Ontario Court of Appeal in 2007 upheld the decision but said the *Citizen* could have won if it had invoked a new defence of "responsible journalism." So, now it's up to the Supreme Court where the *Citizen,* joined by a media coalition including the CBC, argued that reporters should not be required to show that every detail was true if the story was in the public interest and if you did a responsible job of trying to get it right.

So, if the Supremes buy it, there would be a new defamation defence, in addition to truth, fair comment, privilege and consent. It's called "public interest responsible journalism" and this new defence would do much to remove the "chill" from the law of defamation in Canada. Reputations would still have to be protected but, as the Ontario court said, the balance is tilted against the news media without that defence. In the ruling, Mr. Justice Robert Sharpe said: "A newspaper that has properly investigated the story and has every reason to believe it to be true still walks on thin ice. The fear or risk of being unable to prove the truth of controversial matters is bound to discourage the publication of information the public has a legitimate interest in hearing."

Of course, you can catch a chill by other means than a defamation suit.

A second case that's instructive is the effort by the RCMP to get Andrew McIntosh of the *National Post* to hand over a leaked document in the Shawinigate story so that the Mounties can check the saliva on the envelope and find the alleged forger who, it thinks, fabricated a smear placing Jean Chrétien in a conflict of interest. McIntosh says it was not a forgery, but never mind. The lower court says the RCMP have a right to get that envelope in order to fight crime, and that takes precedence over McIntosh's right to protect his source. In that case, we are waiting to discover whether the media is going to be drafted as an investigative arm of the state.

There's also the weird case of Daniel Leblanc of *The Globe and Mail,* who's been ordered by the Quebec Superior Court to name a source for his fine work on the sponsorship scandal. Leblanc could be charged with contempt and fined or even jailed if he fails to answer the court's questions. In this, he's not so much being drafted as a servant of the state but of the ad agency, Groupe Polygone, which got a cool $35 million in sponsorship loot. Yes, weird.

Are these excuses to be timid? Perhaps. But there are also reasons to be bold.

Start with the fascinating case of Rafe Mair, the veteran open-line host in B.C. who made his name railing entertainingly about politics, fish farms, Charlottetown . . . and who accused one Kari Simpson of bigotry. And thereby hangs an encouraging tale.

The background is that Kari Simpson campaigned against the inclusion of gay literature in schools—gay-positive literature like *Heather Has Two Mommies.* Simpson took issue not just with gay literature but, it seemed, with gay people. She said, "These people want your children. . . . [W]hen homosexuality takes on all the aspects of a political movement it too becomes a war . . . And the spoils turn out to be our children . . . We're in a war for the identity of this nation . . ."

And so on. Now, Rafe Mair went on the air and he was not timid. He compared her speeches to those of Hitler and the KKK. He said of Kari Simpson's speeches "For Kari's homosexual one could easily substitute Jew. . . . It could have been Blacks . . . just as easily as gays. Now I'm not suggesting that Kari was proposing or supporting any kind of holocaust or violence but neither really . . . did Hitler or Governor Wallace . . . They were simply declaring their hostility to a minority. Let the mob do as they wished."

Kari Simpson sued. And, after years of costly wrangling, in June of last year, the Supreme Court of Canada delivered a resounding 9-to-nothing ruling against her. And it made it quite clear that it was deliberately expanding the safe zone for commentary.

Rafe himself isn't so keen on the wording of the ruling, written by Justice Ian Binnie, who called him a "shock jock"—for which Rafe demanded an apology. But he really should be happy with the core of Justice Binnie's reasoning. Here's the quote: "There is concern that matters of public interest go unreported because publishers fear the ballooning cost and disruption of defending a defamation action. Investigative reports get 'spiked,' it is contended, because, while true, they are based on facts that are difficult to establish according to rules of evidence. When controversies erupt, statements of claim often follow as night follows day, not only in serious claims (as here) but in actions launched simply for the purpose of intimidation. 'Chilling' false and defamatory speech is not a bad thing in itself, but chilling debate on matters of legitimate public interest raises issues of inappropriate censorship and self-censorship. Public controversy can be a rough trade, and the law needs to accommodate its requirements."

End of quote, and we should pin that one up. The two points I wish to make about this are, first, that these are very important words protecting robust, even rude commentary in Canada. Second, we often seem to act as though we did not have this liberty.

Of course, in courts of law, we do have that liberty—but remember that Canada's Human Rights Commissions are not courts of law. And, although widely condemned, they are still a problem—and Section 13 of the Act still allows them to police the Internet. It seems to me that, if someone's going to police the Internet, they need to do it under the Criminal Code, under normal rules of evidence, and not in a tribunal where truth is not a defence and where the complainant doesn't pay anything but the defendant gets huge legal bills—which is what happened to Ezra Levant and to *Maclean's* in the Mark Steyn case.

No doubt enough has been said about those cases elsewhere but I think the President of the Canadian Association of Journalists, Mary Agnes Welch, summed it up well. She said, "Human rights commissions were never meant to act as language nannies ... The current system allows complainants to chill the speech of those they disagree with by entangling targets in a human rights bureaucracy that doesn't have to operate under the same strict rules of defence as a court."

All of this suggests to me that there is a challenging legal environment—but not one that we can't change by fighting—as we've been doing successfully in many cases.

There's certainly a challenging business environment—but the race goes to the swift and the swiftest will figure out how to make journalism pay in the vast and expanding universe of the Internet.

And there is a challenging internal environment—the reluctance to give offence or to generate complaints. So I don't envy journalism students today trying to find jobs and make a go of this fascinating line of work. All I can tell you is that you'd better try, and you'd better succeed—or the loony bloggers and celebrity recipes will be all we have.

Thank you and good luck.

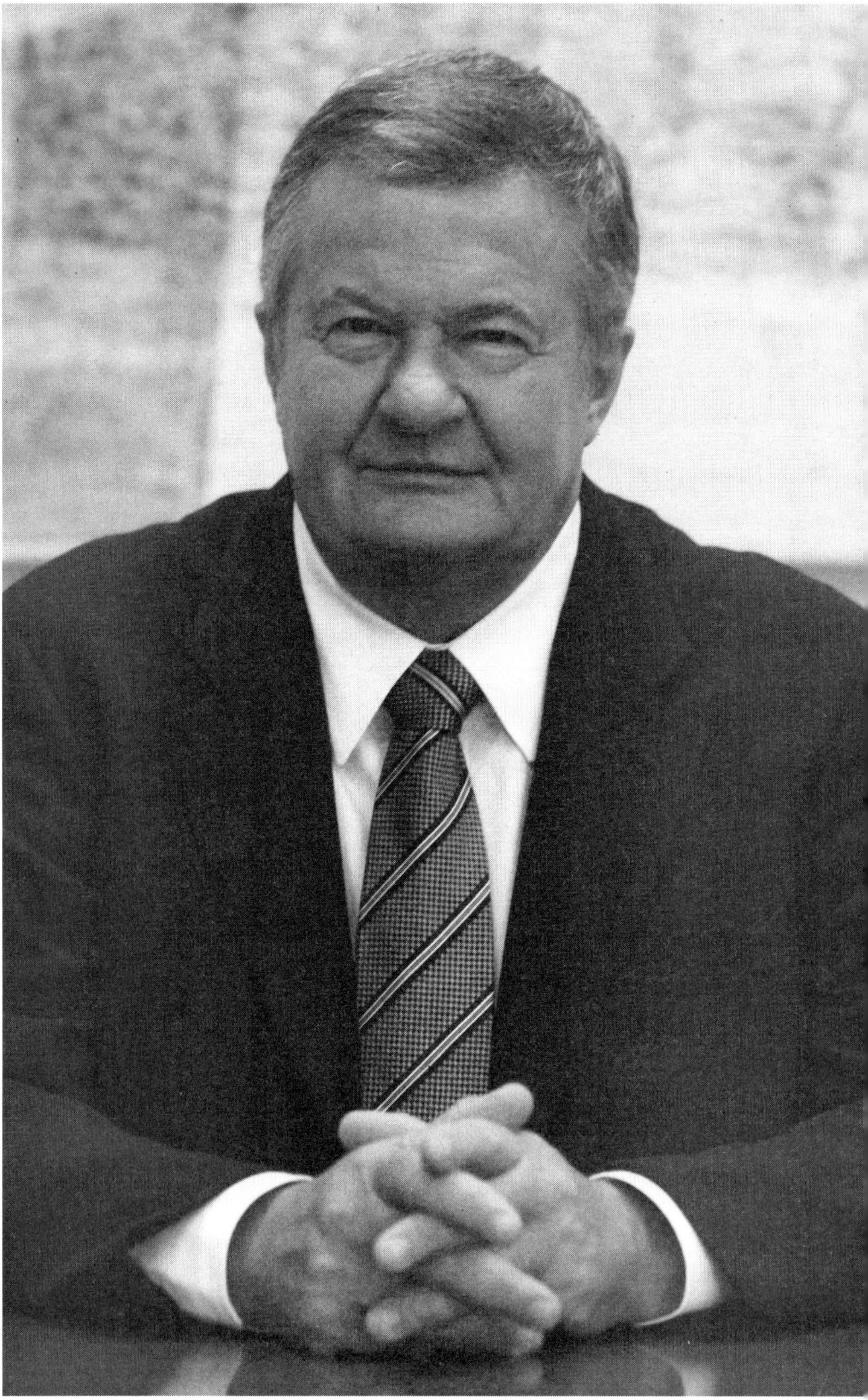

−2010−

TONY BURMAN

Tony Burman has been Managing Director of Al Jazeera's English-language international news channel since May, 2008. During this period, AJE—currently being broadcast in 150 million households in more than 100 countries—has provided exclusive coverage of the Israeli/Gaza conflict as well as groundbreaking news and programming from Asia, Africa, the Middle East and the Americas. Between 2000–2007, he was editor-in-chief and executive director of the Canadian Broadcasting Corporation (CBC News) and initiated the successful integration of CBC's radio, TV and online operations. In a 35-year career with the CBC, he was an award-winning news and documentary producer with field experience in 30 countries. His programs have been seen in a dozen countries, and he has received more than 100 awards for programming and network achievements in Canada, the US, the UK, France, Monaco and Argentina.

TURNING THE WORLD BACK ON:
Journalism and the New Global Reality

I never met James Minifie, although I feel I knew him. I remember his meticulous reporting on CBC radio and television, and I remember his books. I was a university student in Montreal during the turbulent 1960s. For me, he was one of the first Canadian writers who clearly saw Canada's wider role in the world and the obligation of Canadian journalists to help make this world a better place.

Twenty years later, in the barren highlands of Ethiopia, I remembered his message. I was the producer of the CBC's coverage of the horrific Ethiopian famine in 1984 and 1985. The Ethiopian borders had been closed to foreigners, and Brian Stewart and I were the first North American journalists to get in to cover the story. The Canadian response to our coverage was breath-taking. It was a remarkable time when Canadians from every corner of this country seemed engaged and involved in global issues.

A year later, I was back in Toronto, working with Joe Schlesinger on a documentary marking the 50th anniversary of the beginning of the Spanish Civil War. In my research, I was surprised to be reading the writings of James M. Minifie once again. In the 1930s, he covered the Spanish Civil War as the Paris correspondent of the *New York Herald Tribune*; in fact, he was captured by Franco's forces at one point. His reporting focused on what intrigued both Joe Schlesinger and me. What drew thousands of young Canadians, many of them prairie boys from communities such as Regina, to risk their lives and fight fascism on the far-off battlefields of Spain? I remember Minifie's answer. He wrote that it mattered to Canada, and it mattered to Canadians, so it mattered to him. Of course, he was right.

If this were a few years ago, I would be standing in front of you as a proud representative of Canada's public broadcaster. Today, I am equally proud now to be standing in front of you—as a Canadian journalist, still—but on behalf of another proud public broadcaster, Al Jazeera English.

I currently live in Doha, the capital city of Qatar. It's a quiet place.... nothing as racy as Dubai. In fact, it reminds me a lot of Regina, although it's 40 Celsius in Doha. And that doesn't remind me of Regina. Qatar is a tiny country that sits right beside Saudi Arabia. It juts onto a peninsula in the Arabian Gulf. That's what Al Jazeera stands for in English: "peninsula." I live in a condominium overlooking the Gulf, right across from Iran. In fact, from my balcony, after several glasses of wine—inspired by Sarah Palin and her proximity to Russia—I sometimes imagine that if I squint I can actually see Iran, and speak Farsi, all at the same time. But I'm not sure I can.

We live in a very challenging world. I suspect historians will one day judge this as a defining period in this twenty-first century. The centres of global power are shifting. In historic, even epic terms, the ground is moving beneath our feet. Power is shifting from the West.... from the United States.... to China, India and other parts of the developing world where the world's new twenty-first century economy is taking shape. Not coincidentally, that is where Al Jazeera largely resides. After the rise of the West ... for the past hundreds of years ... it's now "*the rise of the rest,*" as one writer put it. That doesn't mean we're entering an *anti-*American world, but we are moving into a world that is defined and directed from many places and by many people.

For Canadians—living in perhaps the most multicultural nation on earth-this will have special resonance. But that will only happen if we strengthen, not weaken, our connections to the wider world. The world's current financial crisis is not helping. Its aftershocks are having a devastating effect on many news organizations, including here in Canada. At a time when coverage of the world is more important than ever—and "global" is becoming the new "local"—our window on the world is increasingly being closed. Throughout North America, and Western Europe, journalists are being laid off. Media companies—many of them still quite rich—are cutting back. International coverage and investigative journalism are at risk. Surveys conducted in 2008 of American news media indicated the percentage of news devoted to international stories was the lowest in more than 20 years. The trend here in Canada is likely the same. This, sadly, comes at a time when people have never been more in need of fearless, independent, public-service journalism—particularly coverage of the world.

My message today is to urge that we do what we can to halt this slide. In adversity, there *is* opportunity, and I think there is an opportunity for Canadian journalists to step in and help fill the vacuum being left by the retreat of the world's media monoliths. But to work out the road ahead, we need to clearly understand the road that brought us here.

This century is only ten years old but it has had a very rocky ride so far. For many of us, the events of September 11, 2001 and their aftermath have defined this first decade of the twenty-first century. But that is not how this stage of history was expected to be.

In the twentieth century, we survived two world wars and many smaller ones. We survived the twin scourges of fascism and communism. We lived through a potential nuclear catastrophe during the Cold War. Given this, much of the world had hoped the beginning of this new century would be marked by relative peace and stability. Even better, many thought, it would be an opportunity to finally deal with the many pressing North-South issues that had been evaded during decades of East-West tensions. The conditions seemed right. The world was weary from the battering it took throughout most of the twentieth century. It appeared more inter-dependent than ever before, and so vulnerable and small.

In much of it, an information and technology revolution had begun which promised unprecedented access to places and ideas that up until now had been closed to us. At the centre of this—or at least this is what many journalists hoped—would be the world's proliferating news media. They would spread high-minded ideas and, perhaps, even a semblance of democracy to all corners of the planet. For example, if there were only three major all-news television networks at the end of the 1980s—CNN, Britain's Sky TV and Canada's CBC Newsworld—there were hundreds of channels worldwide a decade later. And this gave rise to high expectations.

Famed American journalist Walter Lippmann once wrote that the press should be "like the beam of a searchlight that moves restlessly about, bringing one episode and then another out of darkness into vision." As we entered the twenty-first century, the worldwide information explosion raised hopes that journalism's noblest goals were actually attainable. But this was premature. The turbulence of this decade, not its tranquility, has defined this period. In many cases, the news media have been passive, at best, or even complicit, as world events spiraled out of control.

The list of these events has been long: Growing conflict in the Middle East. Religious and political extremism. Increased worries about climate change. Immigration and vanishing borders. The spectre once again of potential nuclear conflict. And, of course, the current financial meltdown that threatens to deepen poverty and despair in many developing countries. As a consequence, many in the world's industrialized countries have turned inward. Instead of greeting this new century with openness and hope, they have become more protective of what they have and more fearful that in this uncertain future they may lose it.

The response by the world's news media to these events has been mixed, even contradictory.

In the developing world, there have been aggressive efforts to *expand* coverage of the world. These have provided alternative voices to the Anglo-American monopoly of CNN and the BBC that has long dominated the world of international journalism. The most notable example has been in the Middle East with the creation of the Al Jazeera network and its newer competitors, a development that is inspiring similar initiatives in Africa and Asia.

In contrast, many of the world's largest commercial news organizations—still rich by most measurements—have gone the opposite way. They have mirrored their sense of the public mood by *reducing* world coverage. Reacting to pressure from shareholders, they have drastically cut back their international bureaus, and shrunk the relatively small amount of space and airtime they still devote to 'foreign news.'

The late CBS news anchor Walter Cronkite gave a somber warning shortly before his death. He said that pressures by media companies to generate ever-greater profits threaten the very freedom the U.S. was built upon. He said today's journalists face greater challenges than those from his generation. No longer could journalists count on their employers to provide the necessary resources, he said, "to expose truths that powerful politicians and special interests often did not want exposed." Instead, he concluded, "they face rounds and rounds of job cuts and cost cuts that require them to do ever more with ever less."

In the full sweep of history, one could argue this is precisely the time when understanding other cultures is a necessary prerequisite to truly understanding your own. If information is power, ignorance can be dangerous. As recently as July 2007, a national public opinion poll in the U.S. indicated that as many as four in 10 Americans still believed Saddam Hussein was directly involved in the Al Qaeda attacks on 9/11—even though all evidence pointed to the contrary.

As a justification for reducing costly international coverage, it has been irresistible for some media companies to blame the victim—in this case, the audience—as in '... *people don't actually care about foreign news.*' But this is self-serving. It tries to absolve journalists and programmers from blame for boring or confusing their audiences. There is considerable research in North America suggesting that superficial coverage of the world is the most important contributor to public apathy.

What is also being ignored is another crucial role of news organizations: to provide news they believe the public *needs* to know to become better informed citizens. There used to be a time when major American media companies were motivated by a sense of public duty. They maintained strong, well-resourced news divisions as a form of '*pay-back*' for access to the public airwaves and the immense profits this produced. This was perhaps best summed up in the 1950s in the United States when Bill Paley, founder of CBS, was once quoted as saying, in effect: "I make money on Jack Benny so I can afford to do the *best* news."

So what is the *best* news, the news the public *needs* to know? Well, we know what *isn't*. A consistent drumbeat of '*good guys, bad guys, those who are with us and those who aren't*' is cited by many in surveys as a major negative in the coverage of world affairs. Beyond labels and name-calling, the public needs to know—and, arguably, *wants* to know—who these leaders are and how they gained power. And what can we learn from this?

Turning the world off may be therapeutic to some, but it is no long-term solution. The long march of history shows us that. There are signs that interest in global news coverage is increasing in the developing world, in Europe and perhaps in Canada—but not yet, it appears, in the United States. And this is ironic given the ubiquitous international influence of the world's last remaining superpower. So what's going on? Why would one of the world's most educated and sophisticated countries—with so much at stake in major international issues—be seemingly so disinterested in world affairs?

In June 2002, the Pew Research Center for People and the Press published a revealing analysis that offered an answer. It argued that the media, not their audience, should take the rap. The survey offered powerful evidence that broad interest in international news is most limited by the public's lack of background in this area. They simply don't understand why these stories are important, and the media mostly make little effort to help them.

CANADA AND THE WORLD

In 2003, CBC News undertook a major study into Canadians' attitudes towards 'news' and 'information' in this new century. It was the most extensive of its kind in Canada. The surprising headline in the study was that, contrary to conventional wisdom, a majority of Canadians indicated they want *more* international news, not *less,* and believe more than ever that what happens beyond their borders matters a lot. But they want *'international made local'*—global stories told in more relevant, local, accessible ways.

The study also identified general weaknesses in news presentation—including with international coverage—that was associated with all media, not just television. News is often defined too narrowly, focusing on 'bad' news that is of little relevance to most people. Journalists use language that is often confusing, and frequently choose stories that interest them more than their audience. News is often presented as a *passive* act instead of focusing on those stories which reveal *meaningful change* that can stimulate a *meaningful response.* Too much of today's news is only 'of passing interest,' or like 'ambient static.' And the audience is saying it wants to hear *all* sides of the story, not just two. They want an end to a simple black-and-white world, and want increased exposure to more divergent views and perspectives.

The study showed that many people are becoming as interested in the world as they are in their back yards, and that is because so many things have changed.

The world has changed. In a post-9/11 environment, people seem to increasingly value world news and its impact on their lives. Look at the global interest in coverage of the financial meltdown. They distrust any effort at short-changing coverage. Audiences expect both context and dramatic story-telling, and want journalists to make world issues as familiar to them as what is happening in their own communities. They want it made as real as if it were 'local.'

Society has changed. Increasingly, it is becoming a multicultural world with people having ties all over the globe. Immigrants are anxious to hear 'news from home.' Families often move back and forth from their home of origin. And world conflicts are often reflected in the tensions, aspirations and struggles evident in our towns and cities.

And audiences have changed. More than ever, people talk about their desire to know about meaningful change at home and around the world. They want to know what people around the world are thinking and what motivates them. They want to know in a more insightful way than what is currently offered.

But in spite of this, there is a circular pattern that becomes evident when examining the treatment of international news by many news organizations.

Coverage is very costly, therefore it is limited. Being limited, it is superficial and often confusing. Being all of that, the public turns off. Since the public turns off, coverage is even more reduced. And the self-fulfilling pattern plays on.

As we scan the wreckage of this first decade of the twenty-first century, there is an issue that urgently needs debate: Whose interests should journalists serve in deciding how much of the 'world' will be presented to the public? For those of us who believe that this shrinking world is crashing down upon us—in a way that affects everyone's day-to-day life—these are challenging times. We are now part of a 'news culture' where stories about celebrities like Paris Hilton receive more coverage than staggering tragedies such as Darfur. It is about time that we all reflect on 'why?.'

A Pew survey in 2007 listed "Tabloid" and "Foreign" news as the areas of *least* interest to the American public over the two-decade period, 1986–2006. Coverage of 'foreign' news has certainly shrunk in recent years, but not so 'tabloid.' It has significantly *increased* across the board. But in spite of this, public interest in 'tabloid' stories is still small and has not grown in recent years. So why the increased coverage? The study concludes that the motivation for more tabloid coverage was not to respond to widespread public appetite, but was due to commercial and competitive reasons. In other words, to appeal to smaller "niche" audiences that will improve ratings and please advertisers.

It examined the three-week saga in 2007 involving the death and internment of American celebrity Anna Nicole Smith. Many news organizations, particularly U.S. cable, blanketed that story, devoting 22 percent of their entire news programming to her. On the day of Smith's death, CNN 'tripled' its audience over the day before and this was hailed by beaming TV executives as a response to public interest.

However, the Pew study presented a different interpretation. It revealed that the increase in ratings was only about a million people—less than a single Nielsen ratings point. In other words, a tabloid story which increased ratings by a mere million people—in a country with a population of 330 million—ended up filling nearly a quarter of U.S. cable's news programming for that period.

In whose interests are these editorial decisions being made? Is it a mystery, therefore, that surveys in the United States indicate the current credibility of news organizations with the public is lower than it has been in memory?

A survey released last September in the u.s. indicated that American trust in the news media was at a record low. Nearly two-thirds of Americans think the news stories they read, hear and watch are frequently inaccurate. A similar survey in Canada in 2008 revealed a slightly more positive outlook—50 percent of Canadians, not two thirds, believe the news media are often inaccurate, but distrust here in still growing.

This probably would have come as no surprise to the late Neil Postman. He was the American media and cultural critic who in 1985 wrote his provocative analysis of television, *Amusing Ourselves to Death*. In that book, Mr. Postman argued that television—particularly TV news—treats serious issues as entertainment. It demeans political discourse by making it less about ideas and more about image. As he put it:

"When a population becomes distracted by trivia, when cultural life is redefined as a perpetual round of entertainment, when serious public conversation becomes a form of baby-talk, when, in short, a people become an audience and their public business a vaudeville act, then a nation finds itself at risk: culture-death is a clear possibility."

Many years from now, when historians reflect on this decade, I believe their judgment of the media's performance during these years will be harsh. Looking at the current state of the world, it is difficult not to conclude that disastrous decisions have been made by political leaders in an environment of ignorance and arrogance. And these disasters were condoned by a public that largely chose to look the other way and a news media that was at various times complicit or incompetent. That's certainly not how this decade was supposed to turn out and as the world becomes more dangerous, this should give us all motivation to set it right.

LESSONS FROM ABROAD

Not surprisingly, there are lessons from abroad. One of those places is the Middle East. As a Canadian journalist, whose career has mainly focused on how to help people navigate this ever-complicated world, I feel very privileged to be where I am—as Managing Director of Al Jazeera English. In my 35-year career as a journalist, mainly at the CBC, I've had the opportunity to visit and work in the Middle East often. I have always found it fascinating, but my perspective has been as an outsider-looking-in. But, as a resident of the Gulf, I now see it differently.

The English-laguage international channel of Al Jazeera has been on the air for three years now. In addition to its popular website, it is broadcast in more than 180 million households in more than 100 countries, which is a level that both CNN and the BBC took many more years to reach. It has received dozens of awards and nominations for its news and documentary excellence from every major TV festival in the world. It is finally making significant breakthroughs in

North America. This includes Washington, DC—where, we're told, we're the number one News Channel at the Pentagon and the State Department!

AJE has a worldwide staff of about 1000 employees, drawn from more than 50 nationalities. It constitutes the most diverse news service in the world. There are many of us from the BBC, CNN, European networks and, yes, the CBC in Canada—but many more come from Africa, Asia, Latin America and the Middle East.

The key aspect of Al Jazeera English is its global perspective. Our 'home team' is not in London, Atlanta, New York.... or Toronto, for that matter. We have no 'home team.' As the day unfolds, our broadcast schedule follows the sun: AJE broadcasts from its centres in Asia, the Middle East, Europe and then—finally—the Americas. Our objective is to let "the world report on itself." We try to cover every story from every side, from as many angles as we can. This is exemplified by our journalistic perspective, which sees the world through the lens of the global South.

In my view, this is in contrast to other international channels, such as CNN and the BBC, which focus on the Western centres of power and inevitably reflect their own national American and British agendas in their reporting. I'm not being critical when I say this. I respect the BBC and CNN. They know their audience and they serve it well. But their interests, and the interests of their largely Western audience, are not universal interests.

At Al Jazeera, we have our flaws, and we sometimes don't live up to our ambitions, but we think we know where we should be going. We try to tap into something different. That has been the approach since Al Jazeera Arabic was created in 1996. We are the only international news network rooted in the global South- in the developing world. Most of our news bureaus are located there. We know there's a large international audience that is tired—and skeptical—of mainstream Western media whose starting point often seems to be the Western centres of power. Coverage of the Middle East is only one example of where our approaches diverge.

In a recent academic study of BBC, CNN, and AJE, it was shown that, in the period examined, 81 percent of AJE's news items were about the news and stories of the South—Africa, Asia, Middle East and Latin America. This was nearly double that of the BBC and CNN whose 'news' focused more on Western Europe and the U.S.

AJE is firmly rooted in regions well beyond the traditional Western power centres, letting the world tell its own story. As a result, it has quickly become a leading international news service in Africa, key markets in Asia, as well as the Middle East. AJE provides news and information not available elsewhere and from parts of the world that go unreported. There is also evidence that it serves as a 'bridge' to understand other cultures. As George Clooney once described it: "Al Jazeera English TV is a perfect example of how we can open up the doors to see what these cultures are and that our differences with them are not so many." As evidence of this, there was a 2008 American academic study of AJE's impact in six countries in Asia, Europe, the Middle East and the United States. It revealed that in contrast to other channels AJE's viewers "found it to function as a 'conciliatory media'... more likely to cover contentious issues in a way that contributes to... cooperation, negotiation and reconciliation."

AJE is fiercely proud to be a central part of the Al Jazeera 'family,' and is influenced by that fact. However, it is also a stand-alone channel within Al Jazeera— separate in staff and editorial direction from Al Jazeera Arabic. AJE is a part of the Al Jazeera broadcast group, but an independent member of it. In that way, it operates in a similar manner to Rupert Murdoch's News Corporation. Just as *The Times* of London, Sun newspapers, Sky News and the Fox TV network all have independent voices, priorities and brands within one international multimedia company—so does Al Jazeera English.

I am sometimes asked whether there is ever any interference from the Government of Qatar, which provides most of the funds for Al Jazeera. The answer is 'no—not a hint of interference.' Al Jazeera is a public broadcaster in the same sense that the CBC in Canada is, and the BBC in Britain. And, in my experience so far, there has been a solid firewall between the Government of Qatar and Al Jazeera. In 18 months in my job, I have not heard anything from the Government of Qatar about what they want on Al Jazeera. In fact, in Canada, where I was Editor-in-Chief of the CBC for eight years, I had a clearer idea of what that government wanted out of its public broadcaster than I do in Qatar.

Al Jazeera English is available and popular in Britain, and it is regulated by Ofcom, the respected UK body which oversees that country's media organizations. AJE is required to adhere to Ofcom's very strict Broadcast Code that deals with issues of impartiality and fairness. In three years of broadcasting, AJE has never experienced a significant problem. AJE journalists are also required to follow Al Jazeera's Code of Ethics, which is available on our website: *www.aljazeera.net/english*. It is precisely the same type of code which governs journalistic quality and integrity at the BBC and CBC. In three years of broadcasting, AJE has never experienced a significant problem.

Not surprisingly, AJE has special pride in its coverage of the Middle East. Again, the goal here is not to push a line or cater to a bias. The goal is far more revolutionary: we simply want people to understand the full story, not a narrow one. At the beginning of this year, AJE gained international acclaim through its coverage of the Israeli-Gaza war. We were the only international English-language news channel that covered both sides of the conflict. We reported exclusively, from within Gaza... but also from throughout Israel—including southern Israel where the rockets out of Gaza landed. It is not surprising, therefore, that both of Al Jazeera's channels—Arabic and English—are broadcast in Israel, and we know that AJE in particular is widely watched.

Praise for AJE's coverage of the Israeli/Gaza conflict came from *The Financial Times, The Economist, The Guardian, Le Monde* in Paris, the *Columbia Journalism Review, The New York Times*. . . and the *Haaretz* newspaper in Israel. The *Haaretz* piece—titled *"My Hero of the Gaza War"*—includes this paragraph:

"My war hero is Ayman Mohyeldin, the young correspondent for Al Jazeera English and the only foreign network broadcasting during these awful days in a Gaza Strip closed off to the media. Al Jazeera English is not what you might think. It offers balanced, professional reporting from correspondents both in Israel and Gaza."

Day in and day out, Israeli politicians speak directly on Al Jazeera—on both its Arabic and English channels—more than on any other network in the world outside of Israel. That actually was one of the first notable achievements of Al Jazeera Arabic when it was created in 1996 by the Emir of Qatar. For the first time in history, the Arab world directly saw and heard Israelis—speaking freely, frequently, live and unedited. That was ground-breaking. Until then, traditional Arab journalism has been limited to state-run propaganda machines, usually serving very narrow interests.

Al Jazeera's hallmark has always been fearless reporting and wide-open debate—regardless of what controversy this triggers. This often challenges the rich and the powerful, and it has enraged dictatorial Arab governments throughout Al Jazeera's 13-year history. Its journalists, at one time or another, have been temporarily thrown out of many Arab countries. In fact as recently as last March, at the Arab summit, several governments denounced Al Jazeera for being too critical of the Arab world.

You probably think of Al Jazeera as the hated nemesis of the American government. In fact, Al Jazeera—until 9/11 in 2001—was widely praised by Western governments, including the Clinton White House in the U.S. . It was seen as the poster child for the strengthening of Arab democracy, but then it changed. Shortly after 9/11, in November 2001, the U.S. government attacked the Taliban in Afghanistan. It claimed no civilians were being killed in the bombing. Al Jazeera, not surprisingly, was the only news organization inside Afghanistan. And it had the temerity to report that, yes, civilians were being killed. It was then that the American government—the charming trio of Bush, Rumsfeld and Cheney—turned on Al Jazeera.

An irony long forgotten in this saga concerns the first interview Bin Laden gave after 9/11, in October, 2001. It was given to Al Jazeera, which is not surprising given its dominant position in the Arab world, but it was never broadcast on Al Jazeera. The network's leadership in Doha refused to air the interview because of the restrictions placed by Al Qaeda on Al Jazeera's interview. A week went by, nothing happened and Al Qaeda got very upset. It released its video copy of the interview on the Internet. And CNN was the first broadcaster to air it. Donald Rumsfeld was asked for his reaction to the interview and he denounced Al Jazeera for being sympathetic to Bin Laden. Go figure.

The year 2010 will undoubtedly turn out to be a crucial period in international affairs, and Canadians should be in the thick of it. As the centre of global power shifts to new regions and new rising powers, Al Jazeera's 70 news bureaus are intensely tracking those developments. Many of those journalists are Canadians. We believe that AJE's unique mix of news, current affairs and documentaries is appealing to many Canadians.

As James M. Minifie would remind us, we should never forget that there is a profound and genuine interest—rarely acknowledged by our media bosses—on the part of many Canadians towards comprehensive coverage of the world. There is a deep respect worldwide for the Canadian values of fair-mindedness, inclusiveness and bridge-building. As a Canadian now working in the middle of the Gulf, I'm humbled by how Canadians and Canadian journalism are held in such high-regard. But this takes hard work and commitment, and we can take neither for granted.

Canada—and the world—need to be exposed to *more* perspectives, *more* diversity and *more* choice. The windows need to be blown open, not shut closed.

Photo Credits

Pages v, x, 30, 276, 310, 320, 332, 350 and 360: courtesy University of Regina School of Journalism.

Pages xxxiv, 58, 80, 90, 98, 116, 128, 142, 186, 200, 224, 238, 252, 262 and 298: courtesy CBC Still Photo Collection.

Page 18: "Clark W. Davey, June 13, 1989" (Montreal Gazette), courtesy Canadian Press Images.

Page 46: by Don Hall, Photography Department, University of Regina.

Pages 68 and 212: courtesy CTVglobemedia Inc.

Page 160: by Irene Borins Ash M.S.W., R.S.W., from *Treasured Legacies—Older & Still Great*, Second Story Press, 2003.

Page 172: courtesy Arthur Kent.

Page 286: by Pete Paterson, courtesy Alanna Mitchell.

Page 374: courtesy Al Jazeera Network.

Index

—A—
Aberhart, William, 174
accountability: by government, 264, 265; of media for themselves, 11, 14–15, 27–28; in modern times, 139, 266–67; and ombudsmen, 27; in reporting, 92–95, 256–57; during war, 323. *see also* credibility
accuracy: and admitting error, 110–12; and distance from subject, 104, 139; and errors of fact and tone, 24–26; and finding the facts, 303–4, 316; as journalistic goal, 2, 21, 25
adversarial journalism, 13
advertisers: and CBC, 220, 257; and focus on children, 154, 305; and internet, 364, 365; relations with media, 8, 56, 278; and television economics, 147, 156, 204, 220, 278
advocacy journalism: benefits of, 163, 164–69; opposition to, 11, 13, 96–97
Afghanistan War, 330, 338, 352, 354, 355, 385
Agnew, Spiro, 139
AIDS, 79
Air India bombing, 368
Al Jazeera English (AJE), 375, 376, 382–86
Al Qaeda, 386
Alar, 133
Allen, Ralph, 100, 103
Alterman, Eric, 323
Amanpour, Christiane, 329
Amazon rainforest, 288
Ames, Bruce, 133
Amusing Ourselves to Death (Postman), 382
Anderson, Scott, 345
Andrews, Julie, 193
Angus Reid polls, 209
anonymous sources, 345–46, 370
APEC Summit fiasco, 366

Arar, Maher, 338, 343–46
Asper brothers, 280; 282
Atwan, Bari, 326
Auletta, Ken, 149, 178
authoritarianism, 176
Axworthy, Chris, 268, 275

—B—
Baden-Powell, Robert, 292
Baird, John, 355
Baldwin, Stanley, 4
Balkans War, 178–79, 181, 353–55
Banks, Elizabeth, 190
Barber, Lloyd, 100
Barker, Bob, 318–19
Batten, James K., 21
BBC (British Broadcasting Corporation), 5, 218, 327, 366, 383
Bell, Edward Price, 188
Bennett, Bill, 82
Bennett, R. B., 169
Bennett, Sr., James G., 189
Bennett, W. A. C., 82
Bentham, Jeremy, 274
Berlusconi, Silvio, 222
Bettag, Tom, 315
Bin Laden, Osama, 325–26, 385–86
Binnie, Ian, 371
Black, Conrad, 279–80
Black, David, 280
Bly, Nellie, 221
Bok, Sissela, 271
Bolan, Kim, 368, 369
Boorstin, Daniel, 301–3
Borsellino, Paolo, 183
Bosnian War, 178–79, 181
Bouchard, Lucien, 192, 234
Brown, Laurie, 207
Brown, Les, 218, 222
Brownell, Kelly, 305
Buchanan, Patrick, 347
Burgess, Anthony, 101
Burke, Edmund, 6
Burman, Tony, 346
Bush, George H. W., 92, 154

Bush, George W., 294, 323–24, 326, 329, 347, 348
Byfield, Ted, 137

—C—
Callaghan, Morley, 165
Calvin, Jim, 354
Cambodia, 62–63
Cameron, Bill, 194
Camp, Dalton, 268
Campbell, Kim, 191–92
Camus, Albert, 166
Canada: celebrating its culture, 122–23; changing self-image of, 353, 356–59; experience of travelling around, 101–2; and idea of moral authority, 352–53; importance of CBC to, 202–3, 205–8, 209–10; problems of, 130, 353; and reasonable contentedness, 228–29; and separatism debate, 229–31, 232–37
Canada-US relationship: and 9/11, 284–85; based on ignorance, 87–89; and CBC, 204, 205–6, 208; and fading of Canadian identity, 222; and international news, 66, 206, 330; and Kyoto Protocol, 295; and politics, 356–57; and sense of scandal, 226, 227; and use of star reporters, 95
Canadair, 132
Canadian constitution, 51, 150
Canadian Daily Newspaper Publishers Association, 28–29
Canadian International Development Agency (CIDA), 40
Canadian Press, 330
Canadian Radio-television Telecommunications Commission (CRTC), 281
Canwest Global: and debt, 362; firing Russell Mills, 366; foreign correspondents at, 330; and libel chill, 369; and

INDEX

media concentration, 281; reliance on US programming, 208; respect for, 203
Capra, Frank, 319
Carey, Mariah, 193
Carman, John, 179
Carney, Pat, 70, 84
CBC (Canadian Broadcasting Corporation): and Canadian culture, 123, 182, 208; and censorship, 39–40, 366–67; and climate change, 290; detractors of, 204, 207–8, 281; economics of, 184, 219–20, 257, 274, 362; experience as chairman of, 119–20; government manipulation of, 38–40, 57; international news coverage, 57, 88, 205–7, 211, 330; and libel chill, 369; major news survey of, 380–81; mandate, 203; mistakes of, 210–11; negativism at, 57; news and current affairs on, 205–7; as part of Canadian identity, 202–3, 205–8, 209–10, 278; political coverage, 111–12, 209, 220, 259; programming in 1960s, 203–4; programming in 1990s, 204–5; timidity of, 365–66, 368; women at, 75, 76–77, 107, 249
celebrity journalism: and anchormen, 109, 217; effect of, 49–50, 52, 243; and interviews, 192–93, 196; and use of star reporters, 11–12, 92–95, 114
cell phones, 365
censorship: of bad news, 38, 40, 162; and CBC, 39–40, 366–67; and convergence, 282; of injustice, 168; and libel chill, 169, 368–72; self, 85, 97, 329, 335, 366–67; state, 32–38, 40–41, 337; of television, 151; of violence, 126; during war, 41–42, 43, 341, 342, 347–48

Chalabi, Ahmed, 325
Chalmers, Floyd, 162
Charest, Jean, 227, 228–29, 236
Charlotte's Web (White), 198
Charter of Rights and Freedoms, 338–39
Cheney, Dick, 325
children, effect of television on, 152–54, 305
China, 41
Chrétien, Jean, 121, 259, 268, 366
Chung, Connie, 188
Church v. Darwinism, 291–93
Churchill, Winston, 5, 44, 335, 347
CIDA (Canadian International Development Agency), 40
civic journalism, 273–74
Clark, Greg, 49
Cleroux, Richard, 335
climate change: Canada's record on, 352–53, 355; effect of, 289, 296; evidence for, 289–91; and fight over belief systems, 293–94; and Kyoto Protocol, 294–95
Clinton, Bill, 226
Clooney, George, 383–84
Close Up, 123–24
CNN: and censorship, 366; and Iraq war, 328–29; need for ratings, 381; perceived US bias of, 222, 383; reach and popularity of, 146, 218
Coates, Bob, 136–37
Collister, Ron, 49
communications experts, 269, 270–72, 275
Communism, fall of, 337
confidential sources, 345–46, 370
Connolly Cyril, 241
Connors, Janet, 194
convergence, 281–82
Cooke, Janet, 12
credibility: of media, 4, 10–11, 12, 139, 266; of public institutions, 272–73. *see also* accountability

Cronkite, Walter, 379
Crosbie, John, 121
CRTC (Canadian Radio-television Telecommunications Commission), 281
CTV, 57, 76, 203, 208, 330
Cuba, 37
curiosity, 2, 61, 115, 243–44
Cusson, Danny, 369–70
Cuthand, Doug, 282
cynicism. *see* negativism

–D–

D-Day anniversary, 209
Daniells, Roy, 72
Danielson, Gord, 312–13
Darkness at Noon (Koestler), 251
Darwin, Charles, 291–92, 293
Dateline, 314
Davey, Clark, 84, 102, 105
Davey, Keith, 14
Davies, Robertson, 101, 206
De Cosmos, Amor, 169
democracy, xvi–xvii, xxiii–xxv, 43–44, 110, 168, 316, 348–49
DePoe, Norman, 49, 175
desensitization, 151–52
Dewar, Elaine, 169
Di Pietro, Antonio, 183
Diefenbaker, John, 20, 132
Dion, Stéphane, 369
Domet, Stephanie, 282
Donahue, Phil, 328
Douglass, Frederick, 231
Dunne, John Gregory, 170
Duskin, Ruthie, 73

–E–

Eaton, John Craig, 8
Edgell, Mike, 317
editorializing, 11, 97
education, 152, 243
Edwards, Bob, 169
Egypt, 38
empathy, 307
Endangered Minds: Why Our Children Don't Think (Healey), 152

INDEX

entertainment: and celebrity journalism, 52; and choices on television, 52, 148–49, 151, 179–81, 217, 302; and television news, 11–12, 114
environmentalists, 132–36
ethics: statement of principles, 28–29; suggestions for, 16–17; of television journalism, 154–55, 157–58; television's replacement for, 150–51; and weighing up stories, 249–50
Ethiopian famine, 376

— F —

fairness, 26, 27, 28–29
Falcone, Giovanni, 182–83
Fears, Aileen, 174
feeding the bear, 216
Fife, Bob, 259
the fifth estate: A. Clarkson at, 242, 248; L. Macintyre at, 264, 265, 266, 268–69, 275
Fillmore, Nick, 168
financial crisis of 2009, 377
The First Casualty (Knightley), 341
Fleischer, Ari, 323
Food Lion v. ABC, 220–21
Ford, Richard, 300, 308
foreign correspondence, 61–65, 65–67, 182, 183, 184, 330. see also international news
Fotheringham, Allan, 49, 51
Fox News Channel, 328
Francis, Anne, 73–74
Frank, Anne, 284
Fraser, John, 137
free trade negotiations, 88, 111–12
Friendly, Fred, 49, 315
Fromm, Erich, 268
Frost, Robert, 189
Frum, Barbara, 188, 196, 197

— G —

Gandhi, Indira, 37–38
Gannon, Jeff, 324
Gardiner, Jimmy, 56

Gartner, Michael, 177–78
General Westmoreland v. CBS Reports, 93
Geneva Summit, 72
Genius, 363–64
Gibson Guitar Company, 177
Gilmarten, Bob, 180
Global National, 317
globalism, 125, 222, 377, 378–81, 386
The Globe and Mail: and advocacy, 166; and Arar case, 344; ethical issues, 111, 366–67, 370; international coverage, 88, 330; Nation Builder awards, 338; and objectivity, 165; police stories, 335–36; politics of, 328; women hired at, 161
Goddard, Nichola, 338
Goddard, Tim, 338
Goldenberg, Eddie, 355
Goldhawk, Dale, 111–12
good news/bad news balance, 8–9, 264–65, 329–30
Google, 274
Google News, 363
Gore, Al, 352
Gotlieb, Sondra, 82
Gould, Tom, 49
Gouzenko, Igor, 33–34
Grant, Ulysses S., 190–91
Greeley, Horace, 189, 303
Greene, Lorne, 101
greenhouse effect, 113
Gretzky, Wayne, 102
GST (Goods and Services Tax), 136
Guatemala, 355–56
Gubbins, General, 35
Guckert, James, 324
Gulf War, 154, 155
Gwyn, Richard, 49
Gzowski, Alison, 106
Gzowski, Peter, 191, 196

— H —

Halton, David, 240
Halton, Matthew, 48, 240
Harding, Tonya, 180

Harper government, 339–40, 352–53, 357
Harrison, Rex, 240
Healey, Jane, 152
Hearst, Randolph, 302
Henry, Frances, 283
Hersey, John, 170
Hillier, Rick, 352, 354
Hitchens, Christopher, 367
Hitler, Adolf, 32, 174
hockey, 104–5
Homer-Dixon, Thomas, 305
Honderich, Beland, 104
HonestReporting.com, 368
hostages in Iran, 343
Howe, Joseph, 169
Human Rights Commissions, 371–72
Hume, David, 270
Hunter, Holly, 196
Hutchinson, Helen, 84
Hutchison, Bruce, 104
Huxley, T. H., 292

— I —

Ignatieff, Michael, 357
The Image: A Guide to Pseudo-events in America (Boorstin), 301–3
independence, 29
India, 37–38
Indonesia, 40–41
information, 144–45, 151, 216, 242, 339–40, 366
Ingenuity Project, 308
international news: on Al Jazeera, 382–86; Canada's views on, 380–81; on CBC, 57, 88, 205–7, 211, 330; cutbacks in, 377, 378–80; in *Globe and Mail*, 88, 330; increased sources for, 378; US views on, 379–80, 381–82. see also foreign correspondence
internet, 274, 316, 363–65, 366, 371
interviews/interviewing: goal of, 188–89, 198; history of, 189–91, 302–3; politicians,

INDEX

191–92, 195, 267; popularity of, 197–98; tips for, 194–97, 244–45, 300; types of, 191–94
investigative reporting, 12–13, 86, 221, 248–49, 267
Iran-Contra, 92, 96
Iranian hostages, 343
Iraq War, 322–27, 328–30
Irving, K. C., 270
Israel-Gaza war, 384–85

– J –

Jackson, Janet, 301
Jefferson, Thomas, 6
Jensen, Monika, 40
Jessop, Ken, 194
Johnson, Lyndon, 8, 214–15
Johnstone, Bruce, 295
Jones, Hal, 88
Jones, Phillip, 135, 136
The Journal, 94–95, 133, 194–95
journalism: and ability to listen, 85–86, 194–95; admitting error, 110–12, 248; and anonymous sources, 345–46; for a cause, 165–66, 169, 344; and compassion, 251, 307, 358; competitive instincts within, 336–37; and context, 64, 72, 242; and dealing with public relations, 258, 260; deep pool of talent in, 105, 316; description of, 301, 318–19; economics of, 53, 76–77, 272, 330, 362–63, 377; and fashionableness of issues, 113–14, 133, 137; and finding the facts, 303–4, 316; generosity received in, 78–79; history of, xxiii–xxiv, 5–6, 55–56, 169, 301–2; importance of life experience to, 245–47; insiders' view of, 313–14, 315, 318, 335; investigating itself, 53–54, 258–59, 312; and Iraq War, 322–27, 328–29; and knowing yourself, 248–50; necessities for career in, 87, 115, 214, 243, 250, 256; and need to challenge elites, 317, 318, 340; and political intimidation, 168, 347–48; and pressure from advertisers, 220; and providing meaning to events, 306–7; and pseudo-events, 302, 303, 317; public's view of, 221, 256, 260, 317–18, 349, 381–82; as reflection of public, 26–27, 29, 139, 222, 273, 318; responsibilities of, 15, 16–17, 28, 157–58, 170, 219, 341; satisfactions of, 61, 170, 259, 315, 318, 349; and seeking practical solutions, 138, 140–41, 308; and selling a story, 156, 219, 256, 302; shortcomings of, 21–23, 87, 112, 163; suggested exercises for, 24–25, 102–3; and timidity, 365–68; training for, 106–7; treatment of critics of, 23, 26, 219; and trivial stories, 140, 156, 179–81, 260, 301, 314; and use of subject experts, 109–10, 167–68, 193, 317; and willingness to be humiliated, 62–63, 245–46. *see also* advocacy journalism; celebrity journalism; censorship; good news/bad news balance; investigative reporting; media freedom; objectivity; political coverage; political manipulation; public trust; right to know
journalism schools: and advocacy, 166; in Canada, 181–82; experience at, 254–55; history, xxi; importance of, 312; interns from, 20–21; University of Regina, xx, xxi–xxii
Juscovitz, Henry, 177

– K –

Kain, Karen, 102
Kay, Jonathan, 369
Keate, Stuart, 87
Keenleyside, Hugh, 79
Keller, Bill, 329, 347, 348, 365
Kelly, Walt, 29
Kennedy, John F., 126
Kennedy Jr., John F., 316–17
Kent, Adele, 175
Kent, James, 174
Kent, Norma, 175
Kent, Parker, 174
Kent, Peter, 175
Kent, Susan, 175
Kent Commission, 6, 27, 54, 57
Khrushchev, Nikita, 39–40, 175
Kimber, Stephen, 282
Kirk, Harvey, 215
Klein, Ralph, 294–95
Knightley, Philip, 82–83, 341
knowledge, 144–45, 242
Koffman, Jeffrey, 327
Koppel, Ted, 158
Korean War, 34
Kumar, Sat, 112
Kurosawa, Akira, 251
Kyoto Protocol, 294–95, 352–53, 355

– L –

Lack, Andrew, 177–78
Landry, Bernard, 284
languages, learning, 246–47
LaPierre, Laurier, 119, 184
Larsen, Bruce, 20
Leblanc, Daniel, 370
libel chill, 169, 368–72
Liebling, A. J., 103, 190
Limbaugh, Rush, 327–28
Lincoln, Abraham, 231–32
literacy, 147
Lon Nol, Marshal, 62
Loney, James, 343
Lore, Louise, 181
Los Angeles Times, 348
Luedtke, Kurt M., 21–23
Lynch, Charles, 84, 112
Lynch, Jessica, 327
Lyons, Eugene, 190

– M –

Macdonald, John A., 203
Mackenzie, William Lyon, 169
Maclean's, 103, 106, 107, 110

INDEX

Madagascar, 289, 296
Mafia, 182–83
Mailer, Norman, 335
Mair, Rafe, 370–71
Makin, Kirk, 165
Malaysia, 41, 42
Malling, Eric, 191
Man Alive, 118
March, Peter, 282
Marsden, Bill, 282
Martin, Paul, 259
Mazankowski, Don, 121
McIntosh, Andrew, 370
McKenna, Brian, 250
McLean, Ross, 123–24
McLellan, Scott, 324
McLuhan, Marshall, 121
media freedom: benefits of, 54–55; in Canada, 38–40, 43–44; international, 9, 36–38, 40–41; as principle, 28; and public opinion, 279; and secret intelligence, 32–34, 36; in war, 41–42, 337
media ownership: and advertisers, 278; and commitment to journalism, 272; concentration of, 279–81, 314; and convergence, 281–82; and editorial interference, 56; lack of investigation of, 53–54; and monopolies, 54, 56–57; and press freedom, 43
Meech Lake Accord, 312–13
Middle East, 368, 384–85
Mill, John Stuart, 168
Miller, Arthur, 340
Miller, Judith, 324–25
Milman, H. H., 293
Milton, John, 5
Minifie, James M.: attitude to US, 48–49, 126, 215; background of, xviii, 33, 35, 242; as reporter, 2, 89, 175–76, 202, 243; testimonials to, 20, 100, 130, 188, 202; as thinker, 79, 147, 157, 241–42, 376
Mitrovica, Andrew, 344, 345–46
Mittermeier, Russ, 288

Monbiot, George, 352–53
Moran, Terry, 323
Morea, Jim, 180
Morenz, Howie, 105
Morin, Guy Paul, 165
Morris, Dick, 226
Moses, Ted, 284
Moyer, Janice, 144
MSNBC, 328
Muhammad cartoons, 366–67
Mulroney, Brian, 120–21, 192
multiculturalism, 283–84, 358
Munro, Ross, 49
Munson, Jim, 362
Murray, Don, 184, 206
Murrow, Edward R., 156, 158, 315

–N–

Naples earthquake, 78
Napoleon, 6
Nash, Knowlton, 21, 49, 89, 162–63, 249, 334
The National, 205–7, 210
National Post, 281–82, 344, 370
national unity crisis, 55
Natives, 137–38
NBC News, 177–78
negativism: and CBC, 57; and fascination with trauma, 138–39; popularity of, 14, 50–51, 114, 132, 134
new journalism, 13
New York Times, 324–25, 342–43, 347–48, 364, 365
Newans, Ken, 83
news organizations, 64, 95, 164, 220–21, 377, 378–79
Newsmagazine, 175–76
Newspaper Act, 27, 54
Niedzviecki, Hal, 303
9/11. *see* September 11th
Nixon administration, 342
Noble, Kimberley, 169

–O–

objectivity: difficulties of, 267–68; importance of, 13, 256–57, 303–4; myth of, 71, 164–65, 279

Ockrent, Christina, 222
off-the-record conversations, 43
Okrent, Daniel, 325
Oliver, Charlie, 166
ombudsmen, 27
O'Neill, Juliet, 344–45
opinion, 11
ordinary people, 193–94, 206–7
O'Reilly, Bill, 328
Orwell, George, 35
Ottawa Citizen, 136, 344–45, 366, 369–70

–P–

Paley, Bill, 379
Parker, Richard, 218
Partan, James, 301
PCBs, 135
Pearson, Drew, 86
Pearson, Lester, 48–49, 101
Pelletier, Jean, 343
Pentagon Papers case, 342–43
Pepin, Marcel, 366
Philip, Prince, 289
Phillips, Bruce, 49
Pioneer Trust, 132
political correctness, 270, 284
political coverage: and advocacy, 166; on CBC, 111–12, 209, 220, 259; changes in, 56; on *the fifth estate,* 264, 265, 268–69, 275; and interviews, 191–92; and Iraq War, 323–25; lapses in, 134, 149; misplaced focus of, 139–40; and public relations, 255–56; on television, 147–48, 150
political manipulation: of Al Jazeera, 384, 385; of CBC, 38–40, 57; and Hitler, 32; of information in Canada, 339–40, 366; internationally, 9; and Iraq War, 323–27, 329–30; and libel chill, 169, 368–72; of news, 7–8, 56; spin, 7–8, 269; through language, 35; and war, 96–97. *see also* censorship
Postman, Neil, 114, 305, 382

Potter, Mitch, 327, 348–49
Powell, Jody, 271
press freedom. *see* media freedom
Prime Time, 314
prisons, 167
private industry: and communications experts, 270, 271–72; dealing with media, 8, 220, 257–58; and financial control of broadcasting, 176–77; and journalism schools, 181–82; and Kyoto Protocol, 294, 295; taking media to court, 220–21
private networks, 208, 210, 220. *see also* CNN; CTV
public broadcasting, 32, 124, 273–74, 304. *see also* CBC (Canadian Broadcasting Corporation)
public relations, 255–56, 257, 258, 260, 269–70
public trust: and accountability of reporting, 92–95, 256–57; changing view of, 264, 265; keeping public informed, xvi, 3, 4–5; mandate for all media, 124–25; news organizations' sense of, 379; and notion of privilege, 22

– Q –

Qatar, 384
Quebec referendum, 235–36, 237

– R –

race/racism and media, 283–85
radio, 73, 130, 266
Raines, Howell, 325
Ramsay, Donald, 12
Rather, Dan, 92, 95–96, 97
Ratushney, Lynn, 345
Regina *Leader-Post*, 335–36
Reich, Robert, 176–77, 306
Reichmann brothers, 169
reporting/reporters. *see* journalism

The Resin, 336–37
right to know: v. lives in danger, 343; v. national security, 42–43, 347–48; v. right to privacy, 14, 22, 29, 136–37, 157
Robbins, Ron, xxi–xxii, 32, 126, 214, 334
Robichaud, Louis, 48
Rosenberg, Jonathan, 364, 365
Rosenstiel, Tom, 323
Rumsfeld, Donald, 327, 329–30, 386
Russell, William H., 341, 342

– S –

Saddam Hussein, 325–26, 329, 379
Safer, Morley, 8, 76
Sarnoff, David, 306
Sarnoff, Robert, 146
Sawatsky, John, 86–87
Scarborough, Joe, 328
Schlesinger, Joe, 84, 88, 376
Scott, C. P., 9
Sears, Val, 131, 132
secrecy, 274–75. *see also* censorship
Segal, Lynn, 307
sensationalism, 167, 219
separatism debate, 229–31, 232–37
September 11th, 284–85, 338, 377, 379, 385
Sharpe, Robert, 370
Shaw, George Bernard, 7
shooting the messenger, 3, 8, 150, 366
Sifton, Michael, 280
Sikh separatism, 368–69
Simpson, Jeffrey, 258–59
Simpson, Kari, 370–71
Sinclair, Gordon, 49
60 Minutes, 133
Skyé Resources, 355–56
Slavco (Bosnian journalist), 179
Smith, Anna Nicole, 381
Smythe, Dallas, xix–xxi, 278
Soharwardy, Syed, 367

Somalia Affair, 354
Southam News, 53, 54, 57, 88, 330
Spanish Civil War, 56
Sparkes, Paul, 362
Spears, Borden, 140
special interest groups, 27, 130, 131, 132–36, 138, 149–50
Sperling, Gerry, 164
spin of news, 7–8, 269
Sports Illustrated, 114
Sprow, Frank, 294
Spry, Graham, xix, 7
St. Augustine, 271
Stalin, Joseph, 190
Steib, Charles, 27
Stephenson, William, 33, 35
Steuart, Davey, 136–37
Stewart, Brian, 376
Stewart, Jon, 318
Stewart, Potter, 343
Stone, I. F., 271
Straight, Hal, 84
Stringer, Howard, 92
Stusiak, Marilyn, 86
Sudan, 356
Sukarno, President, 40–41
Sun newspapers, 53
Suzuki, David, 109

– T –

tabloid news, 179–81, 381. *see* entertainment
Talisman Energy, 356
talk radio, 327–28
Tanzania, 40
Tator, Carol, 283
Taylor, James, 193
Taylor, Maxwell, 348
technology: and deeper efficiency, 306; and democracy, 316; increase of, 144–45; and journalist's work, 86, 214; and press freedom, 43; and television choices, 149, 218, 378
television: and advertisers, 147, 156, 204, 220, 278; and celebrity journalism, 11–12, 114; current affairs

programs, 123–24; and desensitization, 151–52; economics of, 147, 148–49, 218, 219–20, 272, 314, 315; effect on children, 152–54, 305; as entertainment medium, 52, 148–49, 151, 179–81, 217, 302; and foreign correspondence, 182, 183, 184, 330; and golden age of news, 216–18; how it is watched, 155–56; and influence of cable, 147, 218, 378; and journalism ethics, 150–51, 154–55, 157–58; popularity of news on, 6–7, 131, 155; power and scope of, 145–46, 147, 150, 154, 243; as reflection of public, 148, 151; responsibilities of, 15–16; and simplification of issues, 71, 131, 156, 219; and sterile perfectionism, 247–48; and tabloid news, 179–81. *see also* Canwest Global; CBC; CNN; CTV
Thatcher, Margaret, 195, 197, 271
Thatcher, Ross, 110–11
This Hour Has Seven Days, 50, 365
Thomas, Helen, 323
Thompson, Allan, 345
Thomson newspapers, 54, 56, 106
Three Blind Mice (Auletta), 149
Timmins Daily Press, 108
Toffler, Alvin, 218
Toronto Sun raid, 43
Tower, Patrick, 338
travel, 245–46
Trudeau, Pierre, 39, 51, 120–21
truth: and adversarial journalism, 14–15; finding it, 188–89, 192; ruthless search for, 110, 156–58, 316–18; as unattainable goal, 242, 272–73
Tutu, Desmond, 137
20/20, 314

–U–
Undercurrents, 257–58
UNESCO, 9–10
United Nations, 36–37
University of Regina Journalism School, xx, xxi–xxii
The Unreality Industry (Mitroff), 151
US Civil War, 231–32
US Fairness Doctrine, 327
USA Today, 114
Ustinov, Peter, 78–79

–V–
The Valour and the Horror, 365–66
values, 304–5
Vander Zalm, Bill, 82
VE-Day anniversary, 209–10
Veilleux, Girard, 119–20
Vietnam War, 8, 41–42, 96–97, 324, 347
violence, 125–26
visible minorities, 283–84

–W–
W5, 76, 79, 141, 314
Waite, Terry, 97
Wallace, Alfred R., 292
Wallace, Mike, 93
Walters, Barbara, 93, 314
Watergate, 12, 132, 336
Watson, Robert, 294
Weaver, Andrew, 289–90
Welch, Mary Agnes, 371–72
Wells, Clyde, 195
Westell, Tony, 132
White, E. B., 164
Whitton, Charlotte, 77
Williams, Robin, 193
Williams, Tannis MacBeth, 153
Winfrey, Oprah, 226
women: in broadcasting, 73–74, 75–77, 148; as interviewers, 190; in journalism, 107, 161, 249; working to men's stereotypes, 77, 78

women's issues, 74–75
World Sikh Organization (WSO), 369
Worthington, Peter, 282
Wortley, Scot, 284

–Y–
Young, Brigham, 303
Young, Donzel, 194
Young, Yvonne, 194

–Z–
Zolf, Larry, 119

A NOTE ABOUT THE TYPE

This book is set in *Minion Pro*, an Adobe Original typeface designed by Robert Slimbach. *Minion Pro* is inspired by classical, old-style typefaces of the late Renaissance, a period of elegant, beautiful, and highly readable type designs. *Minion Pro* combines the aesthetic and functional qualities that make text type highly readable with the versatility of OpenType digital technology, yielding unprecedented flexibility and typographic control, whether for lengthy text or display settings. With its many ligatures, small caps, old-style figures, swashes, and other added glyphs, *Minion Pro* is ideal for uses ranging from limited-edition books to newsletters to packaging.

The accents in this book are set in *Franklin Gothic*. Morris Fuller Benton designed *Franklin Gothic* for the American Type Founders Company in 1903–1912. Just as early types without serifs were known by the misnomer "grotesque" in Britain, and "grotesk" in Germany, they came to be described as "gothic" in America. There were already many "gothic" typefaces in North America by the early 1900s, but Benton's design was probably influenced by popular "grotesks" from Germany, like *Basic Commercial*, or D. Stempel AG's *Reform*. *Franklin Gothic* may have been named for Benjamin Franklin; however, the design has no historical relationship to that famous early American printer and statesman. *Franklin Gothic* is still one of the most widely used sans serifs; it is a suitable choice for newspapers, advertising and posters.

ENVIRONMENTAL BENEFITS STATEMENT

Canadian Plains Research Center saved the following resources by printing the pages of this book on chlorine free paper made with 100% post-consumer waste.

TREES	WATER	SOLID WASTE	GREENHOUSE GASES
19	8,720	529	1,810
FULLY GROWN	GALLONS	POUNDS	POUNDS

 Calculations based on research by Environmental Defense and the Paper Task Force.
Manufactured at Friesens Corporation

KNOWLTON NASH • CLARK DAVEY • WILLIAM STEVENSON • CHARLES LYNCH • PETER GZOWSKI • PATRICK WATSON • ERIC MALLING • PAMELA WALLIN • LLOYD ROBERTSON • REX MURPHY • ADRIENNE CLARKSON • WENDY MESLEY • KEVIN NEWMAN • DAVID HALTON • EDWARD GREENSPON • CAROL OFF • WILLIAM STEVENSON • CHARLES LYNCH • JOE SCHLESINGER • HELEN HUTCHINSON • ERIC MALLING • PAMELA WALLIN • JUNE CALLWOOD • ARTHUR KENT • ADRIENNE CLARKSON • WENDY MESLEY • LINDEN MACINTYRE • HAROON SIDDIQUI • EDWARD GREENSPON • CAROL OFF • TERRY MILEWSKI • TONY BURMAN • JOE SCHLESINGER • HELEN HUTCHINSON • ALLAN FOTHERINGHAM • ANN MEDINA • JUNE CALLWOOD • ARTHUR KENT • VALERIE PRINGLE • PETER MANSBRIDGE • LINDEN MACINTYRE • HAROON SIDDIQUI • ALANNA MITCHELL • EVAN SOLOMON • TERRY MILEWSKI • TONY BURMAN • KNOWLTON NASH • CLARK DAVEY • W ALLAN FOTHERINGHAM • ANN MEDINA • PETER GZOWSKI • PATRICK WATSON • VALERIE PRINGLE • PETER MANSBRIDGE • LLOYD ROBERTSON • REX MURPHY • ALANNA MITCHELL • EVAN SOLOMON • KEVIN NEWMAN • DAVID HALTON • KNOWLTON NASH • CLARK DAVEY • WILLIAM STEVENSON • CHARLES LYNCH • PETER GZOWSKI • PATRICK WATSON • ERIC MALLING • PAMELA WALLIN • LLOYD ROBERTSON • REX MURPHY • ADRIENNE CLARKSON • WENDY MESLEY • KEVIN NEWMAN • DAVID HALTON • EDWARD GREENSPON • CAROL OFF • WILLIAM STEVENSON • CHARLES LYNCH • JOE SCHLESINGER • HELEN HUTCHINSON • ERIC MALLING • PAMELA WALLIN • JUNE CALLWOOD • ARTHUR KENT • ADRIENNE CLARKSON • WENDY MESLEY • LINDEN MACINTYRE • HAROON SIDDIQUI • EDWARD GREENSPON • CAROL OFF • TERRY MILEWSKI • TONY BURMAN • JOE SCHLESINGER • HELEN HUTCHINSON • ALLAN FOTHERINGHAM • ANN MEDINA • JUNE CALLWOOD • ARTHUR KENT • VALERIE PRINGLE • PETER MANSBRIDGE • LINDEN MACINTYRE • HAROON SIDDIQUI • ALANNA MITCHELL • EVAN SOLOMON • TERRY MILEWSKI • TONY BURMAN • KNOWLTON NASH • CLARK DAVEY • W ALLAN FOTHERINGHAM • ANN MEDINA • PETER GZOWSKI • PATRICK WATSON • VALERIE PRINGLE • PETER MANSBRIDGE • LLOYD ROBERTSON • REX MURPHY • ALANNA MITCHELL • EVAN SOLOMON • KEVIN NEWMAN • DAVID HALTON